MyManagementLab®: Improves Student Engagement Before, During, and After Class

Prep and Engagement

- **Personal Inventory Assessments (PIA) – NEW!** Online questionnaires designed to promote self-reflection and engagement in students, because students learn better when they can connect what they are learning to their personal experience. Student results include a written explanation along with a graphic display that shows how their results compared to the class as a whole. Instructors will also have access to this graphic representation of results to promote classroom discussion.

- **NEW! VIDEO LIBRARY –** Robust video library with over 100 new book-specific videos that include easy-to-assign assessments, the ability for instructors to add YouTube or other sources, the ability for students to upload video submissions, and the ability for polling and teamwork.

- **Decision-making simulations – NEW and improved feedback for students.** Place your students in the role of a key decision-maker! Simulations branch based on the decisions students make, providing a variation of scenario paths. Upon completion students receive a grade, as well as a detailed report of the choices and the associated consequences of those decisions.

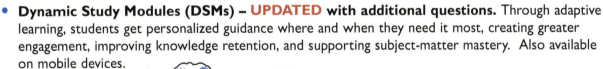

Decision Making

- **Video exercises – UPDATED with new exercises.** Engaging videos that bring business concepts to life and explore business topics related to the theory students are learning in class. Quizzes then assess students' comprehension of the concepts covered in each video.

- **Learning Catalytics –** A "bring your own device" student engagement, assessment, and classroom intelligence system helps instructors analyze students' critical-thinking skills during lecture.

- **Dynamic Study Modules (DSMs) – UPDATED with additional questions.** Through adaptive learning, students get personalized guidance where and when they need it most, creating greater engagement, improving knowledge retention, and supporting subject-matter mastery. Also available on mobile devices.

Critical Thinking

- **Writing Space – UPDATED with new commenting tabs, new prompts, and a new tool for students called Pearson Writer.** A single location to develop and assess concept mastery and critical thinking, the Writing Space offers automatic graded, assisted graded, and create your own writing assignments, allowing you to exchange personalized feedback with students quickly and easily.

Writing Space can also check students' work for improper citation or plagiarism by comparing it against the world's most accurate text comparison database available from **Turnitin**.

http://www.pearsonmylabandmastering.com

PEARSON

Fundamentals of Management

TENTH EDITION

STEPHEN P. ROBBINS

San Diego State University

MARY COULTER

Missouri State University

DAVID A. DECENZO

Coastal Carolina University

PEARSON

Boston   Columbus   Indianapolis   New York   San Francisco   Amsterdam
Cape Town   Dubai   London   Madrid   Milan   Munich   Paris   Montreal   Toronto
Delhi   Mexico City   São Paulo   Sydney   Hong Kong   Seoul   Singapore   Taipei   Tokyo

Vice President, Business Publishing: Donna Battista
Editor-in-Chief: Stephanie Wall
Senior Acquisitions Editor: Kris Ellis-Levy
Editorial Assistant: Lauren Russell
Vice President, Product Marketing: Maggie Moylan
Director of Marketing, Digital Services and Products: Jeanette Koskinas
Executive Field Marketing Manager: Adam Goldstein
Field Marketing Manager: Lenny Ann Kucenski
Product Marketing Assistant: Jessica Quazza
Team Lead, Program Management: Ashley Santora
Program Manager: Sarah Holle
Team Lead, Project Management: Jeff Holcomb
Project Manager: Kelly Warsak
Senior Operations Specialist: Diane Peirano

Creative Director: Blair Brown
Art Director: Janet Slowik
Vice President, Director of Digital Strategy and Assessment: Paul Gentile
Manager of Learning Applications: Paul DeLuca
Digital Editor: Brian Surette
Director, Digital Studio: Sacha Laustsen
Digital Studio Manager: Diane Lombardo
Digital Studio Project Manager: Monique Lawrence
Digital Studio Project Manager: Alana Coles
Digital Studio Project Manager: Robin Lazrus
Full-Service Project Management, Composition, Interior Design, Cover Design: Integra
Printer/Binder: LSC Communications

Library of Congress Cataloging-in-Publication Data

Robbins, Stephen P.
  Fundamentals of management/Stephen P. Robbins, Mary Coulter, David A. Decenzo.—10 Edition.
    pages cm
  Revised edition of Fundamentals of management, 2015.
  Includes bibliographical references and index.
  ISBN 978-0-13-423747-3
  1. Management. I. Coulter, Mary K. II. DeCenzo, David A. III. Title.
  HD31.R5643 2017
  658—dc23
                                                                          2015035514

10 2020

ISBN 10:   0-13-423747-1
ISBN 13: 978-0-13-423747-3

To my wife, Laura

Steve

....

To Brooklynn and Blake... with much love, Grandma.

Mary

....

To my family who stands by me through thick and thin;
whose unwavering support is the best gift anyone could receive.
Thanks for all you do to support me.

Dave

Brief Contents

Contents

Content highlighted in green indicates that it is presented via a visual spread.

Career Module: Building Your Career 232

Chapter 8   Managing Change and Innovation 236

Part 4   Leading 264

Chapter 9   Foundations of Individual Behavior 264

Preface

Welcome to the Tenth Edition of *Fundamentals of Management!* Although much has changed in the world since *FOM* was first published over twenty years ago, we haven't changed our commitment to providing you with the most engaging and up-to-date introduction to management paperback on the market. And how do we do this? By covering the essential concepts of management; providing a sound foundation for understanding the key issues; offering a strong, practical focus, including the latest research on what works for managers and what doesn't; and doing these with a writing style that you and your students will find interesting and straightforward.

This edition continues our exciting design. We love the way it looks and the way management concepts are presented! And we hope you do, too! It's a self-contained learning package. In addition to the end-of-chapter summaries and review questions, you can choose from the chapter self-assessments, skills modules, hands-on manager's inbox exercises, and case applications. In addition, the text is supported by the most comprehensive Web site and supplement package, although your students will find the essential elements they need to understand and apply management concepts within the text itself. You have the choice about how best to use the materials: text only, online only, or text and online. It's your decision!

What Key Changes Have We Made in the Tenth Edition?

You might think that there wouldn't be much new information to put in a book…especially a Tenth Edition! But that's the great thing about a book that discusses managers and management! It's always easy to find new material just by paying attention to what's happening in the news! New issues and ideas are always confronting managers and we've made sure to cover hot topics such as holacracy, the sharing economy, gamification, data analytics/big data, BYOD (bring your own device), and wearable technology, to name a few. In addition to new topics, we've done some other BIG things!

Book-Specific Videos

Today's students have "grown up" in a visual-based learning environment. They're comfortable with and enjoy video clips, and even expect them as part of their learning. That's why we created a series of videos for this tenth edition.

Our *Bust This Myth* videos reinforce and expand upon the chapter-opening Management Myth and Debunking the Myth. We debuted the "Myth" openers in the previous edition and have had positive feedback from them. This was…and *is*…a unique feature among management texts and was created as an answer to one of the most vexing problems that instructors face: unmotivated students who think there is nothing for them to learn in this course. Now, we've taken it a step further by creating fun videos that highlight the myths and why they are just that…a myth…and then explaining why.

Sustainability Emphasized

Sustainability is an important topic and it's critical for our students…our future business leaders…to be familiar with it. So we added an icon ♻ to help you and your students recognize how pervasive sustainability is. Throughout the book, you'll find this sustainability icon used wherever chapter discussion, a photo example, or an end-of-chapter exercise covers an aspect of sustainability. You yourself may be surprised at how much sustainability permeates what we're teaching in management.

MyManagementLab® Suggested Activities

The final change in this edition we want you know about is that we've fully integrated Pearson's MyManagementLab into the text. The new features are outlined below. Making assessment activities available online for students to complete before coming to class will allow you, the professor, more discussion time during class to review areas students are having difficulty comprehending.

WATCH IT Recommends a video clip that can be assigned to students for outside classroom viewing or that can be watched in the classroom. The video corresponds to the chapter material and is accompanied by multiple-choice questions that reinforce students' comprehension of chapter content.

TRY IT Recommends a mini simulation that can be assigned to students as an outside activity or be done in the classroom. As students watch the simulation, they will be asked to make choices based on the scenario presented in the simulation. At the end of the simulation, the student will receive immediate feedback based on the answers they gave. These simulations reinforce chapter concepts and students' comprehension of those concepts.

TALK ABOUT IT Students can be assigned these broad-based, critical-thinking discussion questions that will challenge them to assimilate information that they've read in the chapter.

WRITE IT: ASSISTED GRADED WRITING QUESTIONS These are short essay questions that students can complete as an assignment and submit to the professor for grading.

PERSONAL INVENTORY ASSESSMENTS (PIA) Students learn better when they can connect what they're learning to their personal experience. PIA (Personal Inventory Assessments) is a collection of online exercises designed to promote self-reflection and student engagement, enhancing their ability to connect with concepts taught in principles of management, organizational behavior, and human resource management classes. Assessments are assignable by instructors who can then track students' completions. Student results include a written explanation along with a graphic display that shows how their results compare to the class as a whole. Instructors will also have access to this graphic representation of results to promote classroom discussion.

Continued and Improved Features

The exciting and innovative chapter openers—a common Management Myth and how this myth is just that…a myth—have been updated and we've replaced a few. We've found that students often think that they already know a lot about management…after all, it's just common sense, right? But management isn't just common sense! When it comes to managing, much of what passes for common sense is just plain wrong…a myth! So we kept and improved these chapter openers! We think you'll like the student discussion these "myths" and "debunking" generate! And be sure to use the *Bust This Myth* videos in class or outside of class.

We also kept the three (yes, you read that right, THREE!) Case Applications, many of which are new or updated. These Case Applications are a great way to tell a current story about managers, management, and organizations *and* to involve students in assessing a situation and answering questions about "how" and "why" and "what would you do." These Case Applications cover the gamut from Google and Target to Zara and Keurig.

Also, we retained our complete, self-contained section on developing management skills in each chapter and tried to make them more practical. It's one thing to *know* something. It's another to be able to *use* that knowledge. The skill-building exercises included at the end of each chapter help you apply and use management concepts. We chose these 18 skills (some chapters have more than one) because of their relevance to developing management competence and their linkage to one or more of the topic areas in this book.

Finally, we kept our one section in each chapter that has a contemporary and visually appealing look. The design of this selected material helps reinforce key topics and ideas and makes it easy for students to read and to know what's important from that particular chapter section. Also, because today's students are accustomed to visually rich environments, we've kept additional visual presentations of material throughout the chapters to help engage students with the material.

In addition to all these major changes, here is a chapter-by-chapter list of the topic additions and changes in the Tenth Edition:

Chapter 1

- Statistics tied to chapter material
- Added author recommended MyManagementLab Assignments
- New PIA Assessment titled Using Influence Strategies
- Revised Management Skill Builder to make it more applications-oriented
- New Case Application—Zappos "holacracy"

Chapter 2

- New Management Myth
- New statistics on economy
- New discussion on sharing economy
- New discussion on Internet of Things
- Expanded discussion on Gen Z
- New ethics dilemma
- Revised Content for Learning Objective 2-3
- Added author recommended MyManagementLab Assignments
- New PIA Assessment titled Company Culture Assessment
- Revised Management Skill Builder to make it more applications-oriented.
- New Case Application—Target Corp.

Chapter 3

- Updated Management Myth opener
- Updated statistics
- New Technology and the Manager's Job box on "The Ethics of Data Analysis"
- Added author recommended MyManagementLab Assignments
- New PIA Assessment titled Ethical Leadership Assessment
- Revised Management Skill Builder to make it more applications-oriented.
- New Case Application—Nomura Holdings and Lehman
- New Case Application—Keurig K-cups (Sustainability)

Chapter 4

- New Management Myth
- New statistic
- Added author recommended MyManagementLab Assignments
- New Ethics box
- New PIA Assessment titled Problem Solving, Creativity, and Innovation
- Revised Management Skill Builder to make it more applications-oriented.
- New Case Application—UPS

Chapter 5

- New examples in strategic management introductory section
- Updated other examples, as needed
- Added author recommended MyManagementLab Assignments
- New Ethics box
- New PIA Assessment titled Tolerance of Ambiguity Scale
- New Case Application—Live**Strong** Foundation
- New Case Application—Warby Parker

Chapter 6

- Updated Management Myth opener
- Added author recommended MyManagementLab Assignments
- New PIA Assessment titled Gaining Power and Influence
- New Case Application—NASA

Chapter 7

- Revised chapter-opening Debunked Management Myth.
- Updated statistics/information throughout chapter.
- Added author recommended MyManagementLab Assignments
- New Ethics box
- New Skill Builder—Providing Good Feedback

- New PIA Assessment titled Work Performance Assessment
- New Case Application—Talent Spotting at tech firms

Chapter 8

- Revised chapter-opening Debunked Management Myth.
- Added author recommended MyManagementLab Assignments
- New Technology and the Manager's Job box
- New PIA Assessment titled Controlling Workplace Stress
- Updated cases
- New Case Application—Making Over Avon

Chapter 9

- New Management Myth
- New ethics box
- New Technology and the Manager's Job box
- Added author recommended MyManagementLab Assignments
- New PIA Assessment titled Understanding Employee Emotions
- Update cases
- New Case Application—Getting Emotional at Google

Chapter 10

- Updated Management Myth opener
- Updated technology box
- Added author recommended MyManagementLab Assignments
- New Skill Builder—Developing Your Coaching Skills
- New PIA Assessment titled Diagnosing the Need for Team Building
- New Case Application—Rx: Teamwork
- New Case Application—The Cardinal Way

Chapter 11

- Updated Management Myth opener
- New ethics box
- New technology box
- Introduced concept of gamification
- Added author recommended MyManagementLab Assignments

- New PIA Assessment titled Work Motivation Indicator
- New Case Application—One for the Money

Chapter 12

- Tightened up Management Myth/Debunked
- Added new statistics
- Added author recommended MyManagementLab Assignments
- New PIA Assessment titled Leadership Style Indicator
- New Case Application—Developing Gen Y Leaders

Chapter 13

- Added new statistics
- Updated Technology box
- New ethics box
- Added author recommended MyManagementLab Assignments
- New PIA Assessment titled Communication Styles
- New Case Application—Delivering Bad News
- Updated other two Case Applications

Chapter 14

- New Management Myth/Debunked
- New ethics box
- Added new statistics
- Added author recommended MyManagementLab Assignments
- New PIA Assessment titled Workplace Discipline Indicator
- New Case Application—If You Can't Say Something Nice, Don't Say Anything At All
- New Case Application—Too Relaxed
- Updated other Case Application

Chapter 15

- Tightened up Management Myth/Debunked.
- Added author recommended MyManagementLab Assignments
- New Management Skill—Being A Good Conflict Manager
- New PIA Assessment titled Strategies for Handling Conflict
- Updated Case Applications

Instructor Resources

At the Instructor Resource Center, www.pearsonhighered.com/irc, instructors can easily register to gain access to a variety of instructor resources available with this text in downloadable format. If assistance is needed, our dedicated technical support team is ready to help with the media supplements that accompany this text. Visit http://247.pearsoned.com for answers to frequently asked questions and toll-free user support phone numbers.

The following supplements are available with this text:

- **Instructor's Resource Manual**
- **Test Bank**
- **TestGen® Computerized Test Bank**
- **PowerPoint Presentation**

Video Library

Videos illustrating the most important subject topics are available In MyManagementLab. Contact your local Pearson representative to request access.

AACSB Learning Standards Tags in the Test Item File

Questions that test skills relevant to AACSB standards are tagged with the appropriate standard. For example, a question testing the moral issues associated with externalities would receive the ethical understanding and reasoning abilities tag from the AACSB categories. In addition, the tagged questions may help to identify potential applications of these skills. This, in turn, may suggest enrichment activities or other educational experiences to help students achieve these goals.

Acknowledgments

Writing and publishing a textbook requires the talents of a number of people whose names never appear on the cover. We'd like to recognize and thank a phenomenal team of talented people who provided their skills and abilities in making this book a reality. This team includes Kris Ellis-Levy, our senior acquisitions editor; Sarah Holle, our program manager; Kelly Warsak, our project manager; Lenny Ann Kucenski, our senior marketing manager; Stephanie Wall, our editor in chief; Nancy Moudry, our highly talented and gifted photo researcher; Lauren Cook, our talented digital media whiz who co-created the "Bust The Myth" videos, and Allison Campbell, Associate Managing Editor, Integra-Chicago.

We also want to thank our reviewers—past and present—for the insights they have provided us:

David Adams, *Manhattanville College*

Lorraine P. Anderson, *Marshall University*

Maria Aria, *Camden Community College*

Marcia Marie Bear, *University of Tampa*

Barbara Ann Boyington, *Brookdale Community College*

Reginald Bruce, *University of Louisville*

Jon Bryan, *Bridgewater State University*

Elena Capella, *University of San Francisco*

James Carlson, *Manatee Community College*

Pam Carstens, *Coe College*

Casey Cegielski, *Auburn University*

Michael Cicero, *Highline Community College*

Evelyn Delanee, *Daytona Beach Community College*

Kathleen DeNisco, *Erie Community College, South Campus*

Jack Dilbeck, *Ivy Tech State College*

Fred J. Dorn, *University of Mississippi*

Michael Drafke, *College of DuPage*

Myra Ellen Edelstein, *Salve Regina University*

Deborah Gilliard, *Metropolitan State College, Denver*

Robert Girling, *Sonoma State University*

Patricia Green, *Nassau Community College*

Gary Greene, *Manatee Community College, Venice Campus*

Kenneth Gross, *The University of Oklahoma*

Jamey Halleck, *Marshall University*

Aaron Hines, *SUNY New Paltz*

Robyn Hulsart, *Austin Peavy State University*

Todd E. Jamison, *Chadron State College*

Edward A. Johnson, *University of North Florida*

Kayvan Miri Lavassani, *North Carolina Central*

Kim Lukaszewski, *SUNY New Paltz*

Brian Maruffi, *Fordham University*

Mantha Vlahos Mehallis, *Florida Atlantic University*

Christine Miller, *Tennessee Technological University*

Diane Minger, *Cedar Valley College*

Kimberly K. Montney, *Kellogg Community College*

James H. Moore, *Arizona State University*

Dr. Clara Munson, *Albertus Magnus College*

Jane Murtaugh, *College of DuPage*

Francine Newth, *Providence College*

Leroy Plumlee, *Western Washington University*

Pollis Robertson, *Kellogg Community College*

Cynthia Ruszkowski, *Illinois State University*

Thomas J. Shaughnessy, *Illinois Central College*

Andrea Smith-Hunter, *Siena College*

Martha Spears, *Winthrop University*
Jeff Stauffer, *Ventura College*
Kenneth R. Tillery, *Middle Tennessee State University*
Robert Trumble, *Virginia Commonwealth University*
Philip Varca, *University of Wyoming*

Margaret Viets, *University of Vermont*
Brad Ward, *Kellogg Community College*
Lucia Worthington, *University of Maryland University College*
Seokhwa Yun, *Montclair State University*

Thank You!

Steve, Dave, and I would like to thank you for considering and choosing our book for your management course. All of us have several years of teaching under our belt, and we know how challenging yet rewarding it can be. Our goal is to provide you with the best resources available to help you excel in the classroom!

About the Authors

STEPHEN P. ROBBINS received his Ph.D. from the University of Arizona. He previously worked for the Shell Oil Company and Reynolds Metals Company and has taught at the University of Nebraska at Omaha, Concordia University in Montreal, the University of Baltimore, Southern Illinois University at Edwardsville, and San Diego State University. He is currently professor emeritus in management at San Diego State.

Dr. Robbins's research interests have focused on conflict, power, and politics in organizations, behavioral decision making, and the development of effective interpersonal skills. His articles on these and other topics have appeared in such journals as *Business Horizons*, the *California Management Review, Business and Economic Perspectives, International Management, Management Review, Canadian Personnel and Industrial Relations*, and *The Journal of Management Education*.

Dr. Robbins is the world's best-selling textbook author in the areas of management and organizational behavior. His books have sold more than 7 million copies and have been translated into 20 languages. His books are currently used at more than 1,500 U.S. colleges and universities, as well as hundreds of schools throughout Canada, Latin America, Australia, New Zealand, Asia, and Europe.

Dr. Robbins also participates in masters track competition. Since turning 50 in 1993, he's won 23 national championships and 14 world titles. He was inducted into the U.S. Masters Track & Field Hall of Fame in 2005.

MARY COULTER (Ph.D., University of Arkansas) held different jobs including high school teacher, legal assistant, and city government program planner before completing her graduate work. She has taught at Drury University, the University of Arkansas, Trinity University, and Missouri State University. She is currently professor emeritus of management at Missouri State University. In addition to *Fundamentals of Management,* Dr. Coulter has published other books with Pearson including *Management* (with Stephen P. Robbins), *Strategic Management in Action,* and *Entrepreneurship in Action.*

When she's not busy writing, Dr. Coulter enjoys puttering around in her flower gardens, trying new recipes, reading all different types of books, and enjoying many different activities with husband Ron, daughters and sons-in-law Sarah and James, and Katie and Matt, and most especially with her two grandkids, Brooklynn and Blake, who are the delights of her life!

DAVID A. DECENZO (Ph.D., West Virginia University) is president of Coastal Carolina University in Conway, South Carolina. He has been at Coastal since 2002 when he took over leadership of the E. Craig Wall Sr. College of Business. As president, Dr. DeCenzo has implemented a comprehensive strategic planning process, ensured fiscal accountability through policy and practice, and promoted assessment and transparency throughout the University. Before joining the Coastal faculty in 2002, he served as director of partnership development in the College of Business and Economics at Towson University in Maryland. He is an experienced industry consultant, corporate trainer, public speaker, and board member. Dr. DeCenzo is the author of numerous textbooks that are used widely at colleges and universities throughout the United States and the world. Dr. DeCenzo and his wife, Terri, have four children: Mark, Meredith, Gabriella, and Natalie, and reside in Pawleys Island, South Carolina.

Managers and Management

Management Myth **Myth**

Only those who want to be managers need to take a course in management.

Anyone who works
in an organization
—not just managers—
can gain insight into how
organizations work and the
behaviors of their boss and
coworkers by taking a course
in management.

ASSUME

for a moment that it's your first day in an introductory physics class. Your instructor asks you to take out a piece of paper and "describe Newton's second law of motion." How would you react? I expect most students would respond with something like "How would I know? That's why I'm taking this course!"

Now let's change the situation to the first day in an introductory management class. Your instructor asks you to write an answer to the question: "What traits does one need to be an effective leader?" When we've done this on the first day, we find that students always have an answer. Everyone seems to think they know what makes a good leader.

This example illustrates a popular myth about the study of management: It's just common sense. Well, we can assure you... it's not! When it comes to managing, much of what passes for common sense is just plain wrong. You might be surprised to know that the *academic* study of management is filled with insights, based on extensive research, which often run counter to what seems to be common sense. That's why we decided to tackle head-on this common-sense perception by opening each chapter with a particular "management myth" and then "debunking" this myth by explaining how it *is* just a common-sense myth.

Take a minute to re-look at this chapter's "management myth" and "management myth debunked." This "debunked" myth often surprises students majoring in subjects like accounting, finance, statistics, information technology, or advertising. Since they don't expect to be managers, they see spending a semester studying management as a waste of time and irrelevant to their career goals. Later in this chapter, we'll explain why the study of management is valuable to *every* student, no matter what you're majoring in or whether you are a manager or aspire to be a manager. •

Learning Outcomes

1-1 Tell who managers are and where they work. p. 5

1-2 Define management. p. 7

1-3 Describe what managers do. p. 9

1-4 Explain why it's important to study management. p. 14

1-5 Describe the factors that are reshaping and redefining management. p. 15

Although we'd like to think that all managers are good at what they do, you may have discovered through jobs you've had that managers can be good at what they do or maybe not so good, or even good one day and not so good the next! One thing you need to understand is that all managers—good or not so good—have important jobs to do. And this book is about the work managers do. In this chapter, we introduce you to managers and management: who they are, where they work, what management is, what they do, and why you should spend your time studying management. Finally, we'll wrap up the chapter by looking at some key factors reshaping and redefining organizations *and* the way managers manage.

Who Are Managers and Where Do They Work?

1-1 Tell who managers are and where they work.

There's no pattern or prototype or standard criteria as to who can be a manager. Managers today can be under age 18 or over age 80. They may be women as well as men, and they can be found in all industries and in all countries. They manage entrepreneurial businesses, large corporations, government agencies, hospitals, museums, schools, and not-for-profit enterprises. Some hold top-level management jobs while others are supervisors or team leaders. However, all managers share one common element: They work in an organizational setting. An **organization** is a deliberate arrangement of people brought together to accomplish some specific purpose. For instance, your college or university is an organization, as are the United Way, your neighborhood convenience store, the New Orleans Saints football team, fraternities and sororities, the Cleveland Clinic, and global companies such as Nestlé, Lego, and Samsung. These and all organizations share three common characteristics. (See Exhibit 1–1.)

organization
A systematic arrangement of people brought together to accomplish some specific purpose

What Three Characteristics Do All Organizations Share?

The *first* characteristic of an organization is that it has a distinct purpose, which is typically expressed as a goal or set of goals. For example, Bob Iger, Walt Disney Company's president and CEO, has said his company's goal is to create amazing family entertainment and to provide customers extraordinary experiences, which will lead to increasing shareholder value.[1] The *second* characteristic is that people in an organization work to achieve those goals. How? By making decisions and engaging in work activities to make the desired goal(s) a reality. For instance, at Disney, many employees work to create the content and experiences that are so important to the company's businesses. Others provide supporting services or interact with guests (customers) directly. Finally, the *third* characteristic is that an organization is structured in some way that defines and limits the behavior of its members. Disney, like most large organizations, has a fairly complex structure with different businesses, departments, and functional areas. Within that structure, rules, regulations, and policies might guide what people can or cannot do; some members will supervise other members; work teams might be formed or disbanded; or job descriptions might be created or changed so organizational members know what they're supposed to do. That structure is the setting within which managers manage.

Exhibit 1–1 Three Characteristics of Organizations

Goals | People | Structure

Exhibit 1–2 Management Levels

Top Managers

Middle Managers

First-Line Managers

Team Leaders

nonmanagerial employees
People who work directly on a job or task and have no responsibility for overseeing the work of others

managers
Individuals in an organization who direct the activities of others

top managers
Individuals who are responsible for making decisions about the direction of the organization and establishing policies that affect all organizational members

middle managers
Individuals who are typically responsible for translating goals set by top managers into specific details that lower-level managers will see get done

How Are Managers Different from Nonmanagerial Employees?

Although managers work in organizations, not everyone who works in an organization is a manager. For simplicity's sake, we'll divide organizational members into two categories: nonmanagerial employees and managers. **Nonmanagerial employees** are people who work directly on a job or task and have no responsibility for overseeing the work of others. The employees who ring up your sale at Home Depot, take your order at the Starbucks drive-through, or process your class registration forms are all nonmanagerial employees. These nonmanagerial employees may be called associates, team members, contributors, or even employee partners. **Managers**, on the other hand, are individuals in an organization who direct and oversee the activities of other people in the organization so organizational goals can be accomplished. A manager's job isn't about *personal* achievement—it's about helping *others* do their work. That may mean coordinating the work of a departmental group, leading an entire organization, or supervising a single person. It could involve coordinating the work activities of a team with people from different departments or even people outside the organization, such as temporary employees or individuals who work for the organization's suppliers. This distinction doesn't mean, however, that managers don't ever work directly on tasks. Some managers do have work duties not directly related to overseeing the activities of others. For example, an insurance claims supervisor might process claims in addition to coordinating the work activities of other claims employees.

Ajiti Banga is an associate product manager at Pocket Gems, a firm in San Francisco that makes and publishes mobile games such as Pet Tap Hotel and Paradise Cove. Collaborating with multiple teams of engineers and designers, she manages games from initial concept through development to product launch.

What Titles Do Managers Have?

Although they can have a variety of titles, identifying exactly who the managers are in an organization shouldn't be difficult. In a broad sense, managers can be classified as top, middle, first-line, or team leaders. (See Exhibit 1–2.) **Top managers** are those at or near the top of an organization. They're usually responsible for making decisions about the direction of the organization and defining policies and values that affect all organizational members. Top managers typically have titles such as vice president, president, chancellor, managing director, chief operating officer, chief executive officer, or chairperson of the board. **Middle managers** are those managers found between the lowest and top levels of the organization. These individuals often manage other managers and maybe some nonmanagerial employees and are typically responsible for translating the goals set by top managers

◄◄◄ From the Past to the Present ▶▶▶

The terms *management* and *manager* are actually centuries old.[2] One source says that the word *manager* originated in 1588 to describe one who manages. The specific use of the word as a person who oversees a business or public organization is believed to have originated in the early part of the 18th century. However, used in the way we're defining it in terms of overseeing and directing organizational members, *management* and *manager* are more appropriate to the early-twentieth-century time period. The word *management* was first popularized by Frederick Winslow Taylor. Taylor is a "biggie" in management history, so let's look at his contributions to how management is practiced today.

- In 1911, Taylor's book *Principles of Scientific Management* took the business world by storm—his ideas spread in the United States and to other countries and inspired others.

- Why? His theory of **scientific management**: the use of scientific methods to define the *"one best way"* for a job to be done.

- Taylor, a mechanical engineer in Pennsylvania steel companies, observed workers and was continually shocked by how inefficient they were:

  — Employees used vastly different techniques to do the same job and often "took it easy" on the job.

  — Few, if any, work standards existed.

  — Workers were placed in jobs with little or no concern for matching their abilities and aptitudes with the tasks they were required to do.

  - The result was worker output only about *one-third* of what was possible.

- Taylor's remedy? Apply scientific management to these manual shop-floor jobs.

  - The result was phenomenal increases in worker output and efficiency—in the range of *200 percent or more!*

  - Because of his work, Taylor is known as the "father" of scientific management.

Want to try your hand at using scientific management principles to be more efficient? Choose a task you do regularly (think…laundry, grocery shopping, studying for exams, cooking dinner, etc.). Analyze that task by writing down the steps involved in completing it. What activities could be combined or eliminated? Find the "one best way" to do this task. See if you can become more efficient—keeping in mind that changing habits isn't easy to do.

If your professor has assigned this, go to the Assignments section of **mymanagementlab.com** *to complete these discussion questions.*

⭐ **Talk About It 1:** What would a "Taylor" workplace be like?

⭐ **Talk About It 2:** How do Taylor's views contribute to how management is practiced today?

> Management: Finding one best way to do a job?

---

into specific details that lower-level managers will see get done. Middle managers may have such titles as department or agency head, project leader, unit chief, district manager, division manager, or store manager. **First-line managers** are those individuals responsible for directing the day-to-day activities of nonmanagerial employees. First-line managers are often called supervisors, shift managers, office managers, department managers, or unit coordinators. We want to point out a special type of manager that has become more common as organizations use employee work teams. These managers, or **team leaders**, are individuals who are responsible for managing and facilitating the activities of a work team.

What Is Management?

1-2 Define management.

Simply speaking, management is what managers do. But that simple statement doesn't tell us much. A better explanation is that **management** is the process of getting things done, effectively and efficiently, with and through other people. We need to look closer at some key words in this definition.

scientific management
The use of scientific methods to define the "one best way" for a job to be done

first-line managers
Supervisors responsible for directing the day-to-day activities of nonmanagerial employees

team leaders
Individuals who are responsible for managing and facilitating the activities of a work team

management
The process of getting things done, effectively and efficiently, through and with other people

efficiency
Doing things right, or getting the most output from the least amount of inputs

effectiveness
Doing the right things, or completing activities so that organizational goals are attained

A *process* refers to a set of ongoing and interrelated activities. In our definition of management, it refers to the primary activities or functions that managers perform—functions that we'll discuss in more detail in the next section.

Talk about new ways to be efficient!

ROWE—or results-only work environment—was a radical experiment tried at Best Buy headquarters. In this flexible work program, employees were judged only on tasks completed or results, not on how many hours they spent at work. Employees couldn't say whether they worked fewer hours because they stopped counting, BUT **employee productivity jumped 41 percent!**[3]

Efficiency and effectiveness have to do with the work being done and how it's being done. **Efficiency** means doing a task correctly ("doing things right") and getting the most output from the least amount of inputs. Because managers deal with scarce inputs—including resources such as people, money, and equipment—they're concerned with the efficient use of those resources. Managers want to minimize resource usage and costs.

It's not enough, however, just to be efficient. Managers are also concerned with completing important activities. In management terms, we call this **effectiveness**. Effectiveness means "doing the right things" by doing those work tasks that help the organization reach its goals. Whereas efficiency is concerned with the *means* of getting things done, effectiveness is concerned with the *ends*, or attainment of organizational goals. (See Exhibit 1–3.)

A quick overview of managers and **efficiency & effectiveness**

- The concepts are different, but interrelated.
- It's easier to be effective if you ignore efficiency.
- Poor managers often allow
  — both inefficiency and ineffectiveness OR effectiveness achieved without regard for efficiency.
- Good managers are concerned with
  — both attaining goals (effectiveness) and doing so as efficiently as possible.

✪ Write It!

If your professor has assigned this, go to the Assignments section of **mymanagementlab.com** to complete *MGMT 1: Management Skills*.

Exhibit 1–3 Efficiency and Effectiveness

3 Ways to Look at What Managers Do

1-3 Describe what managers do.

NO TWO ORGANIZATIONS ARE ALIKE, and neither are managers' jobs. But their jobs do share some common elements, as you'll see in these three approaches to describing what managers do.

1

4 Functions Approach

- Says that managers perform certain activities, tasks, or functions as they direct and oversee others' work.

- WHAT Fayol said managers do: First person to identify five common activities managers engage in: plan, organize, command, coordinate, and control (POCCC).[4]

- Today, the management functions have been condensed to four: **planning**, **organizing**, **leading**, and **controlling**.

- See Exhibit 1–4 for what managers do when they P-O-L-C.

Exhibit 1–4 Four Management Functions

PLANNING Includes defining goals, establishing strategy, and developing plans to coordinate activities

ORGANIZING Includes determining what tasks are to be done, who is to do them, how the tasks are to be grouped, who reports to whom, and who will make decisions

LEADING Includes motivating employees, directing the activities of others, selecting the most effective communication channel, and resolving conflicts

CONTROLLING Includes monitoring performance, comparing it with goals, and correcting any significant deviations

Achieving the organization's stated purpose

⭐ **Try It!**

If your professor has assigned this, go to the Assignments section of **mymanagementlab.com** to complete the **Simulation: *What Is Management?***

THEN | **P O C C C**

plan · organize · command · coordinate · control

NOW | **P O L C**

planning · organizing · leading · controlling

Jacques Boyer/Roger-Violiet/The Image Works

Who: Henri Fayol—an engineer/executive at a large French mining company

When: Early 1900s

How: Personal experience and observations.

---

planning
Defining goals, establishing strategy, and developing plans to coordinate activities

organizing
Determining what needs to be done, how it will be done, and who is to do it

leading
Directing and coordinating the work activities of an organization's people

controlling
Monitoring activities to ensure that they are accomplished as planned

Management Roles Approach

- Says that managers engage in certain "roles" as they manage others.

- WHAT Mintzberg said managers do: He identified and defined **managerial roles**—specific categories of managerial actions or behaviors expected of a manager. (Not sure what a "role" is? Think of the different roles you play—such as student, employee, volunteer, bowling team member, boyfriend/girlfriend, sibling, and so forth—and the different things you're expected to do in those roles.)

- Exhibit 1–5 shows Mintzberg's ten separate, but interrelated roles.

Who: Henry Mintzberg
When: late 1960s
How: Empirical study of five chief executives at work.[5]

32 Muschi/Getty Images

Exhibit 1–5 Mintzberg's Managerial Roles

Source: Based on Mintzberg, Henry, *The Nature of Managerial Work*, 1st edition, © 1973.

Which Approach—Functions or Roles—Is Better at Defining What Managers Do?

— Both approaches appear to do a good job of describing what managers do.

— However, the *functions* approach stands out! It continues to be popular due to its clarity and simplicity.[6] But, don't disregard the roles approach; it offers another way to understand and appreciate what managers do.

---

managerial roles
Specific categories of managerial behavior; often grouped around interpersonal relationships, information transfer, and decision making

interpersonal roles
Involving people (subordinates and persons outside the organization) and other duties that are ceremonial and symbolic in nature

decisional roles
Entailing making decisions or choices

informational roles
Involving collecting, receiving, and disseminating information

3

Skills and Competencies

Source: Simon/Fotolia

- Says that managers need certain skills and competencies as they manage others.

- WHAT these researchers say managers do: Identified four general management skills including:[7]

  — **CONCEPTUAL SKILLS:** Analyzing and diagnosing complex situations to see how things fit together and to facilitate making good decisions.

Analyze and diagnose

  — **INTERPERSONAL SKILLS:** Working well with other people both individually and in groups by communicating, motivating, mentoring, delegating, etc.

Working well with others

  — **TECHNICAL SKILLS:** Job-specific knowledge, expertise, and techniques needed to perform work tasks. (For *top-level managers*—knowledge of the industry and a general understanding of the organization's processes and products; For *middle- and lower-level managers*—specialized knowledge required in the areas where they work—finance, human resources, marketing, computer systems, manufacturing, information technology.)

Possessing expert job knowledge

  — **POLITICAL SKILLS:** Building a power base and establishing the right connections to get needed resources for their groups. *Want to learn more?* Assess and develop *your* political skill by completing the PIA and the Management Skill Builder found at the end of the chapter on p. 20.

Political adeptness

- Other important managerial competencies:[8] decision making, team building, decisiveness, assertiveness, politeness, personal responsibility, trustworthiness, loyalty, professionalism, tolerance, adaptability, creative thinking, resilience, listening, self-development.

> **Who:** Robert Katz and others
> **When:** 1970s to present
> **How:** Studies by various researchers

Is the Manager's Job Universal?

So far, we've discussed the manager's job as if it were a generic activity. If management is truly a generic discipline, then what a manager does should be the same whether he or she is a top-level executive or a first-line supervisor; in a business firm or a government agency; in a large corporation or a small business; or located in Paris, Texas, or Paris, France. Is that the case? Let's take a closer look.

Is a manager **a manager no matter** where or what he or she manages?

LEVEL IN THE ORGANIZATION. Although a supervisor of the Genius Bar in an Apple Store may not do exactly the same things that Apple's CEO Tim Cook does, it doesn't mean that their jobs are inherently different. The differences are of degree and emphasis but not of activity.

As managers move up in the organization, they do more planning and less direct overseeing of others. (See Exhibit 1–6.) All managers, regardless of level, make decisions. They plan, organize, lead, and control, but the amount of time they spend on each activity is not

conceptual skills
A manager's ability to analyze and diagnose complex situations

interpersonal skills
A manager's ability to work with, understand, mentor, and motivate others, both individually and in groups

technical skills
Job-specific knowledge and techniques needed to perform work tasks

political skills
A manager's ability to build a power base and establish the right connections

Exhibit 1–6 Management Activities by Organizational Level

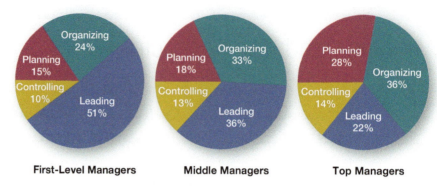

| First-Level Managers | Middle Managers | Top Managers |

Source: Based on T. A. Mahoney, T. H. Jerdee, and S. J. Carroll, "The Job(s) of Management," *Industrial Relations* 4, no. 2 (1965), p. 103.

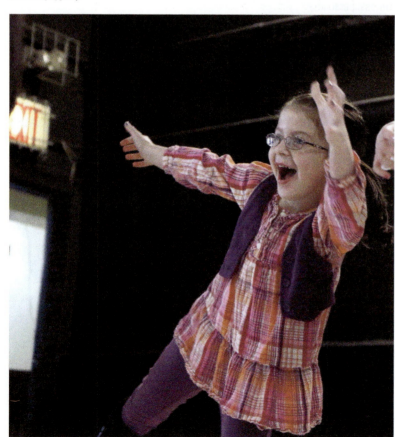

> **small business**
> An independent business having fewer than 500 employees that doesn't necessarily engage in any new or innovative practices and has relatively little impact on its industry

This first-grader participates in a 10-week circus arts program offered by Marquis Studios, a not-for-profit group that offers arts-in-education services to New York City public schools. Managed in much the same way as for-profit firms, Marquis provides programs that encourage students to explore visual arts, theater, music, dance, architecture, circus arts, and puppetry.

necessarily constant. In addition, "what" they plan, organize, lead, and control changes with the manager's level. For example, as we'll demonstrate in Chapter 6, top managers are concerned with designing the overall organization's structure, whereas lower-level managers focus on designing the jobs of individuals and work groups.

PROFIT VERSUS NOT-FOR-PROFIT. Does a manager who works for the U.S. Postal Service, the Memorial Sloan-Kettering Cancer Center, or the Red Cross do the same things that a manager at Amazon or Symantec does? That is, is the manager's job the same in both profit and not-for-profit organizations? The answer, for the most part, is yes. All managers make decisions, set goals, create workable organization structures, hire and motivate employees, secure legitimacy for their organization's existence, and develop internal political support in order to implement programs. Of course, the most important difference between the two is how performance is measured. Profit—the "bottom line"—is an unambiguous measure of a business organization's effectiveness. Not-for-profit organizations don't have such a universal measure, which makes performance measurement more difficult. But don't think this means that managers in those organizations can ignore finances. Even not-for-profit organizations need to make money to continue operating. However, in not-for-profit organizations, "making a profit" for the "owners" is not the primary focus.

SIZE OF ORGANIZATION. Would you expect the job of a manager in a local FedEx store that employs 12 people to be different from that of a manager who runs the FedEx global distribution center in Memphis? This question is best answered by looking at the jobs of managers in small businesses and comparing them with our previous discussion of managerial roles. First, however, let's define a small business.

No commonly agreed-upon definition of a small business is available because different criteria are used to define *small*. For example, an organization can be classified as a small business using such criteria as number of employees, annual sales, or total assets. For our purposes, we'll describe a **small business** as an independent business having fewer than 500 employees that doesn't necessarily engage in any new or innovative practices and has relatively little impact on its industry.[9] So, *is* the job of managing a small business different from that of managing a large one? Yes, some

Exhibit 1–7 Managerial Roles in Small and Large Businesses

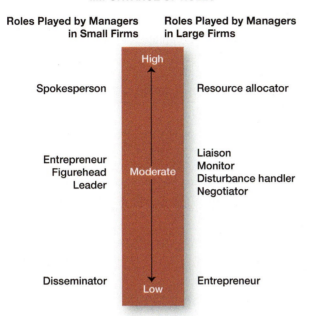

IMPORTANT OF ROLES

Roles Played by Managers in Small Firms		Roles Played by Managers in Large Firms
	High	
Spokesperson		Resource allocator
Entrepreneur Figurehead Leader	Moderate	Liaison Monitor Disturbance handler Negotiator
Disseminator	Low	Entrepreneur

Source: Based on J. G. P. Paolillo, "The Manager's Self-Assessments of Managerial Roles: Small vs. Large Firms," *American Journal of Small Business* (January–March 1984), pp. 61–62.

differences appear to exist. As Exhibit 1–7 shows, the small business manager's most important role is that of spokesperson. He or she spends a great deal of time performing outwardly directed actions such as meeting with customers, arranging financing with bankers, searching for new opportunities, and stimulating change. In contrast, the most important concerns of a manager in a large organization are directed internally—deciding which organizational units get what available resources and how much of them. Accordingly, the entrepreneurial role—looking for business opportunities and planning activities for performance improvement—appears to be least important to managers in large firms, especially among first-level and middle managers.

Compared with a manager in a large organization, a small business manager is more likely to be a generalist. His or her job will combine the activities of a large corporation's chief executive with many of the day-to-day activities undertaken by a first-line supervisor. Moreover, the structure and formality that characterize a manager's job in a large organization tend to give way to informality in small firms. Planning is less likely to be a carefully orchestrated ritual. The organization's design will be less complex and structured, and control in the small business will rely more on direct observation than on sophisticated, computerized monitoring systems. Again, as with organizational level, we see differences in degree and emphasis but not in the activities that managers do. Managers in both small and large organizations perform essentially the same activities, but how they go about those activities and the proportion of time they spend on each are different. (You can find more information on managing small, entrepreneurial organizations in the Entrepreneurship Module at the end of the book.)

MANAGEMENT CONCEPTS AND NATIONAL BORDERS. The last generic issue concerns whether management concepts are transferable across national borders. If managerial concepts were completely generic, they would also apply universally in any country in the world, regardless of economic, social, political, or cultural differences. Studies that have compared managerial practices among countries have not generally supported the universality of management concepts. In Chapter 3, we'll examine some specific differences between countries and describe their effect on managing. At this point, it's important for you to understand that most of the concepts discussed in the rest of the book primarily apply to the United States, Canada, Great Britain, Australia, and other English-speaking countries. Managers likely will have to modify these concepts if they want to apply them in India, China, Chile, or other countries whose economic, political, social, or cultural environments differ from that of the so-called free-market democracies.

Why Study Management?

1-4 Explain why it's important to study management.

Good managers are important because:

- Organizations need their skills and abilities, especially in today's uncertain, complex, and chaotic environment.
- They're critical to getting things done.
- They play a crucial role in employee satisfaction and engagement.

A Question of Ethics

▶ **26%** of new managers feel they're unprepared to transition into management roles.

▶ **58%** of new managers don't receive any training to help them make the transition.

▶ **48%** of first-time managers fail in that transition.

Moving to a management position isn't easy, as these statistics indicate.[10]

If your professor has assigned this, go to the Assignments section of mymanagementlab.com to complete these discussion questions.

⭐ **Talk About It 3:** Does an organization have an ethical responsibility to assist its new managers in their new positions? Why or why not?

⭐ **Talk About It 4:** What could organizations do to make this transition easier?

Well…we're finally at the point where we're going to address the chapter-opening myth! You may still be wondering *why* you need to take a management class. Especially if you're majoring in accounting or marketing or information technology and may not see how studying management is going to help you in your career. Let's look at some reasons why you may want to understand more about management.

Eighty-two percent of Millennials surveyed by a staffing firm expressed an interest in being a manager.[11]

First, all of us have a vested interest in improving the way organizations are managed. Why? Because we interact with them every day of our lives and an understanding of management offers insights into many organizational aspects. When you renew your driver's license or get your car tags, are you frustrated that a seemingly simple task takes so long? Were you surprised when well-known businesses you thought would never fail went bankrupt or were you angry when entire industries had to rely on government bailout money to survive declining economic conditions? Are you annoyed when you use a drive-through and get ready to enjoy your food or drink and realize something is missing or that it's not what you ordered? Such problems are mostly the result of managers doing a poor job of managing.

Organizations that are well managed—such as Apple, Tata, Starbucks, Nike, Singapore Airlines, and Google—develop a loyal following and find ways to prosper even when the economy stinks. Poorly managed organizations may find themselves with a declining customer base and reduced revenues and may have to file for bankruptcy protection even in a strong economy. For instance, Gimbel's, W. T. Grant, Hollywood Video, Dave & Barry's, Circuit City, Eastern Airlines, and Enron were once thriving corporations. They employed tens of thousands of people and provided goods and services on a daily basis to hundreds of thousands of customers. You may not recognize some of these names because these companies no longer exist. Poor management did them in. You can begin to recognize poor management and know what good managers should be doing by studying management.

What can a great boss do?

- Inspire you professionally *and* personally
- Energize you and your coworkers to do things together that you couldn't do alone
- Provide you feedback on how you're doing
- Provide coaching and guidance with problems
- Change your life[12]

The *second* reason for studying management is the *reality that for most of you, once you graduate from college and begin your career, you will either manage or be managed.* For those who plan to be managers, an understanding of management forms the foundation on which to build your own management skills and abilities. For those of you who don't see yourself managing, you're still likely to have to work with managers. Also, assuming that you'll have to work for a living and recognizing that you're likely to work in an organization, you're likely to have some managerial responsibilities even if you're not a manager. Our experience tells us that you can gain a great deal of insight into the way your boss (and coworkers) behave and how organizations function by studying management. Our point is that you don't have to aspire to be a manager to gain valuable information from a course in management.

What Factors Are Reshaping and Redefining Management?

1-5 Describe the factors that are reshaping and redefining management.

Welcome to the **new world of management!**

Changing Workplaces + Changing Workforce

- Not surprisingly, every business is now a technology business. Technology is changing the way we work *and* play.
- As mobile and social technologies continue to proliferate, more organizations are using apps and mobile-enhanced Web sites for managing their workforces and for other organizational work.
- Distributed labor companies like Uber, TaskRabbit, Gigwalk, and IAmExec are changing the face of temporary work.
- About 58 percent of workers ages 60 and older are currently delaying retirement.[13]
- Some 30 to 45 percent of employees work from home or are virtual employees.[14] The CEO of a New Jersey–based social media management company never sees her team members because they're part of a virtual workforce.[15]
- About 3 percent of U.S. businesses currently offer unlimited vacation time to employees—a percentage that's likely to grow.[16]

In today's world, managers are dealing with changing workplaces, a changing workforce, changing technology, and global uncertainties. For example, grocery stores continue to struggle to retain their customer base and to keep costs down. At Publix Super Markets, the large grocery chain in the southeastern United States, everyone, including managers, is looking for ways to better serve customers. The company's president, Todd Jones, who started his career bagging groceries at a Publix in New Smyrna Beach, Florida, is guiding the company through these challenges by keeping everyone's focus—from baggers to checkers to stockers—on exceptional customer service.[17] Or consider the management challenges faced by the *Seattle Post-Intelligencer* (P-I) when it, like many other newspapers, struggled to find a way to be successful in an industry that was losing readers and revenues at an alarming rate. Managers made the decision to go all-digital and the P-I became an Internet-only news source. Difficult actions followed as the news staff was reduced from 165 to less than 20 people. In its new "life" as a digital news source, the organization faces other challenges—challenges for the manager who needs to plan, organize, lead, and control in this changed environment.[18] Managers everywhere are likely to have to manage in changing circumstances, and the fact is that *how* managers manage is changing. Throughout the rest of this book, we'll be

Claire Hobean, operations manager for Re-Time Pty. Ltd., models the Australian firm's innovative Re-Timer glasses at a consumer electronics show. The medical device innovation uses bright light therapy to assist in the treatment of insomnia, jet lag, and Seasonal Affective Disorder by helping reset a person's natural body clock.

Steve Marcus/Reuters

discussing these changes and how they're affecting the way managers plan, organize, lead, and control. We want to highlight four specific changes that are increasingly important to organizations and managers everywhere: customers, innovation, social media, and sustainability.

Why Are Customers Important to the Manager's Job?

John Chambers, CEO of Cisco Systems, likes to listen to voice mails forwarded to him from dissatisfied customers because he wants to hear firsthand the emotions and frustrations they're experiencing. He can't get that type of insight by reading an e-mail.[19] This is a manager who understands the importance of customers. Organizations need customers. Without them, most organizations would cease to exist. Yet, focusing on the customer has long been thought by many managers to be the responsibility of the marketers. We're discovering, however, that employee attitudes and behaviors play a big role in customer satisfaction. Think of the times you've been treated poorly (or superbly) by an employee during a service encounter and how that affected the way you felt about the situation.

Managers are recognizing that delivering consistent high-quality customer service is essential for survival and success in today's competitive environment and that employees are an important part of that equation.[20] The implication is clear—they must create a customer-responsive organization where employees are friendly and courteous, accessible, knowledgeable, prompt in responding to customer needs, and willing to do what's necessary to please the customer.[21]

⭐ Watch It!

If your professor has assigned this, go to the Assignments section of **mymanagementlab.com** to complete the video exercise titled *Zane's Cycles: The Management Environment*.

⋮⋮ Technology and the Manager's Job ⋮⋮
IS IT STILL MANAGING WHEN WHAT YOU'RE MANAGING ARE ROBOTS?

The office of tomorrow is likely to include workers that are faster, smarter, more responsible—and who just happen to be robots.[22] Surprised? Although robots have been used in factory and industrial settings for a long time, it's becoming more common to find robots in the office and it's bringing about new ways of looking at how work is done and at what and how managers manage. So what *would* a manager's job be like managing robots? And even more intriguing is how these "workers" might affect how human coworkers interact with them.

As machines have become smarter and smarter, researchers have been exploring the human-machine interaction and how people interact with the smart devices that are now such an integral part of our professional and personal lives. One insight is that people find it easy to bond with a robot, even one that doesn't look or sound anything like a real person. In a workplace setting, if a robot moves around in a "purposeful way," people tend to view it, in some ways, as a coworker. People name their robots and can even describe the robot's moods and tendencies. As telepresence robots become more common, the humanness becomes even more evident. For example, when Erwin Deininger, the electrical engineer at Reimers Electra Steam, a small company in Clear Brook, Virginia, moved to

the Dominican Republic when his wife's job transferred her there, he was able to still be "present" at the company via his VGo robot. Now "robot" Deininger moves easily around the office and shop floor, allowing the "real" Deininger to do his job just as if he were there in person. The company's president, satisfied with how the robot solution has worked out, has been surprised at how he acts around it, feeling at times that he's interacting with Deininger himself.

There's no doubt that robotic technology will continue to be incorporated into organizational settings. The manager's job will become even more exciting and challenging as humans and machines work together to accomplish the organization's goals.

If your professor has assigned this, go to the Assignments section of **mymanagementlab.com** *to complete these discussion questions.*

⭐ **TALK ABOUT IT 5:** What's your response to the title of this box: *Is* it still managing when what you're managing are robots? Discuss.

⭐ **TALK ABOUT IT 6:** If you had to manage people and robots, how do you think your job as manager might be different than what the chapter describes? (Think in terms of functions, roles, and skills/competencies.)

Why Is Innovation Important to the Manager's Job?

Success in business today demands innovation. Innovation means doing things differently, exploring new territory, and taking risks. And innovation isn't just for high-tech or other technologically sophisticated organizations; innovative efforts are needed in all types, all levels, all areas, and all sizes of organizations. You'd expect companies like Apple, Google, Toyota, and Instagram to be on a list of the world's 50 most innovative companies.[23] But what about the likes of Panera Bread? Here's a company that's using technology to improve everything it does. It's installing a new master system across its North American locations (over 1,800) that will provide customers with new ways to order their food (and even entertain themselves) and kitchen staff with capabilities to better handle custom orders. Or how about Kickstarter, which created the crowdfunding phenomenon? Now, it's looking at ways to better encourage creativity among potential projects and startups and is also expanding its business beyond fundraising into publishing and distribution. In today's challenging environment, innovation *is* critical and managers need to understand what, when, where, how, and why innovation can be fostered and encouraged throughout an organization. In a presentation a few years ago, a manager in charge of Walmart's global business explained his recipe for success (personal and organizational): continually look for new ways to do your job better; that is, be innovative. Managers not only need to be innovative personally, but also encourage their employees to be innovative. We'll share stories of innovative practices and approaches throughout the book.

Importance of Social Media to the Manager's Job

You probably can't imagine a time when employees did their work without e-mail or Internet access. Yet, some 20 years ago, as these communication tools were becoming more common in workplaces, managers struggled with the challenges of providing guidelines for using them. Today, it's all about **social media**, which are forms of electronic communication through which users create online communities to share ideas, information, personal messages, and other content. Social platforms such as Facebook, Twitter, LinkedIn, Tumblr, Instagram, and others are used by more than a billion people.[24] And employees don't just use these on their personal time, but also for work purposes. That's why managers again are struggling with guidelines for employee use as they attempt to navigate the power and peril of social media. For example, at grocery chain SuperValu, managers realized that keeping 135,000-plus employees connected and engaged was imperative to continued success.[25] They decided to adopt an internal social media tool to foster cooperation and collaboration among its 10 distinct store brands operating in 44 states. And they're not alone. More and more businesses are turning to social media not just as a way to connect with customers, but also as a way to manage their human resources and tap into their innovation and talent. That's the potential power of social media. But the potential peril is in how it's used. When the social media platform becomes a way for boastful employees to brag about their accomplishments, for managers to publish one-way messages to employees, or for employees to argue or gripe about something or someone they don't like at work, then it's lost its usefulness. To avoid this, managers need to remember that social media is a tool that needs to be managed to be beneficial. At SuperValu, about 9,000 store managers and assistant managers use the social media system. Although sources say it's too early to draw any conclusions, it appears that managers who actively make use of the system are having better store sales revenues than those who don't. In the remainder of

social media
Forms of electronic communication through which users create online communities to share ideas, information, personal messages, and other content

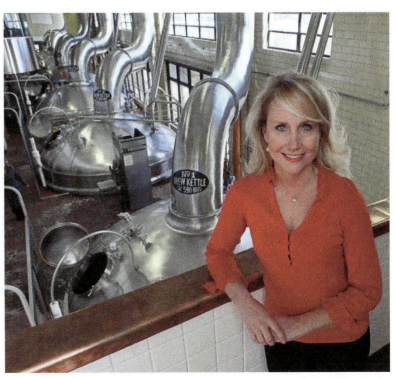

Managing in a sustainable way is important to Kim Marotta, Director of Sustainability at MillerCoors. As part of her role in achieving the company's water conservation goals, she manages initiatives to reduce water usage throughout MillerCoors' brewery processes and supply chain and to include water stewardship messages in the firm's marketing campaigns.

Milwaukee Journal Sentinel/MCT/Landov

the book, we'll look at how social media is impacting how managers manage, especially in the areas of human resource management, communication, teams, and strategy.

Importance of Sustainability to the Manager's Job

BMW is probably not a company that would come to mind in a section describing sustainability. Yet, BMW, the iconic German manufacturer of high-performance luxury autos, is making a huge bet on green, wired cars for those who reside in cities.[26] Its all-electric car, called the i3, is unlike anything that BMW—or any other car manufacturer—has made. The car's weight-saving, carbon-fiber body is layered with electronic services and smartphone apps ready to make life simpler and more efficient for the owner and better for the planet. Company executives recognized that it had to add products that would meet the challenges of a changing world. This corporate action by a well-known global company affirms that sustainability and green management have become mainstream issues for managers.

What's emerging in the twenty-first century is the concept of managing in a sustainable way, which has had the effect of widening corporate responsibility not only to managing in an efficient and effective way, but also to responding strategically to a wide range of environmental and societal challenges.[27] Although "sustainability" may mean different things to different people, the World Business Council for Sustainable Development describes a scenario where all earth's inhabitants can live well with adequate resources.[28] From a business perspective, **sustainability** has been defined as a company's ability to achieve its business goals and increase long-term shareholder value by integrating economic, environmental, and social opportunities into its business strategies.[29] Sustainability issues are now moving up the business agenda. Managers at BMW, Walmart, and other global businesses are discovering that running an organization in a more sustainable way will mean making informed business decisions based on (1) communicating openly with various stakeholders and understanding their requirements, and (2) factoring economic, environmental, and social aspects into how they pursue their business goals. Throughout the rest of the book, we'll explore sustainability as it relates to various aspects of managing. Just look for this for those conversations.

Managers Matter!

Wrapping It Up...

As you can see, being a manager is both challenging and exciting! One thing we know for sure is that *managers do matter* to organizations. The Gallup Organization, which has polled millions of employees and tens of thousands of managers, has found that *the single most important variable in employee productivity and loyalty isn't pay or benefits or workplace environment; it's the quality of the relationship between employees and their direct supervisors*. Gallup also found that employees' relationship with their manager is the largest factor in **employee engagement**—which is when employees are connected to, satisfied with, and enthusiastic about their jobs—accounting for at least 70 percent of an employee's level of engagement.[30] And Gallup found that when companies increase their number of talented managers and double the rate of engaged employees, their EPS (earnings per share) is 147 percent higher than their competitors.[31] That's significant! This same research also showed that talented managers contribute about 48 percent higher profit to their companies than do average managers.[32] Finally, a different study found that when a poor manager was replaced with a great one, employee productivity increased by 12 percent.[33] What can we conclude from such reports? That talented managers *do* matter and will continue to matter to organizations!

sustainability
A company's ability to achieve its business goals and increase long-term shareholder value by integrating economic, environmental, and social opportunities into its business strategies

employee engagement
When employees are connected to, satisfied with, and enthusiastic about their jobs

MyManagementLab®

Go to **mymanagementlab.com** to complete the problems marked with this icon

1 Review

CHAPTER SUMMARY

1-1 Tell who managers are and where they work.

Managers are individuals who work in an organization directing and overseeing the activities of other people. Managers are usually classified as top, middle, first-line, or team leader. Organizations, which are where managers work, have three characteristics: goals, people, and a deliberate structure.

1-2 Define management.

Management is the process of getting things done, effectively and efficiently, with and through other people. Efficiency means doing a task correctly ("doing things right") and getting the most output from the least amount of inputs. Effectiveness means "doing the right things" by doing those work tasks that help the organization reach its goals.

1-3 Describe what managers do.

What managers do can be described using three approaches: functions, roles, and skills/competencies. The functions approach says that managers perform four functions: planning, organizing, leading, and controlling. Mintzberg's roles approach says that what managers do is based on the 10 roles they use at work, which are grouped around interpersonal relationships, the transfer of information, and decision making. The skills/competencies approach looks at what managers do in terms of the skills and competencies they need and use. Four critical management skills are conceptual, interpersonal, technical, and

political. Additional managerial competencies include aspects such as dependability, personal orientation, emotional control, communication, and so forth. All managers plan, organize, lead, and control although how they do these activities and how often they do them may vary according to level in the organization, whether the organization is profit or not-for-profit, the size of the organization, and the geographic location of the organization.

1-4 Explain why it's important to study management.

One reason it's important to study management is that all of us interact with organizations daily so we have a vested interest in seeing that organizations are well managed. Another reason is the reality that in your career you will either manage or be managed. By studying management you can gain insights into the way your boss and fellow employees behave and how organizations function.

1-5 Describe the factors that are reshaping and redefining management.

In today's world, managers are dealing with changing workplaces, a changing workforce, global economic and political uncertainties, and changing technology. Four areas of critical importance to managers are delivering high-quality customer service, encouraging innovative efforts, using social media efficiently and effectively, and recognizing how sustainability contributes to an organization's effectiveness.

DISCUSSION QUESTIONS

1-1 What is an organization and what characteristics do organizations share?

1-2 How do managers differ from nonmanagerial employees?

1-3 In today's environment, which is more important to organizations—efficiency or effectiveness? Explain your choice.

⭐ 1-4 What similarities and differences do you see among the four management functions?

1-5 Using any of the popular business periodicals (such as *Bloomberg BusinessWeek, Fortune, Wall Street Journal, Fast Company*), find examples of managers doing each of the four management functions. Write up a

description and explain how these are examples of that function.

1-6 Is your course instructor a manager? Discuss in terms of planning, organizing, leading, and controlling. Also discuss using Mintzberg's managerial roles approach.

1-7 Can business management be called a profession? Why or why not? Do some external research in answering this question.

⭐ 1-8 Is there one best "style" of management? Why or why not?

1-9 In what ways can managers at each of the four levels of management contribute to efficiency and effectiveness?

Writing Assignments

1-10 Do all organizations need managers? Explain.

1-11 Explain how the 4 functions approach is better than the roles approach and the skills and competencies approach for describing what managers do.

Management Skill Builder | **BECOMING POLITICALLY ADEPT**

Anyone who has had much work experience knows that organizational politics exists everywhere. That is, people try to influence the distribution of advantages and disadvantages within the organization in their favor. Those who understand organizational politics typically thrive. Those who don't, regardless of how good their actual job skills are, often suffer by receiving less positive performance reviews, fewer promotions, and smaller salary increases. If you want to succeed as a manager, it helps to be politically adept. Research has shown that people differ in their political skills.[34] Those who are politically skilled are more effective in their use of influence tactics. Political skill also appears to be more effective when the stakes are high. Finally, politically skilled individuals are able to exert their influence without others detecting it, which is important in being effective so that you're not labeled as playing politics. A person's political skill is determined by (1) his or her networking ability, (2) interpersonal influence, (3) social astuteness, and (4) apparent sincerity.

⭐ PERSONAL INVENTORY ASSESSMENT   PERSONAL INVENTORY ASSESSMENT

Using Influence Strategies

Take a look at how well you use influence strategies. This PIA will help you determine how skillfully you do that and what you need to work on.

Skill Basics

Forget, for a moment, the ethics of politicking and any negative impressions you might have of people who engage in organizational politics. If you want to become more politically adept in your organization, follow these steps:

- *Develop your networking ability.* A good network can be a powerful tool. You can begin building a network by getting to know important people in your work area and the organization and then developing relationships with individuals in positions of power. Volunteer for committees or offer your help on projects that will be noticed by those in positions of power. Attend important organizational functions so that you can be seen as a team player and someone who's interested in the organization's success. Start a file list of individuals that you meet, even if for a brief moment. Then, when you need advice on work, use your connections and network with others throughout the organization.

- *Work on gaining interpersonal influence.* People will listen to you when they're comfortable and feel at ease around you. Work on your communication skills so that you can communicate easily and effectively with others. Work on developing a good rapport with people in all areas and at all levels of your organization. Be open, friendly, and willing to pitch in. The amount of interpersonal influence you have will be affected by how well people like you.

- *Develop your social astuteness.* Some people have an innate ability to understand people and sense what they're thinking. If you don't have that ability, you'll have to work at developing your social astuteness by doing things such as saying the right things at the right time, paying close attention to people's facial expressions, and trying to determine whether others have hidden agendas.

- *Be sincere.* Sincerity is important to getting people to want to associate with you. Be genuine in what you say and do. And show a genuine interest in others and their situations.

Practicing the Skill

Take each of the components of political skill and spend one week working on it as you navigate your school life and work life. Keep a brief set of notes describing your experiences—good and bad. Were you able to begin developing a network of people you could rely on or connect with for school or work commitments? How did you try to become better at influencing those around you? Did you work at communicating better or at developing a good rapport with coworkers or class project team members? Did you work at developing your social astuteness, maybe by starting to recognize and interpret people's facial expressions and the meaning behind those expressions? Did you make a conscious effort to be more sincere in your relationships with others, especially those that are not close friends? What could you have done differently to be more politically skilled? Once you begin to recognize what's involved with political skills, you should find yourself becoming more connected and better able to influence others—that is, more politically adept.

Experiential Exercise

Heartland's Traditional Fragrances

To: Eric Kim, Training Coordinator

From: Helen Merkin, Human Resources Director

Re: Supervisory Training and Management Certification Program

The good news: our sales numbers continue to grow. The bad news: it's putting a strain on our manufacturing supervisors. They're finding it difficult to keep our line employees motivated. We need to get some training in place to help them deal with this demanding pace or our line employees are likely to get even more stressed and we may see product quality go down.

I need you to look into two issues for me. One is a training program that focuses on important supervisory skills. Do some research and put together a list of the skills you think are most important for our supervisors to have, together with a justification for why you think these skills are important.

The second issue is how we could help our supervisors achieve certification that verifies their skills, knowledge, and professionalism. One certification program that I'm aware of is the Certified Professional Manager. Please research this program and prepare a brief (no more than half a page) bulleted list of what's involved. And get me the information as soon as possible. Thnx!

This fictionalized company and message were created for educational purposes only, and not meant to reflect positively or negatively on management practices by any company that may share this name.

CASE APPLICATION #1

Who Needs a Boss?

"Holacracy."[35] That's the word of the day at Zappos, the Nevada-based online shoe and apparel retailer. During a four-hour, year-end employee meeting in 2013, CEO Tony Hsieh announced that he was eliminating the company's traditional managerial and structural hierarchy to implement a holacracy. What is a holacracy, you ask? In a nutshell, it's an organizational system with no job titles, no managers, and no top-down hierarchy with upper, middle, or lower levels where decisions can get hung up. The idea behind this new type of arrangement is to focus on the work that needs to be done and not on some hierarchical structure where great ideas and suggestions can get lost in the channels of reporting. The holacracy concept was dreamed up by Brian Robertson, the founder of a Pennsylvania software startup. Its name comes from the Greek word *holos,* a single, autonomous, self-sufficient unit that's also dependent on a larger unit.[36] A simple explanation of Robertson's vision of a holacracy is: workers as partners, job descriptions as roles, and partners organized into circles.[37]

At Zappos, work (and the 1,500 employees who do it) will be organized around self-governing employee circles—around 400 of these circles. (It might help you grasp this idea by thinking of these employee circles as types of overlapping employee "groups" but with more fluid membership and individual roles/responsibilities.) In these circles, employees can take on any number of roles, and the expectation is that each

At Zappos, they're learning how to manage without managers!

employee will help out wherever he or she can. Without titles or a hierarchy, anyone can initiate a project and implement innovative ideas. The hope is that circle members will pool ideas and watch out for each other. The goal is radical transparency and to get more people to take charge. Yet, trusting individuals who probably know the details of the job better than any "manager" to work conscientiously, creatively, and efficiently is good as long as there is a way to keep standards high. The last thing Zappos wants is for a "slacker" mentality to take hold.

Hsieh has always approached leading his business in unique and radical ways. He strongly believes in the power of the individual and has created a highly successful organization (which is now part of Amazon) that's known for its zany culture, where corporate values are matched with personal values, and where "weirdness and humility" are celebrated.[38] However, as the company moves away from the traditional work model to this new system, it may face some challenges. Both Zappos and Robertson caution that while a holacracy might eliminate the traditional manager's job, there is still structure and accountability. Poor performers will be obvious because they won't have enough "roles" to fill their time, or a circle charged with monitoring the company's culture may decide they're not a good fit. Also, just because there are no "traditional" managers doesn't mean that leaders won't emerge. But it will be important to watch for dominant personalities emerging as authority figures, which could potentially cause other employees to be resentful or to rebel. Zappos says that it will not be leaderless. Some individuals will have a bigger role and scope of purpose, but leadership

is also distributed and expected in each role. "Everybody is expected to lead and be an entrepreneur in their own roles, and holacracy empowers them to do so."[39] Also, there will be some structure arrangement where "the broadest circles can to some extent tell sub-groups what they're accountable for doing."[40] But accountability, rather than flowing only up, will flow throughout the organization in different paths. Other challenges they're still trying to figure out include who has the ultimate authority to hire, fire, and decide pay. The hope is that eventually the authority for each of these roles will be done within the holacratic framework as well. So, if no one has a title and there are no bosses, is Tony Hsieh still the CEO? So far, he hasn't publicly commented about how his own role is impacted.

In March 2015, Hsieh sent a memo to employees stating it was taking too long to make the transition to the new management system.[41] He offered all employees who felt they couldn't work under this radically new management system until April 30 to decide whether they wanted to stay or to leave with three months' severance. About 14 percent of the company's workforce (210 employees) chose to leave. Obviously, those individuals felt that holacracy was not for them.

Discussion Questions

 1-13 What is a holacracy?

 1-14 What benefits do you see to an organization where there are no job titles, no managers, and no hierarchy?

1-15 What challenges does a holacratic approach have?

1-16 Discuss why you would or would not like to work in an organization like this.

CASE APPLICATION #2

Building a Better Boss

Google doesn't do anything halfway. So when it decided to "build a better boss," it did what it does best: look at data.[42] Using data from performance reviews, feedback surveys, and supporting papers turned in for individuals being nominated for top-manager awards, Google tried to find what a great boss is and does. The project, dubbed Project Oxygen, examined some 100 variables and ultimately identified eight characteristics or habits of Google's most effective managers. Here are the "big eight":

- Provide an unambiguous vision of the future;
- Help individuals to reach their long-term work goals;

- Express interest in employees' well-being;
- Ensure you have the necessary technical abilities to support employee efforts;
- Display effective communication skills, especially listening;
- Provide coaching support when needed;
- Focus on being productive and on end results; and
- Avoid over-managing; let your team be responsible.

At first glance, you're probably thinking that these eight attributes seem pretty simplistic and obvious and you may be wondering why Google spent all this time and effort to uncover these. Even Google's vice president for people operations,

Laszlo Bock, said, "My first reaction was, that's it?" Another writer described it as "reading like a whiteboard gag from an episode of *The Office*." But, as the old saying goes, there *was* more to this list than meets the eye.

When Bock and his team began looking closer and rank ordering the eight items by importance, Project Oxygen got interesting—a lot more interesting! And to understand this, you have to understand something about Google's approach to management since its founding in 1999. Plain and simple, managers were encouraged to "leave people alone. Let the engineers do their stuff. If they become stuck, they'll ask their bosses, whose deep technical expertise propelled them to management in the first place." It's not hard to see what Google wanted its managers to be—outstanding technical specialists. Mr. Bock explains, "In the Google context, we'd always believed that to be a manager, particularly on the engineering side, you need to be as deep or deeper a technical expert than the people who work for you." However, Project Oxygen revealed that technical expertise was ranked number eight (very last) on the list. So, here's the complete list from most important to least important, along with what each characteristic entails:

- *Provide coaching support when needed* (provide specific feedback and have regular one-on-one meetings with employees; offer solutions tailored to each employee's strengths)
- *Avoid over-managing; let your team be responsible* (give employees space to tackle problems themselves, but be available to offer advice)
- *Express interest in employees' well-being* (make new team members feel welcome and get to know your employees as people)
- *Focus on being productive and on end results* (focus on helping the team achieve its goals by prioritizing work and getting rid of obstacles)

- *Display good communication skills, especially listening* (learn to listen and to share information; encourage open dialogue and pay attention to the team's concerns)
- *Help individuals to reach their long-term work goals* (notice employees' efforts so they can see how their hard work is furthering their careers; appreciate employees' efforts and make that appreciation known)
- *Provide an unambiguous vision of the future* (lead the team but keep everyone involved in developing and working toward the team's vision)
- *Ensure you have the necessary technical abilities to support employee efforts* (understand the challenges facing the team and be able to help team members solve problems)

Now, managers at Google aren't just encouraged to be great managers, they know what being a great manager involves. And the company is doing its part, as well. Using the list, Google started training managers, as well as providing individual coaching and performance review sessions. You can say that Project Oxygen breathed new life into Google's managers. Bock says the company's efforts paid off quickly. "We were able to have a statistically significant improvement in manager quality for 75 percent of our worst-performing managers."

> Data cruncher **Google crunched data** to find out what being a great manager involves.

Discussion Questions

⭐ **1-17** Describe the findings of Project Oxygen using the functions approach, Mintzberg's roles approach, and the skills approach.

⭐ **1-18** Are you surprised at what Google found out about "building a better boss?" Explain your answer.

⭐ **1-19** What's the difference between encouraging managers to be great managers and knowing what being a great manager involves?

1-20 What could other companies learn from Google's experiences?

1-21 Would you want to work for a company like Google? Why or why not?

CASE APPLICATION #3

Saving the World

You used to be able to tell who the bad guys were. But in our digital online world, those days are long gone.[43] Now, the bad guys are faceless and anonymous. And they can and do inflict all kinds of damage on individuals, businesses, governments, and other organizations. Surveys show that data breach attacks are happening with alarming regularity. And while your home and school PCs are hopefully well protected from data theft and viruses, don't think that you're in the clear. The newest targets for data thieves are smartphones and other mobile devices. However, the good guys are fighting back. For instance, security technology company Symantec Corporation set up a sting called Operation HoneyStick, in which it distributed 50 smartphones in Silicon Valley; Washington, DC; New York; Los Angeles; and Ottawa, Canada. The phones were loaded with a lot of important but fake data and left in locations where thieves would be tempted to pick them up, such as restaurants, elevators, convenience stores, and college student gathering places. Oh, and one other thing: the smartphones were equipped with monitoring software so the security experts could track where the devices were taken once found and what type of information was accessed by the finders. This is just one example of how Symantec's employees are trying to "save the world" one step at a time—not an easy thing to do.

"Imagine what life would be like if your product were never finished, if your work were never done, if your market shifted 30 times a day." Sounds pretty crazy, doesn't it? However, the computer-virus hunters and security experts at Symantec don't have to imagine—that's the reality of their daily work. For instance, at the company's well-obscured Dublin facility (one of three around the globe), operations manager Patrick Fitzgerald must keep his engineers and researchers focused 24/7 on identifying and combating what the bad guys are throwing out there. Right now, they're trying to stay ahead of a big virus threat, Stuxnet, which targets computer systems running the environmental controls in industrial facilities, such as temperature in power plants, pressure in pipelines, automated timing, and so forth. The consequences of someone intent on doing evil getting control over such critical functions could be disastrous.

Symantec, which designs content and network security software for both consumers and businesses, reflects the realities facing many organizations today—quickly shifting customer expectations and continuously emerging global competitors and global threats. Managing talented people in such an environment can be quite challenging.

Symantec's virus hunters around the world deal with some 20,000 virus samples each month, not all of which are unique, stand-alone viruses. To make the hunters' jobs even more interesting is that computer attacks are increasingly being spread by criminals around the world wanting to steal information, whether corporate data or personal user account information that can be used in fraud. Dealing with these critical and time-sensitive

issues requires special talents. The response-center team is a diverse group whose members weren't easy to find. "It's not as if colleges are creating thousands of anti-malware or security experts every year that we can hire. If you find them in any part of the world, you just go after them." The response-center team's makeup reflects that. For instance, one senior researcher is from Hungary; another is from Iceland; and another works out of her home in Melbourne, Florida. But they all share something in common: They're all motivated by solving problems.

The launch of the Blaster-B worm, a particularly nasty virus, in late summer 2003 changed the company's approach to dealing with viruses. The domino effect of Blaster-B and other viruses spawned by it meant that frontline software analysts were working around the clock for almost two weeks. The "employee burn-out" potential made the company realize that its virus-hunting team would now have to be much deeper talent-wise. Now, the response center's team numbers in the hundreds and managers can rotate people from the front lines—where they're responsible for responding to new security threats that crop up—into groups where they can help with new-product development. Others write internal research papers. Still others are assigned to develop new tools that will help their colleagues battle the next wave of threats. There's even an individual who tries to figure out what makes the virus writers tick—and the day never ends for these virus hunters. When Dublin's team finishes its day, colleagues in Santa Monica take over. When the U.S. team finishes its day, it hands off to the team in Tokyo, who then hands back to Dublin for the new day. It's a frenetic, chaotic, challenging work environment that spans the entire globe. But the goals for managing the virus hunters are to "try to take the chaos out, to make the exciting boring," to have a predictable and well-defined process for dealing with the virus threats, and to spread work evenly to the company's facilities around the world. It's a managerial challenge that company managers have embraced.

> Managing talented people in a **work environment that's quickly shifting can be quite** challenging!

Discussion Questions

⭐ **1-22** Keeping professionals excited about work that is routine, standardized, *and* chaotic is a major challenge for Symantec's managers. How could they use technical, human, and conceptual skills to maintain an environment that encourages innovation and professionalism among the virus hunters?

⭐ **1-23** What managerial competencies might be important for these managers and why are these important?

1-24 What management roles would operations manager Patrick Fitzgerald be playing as he (a) held weekly security briefing conference calls with coworkers around the globe, (b) assessed the feasibility of adding a new network security consulting service, and (c) kept employees focused on the company's commitments to customers?

1-25 Go to Symantec's Web site (www.symantec.com) and look up information about the company. What can you tell about its emphasis on customer service and innovation? In what ways does the organization support its employees in servicing customers and in being innovative?

Endnotes

1. The Walt Disney Company, Letter to Shareholders, *2012 Annual Report*, 1–3.
2. From the Past to the Present box based on Dictionary.com Unabridged, based on the Random House Dictionary, © Random House, Inc. 2009, http://dictionary.reference.com/browse/manage; Online Etymology Dictionary, www.etymonline.com (June 5, 2009); P. F. Drucker, *Management: Revised Edition* (New York: HarperCollins Publishers, 2008); and F. W. Taylor, *Principles of Scientific Management* (New York: Harper, 1911), 44. For other information on Taylor, see S. Wagner-Tsukamoto, "An Institutional Economic Reconstruction of Scientific Management: On the Lost Theoretical Logic of Taylorism," *Academy of Management Review*, January 2007, 105–17; R. Kanigel, *The One Best Way: Frederick Winslow Taylor and the Enigma of Efficiency* (New York: Viking, 1997); and M. Banta, *Taylored Lives: Narrative Productions in the Age of Taylor, Veblen, and Ford* (Chicago: University of Chicago Press, 1993).
3. S. Stevenson, "Don't Go to Work," http://www.slate.com/articles/business/psychology_of_management/2014/05/best_buy_s_rowe_experiment_can_results_only_work_environments_actually_be.html, May 11, 2014; S. Miller, "Study: Flexible Schedules Reduce Conflict, Lower Turnover," www.shrm.org, April 13, 2011; K. M. Butler, "We Can ROWE Our Way to a Better Work Environment," EBN.BenefitNews.com, April 1, 2011, p. 8; P. Moen, E. L. Kelly, and R. Hill, "Does Enhancing Work-Time Control and Flexibility Reduce Turnover? A Naturally Occurring Experiment," *Social Problems*, February 2011, 69–98; and R. J. Erickson, "Task, Not Time: Profile of a Gen Y Job," *Harvard Business Review*, February 2008, 19.
4. H. Fayol, *Industrial and General Administration* (Paris: Dunod, 1916).
5. H. Mintzberg, *The Nature of Managerial Work* (New York: Harper & Row, 1973).
6. S. J. Carroll and D. A. Gillen, "Are the Classical Management Functions Useful in Describing Managerial Work?" *Academy of Management Review*, January 1987, 48.
7. See, for example, J. G. Harris, D. W. DeLong, and A. Donnellon, "Do You Have What It Takes to Be an E-Manager?" *Strategy and Leadership* (August 2001): 10–14; C. Fletcher and C. Baldry, "A Study of Individual Differences and Self-Awareness in the Context of Multi-Source Feedback," *Journal of Occupational and Organizational Psychology* (September 2000): 303–19; and R. L. Katz, "Skills of an Effective Administrator," *Harvard Business Review*, September–October 1974, 90–102.
8. R. P. Tett, H. A. Guterman, A. Bleier, and P. J. Murphy, "Development and Content Validation of a 'Hyperdimensional' Taxonomy of Managerial Competence," *Human Performance* 13, no. 3 (2000): 205–51.
9. "Frequently Asked Questions," *U.S. Small Business Administration*, www.sba.gov/advo (September 2008); T. L. Hatten, *Small Business: Entrepreneurship and Beyond* (Upper Saddle River, NJ: Prentice Hall, 1997), 5; L. W. Busenitz, "Research on Entrepreneurial Alertness," *Journal of Small Business Management* (October 1996): 35–44; and J. W. Carland, F. Hoy, W. R. Boulton, and J. C. Carland, "Differentiating Entrepreneurs from Small Business Owners: A Conceptualization," *Academy of Management Review* 9, no. 2 (1984): 354–59.
10. A Question of Ethics box based on M. S. Plakhotnik and T. S. Rocco, "A Succession Plan for First-Time Managers," *T&D*, December 2011, 42–45; P. Brotherton, "New Managers Feeling Lost at Sea," *T&D*, June 2011, 25; and "How Do We Help a New Manager Manage?" *Workforce Management Online*, June 16, 2011.
11. "A New Millennium of Managers," *TD*, February 2015, 19.
12. J. Welch and S. Welch, "An Employee Bill of Rights," *Bloomberg BusinessWeek*, March 16, 2009, 72.
13. N. Hellmich, "Many Delay Retiring: Need More Money, Enjoy Their Jobs," http://www.usatoday.com/story/money/personalfinance/2014/02/27/delay-retirement-money/5785373/, February 27, 2014.
14. M. M. Biro, "Telecommuting Is the Future of Work," www.forbes.com, January 12, 2014.
15. L. Vankam, "Virtual Workforce Stands Ready," *USA Today*, January 8, 2013, 11A.
16. The Muse, "Could Unlimited Vacation Time Work for Your Company?" http://www.forbes.com/sites/dailymuse/2014/10/29/could-unlimited-vacation-time-work-for-your-company/, October 29, 2014.
17. T. W. Martin, "May I Help You?" *Wall Street Journal*, April 23, 2009, R4.
18. "Contact the Staff of seattlepi.com," http://www.seattlepi.com/pistaff/; and W. Yardley and R. Perez-Peña, "Seattle Paper Shifts Entirely to the Web," *New York Times Online* (March 17, 2009).
19. F. F. Reichheld, "Lead for Loyalty," *Harvard Business Review*, July–August 2001, 76.
20. See, for instance, H. Ernst, W. D. Hoyer, M. Krafft, and K. Krieger, "Customer Relationship Management and Company Performance—The Mediating Role of New Product Performance," *Journal of the Academy of Marketing Science* (April 2011): 290–306; J. P. Dotson and G. M. Allenby, "Investigating the Strategic Influence of Customer and Employee Satisfaction on Firm Financial Performance," *Marketing Science* (September–October 2010): 895–908; R. Grewal, M. Chandrashekaran, and A. V. Citrin, "Customer Satisfaction Heterogeneity and Shareholder Value," *Journal of Marketing Research* (August 2010): 612–26; M. Riemann, O. Schilke, and J. S. Thomas, "Customer Relationship Management and Firm Performance: The Mediating Role of Business Strategy," *Journal of the Academy of Marketing Science* (Summer 2010): 326–46; and K. A. Eddleston, D. L. Kidder, and B. E. Litzky, "Who's the Boss? Contending with Competing Expectations from Customers and Management," *Academy of Management Executive* (November 2002): 85–95.
21. See, for instance, C. B. Blocker, D. J. Flint, M. B. Myers, and S. F. Slater, "Proactive Customer Orientation and Its Role for Creating Customer Value in Global Markets," *Journal of the Academy of Marketing Science* (April 2011): 216–33; G. A. Gorry and R. A. Westbrook, "Once More, with Feeling: Empathy and Technology in Customer Care," *Business Horizons* (March–April 2011): 125–34; M. Dixon, K. Freeman, and N. Toman, "Stop Trying to Delight Your Customers," *Harvard Business Review*, July–August 2010, 116–22; D. M. Mayer, M. G. Ehrhart, and B. Schneider, "Service Attribute Boundary Conditions of the Service Climate-Customer Satisfaction Link," *Academy of Management Journal* (October 2009): 1034–50; B. A. Gutek, M. Groth, and B. Cherry, "Achieving Service Success Through Relationships and Enhanced Encounters," *Academy of Management Executive* (November 2002): 132–44; Eddleston, Kidder, and Litzky, "Who's the Boss? Contending with Competing Expectations from Customers and Management"; S. D. Pugh, J. Dietz, J. W. Wiley, and S. M. Brooks, "Driving Service Effectiveness Through Employee-Customer Linkages," *Academy of Management Executive* (November 2002): 73–84; S. D. Pugh, "Service with a Smile: Emotional Contagion in the Service Encounter," *Academy of Management Journal* (October 2001): 1018–27; W. C. Tsai, "Determinants and Consequences of Employee Displayed Positive Emotions," *Journal of Management* 27, no. 4 (2001): 497–512; Naumann and Jackson, Jr., "One More Time: How Do You Satisfy Customers?"; and M. D. Hartline and O. C. Ferrell, "The Management of Customer-Contact Service Employees: An Empirical Investigation," *Journal of Marketing* (October 1996): 52–70.
22. Technology and the Manager's Job box based on D. Bennett, "I'll Have My Robots Talk to Your Robots," *Bloomberg BusinessWeek*

(February 21–27, 2011): 52–62; E. Spitznagel, "The Robot Revolution Is Coming," *Bloomberg BusinessWeek,* January 17–23, 2011, 69–71; G. A. Fowler, "Holiday Hiring Call: People vs. Robots," *Wall Street Journal,* December 20, 2010, B1+; A. Schwartz, "Bring Your Robot to Work Day," *Fast Company.com* (November 2010): 72–74; and P. J. Hinds, T. L. Roberts, and H. Jones, "Whose Job Is It Anyway? A Study of Human-Robot Interaction in a Collaborative Task," *Human-Computer Interaction* (March 2004): 151–81.

23. *Fast Company* Staff, "World's 50 Most Innovative Companies," *Fast Company,* March 2015, 66+.

24. "Top 15 Most Popular Social Networking Sites," http://www.ebizmba.com/articles/social-networking-websites, February 2015; and "Social Media Update 2014," Pew Research Center, http://www.pewinternet.org/2015/01/09/social-media-update-2014/, January 9, 2015.

25. D. Ferris, "Social Studies: How to Use Social Media to Build a Better Organization," *Workforce Online,* February 12, 2012.

26. A. Taylor III, "BMW Gets Plugged In," *Fortune,* March 18, 2013, 150–56.

27. KPMG Global Sustainability Services, *Sustainability Insights,* October 2007.

28. *Vision 2050* Report, Overview, www.wbcsd.org/vision2050.aspx.

29. *Symposium on Sustainability—Profiles in Leadership,* New York, October 2001.

30. J. Harter and A. Adkins, "Employees Want a Lot More From Their Managers," www.gallup.com/businessjournal, April 8, 2015.

31. R. Beck and J. Harter, "Why Great Managers Are So Rare," www.gallup.com/businessjournal, March 26, 2014.

32. Ibid.

33. S. Bailey, "No Manager Left Behind," *Chief Learning Officer,* February 2015, 30.

34. S. Y. Todd, K. J. Harris, R. B. Harris, and A. R. Wheeler, "Career Success Implications of Political Skill," *Journal of Social Psychology,* June 2009, 179–204; G. R. Ferris, D. C. Treadway, P. L. Perrewé, R. L. Brouer, C. Douglas, and S. Lux, "Political Skill in Organizations," *Journal of Management,* June 2007, 290–329; K. J. Harris, K. M. Kacmar, S. Zivnuska, and J. D. Shaw, "The Impact of Political Skill on Impression Management Effectiveness," *Journal of Applied Psychology,* January 2007, 278–85; and G. R. Ferris, D. C. Treadway, R. W. Kolodinsky, W. A. Hochwarter, C. J. Kacmar, C. Douglas, and D. D. Frink, "Development and Validation of the Political Skill Inventory," *Journal of Management,* February 2005, 126–52.

35. R. Trikha, "Zappos Says Bye to Managers—What if You Had No Boss?" www.cybercoders.com/insights/, January 7, 2014; G. Anders, "No More Bosses for Zappos (A Cautionary Tale)," jobs.aol.com/articles/, January 7, 2014; M. Wohlsen, "The Next Big Thing You Missed: Companies That Work Better without Bosses," www.wired.com/business/, January 7, 2014; C. Sweeney and J. Gosfield, "No Managers Required: How Zappos Ditched the Old Corporate Structure for Something New," www.fastcompany.com, January 6, 2014; J. McGregor, "Zappos Says Goodbye to Bosses," www.washingtonpost.com/blogs/on-leadership/, January 3, 2014; J. Edwards, "Zappos Is Getting Rid of All Job Titles and Managers, but Some Bosses Will Still Decide Who Gets Paid What," www.businessinsider.com/, January 2, 2014; A. Groth, "Zappos Is Going Holacratic: No Job Titles, No Managers, No Hierarchy," qz.com/, December 30, 2013; R. E. Silverman, "Managers? Who Needs Those?" *Wall Street Journal,* August 7, 2013, B1+; M. Shaer, "The Boss Stops Here," nymag.com/news/features/, June 16, 2013; S. Wagreich, "A Billion Dollar Company with *No* Bosses? Yes, It Exists," www.inc.com/, March 14, 2013; R. E. Silverman, "Who's the Boss? There Isn't One," *Wall Street Journal,* June 20, 2012, B1+; G. Hamel, "First, Let's Fire All the Managers"; and J. Badal, "Can a Company Be Run as a Democracy?" *Wall Street Journal,* April 23, 2007, B1.

36. C. Sweeney and J. Gosfield, "No Managers Required: How Zappos Ditched the Old Corporate Structure for Something New."

37. Ibid.

38. D. Richards, "At Zappos, Culture Pays," www.strategy-business.com/article, August 24, 2010.

39. A. Groth, "Zappos Is Going Holacratic: No Job Titles, No Managers, No Hierarchy."

40. G. Anders, "No More Bosses for Zappos (A Cautionary Tale)."

41. R. E. Silverman, "At Zappos, Some Employees Find Offer to Leave Too Good to Refuse," *Wall Street Journal Online,* May 7, 2015.

42. R. D'Aprix, "A Simple Effective Formula for Leadership," *Strategic Communication Management,* May 2011, 14; R. Jaish, "Pieces of Eight," *e-learning age,* May 2011, 6; M. L. Stallard, "Google's Project Oxygen: A Case-Study in Connection Culture," www.humanresourcesiq.com, March 25, 2011; J. Aquino, "8 Traits of Stellar Managers, Defined by Googlers," www.businessinsider.com, March 15, 2011; and A. Bryant, "Google's Quest to Build a Better Boss," *New York Times Online,* March 12, 2011.

43. N. Perlroth, "Outmaneuvered at Their Own Game, Anti-Virus Makers Struggle to Adapt," *New York Times Online,* December 31, 2012; A. Vance, "Have You Seen This Android?" *Bloomberg BusinessWeek,* March 12–18, 2012, 37–38; "Are We Winning the Cybersecurity War?" www.networkworld.com, February 13, 2012, 19–20; "Symantec Corporation: Company Profile," *Datamonitor,* February 10, 2012; A. Greenberg, "As Hackers Leak Symantec's Source Code, Firm Says Cops Set Up Extortion Sting Operation," Forbes.com, February 7, 2012, 8; "Under Siege," *Best's Review,* January 2012, 77; E. Savits and A. K. Ghosh, "Cyber Spies Are Winning: Time to Reinvent Online Security," Forbes.com, November 18, 2011, 3; and "The Virus Hunters," *Management Today,* December 2010, 98.

History Module
A BRIEF HISTORY OF MANAGEMENT'S ROOTS

Henry Ford once said, "History is more or less bunk." Well…Henry Ford was wrong! History is important because it can put current activities in perspective. We propose that you need to know management history because it can help you understand what today's managers do. In this module, you'll find an annotated timeline that discusses key milestones in management theory. *Check out each chapter's "From the Past to the Present" box feature where we highlight a key person and his or her contributions or a key historical factor and its effect on contemporary management concepts.* We believe this approach will help you better understand the origins of many contemporary management concepts.

Early Management
Management has been practiced a long time. Organized endeavors directed by people responsible for planning, organizing, leading, and controlling activities have existed for thousands of years. Regardless of what these individuals were called, someone had to perform those functions.

● 3000 BCE–1776	1911–1947	Late 1700s–1950s	1940s–1950s	1960s–present
Early Management	Classical Approaches	Behavioral Approach	Quantitative Approach	Contemporary Approaches

Stephen Studd/Getty Images

3000–2500 BCE
The Egyptian pyramids are proof that projects of tremendous scope, employing tens of thousands of people, were completed in ancient times.[1] It took more than 100,000 workers some 20 years to construct a single pyramid. Someone had to plan what was to be done, organize people and materials to do it, make sure those workers got the work done, and impose some controls to ensure that everything was done as planned. That someone was managers.

Antonio Natale/Getty Images

1400s
At the arsenal of Venice, warships were floated along the canals, and at each stop, materials and riggings were added to the ship.[2] Sounds a lot like a car "floating" along an assembly line, doesn't it? In addition, the Venetians used warehouse and inventory systems to keep track of materials, human resource management functions to manage the labor force (including wine breaks), and an accounting system to keep track of revenues and costs.

1776
Although this is an important date in U.S. history, it's also important because it's the year Adam Smith's *Wealth of Nations* was published. In it, he argued the economic advantages of the **division of labor** (or **job specialization**)—that is, breaking down jobs into narrow, repetitive tasks. Using division of labor, individual productivity could be increased dramatically. Job specialization continues to be a popular way to determine how work gets done in organizations. As you'll see in Chapter 6, it does have its drawbacks.

Fotosearch/Getty Images

Transcendental Graphics/Getty Images

1780s–Mid-1800s
The **Industrial Revolution** may be the most important pre-twentieth-century influence on management. Why? Because with the industrial age came the birth of the corporation. With large, efficient factories pumping out products, someone needed to forecast demand, make sure adequate supplies of materials were available, assign tasks to workers, and so forth. Again, that someone was managers! It was indeed a historic event for two reasons: (1) because of all the organizational aspects (hierarchy, control, job specialization, and so forth) that became a part of the way work was done, and (2) because management had become a necessary component to ensure the success of the enterprise.

Classical Approaches

Beginning around the turn of the twentieth century, the discipline of management began to evolve as a unified body of knowledge. Rules and principles were developed that could be taught and used in a variety of settings. These early management proponents were called classical theorists.

3000 BCE–1776	● 1911–1947	Late 1700s–1950s	1940s–1950s	1960s–present
Early Management	Classical Approaches	Behavioral Approach	Quantitative Approach	Contemporary Approaches

Bettmann/CORBIS

1911

That's the year Frederick W. Taylor's *Principles of Scientific Management* was published. His groundbreaking book described a theory of **scientific management**—the use of scientific methods to determine the "one best way" for a job to be done. His theories were widely accepted and used by managers around the world, and Taylor became known as the "father" of scientific management.[3] (Taylor's work is profiled in Chapter 1's "From the Past to the Present" box.) Other major contributors to scientific management were Frank and Lillian Gilbreth (early proponents of time-and-motion studies and parents of the large family described in the original book *Cheaper by the Dozen*) and Henry Gantt (whose work on scheduling charts was the foundation for today's project management).

Hulton Archive/Getty Images

1916–1947

Unlike Taylor, who focused on an individual production worker's job, Henri Fayol and Max Weber (depicted in the photo) looked at organizational practices by focusing on what managers do and what constituted good management. This approach is known as **general administrative theory**. Fayol was introduced in Chapter 1 as the person who first identified five management functions. He also identified 14 **principles of management**—fundamental rules of management that could be applied to all organizations.[4] (See Exhibit HM–1 for a list of these 14 principles.) Weber is known for his description and analysis of bureaucracy, which he believed was an ideal, rational form of organization structure, especially for large organizations. In Chapter 6, we elaborate on these two important management pioneers.

Exhibit HM–1 Fayol's 14 Principles of Management

1 **Division of Work.** This principle is the same as Adam Smith's "division of labor." Specialization increases output by making employees more efficient.

2 **Authority.** Managers must be able to give orders. Authority gives them this right. Along with authority, however, goes responsibility. Whenever authority is exercised, responsibility arises.

3 **Discipline.** Employees must obey and respect the rules that govern the organization. Good discipline is the result of effective leadership, a clear understanding between management and workers regarding the organization's rules, and the judicious use of penalties for infractions of the rules.

4 **Unity of Command.** Every employee should receive orders from only one superior.

5 **Unity of Direction.** Each group of organizational activities that have the same objective should be directed by one manager using one plan.

6 **Subordination of Individual Interests to the General Interest.** The interests of any one employee or group of employees should not take precedence over the interests of the organization as a whole.

7 **Remuneration.** Workers must be paid a fair wage for their services.

8 **Centralization.** Centralization refers to the degree to which subordinates are involved in decision making. Whether decision making is centralized (to management) or decentralized (to subordinates) is a question of proper proportion. The task is to find the optimum degree of centralization for each situation.

9 **Scalar Chain.** The line of authority from top management to the lowest ranks represents the scalar chain. Communications should follow this chain. However, if following the chain creates delays, cross-communications can be allowed if agreed to by all parties and if superiors are kept informed. Also called chain of command.

10 **Order.** People and materials should be in the right place at the right time.

11 **Equity.** Managers should be kind and fair to their subordinates.

12 **Stability of Tenure of Personnel.** High employee turnover is inefficient. Management should provide orderly personnel planning and ensure that replacements are available to fill vacancies.

13 **Initiative.** Employees who are allowed to originate and carry out plans will exert high levels of effort.

14 **Esprit de Corps.** Promoting team spirit will build harmony and unity within the organization.

Behavioral Approach

The behavioral approach to management focused on the actions of workers. How do you motivate and lead employees in order to get high levels of performance?

3000 BCE–1776	1911–1947	● Late 1700s–1950s	1940s–1950s	1960s–present
Early Management	Classical Approaches	Behavioral Approach	Quantitative Approach	Contemporary Approaches

Late 1700s–Early 1900s

Managers get things done by working with people. Several early management writers recognized how important people are to an organization's success.[5] For instance, Robert Owen, who was concerned about deplorable working conditions, proposed an idealistic workplace. Hugo Munsterberg, a pioneer in the field of industrial psychology, suggested using psychological tests for employee selection, learning theory concepts for employee training, and studies of human behavior for employee motivation. Mary Parker Follett was one of the first to recognize that organizations could be viewed from both individual *and* group behavior. She thought that organizations should be based on a group ethic rather than on individualism.

Hawthorne Works Factory of Morton College

1924–Mid-1930s

The **Hawthorne studies**, a series of studies that provided new insights into individual and group behavior, were without question the most important contribution to the behavioral approach to management.[6] Conducted at the Hawthorne (Cicero, Illinois) Works of the Western Electric Company, the studies were initially designed as a scientific management experiment. Company engineers wanted to see the effect of various lighting levels on worker productivity. Using control and experimental groups of workers, they expected to find that individual output in the experimental group would be directly related to the intensity of the light. However, much to their surprise, they found that productivity in both groups varied with the level of lighting. Not able to explain it, the engineers called in Harvard professor Elton Mayo. Thus began a relationship that lasted until 1932 and encompassed numerous experiments in the behavior of people at work. What were some of their conclusions? Group pressures can significantly affect individual productivity, and people behave differently when they're being observed. Scholars generally agree that the Hawthorne studies had a dramatic impact on management beliefs about the role of people in organizations and led to a new emphasis on the human behavior factor in managing organizations.

1930s–1950s

The human relations movement is important to management history because its supporters never wavered from their commitment to making management practices more humane. Proponents of this movement uniformly believed in the importance of employee satisfaction—a satisfied worker was believed to be a productive worker.[7] So they offered suggestions like employee participation, praise, and being nice to people to increase employee satisfaction. For instance, Abraham Maslow, a humanistic psychologist, who's best known for his description of a hierarchy of five needs (a well-known theory of employee motivation), said that once a need was substantially satisfied, it no longer served to motivate behavior. Douglas McGregor developed Theory X and Theory Y assumptions, which related to a manager's beliefs about an employee's motivation to work. Even though both Maslow's and McGregor's theories were never fully supported by research, they're important because they represent the foundation from which contemporary motivation theories were developed. Both are described more fully in Chapter 11.

1960s–Today

An organization's people continue to be an important focus of management research. The field of study that researches the actions (behaviors) of people at work is called **organizational behavior (OB)**. OB researchers do empirical research on human behavior in organizations. Much of what managers do today when managing people—motivating, leading, building trust, working with a team, managing conflict, and so forth—has come out of OB research. These topics are explored in depth in Chapters 9–13.

Quantitative Approach

The quantitative approach, which focuses on the application of statistics, optimization models, information models, computer simulations, and other quantitative techniques to management activities, provided tools for managers to make their jobs easier.

3000 BCE–1776	1911–1947	Late 1700s–1950s	● 1940s–1950s	1960s–present
Early Management	Classical Approaches	Behavioral Approach	Quantitative Approach	Contemporary Approaches

Bert Hardy/Getty Images

1940s

The **quantitative approach** to management—which is the use of quantitative techniques to improve decision making—evolved from mathematical and statistical solutions developed for military problems during World War II. After the war was over, many of these techniques used for military problems were applied to businesses.[8] For instance, one group of military officers, dubbed the "Whiz Kids," joined Ford Motor Company in the mid-1940s and immediately began using statistical methods to improve decision making at Ford. You'll find more information on these quantitative applications in Chapter 15.

Richard Drew/AP Images

1950s

After World War II, Japanese organizations enthusiastically embraced the concepts espoused by a small group of quality experts, the most famous being W. Edwards Deming (photo below) and Joseph M. Juran. As these Japanese manufacturers began beating U.S. competitors in quality comparisons, Western managers soon took a more serious look at Deming's and Juran's ideas.[9] Their ideas became the basis for **total quality management (TQM)**, which is a management philosophy devoted to continual improvement and responding to customer needs and expectations. We'll look more closely at Deming and his beliefs about TQM in Chapter 15.

Contemporary Approaches

Most of the early approaches to management focused on managers' concerns inside the organization. Starting in the 1960s, management researchers began to look at what was happening in the external environment outside the organization.

3000 BCE-1776	1911-1947	Late 1700s-1950s	1940s-1950s	● 1960s-present
Early Management	Classical Approaches	Behavioral Approach	Quantitative Approach	Contemporary Approaches

Frederic J. Brown/Newscom

1960s

Although Chester Barnard, a telephone company executive, wrote in his 1938 book *The Functions of the Executive* that an organization functioned as a cooperative system, it wasn't until the 1960s that management researchers began to look more carefully at systems theory and how it related to organizations.[10] The idea of a system is a basic concept in the physical sciences. As related to organizations, the **systems approach** views systems as a set of interrelated and interdependent parts arranged in a manner that produces a unified whole. Organizations function as **open systems**, which means they are influenced by and interact with their environment. Exhibit HM–2 illustrates an organization as an open system. A manager has to efficiently and effectively manage all parts of the system in order to achieve established goals. See Chapter 2 for additional information on the external and internal factors that affect how organizations are managed.

Exhibit HM–2 Organization as an Open System

○ Contemporary Approaches

1960s

Early management theorists proposed management principles that they generally assumed to be universally applicable. Later research found exceptions to many of these principles. The **contingency approach (or situational approach)** says that organizations, employees, and situations are different and require different ways of managing. A good way to describe contingency is "if…then." *If* this is the way my situation is, *then* this is the best way for me to manage in this situation. One of the earliest contingency studies was done by Fred Fiedler and looked at what style of leadership was most effective in what situation.[11] Popular contingency variables have been found to include organization size, the routineness of task technology, environmental uncertainty, and individual differences.

Image Source/Getty Images

1980s–Present

Although the dawn of the information age is said to have begun with Samuel Morse's telegraph in 1837, the most dramatic changes in information technology have occurred in the latter part of the twentieth century and have directly affected the manager's job.[12] Managers now may manage employees who are working from home or working halfway around the world. An organization's computing resources used to be mainframe computers locked away in temperature-controlled rooms and only accessed by the experts. Now, practically everyone in an organization is connected—wired or wireless—with devices no larger than the palm of the hand. Just like the impact of the Industrial Revolution in the 1700s on the emergence of management, the information age has brought dramatic changes that continue to influence the way organizations are managed. The impact of information technology on how managers do their work is so profound that we've included in several chapters a boxed feature on "Technology and the Manager's Job."

Industrial Revolution
The advent of machine power, mass production, and efficient transportation beginning in the late eighteenth century in Great Britain

division of labor (or job specialization)
The breakdown of jobs into narrow repetitive tasks

scientific management
The use of the scientific method to define the one best way for a job to be done

general administrative theory
Descriptions of what managers do and what constitutes good management practice

principles of management
Fayol's fundamental or universal principles of management practice

Hawthorne studies
Research done in the late 1920s and early 1930s devised by Western Electric industrial engineers to examine the effect of different work environment changes on worker productivity, which led to a new emphasis on the human factor in the functioning of organizations and the attainment of their goals

organizational behavior (OB)
The field of study that researches the actions (behaviors) of people at work

quantitative approach
The use of quantitative techniques to improve decision making

total quality management (TQM)
A managerial philosophy devoted to continual improvement and responding to customer needs and expectations

systems approach
An approach to management that views an organization as a system, which is a set of interrelated and interdependent parts arranged in a manner that produces a unified whole

open systems
Systems that dynamically interact with their environment

contingency approach (or situational approach)
An approach to management that says that individual organizations, employees, and situations are different and require different ways of managing

Endnotes

1. C. S. George, Jr., *The History of Management Thought,* 2d ed. (Upper Saddle River, NJ: Prentice Hall, 1972), p. 4.

2. Ibid., pp. 35–41.

3. F. W. Taylor, *Principles of Scientific Management* (New York: Harper, 1911), p. 44. For other information on Taylor, see S. Wagner-Tsukamoto, "An Institutional Economic Reconstruction of Scientific Management: On the Lost Theoretical Logic of Taylorism," *Academy of Management Review,* January 2007, pp. 105–117; R. Kanigel, *The One Best Way: Frederick Winslow Taylor and the Enigma of Efficiency* (New York: Viking, 1997); and M. Banta, *Taylored Lives: Narrative Productions in the Age of Taylor, Veblen, and Ford* (Chicago: University of Chicago Press, 1993).

4. H. Fayol, *Industrial and General Administration* (Paris: Dunod, 1916); M. Weber, *The Theory of Social and Economic Organizations,* ed. T. Parsons, trans. A. M. Henderson and T. Parsons (New York: Free Press, 1947); and M. Lounsbury and E. J. Carberry, "From King to Court Jester? Weber's Fall from Grace in Organizational Theory," *Organization Studies,* vol. 26, no. 4 (2005), pp. 501–525.

5. R. A. Owen, *A New View of Society* (New York: E. Bliss and White, 1825); H. Munsterberg, *Psychology and Industrial Efficiency* (Boston: Houghton Mifflin, 1913); and M. P. Follett, *The New State: Group Organization the Solution of Popular Government* (London: Longmans, Green, 1918).

6. E. Mayo, *The Human Problems of an Industrial Civilization* (New York: Macmillan, 1933); and F. J. Roethlisberger and W. J. Dickson, *Management and the Worker* (Cambridge, MA: Harvard University Press, 1939). Also see G. W. Yunker, "An Explanation of Positive and Negative Hawthorne Effects: Evidence from the Relay Assembly Test Room and Bank Wiring Observation Room Studies," paper presented, Academy of Management Annual Meeting, August 1993, Atlanta, Georgia; S. R. Jones, "Was There a Hawthorne Effect?" *American Sociological Review,* November 1992, pp. 451–468; and S. R. G. Jones, "Worker Interdependence and Output: The Hawthorne Studies Reevaluated," *American Sociological Review,* April 1990, pp. 176–190; J. A. Sonnenfeld, "Shedding Light on the Hawthorne Studies," *Journal of Occupational Behavior* (April 1985), pp. 111–130; B. Rice, "The Hawthorne Defect: Persistence of a Flawed Theory," *Psychology Today,* February 1982, pp. 70–74; R. H. Franke and J. Kaul, "The Hawthorne Experiments: First Statistical Interpretations," *American Sociological Review,* October 1978, pp. 623–643; and A. Carey, "The Hawthorne Studies: A Radical Criticism," *American Sociological Review,* June 1967, pp. 403–416.

7. A. Maslow, "A Theory of Human Motivation," *Psychological Review,* July 1943, pp. 370–396; see also A. Maslow, *Motivation and Personality* (New York: Harper & Row, 1954); and D. McGregor, *The Human Side of Enterprise* (New York: McGraw-Hill, 1960).

8. P. Rosenzweig, "Robert S. McNamara and the Evolution of Management," *Harvard Business Review,* December 2010, pp. 86–93; and C. C. Holt, "Learning How to Plan Production, Inventories, and Work Force," *Operations Research,* January–February 2002, pp. 96–99.

9. T. A. Stewart, "A Conversation with Joseph Juran," *Fortune,* January 11, 1999, pp. 168–170; J. R. Hackman and R. Wageman, "Total Quality Management: Empirical, Conceptual, and Practical Issues," *Administrative Science Quarterly,* June 1995, pp. 309–342; B. Krone, "Total Quality Management: An American Odyssey," *The Bureaucrat,* Fall 1990, pp. 35–38; and A. Gabor, *The Man Who Discovered Quality* (New York: Random House, 1990).

10. C. I. Barnard, *The Functions of the Executive* (Cambridge: Harvard University Press, 1938); and K. B. DeGreene, *Sociotechnical Systems: Factors in Analysis, Design, and Management* (Upper Saddle River, NJ: Prentice Hall, 1973), p. 13.

11. F. E. Fiedler, *A Theory of Leadership Effectiveness* (New York: McGraw-Hill, 1967).

12. "Information Age: People, Information & Technology—An Exhibition at the National Museum of American History," *Smithsonian Institution,* http://photo2.si.edu/infoage/infoage.html (June 11, 2009); and P. F. Drucker, *Management, Revised Edition* (New York: HarperCollins Publishers, 2008).

The Management Environment

2

Management Myth

It doesn't matter what an organization's culture is like. I can be happy working anywhere.

Anyone who thinks they can be happy working in any type of organizational setting might be in for a big surprise! Even working at a company rated as "a best company to work for" won't be for everyone. To be happy, don't just "settle" for a job…find a workplace and a culture that "fit" you!

WOULDN'T

it be nice to one day find a job you enjoy in an organization you're excited to go to every day (or at least most days!)? Although other factors influence job choice, an organization's culture can be an important indicator of "fit"—will I like working here and does this seem like a place where I can fit in and contribute? Organizational cultures differ and so do people. In the second part of this chapter, we'll look at what organizational culture is and what elements make up an organization's culture. Before that, however, we need to look at the external environment organizations face.

"Dynamic forces are sweeping across the globe, reshaping our lives and creating a wave of opportunities...."[1] No successful organization, or its managers, can operate without understanding the dynamic external environment that surrounds it. To better understand this external environment, we need to look at the important forces that are affecting the way organizations are managed today. ●

Learning Outcomes

2-1 Explain what the external environment is and why it's important. p. 37

2-2 Discuss how the external environment affects managers. p. 41

2-3 Define what organizational culture is and explain why it's important. p. 45

2-4 Describe how organizational culture affects managers. p. 47

What Is the External Environment and Why Is It Important?

2-1 Explain what the external environment is and why it's important.

One of the biggest mistakes managers make today is **failing to adapt** to the changing world.

external environment
Factors, forces, situations, and events outside the organization that affect its performance

When the Eyjafjallajökull volcano erupted in Iceland, who would have thought that it would lead to a shutdown at the BMW plant in Spartanburg, South Carolina, or the Nissan Motor auto assembly facility in Japan?[2] Yet, in our globalized and interconnected world, such an occurrence shouldn't be surprising at all. As volcanic ash grounded planes across Europe, supplies of tire-pressure sensors from a company in Ireland couldn't be delivered on time to the BMW plant or to the Nissan plant. Because we live in a "connected" world, managers need to be aware of the impact of the external environment on their organization.

The term **external environment** refers to factors, forces, situations, and events outside the organization that affect its performance. As shown in Exhibit 2–1, it includes several different components. The economic component encompasses factors such as interest rates, inflation, employment/unemployment rates, disposable income levels, stock market fluctuations, and business cycle stages. The demographic component is concerned with trends in population characteristics such as age, race, gender, education level, geographic location, and family composition. The technological component is concerned with scientific or industrial innovations. The sociocultural component is concerned with societal and cultural factors such as values, attitudes, trends, traditions, lifestyles, beliefs, tastes, and patterns of behavior. The political/legal component looks at federal, state, and local laws, as well as laws of other countries and global laws. It also includes a country's political conditions and stability. And the global component encompasses those issues (like a volcano eruption, political instability, terrorist attack, etc.) associated with globalization and a world economy. Although *all* these components potentially constrain managers' decisions and actions, we're going to take a more in-depth look at just two—economic and demographic.

What Is the Economy Like Today?

Snapshots of the **economic context**:

- A blue-ribbon company like General Motors goes bankrupt and then new management leads it back to profitability.
- Global news stories are reporting signs that deflation might be making a return in some countries.
- Entry-level jobs now are more "thinking" oriented and include more sophisticated responsibilities.
- Climate change is reshaping supply networks, manufacturing processes, and resource availability.

Exhibit 2–1 Components of the External Environment

Source: Robbins, Stephen P., Coulter, Mary, *Management*, 13th Ed., © 2016, p. 73. Reprinted and electronically reproduced by permission of Pearson Education, Inc., New York, NY.

After several years in crisis mode, the U.S. economy and other global economies seem to have turned the corner. However, it's not now, nor will it ever be, smooth sailing in the economic arena for managers. After all, when you're dealing with important factors such as jobs, incomes, prices of natural resources and consumer goods, stock market valuations, and business cycle stages, managers have to pay attention to those that could constrain organizational decisions and actions. Here's a quick overview of some of the more interesting characteristics of today's economy that have the potential to influence a manager's planning, organizing, leading, and controlling:

- The slowdown in productivity has moderated globally although it continues to lag in the United States. Productivity (how much a worker produces in a hour) is an important measure of how well an economy is doing. Factors that affect productivity include types and pace of innovation, changes in work practices, technology, levels of workforce education/training/skill, etc.[3]
- Global trade, which grew strongly from the late 1970s through 2008, collapsed during the last global recession and has continued to be sluggish. Some analysts are wondering if this is an indicator of a potentially major macroeconomic change where the world economy is becoming *less* connected.[4]
- Total U.S. employment is up. The 5.5 percent unemployment rate was the lowest level in over seven years. However, the downside is that the strongest employment growth has been in *low-wage* jobs.[5]
- Many U.S. workers (nearly seven million) are trapped in part-time jobs, unable to find full-time work.[6]
- Many businesses in low-wage industries (restaurants, retail, warehousing, and other services) are using part-time workers to soften the impact of health-care law mandates.[7]
- According to a *New York Times* poll, only 64 percent of Americans state that they still believe in the American dream—work hard and you can achieve success and riches. This is the lowest number in two decades.[8]

These low poll numbers possibly reflect a significant risk identified by the World Economic Forum facing business leaders and policy makers over the next decade: "severe income disparity."[9] Let's briefly look at this issue to show that managers are constrained not just by the actual economic numbers, but also by societal attitudes about the economy.

ECONOMIC INEQUALITY AND THE ECONOMIC CONTEXT. A Harris Interactive Poll found that only 10 percent of adults think that economic inequality is "*not* a problem at all." Most survey respondents believed that it is either a major problem (57 percent) or a minor problem (23 percent).[10] Why has this issue become so sensitive? After all, individuals who worked hard, took risks, and were rewarded because of their hard work or creativity have long been admired. And yes, an income gap has always existed. In the United States, that gap between the rich and the rest has been much wider than in other developed nations for decades and was accepted as part of our country's values and way of doing things. However, our acceptance of an ever-increasing income gap may be diminishing.[11] As economic growth languished and sputtered, and as people's belief that anyone could grab hold of an opportunity and have a decent shot at prosperity wavered, social discontent over growing income gaps increased. The bottom line is that business leaders need to recognize how societal attitudes in the economic context also may create constraints as they make decisions and manage their businesses.

Lastly, in this section on the economy, we want to take a look at an interesting phenomenon taking place in the United States and around the globe—the sharing economy.

sharing economy
An economic environment in which asset owners share with other individuals through a peer-to-peer service, for a set fee, their underutilized physical assets or their knowledge, expertise, skills, or time

THE SHARING ECONOMY. Have you heard of Airbnb, Uber, Zipcar, SnapGoods? These are just a few of the companies—maybe you've used one—that are part of a fast-growing phenomenon called the "sharing economy." What is the sharing economy? It's an economic environment in which asset owners share with other individuals through a peer-to-peer service, for a fee, their underutilized physical assets (such as a home, car, clothing, tools, or other physical assets). Some analysts have included the sharing of knowledge, expertise, skills, or time, as well.[12] The concept behind the sharing economy (or collaborative consumption) is putting underutilized assets to good use. Asset owners "rent out" assets they're not using to consumers who need those assets but who don't want to or who can't afford to purchase them. For instance, SnapGoods is a service through which individuals lend and borrow expensive household items, such as cameras, musical instruments, kitchenware, etc., for a fee.[13] A new startup called Kitsplit has set up a sharing arrangement between customers looking for sophisticated, high-end, creative-type equipment such as drones, Google Glass headsets, Oculus Rift systems, or expensive cameras and production companies, studios, and individuals looking to lease their unused equipment for short time periods.[14] Some economics experts have said that these arrangements aren't really "sharing" but better described as market-mediated, since there's a service or company that mediates the exchange between consumers. They suggest that the arrangement is more like an "access economy," because what consumers are looking for is convenient access to assets they need but don't have and they're not concerned with developing a business or social relationship with the asset owner.[15] Whatever form or definition it takes, the concept is likely to remain a component of our economic system.

The other external component we want to specifically look at is demographics. Why? Changes and trends in this component tend to be closely linked to the workplace and managing.

omnipotent view of management
The view that managers are directly responsible for an organization's success or failure

symbolic view of management
The view that much of an organization's success or failure is due to external forces outside managers' control

---

◄◄◄ From the Past to the Present ►►►

Just how much **difference does a manager make** in how an organization performs?

Management theory proposes two perspectives in answering this question: the omnipotent view and the symbolic view.

Omnipotent view of management:

- Managers are directly responsible for an organization's success or failure.
- Differences in performance are due to decisions and actions of managers.
- Good managers: anticipate change, exploit opportunities, correct poor performance, lead their organizations.
- Profits ↑. Managers get the credit and rewards.
  Profits ↓. Managers often get fired.
- Someone—*the manager*—is held accountable for poor performance.
- This view helps explain turnover among college and professional sports coaches.

Managers: All-powerful or helpless?

Symbolic view of management:

- Manager's ability to affect performance outcomes is constrained by external factors.
- Managers don't have a significant effect on organization's performance.
- Performance is influenced by factors over which managers have little control (economy, customers, governmental policies, competitors' actions, etc.).
- Managers *symbolize* control and influence by developing plans, making decisions, and engaging in other managerial activities to make sense out of random, confusing, and ambiguous situations.
- Manager's part in organizational success or failure is limited.

In reality, managers are neither all-powerful nor helpless. But their decisions and actions are constrained. *External* constraints come from the organization's external environment and *internal* constraints come from the organization's culture.

If your professor has assigned this, go to the Assignments section of **mymanagementlab.com** *to complete these discussion questions.*

⭐ **Talk About It 1:** Why do you think these two perspectives on management are important?

⭐ **Talk About It 2:** How are these views similar? Different?

Martin Meissner/AP Images

Age is an important demographic for managers of Apple retail stores. The company values its Gen Y employees, such as the young men and women shown here greeting customers at a store in Oberhausen, Germany, who are passionate about sharing their technical knowledge of Apple products with customers.

What Role Do Demographics Play?

Demography is destiny. Have you ever heard this phrase? What it means is that the size and characteristics of a country's population can have a significant effect on what it's able to achieve. For instance, experts say that by 2050, "emerging economies led by India and China will collectively be larger than the developed economies. Small European nations with low birthrates such as Austria, Belgium, Denmark, Norway, and Sweden will drop off the list of the 30 biggest economies."[16] **Demographics**—the characteristics of a population used for purposes of social studies—can and do have a significant impact on how managers manage. Those population characteristics include things such as age, income, sex, race, education level, ethnic makeup, employment status, geographic location, and so forth—pretty much the types of information collected on governmental census surveys.

Age is a **particularly important demographic** for managers.

Age is a particularly important demographic since the workplace often has different age groups all working together. *Baby Boomers. Gen X. Gen Y. Gen Z.* Ever heard or seen these terms? They're names given by population researchers to four well-known age groups found in the U.S. population. *Baby Boomers* are those individuals born between 1946 and 1964. You've heard so much about "boomers" because there are so many of them. The sheer number of people in that cohort has meant they've had a significant impact on every aspect of the external environment (from the educational system and entertainment/lifestyle choices to the Social Security system, health care choices, and so forth) as they've gone through various life cycle stages. *Gen X* is used to describe those individuals born between 1965 and 1977. This age group has been called the baby bust generation since it followed the baby boom and is one of the smaller age cohorts. *Gen Y* (or the "Millennials") is an age group typically considered to encompass those individuals born between 1978 and 1994. As the children of the Baby Boomers, this age group is also large in number and making its imprint on external environmental conditions as well. From technology to clothing styles to work attitudes, Gen Y, now the majority age group in the workforce, is helping shape today's workplaces.[17] Then, we have *Gen Z*—the youngest identified age group. Although demographers don't agree on the exact range of birth years for Gen Z, most group them as being born between 1995 and 2010. Gen Z is huge; those under age 20 represent 25.9 percent of the U.S. population.[18] One thing that characterizes Gen Z is that it is the most diverse and multicultural of any generation in the United States.[19] Another thing that characterizes this group is that their primary means of social interaction is online, where they freely express their opinions and attitudes. It's the first group whose only reality revolves around the "Internet, mobile devices, and social networking."[20]

Demographic age cohorts are important to our study of management because large numbers of people at certain stages in the life cycle can constrain decisions and actions taken by managers of businesses, governments, educational institutions, and other organizations. Studying demographics involves looking not only at current statistics but also at future trends. What *are* some future trends?

- Recent analysis of birth rates shows that more than 80 percent of babies being born worldwide are from Africa and Asia.[21]
- India will be the youngest country by 2020; the median age will be 29 years.[22]
- By 2050, it's predicted that China will have more people age 65 and older than the rest of the world combined.[23]
- For most of human history, individuals over the age of 65 have never exceeded 3 or 4 percent of a country's population. By 2050, however, this number could potentially reach 25 percent, on average.[24]

demographics
The characteristics of a population used for purposes of social studies

Just imagine how these population trends are likely to impact global organizations and the way managers manage.

technology
Any equipment, tools, or operating methods that are designed to make work more efficient

How Does the External Environment Affect Managers?

2-2 Discuss how the external environment affects managers.

Knowing *what* the various components of the external environment are and examining certain aspects of that environment are important for managers. However, understanding *how* the environment affects managers is equally as important. We're going to look at three ways the external environment constrains and challenges managers: (1) through its impact on jobs and employment, (2) through the environmental uncertainty that is present, and (3) through the various stakeholder relationships that exist between an organization and its external constituencies.

JOBS AND EMPLOYMENT. As any or all of the external environmental conditions change, one of the most powerful constraints managers face is the impact of such changes on jobs and employment—both in poor conditions and in good conditions. The power

---

⦂⦂⦂ Technology and the Manager's Job ⦂⦂⦂
CAN TECHNOLOGY IMPROVE THE WAY MANAGERS MANAGE?

Continuing advancements in technology offer many exciting possibilities for how workers work and managers manage. **Technology** includes any equipment, tools, or operating methods that are designed to make work more efficient. One area where technology has had an impact is in the process where inputs (labor, raw materials, and the like) are transformed into outputs (goods and services to be sold). In years past, this transformation was usually performed by human labor. With technology, however, human labor has been replaced with electronic and computer equipment. From robots in offices to online banking systems to social networks where employees interact with customers, technology has made the work of creating and delivering goods and services more efficient and effective.

Another area where technology has had a major impact is in information. Information technology (IT) has created the ability to circumvent the physical confines of working only in a specified organizational location. With notebook and desktop computers, tablets,

> Twenty-five billion. That's the number of "things" (smartphones, smartwatches, climate-control system sensors, kitchen refrigerators, cars, etc.) Gartner Inc. predicts will be connected **to the Internet by 2020**. This **Internet of Things (IoT)** is transforming businesses and disrupting industries and societies around the world.[25]

smartphones, organizational intranets, and other IT tools, organizational members who work mainly with information can do that work from any place at any time.

Finally, technology is also changing the way managers manage, especially in terms of how they interact with employees who may be working anywhere and anytime. Effectively communicating with telecommuting individuals who may simply be working from home or who may be working halfway around the world and ensuring that work goals are being met are challenges that managers must address. Throughout the rest of the book, we'll look at how managers are meeting those challenges in the ways they plan, organize, lead, and control.

*If your professor has assigned this, go to the Assignments section of **mymanagementlab.com** to complete these discussion questions.*

⭐ **TALK ABOUT IT 3:** Is management easier or harder with all the available technology? Explain your position.

⭐ **TALK ABOUT IT 4:** What benefits does technology provide and what problems does technology pose for (a) employees and (b) managers?

environmental uncertainty
The degree of change and complexity in an organization's environment

environmental complexity
The number of components in an organization's environment and the extent of knowledge that the organization has about those components

stakeholders
Any constituencies in an organization's environment that are affected by that organization's decisions and actions

of this constraint became painfully obvious during the past global recession as millions of jobs were eliminated and unemployment rates rose to levels not seen in many years. Although things have improved, economists predict that about a quarter of the 8.4 million jobs eliminated in the United States during this last economic downturn won't come back and have been replaced by other types of work in growing industries.[26] Other countries face the same issues. Although such readjustments aren't bad in and of themselves, they do create challenges for managers who must balance work demands and having enough people with the right skills to do an organization's work.

Flex Work Success Story: Verizon's experiment with organizational "volunteers" who answer customers' technical questions on a company-sponsored customer service Web site has been a success.

Not only do changes in external conditions affect the types of jobs that are available, they affect how those jobs are created and managed. For instance, many employers are using flexible work arrangements with tasks done by freelancers hired on an as-needed basis, or by temporary workers who work full-time but are not permanent employees, or by individuals who share jobs. Some organizations, like Verizon, are even using organizational "volunteers" to do work.[27] Keep in mind that these approaches are used because of the constraints from the external environment. As a manager, you'll need to recognize how such work arrangements affect the way you plan, organize, lead, and control. Flexible work arrangements have become so prevalent and such an important management approach today that we'll discuss them in other chapters as well.

ASSESSING ENVIRONMENTAL UNCERTAINTY. Another constraint posed by external environments is the amount of uncertainty found in that environment, which can affect organizational outcomes. **Environmental uncertainty** refers to the degree of change and complexity in an organization's environment. The matrix in Exhibit 2–2 shows these two aspects.

The first dimension of uncertainty is the degree of unpredictable change. If the components in an organization's environment change frequently, it's a *dynamic* environment. If change is minimal, it's a *stable* one. A stable environment might be one in which there are no new competitors, few technological breakthroughs by current competitors, little activity

Exhibit 2–2 Environmental Uncertainty Matrix

	Degree of Change	
	Stable	**Dynamic**
Simple	**Cell 1** Stable and predictable environment Few components in environment Components are somewhat similar and remain basically the same Minimal need for sophisticated knowledge of components	**Cell 2** Dynamic and unpredictable environment Few components in environment Components are somewhat similar but are continually changing Minimal need for sophisticated knowledge of components
Complex	**Cell 3** Stable and predictable environment Many components in environment Components are not similar to one another and remain basically the same High need for sophisticated knowledge of components	**Cell 4** Dynamic and unpredictable environment Many components in environment Components are not similar to one another and are continually changing High need for sophisticated knowledge of components

Degree of Complexity (vertical axis label)

by pressure groups to influence the organization, and so forth. For instance, Zippo Manufacturing, best known for its Zippo lighters, faces a relatively stable environment. There are few competitors and little technological change. The main external concern for the company is probably the declining trend in tobacco usage. In contrast, the recorded music industry faces a dynamic (highly uncertain and unpredictable) environment. Digital formats, apps, music-streaming sites, and artists releasing selected songs on their personal social media accounts have turned the industry upside down and brought high levels of uncertainty.

The other dimension of uncertainty describes the degree of **environmental complexity**, which looks at the number of components in an organization's environment and the extent of the knowledge that the organization has about those components. An organization that has few competitors, customers, suppliers, or government agencies to deal with, or that needs little information about its environment, has a less complex and thus less uncertain environment.

Software developers and designers from communities throughout the world are valuable stakeholders for Yahoo. The company builds relationships with these computer experts by staging hacking events, like the one shown here in Bangalore, India, that may result in technological innovations.

How does the concept of environmental uncertainty influence managers? Looking again at Exhibit 2–2, each of the four cells represents different combinations of degree of complexity and degree of change. Cell 1 (stable-simple environment) represents the lowest level of environmental uncertainty and cell 4 (dynamic and complex environment) the highest. Not surprisingly, managers have the greatest influence on organizational outcomes in cell 1 and the least in cell 4. Because uncertainty is a threat to an organization's effectiveness, managers try to minimize it. Given a choice, managers would prefer to operate in the least uncertain environments, but they rarely control that choice. In addition, the nature of the external environment today is that most industries are facing more dynamic change, making their environments more uncertain.

MANAGING STAKEHOLDER RELATIONSHIPS. What has made MTV a popular TV channel for young adults year after year? One reason for its popularity is that MTV understands the importance of building relationships with its various stakeholders: viewers (the network is relentless in monitoring its target-audience preferences), reality show participants, celebrities, advertisers, affiliate TV stations, public service groups, and others.[28] The nature of stakeholder relationships is another way in which the environment influences managers. The more obvious and secure these relationships, the more influence managers will have over organizational outcomes.

Stakeholders are any constituencies in an organization's environment that are affected by that organization's decisions and actions. These groups have a stake in or are significantly influenced by what the organization does. In turn, these groups can influence the organization. For example, think of the groups that might be affected by the decisions and actions of Starbucks—coffee bean farmers, employees, specialty coffee competitors, local communities, and so forth. Some of these stakeholders, in turn, may impact the decisions and actions of

A Question of Ethics

Ever heard of Waze? It's an extremely popular mobile traffic software app by Google that provides real-time traffic guidance and warnings about traffic congestion, construction zones, speed traps, stalled vehicles, unsafe weather conditions, etc. However, there's one feature that has law enforcement officers across the United States very worried.[29] Police are pleading with Google to turn off the feature that warns drivers when police are nearby, fearing that making their location known is an officer-safety threat and possibly even a public-safety threat. Although there are no known connections between any attacks on police and the use of Waze, law enforcement trade groups are concerned that it's only a matter of time before a would-be terrorist or cop killer uses the app to find where a police officer target is parked. A Waze spokesperson said that the company is very conscious of safety and security concerns and has worked with the New York City Police Department and others by sharing information.

*If your professor has assigned this, go to the Assignments section of **mymanagementlab.com** to complete these discussion questions.*

⭐ **Talk About It 5:** Is there an ethical issue here? Why or why not?

⭐ **Talk About It 6:** What stakeholders might have a vested interest in this issue and what do you think their position might be? How can identifying stakeholders help a manager decide the most responsible approach?

⭐ **Watch It 1!**

If your professor has assigned this, go to the Assignments section of **www.mymanagementlab.com** to complete the video exercise titled ***Rudi's Bakery: Organizational Culture***.

Starbucks' managers. The idea that organizations have stakeholders is now widely accepted by both management academics and practicing managers.[30]

Exhibit 2–3 identifies the most common stakeholders that an organization might have to deal with. Note that these stakeholders include internal and external groups. Why? Because both can affect what an organization does and how it operates.

Why should managers even care about managing stakeholder relationships? For one thing, it can lead to desirable organizational outcomes such as improved predictability of environmental changes, more successful innovations, greater degree of trust among stakeholders, and greater organizational flexibility to reduce the impact of change. For instance, social media company Facebook is spending more on lobbying and meeting with government officials as lawmakers and regulators look at sweeping changes to online privacy law. The company is "working to shape its image on Capitol Hill and avert measures potentially damaging to its information-sharing business."[31]

Can stakeholder management affect organizational performance? The answer is yes! Management researchers who have looked at this issue are finding that managers of high-performing companies tend to consider the interests of all major stakeholder groups as they make decisions.[32]

Another reason for managing external stakeholder relationships is that it's the "right" thing to do. Because an organization depends on these external groups as sources of inputs (resources) and as outlets for outputs (goods and services), managers should consider the interests of stakeholders as they make decisions. We'll address this issue in more detail in the next chapter when we look at corporate social responsibility.

As we've tried to make clear throughout this section, it's not going to be "business as usual" for organizations or for managers. Managers will always have hard decisions to make about how they do business and about their people. It's important that you understand how changes in the external environment will affect your organizational and management experiences. Now, we need to switch gears and look at the internal aspects of the organization—specifically, its culture.

Exhibit 2–3 Organizational Stakeholders

What Is Organizational Culture?

EACH OF US HAS A UNIQUE PERSONALITY that influences the way we act and interact. An organization has a personality too—we call it **CULTURE**. Here's what **YOU** need to know about **organizational culture**!

2-3 Define what organizational culture is and explain why it's important.

1 **Culture is perceived**. It's not something that can be physically touched or seen, but employees perceive it on the basis of what they experience within the organization.

2 **Culture is descriptive**. It's concerned with how members perceive or describe the culture, not with whether they like it.

3 **Culture is shared**. Even though individuals may have different backgrounds or work at different organizational levels, they tend to describe the organization's culture in similar terms.

SiliconValleyStock/Alamy

Lynn Johnson/Alamy

Google has created a creative and innovative culture at their headquarters in California with an android googleplex, bikes, and bringing your dog to work.

Kristoffer Tripplaar/Alamy

organizational culture
The shared values, principles, traditions, and ways of doing things that influence the way organizational members act

45

Dimensions of Organizational Culture

Exhibit 2–4

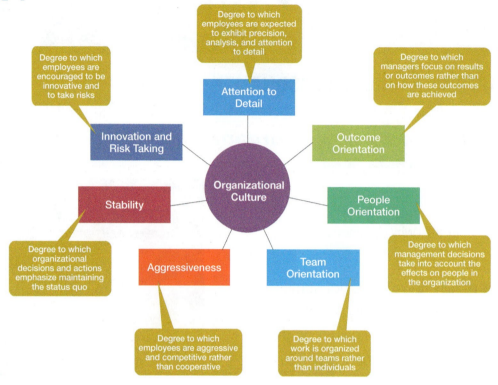

How Can Culture Be Described?

The seven dimensions (shown in Exhibit 2–4):[33]

- Range from *low* (not typical of the culture) to *high* (especially typical of the culture).
- Provide a composite picture of the organization's culture.

    An organization's culture may be shaped by one particular cultural dimension more than the others, thus influencing the organization's personality and the way organizational members work. For example:

    —*Apple's* focus is product innovation (innovation and risk taking). The company "lives and breathes" new product development and employees' work behaviors support that goal.

    —*Southwest Airlines* has made its employees a central part of its culture (people orientation) and shows this through the way it treats them.

Where Does Culture Come From?	How Do Employees Learn the Culture?
Usually reflects the vision or **mission** of founders.	Organizational stories: narrative tales of significant events or people.
Founders project an image of *what the organization should be* and *what its values are*.	**Corporate rituals**: repetitive sequences of activities that express and reinforce important organizational values and goals.
Founders can "impose" their vision on employees because of new organization's small size.	**Material symbols or artifacts**: layout of facilities, how employees dress, size of offices, material perks provided to executives, furnishings, and so forth.
Organizational members *create a shared history* that binds them into a community and reminds them of "who we are."	**Language**: special acronyms; unique terms to describe equipment, key personnel, customers, suppliers, processes, products.

How Does Organizational Culture Affect Managers?

2-4 Describe how organizational culture affects managers.

Ambrosia Humphrey, vice president of talent at Hootsuite, understands the power of organizational culture and how it affects her as a manager. Nurturing and nourishing the company's culture is one of her top priorities. And she does this by continually creating employee experiences that reflect an important company value—transparency. For instance, she's organized all-staff "Ask Me Anything" discussions with the company's CEO. Another tactic she's used is employee "hackathons" in which staff members get together to tackle problems. And, of course, she embraces social media as part of her commitment to transparency to employees, customers, and the community. Employees are encouraged to tweet about their perspectives on what it's like to work at Hootsuite. Those postings have ranged from pictures taken at rooftop meetings to employees complimenting other employees for their hard work to links to media reports about the company as a great place to work.[34]

The two main ways that an organization's culture affects managers are (1) its effect on what employees do and how they behave, and (2) its effect on what managers do.

> ⭐ **Watch It 2!**
>
> If your professor has assigned this, go to the Assignments section of **mymanagementlab.com** to complete the video exercise titled **CH2M Hill: Organizational Culture**.

How Does Culture Affect What Employees Do?

"I think of culture as guardrails...what you stand for, essentially the ground rules so that people know how to operate."[35]

An organization's culture has an effect on what employees do, depending on how strong, or weak, the culture is. **Strong cultures**—those in which the key values are deeply held and widely shared—have a greater influence on employees than do weaker cultures. The more employees accept the organization's key values and the greater their commitment to those values, the stronger the culture is. Most organizations have moderate to strong cultures; that is, there is relatively high agreement on what's important, what defines "good" employee behavior, what it takes to get ahead, and so forth. The stronger a culture becomes, the more it affects what employees do and the way managers plan, organize, lead, and control.[36]

Also, in organizations with a strong culture, that culture can substitute for the rules and regulations that formally guide employees. In essence, strong cultures can create predictability, orderliness, and consistency without the need for written documentation. Therefore, the stronger an organization's culture, the less managers need to be concerned with developing formal rules and regulations. Instead, those guides will be internalized in employees when they accept the organization's culture. If, on the other hand, an organization's culture is weak—if no dominant shared values are present—its effect on employee behavior is less clear.

Twitter employees give their company high marks for a strong culture of collaboration, learning, and open communication that allows them to share ideas and information in solving difficult problems. Employees value a work environment, including a rooftop garden at Twitter headquarters in San Francisco, where they can easily connect and work closely with colleagues.

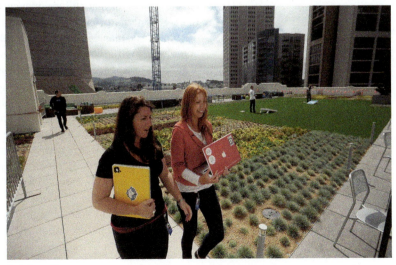

Noah Berger/Reuters

> ### ✪ Try It!
> If your professor has assigned this, go to the Assignments section of **mymanagementlab.com** to complete the **Simulation:** *Organizational Culture*.

How Does Culture Affect What Managers Do?

Say What? Ten percent of executives say they *have not* identified or communicated an organizational culture.[37]

Houston-based Apache Corp. has become one of the best performers in the independent oil drilling business because it has fashioned a culture that values risk taking and quick decision making. Potential hires are judged on how much initiative they've shown in getting projects done at other companies. And company employees are handsomely rewarded if they meet profit and production goals.[38] Because an organization's culture constrains what they can and cannot do and how they manage, it's particularly relevant to managers. Such constraints are rarely explicit. They're not written down. It's unlikely they'll even be spoken. But they're there, and all managers quickly learn *what to do* and *not do* in their organization. For instance, you won't find the following values written down, but each comes from a real organization:

- Look busy even if you're not.
- If you take risks and fail around here, you'll pay dearly for it.
- Before you make a decision, run it by your boss so that he or she is never surprised.
- We make our product only as good as the competition forces us to.
- What made us successful in the past will make us successful in the future.
- If you want to get to the top here, you have to be a team player.

The link between values such as these and managerial behavior is fairly straightforward. Take, for example, a so-called "ready-aim-fire" culture. In such an organization, managers will study and analyze proposed projects endlessly before committing to them. However, in a "ready-fire-aim" culture, managers take action and then analyze what has been done. Or, say an organization's culture supports the belief that profits can be increased by cost cutting and that the company's best interests are served by achieving slow but steady increases in quarterly earnings. In that culture, managers are unlikely to pursue programs that are innovative, risky, long term, or expansionary. In an organization whose culture conveys a basic distrust of employees, managers are more likely to use an authoritarian leadership style than a democratic one. Why? The culture establishes for managers appropriate and expected behavior. You can see this in action at Winegardner & Hammons, a hotel management firm, where company leaders have built a "Winning Workplace Culture" with four characteristics: a positive work environment in which managers are encouraged to make employees feel cared for and valued; an employee selection process that encourages managers to focus on selecting the "right" employees; an employee engagement program that's based on training managers so they have the right skills, knowledge, and experience to nurture an engaging work environment; and a strengths-based workplace in which managers continually reinforce employees' strengths. What has this cultural focus led to? *Thirty-four percent lower employee turnover* and *11 percent higher profitability*.[39] That's the kind of outcomes that can be achieved *if* you pay attention to your organizational culture and *if* managers recognize appropriate and expected behavior in that culture.

Exhibit 2–5 Managerial Decisions Affected by Culture

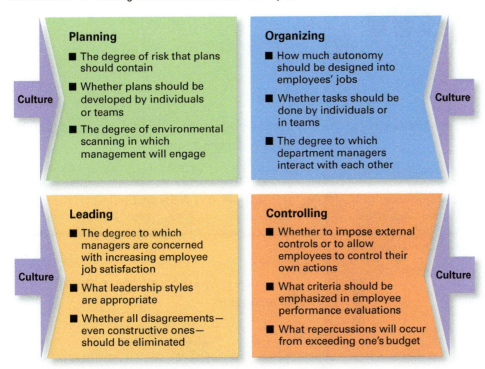

Planning
- The degree of risk that plans should contain
- Whether plans should be developed by individuals or teams
- The degree of environmental scanning in which management will engage

Culture

Organizing
- How much autonomy should be designed into employees' jobs
- Whether tasks should be done by individuals or in teams
- The degree to which department managers interact with each other

Culture

Leading
- The degree to which managers are concerned with increasing employee job satisfaction
- What leadership styles are appropriate
- Whether all disagreements— even constructive ones— should be eliminated

Culture

Controlling
- Whether to impose external controls or to allow employees to control their own actions
- What criteria should be emphasized in employee performance evaluations
- What repercussions will occur from exceeding one's budget

Culture

Source: Robbins, Stephen P., Coulter, Mary, *Management*, 13th Ed., © 2016, p. 86. Reprinted and electronically reproduced by permission of Pearson Education, Inc., New York, NY.

As shown in Exhibit 2–5, a manager's decisions are influenced by the culture in which he or she operates. An organization's culture, especially a strong one, influences and constrains the way managers plan, organize, lead, and control.

MyManagementLab®

Go to **mymanagementlab.com** to complete the problems marked with this icon ⭐.

2 Review

CHAPTER SUMMARY

2-1 Explain what the external environment is and why it's important.

The external environment refers to factors, forces, situations, and events outside the organization that affect its performance. It includes economic, demographic, political/legal, sociocultural, technological, and global components. The external environment is important because it poses constraints and challenges to managers.

2-2 Discuss how the external environment affects managers.

There are three ways that the external environment affects managers: its impact on jobs and employment, the amount of environmental uncertainty, and the nature of stakeholder relationships.

2-3 Define what organizational culture is and explain why it's important.

Organizational culture is the shared values, principles, traditions, and ways of doing things that influence the way organizational members act. It's important because of the impact it has on decisions, behaviors, and actions of organizational employees.

2-4 Describe how organizational culture affects managers.

Organizational culture affects managers in two ways: through its effect on what employees do and how they behave, and through its effect on what managers do as they plan, organize, lead, and control.

DISCUSSION QUESTIONS

2-1 How much impact do managers actually have on an organization's success or failure?

⭐ 2-2 What are the six external environment components and why is it important for managers to understand these components?

2-3 How has the changed economy affected what managers do? Find two or three examples in current business periodicals of activities and practices that organizations are using. Discuss them in light of the changed environment.

2-4 Why is it important for managers to pay attention to demographic trends and shifts?

2-5 What is environmental uncertainty? What impact does it have on managers and organizations? Find two examples in current business periodicals that illustrate how environmental uncertainty affects organizations.

2-6 "Businesses are built on relationships." What do you think this statement means? What are the implications for managing the external environment?

2-7 Is organizational culture an asset to an organization? Explain. Can it ever be a liability? Explain.

⭐ 2-8 How is an organization's culture formed and maintained?

2-9 Discuss the impact of a strong culture on organizations and managers.

2-10 Pick two organizations that you interact with frequently (as an employee or as a customer) and assess their culture according to the dimensions shown in Exhibit 2–4.

Writing Assignments

2-11 How can managers best deal with environmental uncertainty?

2-12 Explain how an organization's culture can help it be successful AND how it can keep it from being successful.

Management Skill Builder | UNDERSTANDING CULTURE

An organization's culture is a system of shared meaning. When you understand your organization's culture, you know, for example, whether it encourages teamwork, rewards innovation, or stifles initiative. When interviewing for a job, the more accurate you are at assessing the culture, the more likely you are to find a good person-organization fit. And once inside an organization, understanding the culture allows you to know what behaviors are likely to be rewarded and which are likely to be punished.[40]

⊛ PERSONAL INVENTORY ASSESSMENT

Company Culture Assessment

Want to know what a company's culture is like? This PIA will show you what's involved with assessing a company's culture.

Skill Basics

Organizational cultures differ. So do individuals. The better you're able to match your personal preferences to an organization's culture, the more likely you are to find satisfaction in your work, the less likely you are to leave, and the greater the probability that you'll receive positive performance evaluations.

The ability to read an organization's culture can be a valuable skill. For instance, if you're looking for a job, you'll want to choose an employer whose culture is compatible with your values and in which you'll feel comfortable. If you can accurately assess a potential employer's culture before you make your job decision, you may be able to save yourself a lot of grief and reduce the likelihood of making a poor choice. Similarly, you'll undoubtedly have business transactions with numerous organizations during your professional career, such as selling a product or service, negotiating a contract, arranging a joint work project, or merely seeking out who controls certain decisions in an organization. The ability to assess another organization's culture can be a definite plus in successfully performing those pursuits.

For the sake of simplicity, we're going to look at this skill from the perspective of a job applicant. We'll assume you're interviewing for a job, although these skills are generalizable to many situations. Here's a list of things you can do to help learn about an organization's culture:

- *Do background work.* Get the names of former employees from friends or acquaintances, and talk with them. Also talk with members of professional trade associations to which the organization's employees belong and executive recruiters who deal with the organization. Look for clues in stories told in annual reports and other organizational literature, and check out the organization's Web sites for evidence of high turnover or recent management shake-ups.

- *Observe the physical surroundings.* Pay attention to signs, posters, pictures, photos, style of dress, length of hair, de-

gree of openness between offices, and office furnishings and arrangements.

- *Make note about those with whom you met.* Whom did you meet? How did they expect to be addressed?

- *How would you characterize the style of the people you met?* Are they formal? Casual? Serious? Jovial? Open? Reticent about providing information?

- *Look at the organization's human resources manual.* Are there formal rules and regulations printed there? If so, how detailed are they? What do they cover?

- *Ask questions of the people with whom you meet.* The most valid and reliable information tends to come from asking the same questions of many people (to see how closely their responses align). Questions that will give you insights into organizational processes and practices might include: What's the background of the founders? What's the background of current senior managers? What are these managers' functional specialties, and were they promoted from within or hired from outside? How does the organization integrate new employees? Is there a formal orientation program? Are there formal employee training programs and, if so, how are they structured? How does your boss define his or her job success? How would you define fairness in terms of reward allocations? Can you identify some people here who are on the "fast track"? What do you think has put them on the fast track? Can you identify someone in the organization who seems to be considered a deviant, and how has the organization responded to this person? Can you describe a decision that someone made that was well received? Can you describe a decision that didn't work out well, and what were the consequences for that decision maker? Could you describe a crisis or critical event that has occurred recently in the organization, and how did top management respond?

Practicing the Skill

After spending your first three years after college graduation as a freelance graphic designer, you're looking at pursuing a job as an account executive at a graphic design firm. You feel that the scope of assignments and potential for technical training far exceed what you'd be able to do on your own, and you're looking to expand your skills and meet a brand-new set of challenges. However, you want to make sure you "fit" into the organization where you're going to be spending more than eight hours every workday. Write a brief paper describing how you would find a place where you'll be happy and where your style and personality will be appreciated.

Experiential Exercise

Speedy Car Wash Services, Inc.

To: Michelle Bradley, Employee Care Manager

From: Alex Bilyeu, President

Re: Creating a Fun Workplace

Michelle, I saw an article the other day explaining the results of a survey that said only 8 percent of employers use fun to reduce employee stress at work. That same article said that research has shown that people who have fun at work are more creative, more productive, work better with others, and call in sick less often. I'm sold! So how and where do we start? Get me a bulleted list of ideas on how we can create a workplace here at Speedy that's both fun and yet still focused on work. I'm sure you'll have to do some research on this. And have fun with it!

This fictionalized company and message were created for educational purposes only, and are not meant to reflect positively or negatively on management practices by any company that may share this name.

CASE APPLICATION #1

Getting Back on Target

You could say the tipping point for Target Corp. was the massive credit-card hack in November.

- The biggest retail breach in U.S. history.
- Some 110 million customer records compromised.[41]

Even before this major fiasco, however, things were not good at Target, the nation's second-largest retailer. The company had lost its way under the leadership of former CEO Gregg Steinhafel. Target, a superb marketing machine, had always been viewed as hip and "fun, fresh, and energetic."[42] But that wasn't who Steinhafel was. As the former chief financial officer, Steinhafel's skills, personality, and demeanor set a tone that was numbers-driven, not people-driven. The culture he fostered at Target was one oriented around rigid performance measures. Creativity and quirkiness (remember the fun Target ads with the company's mascot dog) were no longer rewarded or encouraged. Instead, company buyers were less willing to take risks on the newest and most unique merchandise items, product vendors were pressured on costs, and things that used to make the company one of the most exciting merchandisers were downplayed or ignored. For example, a plan to use mannequins in stores for the first time ever stalled after months of testing and review.[43] Then came the data breach, which affected both employee and customer morale. The workplace culture at the company's Minneapolis headquarters, already struggling, deteriorated even further.

In early May 2014, an anonymous mid-level employee at headquarters let loose a rant on Gawker that was aimed at the company's leadership (Steinhafel) and the company's future.[44] The employee rant also described a culture that was very insular and resistant to change.[45] Target's chief marketing officer, Jeff Jones, responded to the post. Although initially quite outraged, Jones responded with honesty and openness. He acknowledged that a lot of work needed to be done on the company's cultural approach and a new truth created about what Target is and what it stands for. Not long after, Target's board fired Steinhafel. Although the company's cultural issues and the massive data breach were partly the reason, there was other ample evidence that the organization's performance was

Bull's-eye—Target's Culture

suffering, especially in its Canadian division. But when a company's top leader is viewed so negatively, it's next to impossible for needed changes to take place. Those changes would have to come from new leadership.

Target Corp.'s new CEO, Brian Cornell, took over in August 2014. Since his arrival, there appears to have been a significant shift in culture. A company that was once described as very insular and resistant to change is now embracing transparency, openness, and change. Cornell has been described as very enthusiastic about customers and Target's businesses.[46] That type of enthusiasm is contagious for not only headquarter employees but employees throughout the organization. Other cultural changes are happening in the expectations for Target's employees. Innovation is accelerating, decision making is being simplified, and old "cultural symbols of unacceptable behavior"[47] are being obliterated. Target executives aren't

underestimating the hard work that's ahead of them. But by staying focused on the bull's-eye—Target's "guests" (customers)—they intend to be united in their return to Target's "cheap-chic roots."[48]

Discussion Questions

2-14 What role does a CEO play in an organization's culture? What role do other leaders/managers play?

2-15 Describe Target's culture under its previous CEO. Describe Target's culture under its current CEO.

2-16 What are the benefits and challenges of social media in managing organizational culture?

2-17 Which view of management do you see played out here? The omnipotent or the symbolic? Explain.

2-18 What advice about organizational culture would you give the new CEO?

CASE APPLICATION #2

Not Sold Out

Competitors in the movie theater industry had hoped that they were through the challenges they'd faced during the economic downturn.[49] Ticket sales revenue has been on a roller coaster: 2011, it fell 4 percent from the previous year; 2012, it was up 6.1 percent; 2013, it was up, but just barely, by not even 1 percent; and 2014, it was down about 5 percent. The numbers of people going to see a movie continue to stall. So, the industry has tried to pump up revenue with high-profile movies, higher ticket prices, and premium amenities.

The number of movie screens in the United States totals almost 40,000. Together, the four largest movie theater chains in the United States have a little over 20,100 screens—and a lot of seats to fill. The largest, Regal Entertainment Group (based in Knoxville, Tennessee), has almost 7,400 screens. AMC Entertainment (based in Kansas City, Missouri) has 5,000 screens. The other two major competitors are Cinemark (based in Plano, Texas—about 5,200 screens) and Carmike Cinemas (based in Columbus, Georgia—more than 2,500 screens). The challenge for these companies is getting people to watch movies on all those screens; a decision that encompasses many factors.

What **WILL** get customers into movie theaters?

One important factor, according to industry analysts, is the uncertainty over how people want their movies delivered, which is largely a trade-off between convenience and quality (or what the experts call fidelity experience). Will consumers choose convenience over quality and use mobile devices such as iPads? Will they trade some quality for convenience and watch at home using streaming services on surround-sound, flat-screen, high-definition home theater systems? Or will they go to a movie theater with wide screens, high-quality sound systems, and the social experience of being with other moviegoers and enjoy the highest-fidelity experience—even with the inconveniences? Movie theater managers believe that mobile devices aren't much of a threat, even though they may be convenient. On the other hand, home theater systems may be more of a threat as they've become extremely affordable and have "acceptable" quality. Although not likely to replace any of these higher-quality offerings, drive-in theaters, analysts note, are experiencing a resurgence, especially in geographic locations where they can be open year-round. The movie theater chains are also battling IMAX Corporation for customers as movie screens get bigger and bigger. The number of these oversized screens built by the five largest theater companies has grown to the point where it almost equals the number of IMAX locations. The movie theater chains have invested in these formats because it can add several extra dollars to the ticket price, resulting in increased revenues.

Another factor managers need to wrestle with is the impression consumers have of the movie-going experience. A consumer lifestyle poll showed that the major dislike about going to the movies was the cost, a drawback cited by 36 percent of the respondents. Other factors noted included the noise, uncomfortable seats, the inconvenience, the crowds, and too many previews/commercials before the movie.

A final question facing the movie theater industry *and* the major film studios is how to be proactive in avoiding the problems that the recorded music industry faced with the illegal downloading of songs. The amount of entertainment streamed online (which includes both music and video) continues to experience double-digit growth. The biggest threat so far has been YouTube, which has become a powerful force in the media world with owner Google's backing. But now Amazon, Netflix, and other competitors are flexing their movie muscles as well. To counter that threat, industry executives have asked for filtering mechanisms to keep unlawful material off these sites and to develop some type of licensing arrangements whereby the industry has some protection over its copyrighted film content.

Given these factors, what are the movie theater chains doing? They're finding ways to make the movie-going experience something special by providing expensive presentation formats that can't be replicated or accessed in the home, comfortable surroundings (think reclining seats and blankets plus gourmet food brought to you), valet parking, babysitting, beefed-up concession stands, and so forth. These are just some of the ways that movie theaters are working to keep their seats filled.

Discussion Questions

2-19 Using Exhibit 2–1, what external components might be most important for managers in movie theater chains to know about? Why?

2-20 According to the case, what external trends do managers at the movie theater chains have to deal with?

2-21 How do you think these trends might constrain decisions made by managers at the movie theater chains?

2-22 What stakeholders do you think might be most important to movie theater chains? What interests might these stakeholders have?

CASE APPLICATION #3

Going to Extremes

Number one best e-retailer: For those of you who have shopped on Zappos.com, that ranking probably isn't a surprise.[50] For those of you who haven't shopped on Zappos.com, it wouldn't take long for you to see why Zappos deserves that accolade. And it's more than the fact that Zappos has a great selection of products, superfast shipping, and free returns. The real secret to its success is its people, who make the Zappos shopping experience truly unique and outstanding. The company, which began selling shoes and other products online in 1999, has put "extraordinary effort into building a desirable organizational culture, which has provided a sure path to business success." As part of its culture, Zappos espouses 10 corporate values. At the top of that list is "Deliver WOW through service." And do they ever deliver the WOW! Even through the recent economic challenges, Zappos has continued to thrive—a sure sign its emphasis on organizational culture is paying off.

Zappos is not only the number one e-retailer but also one of the 100 best companies to work for. Okay. So what is it *really* that makes Zappos' culture so great? Let's take a closer look. (Also, look back at Case Application #1 in Chapter 1 about Zappos' move to a holacracy.)

Zappos began selling shoes and other products online in 1999. Four years later, it was profitable, and it reached more than $1 billion in sales by 2009. Zappos was named *Business Week*'s Customer Service Champ and was given an A+ rating by the Better Business Bureau in 2009. Also, that year, Amazon (yeah, that Amazon) purchased Zappos for 10 million Amazon shares, worth almost $928 million at the time. Zappos' employees divided up $40 million in cash and

Zappos ... **delivering the WOW** through service.

restricted stock and were assured that Zappos management would remain in place.

Tony Hsieh (pronounced *Shay)* became Zappos CEO in 2000. His personality has been best described as a blend of "weirdness and humility." And those same characteristics are what Hsieh wanted Zappos culture to look like. Before joining Zappos, Hsieh had been co-founder of the Internet advertising network LinkExchange and had seen firsthand the problems that crop up when you have a company where people's technical skills are the only thing that matters. He was determined to do it differently at Zappos. Hsieh first invited Zappos' 300 employees to list the core values the culture should be based on. That process led to the 10 values that continue to drive the organization, which now employs about 1,400 people.

Another thing that distinguishes Zappos' culture is the recognition that organizational culture is more than a list of written values. The culture has to be "lived." And Zappos does this by maintaining a culture that's focused on creating ways for employees to interact. At Zappos, social media is used liberally to link employees with one another and with the company's customers. For instance, in one recent tweet, an employee wanted to know if anyone had brought a hairdryer to work that day. (Must have been a bad hair day!) This kind of camaraderie can maintain and sustain employee commitment to the company.

Also, at Zappos, the company's "pulse" or "health" of the culture is surveyed monthly. In these happiness surveys, employees answer questions such as whether they enjoy their jobs, whether the company is too focused on profits, whether they feel their job is meaningful, if they feel they make the

decisions about their own career path, and if colleagues are friendly and like family to them. Survey results are broken down by department, and opportunities for "development" are identified and acted on. For example, when one month's survey showed that a particular department seemed isolated and cut off from other departments, actions were taken to show employees how integral their work was to the rest of the company.

Oh, and one other thing about Zappos: Every year, to celebrate its accomplishments, it publishes a *Culture Book,* a testimonial to the power of its culture. Zappos feels strongly that when you have an appropriate culture with appropriate values, that's when you achieve the best organizational performance. And such confidence about what and how it's doing business is ultimately what Zappos is all about.

Discussion Questions

2-23 Find a list of all 10 of Zappos' corporate values. Pick two of the values and explain how you think those values would influence the way employees do their work.

2-24 Using this list of corporate values and Exhibit 2–4, describe Zappos' organizational culture. In which areas would you say that Zappos' culture is very high (or typical)? Explain.

2-25 How did Zappos' corporate culture begin? How is Zappos' corporate culture maintained?

2-26 The right culture with the right values will always produce the best organizational performance. Do you agree or disagree with this statement? Why?

2-27 What could other companies learn from Tony Hsieh and Zappos' experiences?

Endnotes

1. "A Transforming World," Report by Merrill Lynch Wealth Management, http://www.ml.com/publish/content/application/pdf/GWMOL/AR9D50CF-MLWM.pdf, May 2014.

2. C. Matlack, "The Growing Peril of a Connected World," *Bloomberg BusinessWeek*, December 6–12, 2010, 63–64.

3. G. Ip, "Sluggish Productivity Hampers Wage Gains," *Wall Street Journal*, March 7–8, 2015, A1+; R. Miller, "How Productive Is the U.S.?" *Bloomberg BusinessWeek*, March 2, 2015, 16–17; and "Global Productivity Slowdown Moderated in 2013—2014 May See Better Performance," The Conference Board, https://www.conference-board.org/pdf_free/economics/TED3.pdf, 2014.

4. D. Weldon, "Has the Global Economy Slowed Down?" BBC News, http://www.bbc.com/news/explainers-31661078, March 1, 2015; and P. Davidson, "Global Growth Appears Stunted, IMF Chief Says," *USA Today*, April 3, 2014, 2B.

5. E. Morath, "Brisk Jobs Growth Puts Fed on Notice," *Wall Street Journal*, March 7–8, 2015, A1+; "United States Unemployment Rate," Trading Economics, http://www.tradingeconomics.com/united-states/unemployment-rate, January 2015; and A. Lowrey, "Recovery Has Created Far More Low-Wage Jobs Than Better-Paid Ones," *New York Times Online*, April 27, 2014.

6. N. Timiraos, "Many Face New Normal: Part-Time Pay, Full-Time Bills," *Wall Street Journal*, November 13, 2014, A1+.

7. P. Davidson, "Firms Go with Part-Timers to Get around Health Law," *USA Today*, December 31, 2014, 3B.

8. A. R. Sorkin and M. Thee-Brenan, "Many Feel the American Dream Is out of Reach, Poll Shows," *New York Times Online*, December 10, 2014.

9. E. Pfanner, "Economic Troubles Cited as the Top Risks in 2012," *New York Times Online*, January 11, 2012; and E. Pfanner, "Divining the Business and Political Risks of 2012," *New York Times Online*, January 11, 2012.

10. C. Hausman, "Americans See Inequality as a Major Problem," *Ethics Newsline*, www.globalethics.org/news-line, April 9, 2012.

11. E. Porter, "Inequality Undermines Democracy," *New York Times Online*, March 20, 2012.

12. T. Meelen and K. Frenken, "Stop Saying Uber Is Part of the Sharing Economy," http://www.fastcoexist.com/3040863/stop-saying-uber-is-part-of-the-sharing-economy, January 14, 2015; and "The Rise of the Sharing Economy," *The Economist*, http://www.economist.com/news/leaders/21573104-internet-everything-hire-rise-sharing-economy, March 9, 2013.

13. "Airbnb, Snapgoods and 12 More Pioneers of the 'Share Economy,'" http://www.forbes.com/pictures/eeji45emgkh/airbnb-snapgoods-and-12-more-pioneers-of-the-share-economy/, 2015.

14. N. Ungerleider, "This 'Airbnb for Creative Equipment' Will Rent You Drones, Oculus Rifts, Google Glass, More," *Fast Company*, http://www.fastcompany.com/3043160/tech-forecast/this-airbnb-for-creative-equipment-will-rent-you-drones-oculus-rifts-google-gl, March 6, 2015.

15. G. M. Eckhardt and F. Bardhi, "The Sharing Economy Isn't about Sharing at All," *Harvard Business Review*, https://hbr.org/2015/01/the-sharing-economy-isnt-about-sharing-at-all, January 28, 2015.

16. P. Coy, "If Demography Is Destiny, Then India Has the Edge," *Bloomberg BusinessWeek*, January 17–23, 2011, 9–10.

17. S. Brownstone, "Millennials Will Become the Majority in the Workforce in 2015. Is Your Company Ready?" http://www.fastcoexist.com/3037823/millennials-will-become-the-majority-in-the-workforce-in-2015-is-your-company-ready, November 4, 2014.

18. J. Villa, "How Hispanic Gen Z Will Change Everything," www.media.post, March 4, 2015.

19. R. Bernstein, "Move over Millennials—Here Comes Gen Z," *Ad Age*, http://adage.com/article/cmo-strategy/move-millennials-gen-z/296577/, January 21, 2015.

20. R. Friedrich, M. Peterson, and A. Koster, "The Rise of Generation C," *Strategy+Business*, Spring 2011, 1–8.

21. S. Cardwell, "Where Do Babies Come From?" *Newsweek*, October 19, 2009, 56.

22. G. Shivakumar, "India Is Set to Become the Youngest Country by 2020," *The Hindu*, http://www.thehindu.com/news/national/india-is-set-to-become-the-youngest-country-by-2020/article4624347.ece, April 17, 2013.

23. Y. Hori, J-P. Lehmann, T. Ma Kam Wah, and V. Wang, "Facing up to the Demographic Dilemma," *Strategy+Business Online*, Spring 2010; and E. E. Gordon, "Job Meltdown or Talent Crunch?" *Training* (January 2010): 10.

24. M. Chand and R. L. Tung, "The Aging of the World's Population and Its Effects on Global Business," *Academy of Management Perspectives*, November 2014. 409–29.

25. R. Hampson, "The Changing Face of American Jobs," *USA Today*, January 13, 2011, 1A+; P. Izzo, "Economists Expect Shifting Work Force," *Wall Street Journal Online*, February 11, 2010; and J. Lanhart, "Even in a Recovery, Some Jobs Won't Return," *Wall Street Journal*, January 12, 2010, A15.

26. "Gartner Says 4.9 Billion Connected 'Things' Will Be in Use in 2015," Press Release, www.gartner.com/newsroom/id/2905717, November 11, 2014.

27. E. Frauenheim, "Companies Focus Their Attention on Flexibility," *Workforce Management Online*, February 2011; P. Davidson, "Companies Do More with Fewer Workers," *USA Today*, February 23, 2011, 1B+; K. Bennhold, "Working Part-Time in the 21st Century," *New York Times Online*, December 29, 2010; M. Rich, "Weighing Costs, Companies Favor Temporary Help," *New York Times Online*, December 19, 2010; P. Davidson, "Temporary Workers Reshape Companies, Jobs," *USA Today*, October 13, 2010, 1A+; A. Fox, "Pave the Way for Volunteers," *HR Magazine*, June 2010, 70–74; P. Davidson, "More Temp Workers Are Getting Hired," *USA Today*, March 8, 2010, 1B; S. Reddy, "Wary Companies Rely on Temporary Workers," *Wall Street Journal*, March 6–7, 2010, A4; P. Davidson, "Cuts in Hours versus Cuts in Jobs," *USA Today*, February 25, 2010, 1B; and S. A. Hewlett, L. Sherbin, and K. Sumberg, "How Gen Y and Boomers Will Reshape Your Agenda," *Harvard Business Review*, July–August 2009, 71–76; and S. Lohr, "Customer Service? Ask a Volunteer," *New York Times Online*, April 26, 2009.

28. D. Bauder, Associated Press, "Programming Vet Guiding Changes at MTV," *Springfield, Missouri News-Leader*, May 7, 2014, 5C.

29. A Question of Ethics box based on "Police Are Pleading with Google to Ditch a Feature in Its Waze App That Could Help Terrorists," *Business Insider*, http://www.businessinsider.com/police-google-change-waze-app-2015-2, February 7, 2015; The Associated Press, "Police Say Waze Cop-Tracker Is Threat to Officers," CBS News.com, http://www.cbsnews.com/news/police-say-waze-cop-tracker-is-threat-to-officers/, January 26, 2015; and J. Wells, "LA Residents Complain about 'Waze Craze'," www.cnbc.co/id/102261534, December 11, 2014.

30. J. S. Harrison and C. H. St. John, "Managing and Partnering with External Stakeholders," *Academy of Management Executive*, May 1996, 46–60.

31. J. Swartz, "Facebook Changes Its Status in Washington," *USA Today*, January 13, 2011, 1B+.

32. S. L. Berman, R. A. Phillips, and A. C. Wicks, "Resource Dependence, Managerial Discretion, and Stakeholder Performance," Academy of Management Proceedings Best Conference Paper, August 2005; A. J. Hillman and G. D. Keim, "Shareholder Value, Stakeholder Management, and Social Issues: What's the Bottom Line?" *Strategic Management Journal* (March 2001): 125–39; J. S. Harrison and R. E. Freeman, "Stakeholders, Social Responsibility, and Performance: Empirical Evidence and Theoretical Perspectives," *Academy of Management Journal* (July 1999): 479–87; and J. Kotter and J. Heskett, *Corporate Culture and Performance* (New York: The Free Press, 1992).

33. J. A. Chatman and K. A. Jehn, "Assessing the Relationship between Industry Characteristics and Organizational Culture: How Different Can You Be?" *Academy of Management Journal* (June 1994): 522–53; and C. A. O'Reilly III, J. Chatman, and D. F. Caldwell, "People and Organizational Culture: A Profile Comparison Approach to Assessing Person-Organization Fit," *Academy of Management Journal* (September 1991): 487–516.

34. T. Lytle, "Social Work," *HR Magazine*, August 2014, 40–42.

35. A. Bryant, "On a Busy Road, a Company Needs Guardrails, an interview with Christopher J. Nassetta, president and chief executive of Hilton Worldwide," *New York Times Online*, October 13, 2012.

36. E. H. Schein, *Organizational Culture and Leadership* (San Francisco: Jossey-Bass, 1985), 314–15.

37. "Executive Views on Organizational Culture," *T&D*, November 2014, 19.

38. C. Palmeri, "The Fastest Drill in the West," *BusinessWeek*, October 24, 2005, 86–88.

39. C. Kenkel and S. Sorenson, "How Winegardner & Hammons Built a Winning Culture," *Gallup Business Journal*, http://www.gallup.com/businessjournal/175394/winegardner-hammons-built-winning-workplace-culture.aspx, September 18, 2014.

40. Based on A. L. Wilkins, "The Culture Audit: A Tool for Understanding Organizations," *Organizational Dynamics*, Autumn 1983, 24–38; H. M. Trice and J. M. Beyer, *The Culture of Work Organizations* (Upper Saddle River, NJ: Prentice Hall, 1993), 358–62; and D. M. Cable, L. Aiman-Smith, P. W. Mulvey, and J. R. Edwards, "The Sources and Accuracy of Job Applicants' Beliefs about Organizational Culture," *Academy of Management Journal* (December 2000): 1076–85.

41. E. Palermo, "10 Worst Data Breaches of All Time," http://www.tomsguide.com/us/biggest-data-breaches,news-19083.html, February 6, 2015.

42. T. Lee, "Target's Culture Contributed to Gregg Steinhafel's Downfall," *SFGate,* http://www.sfgate.com/business/article/Target-s-culture-contributed-to-Gregg-5458122.php, May 7, 2014.

43. P. Ziobro and S. Ng, "Retailer Target Lost Its Way under Ousted CEO Gregg Steinhafel," *Wall Street Journal,* http://www.wsj.com/articles/retailer-target-lost-its-way-under-ousted-ceo-gregg-steinhafel-1403577233, June 23, 2014.

44. "Target CMO Acknowledges Culture Crisis after Employee Rant Posted on Gawker," http://www.buzzfeed.com/sapna/target-cmo-acknowledges-culture-crisis-after-employee-rant-p.tvox6lwle4, May 14, 2014.

45. H. Malcolm and B. Horovitz, "Target CMO Responds to Employee Rant over Culture," http://www.usatoday.com/story/money/business/2014/05/14/target-cmo-response-employee-rant/9075327/, May 14, 2014.

46. J. Reingold, "What's behind Target's New Openness?" http://fortune.com/2014/11/21/whats-behind-targets-new-openness/, November 22, 2014.

47. "Target CMO Acknowledges Culture Crisis after Employee Rant Posted on Gawker."

48. P. Ziobro, "Target to Cut Several Thousand Jobs," *Wall Street Journal,* http://www.wsj.com/articles/target-ceo-plans-digital-small-store-investments-to-fuel-growth-1425416165, March 4, 2015.

49. E. Schwartzel, "Crowds Return to Movie Theaters," *Wall Street Journal,* February 28, 2015, B2; "Yearly Box Office," boxofficemojo.com/yearly/, March 7, 2014; E. Schwartzel, "Movie-Theater Chains Take on IMAX," *Wall Street Journal,* December 13, 2013, B6; A. Sharma, "Hollywood Feels Netflix's Influence," *Wall Street Journal,* July 8, 2013, B1+; C. Bialik, "Studios Struggle for Focus on Film Pirates' Booty," *Wall Street Journal,* April 6–7, 2013, A2; M. Rosenbaum, "Box Office Bust: Movie Attendance Hits 16-Year Low," ABCNews.com, December 28, 2011; M. Cieply, "Charging a Premium for Movies, at a Cost," *New York Times Online,* July 31, 2011; B. Barnes and M. Cieply, "Graying Audience Returns to Movies," *New York Times Online,* February 25, 2011; L. A. E. Schuker, "Double Feature: Dinner and a Movie," *Wall Street Journal,* January 5, 2011, D1+; J. O'Donnell, "Going to the Movies at Home," *USA Today,* January 5, 2011, 3B; M. DeCuir, "Some Food and Alcohol with Your Flick? Cinemas Hope So," *USA Today,* March 27, 2008, 3A; B. Barnes, "At Cineplexes, Sports, Opera, Maybe a Movie," *New York Times Online,* March 23, 2008; D. Stuckey and K. Gelles, "Entertainment Sold Online," *USA Today,* February 26, 2008; and J. Carroll, "Americans Dislike the Cost of Going to the Movies," *Gallup News Service,* December 22, 2006.

50. M. Moskowitz, R. Levering, C. Tkaczyk, C. Keating, A. Konrad, A. Vandermey, and C. Kapelke, "The 100 Best Companies to Work For," *Fortune,* February 6, 2012, 117+; K. Gurchiek, "Delivering HR at Zappos," *HRMagazine,* June 2011, 44–45; V. Nayar, "Employee Happiness: Zappos vs. HCL," Businessweek.com, January 5, 2011; D. Richards, "At Zappos, Culture Pays," *Strategy+Business Online,* August 2010; T. Hseih, "Zappos's CEO on Going to Extremes for Customers," *Harvard Business Review,* July–August 2010, 41–45; A. Perschel, "Work-Life Flow: How Individuals, Zappos, and Other Innovative Companies Achieve High Engagement," *Global Business & Organizational Excellence,* July 2010, 17–30; T. Hseih, "Why I Sold Zappos," *Inc.,* June 2010, 100–04; T. Hseih, "Happy Feet," *Newsweek,* June 21, 2010, 10; M. Betts, "Zappos Earns No. 1 Ranking for E-retailing," *Computerworld,* June 7, 2010, 4; S. Elliott, "Tireless Employees Get Their Tribute, Even if It's in Felt and Polyester," *New York Times Online,* March 4, 2010; C. Palmeri, "Now for Sale, Zappos Culture," *Bloomberg BusinessWeek,* January 11, 2010, 57; E. Frauenheim, "Can Zappos Culture Survive the Amazon Jungle?"; and Zappos, *Culture Book. Workforce Management Online,* September 14, 2009.

Management **Myth** Myth

Employees are less ethical today than in the past.

Management **DEBUNKED!** Myth

The reality is that the percentage of employees who witnessed ethical misconduct at work is at an all-time low—41 percent.[1] Organizations have been quick to penalize or even fire employees (including managers) who have been found to act unethically, demonstrating that such practices won't be tolerated. And large companies have been particularly conscientious about improving their ethical standards—97 percent have codes of ethics.

IF you relied on TV, newspapers, and other media to shape your perceptions, you might rightly assume that today's executives are far more unethical than their peers of 20 or 30 years ago. For instance, in one recent six-month period we found media coverage of a wide range of unethical business practices—including insider trading, lying, bribery, conflicts of interest, sexual harassment, product deficiency cover-ups, expense account abuses, and environmental violations.

But don't confuse publicity with actual practices. Although it *seems* that unethical practices are increasing, the reason may be that there are vastly more media outlets today—online *and* physical—and they're actively competing for your attention. The media give their readers what they want, which seems to be the "juicy," negative stuff. So, networks, cable, online news sites, blogs, and newspapers highlight stories of managers who lied, cheated, or rigged the system.

However, the issue of employees behaving ethically *is* an important one for today's managers. And managers also face other important issues associated with globalization and with employing and engaging a diverse global workforce. Because each of these topics—diversity, globalization, and ethics/social responsibility—are integrated throughout many aspects of what managers do and how they manage, we're going to look at each in this chapter. ●

Learning Outcomes

3-1 Explain globalization and its impact on organizations. p. 61

3-2 Discuss how society's expectations are influencing managers and organizations.
p. 67

3-3 Discuss the factors that lead to ethical and unethical behavior in organizations. p. 70

3-4 Describe how the workforce is changing and its impact on the way organizations are managed. p. 74

What Is Globalization and How Does It Affect Organizations?

3-1 Explain globalization and its impact on organizations.

> "It's like being in **an emergency room**, doing triage."

That was the reaction of Hewlett-Packard's senior vice president for operations after learning that a catastrophic earthquake and tsunami had hit Japan.[2] Not long after getting the news, company managers in Japan, Taiwan, and the United States gathered in a "virtual situation room" to instantly share information. This analogy of an emergency room is very apt, according to experts, because today's global supply chains are like intricate interconnected biological systems. They can respond and self-heal as needed, but they're also susceptible to weaknesses. Normally, the global flow of goods will adapt, day in and day out, to all kinds of glitches and setbacks. However, when a disaster strikes (for instance, an earthquake, a volcano eruption, labor unrest, political upheavals, floods or hurricanes or tornadoes or blizzards anywhere in the world), you really grasp the fragility of the global supply chain.[3]

An important issue that managers must deal with is globalization. (Remember our discussion of the global arena in Chapter 2 as one component of the external environment.) Major events such as catastrophic natural disasters, global economic meltdowns, or terrorist threats have created challenges for managers doing business globally. Despite such challenges, globalization isn't about to disappear. Nations and businesses have been trading with each other for centuries through all kinds of disasters and economic ups and downs. Over the last couple of decades, we've seen an explosion of companies—big *and* small—operating almost anywhere in the world. Geographic borders mean little when it comes to doing business. For instance, BMW, a German firm, builds cars in South Carolina. McDonald's sells hamburgers in China. Tata, an Indian company, purchased the Jaguar brand—which started as a British company—from Ford Motor Company, a U.S. company. And look at these so-called American companies that get well over half of their annual revenues from sales outside the United States.

Global Sales (outside the United States) for:

Avon—89 percent
McDonald's—63 percent
IBM—58 percent
Coke—56 percent
GE—52 percent
Apple—52 percent[4]

Although the world is still a **global village**—that is, a boundaryless world where goods and services are produced and marketed worldwide—how managers do business in that global village is changing. To be effective in this boundaryless world, managers need to adapt to this changed environment, as well as be more understanding of cultures, systems, and techniques that are different from their own.

What Does It Mean to Be "Global"?

There are three different ways for organizations to be considered "global." For instance, organizations are considered global if they exchange goods and services with consumers in other countries. Such ❶ *marketplace globalization* is the most common approach to being global. However, many organizations, especially high-tech organizations, are considered global because they ❷ *use managerial and technical employee talent from other countries*. One factor

global village
A boundaryless world where goods and services are produced and marketed worldwide

global sourcing
Purchasing materials or labor from around the world, wherever it is cheapest

exporting
Making products domestically and selling them abroad

importing
Acquiring products made abroad and selling them domestically

licensing
An agreement in which an organization gives another the right, for a fee, to make or sell its products, using its technology or product specifications

franchising
An agreement in which an organization gives another organization the right, for a fee, to use its name and operating methods

MNC (multinational corporation)
Any type of international company that maintains operations in multiple countries.

multidomestic corporation
An MNC that decentralizes management and other decisions to the local country where it's doing business

transnational (borderless) organization
An MNC where artificial geographic boundaries are eliminated

global corporation
An MNC that centralizes management and other decisions in the home country

that affects *talent globalization* is immigration laws and regulations. Managers must be alert to changes in those laws. Finally, an organization can be considered global if it ③ *uses financial sources and resources outside its home country, which is known as financial globalization.*[5] As might be expected, the global economic slowdown severely affected the availability of financial resources globally. And even as countries' economies began the slow process of recovery, the impact continued to be felt globally.

How Do Organizations Go Global?

As organizations go global, they often use different approaches. (See Exhibit 3–1.) At first, managers may want to get into a global market with minimal investment. At this stage, they may start with **global sourcing** (also called global outsourcing), which is purchasing materials or labor from around the world wherever it is cheapest. The goal: take advantage of lower costs in order to be more competitive. For instance, Massachusetts General Hospital uses radiologists in India to interpret CT scans.[6] Although global sourcing may be the first step to going international for many companies, they often continue using this approach because of the competitive advantages it offers. However, during the last economic crisis, many organizations reconsidered their decisions to source globally. For instance, Dell, Apple, and American Express were just a few U.S. companies that scaled back some of their offshore customer service operations. Others brought manufacturing back home. For instance, Apple decided to build some Mac computers in the United States for the first time in about a decade. The company had faced political pressure to hire U.S. workers and to "reduce its reliance on foreign subcontractors whose treatment of workers" has been strongly criticized.[7] As companies think about the best places to do business, they face choices of offshore (in another global location), onshore (at home), or nearshore (in countries close to home).[8] Then, as a company takes that next step in going global, each successive stage beyond global sourcing requires more investment and thus entails more risk for the organization.

The next step in going global may involve **exporting** the organization's products to other countries—that is, making products domestically and selling them abroad. In addition, an organization might do **importing**, which involves acquiring products made abroad and selling them domestically. Both usually entail minimal investment and risk, which is why many small businesses often use these approaches to doing business globally.

Finally, managers might use **licensing** or **franchising**, which are similar approaches involving one organization giving another organization the right to use its brand name, technology, or product specifications in return for a lump-sum payment or a fee that is usually based on sales. The only difference is that licensing is primarily used by manufacturing organizations that make or sell another company's products, and franchising is primarily used by service organizations that want to use another company's name and operating

Exhibit 3–1 How Organizations Go Global

Global Investment	
Significant ▲	Foreign Subsidiary
	Strategic Alliance – Joint Venture
	Franchising
	Licensing
	Exporting and Importing
Minimal	Global Sourcing

Source: Robbins, Stephen P., Coulter, Mary, *Management*, 13th Ed., © 2016, p. 106. Reprinted and electronically reproduced by permission of Pearson Education, Inc., New York, NY.

What Are the Different Types of Global Organizations?

MNC
(multinational corporation)
Any type of international company that maintains operations in multiple countries

---

"Which product is right for you?"

Multidomestic corporation:
An MNC in which management and other decisions are *decentralized* to the *local* country in which it is operating.

- Rely on local employees to manage the business.
- Tailor strategies to each country's unique characteristics.
- Used by many consumer product companies.

Lyroky/Alamy

John Deere's green-and-yellow tractors are a familiar sight in farm country. Although John Deere once struggled selling its farm equipment overseas, its line of *highly customizable products* has made the company a ton of profits.

"We don't want people to think we're based in any one place."

Transnational (borderless) organization:
An MNC where artificial *geographical boundaries are eliminated*.

- Country of origin or where business is conducted becomes irrelevant.
- Increases efficiency and effectiveness in a competitive global marketplace.

A sport utility vehicle has changed the way Ford develops and makes cars. Ford's Escape is made from a *common set of components* that are used in Ford cars around the world.

Oleksiy Maksymenko Photography/Alamy

"This decision we're making at headquarters has company-wide, world-wide implications."

Global corporation:
An MNC in which management and other decisions are *centralized* in the *home* country.

- World market is treated as an integrated whole.
- Focus is on control and global efficiency.

Mouse in the House/Alamy

Sony Corporation's strengths in product innovation are legendary: the Walkman, the Handycam, the PlayStation. New products are developed and launched globally *under the guidance and oversight of corporate headquarters*.

TATA STARBUCKS LTD.

Danish Siddiqui/Reuters

Top managers of India's Tata Global Beverages and Starbucks Coffee Company, shown here, announced a joint venture that will own and operate Starbucks cafes in cities throughout India. The new organization, TATA Starbucks Ltd., will give Indian consumers an expanded range of coffee, tea, and innovative beverages.

methods. For example, New Delhi consumers can enjoy Subway sandwiches, Namibians can dine on KFC fried chicken, and Russians can consume Dunkin' Donuts—all because of *franchises* in these countries. On the other hand, Anheuser-Busch InBev *licensed* the right to brew and market its Budweiser beer to brewers such as Labatt in Canada, Modelo in Mexico, and Kirin in Japan.

Once an organization has been doing business internationally for a while and has gained experience in international markets, managers may decide to make more of a direct investment. One way to do this is through a **global strategic alliance**, which is a partnership between an organization and a foreign company partner or partners in which both share resources and knowledge in developing new products or building production facilities. For example, Honda Motor and General Electric teamed up to produce a new jet engine. A specific type of strategic alliance in which the partners form a separate, independent organization for some business purpose is called a **joint venture**. For example, Hewlett-Packard—the company we mentioned at the beginning of this section—has had numerous joint ventures with various suppliers around the globe to develop different components for its computer equipment. These partnerships provide a relatively easy way for companies to compete globally.

Finally, managers may choose to directly invest in a foreign country by setting up a **foreign subsidiary** as a separate and independent facility or office. This subsidiary can be managed as a multidomestic organization (local control) or as a global organization (centralized control). As you can probably guess, this arrangement involves the greatest commitment of resources and poses the greatest amount of risk. For instance, United Plastics Group of Westmont, Illinois, built three injection-molding facilities in Suzhou, China. The company's executive vice president for business development says that level of investment was necessary because "it fulfilled our mission of being a global supplier to our global accounts."[9]

✪ **Write It 1!**

If your professor has assigned this, go to the Assignments section of **mymanagementlab.com** to complete *MGMT 5: The Global Marketplace*.

---

global strategic alliance
A partnership between an organization and foreign company partner(s) in which both share resources and knowledge in developing new products or building production facilities

joint venture
A specific type of strategic alliance in which the partners agree to form a separate, independent organization for some business purpose

foreign subsidiary
A direct investment in a foreign country that involves setting up a separate and independent facility or office

parochialism
A narrow focus in which managers see things only through their own eyes and from their own perspective

What Do Managers Need to Know About Managing in a Global Organization?

A global world brings new challenges for managers, especially in managing in a country with a different national culture.[10] A specific challenge comes from the need to recognize the differences that might exist and then find ways to make interactions effective.

U.S. managers once held (and some still hold) a rather parochial view of the world of business. **Parochialism** is a narrow focus in which managers see things only through their own eyes and from their own perspectives; they don't recognize that people from other countries have different ways of doing things or that they live differently from Americans. This view can't succeed in a global village—nor is it the dominant view held today. Changing such perceptions requires understanding that countries have different cultures and environments.

A person with a **parochial attitude** cannot succeed in today's world.

◄◄◄ **From the Past to the Present** ►►►

Hofstede's 5 Dimensions of National Culture

An illuminating study of the differences in cultural environments was conducted by Geert Hofstede in the 1970s and 1980s.[11] He surveyed more than 116,000 IBM employees in 40 countries about their work-related values and found that managers and employees vary on five dimensions of national culture:

- *Power distance.* The degree to which people in a country accept that power in institutions and organizations is distributed unequally. It ranges from relatively equal (low power distance) to extremely unequal (high power distance).

- *Individualism versus collectivism.* Individualism is the degree to which people in a country prefer to act as individuals rather than as members of groups. Collectivism is the equivalent of low individualism.

- *Achievement versus nurturing.* Quantity of life is the degree to which values such as assertiveness, the acquisition of money and material goods, and competition are important. Quality of life is the degree to which people value relationships and show sensitivity and concern for the welfare of others.

- *Uncertainty avoidance.* This dimension assesses the degree to which people in a country prefer structured over unstructured situations and whether people are willing to take risks.

- *Long-term versus short-term orientation.* People in cultures with long-term orientations look to the future and value thrift and persistence. A short-term orientation values the past and present and emphasizes respect for tradition and fulfilling social obligations.

The table below shows a few highlights of four of Hofstede's cultural dimensions and how different countries rank on those dimensions.

If your professor has assigned this, go to the Assignments section of **mymanagementlab.com** *to complete these discussion questions.*

Here's one way to UNDERSTAND CULTURAL DIFFERENCES!

⭐ **Talk About It 1:** Using Hofstede's data for Mexico and the United States, how do you think employees in each country (a) might react to a team-based rewards program; (b) would be likely to view their relationship with their boss; and (c) might react to a change in work processes?

⭐ **Talk About It 2:** What does this example tell you about the importance of understanding cultural differences?

Country	Individualism/ Collectivism	Power Distance	Uncertainty Avoidance	Achievement/ Nurturing[a]
Australia	Individual	Small	Moderate	Strong
Canada	Individual	Moderate	Low	Moderate
England	Individual	Small	Moderate	Strong
France	Individual	Large	High	Weak
Greece	Collective	Large	High	Moderate
Italy	Individual	Moderate	High	Strong
Japan	Collective	Moderate	High	Strong
Mexico	Collective	Large	High	Strong
Singapore	Collective	Large	Low	Moderate
Sweden	Individual	Small	Low	Weak
United States	Individual	Small	Low	Strong
Venezuela	Collective	Large	High	Strong

[a]A weak achievement score is equivalent to high nurturing.

Source: Based on G. Hofstede, "Motivation, Leadership, and Organization: Do American Theories Apply Abroad?" *Organizational Dynamics* (Summer 1980): 42–63.

All countries have different values, morals, customs, political and economic systems, and laws, all of which can affect how a business is managed. For instance, in the United States, laws guard against employers taking action against employees solely on the basis of their age. Similar laws can't be found in all other countries. Thus, managers must be aware of a country's laws when doing business there.

The most important and challenging differences for managers to understand, however, are those related to a country's social context or culture. For example, status is perceived differently in different countries. In France, status is often the result of factors important to the organization, such as seniority, education, and the like. In the United States, status is more a function of what individuals have accomplished personally. Managers need to understand societal issues (such as status) that might affect business operations in another country and recognize that organizational success can come from a variety of managerial practices. Fortunately, managers have help in this regard by turning to the research that is being done on the differences in cultural environments.

HOFSTEDE'S FRAMEWORK. Geert Hofstede's framework is one of the most widely referenced approaches for analyzing cultural variations. His work has had a major impact on what we know about cultural differences among countries and is highlighted in our "From the Past to the Present" box.

GLOBE FINDINGS. Although Hofstede's work has provided the basic framework for differentiating among national cultures, most of the data are over 30 years old. Another more recent research program, called **Global Leadership and Organizational Behavior Effectiveness (GLOBE)**, is an ongoing cross-cultural investigation of leadership and national culture. Using data from more than 17,000 managers in 62 societies around the world, the GLOBE research team (led by Robert House) has identified nine dimensions on which national cultures differ.[12] For each of these dimensions, we have indicated which countries rated high, which rated moderate, and which rated low.

- *Assertiveness.* The extent to which a society encourages people to be tough, confrontational, assertive, and competitive versus modest and tender. (*High:* Spain, United States, and Greece. *Moderate:* Egypt, Ireland, and Philippines. *Low:* Sweden, New Zealand, and Switzerland.)
- *Future orientation.* The extent to which a society encourages and rewards future-oriented behavior such as planning, investing in the future, and delaying gratification. (*High:* Denmark, Canada, and Netherlands. *Moderate:* Slovenia, Egypt, and Ireland. *Low:* Russia, Argentina, and Poland.)
- *Gender differentiation.* The extent to which a society maximizes gender role differences. (*High:* South Korea, Egypt, and Morocco. *Moderate:* Italy, Brazil, and Argentina. *Low:* Sweden, Denmark, and Slovenia.)
- *Uncertainty avoidance.* As defined in Hofstede's landmark research, the GLOBE team defined this term as a society's reliance on social norms and procedures to alleviate the unpredictability of future events. (*High:* Austria, Denmark, and Germany. *Moderate:* Israel, United States, and Mexico. *Low:* Russia, Hungary, and Bolivia.)
- *Power distance.* As in the original research, the GLOBE team defined this as the degree to which members of a society expect power to be unequally shared. (*High:* Russia, Spain, and Thailand. *Moderate:* England, France, and Brazil. *Low:* Denmark, Netherlands, and South Africa.)
- *Individualism/collectivism.* Again, this term was defined similarly to the original research as the degree to which individuals are encouraged by societal institutions to be integrated into groups within organizations and society. A low score is synonymous with collectivism. (*High:* Greece, Hungary, and Germany. *Moderate:* Hong Kong, United States, and Egypt. *Low:* Denmark, Singapore, and Japan.)
- *In-group collectivism.* In contrast to focusing on societal institutions, this dimension encompasses the extent to which members of a society take pride in membership in small groups such as their family and circle of close friends and the organizations in which they

GLOBE
The Global Leadership and Organizational Behavior Effectiveness research program, a program that studies cross-cultural leadership behaviors

are employed. (*High:* Egypt, China, and Morocco. *Moderate:* Japan, Israel, and Qatar. *Low:* Denmark, Sweden, and New Zealand.)

- *Performance orientation.* This dimension refers to the degree to which a society encourages and rewards group members for performance improvement and excellence. (*High:* United States, Taiwan, and New Zealand. *Moderate:* Sweden, Israel, and Spain. *Low:* Russia, Argentina, and Greece.)
- *Humane orientation.* This cultural aspect is the degree to which a society encourages and rewards individuals for being fair, altruistic, generous, caring, and kind to others. (*High:* Indonesia, Egypt, and Malaysia. *Moderate:* Hong Kong, Sweden, and Taiwan. *Low:* Germany, Spain, and France.)

The GLOBE studies confirm the validity of Hofstede's dimensions and extend his research rather than replace it. GLOBE's added dimensions provide an expanded and updated measure of countries' cultural differences. It's likely that cross-cultural studies of human behavior and organizational practices will increasingly use the GLOBE dimensions to assess differences between countries.

 Try It 1!

If your professor has assigned this, go to the Assignments section of **mymanagementlab.com** to complete the **Simulation:** *Managing in the Global Environment.*

What Does Society Expect from Organizations and Managers?

3-2 Discuss how society's expectations are influencing managers and organizations.

It's an **incredibly simple but potentially world-changing** idea.

What is *it*? The business model followed by TOMS shoes: For each pair of shoes sold, a pair is donated to a child in need. As a contestant on the CBS reality show *The Amazing Race,* Blake Mycoskie, founder of TOMS, visited Argentina and "saw lots of kids with no shoes who were suffering from injuries to their feet." He was so moved by the experience that he wanted to do something. That *something* is what TOMS Shoes does now by blending charity with commerce. Those shoe donations—now over 35 million pairs—have been central to the success of the TOMS brand.

What *does* society expect from organizations and managers? That may seem like a hard question to answer, but not for Blake Mycoskie. He believes that society expects organizations and managers to be responsible and ethical *and* to give something back. However, as we saw in the highly publicized stories of notorious financial scandals at Enron, Bernard Madoff Investment Securities, HealthSouth, and others, some managers *don't* act responsibly or ethically.

How Can Organizations Demonstrate Socially Responsible Actions?

Few terms have been defined in as many different ways as *social responsibility*—profit maximization, going beyond profit making, voluntary activities, and concern for the broader social system are but a few.[13] These descriptions fall into two camps. On one side is the classical—or purely economic—view that management's only social responsibility is to maximize profits.[14]

Happiness goes from heart to heart

Artsana, the Italian maker of Chicco baby care products, invests in social responsibility initiatives that help children in need both in Italy and in the poorest regions of the world. Chicco's global "Happiness Goes from Heart to Heart" project is aimed at treating childhood heart disease and supports the brand's mission of "making children happy and giving them something to smile about".

social responsibility (corporate social responsibility, or CSR)
A business firm's intention, beyond its legal and economic obligations, to do the right things and act in ways that are good for society

social obligation
When a business firm engages in social actions because of its obligation to meet certain economic and legal responsibilities

social responsiveness
When a business firm engages in social actions in response to some popular social need

On the other side is the socioeconomic position, which holds that management's responsibility goes beyond making profits to include protecting and improving society's welfare.[15]

When *we* talk about social responsibility (also known as corporate social responsibility, or CSR), we mean a business firm's intention, beyond its legal and economic obligations, to do the right things and act in ways that are good for society. Note that this definition assumes that a business ❶ obeys the law and ❷ pursues economic interests. But also note that this definition ❸ views a business as a moral agent. *In its effort to do good for society, it must differentiate between right and wrong.*

We can understand social responsibility better if we compare it to two similar concepts. Social obligations are those activities a business firm engages in to meet certain economic and legal responsibilities. It does the minimum that the law requires and only pursues social goals to the extent that they contribute to its economic goals. Social responsiveness is characteristic of the business firm that engages in social actions in response to some popular social need. Managers in these companies are guided by social norms and values and make practical, market-oriented decisions about their actions.[16] A U.S. business that meets federal pollution standards or safe packaging regulations is meeting its social obligation because laws mandate these actions. However, when it provides on-site child-care facilities for employees or packages products using recycled paper, it's being socially responsive to working parents and environmentalists who have voiced these social concerns and demanded such actions. For many businesses, their social actions are probably better viewed as being socially responsive rather than socially responsible, at least according to our definitions. However, such actions are still good for society. Social responsibility adds an ethical imperative to do those things that make society better and to not do those that could make it worse.

✪ Watch It 1!

If your professor has assigned this, go to the Assignments section of **mymanagementlab.com** to complete the video exercise titled *Honest Tea: Corporate Social Responsibility*.

Should Organizations Be Socially Involved?

Managers regularly **confront decisions where social responsibility** is a factor.

The importance of corporate social responsibility surfaced in the 1960s when social activists questioned the singular economic objective of business. Even today, good arguments can be made for and against businesses being socially responsible. (See Exhibit 3–2.) Yet, arguments aside, times have changed. Managers regularly confront decisions that have a dimension of social responsibility: philanthropy, pricing, employee relations, resource conservation, product quality, and doing business in countries with oppressive governments are just a few. To address these issues, managers may reassess packaging design, recyclability of products, environmental safety practices, outsourcing decisions, foreign supplier practices, employee policies, and the like.

Exhibit 3–2 Arguments For and Against Social Responsibility

FOR

Public expectations
Public opinion now supports businesses pursuing economic and social goals.

Long-run profits
Socially responsible companies tend to have more secure long-run profits.

Ethical obligation
Businesses should be socially responsible because responsible actions are the right thing to do.

Public image
Businesses can create a favorable public image by pursuing social goals.

Better environment
Business involvement can help solve difficult social problems.

Discouragement of further governmental regulation
By becoming socially responsible, businesses can expect less government regulation.

Balance of responsibility and power
Businesses have a lot of power and an equally large amount of responsibility is needed to balance against that power.

Stockholder interests
Social responsibility will improve a business's stock price in the long run.

Possession of resources
Businesses have the resources to support public and charitable projects that need assistance.

Superiority of prevention over cures
Businesses should address social problems before they become serious and costly to correct.

AGAINST

Violation of profit maximization
Business is being socially responsible only when it pursues its economic interests.

Dilution of purpose
Pursuing social goals dilutes business's primary purpose—economic productivity.

Costs
Many socially responsible actions do not cover their costs and someone must pay those costs.

Too much power
Businesses have a lot of power already; if they pursue social goals, they will have even more.

Lack of skills
Business leaders lack the necessary skills to address social issues.

Lack of accountability
There are no direct lines of accountability for social actions.

Source: Robbins, Stephen P., Coulter, Mary, *Management*, 13th Ed., © 2016, p. 154. Reprinted and electronically reproduced by permission of Pearson Education, Inc., New York, NY.

Another way to look at this issue is whether social involvement affects a company's economic performance, which numerous studies have done.[17] Although most found a small positive relationship between social involvement and economic performance, no generalizable conclusions can be made because these studies have shown that the relationship is affected by various contextual factors such as firm size, industry, economic conditions, and regulatory environment.[18] Other researchers have questioned causation. If a study showed that social involvement and economic performance were positively related, this didn't necessarily mean that social involvement *caused* higher economic performance. It could simply mean that high profits afforded companies the "luxury" of being socially involved.[19] Such concerns can't be taken lightly. In fact, one study found that if the flawed empirical analyses in these studies were "corrected," social responsibility had a neutral impact on a company's financial performance.[20] Another found that participating in social issues not related to the

sustainability
A company's ability to achieve its business goals and increase long-term shareholder value by integrating economic, environmental, and social opportunities into its business strategies

organization's primary stakeholders had a negative effect on shareholder value.[21] Despite all these concerns, after reanalyzing several studies, other researchers have concluded that *managers can afford to be (and should be) socially responsible.*[22]

What Is Sustainability and Why Is It Important?

Being **green** at the world's largest retailer

- $482.2 billion in revenues
- 2.2 million employees
- 11,400+ stores

Sustainability goal:

Remove 20 million metric tons of greenhouse gas emissions from supply chains—the equivalent of removing more than 3.8 million cars from the road for a year.

Yes, we're talking about Walmart. And considering its size, Walmart is probably the last company you'd think of for being highlighted in a section describing sustainability. However, Walmart has committed to improving its sustainability efforts. In fact, it now reuses or recycles more than 80 percent of the waste produced in its domestic stores and in other U.S. operations.[23] This corporate action affirms that sustainability has definitely become a mainstream issue for managers.

We introduced you to sustainability in Chapter 1 as we discussed factors reshaping management in today's organizations. Just a refresher: We defined sustainability as a company's ability to achieve its business goals and increase long-term shareholder value by integrating economic, environmental, and social opportunities into its business strategies.[24] Organizations are widening their responsibility not just to managing in an efficient and effective way, but also to responding strategically to a wide range of environmental and societal challenges.[25] Like the managers at Walmart (and others committed to being sustainable) are discovering, running an organization in a more sustainable way means making informed business decisions based on thorough and ongoing communication with various stakeholders, understanding their requirements, and factoring economic, environmental, and social aspects into how they pursue their business goals.

Seventy-five percent of workplaces have at least one green technology practice.[26]

The idea of practicing sustainability affects many aspects of business, from the creation of products and services to their use and subsequent disposal by consumers. (Check out Case Application #2 on Keurig Green Mountain Inc. at the end of the chapter.) Following sustainability practices is one way in which organizations can show their commitment to being responsible. *In today's world where many individuals have diminishing respect for businesses, few organizations can afford the bad press or potential economic ramifications of being seen as socially irresponsible.* Managers also want to be seen as ethical, which is the topic we're going to look at next.

What Factors Determine Ethical and Unethical Behavior?

3-3 Discuss the factors that lead to ethical and unethical behavior in organizations.

- Employees at a law firm in Florida that handled foreclosures for Freddie Mac and Fannie Mae changed thousands of documents and hid them when company officials came to conduct audits.[27]
- A Paris court found Jérôme Kerviel, a former financial trader at French bank Société Générale, guilty of triggering a massive trading scandal that created severe financial problems for his employer. Mr. Kerviel claims that the company turned a blind eye to his questionable but hugely profitable methods.[28]

- The National Football League finally admitted recently in federal court documents that it "expects nearly a third of retired players to develop long-term cognitive problems" and that players may see the problems happening at noticeably younger ages.[29]

You might be wondering about the connection among these three unrelated stories. When you read about these decisions, behaviors, and outcomes, you might be tempted to conclude that businesses just aren't ethical. Although that isn't the case, *managers do face ethical issues*, as the above examples show.

Ethics commonly refers to a set of rules or principles that defines right and wrong conduct.[30] Right or wrong behavior, though, may at times be difficult to determine. Most recognize that something illegal is also unethical. But what about questionable "legal" areas or strict organizational policies? For instance, what if you managed an employee who worked all weekend on a rush project and you told him to take off two days sometime later and mark it down as "sick days" because your company had a clear policy that overtime would not be compensated for any reason?[31] Would that be wrong? As a manager, how will you handle such situations?

In What Ways Can Ethics Be Viewed?

To better understand what's involved with managerial ethics, we need to first look at three different perspectives on how managers make ethical decisions.[32] The **utilitarian view of ethics** says that ethical decisions are made solely on the basis of their outcomes or consequences. The goal of utilitarianism is to provide the greatest good for the greatest number. In the **rights view of ethics**, individuals are concerned with respecting and protecting individual liberties and privileges such as the right of free consent, the right to privacy, the right of free speech, and so forth. Making ethical decisions under this view is fairly simple because the goal is to avoid interfering with the rights of others who might be affected by the decision. Finally, under the **theory of justice view of ethics**, an individual imposes and enforces rules fairly and impartially. For instance, a manager would be using the theory of justice perspective by deciding to pay individuals who are similar in their levels of skills, performance, or responsibility the same and not base that decision on arbitrary differences such as gender, personality, or personal favorites. The goal of this approach is to be equitable, fair, and impartial in making decisions.

Whether a manager (or any employee, for that matter) acts **ethically or unethically will depend** on several factors.

These factors include an individual's morality, values, personality, and experiences; the organization's culture; and the ethical issue being faced.[33] People who lack a strong moral sense are much less likely to do the wrong things if they are constrained by rules, policies, job descriptions, or strong cultural norms that discourage such behaviors. For example, suppose that someone in your class stole the final exam and is selling a copy for $50. You need to do well on the exam or risk failing the course. You suspect that some classmates have bought copies, which could affect any results because your professor grades on a curve. Do you buy a copy because you fear that without it you'll be disadvantaged, do you refuse to buy a copy and try your best, or do you report your knowledge to your instructor? This example of the stolen final exam illustrates how ambiguity over what is ethical can be a problem for managers.

How Can Managers Encourage Ethical Behavior?

At a Senate hearing exploring the accusations that Wall Street firm Goldman Sachs deceived its clients during the housing-market meltdown, Arizona senator John McCain said, "I don't know if Goldman has done anything *illegal*, but there's no doubt their behavior was *unethical*."[34] You have to wonder what the firm's managers were thinking or doing while such ethically questionable decisions and actions were occurring. It's pretty obvious that they weren't encouraging ethical behaviors!

ethics
A set of rules or principles that defines right and wrong conduct

utilitarian view of ethics
View that says ethical decisions are made solely on the basis of their outcomes or consequences

rights view of ethics
View that says ethical decisions are made in order to respect and protect individual liberties and privileges

theory of justice view of ethics
View that says ethical decisions are made in order to enforce rules fairly and impartially

Technology and the Manager's Job
THE ETHICS OF DATA ANALYTICS

Every time you click on anything in Facebook or do a search in Google or purchase anything on Amazon or post anything on Instagram, data is being collected about you. Technology has evolved to the point where companies can capture data about consumer habits anytime they access a Web site, post on social media, do a search, or purchase something online. But it's not just on external Web sites that data is being collected and analyzed. A recent article in the *Wall Street Journal* discussed how certain companies have been analyzing a wide variety of data points on employees to try to pinpoint who is likely to leave the organization.[35] Since employee turnover costs money and time, companies want to try to get an early handle on it so managers can take action before an employee—and especially a good employee—decides to leave.

Statisticians and data scientists have expressed misgivings about the lack of ethical guidelines for big data research and analytics, especially online. Just because we have the technology to collect these vast amounts of quantifiable information that can

be analyzed by highly sophisticated data processing, should we? *And* should organizations (managers) be using it? When it was discovered that Facebook had manipulated news feeds either positively or negatively of more than half a million randomly selected users to see how emotions spread on social media, people were outraged. But Facebook isn't the only one that manipulates and analyzes user data. Google, Yahoo, Amazon, and others also manipulate and analyze this data, all under the guise of "improving the user experience."[36] The technology of data analytics itself is ethics-free; it's neither good nor bad. But it's in *how* the technology is used that ethical concerns can arise.

If your professor has assigned this, go to the Assignments section of mymanagementlab.com to complete these discussion questions.

✪ **TALK ABOUT IT 3:** What does it mean that the technology of data analytics is ethics-free?

✪ **TALK ABOUT IT 4:** How could managers ethically use big data?

If managers are serious about **encouraging ethical behaviors**, there are a number of things they can do.

Like what? Hire employees with high ethical standards, establish codes of ethics, lead by example, link job goals and performance appraisal, provide ethics training, and implement protective mechanisms for employees who face ethical dilemmas. By themselves, such actions won't have much of an impact. But if an organization has a comprehensive ethics program in place, it can potentially improve an organization's ethical climate. The key variable, however, is *potentially*. A well-designed ethics program does not guarantee the desired outcome. Sometimes corporate ethics programs are mostly public relations gestures that do little to influence managers and employees. For instance, even Enron, often thought of as the "poster child" of corporate wrongdoing, outlined values in its final annual report that most would consider ethical—communication, respect, integrity, and excellence. Yet the way top managers behaved didn't reflect those values at all.[37] We want to look at three ways that managers can encourage ethical behavior and create a comprehensive ethics program.

CODES OF ETHICS.   Codes of ethics are popular tools for attempting to reduce employee ambiguity about what's ethical and what's not.[38] A **code of ethics** is a formal document that states an organization's primary values and the ethical rules it expects managers and nonmanagerial employees to follow. Ideally, these codes should be specific enough to guide organizational members in what they're supposed to do yet loose enough to allow for freedom of judgment. Research shows that 97 percent of organizations with more than 10,000 employees have written codes of ethics. Even in smaller organizations, nearly 93 percent have them.[39] And codes of ethics are becoming more popular globally. Research by the Institute for Global Ethics says that shared values such as honesty, fairness, respect, responsibility, and caring are embraced worldwide.[40]

code of ethics
A formal document that states an organization's primary values and the ethical rules it expects managers and nonmanagerial employees to follow

Exhibit 3–3 Being an Ethical Leader

- Be a good role model by being ethical and honest.
- Tell the truth always.
- Don't hide or manipulate information.
- Be willing to admit your failures.
- Share your personal values by regularly communicating them to employees.
- Stress the organization's or team's important shared values.
- Use the reward system to hold everyone accountable to the values.

The effectiveness of such codes depends heavily on whether management supports them and ingrains them into the corporate culture, and how individuals who break the codes are treated.[41] If management considers them to be important, regularly reaffirms their content, follows the rules itself, and publicly reprimands rule breakers, ethics codes can be a strong foundation for an effective corporate ethics program.[42]

ETHICAL LEADERSHIP. In 2011, Tim Cook was named CEO of Apple Inc. Although it's an extremely successful company, Apple is viewed by some as the epitome of greedy capitalism with no concern for how its products are manufactured. Cook, who was named one of the 100 Most Influential People in Business Ethics by *Ethisphere*, has increased the company's focus on supply chain ethics and compliance issues. It was the first technology company to join the Fair Labor Association, which means that organization can now review the company's labor practices within the supply chain. In addition, at a recent annual stockholders' meeting with investors and journalists, Cook, who was challenged by a spokesperson from a conservative think tank to explain how the company's sustainability efforts were in the best interests of shareholders, bluntly and clearly said that Apple wasn't just about making a profit and that "We want to leave the world better than we found it."[43]

Doing business ethically requires a commitment from managers. Why? Because they're the ones who uphold the shared values and set the cultural tone. Managers must be good ethical role models both in words *and,* more importantly, in actions. For example, if managers take company resources for their personal use, inflate their expense accounts, or give favored treatment to friends, they imply that such behavior is acceptable for all employees.

> Through his words and actions, L'Oreal's CEO and chairman Jean-Paul Agon is committed to doing business ethically. Leading by example, he expects all managers and employees to model ethical behavior and integrates ethical principles into all of L'Oreal's business practices that build relationships of trust with the company's customers.

What you **DO is *far more important* than what you SAY** in getting employees to act ethically!

Managers also set the tone through their reward and punishment practices. The choices of when to reward with pay increases and promotions send a strong signal to employees. As we said earlier, when an employee is rewarded for achieving impressive results in an ethically questionable manner, it indicates to others that those ways are acceptable. When an employee does something unethical, managers must punish the offender and publicize the fact by making the outcome visible to everyone in the organization. This practice sends a message that doing wrong has a price and it's not in employees' best interests to act unethically! (See Exhibit 3–3 for suggestions on being an ethical leader.)

ETHICS TRAINING. Yahoo! used an off-the-shelf online ethics training package, but employees said

Charles Platiau/Reuters

> ✪ **Write It 2!**
> If your professor has assigned this, go to the Assignments section of **mymanagementlab.com** to complete *MGMT 4: Ethics*.

that the scenarios used to demonstrate different concepts didn't resemble those that might come up at Yahoo! and were too middle-American and middle-aged for the global company with a youthful workforce. So the company changed its ethics training! The new ethics training package is more animated and interactive and has more realistic storylines for the industry. The 45-minute training module covers the company's code of conduct and resources available to help employees understand it.[44]

Like Yahoo!, more and more organizations are setting up seminars, workshops, and similar ethics training programs to encourage ethical behavior. Such training programs aren't without controversy; the primary concern is whether ethics can be taught. Critics stress that the effort is pointless because people establish their individual value systems when they're young. Proponents note, however, that several studies have shown that values can be learned after early childhood. In addition, they cite evidence that shows that teaching ethical problem solving can make an actual difference in ethical behaviors;[45] that training has increased individuals' level of moral development;[46] and that, if nothing else, ethics training increases awareness of ethical issues in business.[47]

> ✪ **Try It 2!**
> If your professor has assigned this, go to the Assignments section of **mymanagementlab.com** to complete the **Simulation:** *Management Ethics*.

What Is Today's Workforce Like and How Does It Affect the Way Organizations Are Managed?

3-4 Describe how the workforce is changing and its impact on the way organizations are managed.

It's amazing all the different languages you can hear in **the lobby of one of MGM Mirage's hotels**. Because guests come from all over the world, the company is committed to reflecting that diversity in its workplace.

MGM Mirage has implemented a program that is devoted to making sure that everyone in the organization feels included.[48] Such diversity can be found in many organizational workplaces domestically and globally, and managers in those workplaces are looking for ways to value and develop that diversity.

What Is Workplace Diversity?

Look around your classroom (or your workplace). You're likely to see young/old, male/female, tall/short, blonde/brunette, blue-eyed/brown-eyed, any number of races, and any variety of dress styles. You'll see people who speak up in class and others who are content to keep their attention on taking notes or daydreaming. Have you ever noticed your own little world of diversity where you are right now? Many of you may have grown up in an environment that included diverse individuals, while others may have not had that experience. We want to focus on *workplace* diversity, so let's look at what it is.

Diversity has been "one of the most popular business topics over the last two decades. It ranks with modern business disciplines such as quality, leadership, and ethics. Despite this popularity, it's also one of the most controversial and least understood topics."[49] With its basis in civil rights legislation and social justice, the word "diversity" often invokes a variety of attitudes and emotional responses in people. Diversity has traditionally been considered a term used by human resources departments, associated with fair hiring practices, discrimination, and inequality. But diversity today is considered to be so much more.

We're defining **workforce diversity** as the ways in which people in an organization are different from and similar to one another. Notice that our definition not only focuses on the differences but also the similarities of employees, reinforcing our belief that managers and organizations should view employees as having qualities in common as well as differences that separate them. It doesn't mean that those differences are any less important, but rather that our focus as managers is in finding ways to develop strong relationships with and engage our entire workforce.

workforce diversity
Ways in which people in a workforce are similar and different from one another in terms of gender, age, race, sexual orientation, ethnicity, cultural background, and physical abilities and disabilities

---

⭐ **Watch It 2!**

If your professor has assigned this, go to the Assignments section of **mymanagementlab.com** to complete the video exercise titled *CH2MHill: Diversity*.

What Types of Diversity Are Found in Workplaces?

Diversity is a big issue, and an important issue, in today's workplaces. What types of diversity do we find in those workplaces? Exhibit 3–4 lists several types of workplace diversity.

AGE.   The aging of the population is a major critical shift taking place in the workforce. With many of the nearly 85 million baby boomers still employed and active in the workforce, managers must ensure that those employees are not discriminated against because of age. Both Title VII of the Civil Rights Act of 1964 and the Age Discrimination in Employment Act of 1967 prohibit age discrimination. The Age Discrimination Act also restricts mandatory retirement at specific ages. In addition to complying with these laws, organizations need programs and policies in place that provide for fair and equal treatment of their older employees.

Exhibit 3–4 Types of Diversity Found in Workplaces

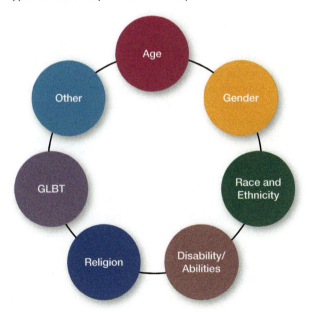

race
The biological heritage (including physical characteristics, such as one's skin color and associated traits) that people use to identify themselves

ethnicity
Social traits, such as one's cultural background or allegiance, that are shared by a human population

GENDER. Women (49.8 percent) and men (50.2 percent) now each make up almost half of the workforce.[50] However, gender diversity issues are still quite prevalent in organizations. These issues include the gender pay gap, career start and progress, and misconceptions about whether women perform their jobs as well as men do. It's important for managers and organizations to explore the strengths that both women and men bring to an organization and the barriers they face in contributing fully to organizational efforts.

RACE AND ETHNICITY. There's a long and controversial history in the United States and in other parts of the world over race and, as recent events have shown, how people react to and treat others of a different race. Race and ethnicity are important types of diversity in organizations. We're going to define **race** as the biological heritage (including physical characteristics such as one's skin color and associated traits) that people use to identify themselves. Most people identify themselves as part of a racial group, and such racial classifications are an integral part of a country's cultural, social, and legal environments. **Ethnicity** is related to race, but it refers to social traits—such as one's cultural background or allegiance—that are shared by a human population.

The racial and ethnic diversity of the U.S. population is increasing and at an exponential rate. We're also seeing this same effect in the composition of the workforce. Most of the research on race and ethnicity as they relate to the workplace has looked at hiring decisions, performance evaluations, pay, and workplace discrimination. Managers and organizations need to make race and ethnicity issues a key focus in effectively managing workforce diversity.

DISABILITY/ABILITIES. For persons with disabilities, 1990 was a watershed year—the year the Americans with Disabilities Act (ADA) became law. ADA prohibits discrimination against persons with disabilities and also requires employers to make reasonable accommodations so their workplaces are accessible to people with physical or mental disabilities and enable them to effectively perform their jobs. With the law's enactment, individuals with disabilities became a more representative and integral part of the U.S. workforce.

In effectively managing a workforce with disabled employees, managers need to create and maintain an environment in which employees feel comfortable disclosing their need for accommodation. Those accommodations, by law, enable individuals with disabilities to perform their jobs, but they also need to be perceived as equitable by those not disabled. It's the balancing act that managers face.

A Question of Ethics

Smokers. Overweight individuals. Two groups about whom much has been written and much has been discussed, especially when it comes to workplaces. A Gallup poll found that most Americans said that if they were in a position to hire someone, it would make no difference to them if that person were overweight (79 percent) or smoked (74 percent). However, the majority of Americans (60 percent) said it is justified to set higher health insurance rates for smokers. A majority (57 percent) said it is *un*-justified to set higher insurance rates because someone is very overweight.

*If your professor has assigned this, go to the Assignments section of **mymanagementlab .com** to complete these discussion questions.*

⭐ **Talk About It 5:** What ethical issues might arise in workplaces with employees who fit into these two groups?

⭐ **Talk About It 6:** As a manager, how would you handle such issues?

RELIGION. Hani Khan, a college sophomore, had worked for three months as a stock clerk at a Hollister clothing store in San Francisco.[51] One day, she was told by her supervisors to remove the head scarf that she wears in observance of Islam (known as a *hijab*) because it violated the company's "look policy" (which instructs employees on clothing, hair styles, makeup, and accessories they may wear to work). She refused on religious grounds and was fired one week later. Like a number of other Muslim women, she filed a federal job discrimination complaint. A spokesperson for Abercrombie & Fitch (Hollister's parent company) said that, "If any Abercrombie associate identifies a religious conflict with an Abercrombie policy...the company will work with the associate in an attempt to find an accommodation."

Title VII of the Civil Rights Act prohibits discrimination on the basis of religion (as well as race/ethnicity, country of origin, and sex). However, you'd probably not be surprised to find out that the number of religious discrimination claims has been growing in the United States.[52] In accommodating religious diversity, managers need to recognize and be aware of different religions and their beliefs, paying special attention to when certain religious holidays fall. Businesses benefit when they can accommodate, if possible, employees who have special needs or requests in a way that other employees don't view it as "special treatment."

GLBT—SEXUAL ORIENTATION AND GENDER IDENTITY.   The acronym GLBT—which refers to gay, lesbian, bisexual, and transgender people—is being used more frequently and relates to the diversity of sexual orientation and gender identity.[53] Sexual orientation has been called the "last acceptable bias."[54] We want to emphasize that we're not condoning this perspective; what this comment refers to is that most people understand that racial and ethnic stereotypes are "off-limits." Unfortunately, it's not unusual to hear derogatory comments about gays or lesbians. U.S. federal law does not prohibit discrimination against employees on the basis of sexual orientation, although many states and municipalities do. However, in Europe, the Employment Equality Directive required all European Union member states to introduce legislation making it unlawful to discriminate on grounds of sexual orientation.[55] Despite the progress that's been made in making workplaces more accommodating of gays and lesbians, obviously much more needs to be done. One study found that more than 40 percent of gay and lesbian employees indicated they had been unfairly treated, denied a promotion, or pushed to quit their job because of their sexual orientation.[56]

As with most of the types of diversity we've discussed in this section, managers need to look at how best to meet the needs of their GLBT employees. They need to respond to employees' concerns while also creating a safe and productive work environment for all.

Jane Hobson/Alamy

OTHER TYPES OF DIVERSITY.   As we said earlier, diversity refers to *any* dissimilarities or differences that might be present in a workplace.

Other types of workplace diversity that managers might confront and have to deal with include socioeconomic background (social class and income-related factors), team members from different functional areas or organizational units, physical attractiveness, obesity/thinness, job seniority, or intellectual abilities. Each of these types of diversity also can affect how employees are treated in the workplace. Again, managers need to ensure that all employees—no matter the similarities or dissimilarities—are treated fairly and given the opportunity and support to do their jobs to the best of their abilities.

Increasing gender diversity in senior management is a top priority of Sodexo, a global food and facilities management services firm. Sodexo nurtures high-potential talent like Debbie White, CEO of Sodexo in the United Kingdom and Ireland, through initiatives that include training, mentoring, women's networks, and visible job assignments.

✪ **Try It 3!**

If your professor has assigned this, go to the Assignments section of **mymanagementlab.com** to complete the **Simulation: *HR and Diversity***.

Challenge for Managers: **Blurred lines between employees' work and personal lives.**

How Are Organizations and Managers Adapting to a Changing Workforce?

Since organizations wouldn't be able to do what they're in business to do without employees, managers have to adapt to the changes taking place in the workforce. They're responding with diversity initiatives such as work-life balance programs, contingent jobs, and recognition of generational differences.

WORK-LIFE BALANCE PROGRAMS.   The typical employee in the 1960s or 1970s showed up at the workplace Monday through Friday and did his or her job in eight- or nine-hour chunks of time. The workplace and hours were clearly specified. That's not

Charles Trainor Jr./MCT/Newscom

Employees at Citrix, a cloud computing company that enables mobile work styles, enjoy flexible work schedules that help them balance their work and home life. Citrix gives them the freedom to determine how, when, and where their work gets done and allows them to use their own devices for working at home or at the office, with Windows or Mac OS X.

the case anymore for a large segment of the workforce. Employees are increasingly complaining that the line between work and nonwork time has blurred, creating personal conflicts and stress.[57] Several factors have contributed to this blurring between work and personal life. One is that in a world of global business, work never ends. At any time and on any day, for instance, thousands of Caterpillar employees are working somewhere in the company's facilities. The need to consult with colleagues or customers 8 or 10 time zones away means that many employees of global companies are "on call" 24 hours a day. Another factor is that communication technology allows employees to do their work at home, in their cars, or on the beach in Tahiti. Although this capability allows those in technical and professional jobs to do their work anywhere and at any time, it also means there's no escaping from work. Another factor is that as organizations have had to lay off employees during the economic downturn, "surviving" employees find themselves working longer hours. It's not unusual for employees to work more than 45 hours a week, and some work more than 50. Finally, fewer families today have a single wage earner. Today's married employee is typically part of a dual-career couple, which makes it increasingly difficult for married employees to find time to fulfill commitments to home, spouse, children, parents, and friends.[58]

More and more, employees recognize that work is squeezing out their personal lives, and they're not happy about it. Today's progressive workplaces must accommodate the varied needs of a diverse workforce. In response, many organizations are offering **family-friendly benefits**: benefits that provide a wide range of scheduling options that allow employees more flexibility at work, accommodating their need for work-life balance. They've introduced programs such as on-site child care, summer day camps, flextime, job sharing, time off for school functions, telecommuting, and part-time employment. Younger people, particularly, put a higher priority on family and a lower priority on jobs and are looking for organizations that give them more work flexibility.[59]

CONTINGENT JOBS. "Companies want a workforce they can switch on and off as needed."[60] Although this quote may shock you, the truth is that the labor force already has begun shifting away from traditional full-time jobs toward a **contingent workforce**—part-time, temporary, and contract workers who are available for hire on an as-needed basis. In today's economy, many organizations have responded by converting full-time permanent jobs into contingent jobs. It's predicted that by the end of the next decade the number of contingent employees will have grown to about 40 percent of the workforce. (It's at 30 percent today.)[61] In fact, one compensation and benefits expert says that "a growing a number of workers will need to structure their careers around this model," which could likely include you![62]

What are the implications for managers and organizations? Because contingent employees are not "employees" in the traditional sense of the word, managing them has its own set of challenges and expectations. Managers must recognize that because contingent workers lack the stability and security of permanent employees, they may not identify with the organization or be as committed or motivated. Managers may need to treat contingent workers differently in terms of practices and policies. However, with good communication and leadership, an organization's contingent employees can be just as valuable a resource to an organization as permanent employees are. Today's managers must recognize that it will be their responsibility to motivate their entire workforce, full-time and contingent, and to build their commitment to doing good work!

family-friendly benefits
Benefits that provide a wide range of scheduling options and allow employees more flexibility at work, accommodating their needs for work-life balance

contingent workforce
Part-time, temporary, and contract workers who are available for hire on an as-needed basis

GENERATIONAL DIFFERENCES. Managing generational differences presents some unique challenges, especially for baby boomers and Gen Y. Conflicts and resentment can arise over issues ranging from appearance to technology and management style.

What *is* appropriate office attire? That answer may depend on who you ask, but more importantly, it depends on the type of work being done and the size of the organization. To accommodate generational differences in what is considered appropriate, the key is flexibility. For instance, a guideline might be that when an employee is not interacting with someone outside the organization, more casual wear (with some restrictions) is acceptable.

What about technology? Gen Y has grown up with ATMs, DVDs, cell phones, e-mail, texting, laptops, and the Internet. When they don't have information they need, they just enter a few keystrokes to get it. They're content to meet virtually to solve problems, while baby boomers expect important problems to be solved with in-person meetings. Baby boomers complain about Gen Y's inability to focus on one task, while Gen Y'ers see nothing wrong with multitasking. Again, flexibility and understanding from both are the key to working together effectively and efficiently.

Finally, what about management style? Gen Y employees want bosses who are open-minded; experts in their field, even if they aren't tech savvy; organized; teachers, trainers, and mentors; not authoritarian or paternalistic; respectful of their generation; understanding of their need for work-life balance; providing constant feedback; communicating in vivid and compelling ways; and providing stimulating and novel learning experiences.[63]

Because Gen Y employees have a lot to offer organizations in terms of their knowledge, passion, and abilities, managers have to recognize and understand the behaviors of this group in order to create an environment in which work can be done efficiently, effectively, and without disruptive conflict.

MyManagementLab®

Go to **mymanagementlab.com** to complete the problems marked with this icon ⭐.

3 Review

CHAPTER SUMMARY

3-1 Explain globalization and its impact on organizations.

Organizations are considered global if they exchange goods and services with consumers in other countries, if they use managerial and technical employee talent from other countries, or if they use financial sources and resources outside their home country. Businesses going global are usually referred to as multinational corporations (MNCs). As an MNC, they may operate as a multidomestic corporation, a global corporation, or a transnational or borderless organization. When a business goes global, it may start with global sourcing, move to exporting or importing, use licensing or franchising, pursue a global strategic alliance, or set up a foreign subsidiary. In doing business globally, managers need to be aware of different laws and political and economic systems. But the biggest challenge is in understanding the different country cultures. Two cross-cultural frameworks that managers can use are Hofstede's and GLOBE.

3-2 Discuss how society's expectations are influencing managers and organizations.

Society expects organizations and managers to be responsible and ethical. An organization's social involvement can be from the perspective of social obligation, social responsiveness, or social responsibility. After much analysis, researchers have concluded that managers can afford to be (and should be)

socially responsible. Sustainability has become an important societal issue for managers and organizations.

3-3 Discuss the factors that lead to ethical and unethical behavior in organizations.

Ethics can be viewed from the utilitarian view, the rights view, or the theory of justice view. Whether a manager acts ethically or unethically depends on his or her morality, values, personality, and experiences; the organization's culture; and the ethical issue being faced. Managers can encourage ethical behavior by hiring employees with high ethical standards, establishing a code of ethics, leading by example, linking ethical behavior to job goals and performance appraisal, providing ethics training, and implementing protective mechanisms for employees who face ethical dilemmas.

3-4 Describe how the workforce is changing and its impact on the way organizations are managed.

The workforce continues to reflect increasing diversity. Types of workforce diversity include age, gender, race and ethnicity, disability/abilities, religion, and sexual orientation and gender identity. Organizations and managers are responding to the changing workforce with work-life balance programs, contingent jobs, and recognition of generational differences.

DISCUSSION QUESTIONS

⭐ 3-1 How does the concept of a global village affect organizations and managers?

3-2 Describe the different types of global organizations and the ways that organizations can go global.

3-3 What are the managerial implications of Hofstede's research on cultural environments? The GLOBE study?

⭐ 3-4 How are social responsibility, social obligation, and social responsiveness different? Similar?

3-5 What is sustainability, and how can organizations practice it?

3-6 Describe how a manager would approach ethical decisions according to each of the three views on ethics.

3-7 Discuss specific ways managers can encourage ethical behavior.

3-8 What is workforce diversity, and why is it an important issue for managers?

3-9 Describe the six types of diversity found in workplaces.

3-10 Describe and discuss the three ways that organizations and managers are adapting to a changing workforce.

Writing Assignments

3-11 Why is it important for an organization to have a clear definition of diversity?

3-12 Which do you think would be a manager's best choice for shaping long-term ethical behavior: a written code of ethics combined with ethics training OR strong ethical leadership? Support your position.

Management Skill Builder | BUILDING HIGH ETHICAL STANDARDS

Ethics encompasses the rules and principles we use to define right and wrong conduct. Many organizations have formally written ethical codes to guide managers and employees in their decisions and actions. But individuals need to establish their own personal ethical standards. If managers are to successfully lead others, they need to be seen as trustworthy and ethical.

⭐ PERSONAL INVENTORY ASSESSMENT   PERSONAL INVENTORY ASSESSMENT

Ethical Leadership Assessment

Organizations need ethical leadership from all employees, but especially from managers. In this PIA, you'll see how much thought and effort goes into your being ethical in your workplace behavior.

Skill Basics

To be more ethical in your leadership, focus on what *you* can do and what *your organization* can do. Here are some suggestions on how to do this:

What You Can Do:

- *Know your values.* What's important to you? Where do you draw the line?

- *Think before you act.* Will your actions injure someone? What are your ulterior motives? Will your actions jeopardize your reputation?

- *Consider all consequences.* If you make the wrong decision, what will happen? Every decision comes with consequences and you should be sure you've considered their implications.

- *Apply the "publicity test."* What would your family and friends think if your actions were described in detail on the front page of your local newspaper or on the local TV news?

- *Seek opinions from others. Ask advice from others you respect.* Use their experience and listen to their perspectives.

What Your Organization Can Do:

- *Create a formal ethics code.* Organizations should set down their ethical standards and policies in a formal ethical code. The code should be widely distributed to all employees.

- *Set an ethical culture.* Visibly reward employees who set a high ethical standard and visibly punish those who engage in unethical practices.

- *Ensure managers are role models.* Employees look to their immediate superior and upper management for cues as to what is or is not acceptable behavior. Managers need to be positive ethical role models.

- *Offer ethics workshops.* Employees should participate in regular ethics training to reinforce the importance of high ethical standards, to interpret the organization's ethical code, and to allow employees to clarify what they may see as "gray areas."

- *Appoint an ethics "advisor."* A senior executive should be available for employees to meet and confer with to confidentially discuss ethical concerns.

- *Protect employees who report unethical practices.* Mechanisms need to be put in place that protect employees from retributions or other negative consequences should they reveal unethical practices that are a threat to others.

Based on L. Nash, "Ethics without the Sermon," *Harvard Business Review* (November–December 1981): 78–92; W. D. Hall, *Making the Right Decision: Ethics for Managers* (New York: John Wiley, 1993); and L. K. Trevino and K. A. Nelson, *Managing Business Ethics: Straight Talk about How to Do It Right* (New York: John Wiley, 1995).

Practicing the Skill

We're taking a little different approach with this chapter's skill practice. Form into teams of four or five people. Using a copy of your college's code of conduct, answer the following questions: How many of the team members were aware of the code? How many had read it? Evaluate the code's provisions and policies. Are you uncomfortable with any of the code's provisions? Why? How effective do you think they have been in shaping student and faculty behavior? If they haven't been effective, what could be done to improve them?

Be prepared to present your team's findings to the class.

Experiential Exercise

Delaney Environmental Services

To: Sandy Burk, Director of Operations

From: J. Delaney, Managing Director

Subject: Global Expansion

Sandy, we need to start looking at expanding our global market opportunities. We've had a successful track record here in San Antonio providing environmental consulting and design services, and I believe that with our experience we have a lot to offer the Latin American market, particularly in Mexico.

Please research the potential problems we might face in moving into the Mexican market. Focus on: (1) cultural differences; (2) the current currency rate of exchange and how it's changed over the last three years; and (3) any legal or political situations we need to be aware of. Because this is just an initial analysis, please keep your report to one page or less.

This fictionalized company and message were created for educational purposes only, and are not meant to reflect positively or negatively on management practices by any company that may share this name.

CASE APPLICATION #1

Global Stumble

It's not always easy to do business globally, as executives at Japanese brokerage firm Nomura Holdings Inc. have discovered.[64] Nomura acquired Lehman's international operations after Lehman's parent company sought Chapter 11 bankruptcy protection—an action that added about 8,000 non-Japanese workers. For Nomura, the time seemed right to strengthen its global expansion strategy. However, since the acquisition, cultural and business differences between the two organizations have been a major stumbling block. Although blending two diverse cultures requires intentional efforts when different organizations merge or are acquired, it's particularly challenging when the key assets in the cross-border acquisition are the people employed by the organization being acquired.

Workplace tensions arose over executive compensation, how quickly decisions were made, and how women were

The challenges of **BLENDING TWO CULTURES**

treated. For instance, during Nomura's initial training session for new hires, the men and women were separated. The women—many of whom had earned prestigious degrees from the likes of Harvard—were taught how to wear their hair, serve tea, and choose their clothing according to the season. The company's dress code for women was also strictly interpreted. Women from Lehman were told to remove highlights from their hair, to wear sleeves no shorter than mid-bicep, and to avoid brightly colored clothing. Several women were sent home from the trading floor for dressing "inappropriately." One said, "I was sent home for wearing a short-sleeve dress, even though I was wearing a jacket." A Nomura spokesperson said, "The dress code is displayed on the company's intranet and is intended to ensure that clients and colleagues don't feel uncomfortable."

Lehman bankers also said they found the process for getting approval on deals was "slower and more difficult than it was at Lehman." Also, at Lehman, clients were categorized, in large part, by the fees they paid. At Nomura, more emphasis was placed on other factors, such as the length of the relationship. The bankers at Nomura said that "their new colleagues were too willing to dump loyal clients for a quick profit."

In its defense, Nomura has tried to blend the two cultures. In offices in Europe and in Asia outside of Japan, there's a mix of nationalities. Also, the company has promoted a handful of non-Japanese employees to high-ranking positions. "To reduce the Tokyo-centric nature of the company, Hiromi Yamaji, head of global investment banking, moved to London, and Naoki Matsuba, global head of equities, moved to New York." Until March 2010, Nomura's executive committee was all Japanese men. However, in an attempt to make the company more globally oriented, an ex-Lehman executive and foreigner, Jasjit "Jesse" Bhattal, a native of India, was promoted to the committee. Nomura's deputy president and chief operating officer, Takumi Shibata, said, "When your business is global,

management needs to be global." Two years later, however, unable to garner support from Tokyo for an overhaul of the global wholesale-banking operations, Bhattal resigned as Nomura's highest-ranking foreign executive.

Discussion Questions

3-14 What obvious cultural differences between Nomura and Lehman do you see in this situation?

3-15 What global attitude do you think characterizes Nomura? Be specific in your description. Do you see any evidence of that changing?

3-16 Do some cultural research on Japan and the United States. Compare those cultural characteristics. What similarities and differences exist? How might these cultural differences be affecting the situation at Nomura?

3-17 What could Nomura managers do to support, promote, and encourage cultural awareness among employees? Explain.

3-18 What do you think the statement, "When your business is global, management needs to be global," is saying? In your opinion, is Nomura doing this? Explain.

CASE APPLICATION #2

 Serious about Sustainability?

It's got to be one of the most convenient products ever—especially for consumers who want their coffee (or tea or other hot beverage) efficiently delivered without much hassle. The Keurig K-Cups® were invented in 1992 by John Sylvan. Like any innovator, Sylvan was looking for a better way. For him, it was finding a better way to provide his 30–40 daily cups of coffee in a way that was customizable and easy.[65] The single-serve brewing pod he created became the Keurig K-Cup. Interesting note: Keurig translates to "neat" in Dutch, and the Keurig machine and its ubiquitous K-Cup *are* quite neat. The single-brew machine is a very efficient and convenient alternative to the traditional coffee pot *or* to stopping and picking up drive-through coffee every morning.[66] However, what Sylvan didn't anticipate was (1) the overwhelming popularity of the approach and (2) the amount of waste the single-serve pods would create because of that popularity.

Today, almost one in three homes has a pod-based coffee machine. And the sales of those pods accounted for a vast majority of the revenues of the company that makes them—Keurig Green Mountain. The company's mission is "A

Keurig brewer on every counter and a beverage for every occasion."[67] And the company is taking another step toward that goal of a beverage for *every* occasion through its partnership with Coca-Cola Company. It will begin selling, at the end of 2015, a machine called "Keurig Cold," which will be used to dispense Coke's various brands. The Dr Pepper Snapple group also recently signed on to allow its flavor options for the new machine.[68] Although the Keurig machine is popular and a convenience, it also has a more troubling characteristic: the constant need to buy more K-Cups. They're designed as single-serve, and with 9.8 billion of them sold in 2014, that's a lot of K-Cups hitting landfills, because they are *not* recyclable. Those 9.8 billion K-Cups would circle the globe more than 12 times.[69]

Environmentalists have criticized the company for its slow response to creating and selling a recyclable version of the pod. And it's not that it can't be done. For instance, when the K-Cup design patent expired in 2012, other companies brought out single-serve cups that *are* completely biodegradable and recyclable. To further highlight the sustainability issue, an anonymous

YouTube video called "Kill the K-Cup" hit the Internet in early 2015. The apocalyptic nature of the video highlighted the extreme waste and irresponsibility of continuing to make coffee in a way "that simply cannot be sustained."[70] It was eventually revealed that the creator of the video was a production company in Halifax, Nova Scotia, whose employees loved their Keurig until they began to notice the growing pile of discarded K-Cups that, despite great Canadian recycling programs, could not easily be recycled.

So what does the company say? Keurig's chief sustainability officer, Monique Oxender, says that the company isn't happy with its track record either. In 2014, the company pledged to create a fully recyclable version of the K-Cup by 2020. Of course, the critics have jumped all over the 2020 goal saying that five years is a long time to continue to fill up landfills and pointing out that the plastic used in the K-Cups will never be able to be fully recyclable because of the type of plastic it is. In its annual sustainability report, Keurig Green Mountain describes its efforts to strengthen its global citizenship and sustainability leadership.[71] Others have said that despite the outcry against the K-Cups, there are some sustainability benefits to the Keurig machine and its single-serve pods. For instance, they're

likely to save electricity over a coffee pot that's constantly "on" to keep the coffee warm. Also, the pods have been shown to be a more efficient way of extracting coffee from grounds, thus saving resources. And other approaches to coffee making likely use more water in brewing coffee that may not actually be consumed and then dumped down the drain. So, although "environmental awareness is never a bad thing,"[72] are the critics overreacting to the situation?

Discussion Questions

3-19 What global issues do you see here? What ethical/social responsibility issues do you see here?

3-20 *Are* the critics overreacting to the situation? Do you think Keurig Green Mountain's managers are handling this situation in the best way, ethically and responsibly? What else could they do to be more ethical and responsible?

3-21 Are Keurig's proposed actions best described as social obligation, social responsiveness, or social responsibility? Explain.

3-22 What do you think the statement "environmental awareness is never a bad thing" means?

3-23 What lesson(s) about sustainability and business did you learn from this case application?

CASE APPLICATION #3

From Top to Bottom

Diversity management is the bottom line at professional services company PricewaterhouseCoopers (PwC).[73] And the company's commitment to diversity puts them at the top of the list for Top Companies for Diversity as determined by *DiversityInc*. So what does a company do to be recognized as the number one company for diversity management? Well, it starts at the top.

PwC's chairman and senior partner Bob Moritz is a vocal advocate of diversity and inclusion and says that "it's also the key to sustainable global growth for an organization." Moritz's commitment to diversity stems from his personal experiences. As a young professional, he lived in Japan for three years where he was a minority. He recalls, "If you're overseas or in a country where no one speaks your language—or the cab refuses to pick you up in the middle of the night because you're

Professional service companies prosper or fail because of their human talent.

a foreigner—you get a different perspective." In addition, his work team included individuals from France, Australia, and the United Kingdom, as well as from Japan. He soon recognized that people from different cultures approach problems with differing perspectives—that his way wasn't necessarily the right way and certainly not the only way. That's why now, as the company's top executive, he realizes that to help his company succeed in today's global economy, an inclusive culture that attracts and retains diverse talent is critical.

PwC also has several diversity programs and initiatives in place. The company's first chief diversity officer (CDO) was appointed in 2003 and, like at many organizations, was first "housed" in the human resources department. Now, however, the CDO reports directly to Moritz, giving the position credibility and, more importantly, accountability. Another interesting thing about PwC's CDO position is that it is rotating—that is, partners are rotated in and out of the role every two years. Currently, that position belongs to Maria Castanón Moats, an audit partner who recently was named CDO.

Another diversity commitment that PwC has made is to talent development. Professional services companies, like PwC, prosper or fail because of their human talent. PwC has made it a priority to "find, engage, and promote the best and brightest employees, especially those from underrepresented groups." To attract such outstanding, diverse talent, the company offers employees an enviable array of benefits. Because work at professional services companies can be arduous and demanding, PwC has looked for ways to offer its employees work/life flexibility to deal with personal and professional challenges. Some of the benefits it offers include backup childcare assistance, paid paternity leave, nanny resources and referrals, onsite religious accommodations, well-being rewards, and tax equalization for all domestic partners.

Finally, a major key to PwC's diversity management is its mentoring program, which has been described as "world class." A mentor is a senior employee who sponsors and supports a less-experienced employee, called a protégé. Although half of the company's mentoring pairings are cross-cultural, Moritz has asked each of PwC's 2,500 partners to "consciously diversify their pool of protégés." Part of the partners' evaluations will be based on their advocacy and investment in these individuals. But PwC doesn't just expect its employees to know what to do in mentoring. A toolkit for successful advocacy was created that includes guidelines, suggested readings, and other internal resources. And the most important part of that toolkit? Videos showing real-life examples of partners and staff members sharing their personal experiences with mentoring.

Discussion Questions

3-24 How might population trends affect a professional services organization like PwC? What might it have to do to adapt to these trends?

3-25 What challenges might PwC face in adapting to a more diverse applicant pool of college graduates?

3-26 Businesses often face the dilemma of retaining diverse employees once they're trained. What can PwC do to retain its diverse employees?

3-27 What advantages do you think PwC's mentoring program provides? What potential drawbacks might there be?

3-28 PwC's "rotating" chief diversity officer is an unusual approach. What advantages do you see to such an arrangement? Drawbacks?

Endnotes

1. "National Business Ethics Survey® 2013," Ethics Resource Center, http://www.ethics.org/downloads/2013NBESFinalWeb.pdf, 12.
2. S. Lohr, "Stress Test for the Global Supply Chain," *New York Times Online*, March 19, 2011.
3. S. Lohr, "Stress Test for the Global Supply Chain," *New York Times Online*, March 19, 2011; D. Jolly, "Long Pause for Japanese Industry Raises Concerns about Supply Chain," *New York Times Online*, March 16, 2011; and M. Helft and N. Bunkley, "Disaster in Japan Batters Suppliers," *New York Times Online*, March 14, 2011.
4. Percentages based on Securities and Exchange Commission 10-K filings, Hoovers.com, March 14, 2015.
5. E. Beinhocker, I. Davis, and L. Mendonca, "The 10 Trends You Have to Watch," *Harvard Business Review*, July–August 2009, 55–60.
6. B. Davis, "Migration of Skilled Jobs Abroad Unsettles Global-Economy Fans," *Wall Street Journal*, January 26, 2004, A1.
7. E. Frauenheim, "Bringing the Jobs Back Home: How 'Reshoring' Is Coming to America," www.

workforce.com, February 7, 2013; J. E. Lessin and J. R. Hagerty, "A Mac That's 'Made in U.S.A.'," *Wall Street Journal*, December 7, 2012, B1+; and V. Shannon, "Apple to Resume U.S. Manufacturing," *New York Times Online*, December 6, 2012.
8. A. Pande, "How to Make Onshoring Work," *Harvard Business Review*, March 2011, 30; P. Davidson, "Some Manufacturing Heads Back to USA," *USA Today*, August 6, 2010, 1B+; and V. Couto, A. Divakaran, and M. Mani, "Is Backshoring the New Offshoring?" *Strategy & Business*, October 21, 2008, 1–3.
9. J. Teresko, "United Plastics Picks China's Silicon Valley," *Industry Week*, January 2003, 58.
10. "Global Business: Getting the Frameworks Right," *Organization for Economic Cooperation and Development*, April 2000, 20.
11. From the Past to the Present box based on D. Holtbrügge and A. T. Mohr, "Cultural Determinants of Learning Style Preferences," *Academy of Management Learning & Education*, December 2010, 622–37; G. Hofstede, "The GLOBE Debate: Back to

Relevance," *Journal of International Business Studies* (November 2010): 1339–46; G. A. Gelade, P. Dobson, and K. Auer, "Individualism, Masculinity, and the Sources of Organizational Commitment," *Journal of Cross-Cultural Psychology* (September 2008): 599–617; G. Hofstede, "The Cultural Relativity of Organizational Practices and Theories," *Journal of International Business Studies* (Fall 1983): 75–89; and G. Hofstede, *Culture Consequences: International Differences in Work-Related Values* (Beverly Hills, CA: Sage Publications, 1980), 25–26. For an interesting discussion of collectivism and teams, see C. Gomez, B. L. Kirkman, and D. Shapiro, "The Impact of Collectivism and In-Group Membership on the Evaluation Generosity of Team Members," *Academy of Management Journal* (December 2000): 1097–106. Hofstede's term for what we've called quantity of life and quality of life was actually "masculinity versus femininity," but we've changed his terms because of their strong sexist connotation.

12. R. J. House, N. R. Quigley, and M. S. deLuque, "Insights from Project GLOBE: Extending Advertising Research Through a Contemporary Framework," *International Journal of Advertising* 29, no. 1 (2010): 111–39; R. R. McRae, A. Terracciano, A. Realo, and J. Allik, "Interpreting GLOBE Societal Practices Scale," *Journal of Cross-Cultural Psychology* (November 2008): 805–10; J. S. Chhokar, F. C. Brodbeck, and R. J. House, *Culture and Leadership across the World: The GLOBE Book of In-Depth Studies of 25 Societies* (Philadelphia: Lawrence Erlbaum Associates, 2007); and R. J. House, P. J. Hanges, M. Javidan, P. W. Dorfman, and V. Gupta, *Culture, Leadership, and Organizations: The GLOBE Study of 62 Societies* (Thousand Oaks, CA: Sage Publications, 2004).
13. D. Dearlove and S. Crainer, "Enterprise Goes Social," *Chief Executive*, March 2002, 18; and "Bronze Winner: Ben & Jerry's Citizen Cool," *Brandweek*, March 18, 2002, R-24.
14. M. Friedman, *Capitalism and Freedom* (Chicago: University

of Chicago Press, 1962); and M. Friedman, "The Social Responsibility of Business Is to Increase Profits," *New York Times Magazine*, September 13, 1970, 33.

15. See, for instance, N. A. Ibrahim, J. P. Angelidis, and D. P. Howell, "The Corporate Social Responsiveness Orientation of Hospital Directors: Does Occupational Background Make a Difference?" *Health Care Management Review*, Spring 2000, 85–92.

16. See, for example, D. J. Wood, "Corporate Social Performance Revisited," *Academy of Management Review*, October 1991, 703–08; and S. L. Wartick and P. L. Cochran, "The Evolution of the Corporate Social Performance Model," *Academy of Management Review*, October 1985, 763.

17. See, for instance, R. Lacy and P. A. Kennett-Hensel, "Longitudinal Effects of Corporate Social Responsibility on Customer Relationships," *Journal of Business Ethics* (December 2010): 581–97; S. Arendt and M. Brettel, "Understanding the Influence of Corporate Social Responsibility on Corporate Identity, Image, and Firm Performance," *Management Decision* 48, no. 10 (2010): 1469–92; J. Peloza, "The Challenge of Measuring Financial Impacts from Investments in Corporate Social Performance," *Journal of Management* (December 2009): 1518–41; J. D. Margolis and H. Anger Elfenbein, "Do Well by Doing Good? Don't Count on It," *Harvard Business Review*, January 2008, 19–20; M. L. Barnett, "Stakeholder Influence Capacity and the Variability of Financial Returns to Corporate Social Responsibility," 2007; D. O. Neubaum and S. A. Zahra, "Institutional Ownership and Corporate Social Performance: The Moderating Effects of Investment Horizon, Activism, and Coordination," *Journal of Management* (February 2006): 108–31; B. A. Waddock and S. B. Graves, "The Corporate Social Performance–Financial Performance Link," *Strategic Management Journal* (April 1997): 303–319; J. B. McGuire, A. Sundgren, and T. Schneeweis, "Corporate Social Responsibility and Firm Financial Performance," *Academy of Management Journal* (December 1988): 854–72; K. Aupperle, A. B. Carroll, and J. D. Hatfield, "An Empirical Examination of the Relationship between Corporate Social Responsibility and Profitability," *Academy of Management Journal* (June 1985): 446–63; and P. Cochran and R. A. Wood, "Corporate Social Responsibility and Financial Performance," *Academy of Management Journal* (March 1984): 42–56.

18. Peloza, "The Challenge of Measuring Financial Impacts from

Investments in Corporate Social Performance."

19. B. Seifert, S. A. Morris, and B. R. Bartkus, "Having, Giving, and Getting: Slack Resources, Corporate Philanthropy, and Firm Financial Performance," *Business & Society*, June 2004, 135–61; and McGuire, Sundgren, and Schneeweis, "Corporate Social Responsibility and Firm Financial Performance."

20. A. McWilliams and D. Siegel, "Corporate Social Responsibility and Financial Performance: Correlation or Misspecification?" *Strategic Management Journal* (June 2000): 603–09.

21. A. J. Hillman and G. D. Keim, "Shareholder Value, Stakeholder Management, and Social Issues: What's the Bottom Line?" *Strategic Management Journal* 22 (2001): 125–39.

22. M. Orlitzky, F. L. Schmidt, and S. L. Rynes, "Corporate Social and Financial Performance," *Organization Studies* 24, no. 3 (2003): 403–41.

23. S. Clifford, "Unexpected Ally Helps Wal-Mart Cut Waste," *New York Times Online*, April 13, 2012; and S. Rosenbloom, "Wal-Mart Unveils Plan to Make Supply Chain Greener," *New York Times Online*, February 26, 2010.

24. Symposium on Sustainability: Profiles in Leadership, New York, October 2001.

25. G. Unruh and R. Ettenson, "Growing Green," *Harvard Business Review*, June 2010, 94–100; G. Zoppo, "Corporate Sustainability," *DiversityInc*, May 2010, 76–80; and KPMG Global Sustainability Services, *Sustainability Insights*, October 2007.

26. J. Yang and P. Trap, "Applying Green Tech at Work," *USA Today*, May 13, 2013, 1B.

27. S. Armour and T. Frank, "Ex-Worker: Law Firm Ran 'Foreclosure Mill'," *USA Today*, October 19, 2010, 3B.

28. N. Clark, "Rogue Trader at Societe Generale Gets Jail Term," *New York Times Online*, October 5, 2010.

29. K. Belson, "Brain Trauma to Affect One in Three Players, NFL Agrees," *New York Times Online*, September 12, 2014.

30. S. A. DiPiazza, "Ethics in Action," *Executive Excellence*, January 2002, 15–16.

31. This example is based on J. F. Viega, T. D. Golden, and K. Dechant, "Why Managers Bend Company Rules," *Academy of Management Executive* (May 2004): 84–90.

32. G. F. Cavanaugh, D. J. Moberg, and M. Valasquez, "The Ethics of Organizational Politics," *Academy of Management Journal* (June 1981): 363–74.

33. J. Liedtka, "Ethics and the New Economy," *Business and Society Review*, Spring 2002, 1.

34. R. M. Kidder, "Can Disobedience Save Wall Street?" *Ethics Newsline*, www.globalethics.org, May 3, 2010.

35. R. E. Silverman and N. Waller, "Thinking of Quitting? The Boss Knows," *Wall Street Journal*, March 14, 2015, A1+.

36. V. Goel, "Facebook Tinkers with Users' Emotions in News Feed Experiment, Stirring Outcry," *New York Times Online*, June 29, 2014.

37. P. M. Lencioni, "Make Your Values Mean Something," *Harvard Business Review*, July 2002, 113.

38. D. H. Schepers, "Setting Global Standards: Guidelines for Creating Codes of Conduct in Multinational Corporations," *Business and Society*, December 2003, 496; and B. R. Gaummitz and J. C. Lere, "Contents of Codes of Ethics of Professional Business Organizations in the United States," *Journal of Business Ethics* (January 2002): 35–49.

39. M. Weinstein, "Survey Says: Ethics Training Works," *Training* (November 2005): 15.

40. J. E. Fleming, "Codes of Ethics for Global Corporations," *Academy of Management News*, June 2005, 4.

41. T. F. Shea, "Employees' Report Card on Supervisors' Ethics: No Improvement," *HR Magazine*, April 2002, 29.

42. See also A. G. Peace, J. Weber, K. S. Hartzel, and J. Nightingale, "Ethical Issues in eBusiness: A Proposal for Creating the eBusiness Principles," *Business and Society Review*, Spring 2002, 41–60.

43. L-M. Eleftheriou-Smith, "Apple's Tim Cook: 'Business Isn't Just about Making Profit'"; and P. Elmer-Dewitt, "Apple's Tim Cook Picks a Fight with Climate Change Deniers," tech.fortune.com, March 1, 2014.

44. E. Finkel, "Yahoo Takes New 'Road' on Ethics Training," *Workforce Management Online*, July 2010.

45. T. A. Gavin, "Ethics Education," *Internal Auditor*, April 1989, 54–57.

46. L. Myyry and K. Helkama, "The Role of Value Priorities and Professional Ethics Training in Moral Sensitivity," *Journal of Moral Education* 31, no. 1 (2002): 35–50; W. Penn and B. D. Collier, "Current Research in Moral Development as a Decision Support System," *Journal of Business Ethics* (January 1985): 131–36.

47. J. A. Byrne, "After Enron: The Ideal Corporation," *BusinessWeek*, August 19, 2002, 68–71; D. Rice and C. Dreilinger, "Rights and Wrongs of Ethics Training," *Training & Development Journal* (May 1990): 103–09; and J. Weber, "Measuring the Impact of Teaching Ethics to Future Managers: A Review, Assessment, and Recommendations," *Journal of Business Ethics* (April 1990): 182–90.

48. S. Caminiti, "The Diversity Factor," *Fortune*, October 19, 2007, 95–105; and B. Velez, "People and Places," *DiversityInc Online*, www.diversityinc.com, October 2006.

49. R. Anand and M. Frances Winters, "A Retrospective View of Corporate Diversity Training from 1964 to the Present," *Academy of Management Learning & Education*, September 2008, 356–72.

50. N. Gibbs, "What Women Want Now," *Time*, October 26, 2009, 24–33.

51. M. Bello, *USA Today*, "Controversy Shrouds Scarves," *Springfield, Missouri News-Leader*, April 17, 2010, 8A.

52. "Facts & Figures: Number of Religious Discrimination Complaints Received," *DiversityInc*, November–December 2009, 52.

53. P. Wang and J. L. Schwartz, "Stock Price Reactions to GLBT Nondiscrimination Policies," *Human Resource Management*, March–April 2010, 195–216.

54. L. Sullivan, "Sexual Orientation—The Last 'Acceptable' Bias," *Canadian HR Reporter*, December 20, 2004, 9–11.

55. F. Colgan, T. Wright, C. Creegan, and A. McKearney, "Equality and Diversity in the Public Services: Moving Forward on Lesbian, Gay and Bisexual Equality?" *Human Resource Management Journal* 19, no. 3 (2009): 280–301.

56. J. Hempel, "Coming Out in Corporate America," *BusinessWeek*, December 15, 2003, 64–72.

57. See, for instance, P. Cappelli, J. Constantine, and C. Chadwick, "It Pays to Value Family: Work and Family Trade-Offs Reconsidered," *Industrial Relations*, April 2000, 175–198; R. C. Barnett and D. T. Hall, "How to Use Reduced Hours to Win the War for Talent," *Organizational Dynamics*, March 2001, 42; and M. A. Verespej, "Balancing Act," *Industry Week*, May 15, 2000, 81–85.

58. M. Conlin, "The New Debate over Working Moms," *BusinessWeek*, November 18, 2000, 102–03.

59. M. Elias, "The Family-First Generation," *USA Today*, December 13, 2004, 5D.

60. J. Revell, C. Bigda, and D. Rosato, "The Rise of Freelance Nation," *CNNMoney*, cnnmoney.com, June 12, 2009.

61. Ibid.

62. Ibid.

63. S. Armour, "Generation Y: They've Arrived at Work with a New Attitude," *USA Today*, November 6, 2005, 1B+; B. Moses, "The Challenges of Managing Gen Y," *Globe and Mail*, March 11 2005, C1; and C. A. Martin, *Managing Generation Y* (Amherst, MA: HRD Press, 2001).

64. "Nomura Falls Out of Love with Lehman Dream Team," *Euroweek*, January 13, 2012, 108; A. House and K. Johnson, "Delivering Integrated Global Train-

ing," *Chief Learning Officer,* December 2011, 68–72; A. Tudor, "Bhattal's Goal; Keep Lehman Talent," *Wall Street Journal,* April 19, 2010, C5; A. Tudor, "Lehman Defections Continue at Nomura," *Wall Street Journal,* March 23, 2010, C5; A. Tudor, "Nomura Turns to a Foreigner from Lehman," *Wall Street Journal,* March 18, 2010, C1; A. Or, "More Quit Nomura as Bonuses Lapse," *Wall Street Journal,* March 12, 2010, C2; A. Rozens, "The Return of Nomura," *Invest-*

ment Dealers' Digest, February 12, 2010, 1+; "Nomura Set for Fight on All Fronts," *Euroweek,* December 4, 2009, 49; L. Peacock, untitled, *Personnel Today,* November 10, 2009, 25; and A. Tudor, "Nomura Stumbles in New Global Push," *Wall Street Journal,* July 29, 2009, A1+.

65. J. Hamblin, "A Brewing Problem," *The Atlantic,* http://www.theatlantic.com/technology/archive/2015/03/the-abominable-k-cup-coffee-pod-environment-problem/386501/, March 2015.

66. G. Wallace, "Inventor of K-Cups Regrets the Idea," http://money.cnn.com/2015/03/04/news/k-cups-keurig-inventor-regrets/, March 4, 2015.
67. Hamblin, "A Brewing Problem."
68. R. A. Munarriz, "Keurig Cold Heats Up with Dr Pepper Snapple Deal," http://www.dailyfinance.com/2015/01/13/keurig-dr-pepper-snapple-deal/, January 13, 2015.
69. Hamblin, "A Brewing Problem."
70. Ibid.
71. "Keurig Green Mountain, Inc. Releases 2014 Sustainability

Report, 'Beyond the Cup'," http://investor.keuriggreenmountain.com/releasedetail.cfm?releaseid=897260, February 19, 2015.
72. Hamblin, "A Brewing Problem."
73. "No. 1: PricewaterhouseCoopers," *DiversityInc Online,* April 24, 2012; L. Kwor, "Firms Hail Chiefs (of Diversity)," *Wall Street Journal,* January 5, 2012, B10; S. Ali, "PWC Chairman Bob Moritz Makes Diversity Personal," *DiversityInc,* Fall 2011, 42–43; "PwC Tops Global Ranking of Firms," *Accountancy,* November 2011, 10.

Foundations of Decision Making

4

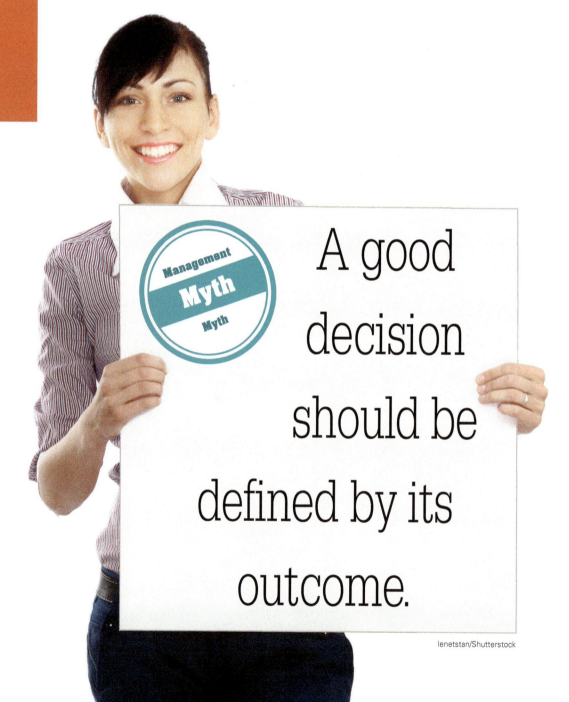

Management Myth

Myth

Myth

A good decision should be defined by its outcome.

lenetstan/Shutterstock

Management **DEBUNKED?** Myth

A good decision should be judged by the process used, not the results achieved. In some cases, a good decision results in an undesirable outcome. As a decision maker, you can control the process. But in the real world, factors outside your control can adversely affect the outcome. Using the right process may not always result in a desirable outcome, but it increases the probability!

MANAGERS

at all organizational levels and in all areas make a lot of decisions—routine and non-routine; minor and major. The overall quality of those decisions goes a long way in determining an organization's success or failure. To be a successful manager—and to be a valued employee—you need to know about decision making. In this chapter, we'll look at types of decisions and how decisions should be made. But we'll also consider some common biases and errors that can undermine the quality of decisions and discuss contemporary issues facing managerial decision makers. ●

Learning Outcomes

How Do Managers Make Decisions?

4-1 Describe the decision-making process.

How do businesses put new ideas into action? Through lots of decisions, that's how. When Bertucci's, a shopping-mall restaurant chain in New England and the mid-Atlantic region, wanted to create a spin-off chain with a more contemporary, "hipper" appeal, managers had lots of decisions to make over a nine-month period from concept to opening. Managers hope, of course, that those decisions prove to be good ones.[1]

decision-making process
A set of eight steps that includes identifying a problem, selecting a solution, and evaluating the effectiveness of the solution

problem
A discrepancy between an existing and a desired state of affairs

Forty hours a week: how often companies expect people to be strong decision makers.[2]

Decision making is typically described as choosing among alternatives, but this view is overly simplistic. Why? Because decision making is a process, not a simple act of choosing among alternatives. Exhibit 4–1 illustrates the **decision-making process** as a set of eight steps that begins with identifying a problem; it moves through selecting an alternative that can alleviate the problem and concludes with evaluating the decision's effectiveness. This process is as applicable to your decision about what you're going to do on spring break as it is to the decisions UPS executives are making as they deal with issues that could affect the organization's future profitability (see Case Application #1 on p. 114). The process can also be used to describe both individual and group decisions. Let's take a closer look at the process in order to understand what each step entails by using a simple example most of us can relate to—the decision to buy a car.

What Defines a Decision Problem?

Step 1. The decision-making process begins with the identification of a **problem** or, more specifically, a discrepancy between an existing and a desired state of affairs.[3] Take the case of a sales manager for Pfizer. The manager is on the road a lot and spent nearly $6,000 on auto repairs over the past few years. Now her car has a blown engine and cost estimates indicate it's not economical to repair. Furthermore, convenient public transportation is unavailable. So, we have a problem—a discrepancy between the manager's need to have a car that works and the fact that her current one doesn't.

Identifying problems is IMPORTANT... and CHALLENGING![4]

In our example, a blown engine is a clear signal to the manager that she needs a new car, but few problems are that obvious. In the real world, most problems don't come with neon signs identifying them as such. And problem identification is subjective. A manager who mistakenly solves the wrong problem perfectly is just as likely to perform poorly as the manager

Exhibit 4–1 The Decision-Making Process

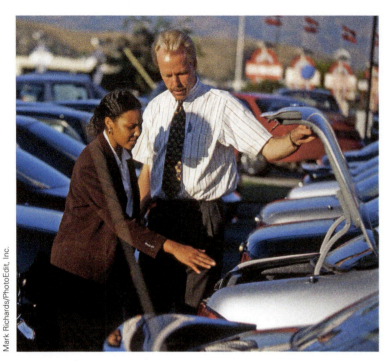

Mark Richards/PhotoEdit, Inc.

The steps involved in buying a vehicle provide a good example of the decision-making process. For this young woman, the process starts with the first step of identifying the problem of needing a car so she can drive to her new job and ends with the last step in the process of evaluating the results of her decision.

who fails to identify the right problem and does nothing. So, how do managers become aware they have a problem? They have to make a comparison between current reality and some standard, which can be (1) past performance, (2) previously set goals, or (3) the performance of some other unit within the organization or in other organizations. In our car-buying example, the standard is past performance—a car that runs.

What Is Relevant in the Decision-Making Process?

Step 2. Once a manager has identified a problem that needs attention, the **decision criteria** that will be important in solving the problem must be identified. In our vehicle-buying example, the sales manager assesses the factors that are relevant in her decision, which might include criteria such as price, model (two-door or four-door), size (compact or intermediate), manufacturer (French, Japanese, South Korean, German, American), optional equipment (navigation system, side-impact protection, leather interior), and repair records. These criteria reflect what she thinks is relevant in her decision. Every decision maker has criteria—whether explicitly stated or not—that guide his or her decision making. Note that in this step in the decision-making process, what's not identified can be as important as what is because it's still guiding the decision. For instance, although the sales manager didn't consider fuel economy to be a criterion and won't use it to influence her choice of car, she had to assess that criteria before choosing to include or not include it in her relevant criteria.

How Does the Decision Maker Weight the Criteria and Analyze Alternatives?

Steps 3, 4, and 5. In many decision-making situations, the criteria are not all equally important.[5] So, the decision maker has to allocate weights to the items listed in step 2 in order to give them their relative priority in the decision (step 3). A simple approach is to give the most important criterion a weight of 10 and then assign weights to the rest against that standard. Thus, in contrast to a criterion that you gave a 5, the highest-rated factor is twice as important. The idea is to use your personal preferences to assign priorities to the relevant criteria in your decision and indicate their degree of importance by assigning a weight to each. Exhibit 4–2 lists the criteria and weights that our manager developed for her vehicle replacement decision. What is the most important criterion in her decision? Price. What has low importance? Performance and handling.

decision criteria
Factors that are relevant in a decision

Exhibit 4–2 Important Criteria and Weights in a Car-Buying Decision

CRITERION	WEIGHT
Price	10
Interior comfort	8
Durability	5
Repair record	5
Performance	3
Handling	1

Exhibit 4–3 Assessment of Possible Car Alternatives

ALTERNATIVES	INITIAL PRICE	INTERIOR COMFORT	DURABILITY	REPAIR RECORD	PERFORMANCE	HANDLING	TOTAL
Jeep Compass	2	10	8	7	5	5	37
Ford Focus	9	6	5	6	8	6	40
Hyundai Elantra	8	5	6	6	4	6	35
Ford Fiesta SES	9	5	6	7	6	5	38
Volkswagen Golf	5	6	9	10	7	7	44
Toyota Prius	10	5	6	4	3	3	31
Mazda 3 MT	4	8	7	6	8	9	42
Kia Soul	7	6	8	6	5	6	38
BMW i3	9	7	6	4	4	7	37
Nissan Cube	5	8	5	4	10	10	42
Toyota Camry	6	5	10	10	6	6	43
Honda Fit Sport MT	8	6	6	5	7	8	40

Then the decision maker lists the alternatives that could successfully resolve the problem (step 4). No attempt is made in this step to evaluate these alternatives, only to list them.[6] Let's assume that our manager identifies 12 cars as viable choices: Jeep Compass, Ford Focus, Hyundai Elantra, Ford Fiesta SES, Volkswagen Golf, Toyota Prius, Mazda 3 MT, Kia Soul, BMW i3, Nissan Cube, Toyota Camry, and Honda Fit Sport MT.

Once the alternatives have been identified, the decision maker critically analyzes each one (step 5). How? By evaluating it against the criteria. The strengths and weaknesses of each alternative become evident as they're compared with the criteria and weights established in steps 2 and 3. Exhibit 4–3 shows the assessed values that the manager assigned each of her 12 alternatives after she had test-driven each car. Keep in mind that the ratings shown in Exhibit 4–3 are based on the assessment made by the sales manager. Again, we're using a scale of 1 to 10. Some assessments can be achieved in a relatively objective fashion. For instance, the purchase price represents the best price the manager can get online or from local dealers, and consumer magazines report data from owners on frequency of repairs. Others, like how well the car handles, are clearly personal judgments.

Most decisions involve **judgments.**

Personal judgments by a decision maker are reflected in (1) the criteria chosen in step 2, (2) the weights given to the criteria, and (3) the evaluation of alternatives. The influence of personal judgment explains why two car buyers with the same amount of money may look at two totally distinct sets of alternatives or even look at the same alternatives and rate them differently.

Exhibit 4–3 shows only an assessment of the 12 alternatives against the decision criteria; it does not reflect the weighting done in step 3. If one choice had scored 10 on every criterion, obviously you wouldn't need to consider the weights. Similarly, if all the weights were equal—that is, all the criteria were equally important to you—each alternative would be evaluated merely by summing up the appropriate lines in Exhibit 4–3. For instance, the Ford Fiesta SES would have a score of 38, and the Toyota Camry a score of 43. But if you multiply each alternative assessment against its weight, you get the figures in Exhibit 4–4. For instance, the Kia Soul scored a 40 on durability, which was determined by multiplying the weight given to durability [5] by the manager's appraisal of the car on this criterion [8]. The sum of these scores represents an evaluation of each alternative against the previously established criteria and weights. Notice that the weighting of the criteria has changed the ranking of alternatives in

Exhibit 4–4 Evaluation of Car Alternatives: Assessment Criteria × Criteria Weight

ALTERNATIVES	INITIAL PRICE [10]		INTERIOR COMFORT [8]		DURABILITY [5]		REPAIR RECORD [5]		PERFORMANCE [3]		HANDLING [1]		TOTAL
Jeep Compass	2	20	10	80	8	40	7	35	5	15	5	5	195
Ford Focus	9	90	6	48	5	25	6	30	8	24	6	6	223
Hyundai Elantra	8	80	5	40	6	30	6	30	4	12	6	6	198
Ford Fiesta SES	9	90	5	40	6	30	7	35	6	18	5	5	218
Volkswagen Golf	5	50	6	48	9	45	10	50	7	21	7	7	221
Toyota Prius	10	100	5	40	6	30	4	20	3	9	3	3	202
Mazda 3 MT	4	40	8	64	7	35	6	30	8	24	9	9	202
Kia Soul	7	70	6	48	8	40	6	30	5	15	6	6	209
BMW i3	9	90	7	56	6	30	4	20	4	12	7	7	215
Nissan Cube	5	50	8	64	5	25	4	20	10	30	10	10	199
Toyota Camry	6	60	5	40	10	50	10	50	6	18	6	6	224
Honda Fit Sport MT	8	80	6	48	6	30	5	25	7	21	8	8	212

our example. The Volkswagen Golf, for example, has gone from first to third. Looking at the analysis, both initial price and interior comfort worked against the Volkswagen.

What Determines the Best Choice?

Step 6. Now it's time to choose the best alternative from among those assessed. Because we determined all the pertinent factors in the decision, weighted them appropriately, and identified and assessed the viable alternatives, this step is fairly simple. We merely choose the alternative that generated the highest score in step 5. In our vehicle example (Exhibit 4–4), the manager would choose the Toyota Camry. On the basis of the criteria identified, the weights given to the criteria, and her assessment of each car on the criteria, the Toyota scored highest [224 points] and, thus, became the best alternative.

What Happens in Decision Implementation?

Step 7. Although the choice process is completed in the previous step, the decision may still fail if it's not implemented properly (step 7). Therefore, this step, **decision implementation**, involves putting the decision into action. If others will be affected by the decision, implementation also includes conveying the decision to those affected and getting their commitment to it.[7] *Want people to be committed to a decision?* Let them participate in the decision-making process. We'll discuss later in the chapter how groups can help a manager do this.

What Is the Last Step in the Decision Process?

Step 8. In the last step in the decision-making process, managers appraise the outcome of the decision to see *whether the problem was resolved.* Did the alternative chosen in step 6 and implemented in step 7 accomplish the desired result? For our sales manager, that means does she have a car that reliably works? Evaluating the results of a decision is part of the managerial control process, which we'll discuss in Chapter 14.

What Common Errors Are Committed in the Decision-Making Process?

When managers make decisions, they use their own particular style, and may use "rules of thumb," or **heuristics**, to simplify their decision making.[8] Rules of thumb can be useful because they help make sense of complex, uncertain, and ambiguous information. However, even though

decision implementation
Putting a decision into action

heuristics
Judgmental shortcuts or "rules of thumb" used to simplify decision making

Exhibit 4–5 Common Decision-Making Errors and Biases

managers may use rules of thumb, that doesn't mean those rules are reliable. Why? Because they may lead to errors and biases in processing and evaluating information. Exhibit 4–5 identifies 12 common decision errors and biases that managers make. Let's look briefly at each.[9]

Which of these **are YOU guilty** of when making decisions?

When decision makers tend to think they know more than they do or hold unrealistically positive views of themselves and their performance, they're exhibiting the *over-confidence bias*. The *immediate gratification bias* describes decision makers who tend to want immediate rewards and to avoid immediate costs. For these individuals, decision choices that provide quick payoffs are more appealing than those in the future. The *anchoring effect* describes when decision makers fixate on initial information as a starting point and then, once set, fail to adequately adjust for subsequent information. First impressions, ideas, prices, and estimates carry unwarranted weight relative to information received later. When decision makers selectively organize and interpret events based on their biased perceptions, they're using the *selective perception bias*. This influences the information they pay attention to, the problems they identify, and the alternatives they develop. Decision makers who seek out information that reaffirms their past choices and discount information that contradicts past judgments exhibit the *confirmation bias*. These people tend to accept at face value information that confirms their preconceived views and are critical and skeptical of information that challenges these views. The *framing bias* happens when decision makers select and highlight certain aspects of a situation while excluding others. By drawing attention to specific aspects of a situation and highlighting them, while at the same time downplaying or omitting other aspects, they distort what they see and create incorrect reference points. The *availability bias* occurs when decision makers tend to remember events that are the most recent and vivid in their memory. The result? It distorts their ability to recall events in an objective manner and results in

(*continues on p. 100*)

✪ **Watch It 1!**

If your professor has assigned this, go to the Assignments section of **mymanagementlab.com** to complete the video exercise titled *Rudi's Bakery: Decision Making*.

What Are the 3 Approaches Managers Can Use to Make Decisions?

4-2 Explain the three approaches managers can use to make decisions.

Decision making is the essence of management.[10]

- Everyone in an organization makes decisions, _but_ it's particularly important to managers.
- Managers _make decisions_—mostly routine ones like which employee will work what shift, what information to include in a report, how to resolve a customer's complaint, etc.—as they **plan, organize, lead,** and **control**. See Exhibit 4–6.

Exhibit 4–6 Decisions Managers May Make

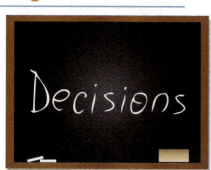
© mihaela1975 0405/Fotolia

Planning	Leading
■ What are the organization's long-term objectives?	■ How do I handle unmotivated employees?
■ What strategies will best achieve those objectives?	■ What is the most effective leadership style in a given situation?
■ What should the organization's short-term objectives be?	■ How will a specific change affect worker productivity?
■ How difficult should individual goals be?	■ When is the right time to stimulate conflict?

Organizing	Controlling
■ How many employees should I have report directly to me?	■ What activities in the organization need to be controlled?
■ How much centralization should there be in an organization?	■ How should those activities be controlled?
■ How should jobs be designed?	■ When is a performance deviation significant?
■ When should the organization implement a different structure?	■ What type of management information system should the organization have?

McCarony/Fotolia

Source: Robbins, Stephen P., Coulter, Mary, _Management_, 13th Ed., © 2016, p. 45. Reprinted and electronically reproduced by permission of Pearson Education, Inc., New York, NY.

- Managers _want to be good decision makers_ and _exhibit good decision-making behaviors_ so they appear **competent** and **intelligent** to their boss, employees, and coworkers.

1 Rational Model

- This approach assumes: Decision makers MUST ACT RATIONALLY.[11]
  How? Use **rational decision making**; that is, make logical and consistent choices to maximize value.[12]

rational decision making
Describes choices that are consistent and value-maximizing within specified constraints

(Check out the two decision-making tools described in the Technology and the Manager's Job box on p. 99.)

- A "rational" decision maker...

Should Be:	Can Ever Be?
Fully objective and logical ········▶	Can we ever be fully objective and logical?
Problem is clear and unambiguous ········▶	Can problems ever be totally clear and unambiguous?
Clear and specific goal regarding decision ········▶	Can a goal ever be made that clear and specific?
All possible alternatives and consequences known ········▶	Can all possible alternatives and consequences ever be known?
Alternative selected maximizes likelihood of achieving goal ········▶	Can any alternative ever really do that?
Organization's best interests are considered ········▶	Managers should do this but may face factors beyond their control.

Rationality is not a very realistic approach.

2 Bounded Rationality

"A. More. Realistic. Approach."

- **Bounded rationality:** Managers make rational decisions, but are limited (bounded) by their ability to process information.[13]
- Most decisions managers make don't fit the assumption of perfect rationality.
- No one can possibly analyze _all_ information on _all_ alternatives so they...
- **satisfice**—that is, accept solutions that are "good enough," rather than spend time and other resources trying to maximize. *(See From **Past to Present** box on p. 98.)*

Example: As a newly graduated finance major, you look for a job as a financial planner—minimum salary of $55k, and within 100 miles of your hometown. After searching several different options, you accept a job as a business credit analyst at a bank 50 miles away at a starting salary of $52k. HOORAY! If, however, you'd *maximized*—that is, continued to search all possible alternatives—you'd have eventually found this financial planning job at a trust company 25 miles away with a starting salary of $57k. However, the first job offer was *satisfactory*—"good enough"—and you took it! Your decision making was still rational...but within the bounds of your abilities to process information!

iQoncept/Fotolia

bounded rationality
Making decisions that are rational within the limits of a manager's ability to process information

satisfice
Accepting solutions that are "good enough"

97

Who: Bounded rationality and satisficing are the work of Herbert A. Simon, who won a Nobel Prize in economics for his work on decision making.

What: His primary concern was how people use logic and psychology to make choices and proposed that individuals were limited in their ability to "grasp the present and anticipate the future." This bounded rationality made it difficult for them to "achieve the best possible decisions," but they made "good enough" or "satisficing" choices.[14]

How: Simon's important contributions to management thinking stemmed from his belief that understanding organizations meant studying the complex network of decisional processes that were inherent.

> When faced with too many choices, we **SATISFICE**!

Why: His work in bounded rationality helps us make sense of how managers can behave rationally and still make satisfactory decisions, even given the limits of their capacity to process information.

If your professor has assigned this, go to the Assignments section of **mymanagementlab.com** *to complete these discussion questions.*

⭐ **Talk About It 1:** Is satisficing settling for second best? Discuss.

⭐ **Talk About It 2:** How does knowing about bounded rationality help managers be better decision makers?

- Most managerial decisions don't fit the assumptions of perfect rationality, but can still be influenced by (1) the organization's culture, (2) internal politics, (3) power considerations, and (4) a phenomenon called:

escalation of commitment An increased commitment to a previous decision despite evidence that it may have been wrong.[15]

- *Why* would anyone—especially managers—escalate commitment to a bad decision?
  - Hate to admit that initial decision may have been flawed.
  - Don't want to search for new alternatives.

3 Intuition and Managerial Decision Making

When deciding yay or nay on new shoe styles, Diego Della Valle, chairman of Tod's luxury shoe empire, doesn't use common decision-making tools like focus groups or poll testing. Nope…he wears the shoes for a few days. If they're not to his liking, his verdict: No! **His intuitive decision approach has helped make Tod's a successful multinational company.**[16]

Smalik/Fotolia

- **Intuitive decision making**—making decisions on the basis of experience, feelings, and accumulated judgment
  - Described as "unconscious reasoning."[17]
  - Five different aspects of intuition: *See Exhibit 4–7.*[18]

Almost **half of managers rely on intuition** more often than formal analysis **to make decisions** about their companies.[19]

Exhibit 4–7 What Is Intuition?

Sources: Based on J. Evans, "Intuition and Reasoning: A Dual-Process Perspective," *Psychological Inquiry*, October–December 2010, pp. 313–326; T. Betsch and A. Blockner, "Intuition in Judgment and Decision Making: Extensive Thinking Without Effort," *Psychological Inquiry*, October–December 2010, pp. 279–294; R. Lange and J. Houran, "A Transliminal View of Intuitions in the Workplace," *North American Journal of Psychology*, 12, no. 3 (2010), pp. 501–516; E. Dane and M. G. Pratt, "Exploring Intuition and Its Role in Managerial Decision Making," *Academy of Management Review*, January 2007, pp. 33–54; M. H. Bazerman and D. Chugh, "Decisions Without Blinders," *Harvard Business Review*, January 2006, pp. 88–97; C. C. Miller and R. D. Ireland, "Intuition in Strategic Decision Making: Friend or Foe in the Fast-Paced 21st Century," *Academy of Management Executive*, February 2005, pp. 19–30; E. Sadler-Smith and E. Shefy, "The Intuitive Executive: Understanding and Applying 'Gut Feel' in Decision-Making," *Academy of Management Executive*, November 2004, pp. 76–91; and L. A. Burke and M. K. Miller, "Taking the Mystery Out of Intuitive Decision Making," *Academy of Management Executive*, October 1999, pp. 91–99.

- Suggestions for using intuitive decision making:
  - — Use it to complement, not replace, other decision-making approaches.[20]
  - — Look to act quickly with limited information because of past experience with a similar problem.
  - — Pay attention to the intense feelings and emotions experienced when making decisions.

    The payoff? Better decisions![21]

Technology and the Manager's Job
MAKING BETTER DECISIONS WITH TECHNOLOGY

Information technology is providing managers with a wealth of decision-making support.[22] Two decision-making tools include: *Expert systems* and *Neural networks*.

EXPERT SYSTEMS:

- Encode relevant expert experience using software programs.
- Act as that expert in analyzing and solving unstructured problems.
- Guide users through problems by asking sequential questions about the situation and drawing conclusions based on answers given.
- Make decisions easier for users through programmed rules modeled on actual reasoning processes of experts.
- Allow employees and lower-level managers to make high-quality decisions normally made only by upper-level managers.

NEURAL NETWORKS:

- Use computer software to imitate the structure of brain cells and connections among them.

- Can distinguish patterns and trends too subtle or complex for human beings.
- Can perceive correlations among hundreds of variables, unlike our limited human brain capacity, which can only easily assimilate no more than two or three variables at once.
- Can perform many operations simultaneously, recognizing patterns, making associations, generalizing about problems not exposed to before, and learning through experience.
- Example: banks using neural network systems to catch fraudulent credit card activities in a matter of hours, not days.

If your professor has assigned this, go to the Assignments section of **mymanagementlab.com** *to complete these discussion questions.*

⭐ **TALK ABOUT IT 3:** Can a manager ever have too much data when making decisions? Explain.

⭐ **TALK ABOUT IT 4:** How can technology help managers make better decisions?

distorted judgments and probability estimates. When decision makers assess the likelihood of an event based on how closely it resembles other events or sets of events, that's the *representation bias*. Managers exhibiting this bias draw analogies and see identical situations where they don't exist. The *randomness bias* describes when decision makers try to create meaning out of random events. They do this because most decision makers have difficulty dealing with chance even though random events happen to everyone and there's nothing that can be done to predict them. The *sunk costs error* takes place when decision makers forget that current choices can't correct the past. They incorrectly fixate on past expenditures of time, money, or effort in assessing choices rather than on future consequences. Instead of ignoring sunk costs, they can't forget them. Decision makers who are quick to take credit for their successes and to blame failure on outside factors are exhibiting the *self-serving bias*. Finally, the *hindsight bias* is the tendency for decision makers to falsely believe that they would have accurately predicted the outcome of an event once that outcome is actually known.

How can managers avoid the negative effects of these decision errors and biases? **1** Be aware of them and then don't use them! **2** Pay attention to "how" decisions are made, try to identify heuristics being used, and critically evaluate how appropriate those are. **3** Ask colleagues to help identify weaknesses in decision-making style and then work on improving those weaknesses.

✪ Watch It 2!

If your professor has assigned this, go to the Assignments section of **mymanagementlab.com** to complete the video exercise titled *CH2MHill: Decision Making*.

What Types of Decisions and Decision-Making Conditions Do Managers Face?

4-3 Describe the types of decisions and decision-making conditions managers face.

Laura Ipsen is a senior vice president and general manager at Smart Grid, a business unit of Cisco Systems, which is working on helping utility companies find ways to build open, interconnected systems. She describes her job as "like having to put together a 1,000-piece puzzle, but with no box top with the picture of what it looks like and with some pieces missing."[23] Decision making in that type of environment is quite different from decision making done by a manager of a local Gap store.

The types of problems managers face in decision-making situations often determine how it's handled. In this section, we describe a categorization scheme for problems and types of decisions and then show how the type of decision making a manager uses should reflect the characteristics of the problem.

How Do Problems Differ?

Some problems are straightforward. The goal of the decision maker is clear, the problem familiar, and information about the problem easily defined and complete. Examples might include a supplier who is late with an important delivery, a customer who wants to return an Internet purchase, a TV news team that has to respond to an unexpected and fast-breaking event, or a university that must help a student who is applying for financial aid. Such situations are called **structured problems**.

Many situations faced by managers, however, are **unstructured problems**. They are new or unusual. Information about such problems is ambiguous or incomplete. Examples of unstructured problems include the decision to enter a new market segment, to hire an architect to design a new office park, or to merge two organizations. So, too, is the decision to invest in a new, unproven technology. For instance, when Takeshi Idezawa founded his mobile messaging app LINE, he faced a situation best described as an unstructured problem.[24]

How Does a Manager Make Programmed Decisions?

Decisions are also divided into two categories: programmed and nonprogrammed (described in the next section). **Programmed,** or routine, **decisions** are the most efficient way to handle structured problems.

An auto mechanic damages a customer's rim while changing a tire. What does the shop manager do? Because the company probably has a standardized method for handling this type of problem, it's considered a programmed decision. For example, the manager may replace the rim at the company's expense. *Decisions are programmed* to the extent that (1) they are repetitive and routine and (2) a specific approach has been worked out for handling them. Because the problem is well structured, the manager does not have to go to the trouble and expense of an involved decision process. Programmed decision making is relatively simple and tends to rely heavily on previous solutions. The develop-the-alternatives stage in the decision-making process is either nonexistent or given little attention. Why? Because once the structured problem is defined, its solution is usually self-evident or at least reduced to only a few alternatives that are familiar and that have proved successful in the past. In many cases, programmed decision making becomes decision making by precedent. Managers simply do what they and others have done previously in the same situation. The damaged rim does not require the manager to identify and weight decision criteria or develop a long list of possible solutions.

> For structured problems, use: — Procedures
> — Rules
> — Policies

PROCEDURES. A **procedure** is a series of interrelated sequential steps that a manager can use when responding to a well-structured problem. The only real difficulty is identifying the problem. Once the problem is clear, so is the procedure. For instance, a purchasing manager receives a request from computing services for licensing arrangements to install 250 copies of Norton Antivirus Software. The purchasing manager knows that a definite procedure is in place for handling this decision. Has the requisition been properly filled out and approved? If not, he can send the requisition back with a note explaining what is deficient. If the request is complete, the approximate costs are estimated. If the total exceeds $8,500, three bids must be obtained. If the total is $8,500 or less, only one vendor need be identified and the order placed. The decision-making process is merely executing a simple series of sequential steps.

RULES. A **rule** is an explicit statement that tells a manager what he or she must—or must not—do. Rules are frequently used by managers who confront a structured problem because they're simple to follow and ensure consistency. In the preceding example, the $8,500 cutoff rule simplifies the purchasing manager's decision about when to use multiple bids.

POLICIES. A third guide for making programmed decisions is a **policy**. It provides guidelines to channel a manager's thinking in

> **programmed decision**
> A repetitive decision that can be handled using a routine approach
>
> **procedure**
> A series of interrelated, sequential steps used to respond to a structured problem
>
> **rule**
> An explicit statement that tells employees what can or cannot be done
>
> **policy**
> A guideline for making decisions

Top managers of Mars Chocolate North America decided to build a new plant for making its M&M brand and other candy in Topeka, Kansas, the first new chocolate facility built by Mars in 35 years. The nonprogrammed decision involved gathering and analyzing demographic and other data for 82 possible locations in 13 states.

Thad ALLTON/AP Images

nonprogrammed decision
A unique and nonrecurring decision that requires a custom-made solution

a specific direction. The statement that "we promote from within, whenever possible" is an example of a policy. In contrast to a rule, a policy establishes parameters for the decision maker rather than specifically stating what should or should not be done. Policies often leave interpretation up to the decision maker. It's in such instances that ethical standards may come into play.

How Do Nonprogrammed Decisions Differ from Programmed Decisions?

When problems are unstructured, managers must rely on **nonprogrammed decisions** in order to develop unique solutions. Examples of nonprogrammed decisions include deciding whether to acquire another organization, deciding which global markets offer the most potential, or deciding whether to sell off an unprofitable division. Such decisions are unique and nonrecurring. When a manager confronts an unstructured problem, no cut-and-dried solution is available. A custom-made, nonprogrammed response is required.

The creation of a new organizational strategy is a nonprogrammed decision. This decision is different from previous organizational decisions because the issue is new; a different set of environmental factors exists, and other conditions have changed. For example, Amazon's strategy to "get big fast" helped the company grow tremendously. But this strategy came at a cost—perennial financial losses. To turn a profit, CEO Jeff Bezos made decisions regarding how to organize orders, anticipate demand, ship more efficiently, establish foreign partnerships, and create a marketplace for other sellers to sell their books on Amazon. As a result, Amazon has moved towards profitability.[25]

How Are Problems, Types of Decisions, and Organizational Level Integrated?

Exhibit 4–8 describes the relationship among types of problems, types of decisions, and level in the organization. Structured problems? Use programmed decision making. Unstructured problems? Use nonprogrammed decision making. Lower-level managers essentially confront familiar and repetitive problems so they most typically rely on programmed decisions such as standard operating procedures. However, as managers move up the organizational hierarchy, the problems they confront are likely to become less structured. Why? Because lower-level managers handle the routine decisions themselves and only pass upward decisions that they find unique or difficult. Similarly, managers pass down routine decisions to their employees so they can spend their time on more problematic issues.

MANAGERIAL DECISIONS: **Real World—Real Advice**

- Few managerial decisions are either fully programmed or fully nonprogrammed. Most fall somewhere in between.
- At the top level, most problems that managers face *are* unique—that is, nonprogrammed.
- Programmed routines may help even in situations requiring a nonprogrammed decision.
- Top-level managers often create policies, standard operating procedures, and rules—that is, programmed decision making—for lower-level managers in order to control costs and other variables.
- Programmed decision making can facilitate organizational efficiency—maybe that's why it's so popular!
- Programmed decisions minimize the need for managers to exercise discretion.
- Discretion—the ability to make sound judgments—costs money because it's an uncommon and valuable quality and managers who have it are paid more.
- Even in some programmed decisions, individual judgment may be needed.

Exhibit 4–8 Types of Problems, Types of Decisions, and Organizational Level

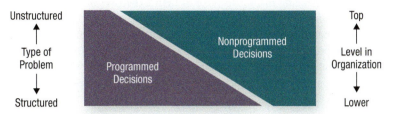

What Decision-Making Conditions Do Managers Face?

When making decisions, managers face three different conditions: certainty, risk, and uncertainty. Let's look at each.

The ideal situation for making decisions is one of **certainty**, which is a situation where a manager can make accurate decisions because the outcome of every alternative is known. For example, when South Dakota's state treasurer decides where to deposit excess state funds, he knows exactly the interest rate being offered by each bank and the amount that will be earned on the funds. He is certain about the outcomes of each alternative. As you might expect, most managerial decisions aren't like this.

Far more common is a situation of **risk**, conditions in which the decision maker is able to estimate the likelihood of certain outcomes. Under risk, managers have historical data from past personal experiences or secondary information that lets them assign probabilities to different alternatives.

What happens if you face a decision where you're not certain about the outcomes and can't even make reasonable probability estimates? We call this condition **uncertainty**. Managers do face decision-making situations of uncertainty. Under these conditions, the choice of alternative is influenced by the limited amount of available information and by the psychological orientation of the decision maker.

certainty
A situation in which a decision maker can make accurate decisions because all outcomes are known

risk
A situation in which a decision maker is able to estimate the likelihood of certain outcomes

uncertainty
A situation in which a decision maker has neither certainty nor reasonable probability estimates available

> ✪ **Write It!**
> If your professor has assigned this, go to the Assignments section of **mymanagementlab.com** to complete *MGMT 8: Decision Making*.

How Do Groups Make Decisions?

4-4 Discuss group decision making.

Work teams are common at Amazon. Jeff Bezos, founder and CEO, uses a **"two-pizza" philosophy**—that is, a team should be small enough that it can be fed with two pizzas.[26]

Do managers make a lot of decisions in groups? You bet they do! Many decisions in organizations, especially important decisions that have far-reaching effects on organizational activities and people, are typically made in groups. It's a rare organization that doesn't at some time use committees, task forces, review panels, work teams, or similar groups as vehicles for making decisions. Why? In many cases, these groups represent the people who will be most affected by the decisions being made. Because of their expertise, these people are often best qualified to make decisions that affect them.

Studies tell us that managers spend a significant portion of their time in meetings. Undoubtedly, a large portion of that time is involved with defining problems, arriving at solutions to those problems, and determining the means for implementing the solutions. It's possible, in fact, for groups to be assigned any of the eight steps in the decision-making process.

What Are the Advantages and Disadvantages of Group Decision Making?

Decisions can be made by individuals or by groups—each approach has its own set of strengths and neither is ideal for all situations.

Advantages of Group Decisions

- *More complete information.*[27]
- *Diversity of experiences and perspectives* brought to the decision process.[28]
- *More alternatives generated* due to greater quantity and diversity of information, especially when group members represent different specialties.
- *Increased acceptance of a solution* by having people who will be affected by a certain solution and who will help implement it participate in the decision.[29]
- *Increased legitimacy* because the group decision-making process is consistent with democratic ideals, and decisions made by groups may be perceived as more legitimate than those made by a single person, which can appear autocratic and arbitrary.

Disadvantages of Group Decisions

- *Time-consuming*—assembling the group, getting decisions made.
- *Minority domination* can unduly influence final decision because group members are never perfectly equal—they differ in rank, experience, knowledge about the problem, influence on other members, verbal skills, assertiveness, etc.[30]
- *Ambiguous responsibility*. Group members share responsibility, BUT who is actually responsible for final outcome?[31] Individual decision—it's clear. Group decision—it's not.
- *Pressures to conform*. Have you ever been in a group where your views didn't match the group's consensus views and you remained silent? Maybe others felt the same way and also remained silent. This is what Irving Janis called **groupthink**, a form of conformity in which group members withhold deviant, minority, or unpopular views in order to give the *appearance of agreement*.[32]

The Tragedy of Groupthink

<u>What It Does</u>

Hinders decision making, possibly jeopardizing the quality of the decision by:

- Undermining critical thinking in the group.
- Affecting a group's ability to objectively appraise alternatives.
- Deterring individuals from critically appraising unusual, minority, or unpopular views.

<u>How Does It Occur?</u> Here are some things to watch out for:

- Group members rationalize resistance to assumptions.
- Members directly pressure those who express doubts or question the majority's views and arguments.
- Members who have doubts or differing points of view avoid deviating from what appears to be group consensus.
- An illusion of unanimity prevails. Full agreement is *assumed* if no one speaks up.

groupthink
When a group exerts extensive pressure on an individual to withhold his or her different views in order to appear to be in agreement

What Can Be Done to Minimize Groupthink?

- Encourage cohesiveness.
- Foster open discussion.
- Have an impartial leader who seeks input from all members.[33]

When Are Groups Most Effective?

Well, that depends on the *criteria you use for defining effectiveness*, such as accuracy, speed, creativity, and acceptance. Group decisions tend to be more accurate. On average, groups tend to make better decisions than individuals, although groupthink may occur.[34] However, if decision effectiveness is defined in terms of speed, individuals are superior. If creativity is important, groups tend to be more effective than individuals. And if effectiveness means the degree of acceptance the final solution achieves, the nod again goes to the group.

The *effectiveness* of group decision making is *also influenced by the size of the group*. The larger the group, the greater the opportunity for heterogeneous representation. On the other hand, a larger group requires more coordination and more time to allow all members to contribute. This means that groups probably shouldn't be too large: A minimum of five to a maximum of about fifteen members is best. Groups of five to seven individuals appear to be the most effective (remember Amazon's "two-pizza" rule!). Because five and seven are odd numbers, decision deadlocks are avoided. You can't consider effectiveness without also assessing efficiency. Groups almost always stack up as a poor second in efficiency to the individual decision maker. Yet, with few exceptions, group decision making consumes more work hours than does individual decision making.

A Question of Ethics

There's no doubt that American college sports is a big business, generating billions for colleges and universities *and* for the NCAA (National Collegiate Athletic Association), the umbrella organization that monitors, oversees, and supports these sports programs.[35] The NCAA, which brought in over a billion dollars in revenue last year, recently reached a $20 million settlement with ex-football and basketball players who had sued about their likenesses being used in videogames made by Electronic Arts. This was hailed as a landmark settlement because it's the first time the NCAA will pay college athletes for their playing a sport. This reflects an ongoing issue: should college athletes be paid? Not surprisingly, there are pros and cons to this decision. And not surprisingly, there are ethical issues associated with the decision.

If your professor has assigned this, go to the Assignments section of mymanagementlab.com to complete these discussion questions.

⭐ **Talk About It 5:** Paying college athletes: Who are the stakeholders in this situation and what stake do they have?

⭐ **Talk About It 6:** How do ethical issues affect decision making and what ethical issues do you see in the decision about whether to pay college athletes for their time and work?

Bottom Line on Groups or Individuals: Do **increases in effectiveness offset losses in efficiency?**

How Can You Improve Group Decision Making?

Use these techniques to make group decisions more creative: (1) brainstorming, (2) the nominal group technique, and (3) electronic meetings.

WHAT IS BRAINSTORMING?   Brainstorming is a relatively simple idea-generating process that specifically encourages any and all alternatives while withholding criticism of those alternatives.[36] In a typical brainstorming session, a half-dozen to a dozen people sit around a table. Of course, technology is changing where that "table" is. The group leader states the problem in a clear manner that is understood by all participants. Members then shout out, offer up, fire off, "freewheel" as many alternatives as they can in a given time. No criticism is allowed, and all the alternatives are recorded for later discussion and analysis.[37]

HOW DOES THE NOMINAL GROUP TECHNIQUE WORK?   The nominal group technique helps groups arrive at a preferred solution by restricting discussion during the decision-making process.[38] Group members must be present, as in a traditional committee meeting, but they're required to operate independently. They secretly write a list of general problem areas or potential solutions to a problem. The chief advantage of this technique is that it permits the group to meet formally but does not restrict independent thinking or lead to groupthink, as can often happen in a traditional interacting group.[39]

brainstorming
An idea-generating process that encourages alternatives while withholding criticism

nominal group technique
A decision-making technique in which group members are physically present but operate independently

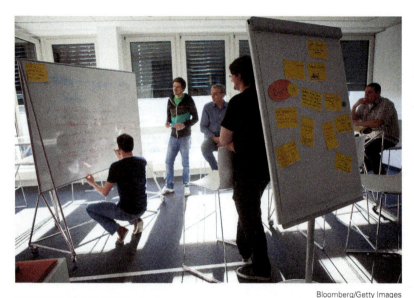

Brainstorming is an important way of improving group decision making at SAP AG, a provider of enterprise software. Employees working at SAP headquarters in Walldorf, Germany, use white boards during a brainstorming session to develop product and service innovations following the company's decision to target the growing online software market.

Bloomberg/Getty Images

HOW CAN ELECTRONIC MEETINGS ENHANCE GROUP DECISION MAKING?   Another approach to group decision making blends the nominal group technique with information technology and is called the **electronic meeting**.

Once the technology is in place, the concept is simple. Numerous people sit around a table with laptops or tablets. Participants are presented issues and type their responses onto their computers. Individual comments, as well as aggregate votes, are displayed on a projection screen in the room.

The major advantages of electronic meetings are anonymity, honesty, and speed.[40] Participants can anonymously type any message they want, and it will flash on the screen for all to see with a keystroke. It allows people to be brutally honest with no penalty. And it's fast—chitchat is eliminated, discussions do not digress, and many participants can "talk" at once without interrupting the others.

Electronic meetings *are* significantly faster and much cheaper than traditional face-to-face meetings.[41] Nestlé, for instance, uses the approach for many of its meetings, especially globally focused meetings.[42] However, as with all other forms of group activities, electronic meetings have some drawbacks. Those who type quickly can outshine those who may be verbally eloquent but lousy typists; those with the best ideas don't get credit for them; and the process lacks the informational richness of face-to-face oral communication. However, group decision making is likely to include extensive usage of electronic meetings.[43]

A variation of the electronic meeting is the videoconference. Using technology to link different locations, people can have face-to-face meetings even when they're thousands of miles apart. This capability has enhanced feedback among the members, saved countless hours of business travel, and ultimately saved companies such as Nestlé and Logitech hundreds of thousands of dollars, especially during the recent global recession. As a result, they're more effective in their meetings and have increased the efficiency with which decisions are made.[44]

What Contemporary Decision-Making Issues Do Managers Face?

4-5 Discuss contemporary issues in managerial decision making.

Bad decisions can cost millions.

Today's business world revolves around making decisions, often risky ones, usually with incomplete or inadequate information, and under intense time pressure. Most managers make one decision after another; and as if that weren't challenging enough, more is at stake than ever before since bad decisions can cost millions. We're going to look at three important issues—❶ national culture, ❷ creativity and design thinking, and ❸ big data—that managers face in today's fast-moving and global world.

How Does National Culture Affect Managers' Decision Making?

Research shows that, to some extent, decision-making practices differ from country to country.[45] The way decisions are made—whether by group, by team members, participatively, or autocratically by an individual manager—and the degree of risk a decision maker is willing to take are just two examples of decision variables that reflect a country's cultural environment.

electronic meeting
A type of nominal group technique in which participants are linked by computer

For example, in India, power distance and uncertainty avoidance (see Chapter 3) are high. There, only very senior-level managers make decisions, and they're likely to make safe decisions. In contrast, in Sweden, power distance and uncertainty avoidance are low. Swedish managers are not afraid to make risky decisions. Senior managers in Sweden also push decisions down to lower levels. They encourage lower-level managers and employees to take part in decisions that affect them. In countries such as Egypt, where time pressures are low, managers make decisions at a slower and more deliberate pace than managers do in the United States. And in Italy, where history and traditions are valued, managers tend to rely on tried and proven alternatives to resolve problems.

Bloomberg/Getty Images

Decision making in Japan is much more group oriented than in the United States.[46] The Japanese value conformity and cooperation. Before making decisions, Japanese CEOs collect a large amount of information, which is then used in consensus-forming group decisions called **ringisei**. Because employees in Japanese organizations have high job security, managerial decisions take a long-term perspective rather than focusing on short-term profits, as is often the practice in the United States.

These senior managers of Mitsubishi Motors, a multinational automaker based in Tokyo, Japan, take a long-term perspective in making decisions rather than focusing on short-term results. In Japan, where conformity and cooperation are valued, managers adapt their decisions to their country's group-oriented culture.

Senior managers in France and Germany also adapt their decision styles to their countries' cultures. In France, for instance, autocratic decision making is widely practiced, and managers avoid risks. Managerial styles in Germany reflect the German culture's concern for structure and order. Consequently, German organizations generally operate under extensive rules and regulations. Managers have well-defined responsibilities and accept that decisions must go through channels.

As managers deal with employees from diverse cultures, they need to recognize common and accepted behavior when asking them to make decisions. Some individuals may not be as comfortable as others with being closely involved in decision making, or they may not be willing to experiment with something radically different. *Managers who accommodate the diversity in decision-making philosophies and practices can expect a high payoff if they capture the perspectives and strengths that a diverse workforce offers.*

Why Are Creativity and Design Thinking Important in Decision Making?

How do most of you take and save photos today? It's highly unlikely that you've ever had to insert film into a camera, shoot the photos you wanted while hoping you "got the shot," remove the film from the camera, take the film to be processed, and then pick up your photos later. When Apple, Facebook, and Instagram wanted to make this process easier and better, someone making decisions about future products had to *be creative* and they had to *use design thinking*. Both are important to decision makers today.

UNDERSTANDING CREATIVITY. A decision maker needs **creativity**: the ability to produce novel and useful ideas. These ideas are different from what's been done before but are also appropriate to the problem or opportunity presented. Why is creativity important to decision making? It allows the decision maker to appraise and understand the problem more fully, including "seeing" problems others can't see. However, creativity's most obvious value is in helping the decision maker identify all viable alternatives.

ringisei
Japanese consensus-forming group decisions

creativity
The ability to produce novel and useful ideas

Most people have creative potential that they can use when confronted with a decision-making problem. But to unleash that potential, they have to get out of the psychological ruts most of us get into and learn how to think about a problem in divergent ways.

Learn to **unleash YOUR** creativity.

We can start with the obvious. People differ in their inherent creativity. Einstein, Edison, Dali, and Mozart were individuals of exceptional creativity. Not surprisingly, exceptional creativity is scarce.

A study of lifetime creativity of 461 men and women found that:

- Fewer than 1 percent were exceptionally creative
- 10 percent were highly creative
- About 60 percent were somewhat creative.

These findings suggest that most of us have some creative potential, *if* we can learn to unleash it.

Given that most people have the capacity to be at least moderately creative, what can individuals and organizations do to stimulate employee creativity? The best answer to this question lies in the three-component model of creativity based on an extensive body of research.[47] This model proposes that individual creativity essentially requires ❶ expertise, ❷ creative-thinking skills, and ❸ intrinsic task motivation. Studies confirm that the higher the level of each of these three components, the higher the creativity.

Expertise is the foundation of all creative work. Dali's understanding of art and Einstein's knowledge of physics were necessary conditions for them to be able to make creative contributions to their fields. And you wouldn't expect someone with a minimal knowledge of programming to be highly creative as a software engineer. The potential for creativity is enhanced when individuals have abilities, knowledge, proficiencies, and similar expertise in their fields of endeavor.

The second component is *creative-thinking skills*. It encompasses personality characteristics associated with creativity, the ability to use analogies, as well as the talent to see the familiar in a different light. For instance, the following individual traits have been found to be associated with the development of creative ideas: intelligence, independence, self-confidence, risk taking, internal locus of control, tolerance for ambiguity, and perseverance in the face of frustration. The effective use of analogies allows decision makers to apply an idea from one context to another. One of the most famous examples in which analogy resulted in a creative breakthrough was Alexander Graham Bell's observation that it might be possible to take concepts that operate in the ear and apply them to his "talking box." He noticed that the bones in the ear are operated by a delicate, thin membrane. He wondered why, then, a thicker and stronger piece of membrane shouldn't be able to move a piece of steel. Out of that analogy the telephone was conceived. Of course, some people have developed their skill at being able to see problems in a new way. They're able to make the strange familiar and the familiar strange. For instance, most of us think of hens laying eggs. But how many of us have considered that a hen is only an egg's way of making another egg?

The final component in our model is *intrinsic task motivation*—the desire to work on something because it's interesting, involving, exciting, satisfying, or personally challenging. This motivational component is what turns creative *potential* into *actual* creative ideas. It determines the extent to which individuals fully engage their expertise and creative skills. So creative people often love their work, to the point of seeming obsessed. Importantly, an individual's work environment and the organization's culture (which we discussed in Chapter 2) can have a significant effect on intrinsic motivation. Five organizational factors have been found that can impede your creativity:

- expected evaluation—focusing on how your work is going to be evaluated
- surveillance—being watched while you're working
- external motivators—emphasizing external, tangible rewards
- competition—facing win–lose situations with your peers
- constrained choices—being given limits on how you can do your work.

⭐ Try It!

If your professor has assigned this, go to the Assignments section of **mymanagementlab.com** to complete the **Simulation:** *Decision Making*.

design thinking
Approaching management problems as designers approach design problems

Apple—a great example of how **design thinking benefits** an organization.

UNDERSTANDING DESIGN THINKING.   The way managers approach decision making—using a rational and analytical mindset in identifying problems, coming up with alternatives, evaluating alternatives, and choosing one of those alternatives—may not be the best and certainly not the only choice in today's environment. That's where design thinking comes in. **Design thinking** has been described as "approaching management problems as designers approach design problems."[48] More organizations are beginning to recognize how design thinking can benefit them.[49] For instance, Apple has long been celebrated for its design thinking. The company's lead designer, Jonathan "Jony" Ive (who was behind some of Apple's most successful products including the iPod and iPhone) had this to say about Apple's design approach, "We try to develop products that seem somehow inevitable. That leave you with the sense that that's the only possible solution that makes sense."[50]

While many managers don't deal specifically with product or process design decisions, they still make decisions about work issues that arise, and design thinking can help them be better decision makers. What can the design thinking approach teach managers about making better decisions? Well, it begins with (1) the first step in the decision-making process of identifying problems. Design thinking says that managers should look at problem identification collaboratively and integratively with the goal of gaining a deep understanding of the situation. They should look not only at the rational aspects, but also at the emotional elements. Then invariably, of course, design thinking would (2) influence how managers identify and evaluate alternatives—steps 2 through 5 in the decision-making process. A traditional manager (educated in a business school, of course) would look at the alternatives, rationally evaluate them, and select the one with the highest payoff. However, using design thinking, a manager would say, "What is something completely new that would be lovely if it existed but doesn't now?"[51] Design thinking means opening up your perspective and gaining insights by using observation and inquiry skills, and not relying simply on rational analysis. We're not saying that rational analysis isn't needed; we are saying that there's more needed in making effective decisions, especially in today's world.

Design thinking leads the strategic decisions of Jack Dorsey, co-founder of Twitter and CEO of Square, a mobile payments processor for smartphones and tablets. Dorsey used observation and inquiry in deciding to start a company based on the idea that people needed an easy way to make payments in person.

Big data is **changing the way** managers make decisions.

Big Data Understood.

- Amazon.com, Earth's biggest online retailer, earns billions of dollars of revenue each year—estimated at one-third of sales—from its "personalization technologies" such as product recommendations and computer-generated e-mails.[52]
- At AutoZone, decision makers are using new software that gleans information from a variety of databases and allows its 5,000-plus local stores to target deals and hopefully reduce the chance that customers will walk away without making a purchase. AutoZone's chief information officer says, "We think this is the direction of the future."[53]

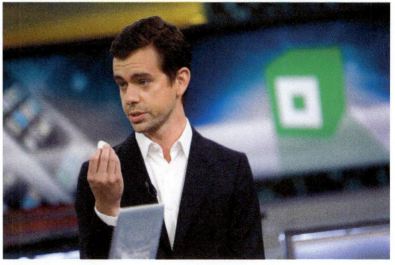

big data
The vast amount of quantifiable information that can be analyzed by highly sophisticated data processing

• It's not just businesses that are exploiting big data. A team of San Francisco researchers was able to predict the magnitude of a disease outbreak halfway around the world by analyzing phone patterns from mobile phone usage.[54]

Yes, there's a ton of information out there—100 petabytes here in the decade of the 2010s, according to experts. (In bytes, that translates to 1 plus 17 zeroes, in case you were wondering!)[55] And businesses—and other organizations—are finally figuring out how to use it. So what is **big data**? It's the vast amount of quantifiable information that can be analyzed by highly sophisticated data processing. One IT expert described big data with "3V's: high volume, high velocity, and/or high variety information assets."[56]

What does big data have to do with decision making? A lot, as you can imagine. With this type of data at hand, decision makers have very powerful tools to help them make decisions. However, experts caution that collecting and analyzing data for data's sake is wasted effort. Goals are needed when collecting and using this type of information. As one individual said, "Big data is a descendant of Taylor's 'scientific management' of more than a century ago."[57] While Taylor used a stopwatch to time and monitor a worker's every movement, big data is using math modeling, predictive algorithms, and artificial intelligence software to measure and monitor people and machines like never before. (See Case Applications #2 and #3 on pp. 115 and 116.) But managers need to really examine and evaluate how big data might contribute to their decision making before jumping in with both feet.

MyManagementLab®

Go to **mymanagementlab.com** to complete the problems marked with this icon .

4 Review

CHAPTER SUMMARY

4-1 Describe the decision-making process.

The decision-making process consists of eight steps: (1) identify a problem, (2) identify decision criteria, (3) weight the criteria, (4) develop alternatives, (5) analyze alternatives, (6) select alternative, (7) implement alternative, and (8) evaluate decision effectiveness. As managers make decisions, they may use heuristics to simplify the process, which can lead to errors and biases in their decision making. The 12 common decision-making errors and biases include overconfidence, immediate gratification, anchoring, selective perception, confirmation, framing, availability, representation, randomness, sunk costs, self-serving bias, and hindsight.

4-2 Explain the three approaches managers can use to make decisions.

The first approach is the rational model. The assumptions of rationality are as follows: the problem is clear and unambiguous; a single, well-defined goal is to be achieved; all alternatives and consequences are known; and the final choice will maximize the payoff. The second approach, bounded rationality, says that managers make rational decisions but are bounded (limited) by their ability to process information. In this approach, managers satisfice, which is when decision makers accept solutions that are good enough. Finally, intuitive decision making is making decisions on the basis of experience, feelings, and accumulated judgment.

4-3 Describe the types of decisions and decision-making conditions managers face.

Programmed decisions are repetitive decisions that can be handled by a routine approach and are used when the problem being resolved is straightforward, familiar, and easily defined (structured). Nonprogrammed decisions are unique decisions that require a custom-made solution and are used when the problems are new or unusual (unstructured) and for which information is ambiguous or incomplete. Certainty involves a situation in which a manager can make accurate decisions because all outcomes are known. With risk, a manager can estimate the likelihood of certain outcomes in a situation. Uncertainty is a situation in which a manager is not certain about the outcomes and can't even make reasonable probability estimates.

4-4 Discuss group decision making.

Groups offer certain advantages when making decisions—more complete information, more alternatives, increased acceptance of a solution, and greater legitimacy. On the other hand, groups are time-consuming, can be dominated by a minority, create pressures to conform, and cloud responsibility. Three ways of improving group decision making are brainstorming (utilizing an idea-generating process that specifically encourages any and all alternatives while withholding any criticism of those alternatives), the nominal group technique (a technique that restricts discussion during the decision-making process), and electronic meetings (the most recent approach to group decision making, which blends the nominal group technique with sophisticated computer technology).

4-5 Discuss contemporary issues in managerial decision making.

As managers deal with employees from diverse cultures, they need to recognize common and accepted behavior when asking them to make decisions. Some individuals may not be as comfortable as others with being closely involved in decision making, or they may not be willing to experiment with something radically different. Also, managers need to be creative in their decision making because creativity allows them to appraise and understand the problem more fully, including "seeing" problems that others can't see. Design thinking also influences the way that managers approach decision making, especially in terms of identifying problems and how they identify and evaluate alternatives. Finally, big data is changing what and how decisions are made, but managers need to evaluate how big data might contribute to their decision making.

DISCUSSION QUESTIONS

⭐ **4-1** Why is decision making often described as the essence of a manager's job?

4-2 Describe the eight steps in the decision-making process.

4-3 All of us bring biases to the decisions we make. What would be the drawbacks of having biases? Could there be any advantages to having biases? Explain. What are the implications for managerial decision making?

4-4 "Because managers have so many powerful decision-making tools to use, they should be able to make more rational decisions." Do you agree or disagree with this statement? Why?

4-5 Is there a difference between wrong decisions and bad decisions? Why do good managers sometimes make wrong decisions? Bad decisions? How might managers improve their decision-making skills?

4-6 Describe a decision you've made that closely aligns with the assumptions of perfect rationality. Compare this decision with the process you used to select your college. Did you depart from the rational model in your college decisions? Explain.

4-7 Explain how a manager might deal with making decisions under conditions of uncertainty.

⭐ **4-8** Why do you think organizations have increased the use of groups for making decisions and when would you recommend using groups to make decisions?

4-9 Find two examples each of procedures, rules, and policies. Bring your examples to class and be prepared to share them.

4-10 Do a Web search on the phrase "dumbest moments in business" and get the most current version of this list. Choose three of the examples and describe what happened. What's your reaction to each example? How could the managers in each have made better decisions?

Writing Assignments

4-11 Today's world is chaotic and fast-paced. How does time pressure affect managerial decision making? What can managers do to still be good decision makers under such conditions?

4-12 Discuss the pros and cons of managers using technology to help make decisions.

Management Skill Builder | BEING A CREATIVE DECISION MAKER

Many decisions that managers make are routine, so they can fall back on experience and "what's worked in the past." But other decisions—especially those made by upper-level managers—are unique and haven't been confronted before. The uniqueness and variety of problems that managers face demand creativity—the ability to produce novel and useful ideas. If managers are to successfully progress upward in an organization, they'll find an increasing need to develop creative decisions. Creativity is partly a frame of mind. You need to expand your mind's capabilities—that is, open yourself up to new ideas. Every individual has the ability to improve his or her creativity, but many people simply don't try to develop that ability.

✪ PERSONAL INVENTORY ASSESSMENT

Problem Solving, Creativity, and Innovation

Making decisions is all about solving problems. Do this PIA and find out about your level of creativity and innovation in problem solving.

Skill Basics

Creativity is a skill you can develop. Here are some suggestions on how you can do this:

- *Think of yourself as creative.* Research shows that if you think you can't be creative, you won't be. Believing in your ability to be creative is the first step in becoming more creative.

- *Pay attention to your intuition.* Every individual has a subconscious mind that works well. Sometimes answers will come to you when you least expect them. Listen to that "inner voice." In fact, most creative people will keep a notepad near their bed and write down ideas when the thoughts come to them.

- *Move away from your comfort zone.* Every individual has a comfort zone in which certainty exists. But creativity and the known often do not mix. To be creative, you need to move away from the status quo and focus your mind on something new.

- *Determine what you want to do.* This includes such things as taking time to understand a problem before beginning to try to resolve it, getting all the facts in mind, and trying to identify the most important facts.

- *Think outside the box.* Use analogies whenever possible (for example, could you approach your problem like a fish out of water and look at what the fish does to cope? Or can you use the things you have to do to find your way when it's foggy to help you solve your problem?). Use different problem-solving strategies such as verbal, visual, mathematical, or theatrical. Look at your problem from a different perspective or ask yourself what someone else, like your grandmother, might do if faced with the same situation.

- *Look for ways to do things better.* This may involve trying consciously to be original, not worrying about looking foolish, keeping an open mind, being alert to odd or puzzling facts, thinking of unconventional ways to use objects and the environment, discarding usual or habitual ways of doing things, and striving for objectivity by being as critical of your own ideas as you would those of someone else.

- *Find several right answers.* Being creative means continuing to look for other solutions even when you think you

have solved the problem. A better, more creative solution just might be found.

- *Believe in finding a workable solution.* Like believing in yourself, you also need to believe in your ideas. If you don't think you can find a solution, you probably won't.

- *Brainstorm with others.* Creativity is not an isolated activity. Bouncing ideas off of others creates a synergistic effect.

- *Turn creative ideas into action.* Coming up with creative ideas is only part of the process. Once the ideas are generated, they must be implemented. Keeping great ideas in your mind, or on papers that no one will read, does little to expand your creative abilities.

Based on J. V. Anderson, "Mind Mapping: A Tool for Creative Thinking," *Business Horizons*, January–February 1993, 42–46; and T. Proctor, *Creative Problem Solving for Managers* (New York: Routledge, 2005).

Practicing the Skill

Read through this scenario and follow the directions at the end of it:

Every time the phone rings, your stomach clenches and your palms start to sweat. And it's no wonder! As sales manager for Brinkers, a machine tool parts manufacturer, you're besieged by calls from customers who are upset about late deliveries. Your boss, Carter Hererra, acts as both production manager and scheduler. Every time your sales representatives negotiate a sale, it's up to Carter to determine whether production can actually meet the delivery date the customer specifies. And Carter invariably says, "No problem." The good thing about this is that you make a lot of initial sales. The bad news is that production hardly ever meets the shipment dates that Carter authorizes. And he doesn't seem to be all that concerned about the aftermath of late deliveries. He says, "Our customers know they're getting outstanding quality at a great price. Just let them try to match that anywhere. It can't be done. So even if they have to wait a couple of extra days or weeks, they're still getting the best deal they can." Somehow the customers don't see it that way. And they let you know about their unhappiness. Then it's up to you to try to soothe the relationship. You know this problem has to be taken care of, but what possible solutions are there? After all, how are you going to keep from making your manager mad or making the customers mad?

Break into groups of three. Assume you're the sales manager. What creative solutions can your group come up with to deal with this problem?

Magic Carpet Software

To: Rajiv Dutta, Research Manager

From: Amanda Schrenk, Vice President of Operations

Re: Software Design Decisions

Rajiv, we have a problem in our software design unit. Our diverse pool of extremely talented and skilled designers is, undoubtedly, one of our company's most important assets. However, I'm concerned that our designers' emotional attachment to the software they've created overshadows other important factors that should be considered in the decision whether to proceed with the new product design. At this point, I'm not sure how to approach this issue. The last thing I want to do is stifle their creativity. But I'm afraid if we don't come up with an action plan soon, the problem may get worse.

I need you to research the role of emotions in decision making. What do the "experts" say? Is it even an issue that we need to be concerned about? What's the best way to deal with it? Please provide me with a one-page bulleted list of the important points you find from your research. And be sure to cite your sources in case I need to do some follow-up.

This fictionalized company and message were created for educational purposes only, and not meant to reflect positively or negatively on management practices by any company that may share this name.

CASE APPLICATION

 Big Brown Numbers

It's the world's largest package delivery company with the instantly recognizable trucks.[58] Every day, United Parcel Service (UPS) transports more than 18 million packages and documents throughout the United States and to more than 220 countries and territories, including every address in North America and Europe. (Total worldwide delivery volume was 4.6 billion packages and documents in 2014.) Delivering those packages efficiently and on time is what UPS gets paid to do, and that takes a massive effort in helping drivers to make decisions about the best routes to follow.

Efficiency and uniformity have always been important to UPS. The importance of work rules, procedures, and analytic tools are continually stressed to drivers through training and retraining. For instance, drivers are taught to hold their keys on a pinky finger so they don't waste time fumbling in their pockets for the keys. And for safety reasons, they're taught no-left turns and no backing up. Now, however, the company has been testing and rolling out a quantum leap in its long-used business model of uniformity and efficiency. It goes by the name ORION, which stands for On-Road Integrated Optimization and Navigation. What it boils down to is helping UPS drivers shave millions of miles off their delivery routes using decision algorithms built by a team of mathematicians.

UPS has been described as an **EFFICIENCY FREAK**.

Consider that each UPS driver makes an average of 120 stops per day. The efficiency challenge is deciding the best order to make all those stops (6,689,502,913,449,135 + 183 zeroes of possible alternatives)—taking into consideration "variables such as special delivery times, road regulations, and the existence of private roads that don't appear on a map?"[59] Another description of the logistics decision challenge: There are more ways to deliver packages along an average driver's route "than there are nanoseconds that Earth has existed."[60] Any way you look at it, that's a lot of alternatives. The human mind can't even begin to figure it out. But the ORION algorithm, which has taken 10 years and an estimated hundreds of millions of dollars to build, is the next best thing. IT experts have described ORION as the largest investment in operations research ever by any company.

So what does ORION do? Instead of searching for the one best answer, ORION is designed to refine itself over time, leading to a balance between an optimum result and consistency to help drivers make the best possible decisions about route delivery. And considering how many miles UPS drivers travel every day, saving a dollar or two here and there can add up quickly. When a driver "logs on" his delivery information acquisition device (DIAD) at the beginning of his shift each workday, what comes up are two possible ways to make the day's package deliveries: one that uses ORION and one that uses the "old" method. The driver can choose to use either one but if ORION is not chosen, the driver is asked to explain the decision. The roll-out of ORION hasn't been without challenges. Some drivers have been reluctant to give up autonomy; others have had trouble understanding ORION's logic—why deliver a package in one neighborhood in the morning and come back to the same neighborhood later in the day. But despite the challenges, the company is committed to ORION, saying that "a driver together with ORION is better than each alone."[61]

Discussion Questions

4-14 Why is efficiency and safety so important to UPS?

4-15 Would you characterize a driver's route decisions as structured or unstructured problems? Programmed or nonprogrammed decisions? Explain.

4-16 How would ORION technology help drivers make better decisions? (Think of the steps in the decision-making process.)

4-17 How is UPS being a sustainable corporation?

CASE APPLICATION #2

The Business of Baseball

Baseball has long been called "America's national pastime" (although according to a Harris Interactive survey, the NFL has been, hands down, the favorite sport of Americans).[62] Now, the game of baseball can probably be better described as America's number crunchers. Take, for instance, Sandy Alderson, the general manager of the New York Mets. He explained the team's decision to let batting champion and free agent shortstop Jose Reyes go to the Miami Marlins. "I'm happy with the analysis we used and the strategy we pursued." As he made this announcement, three members of his baseball operations staff stood by with their laptops open and ready to provide any needed data. A baseball writer has described the sport's move to data analysis this way, "Don't overlook the increasing value of facts, figures, and other data…and the people who interpret them."

As the film *Moneyball* (based on an earlier book by the same name) emphasized, statistics—the "right" statistics—are crucial aspects of effective decision making in the sport of baseball. The central premise of *Moneyball* was that the collected wisdom of baseball insiders (players, managers, coaches, scouts, and the front office) had pretty much been flawed almost from the onset of the game. Commonly used statistics such as stolen bases, runs batted in, and batting averages that were typically used to evaluate players' abilities and performances were inadequate and poor gauges of potential. Rigorous statistical analysis showed that on-base percentages and slugging percentages were better indicators of a player's offensive potential. The goal of all this number crunching? To make better decisions. Team managers want to allocate their limited payroll in the best way possible to help the team be a winner.

The move to more systematic data usage can also be seen in college baseball. At this level, coaches have long used their faces (touching their ears, noses, and chins continually and constantly) to communicate pitch selection to the catcher. Now, however, hundreds of college teams at all levels have abandoned these body signals and are using a system in which the coach yells out a series of numbers. "The catcher decodes the sequence by looking at a chart tucked into a wristband—the kind football quarterbacks have worn since 1965—and then relays the information to the pitcher the way he always has." Coaches say this approach is not only faster and more efficient, it's not decipherable by opponents wanting to steal the signs. Since the method allows for many combinations that can mean many different pitches, the same number sequence won't be used for the rest of the game—and maybe not even for the rest of the season.

> The **GAME** of Baseball…
> number crunching, statistical
> analysis, and data.

Discussion Questions

4-18 In a general sense, what kinds of decisions are made in baseball? Would you characterize these decisions as structured or unstructured problems? Explain. What type(s) of decision-making condition would you consider this to be? Explain.

4-19 Is it appropriate for baseball managers to use only quantitative, objective criteria in evaluating their players? What do you think? Why?

4-20 Describe how baseball front office executives and college coaches could use each of the following to make

better decisions: (a) rationality, (b) bounded rationality, and (c) intuition.

4-21 Can there be too much information in managing the business of baseball? Discuss.

CASE APPLICATION #3

Tasting Success

The Coca-Cola Company (Coke) is in a league by itself.[63] As the world's largest and number one nonalcoholic beverage company, Coke makes or licenses more than 3,500 drinks in more than 200 countries. Coke has built 15 billion-dollar brands and also claims four of the top five soft-drink brands (Coke, Diet Coke, Fanta, and Sprite). Each year since 2001, global brand consulting firm Interbrand, in conjunction with *Bloomberg BusinessWeek,* has identified Coke as the number one best global brand. Coke's executives and managers are focusing on ambitious, long-term growth for the company—doubling Coke's business by 2020. A big part of achieving this goal is building up its Simply Orange juice business into a powerful global juice brand. Decision making is playing a crucial role as managers try to beat rival PepsiCo, which has a 40 percent market share in the not-from-concentrate juice category compared to Coke's 28 percent share. And those managers aren't leaving anything to chance in this hot—umm, cold—pursuit!

Orange Juice and the 1 Quintillion Decisions needed to deliver it!

You'd think that making orange juice (OJ) would be relatively simple—pick, squeeze, pour. While that would probably be the case in your own kitchen, in Coke's case, that glass of 100 percent OJ is possible only through the use of satellite images, complex mathematical algorithms, and a pipeline solely for the purpose of transporting juice. The purchasing director for Coke's massive Florida juice packaging facility says that when you're dealing with "Mother Nature," standardization is a huge problem. Yet, standardization is what it takes for Coke to make this work profitably. And producing a juice beverage is far more complicated than bottling soda.

Using what it calls its "Black Book model," Coke wants to ensure that customers have consistently fresh, tasty OJ 12 months a year despite a peak growing season that's only three months long. To help in this, Coke relies on a consultant experienced with revenue analytics, who has described OJ as "one of the most complex applications of business analytics." How complex? To consistently deliver an optimal blend given the challenges of nature requires some 1 quintillion (that's 1 followed by 18 zeroes) decisions!

There's no secret formula to Black Book, it's simply an algorithm. It includes detailed data about the more than 600 different flavors that make up an orange and about customer preferences. This data is correlated to a profile of each batch of raw juice. The algorithm then determines how to blend batches to match a certain taste and consistency. At the juice bottling plant, "blend technicians" carefully follow the Black Book instructions before beginning the bottling process. The weekly OJ recipe they use is "tweaked" constantly. Black Book also includes data on external factors such as weather patterns, crop yields, and other cost pressures. This is useful for Coke's decision makers as they ensure they'll have enough supplies for at least 15 months. One Coke executive says the company's mathematical modeling means that if a weather catastrophe (hurricane or hard freeze) hits, the business can quickly regroup and replan in a very short time frame: as little as 5 or 10 minutes.

Discussion Questions

4-22 Which decisions in this story could be considered unstructured problems? Structured problems?

4-23 How does the Black Book help Coke's managers and other employees in decision making?

4-24 What does Coke's big data have to do with its goals?

4-25 Do some research on revenue analytics. What is it? How can it help managers make better decisions?

Endnotes

1. J. Zucker, "Proof in the Eating," *Fast Company*, March 2013, 34+.

2. A. Blackman, "Inside the Executive Brain," *Wall Street Journal*, April 28, 2014, R1.

3. See, for example, A. Nagurney, J. Dong, and P. L. Mokhtarian, "Multicriteria Network Equilibrium Modeling with Variable Weights for Decision-Making in the Information Age with Applications to the Telecommuting and Teleshopping," *Journal of Economic Dynamics and Control* (August 2002): 1629–50.

4. J. Flinchbaugh, "Surfacing Problems Daily: Advice for Building a Problem-Solving Culture," *Industry Week*, April 2011, 12; "Business Analysis Training Helps Leaders Achieve an Enterprise-Wide Perspective," *Leader to Leader*, Fall 2010, 63–65; D. Okes, "Common Problems with Basic Problem Solving," *Quality*, September 2010, 36–40; J. Sawyer, "Problem-Solving Success Tips," *Business and Economic Review*, April–June 2002, 23–24.

5. See J. Figueira and B. Ray, "Determining the Weights of Criteria in the Electre Type of Methods with a Revised Simons' Procedure," *European Journal of Operational Research*, June 1, 2002, 317–26.

6. For instance, see M. Elliott, "Breakthrough Thinking," *IIE Solution*, October 2001, 22–25; and B. Fazlollahi and R. Vahidov, "A Method for Generation of Alternatives by Decision Support Systems," *Journal of Management Information Systems* (Fall 2001): 229–50.

7. D. Miller, Q. Hope, R. Eisenstat, N. Foote, and J. Galbraith, "The Problem of Solutions: Balancing Clients and Capabilities," *Business Horizons*, March–April 2002, 3–12.

8. E. Teach, "Avoiding Decision Traps," *CFO*, June 2004, 97–99; and D. Kahneman and A. Tversky, "Judgment Under Uncertainty: Heuristics and Biases," *Science* 185 (1974): 1124–31.

9. Information for this section taken from S. P. Robbins, *Decide & Conquer* (Upper Saddle River, NJ: Financial Times/Prentice Hall, 2004).

10. T. A. Stewart, "Did You Ever Have to Make Up Your Mind?" *Harvard Business Review*, January 2006, 12; and E. Pooley, "Editor's Desk," *Fortune*, June 27, 2005, 16.

11. J. G. March, "Decision-Making Perspective: Decisions in Organizations and Theories of Choice," in A. H. Van de Ven and W. F. Joyce (eds.), *Perspectives on Organization Design and Behavior* (New York: Wiley-Interscience, 1981), 232–33.

12. See T. Shavit and A. M. Adam, "A Preliminary Exploration of the Effects of Rational Factors and Behavioral Biases on the Managerial Choice to Invest in Corporate Responsibility," *Managerial and Decision Economics*, April 2011, 205–13; A. Langley, "In Search of Rationality: The Purposes Behind the Use of Formal Analysis in Organizations," *Administrative Science Quarterly*, December 1989, 598–631; and H. A. Simon, "Rationality in Psychology and Economics," *Journal of Business* (October 1986), 209–24.

13. See D. R. A. Skidd, "Revisiting Bounded Rationality," *Journal of Management Inquiry* (December 1992): 343–47; R. F. Kaufman, "A New Theory of Satisficing," *Journal of Behavioral Economics* (Spring 1990): 35–51; and N. McK. Agnew and J. L. Brown, "Bounded Rationality: Fallible Decisions in Unbounded Decision Space," *Behavioral Science*, July 1986, 148–61.

14. From the Past to the Present box based on M. Ibrahim, "Theory of Bounded Rationality," *Public Management*, June 2009, 3–5; D. A. Wren, *The Evolution of Management Thought*, Fourth Edition (New York: John Wiley & Sons, Inc., 1994), 291; and H. A. Simon, *Administrative Behavior* (New York: Macmillan Company, 1945).

15. See, for example, G. McNamara, H. Moon, and P. Bromiley, "Banking on Commitment: Intended and Unintended Consequences of an Organization's Attempt to Attenuate Escalation of Commitment," *Academy of Management Journal* (April 2002): 443–52; V. S. Rao and A. Monk, "The Effects of Individual Differences and Anonymity on Commitment to Decisions," *Journal of Social Psychology* (August 1999): 496–515; C. F. Camerer and R. A. Weber, "The Econometrics and Behavioral Economics of Escalation of Commitment: A Re-examination of Staw's Theory," *Journal of Economic Behavior and Organization* (May 1999): 59–82; D. R. Bobocel and J. P. Meyer, "Escalating Commitment to a Failing Course of Action: Separating the Roles of Choice and Justification," *Journal of Applied Psychology* (June 1994): 360–63; and B. M. Staw, "The Escalation of Commitment to a Course of Action," *Academy of Management Review*, October 1981, 577–87.

16. L. Alderman, "A Shoemaker That Walks but Never Runs," *New York Times Online*, October 8, 2010.

17. C. Flora, "When to Go with Your Gut," *Women's Health*, June 2009, 68–70.

18. See J. Evans, "Intuition and Reasoning: A Dual-Process Perspective," *Psychological Inquiry*, October–December 2010, 313–26; T. Betsch and A. Blockner, "Intuition in Judgment and Decision Making: Extensive Thinking without Effort," *Psychological Inquiry*, October–December 2010, 279–94; R. Lange and J. Houran, "A Transliminal View of Intuitions in the Workplace," *North American Journal of Psychology* 12, no. 3 (2010): 501–16; E. Dane and M. G. Pratt, "Exploring Intuition and Its Role in Managerial Decision Making," *Academy of Management Review*, January 2007, 33–54; M. H. Bazerman and D. Chugh, "Decisions without Blinders," *Harvard Business Review*, January 2006, 88–97; C. C. Miller and R. D. Ireland, "Intuition in Strategic Decision Making: Friend or Foe in the Fast-Paced 21st Century," *Academy of Management Executive*, February 2005, 19–30; E. Sadler-Smith and E. Shefy, "The Intuitive Executive: Understanding and Applying 'Gut Feel' in Decision-Making," *Academy of Management Executive*, November 2004, 76–91; and L. A. Burke and M. K. Miller, "Taking the Mystery Out of Intuitive Decision Making," *Academy of Management Executive*, October 1999, 91–99.

19. C. C. Miller and R. D. Ireland, "Intuition in Strategic Decision Making: Friend or Foe," 20.

20. E. Sadler-Smith and E. Shefy, "Developing Intuitive Awareness in Management Education," *Academy of Management Learning & Education*, June 2007, 186–205.

21. M. G. Seo and L. Feldman Barrett, "Being Emotional During Decision Making—Good or Bad? An Empirical Investigation," *Academy of Management Journal* (August 2007): 923–40.

22. Technology and the Manager's Job box based on M. Xu, V. Ong, Y. Duan, and B. Mathews, "Intelligent Agent Systems for Executive Information Scanning, Filtering, and Interpretation: Perceptions and Challenges," *Information Processing & Management*, March 2011, 186–201; J. P. Kallunki, E. K. Laitinen, and H. Silvola, "Impact of Enterprise Resource Planning Systems on Management Control Systems and Firm Performance," *International Journal of Accounting Information Systems* (March 2011), 20–39; H. W. K. Chia, C. L. Tan, and S. Y. Sung, "Enhancing Knowledge Discovery via Association-Based Evolution of Neural Logic Networks," *IEEE Transactions on Knowledge and Data Engineering* (July 2006): 889–901; F. Harvey, "A Key Role in Detecting Fraud Patterns: Neural Networks," *Financial Times*, January 23, 2002, 3; D. Mitchell and R. Pavur, "Using Modular Neural Networks for Business Decisions," *Management Decision*, January–February 2002, 58–64; B. L. Killingsworth, M. B. Hayden, and R. Schellenberger, "A Network Expert System Management System of Multiple Domains," *Journal of Information Science* (March–April 2001): 81; and S. Balakrishnan, N. Popplewell, and M. Thomlinson, "Intelligent Robotic Assembly," *Computers & Industrial Engineering*, December 2000, 467.

23. "Next: Big Idea," *Fast Company*, December 2010–January 2011, 39–40.

24. H. McCracken, "50 Most Innovative Companies: LINE," *Fast Company*, March 2015, 84+.

25. And the Survey Says box based on D. Kahneman, D. Lovallo, and O. Siboney, "Before You Make That Big Decision," *Harvard Business Review*, June 2011, 50–60; P. Wang, "To Make Better Choices, Choose Less," *Money*, June 2010, 111–14; B. Dumaine, "The Trouble with Teams," *Fortune*, September 5, 1994, 86–92; A. S. Wellner, "A Perfect Brainstorm," *Inc.*, October 2003, 31–35; "The Poll," *BusinessWeek*, August 21–28, 2006, 44; "Hurry Up and Decide," *BusinessWeek*, May 14, 2001, 16; J. MacIntyre, "Bosses and Bureaucracy," *Springfield, Missouri Business Journal*, August 1–7, 2005, 29; J. Crick, and "On the Road to Invention," *Fast Company*, February 2005, 16.

26. A. Deutschman, "Inside the Mind of Jeff Bezos," *Fast Company*, August 2004, 50–58.

27. See, for instance, S. Schulz-Hardt, A. Mojzisch, F. C. Brodbeck, R. Kerschreiter, and D. Frey, "Group Decision Making in Hidden Profile Situations: Dissent as a Facilitator for Decision Quality," *Journal of Personality and Social Psychology* (December 2006), 1080–83; and C. K. W. DeDreu and M. A. West, "Minority Dissent and Team Innovation: The Importance of Participation in Decision Making," *Journal of Applied Psychology* (December 2001): 1191–1201.

28. S. Mohammed, "Toward an Understanding of Cognitive Consensus in a Group Decision-Making Context," *Journal of Applied Behavioral Science* (December 2001): 408.

29. M. J. Fambrough and S. A. Comerford, "The Changing Epistemological Assumptions of Group Theory," *Journal of Applied Behavioral Science* (September 2006): 330–49.

30. R. A. Meyers, D. E. Brashers, and J. Hanner, "Majority-Minority Influence: Identifying Argumentative Patterns and Predicting Argument-Outcome Links," *Journal of Communication* (Autumn 2000): 3–30.

31. See, for instance, T. Horton, "Groupthink in the Boardroom,"

Directors and Boards, Winter 2002, 9.

32. I. L. Janis, *Groupthink* (Boston: Houghton Mifflin, 1982). See also J. Chapman, "Anxiety and Defective Decision Making: An Elaboration of the Groupthink Mode," *Management Decision*, October 2006, 1391–1404.

33. See, for example, T. W. Costello and S. S. Zalkind, eds., *Psychology in Administration: A Research Orientation* (Upper Saddle River, NJ: Prentice Hall, 1963), 429–30; R. A. Cooke and J. A. Kernaghan, "Estimating the Difference between Group versus Individual Performance on Problem Solving Tasks," *Group and Organization Studies*, September 1987, 319–42; and L. K. Michaelsen, W. E. Watson, and R. H. Black, "A Realistic Test of Individual versus Group Consensus Decision Making," *Journal of Applied Psychology* (October 1989): 834–39. See also J. Hollenbeck, D. R. Ilgen, J. A. Colquitt, and A. Ellis, "Gender Composition, Situational Strength, and Team Decision-Making Accuracy: A Criterion Decomposition Approach," *Organizational Behavior and Human Decision Processes*, May 2002, 445–75.

34. See, for example, L. K. Michaelsen, W. E. Watson, and R. H. Black, "A Realistic Test of Individual versus Group Consensus Decision Making," *Journal of Applied Psychology* (October 1989): 834–39; and P. W. Pease, M. Beiser, and M. E. Tubbs, "Framing Effects and Choice Shifts in Group Decision Making," *Organizational Behavior and Human Decision Processes*, October 1993, 149–65.

35. M. Strachan, "NCAA Schools Can Absolutely Afford to Pay College Athletes, Economists Say," http://www.huffingtonpost.com/2015/03/27/ncaa-pay-student-athletes_n_6940836.html, March 27, 2015; A. Zimbalist, "Paying College Athletes: Take Two," http://www.huffingtonpost.com/andrew-zimbalist/paying-college-athletes-take-two_b_6961314.html, March 28, 2015; S. Terlep,

"NCAA Reaches $20 Million Settlement with Ex-Players over Videogames," *Wall Street Journal*, http://www.wsj.com/articles/ncaa-unveils-20-million-settlement-with-ex-players-over-videogames-1402330931, June 9, 2014; and C. Smith, "The Most Valuable Conferences in College Sports 2014," www.forbes.com, April 15, 2014.

36. J. Wagstaff, "Brainstorming Requires Drinks," *Far Eastern Economic Review*, May 2, 2002, 34.

37. T. Kelley, "Six Ways to Kill a Brainstormer," *Across the Board*, March–April 2002, 12.

38. K. L. Dowling and R. D. St. Louis, "Asynchronous Implementation of the Nominal Group Technique: Is It Effective," *Decision Support Systems*, October 2000, 229–48.

39. See also B. Andersen and T. Fagerhaug, "The Nominal Group Technique," *Quality Progress*, February 2000, 144.

40. J. Burdett, "Changing Channels: Using the Electronic Meeting System to Increase Equity in Decision Making," *Information Technology, Learning, and Performance Journal* (Fall 2000): 3–12.

41. "Fear of Flying," *Business Europe*, October 3, 2001, 2.

42. "VC at Nestlé," *Business Europe*, October 3, 2001, 3.

43. M. Roberti, "Meet Me on the Web," *Fortune: Tech Supplement*, Winter 2002, 10.

44. See also, J. A. Hoxmeier and K. A. Kozar, "Electronic Meetings and Subsequent Meeting Behavior: Systems as Agents of Change," *Journal of Applied Management Studies* (December 2000): 177–95.

45. See, for instance, P. Berthon, L. F. Pitt, and M. T. Ewing, "Corollaries of the Collective: The Influence of Organizational Culture and Memory Development on Perceived Decision-Making Context," *Academy of Marketing Science Journal* (Spring 2001): 135–50.

46. J. de Haan, M. Yamamoto, and G. Lovink, "Production Planning in Japan: Rediscovering Lost Experiences or New Insights," *International Journal of Production Economics* (May 6, 2001): 101–09.

47. T. M. Amabile, "Motivating Creativity in Organizations," *California Management Review* (Fall 1997): 39–58.

48. D. Dunne and R. Martin, "Design Thinking and How It Will Change Management Education: An Interview and Discussion," *Academy of Management Learning & Education*, December 2006, 512.

49. M. Korn and R. E. Silverman, "Forget B-School, D-School Is Hot," *Wall Street Journal*, June 7, 2012, B1+; R. Martin and J. Euchner, "Design Thinking," *Research Technology Management*, May/June 2012, 10–14; T. Larsen and T. Fisher, "Design Thinking: A Solution to Fracture-Critical Systems," *DMI News & Views*, May 2012, 31; T. Berno, "Design Thinking versus Creative Intelligence," *DMI News & Views*, May 2012, 28; J. Liedtka and Tim Ogilvie, "Helping Business Managers Discover Their Appetite for Design Thinking," *Design Management Review*, Issue 1, 2012, 6–13; and T. Brown, "Strategy by Design," *Fast Company*, June 2005, 52–54.

50. C. Guglielmo, "Apple Loop: The Week in Review," *Forbes.com*, May 25, 2012, 2.

51. D. Dunne and R. Martin, "Design Thinking and How It Will Change Management Education: An Interview and Discussion," 512.

52. K. Cukier and V. Mayer-Schönberger, "The Financial Bonanza of Big Data," *Wall Street Journal*, March 8, 2013, A15.

53. R. King and S. Rosenbush, "Big Data Broadens Its Range," *Wall Street Journal*, March 14, 2013, B5.

54. "Big Data, Big Impact: New Possibilities for International Development," *World Economic Forum*, weforum.org, 2012.

55. M. Kassel, "From a Molehill to a Mountain," *Wall Street Journal*, March 11, 2013, R1.

56. D. Laney, "The Importance of 'Big Data': A Definition," www.gartner.com/it-glossary/big-data/, March 22, 2013.

57. S. Lohr, "Sure, Big Data Is Great. But So Is Intuition," *New York Times Online*, December 29, 2012.

58. S. Rosenbush and L. Stevens, "At UPS, the Algorithm Is the Driver," *Wall Street Journal*, February 17, 2015, B1+; D. Zax, "Brown Down: UPS Drivers vs. the UPS Algorithm," http://www.fastcompany.com/3004319/brown-down-ups-drivers-vs-ups-algorithm, January 3, 2013; T. Bingham and P. Galagan, "Delivering 'On-Time, Every Time' Knowledge and Skills to a World of Employees," *T&D*, July 2012, 32–37; J. Levitz, "UPS Thinks Outside the Box on Driver Training," *Wall Street Journal*, April 6, 2010, B1+; and K. Kingsbury, "Road to Recovery," *Time*, March 8, 2010, Global 14–Global 16.

59. Rosenbush and Stevens, "At UPS, the Algorithm Is the Driver."

60. Zax, "Brown Down: UPS Drivers vs. the UPS Algorithm."

61. Rosenbush and Laura Stevens, "At UPS, the Algorithm Is the Driver."

62. T. Caporale and T. C. Collier, "Scouts versus Stats: The Impact of Moneyball on the Major League Baseball Draft," *Applied Economics* vol. 45, issue 15 (2013): 1983–90; B. Cohen, "College Baseball Showing Signs of a Revolution," *Wall Street Journal*, June 22, 2012, D10; T. Van Riper and C. Semmimi, "The New Moneyball," *Forbes*, April 9, 2012, 70–76; D. K. Berman, "So, What's Your Algorithm?" *Wall Street Journal*, January 4, 2012, B1+; P. White, "The Suits Behind the Uniforms," *USA Today*, December 7, 2011, 1C+; K. L. Papps, A. Bryson, and R. Gomez, "Heterogeneous Worker Ability and Team-Based Production: Evidence from Major League Baseball, 1920–2009," *Labour Economics*, June 2011, 310–19; Michael Lewis, *Moneyball*, (W. W. Norton & Co., 2011); and B. Curtis, "Debating America's Pastime(s)," *New York Times Online*, January 2, 2009.

63. D. D. Stanford, "Coke Has a Secret Formula for Orange Juice, Too," *Bloomberg Businessweek*, February 4–10, 2013, 19–20; P. Sellers, "The New Coke," *Fortune*, May 21, 2012, 138–44; and Adi Ignatious, "Shaking Things Up at Coca-Cola," *Harvard Business Review*, October 2011, 94–99.

Quantitative Module
QUANTITATIVE DECISION-MAKING AIDS

In this module we'll look at several decision-making aids and techniques, as well as some popular tools for managing projects.[1] Specifically, we'll introduce you to payoff matrices, decision trees, break-even analysis, ratio analysis, linear programming, queuing theory, and economic order quantity. The purpose of each method is to provide managers with a tool to assist in the decision-making process and to provide more complete information to make better-informed decisions.

Payoff Matrices

In Chapter 4 we introduced you to the topic of uncertainty and how it can affect decision making. Although uncertainty plays a critical role by limiting the amount of information available to managers, another factor is their psychological orientation. For instance, the optimistic manager will typically follow a *maximax* choice (maximizing the maximum possible payoff); the pessimist will often pursue a *maximin* choice (maximizing the minimum possible payoff); and the manager who desires to minimize his "regret" will opt for a *minimax* choice. Let's briefly look at these different approaches using an example.

Consider the case of a marketing manager at Visa International in New York. He has determined four possible strategies (we'll label these S1, S2, S3, and S4) for promoting the Visa card throughout the northeastern United States. However, he is also aware that one of his major competitors, American Express, has three competitive strategies (CA1, CA2, and CA3) for promoting its own card in the same region. In this case, we'll assume that the Visa executive has no previous knowledge that would allow him to place probabilities on the success of any of his four strategies. With these facts, the Visa card manager formulates the matrix in Exhibit QM–1 to show the various Visa strategies and the resulting profit to Visa, depending on the competitive action chosen by American Express.

In this example, if our Visa manager is an optimist, he'll choose S4 because that could produce the largest possible gain ($28 million). Note that this choice maximizes the maximum

Exhibit QM–1 Payoff Matrix for Visa

VISA MARKETING STRATEGY	AMERICAN EXPRESS'S RESPONSE (in $millions)		
	CA1	CA2	CA3
S1	13	14	11
S2	9	15	18
S3	24	21	15
S4	18	14	28

Exhibit QM–2 Regret Matrix for Visa

VISA MARKETING STRATEGY	AMERICAN EXPRESS'S RESPONSE (in $millions)		
	CA1	CA2	CA3
S1	11	7	17
S2	15	6	10
S3	0	0	13
S4	6	7	0

possible gain (maximax choice). If our manager is a pessimist, he'll assume only the worst can occur. The worst outcome for each strategy is as follows: S1 = $11 million; S2 = $9 million; S3 = $15 million; and S4 = $14 million. Following the maximin choice, the pessimistic manager would maximize the minimum payoff—in other words, he'd select S3.

In the third approach, managers recognize that once a decision is made it will not necessarily result in the most profitable payoff. What could occur is a "regret" of profits forgone (given up)—regret referring to the amount of money that could have been made had a different strategy been used. Managers calculate regret by subtracting all possible payoffs in each category from the maximum possible payoff for each given—in this case, for each competitive action. For our Visa manager, the highest payoff, given that American Express engages in CA1, CA2, or CA3, is $24 million, $21 million, or $28 million, respectively (the highest number in each column). Subtracting the payoffs in Exhibit QM–1 from these figures produces the results in Exhibit QM–2.

The maximum regrets are S1 = $17 million; S2 = $15 million; S3 = $13 million; and S4 = $7 million. The minimax choice minimizes the maximum regret, so our Visa manager would choose S4. By making this choice, he'll never have a regret of profits forgone of more than $7 million. This result contrasts, for example, with a regret of $15 million had he chosen S2 and American Express had taken CA1.

Decision Trees

Decision trees are a useful way to analyze hiring, marketing, investment, equipment purchases, pricing, and similar decisions that involve a progression of decisions. They're called decision trees because, when diagrammed, they look a lot like a tree with branches. Typical decision trees encompass expected value analysis by assigning probabilities to each possible outcome and calculating payoffs for each decision path.

Exhibit QM–3 illustrates a decision facing Becky Harrington, the Midwestern region site selection supervisor for Barry's Brews. Becky supervises a small group of specialists who analyze potential locations and make store site recommendations to the Midwestern region's director. The lease on the company's store in Winter Park, Florida, is expiring, and the property owner has decided not to renew it. Becky and her group have to make a relocation recommendation to the regional director. Becky's group has identified an excellent site in a nearby shopping mall in Orlando. The mall owner has offered her two comparable locations: one with 12,000 square feet (the same as she has now) and the other a larger, 20,000-square-foot space. Becky's initial decision concerns whether to recommend renting the larger or smaller location. If she chooses the larger space and the economy is strong, she estimates the store will make a $320,000 profit. However, if the economy is poor, the high operating costs of the larger store will mean that the profit will be only $50,000. With the smaller store, she estimates the profit at $240,000 with a good economy and $130,000 with a poor one.

decision trees

A diagram used to analyze a progression of decisions. When diagrammed, a decision tree looks like a tree with branches.

Exhibit QM–3

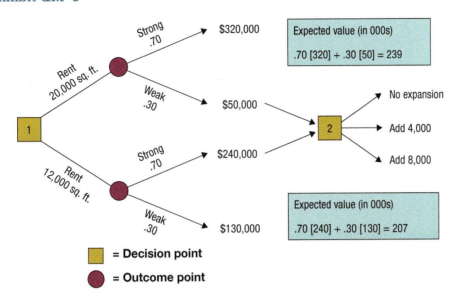

As you can see from Exhibit QM–3, the expected value for the larger store is $239,000 [(.70 × 320) + (.30 × 50)]. The expected value for the smaller store is $207,000 [(.70 × 240) + (.30 × 130)]. Given these projections, Becky is planning to recommend the rental of the larger store space. What if Becky wants to consider the implications of initially renting the smaller space and then expanding if the economy picks up? She can extend the decision tree to include this second decision point. She has calculated three options: no expansion, adding 4,000 square feet, and adding 8,000 square feet. Following the approach used for Decision Point 1, she could calculate the profit potential by extending the branches on the tree and calculating expected values for the various options.

Break-Even Analysis

How many units of a product must an organization sell in order to break even—that is, to have neither profit nor loss? A manager might want to know the minimum number of units that must be sold to achieve his or her profit objective or whether a current product should continue to be sold or should be dropped from the organization's product line. **Break-even analysis** is a widely used technique for helping managers make profit projections.[2]

Break-even analysis is a simplistic formulation, yet it is valuable to managers because it points out the relationship among revenues, costs, and profits. To compute the break-even point (BE), the manager needs to know the unit price of the product being sold (P), the variable cost per unit (VC), and the total fixed costs (TFC).

An organization breaks even when its total revenue is just enough to equal its total costs. But total cost has two parts: a fixed component and a variable component. Fixed costs are expenses that do not change, regardless of volume, such as insurance premiums and property taxes. Fixed costs, of course, are fixed only in the short term because, in the long run, commitments terminate and are, thus, subject to variation. Variable costs change in proportion to output and include raw materials, labor costs, and energy costs.

The break-even point can be computed graphically or by using the following formula:

$$BE = [TFC/(P - VC)]$$

break-even analysis
A technique for identifying the point at which total revenue is just sufficient to cover total costs

Exhibit QM–4

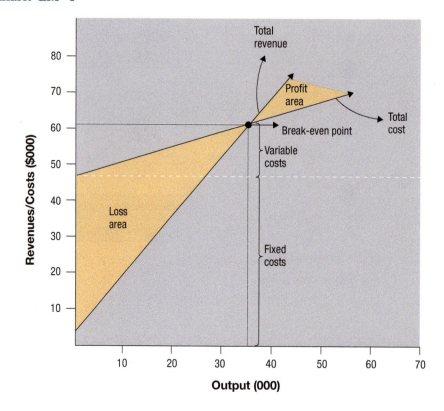

This formula tells us that (1) total revenue will equal total cost when we sell enough units at a price that covers all variable unit costs, and (2) the difference between price and variable costs, when multiplied by the number of units sold, equals the fixed costs.

When is break-even analysis useful? To demonstrate, assume that, at Jose's Bakersfield Espresso, Jose charges $1.75 for an average cup of coffee. If his fixed costs (salary, insurance, etc.) are $47,000 a year and the variable costs for each cup of espresso are $0.40, Jose can compute his break-even point as follows: $47,000/(1.75 − 0.40) = 34,815 (about 670 cups of espresso sold each week), or when annual revenues are approximately $60,926. This same relationship is shown graphically in Exhibit QM–4.

How can break-even analysis serve as a planning and decision-making tool? As a planning tool, break-even analysis could help Jose set his sales objective. For example, he could establish the profit he wants and then work backward to determine what sales level is needed to reach that profit. As a decision-making tool, break-even analysis could also tell Jose how much volume has to increase in order to break even if he is currently operating at a loss, or how much volume he can afford to lose and still break even if he is currently operating profitably. In some cases, such as the management of professional sports franchises, break-even analysis has shown the projected volume of ticket sales required to cover all costs to be so unrealistically high that management's best choice is to sell or close the business.

Ratio Analysis

We know that investors and stock analysts make regular use of an organization's financial documents to assess its worth. These documents can be analyzed by managers as planning and decision-making aids.

Managers often want to examine their organization's balance sheet and income statements to analyze key ratios, that is, to compare two significant figures from the financial statements and express them as a percentage or ratio. This practice allows managers to compare

Exhibit QM–5 Popular Financial Controls

OBJECTIVE	RATIO	CALCULATION	MEANING
Liquidity test	Current ratio	$\dfrac{Current\ assets}{Current\ liabilities}$	Tests the organization's ability to meet short-term obligations
	Acid test	$\dfrac{Current\ assets\ less\ inventories}{Current\ liabilities}$	Tests liquidity more accurately when inventories turn over slowly or are difficult to sell
Leverage test	Debt to assets	$\dfrac{Total\ debt}{Total\ assets}$	The higher the ratio, the more leveraged the organization
	Times interest earned	$\dfrac{Profits\ before\ interest\ and\ taxes}{Total\ interest\ charges}$	Measures how far profits can decline before the organization is unable to meet its interest expenses
Operations test	Inventory turnover	$\dfrac{Cost\ of\ sales}{Inventory}$	The higher the ratio, the more efficiently inventory assets are being used
	Total assets turnover	$\dfrac{Revenues}{Total\ assets}$	The fewer assets used to achieve a given level of sales, the more efficiently management is using the organization's total assets
Profitability	Profit margin on revenues	$\dfrac{Net\ profit\ after\ taxes}{Total\ revenues}$	Identifies the profits that various products are generating
	Return on investment	$\dfrac{Net\ profit\ after\ taxes}{Total\ assets}$	Measures the efficiency of assets to generate profits

current financial performance with that of previous periods and other organizations in the same industry. Some of the more useful ratios evaluate liquidity, leverage, operations, and profitability. These ratios are summarized in Exhibit QM–5.

What are liquidity ratios? *Liquidity* is a measure of the organization's ability to convert assets into cash in order to meet its debt obligations. The most popular liquidity ratios are the current ratio and the acid test ratio.

The *current ratio* is defined as the organization's current assets divided by its current liabilities. Although there is no magic number that is considered safe, the accountant's rule of thumb for the current ratio is 2:1. A significantly higher ratio usually suggests that management is not getting the best return on its assets. A ratio at or below 1:1 indicates potential difficulty in meeting short-term obligations (accounts payable, interest payments, salaries, taxes, etc.).

The *acid test ratio* is the same as the current ratio except that current assets are reduced by the dollar value of inventory held. When inventories turn slowly or are difficult to sell, the acid test ratio may more accurately represent the organization's true liquidity. That is, a high current ratio heavily based on an inventory that is difficult to sell overstates the organization's true liquidity. Accordingly, accountants typically consider an acid test ratio of 1:1 to be reasonable.

Leverage ratios refer to the use of borrowed funds to operate and expand an organization. The advantage of leverage occurs when funds can be used to earn a rate of return well above the cost of those funds. For instance, if management can borrow money at

8 percent and can earn 12 percent on it internally, it makes good sense to borrow, but there are risks to overleveraging. The interest on the debt can be a drain on the organization's cash resources and can, in extreme cases, drive an organization into bankruptcy. The objective, therefore, is to use debt wisely. Leverage ratios such as *debt to assets ratio* (computed by dividing total debt by total assets) or the *times interest earned ratio* (computed as profits before interest and taxes divided by total interest charges) can help managers control debt levels.

Operating ratios describe how efficiently management is using the organization's resources. The most popular operating ratios are inventory turnover and total assets turnover. The *inventory turnover ratio* is defined as revenue divided by inventory. The higher the ratio, the more efficiently inventory assets are being used. Revenue divided by total assets represents an organization's *total assets turnover ratio*. It measures the level of assets needed to generate the organization's revenue. The fewer the assets used to achieve a given level of revenue, the more efficiently management is using the organization's total assets.

Profit-making organizations want to measure their effectiveness and efficiency. Profitability ratios serve such a purpose. The better known of these ratios are profit margin on revenues and return on investment.

Managers of organizations that have a variety of products want to put their efforts into those products that are most profitable. The *profit margin on revenues ratio*, computed as net profit after taxes divided by total revenues, is a measure of profits per dollar revenues.

One of the most widely used measures of a business firm's profitability is the *return on investment ratio*. It's calculated by dividing net profits by total assets. This percentage recognizes that absolute profits must be placed in the context of assets required to generate those profits.

Linear Programming

Matt Free owns a software development company. One product line involves designing and producing software that detects and removes viruses. The software comes in two formats: Windows and Mac versions. He can sell all of these products that he can produce, which is his dilemma. The two formats go through the same production departments. How many of each type should he make to maximize his profits?

A close look at Free's operation tells us he can use a mathematical technique called **linear programming** to solve his resource allocation dilemma. As we will show, linear programming is applicable to his problem, but it cannot be applied to all resource allocation situations. Besides requiring limited resources and the objective of optimization, it requires that there be alternative ways of combining resources to produce a number of output mixes. A linear relationship between variables is also necessary, which means that a change in one variable will be accompanied by an exactly proportional change in the other. For Free's business, this condition would be met if it took exactly twice the time to produce two diskettes—irrespective of format—as it took to produce one.

Many different types of problems can be solved with linear programming. Selecting transportation routes that minimize shipping costs, allocating a limited advertising budget among various product brands, making the optimum assignment of personnel among projects, and determining how much of each product to make with a limited number of resources are just a few. To give you some idea of how linear programming is useful, let's return to Free's situation. Fortunately, his problem is relatively simple, so we can solve it rather quickly. For complex linear programming problems, computer software has been designed specifically to help develop solutions.

First, we need to establish some facts about the business. He has computed the profit margins to be $18 for the Windows format and $24 for the Mac. He can, therefore, express his objective function as maximum profit = $18R + $24S, where R is the number of Windows-based CDs produced and S is the number of Mac CDs. In addition, he knows how long it takes to produce each format and the monthly production capacity for virus software: 2,400 hours

linear programming
A mathematical technique that solves resource allocation problems

Exhibit QM–6   Production Data for Virus Software

	NUMBER OF HOURS REQUIRED PER UNIT		
DEPARTMENT	**WINDOWS VERSION**	**MAC VERSION**	**MONTHLY PRODUCT CAPACITY (hours)**
Design	4	6	2,400
Manufacture	2.0	2.0	900
Profit per unit	$18	$24	

in design and 900 hours in production (see Exhibit QM–6). The production capacity numbers act as constraints on his overall capacity. Now Free can establish his constraint equations:

$$4R + 6S < 2,400$$
$$2R + 2S < 900$$

Of course, because a software format cannot be produced in a volume less than zero, Matt can also state that $R > 0$ and $S > 0$. He has graphed his solution as shown in Exhibit QM–7. The beige shaded area represents the options that do not exceed the capacity of either department. What does the graph mean? We know that total design capacity is 2,400 hours. So if Matt decides to design only the Windows format, the maximum number he can produce is 600 (2,400 hours ÷ 4 hours of design for each Windows version). If he decides to produce all Mac versions, the maximum he can produce is 400 (2,400 hours ÷ 6 hours of design for Mac). This design constraint is shown in Exhibit QM–7 as line BC. The other constraint Matt faces is that of production. The maximum of either format he can produce is 450, because each takes two hours to copy, verify, and package. This production constraint is shown in the exhibit as line DE.

Free's optimal resource allocation will be defined at one of the corners of this feasibility region (area ACFD). Point F provides the maximum profits within the constraints stated. At point A, profits would be zero because neither virus software version is being produced. At points C and D, profits would be $9,600 (400 units @ $24) and $8,100 (450 units @ $18), respectively. At point F profits would be $9,900 (150 Windows units @ $18 + 300 Mac units @ $24).[3]

Exhibit QM–7

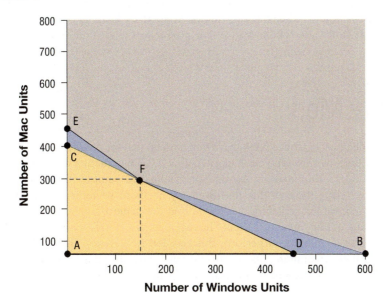

Queuing Theory

You are a supervisor for a branch of Bank of America outside of Cleveland, Ohio. One of the decisions you have to make is how many of the six teller stations to keep open at any given time. **Queuing theory**, or what is frequently referred to as waiting line theory, could help you decide.

A decision that involves balancing the cost of having a waiting line against the cost of service to maintain that line can be made more easily with queuing theory. These types of common situations include determining how many gas pumps are needed at gas stations, tellers at bank windows, toll takers at toll booths, or check-in lines at airline ticket counters. In each situation, management wants to minimize cost by having as few stations open as possible yet not so few as to test the patience of customers. In our teller example, on certain days (such as the first of every month and Fridays) you could open all six windows and keep waiting time to a minimum, or you could open only one, minimize staffing costs, and risk a riot.

The mathematics underlying queuing theory is beyond the scope of this book, but you can see how the theory works in our simple example. You have six tellers working for you, but you want to know whether you can get by with only one window open during an average morning. You consider 12 minutes to be the longest you would expect any customer to wait patiently in line. If it takes 4 minutes, on average, to serve each customer, the line should not be permitted to get longer than three deep (12 minutes ÷ 4 minutes per customer = 3 customers). If you know from past experience that, during the morning, people arrive at the average rate of two per minute, you can calculate the probability (P) of customers waiting in line as follows:

$$P_n = \left[1 - \left(\frac{\text{Arrival rate}}{\text{Service rate}} \right) \right] \times \left[\frac{\text{Arrival rate}}{\text{Service rate}} \right]^n$$

where $n = 3$ customers, arrival rate = 2 per minute, and service rate = 4 minutes per customer.

Putting these numbers into the foregoing formula generates the following:

$$P_n = [1 - 2/4] \times [2/4]^3 = (1/2) \times (8/64) = (8/128) = 0.0625$$

What does a P of 0.0625 mean? It tells you that the likelihood of having more than three customers in line during the average morning is 1 chance in 16. Are you willing to live with four or more customers in line 6 percent of the time? If so, keeping one teller window open will be enough. If not, you will have to assign more tellers to staff more windows.

Economic Order Quantity Model

When you order checks from a bank, have you noticed that the reorder form is placed about two-thirds of the way through your supply of checks? This practice is a simple example of a **fixed-point reordering system**. At some preestablished point in the process, the system is designed to "flag" the fact that the inventory needs to be replenished. The objective is to minimize inventory carrying costs while at the same time limiting the probability of *stocking out* of the inventory item. In recent years, retail stores have increasingly been using their computers to perform this reordering activity. Their cash registers are connected to their computers, and each sale automatically adjusts the store's inventory record. When the inventory of an item hits the critical point, the computer tells management to reorder.

queuing theory
Also known as waiting line theory, it is a way of balancing the cost of having a waiting line versus the cost of maintaining the line. Management wants to have as few stations open as possible to minimize costs without testing the patience of its customers.

fixed-point reordering system
A method for a system to "flag" the need to reorder inventory at some preestablished point in the process

Exhibit QM–8

One of the best-known techniques for mathematically deriving the optimum quantity for a purchase order is the **economic order quantity (EOQ)** model (see Exhibit QM–8). The EOQ model seeks to balance four costs involved in ordering and carrying inventory: the purchase costs (purchase price plus delivery charges less discounts); the ordering costs (paperwork, follow-up, inspection when the item arrives, and other processing costs); carrying costs (money tied up in inventory, storage, insurance, taxes, etc.); and stock-out costs (profits forgone from orders lost, the cost of reestablishing goodwill, and additional expenses incurred to expedite late shipments). When these four costs are known, the model identifies the optimal order size for each purchase.

The objective of the economic order quantity (EOQ) model is to minimize the total costs associated with the carrying and ordering costs. As the amount ordered gets larger, average inventory increases and so do carrying costs. For example, if annual demand for an inventory item is 26,000 units, and a firm orders 500 each time, the firm will place 52 [26,000/500] orders per year. This order frequency gives the organization an average inventory of 250 [500/2] units. If the order quantity is increased to 2,000 units, fewer orders (13) [26,000/2,000] will be placed. However, average inventory on hand will increase to 1,000 [2,000/2] units. Thus, as holding costs go up, ordering costs go down, and vice versa. The optimum economic order quantity is reached at the lowest point on the total cost curve. That's the point at which ordering costs equal carrying costs—or the economic order quantity (see point Q in Exhibit QM–8).

To compute this optimal order quantity, you need the following data: forecasted demand for the item during the period (D); the cost of placing each order (OC); the value or purchase price of the item (V); and the carrying cost (expressed as a percentage) of maintaining the total inventory (CC). Given these data, the formula for EOQ is as follows:

$$EOQ = \sqrt{\frac{2 \times D \times OC}{V \times CC}}$$

economic order quantity (EOQ)
A model that seeks to balance the costs involved in ordering and carrying inventory, thus minimizing total costs associated with carrying and ordering costs

Let's work an example of determining the EOQ. Take, for example, Barnes Electronics, a retailer of high-quality sound and video equipment. The owner, Sam Barnes, wishes to determine the company's economic order quantities of high-quality sound and video equipment. The item in question is a Sony compact voice recorder. Barnes forecasts sales of 4,000 units a year. He believes that the cost for the sound system should be $50. Estimated costs of placing an order for these systems are $35 per order and annual insurance, taxes, and other carrying costs at 20 percent of the recorder's value. Using the EOQ formula, and the preceding information, he can calculate the EOQ as follows:

$$EOQ = \sqrt{\frac{2 \times 4{,}000 \times 35}{50 \times .20}}$$

$$EOQ = \sqrt{28{,}000}$$

$$EOQ = 167.33 \quad \text{or} \quad 168 \text{ units}$$

The inventory model suggests that it's most economical to order in quantities or lots of approximately 168 recorders. Stated differently, Barnes should order about 24 [4,000/168] times a year. However, what would happen if the supplier offers Barnes a 5 percent discount on purchases if he buys in minimum quantities of 250 units? Should he now purchase in quantities of 168 or 250? Without the discount, and ordering 168 each time, the annual costs for these recorders would be as follows:

With the 5 percent discount for ordering 250 units, the item cost [$50 × ($50 × 0.05)] would be $47.5.

Purchase cost:	$50 × $4,000	= $200,000
Carrying cost (average number of inventory units times value of item times percentage):	168/2 × $50 × 0.2 =	840
Ordering costs (number of orders times cost to place order):	24 × $35 =	840
Total cost:		= $201,680

The annual inventory costs would be as follows:

Purchase cost:	$47.50 × $4,000	= $190,000.00
Carrying cost:	250/2 × $47.50 × 0.2 =	1,187.50
Ordering cost:	16 × $35 =	560.00
Total cost:		= $191,747.50

These calculations suggest to Barnes that he should take advantage of the 5 percent discount. Even though he now has to stock larger quantities, the annual savings amounts to nearly $10,000. A word of caution, however, needs to be added. The EOQ model assumes that demand and lead times are known and constant. If these conditions can't be met, the model shouldn't be used. For example, it generally shouldn't be used for manufactured component inventory because the components are taken out of stock all at once, in lumps, or odd lots, rather than at a constant rate. Does this caveat mean that the EOQ model is useless when demand is variable? No. The model can still be of some use in demonstrating trade-offs in costs and the need to control lot sizes. However, more sophisticated lot sizing models are available for handling demand and special situations. The mathematics for EOQ, like the mathematics for queuing theory, go far beyond the scope of this text.

Endnotes

1. Readers are encouraged to see B. Render, R. M. Stair, and M. E. Hanna, *Quantitative Analysis for Management*, 9th ed. (Upper Saddle River, NJ: Prentice Hall, 2005).

2. J. Schmid, "Getting to Breakeven," *Catalog Age*, November 2001, pp. 89–90.

3. We want to acknowledge and thank Professor Jeff Storm of Virginia Western Community College for his assistance in this example.

Foundations of Planning

5

Andresr/Shutterstock

Management
DEBUNKED?
Myth

People say that the future is unpredictable. No matter how well you plan, there's always the unexpected. For managers it might be a sudden recession, a new and innovative product from a competitor, the loss of a key customer, the loss of a key employee, or the breakdown of a long-established business model This logic has led many to conclude that planning is a waste of time. Well, it's not. Flexible planning that includes multiple scenarios can prepare managers for a variety of situations, eliminating some of the unpredictability.

AS we learned in Chapter 1, organizations have a purpose, people, and a structure to support and enable those people in carrying out that purpose. And in those organizations, managers must develop goals, plans, and strategies for how best to achieve that purpose. However, sometimes after evaluating the outcomes of those plans and strategies, managers have to change direction as conditions change. This chapter presents the basics of planning. You'll learn what planning is, how managers use strategic management, and how they set goals and establish plans. Finally, we'll look at some of the contemporary planning issues managers face. ●

Learning Outcomes

What Is Planning and Why Do Managers Need to Plan?

5-1 Discuss the nature and purposes of planning.

All **managers plan.**

Planning is often called the primary management function because it establishes the basis for all the other things managers do as they organize, lead, and control. What is meant by the term *planning?* As we said in Chapter 1, planning involves defining the organization's objectives or goals, establishing an overall strategy for achieving those goals, and developing a comprehensive hierarchy of plans to integrate and coordinate activities. It's concerned with ends (*what* is to be done) as well as with means (*how* it's to be done).

Planning can be further defined in terms of whether it's *formal* or *informal*. All managers plan, even if it's only informally. In informal planning, very little, if anything, is written down. What is to be accomplished is in the heads of one or a few people. Furthermore, the organization's goals are rarely verbalized. Informal planning generally describes the planning that takes place in many smaller businesses. The owner-manager has an idea of where he or she wants to go and how he or she expects to get there. The planning is general and lacks continuity. Of course, you'll see informal planning in some large organizations, while some small businesses will have sophisticated formal plans.

When we use the term *planning* in this book, we're referring to formal planning. Formal planning means (1) defining specific goals covering a specific time period, (2) writing down these goals and making them available to organization members, and (3) using these goals to develop specific plans that clearly define the path the organization will take to get from where it is to where it wants to be.

Why Should Managers Formally Plan?

How does McDonald's—with over 35,000 restaurants in approximately 120 countries serving over 68 million customers every day—do what it does? The key is its Plan to Win, which is built on three components: operational excellence, being the leader in marketing, and continual product innovation. McDonald's managers—from corporate to individual stores—know that planning is vital to the company's continued success. Now, as the company struggles with declining global sales, that plan takes on added importance for managers.

Managers should plan for at least four reasons. (See Exhibit 5–1.) First, planning *establishes coordinated effort*. It gives direction to managers and nonmanagerial employees. When all organizational members understand where the organization is going and what they must contribute to reach the goals, they can begin to coordinate their activities, thus fostering teamwork and cooperation. On the other hand, not planning can cause organizational members or work units to work against one another and keep the organization from moving efficiently toward its goals.

Second, planning *reduces uncertainty* by forcing managers to look ahead, anticipate change, consider the impact of change, and develop appropriate responses. It also clarifies the consequences of the actions managers might take in response to change. Planning, then, is precisely what managers need in a changing environment.

Third, planning *reduces overlapping and wasteful activities*. Coordinating efforts and responsibilities before the fact is likely to uncover waste and redundancy. Furthermore, when means and ends are clear, inefficiencies become obvious.

Finally, planning *establishes the goals or standards* that facilitate control. If organizational members aren't sure what they're working towards, how can they assess whether they've achieved it? When managers plan, they develop goals and plans. When they control, they see whether the plans have been carried out and the goals met. (We'll discuss controlling in depth in Chapter 14.) If significant deviations are identified, corrective action can be taken. Without planning, there are no goals against which to measure or evaluate work efforts.

Exhibit 5–1 Reasons for Planning

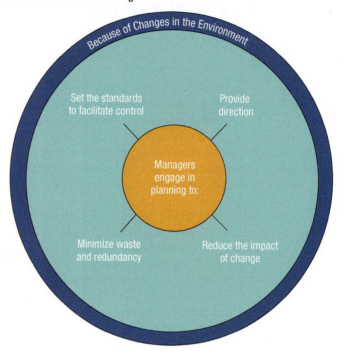

What Are Some Criticisms of Formal Planning and How Should Managers Respond?

It makes sense for an organization to establish goals and direction, but critics have challenged some of the basic assumptions of planning.[1]

Criticism: *Planning may create rigidity.* Formal planning efforts can lock an organization into specific goals to be achieved within specific timetables. Such goals may have been set under the assumption that the environment wouldn't change. Forcing a course of action when the environment is random and unpredictable can be a recipe for disaster.

Manager's Response: Managers need to remain flexible and not be tied to a course of action simply because it's the plan.

Criticism: *Formal plans can't replace intuition and creativity.* Successful organizations are typically the result of someone's vision, but these visions have a tendency to become formalized as they evolve. If formal planning efforts reduce the vision to a programmed routine, that too can lead to disaster.

Manager's Response: Planning should enhance and support intuition and creativity, not replace it.

Criticism: *Planning focuses managers' attention on today's competition, not on tomorrow's survival.* Formal planning, especially strategic planning (which we'll discuss shortly), has a tendency to focus on how to best capitalize on existing business opportunities within the industry. Managers may not look at ways to re-create or reinvent the industry.

Manager's Response: When managers plan, they should be open to forging into uncharted waters if there are untapped opportunities.

Criticism: *Formal planning reinforces success, which may lead to failure.* The American tradition has been that success breeds success. After all, if it's not broken, don't fix it. Right? Well maybe not! Success may, in fact, breed failure in an uncertain environment. It's hard to change or discard successful plans—to leave the comfort of what works for the uncertainty (and anxiety) of the unknown.

Manager's Response: Managers may need to face that unknown and be open to doing things in new ways to be even more successful.

Does Formal Planning Improve Organizational Performance?

DOES it PAY to PLAN?

Does it pay to plan? Or have the critics of planning won the debate? Let's look at the evidence.

Contrary to what the critics of planning say, the evidence generally *supports* the position that organizations should have formal plans. Although most studies that have looked at the relationship between planning and performance have shown generally positive relationships, we can't say that organizations that formally plan always outperform those that don't.[2] But what can we conclude?

- *Formal planning* generally means higher profits, higher return on assets, and other positive financial results.
- The *quality of the planning process* and the *appropriate implementation of the plan* probably contribute more to high performance than does the extent of planning.
- In those organizations where formal planning did not lead to higher performance, the *environment*—for instance, governmental regulations, unforeseen economic challenges, and so forth—was often to blame. Why? Because managers have fewer viable alternatives.

One important aspect of an organization's formal planning is strategic planning, which managers do as part of the strategic management process.

What Do Managers Need To Know About Strategic Management?

5-2 Explain what managers do in the strategic management process.

- The Chicago Cubs have put together a new strategic plan that managers hope will help the team achieve success after many decades of struggling.[3]
- IBM reached a deal with The Weather Company to exploit opportunities for providing and distributing weather data. This type of data partnership is part of IBM's long-term strategy.[4]
- After a three-year freeze on new plant construction, Toyota announced that it would spend over $1 billion to build two new car plants, one in Mexico and one in China.[5]
- For its 20th anniversary, ESPN.com announced a makeover of its highly popular sports Web site and mobile apps. ESPN.com is the most visited sports site, with a record 126.5 million people globally logging on the site in early 2015.[6]
- Taco Bell has fired another volley in its breakfast war against Mickey D's (McDonald's): the Biscuit Taco. It tastes like a biscuit but is shaped like a taco.[7]
- Mercedes-Benz announced plans for its first "luxury" pick-up. Executives said the vehicle is expected to contribute to the company's global growth targets.[8]

These are just a few of the business news stories from a single week, and each one is about a company's strategies. And yes…strategic management is very much a part of what managers do.

What Is Strategic Management?

Strategic management is what managers do to develop an organization's strategies. What are an organization's **strategies**? They're the plans for how the organization will do what it's in business to do, how it will compete successfully, and how it will attract and satisfy its customers in order to achieve its goals.

strategic management
What managers do to develop an organization's strategies

strategies
Plans for how the organization will do what it's in business to do, how it will compete successfully, and how it will attract its customers in order to achieve its goals

Zhang Xin, co-founder and CEO of SOHO China, poses in front of skyscrapers the firm built in Beijing. Xin and her husband started SOHO with a narrowly focused and highly successful strategy of developing commercial real estate in prime locations in Beijing and Shanghai that features architecture reflecting the spirit of a changing modern China.

Why Is Strategic Management Important?

Unlike many other mall-based clothing chains experiencing disastrous sales declines, retailer The Buckle Inc. suffered from weak sales only during the last stages of the most recent economic downturn. And being smart about strategies, it didn't take long for Buckle to regain its footing. One important element was its location strategy. Only a few of its 450 stores were located in states that suffered the worst from the recession. Another part of its strategy was offering customer perks such as custom pants fittings and free hemming on its jeans. Focusing on customer service enhancements like this helped differentiate The Buckle in an overly crowded teen clothing market.[9] These managers obviously understood why strategic management is important!

Why *is* strategic management so important? *One reason is that it can make a difference in how well an organization performs.* Why do some businesses succeed and others fail, even when faced with the same environmental conditions? Research has found a generally positive relationship between strategic planning and performance.[10] Those companies that strategically plan appear to have better financial results than those organizations that don't.

Another reason it's important has to do with the fact that *managers in organizations of all types and sizes face continually changing situations* (recall our discussion in Chapter 2). They cope with this uncertainty by using the strategic management process to examine relevant factors in planning future actions.

Finally, strategic management is important because *organizations are complex and diverse and each part needs to work together to achieve the organization's goals.* Strategic management helps do this. For example, with more than 2.2 million employees worldwide working in various departments, functional areas, and stores, Walmart uses strategic management to help coordinate and focus employees' efforts on what's important.

It's important to note that *strategic management isn't just for business organizations.* Even organizations such as government agencies, hospitals, educational institutions, and social agencies need it. For example, the skyrocketing costs of a college education, competition from for-profit companies offering alternative educational environments, state budgets being slashed because of declining revenues, and cutbacks in federal aid for students and research have led many university administrators to assess their colleges' aspirations and identify a market niche in which they can survive and prosper.

✪ Watch It 1!

If your professor has assigned this, go to the Assignments section of **mymanagementlab.com** to complete the video exercise titled *Rudi's Bakery: Strategic Management*.

What Are the Steps in the Strategic Management Process?

The **strategic management process** (see Exhibit 5–2) is a six-step process that encompasses strategy planning, implementation, and evaluation. The first four steps describe the planning that must take place, but implementation and evaluation are just as important! Even the best strategies can fail if managers don't implement or evaluate them properly.

STEP 1: Identifying the organization's current mission, goals, and strategies. Every organization needs a **mission**—a statement of its purpose. Defining the mission forces managers to identify what it's in business to do. For instance, the mission of Avon is "To be the company that best understands and satisfies the product, service, and self-fulfillment needs of women on a global level."[11] The mission of the National Heart Foundation of Australia is to "reduce suffering and death from

strategic management process
A six-step process that encompasses strategy planning, implementation, and evaluation

mission
A statement of an organization's purpose

Ton Koene/Newscom

Exhibit 5-2 The Strategic Management Process

heart, stroke, and blood vessel disease in Australia." These statements provide clues to what these organizations see as their purpose. What should a mission statement include? Exhibit 5–3 describes some typical components.

✪ Write It 1!

If your professor has assigned this, go to the Assignments section of **mymanagementlab.com** and complete *MGMT 11: Mission Statement*.

It's also important for managers to identify current goals and strategies. Why? So managers have a basis for assessing whether they need to be changed.

STEP 2: Doing an external analysis. We discussed the external environment in Chapter 2. Analyzing that environment is a critical step in the strategic management process. Managers do an external analysis so they know, for instance, what the competition is doing, what pending legislation might affect the organization, or what the labor supply is like in locations where it operates. In an external analysis, managers should examine all components of the environment (economic, demographic, political/legal, sociocultural, technological, and global) to see the trends and changes.

Once they've analyzed the environment, managers need to pinpoint opportunities that the organization can exploit and threats that it must counteract or buffer

Exhibit 5-3 Components of a Mission Statement

Customers:	Who are the firm's customers?
Markets:	Where does the firm compete geographically?
Concern for survival, growth, and profitability:	Is the firm committed to growth and financial stability?
Philosophy:	What are the firm's basic beliefs, values, and ethical priorities?
Concern for public image:	How responsive is the firm to societal and environmental concerns?
Products or services:	What are the firm's major products or services?
Technology:	Is the firm technologically current?
Self-concept:	What are the firm's major competitive advantage and core competencies?
Concern for employees:	Are employees a valuable asset of the firm?

against. **Opportunities** are positive trends in the external environment; **threats** are negative trends.

STEP 3: Doing an internal analysis. Now we move to the internal analysis, which provides important information about an organization's specific resources and capabilities. An organization's **resources** are its assets—financial, physical, human, and intangible—that it uses to develop, manufacture, and deliver products to its customers. They're "what" the organization has. On the other hand, its **capabilities** are the skills and abilities needed to do the work activities in its business—"how" it does its work. The major value-creating capabilities of the organization are known as its **core competencies**.[12] Both resources and core competencies determine the organization's competitive weapons.

After completing an internal analysis, managers should be able to identify organizational strengths and weaknesses. Any activities the organization does well or any unique resources that it has are called **strengths**. **Weaknesses** are activities the organization doesn't do well or resources it needs but doesn't possess.

The combined external and internal analyses are called the **SWOT analysis** because it's an analysis of the organization's *s*trengths, *w*eaknesses, *o*pportunities, and *t*hreats. After completing the SWOT analysis, managers are ready to formulate appropriate strategies—that is, strategies that (1) exploit an organization's strengths and external opportunities, (2) buffer or protect the organization from external threats, or (3) correct critical weaknesses.

> ✪ **Write It 2!**
> If your professor has assigned this, go to the Assignments section of **mymanagementlab.com** to complete *MKTG 2: SWOT Analysis*.

STEP 4: Formulating strategies. As managers formulate strategies, they should consider the realities of the external environment and their available resources and capabilities and design strategies that will help an organization achieve its goals. Managers typically formulate three main types of strategies: corporate, business, and functional. We'll describe each shortly.

STEP 5: Implementing strategies. Once strategies are formulated, they must be implemented. No matter how effectively an organization has planned its strategies, performance will suffer if the strategies aren't implemented properly.

STEP 6: Evaluating results. The final step in the strategic management process is evaluating results. How effective have the strategies been at helping the organization reach its goals? What adjustments are necessary: Do assets need to be acquired or sold? Does the organization need to be reorganized? and so forth.

> ✪ **Write It 3!**
> If your professor has assigned this, go to the Assignments section of **mymanagementlab.com** and complete *MGMT 7: Planning (Business Plan Research)*.

What Strategic Weapons Do Managers Have?

ESPN Digital Media gets some 75.7 million unique users a month on its digital media platforms. Just think of that—75.7 million! That's almost nine times the population of New York City. And its popular online platforms are just one component of ESPN's many businesses. Company president John Skipper "runs one of the most successful and envied franchises in entertainment" and obviously understands how to successfully manage its various strategies in today's environment.[13]

In today's intensely competitive and chaotic marketplace, organizations are looking for whatever "weapons" they can use to do what they're in business to do and to achieve their goals. We think *six strategic "weapons" are important in today's environment*: ❶ customer service,

opportunities
Positive trends in the external environment

threats
Negative trends in the external environment

resources
An organization's assets that it uses to develop, manufacture, and deliver products to its customers

capabilities
An organization's skills and abilities in doing the work activities needed in its business

core competencies
The major value-creating capabilities of an organization

strengths
Any activities the organization does well or any unique resources that it has

weaknesses
Activities the organization doesn't do well or resources it needs but doesn't possess

SWOT analysis
The combined external and internal analyses

2 employee skills and loyalty, **3** innovation, **4** quality, **5** social media, and **6** big data. We've covered customer service in previous chapters and will discuss employee-related matters in Chapters 7 and 9 through 13. Look for a discussion related to innovation and strategy in this chapter's Technology and the Manager's Job box and in Chapter 8. That leaves the last three—quality, social media, and big data—for us to look at.

benchmarking
The search for the best practices among competitors or noncompetitors that lead to their superior performance

QUALITY AS A STRATEGIC WEAPON. When W. K. Kellogg started manufacturing cornflake cereal in 1906, his goal was to provide customers with a high-quality, nutritious product that was enjoyable to eat. That *emphasis on quality is still important* today. Every Kellogg employee is responsible for maintaining the high quality of its products.

Many organizations use quality practices to build competitive advantage and attract and hold a loyal customer base. If implemented properly, *quality can be a way for an organization to create a sustainable competitive advantage.*[14] And if a business is able to continuously improve the quality and reliability of its products, it may have a competitive advantage that can't be taken away.[15] Incremental improvement is something that becomes an integrated part of an organization's operations and can develop into a considerable advantage.

Benchmark the best!

Managers in such diverse industries as health care, education, and financial services are discovering what manufacturers have long recognized—the benefits of **benchmarking**, which is the search for the best practices among competitors or noncompetitors that lead to their superior performance. The basic idea of benchmarking is that managers can improve quality by analyzing and then copying the methods of the leaders in various fields.

> ✪ **Try It 1!**
> If your professor has assigned this, go to the Assignments section of **mymanagementlab.com** to complete the **Simulation:** *Strategic Management*.

Technology and the Manager's Job
INNOVATIVE IT AND STRATEGY

Very important...as two examples will illustrate! Caesars Entertainment (formerly Harrah's Entertainment) is fanatical about customer service, and for good reason. Company research showed that customers who were satisfied with the service they received at a Harrah's casino increased their gaming expenditures by 10 percent, and those who were extremely satisfied increased their gaming expenditures by 24 percent. It discovered this important customer service–expenditures connection because of its incredibly sophisticated information system. But an organization's IT investment may not always have such a positive payoff, as the next example shows! At Prada's Manhattan flagship store, store designers were hoping for a totally different shopping environment that combined "cutting-edge architecture and twenty-first-century customer service." Or at least that was the strategy. Prada invested almost one-fourth of the new store's budget into IT, including wireless networks linked to an inventory database. As envisioned, sales staff would

How important is innovative IT to a company's strategy?

roam the store armed with PDAs so they could check whether items were in stock. Even the dressing rooms would have touch screens so customers could do the same. But the strategy didn't work as planned. The equipment malfunctioned and the staff was overwhelmed with trying to cope with crowds and equipment that didn't work. It's no wonder the multimillion-dollar investment might not have been the best strategy. When an organization's innovative IT "works," it can be a very powerful strategic tool!

*If your professor has assigned this, go to the Assignments section of **mymanagementlab.com** to complete these discussion questions.*

✪ **TALK ABOUT IT 1:** How should managers ensure that their innovative IT efforts contribute to helping strategies succeed?

✪ **TALK ABOUT IT 2:** How do your IT applications (smartphone organizers and calendars, apps, text messaging, etc.) help you be a better planner in your personal life?

What Strategies Do Managers Use?

Exhibit 5–4 **Organizational Strategies**

Corporate	Multibusiness Corporation		
Competitive	Strategic Business Unit 1	Strategic Business Unit 2	Strategic Business Unit 3
Functional	Research and Development • Manufacturing • Marketing • Human Resources • Finance		

1 Corporate Strategy `Multibusiness Corporation`

Specifies *what businesses* to be in and *what to do with those businesses.*

▶▶▶ **Three main corporate strategies**

1 Growth Strategy. Organization expands the number of markets served or products offered, either through its current business(es) or through new business(es).

WAYS to grow:

- **Concentration**: Growing by focusing on primary line of business and increasing the number of products offered or markets served in this primary business.

- **Vertical integration**: Growing by gaining control of inputs or outputs or both.
  - ■ Backward vertical integration—organization gains control of inputs by becoming its own supplier.
  - ■ Forward vertical integration—organization gains control of outputs by becoming its own distributor.

- **Horizontal integration**: Growing by combining with competitors.

- **Diversification**: Growing by moving into a different industry.
  - ■ Related diversification—different, but related, industries. "Strategic fit."
  - ■ Unrelated diversification—different and unrelated industries. "No strategic fit."

Jojje11/ Fotolia

2 Stability Strategy. Organization continues—often during periods of uncertainty—to do what it is currently doing; to maintain things as they are.

- **Examples:** continuing to serve the same clients by offering the same product or service, maintaining market share, and sustaining current business operations.

The organization **doesn't grow**, but **doesn't fall** behind, either.

③ Renewal Strategy. Organization is in trouble and needs to address declining performance.

- **Retrenchment strategy:** Minor performance problems—need to stabilize operations, revitalize organizational resources and capabilities, and prepare organization to compete once again.
- **Turnaround strategy:** More serious performance problems requiring more drastic action.

    In both renewal strategies, managers can (**1**) **cut costs** and (**2**) **restructure organizational operations,** but actions are more extensive in turnaround strategy.

2 Competitive Strategy

| Strategic Business Unit 1 | Strategic Business Unit 2 | Strategic Business Unit 3 |

How an organization will compete in its business(es).

- A small organization in only one line of business OR a large organization that has not diversified:

    Competitive strategy *describes how it will compete in its primary or main market.*

- Organizations in multiple businesses:

    Each business will have its own competitive strategy.

    - Those single businesses that are independent and formulate their own competitive strategies are often called **strategic business units (SBUs)**.

▶ **Important Role of Competitive Advantage:**

Developing an effective competitive strategy requires understanding **competitive advantage**, which is what sets an organization apart; that is, its distinctive edge, which comes from:

- The *organization's core competencies*—doing something that others cannot do or doing it better than others can do it.
- The *company's resources*—having something that its competitors do not.

▼ **Types of Competitive Strategies:**

Porter's **competitive strategies** framework:[16]

1 Cost leadership strategy	**2** Differentiation strategy	**3** Focus strategy	**4** Stuck in the middle
Having the lowest costs in its industry and aimed at broad market.	Offering unique products that are widely valued by customers and aimed at broad market.	A cost advantage (cost focus) or a differentiation advantage (differentiation focus) in a narrow segment or niche (which can be based on product variety, customer type, distribution channel, or geographical location).	What happens if an organization can't develop a cost or differentiation advantage—bad place to be.
<ul><li>Highly efficient.</li><li>Overhead kept to a minimum.</li><li>Does everything it can to cut costs.</li><li>Product must be perceived as comparable in quality to that offered by rivals or at least acceptable to buyers.</li></ul>	<ul><li>Product differences: exceptionally high quality, extraordinary service, innovative design, technological capability, or an unusually positive brand image.</li></ul>	 Artursfoto/Fotolia	

 Use **strategic management** to get a **sustainable competitive advantage.**

3 Functional STRATEGY

| Research and Development | Manufacturing | Marketing | Human Resources | Finance |

Those strategies used by an organization's various functional departments (marketing, operations, finance/accounting, human resources, and so forth) to support the competitive strategy.

corporate strategy
An organizational strategy that specifies what businesses a company is in or wants to be in and what it wants to do with those businesses

growth strategy
A corporate strategy in which an organization expands the number of markets served or products offered either through its current business(es) or through new business(es)

stability strategy
A corporate strategy in which an organization continues to do what it is currently doing

renewal strategy
A corporate strategy that addresses declining organizational performance

competitive strategy
An organizational strategy for how an organization will compete in its business(es)

strategic business units (SBUs)
An organization's single businesses that are independent and formulate their own competitive strategies

competitive advantage
What sets an organization apart; its distinctive edge

cost leadership strategy
When an organization competes on the basis of having the lowest costs in its industry

differentiation strategy
When an organization competes on the basis of having unique products that are widely valued by customers

---

⭐ **Write It 4!**

If your professor has assigned this, go to the Assignments section of **mymanagementlab.com** to complete *MGMT 13: Strategic Decision Making (Competitive Marketing Strategy)*.

Backstory on **BENCHMARKING**

* *What:* First known benchmarking effort by an American company
* *When:* 1979
* *Who:* Xerox
* *How:* Japanese copier competitors had been traveling around, watching what others were doing and then using that knowledge to aggressively replicate their successes. Xerox's managers couldn't figure out how Japanese manufacturers could sell copiers in the United States for considerably less than Xerox's production costs.
* Xerox's head of manufacturing took a team to Japan to do a detailed study of its competitors' costs and processes. SPOILER ALERT! The team found their Japanese rivals light years ahead of Xerox in efficiency.
* Xerox benchmarked those efficiencies and began its strategic turnaround in the copier market.
* And there you have it, the history behind benchmarking!

Today, many organizations use benchmarking practices. For instance, the American Medical Association developed more than 100 standard performance measures to improve medical care. Nissan benchmarked Walmart's operations in purchasing, transportation, and logistics. And Southwest Airlines studied Indy 500 pit crews, who can change a race car's tire in under 15 seconds, to see how their gate crews could make their gate turnaround times even faster.[17]

SOCIAL MEDIA AS A STRATEGIC WEAPON. When Red Robin Gourmet Burgers launched its Tavern Double burger line, everything about the introduction needed to be absolutely on target. So what did company executives do? They utilized social media.[18] Using an internal social network resembling Facebook, managers in the 460-restaurant chain were taught everything from the recipes to tips on efficiently making the burgers. That same internal network has been a great feedback tool. Company chefs have used tips and suggestions from customer feedback and from store managers to tweak the recipe.

Successful social media strategies should (1) help people—inside and outside the organization—connect; and (2) reduce costs or increase revenue possibilities or both. As managers look at how to strategically use social media, it's important to have goals and a plan. For instance, at global banking firm Wells Fargo & Co., executives realized that social media tools could be used to support and develop their business strategy and looked for ways to do just that.[19] Now it's using several social media tools for a variety of specific needs that align with company goals.

Recognized as an innovator in social media marketing, KLM Airlines gathers employees at Amsterdam's Schiphol airport to form words that give live answers to questions asked by followers on Twitter and Facebook. KLM uses social media as a strategic weapon in achieving its goal of giving customers the best service in the airline industry.

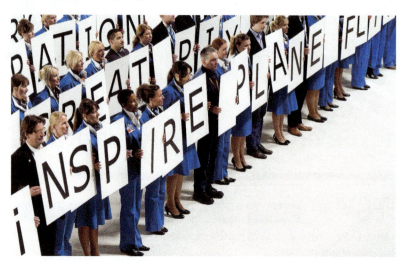

EPA/KOEN VAN WEEL/Landov

> 52 percent of **managers say social media are important/** somewhat important to their business.

It's not just for the social connections that organizations are employing social media strategies. Many are finding that social media tools can boost productivity.[20] For example, many physicians are tapping into online postings and sharing technologies as part of their daily routines. Collaborating with colleagues and experts allows them to improve the speed and efficiency of patient care. At TrunkClub, an online men's clothes shopping service that sends trunks with new clothing items to clients who've requested them, the CEO uses a software tool called Chatter to let the company's personal shoppers know about hot new shipments of shoes or clothes. He says that when he "chats" that information out to the team, he immediately sees the personal shoppers putting the items into customers' "trunks."[21] When used strategically, social media can be a powerful weapon, as can big data!

BIG DATA AS A STRATEGIC WEAPON. Big data can be an effective counterpart to the information exchange generated through social media. All the enormous amounts of data collected about customers, partners, employees, markets, and other quantifiables can be used to respond to the needs of these same stakeholders. With big data, managers can measure and know more about their businesses and "translate that knowledge into improved decision making and performance."[22] Case in point: When Walmart began looking at its enormous database, it noticed that when a hurricane was forecasted, not only did sales of flashlights and batteries increase, but so did sales of Pop-Tarts. Now, when a hurricane is threatening, stores stock Pop-Tarts with other emergency storm supplies at the front entrance. This helps them better serve customers *and* drive sales.[23] By helping a business do what it's in business to do, compete successfully, and attract and satisfy its customers in order to achieve its goals, big data is a critical strategic weapon.

Once managers have the organization's strategies in place, it's time to set goals and develop plans to pursue those strategies.

A Question of Ethics

Do you shop? Well, you might be saying to yourself, that's kind of a stupid question…of course I shop. Well, here's another question: Do you realize the extent to which retail stores are spying on you as you shop?[24] Although most of us "accept" the fact that when we shop online, we're "allowing" the online retailer to install its cookies and to track our every move and click. Now, however, technology is being used more frequently in the physical retail environment. And it's more than cameras watching us. Many retailers are using cell phone tracking technology, personalized advertising, and super spy cams. Why? To track your behavior and to get you (and all those other shoppers) to buy more. Results from a recent survey showed that 80 percent of consumers do not want stores to track their movements via smartphone. And 44 percent said that a tracking program would make them less likely to shop with that store.

*If your professor has assigned this, go to the Assignments section of **mymanagementlab.com** to complete these discussion questions.*

✪ **Talk About It 3:** What ethical dilemmas are involved with the strategy of retail consumer tracking?

✪ **Talk About It 4:** What factors might influence a business's decision to use this strategy? (Think in terms of the various stakeholders who might be affected by this decision.)

How Do Managers Set Goals and Develop Plans?

5-3 Compare and contrast approaches to goal setting and planning.

Planning = Goals + Plans

Planning involves two important aspects: goals and plans. **Goals (objectives)** are desired outcomes or targets. They guide managers' decisions and form the criteria against which work results are measured. **Plans** are documents that outline how goals are going to be met. They usually include resource allocations, budgets, schedules, and other necessary actions to accomplish the goals. As managers plan, they develop both goals and plans.

What Types of Goals Do Organizations Have and How Do They Set Those Goals?

Although it might seem that organizations have a single goal—for businesses, to make a profit, and for not-for-profit organizations, to meet the needs of some constituent group(s)—an organization's success can't be determined by a single goal. In reality, *all organizations have multiple goals.* For instance, businesses may want to increase market share, keep employees motivated, or work toward more environmentally sustainable practices. And a church provides a place for religious practices, but it also assists economically disadvantaged individuals in its community and acts as a social gathering place for church members.

focus strategy
When an organization competes in a narrow segment or niche with either a cost focus or a differentiation focus

functional strategy
Strategy used in an organization's various functional departments to support the competitive strategy

goals (objectives)
Desired outcomes or targets

plans
Documents that outline how goals are going to be met

Amber Miller/Newscom

Pierre-Andre Senizergues, founder and CEO of Sole Technology, set a goal for his company to be the first action sports firm to go carbon neutral by 2020. Shown here planting a tree in honor of his employees, he devised a six-point plan—from reducing water usage to using green production materials—to achieve his goal.

TYPES OF GOALS. Most company goals can be classified as either strategic or financial. Financial goals are related to the financial performance of the organization, while strategic goals are related to all other areas of an organization's performance. For instance, McDonald's financial targets include 3 to 5 percent average annual sales and revenue growth, 6 to 7 percent average annual operating income growth, and returns on invested capital in the high teens.[25] An example of a strategic goal: Nissan's CEO's request for the company's GT-R super sports car: match or beat the performance of Porsche's 911 Turbo.[26] These goals are **stated goals**—official statements of what an organization says, and what it wants its stakeholders to believe, its goals are. However, stated goals—which can be found in an organization's charter, annual report, public relations announcements, or in public statements made by managers—are often conflicting and influenced by what various stakeholders think organizations should do. Such statements can be vague and probably better represent management's public relations skills instead of being meaningful guides to what the organization is actually trying to accomplish. It shouldn't be surprising then to find that an organization's stated goals are often irrelevant to what's actually done.[27]

Stated vs. **Real Goals**

If you want to know an organization's **real goals**—those goals an organization actually pursues—observe what organizational members are doing. *Actions define priorities.* Knowing that real and stated goals may differ is important for recognizing what you might otherwise think are inconsistencies.

SETTING GOALS. As we said earlier, goals provide the direction for all management decisions and actions and form the criterion against which actual accomplishments are measured. Everything organizational members do should be oriented toward achieving goals. These goals can be set either through a process of traditional goal setting or by using management by objectives.

Traditional Goal Setting. In **traditional goal setting**, goals set by top managers flow down through the organization and become subgoals for each organizational area. (See Exhibit 5–5.) This traditional perspective assumes that top managers know what's best because they see the "big picture." And the goals passed down to each succeeding level guide individual employees as they work to achieve those assigned goals. Take a manufacturing business, for example. The president tells the vice president of production what he expects manufacturing costs to be for the coming year and tells the marketing vice president what level he expects sales to reach for the year. These goals are passed to the next organizational level and written to reflect

stated goals
Official statements of what an organization says, and wants its stakeholders to believe, its goals are

real goals
Those goals an organization actually pursues as shown by what the organization's members are doing

traditional goal setting
Goals set by top managers flow down through the organization and become subgoals for each organizational area

Exhibit 5–5 Traditional Goal Setting

"We need to improve the company's performance."

"I want to see a significant improvement in this division's profits."

Top Management's Objective

"Increase profits regardless of the means."

Division Manager's Objective

"Don't worry about quality; just work fast."

Department Manager's Objective

Individual Employee's Objective

the responsibilities of that level, passed to the next level, and so forth. Then, at some later time, performance is evaluated to determine whether the assigned goals have been achieved. Or that's the way it's supposed to happen. But in reality, it doesn't always do so. Turning broad strategic goals into departmental, team, and individual goals can be a difficult and frustrating process.

Another problem with traditional goal setting is that when top managers define the organization's goals in broad terms—such as achieving "sufficient" profits or increasing "market leadership"—these ambiguous goals have to be made more specific as they flow down through the organization. Managers at each level define the goals and apply their own interpretations and biases as they make them more specific. Clarity is often lost as the goals make their way down from the top of the organization to lower levels. But it doesn't have to be that way. For example, at Tijuana-based dj Orthopedics de Mexico, employee teams see the impact of their daily work output on company goals. The company's human resource manager says, "When people get a close connection with the result of their work, when they know every day what they are supposed to do and how they achieved the goals, that makes a strong connection with the company and their job."[28]

When the hierarchy of organizational goals *is* clearly defined, as it is at dj Orthopedics, it forms an integrated network of goals, or a **means-ends chain**. Higher-level goals (or ends) are linked to lower-level goals, which serve as the means for their accomplishment. In other words, the goals achieved at lower levels become the means to reach the goals (ends) at the next level. And the accomplishment of goals at that level becomes the means to achieve the goals (ends) at the next level and on up through the different organizational levels. That's how traditional goal setting is supposed to work.

Management by Objectives. Instead of using traditional goal setting, many organizations use **management by objectives (MBO)**, a process of setting mutually agreed-upon goals and using those goals to evaluate employee performance. If a manager were to use this approach, he or she would sit down with each member of his or her team and set goals and periodically review whether progress was being made toward achieving those goals. MBO programs have four

means-ends chain
An integrated network of goals in which higher-level goals are linked to lower-level goals, which serve as the means for their accomplishment

management by objectives (MBO)
A process of setting mutually agreed-upon goals and using those goals to evaluate employee performance

---

◄◄◄ From the Past to the Present ►►►

All you need to know about MBO!

Management by objectives (MBO) isn't new—it was a popular management approach in the 1960s and 1970s. The concept can be traced back to Peter Drucker, who first popularized the term in his 1954 book *The Practice of Management*.[29] Its appeal lies in its emphasis on converting overall objectives into specific objectives for organizational units and individual members.

How Is MBO Used?

- MBO makes goals practical and operational as they "cascade" down through the organization.

- Overall broad objectives are translated into specific objectives for each succeeding organizational level—division, departmental, and individual.

- Result: a hierarchy that links objectives at one level to those at the next level.

- For each individual employee, MBO provides specific personal performance objectives.

- If all individuals achieve their goals, then the unit's goals will be attained. If all units attain their goals, then the divisional goals will be met until…BOOM…the organization's overall goals are achieved!

Does MBO Work?

- Assessing MBO effectiveness is *not* easy!

- Research on goal-setting gives us some answers:

  + Specific, difficult-to-achieve goals—an important part of MBO—produce a higher level of output than do no goals or generalized goals such as "do your best."

  + Feedback—also an important part of MBO—favorably affects performance because it lets a person know whether his or her level of effort is sufficient or needs to be increased.

  − Participation—also strongly advocated by MBO—has *not* shown any consistent relationship to performance.

ABSOLUTELY CRITICAL TO SUCCESS of MBO program: Top management commitment to the process. When top managers have a high commitment to MBO and are personally involved in its implementation, productivity gains are higher than without that commitment.

*If your professor has assigned this, go to the Assignments section of **mymanagementlab.com** to complete these discussion questions.*

⭐ **Talk About It 5:** Why do you think management commitment is so important to the success of MBO programs?

⭐ **Talk About It 6:** How could you use MBO for your personal goals?

elements: **1** goal specificity, **2** participative decision making, **3** an explicit time period, and **4** performance feedback.[30] Instead of using goals to make sure employees are doing what they're supposed to be doing, MBO uses goals to motivate them as well. The appeal is that *it focuses on employees working to accomplish goals they've had a hand in setting.* (See the From the Past to the Present box for more information on MBO.)

Studies of actual MBO programs have shown that it can increase employee performance and organizational productivity. For example, one review of MBO programs found productivity gains in almost all of them.[31] But is MBO relevant for today's organizations? Yes, if it's viewed as a way of setting goals, because research shows that *goal setting can be an effective tool in motivating employees.*[32]

Characteristics of Well-Written Goals. No matter which approach is used, goals have to be written, and some goals more clearly indicate what the desired outcomes are. Managers should develop well-written goals. Exhibit 5–6 lists the characteristics.[33] With these characteristics in mind, managers are now ready to actually set goals.

Steps in Setting Goals. Managers should follow six steps when setting goals.

1. *Review the organization's mission and employees' key job tasks.* The mission statement provides an overall guide to what's important, and goals should reflect that mission. In addition, it's important to define what you want employees to accomplish as they do their tasks.

2. *Evaluate available resources.* Don't set goals that are impossible to achieve given your available resources. Goals should be challenging, but realistic. After all, if the resources you have to work with won't allow you to achieve a goal no matter how hard you try or how much effort is exerted, you shouldn't set that goal.

3. *Determine the goals individually or with input from others.* Goals reflect desired outcomes and should be congruent with the organizational mission and goals in other organizational areas. These goals should be measurable, specific, and include a time frame for accomplishment.

4. *Make sure goals are well-written and then communicate them to all who need to know.* Writing down and communicating goals forces people to think them through. Written goals become visible evidence of the importance of working toward something.

5. *Build in feedback mechanisms to assess goal progress.* If goals aren't being met, change them as needed.

6. *Link rewards to goal attainment.* Employees want to know "What's in it for me?" Linking rewards to goal achievement will help answer that question.

Once the goals have been established, written down, and communicated, managers are ready to develop plans for pursuing the goals.

What Types of Plans Do Managers Use and How Do They Develop Those Plans?

Managers need plans to help them clarify and specify how goals will be met. Let's look first at the types of plans managers use.

TYPES OF PLANS. The most popular ways to describe plans are in terms of their *breadth* (strategic versus tactical), *time frame* (long term versus short), *specificity* (directional

Exhibit 5–6 Well-Written Goals

- Written in terms of outcomes rather than actions
- Measurable and quantifiable
- Clear as to a time frame
- Challenging yet attainable
- Written down
- Communicated to all necessary organizational members

Source: Robbins, Stephen P., Coulter, Mary, *Management*, 13th Ed., © 2016, p. 222. Reprinted and electronically reproduced by permission of Pearson Education, Inc., New York, NY.

versus specific), and *frequency of use* (single-use versus standing). As Exhibit 5–7 shows, these types of plans aren't independent. That is, strategic plans are usually long term, directional, and single-use. Let's look at each type of plan.

Breadth.   **Strategic plans** are those that apply to an entire organization and encompass the organization's overall goals. **Tactical plans** (sometimes referred to as operational plans) specify the details of how the overall goals are to be achieved. When McDonald's invested in the Redbox kiosk business, it was the result of strategic planning. Deciding when, where, and how to actually operate the business was the result of tactical plans in marketing, logistics, finance, and so forth.

Time Frame.   The number of years used to define short-term and long-term plans has declined considerably due to environmental uncertainty. *Long term* used to mean anything over seven years. Try to imagine what you're likely to be doing in seven years. It seems pretty distant, doesn't it? Now, you can begin to understand how difficult it is for managers to plan that far in the future. Thus, **long-term plans** are now defined as plans with a time frame beyond three years. **Short-term plans** cover one year or less.

Nestlé Japan is using a humanoid robot capable of reading and responding to human emotions to sell its Nescafé coffee machines. This tactical promotional plan devised to encourage consumers to buy products supports Nestlé's strategic plan of improving the company's performance and ensuring its profitable growth.

Specificity.   Intuitively, it would seem that specific plans would be preferable to directional, or loosely guided, plans. **Specific plans** are plans that are clearly defined and leave no room for interpretation. For example, a manager who wants to increase his work unit's output by 8 percent over the next 12 months might establish specific procedures, budget allocations, and work schedules to reach that goal. However, when uncertainty is high and managers must be flexible in order to respond to unexpected changes, they'd likely use **directional plans**, flexible plans that set general guidelines. For example, Sylvia Rhone, president of Motown Records, had a simple goal—to "sign great artists."[34] She could create a specific plan to produce and market 10 albums from new artists this year. Or she might formulate a directional plan to use a network of people around the world to alert her to new and promising talent so she can increase the number of artists she has under contract. Sylvia, and any manager who engages in planning, must keep in mind that you have to weigh the flexibility of directional plans against the clarity you can get from specific plans.

Flexibility ↔ Clarity

Frequency of Use.   Some plans that managers develop are ongoing, while others are used only once. A **single-use plan** is a one-time plan specifically designed to meet the needs of a unique situation. For instance, when Dell began developing a pocket-sized device for getting on the Internet, managers used a single-use plan to guide their decisions. In contrast, **standing plans** are ongoing plans that provide guidance for activities performed repeatedly. For example, when you register for classes for the upcoming semester, you're using a standardized registration plan at your college or university. The dates change, but the process works the same way semester after semester.

Exhibit 5–7 Types of Plans

BREADTH OF USE	TIME FRAME	SPECIFICITY	FREQUENCY OF USE
Strategic	Long term	Directional	Single-use
Tactical	Short term	Specific	Standing

strategic plans
Plans that apply to the entire organization and encompass the organization's overall goals

tactical plans
Plans that specify the details of how the overall goals are to be achieved

long-term plans
Plans with a time frame beyond three years

short-term plans
Plans with a time frame of one year or less

specific plans
Plans that are clearly defined and leave no room for interpretation

directional plans
Plans that are flexible and set general guidelines

single-use plan
A one-time plan specifically designed to meet the needs of a unique situation

standing plans
Plans that are ongoing and provide guidance for activities performed repeatedly

Exhibit 5–8 Planning and Organizational Level

DEVELOPING PLANS.   The process of developing plans is influenced by three contingency factors and by the planning approach followed.

Contingency Factors in Planning.   Three contingency factors affect the choice of plans: (1) organizational level, (2) degree of environmental uncertainty, and (3) length of future commitments.[35]

Exhibit 5–8 shows the relationship between a manager's level in the organization and the type of planning done. For the most part, lower-level managers do operational (or tactical) planning while upper-level managers do strategic planning.

The second contingency factor is environmental uncertainty. When uncertainty is high, plans should be specific, but flexible. Managers must be prepared to change or amend plans as they're implemented. For example, at Continental Airlines (now part of United Airlines), the former CEO and his management team established a specific goal of focusing on what customers wanted most—on-time flights—to help the company become more competitive in the highly uncertain airline industry. Because of that uncertainty, the management team identified a "destination, but not a flight plan," and changed plans as necessary to achieve its goal of on-time service.

The last contingency factor also is related to the time frame of plans. The **commitment concept** says that plans should extend far enough to meet those commitments made when the plans were developed. Planning for too long or too short a time period is inefficient and ineffective. We can see the importance of the commitment concept, for example, with the plans that organizations make to increase their computing capabilities. At the data centers where companies' computers are housed, many have found their "power-hungry computers" generate so much heat that their electric bills have skyrocketed because of the increased need for air conditioning.[36] How does this illustrate the commitment concept? As organizations expand their computing technology, they're "committed" to whatever future expenses are generated by that plan. They have to live with the plan and its consequences.

38 percent of leaders say planning for next
year is a challenge.[37]

Approaches to Planning.   Federal, state, and local government officials are working together on a plan to boost populations of wild salmon in the northwestern United States. Managers in the Global Fleet Graphics division of the 3M Company are developing detailed plans to satisfy increasingly demanding customers and to battle more aggressive competitors. Emilio Azcárraga Jean, chairman, president, and CEO of Grupo Televisa, gets input from many different people before setting company goals and then turns over the planning for achieving the goals to various executives. In each of these situations, planning is done a little differently. *How* an organization plans can best be understood by looking at *who* does the planning.

commitment concept
The idea that plans should extend far enough to meet those commitments made when the plans were developed

In the traditional approach, planning is done entirely by top-level managers who often are assisted by a **formal planning department**, a group of planning specialists whose sole responsibility is to help write the various organizational plans. Under this approach, plans developed by top-level managers flow down through other organizational levels, much like the traditional approach to goal setting. As they flow down through the organization, the plans are tailored to the particular needs of each level. Although this approach makes managerial planning thorough, systematic, and coordinated, all too often the focus is on developing "the plan," a thick binder (or binders) full of meaningless information that's stuck away on a shelf and never used by anyone for guiding or coordinating work efforts.

> **formal planning department**
> A group of planning specialists whose sole responsibility is to help write the various organizational plans

In a survey of managers about formal top-down organizational planning processes, **over 75 percent said that their company's planning approach was unsatisfactory**.[38]

A common complaint was that "plans are documents that you prepare for the corporate planning staff and later forget."[39] Although this traditional top-down approach to planning is used by many organizations, it's effective only if managers understand the importance of creating documents that organizational members actually use, not documents that look impressive but are never used.

Another approach to planning is to involve more organizational members in the process. In this approach, plans aren't handed down from one level to the next, but instead are developed by organizational members at the various levels and in the various work units to meet their specific needs. For instance, at Dell, employees from production, supply management, and channel management meet weekly to make plans based on current product demand and supply. In addition, work teams set their own daily schedules and track their progress against those schedules. If a team falls behind, team members develop "recovery" plans to try to get back on schedule.[40] When organizational members are more actively involved in planning, they see that the plans are more than just something written down on paper. They can actually see that the plans are used in directing and coordinating work.

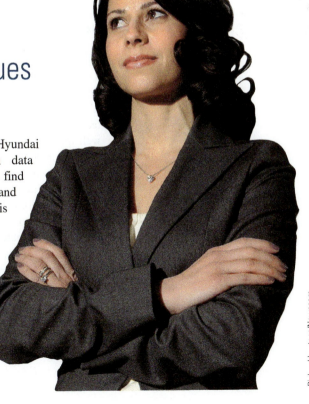

Virginia Poly, founder and CEO of Poly Placements, a Canadian recruiting firm, manages in a dynamic environment where clients continue to use more contingent workers. To succeed, she plans to keep her employees focused on building long-term relationships with customers and serving as consultants rather than transactional salespeople.

What Contemporary Planning Issues Do Managers Face?

5-4 Discuss contemporary issues in planning.

The second floor of the 21-story Hyundai Motor headquarters buzzes with data 24 hours a day. That's where you'd find the company's Global Command and Control Center (GCCC), which is modeled after the CNN newsroom with numerous "computer screens relaying video and data keeping watch on Hyundai operations around the world." Managers get information on parts shipments from suppliers to factories. Cameras watch assembly lines and closely monitor the company's massive Ulsan, Korea, factory looking for competitors' spies and any hints of labor unrest. The GCCC also keeps tabs on the company's R&D activities in Europe, Japan, and North America. Hyundai can identify problems in an instant and react quickly. The company is all about aggressiveness and speed and is representative of how a successful twenty-first-century company approaches planning.[41]

Richard Lautens/Newscom

We conclude this chapter by addressing two contemporary issues in planning. Specifically, we're going to look at planning effectively in dynamic environments and then at how managers can use environmental scanning, especially competitive intelligence.

✪ Try It 2!

If your professor has assigned this, go to the Assignments section of **mymanagementlab.com** to complete the **Simulation: *Planning***.

How Can Managers Plan Effectively in Dynamic Environments?

Dynamic **Environments = Planning** Challenges

As we saw in Chapter 2, the external environment is continually changing. How can managers effectively plan when the external environment is continually changing? We already discussed uncertain environments as one of the contingency factors that affect the types of plans managers develop. Because dynamic environments are more the norm than the exception, let's look at how they can effectively plan in such environments.

In an uncertain environment, *managers should develop plans that are specific, but flexible*. Although this may seem contradictory, it's not. To be useful, plans need some specificity, but the plans should not be set in stone. Managers need to *recognize that planning is an ongoing process*. The plans serve as a road map although the destination may change due to dynamic market conditions. They should be ready to change directions if environmental conditions warrant. This flexibility is particularly important as plans are implemented. Managers need to *stay alert to environmental changes that may impact implementation and respond as needed*. Keep in mind, also, that even when the environment is highly uncertain, it's important to *continue formal planning in order to see any effect on organizational performance*. It's the persistence in planning that contributes to significant performance improvement. Why? It seems that, as with most activities, managers "learn to plan" and the quality of their planning improves when they continue to do it.[42] Finally, *make the organizational hierarchy flatter to effectively plan in dynamic environments*. A flatter hierarchy means lower organizational levels can set goals and develop plans because organizations have little time for goals and plans to flow down from the top. Managers should teach their employees how to set goals and to plan and then trust them to do it. And you need look no further than Bangalore, India, to find a company that effectively understands this. Just a decade ago, Wipro Limited was "an anonymous conglomerate selling cooking oil and personal computers, mostly in India." Today, it's a $6.4 billion-a-year global company with most of its business coming from information-technology services.[43] Accenture, EDS, IBM, and the big U.S. accounting firms know all too well the competitive threat Wipro represents. Not only are Wipro's employees economical, they're knowledgeable and skilled. And they play an important role in the company's planning. Since the information services industry is continually changing, employees are taught to analyze situations and to define the scale and scope of a client's problems in order to offer the best solutions. These employees are the ones on the front line with the clients and it's their responsibility to establish what to do and how to do it. It's an approach that positions Wipro for success no matter how the industry changes.

✪ Watch It 2!

If your professor has assigned this, go to the Assignments section of **mymanagementlab.com** to complete the video exercise titled *CH2MHill: Planning*.

How Can Managers Use Environmental Scanning?

A manager's analysis of the external environment may be improved by **environmental scanning**, which involves screening large amounts of information to detect emerging trends. One of the fastest-growing forms of environmental scanning is **competitive intelligence**, which is accurate information about competitors that allows managers to anticipate competitors' actions rather than merely react to them.[44] It seeks basic information about competitors: Who are they? What are they doing? How will what they're doing affect us?

Many who study competitive intelligence suggest that much of the competitor-related information managers need to make crucial strategic decisions is available and accessible to the public.[45] In other words, competitive intelligence isn't organizational espionage. Advertisements, promotional materials, press releases, reports filed with government agencies, annual reports, want ads, newspaper reports, information on the Internet, and industry studies are readily accessible sources of information. Specific information on an industry and associated organizations is increasingly available through electronic databases. Managers can literally tap into this wealth of competitive information by purchasing access to databases. Attending trade shows and debriefing your own sales staff also can be good sources of information on competitors. In addition, many organizations even regularly buy competitors' products and ask their own employees to evaluate them to learn about new technical innovations.[46]

In a changing global business environment, environmental scanning and obtaining competitive intelligence can be quite complex, especially when information must be gathered from around the world. However, managers could subscribe to news services that review newspapers and magazines from around the globe and provide summaries to client companies.

Managers do need to be careful about the way information, especially competitive intelligence, is gathered to prevent any concerns about whether it's legal or ethical. For instance, Starwood Hotels sued Hilton Hotels alleging that two former employees stole trade secrets and helped Hilton develop a new line of luxury, trendy hotels designed to appeal to a young demographic.[47] The court filing said, "This is the clearest imaginable case of corporate espionage, theft of trade secrets, unfair competition, and computer fraud." Competitive intelligence becomes illegal corporate spying when it involves the theft of proprietary materials or trade secrets by any means. The Economic Espionage Act makes it a crime in the United States to engage in economic espionage or to steal a trade secret.[48] Difficult decisions about competitive intelligence arise because often there's a fine line between what's considered *legal and ethical* and what's considered *legal but unethical*. Although the top manager at one competitive intelligence firm contends that 99.9 percent of intelligence gathering is legal, there's no question that some people or companies will go to any lengths—some unethical—to get information about competitors.[49]

environmental scanning
An analysis of the external environment, which involves screening large amounts of information to detect emerging trends

competitive intelligence
A type of environmental scanning that gives managers accurate information about competitors

MyManagementLab®

Go to **mymanagementlab.com** to complete the problems marked with this icon .

5 Review

CHAPTER SUMMARY

5-1 Discuss the nature and purposes of planning.

As the primary management function, planning establishes the basis for all the other things that managers do. The planning we're concerned with is formal planning; that is, specific goals covering a specific time period are defined and written down and specific plans are developed to make sure those goals are met. There are four reasons why managers should plan: (1) it establishes coordinated efforts; (2) it reduces uncertainty; (3) it reduces overlapping and wasteful activities; and (4) it establishes the goals or standards that are used in controlling work. Although criticisms have been directed at planning, the evidence generally supports the position that organizations benefit from formal planning.

5-2 Explain what managers do in the strategic management process.

Managers develop the organization's strategies in the strategic management process, which is a six-step process encompassing strategy planning, implementation, and evaluation. The six steps are as follows: (1) Identify the organization's current mission, goals, and strategies; (2) do an external analysis; (3) do an internal analysis—steps 2 and 3 together are called SWOT analysis; (4) formulate strategies; (5) implement strategies; and (6) evaluate results. The end result of this process is a set of corporate, competitive, and functional strategies that allow the organization to do what it's in business to do and to achieve its goals. Six strategic weapons are important in today's environment: customer service, employee skills and loyalty, innovation, quality, social media, and big data.

5-3 Compare and contrast approaches to goal setting and planning.

The goals of most companies are classified as either strategic or financial. We can also look at goals as either stated or real. In traditional goal setting, goals set by top managers flow down through the organization and become subgoals for each organizational area. Organizations could also use management by objectives, which is a process of setting mutually agreed-upon goals and using those goals to evaluate employee performance. Plans can be described in terms of their breadth, time frame, specificity, and frequency of use. Plans can be developed by a formal planning department or by involving more organizational members in the process.

5-4 Discuss contemporary issues in planning.

One contemporary planning issue is planning in dynamic environments, which usually means developing plans that are specific but flexible. Also, it's important to continue planning even when the environment is highly uncertain. Finally, because there's little time in a dynamic environment for goals and plans to flow down from the top, lower organizational levels should be allowed to set goals and develop plans. Another contemporary planning issue is using environmental scanning to help do a better analysis of the external environment. One form of environmental scanning, competitive intelligence, can be especially helpful in finding out what competitors are doing.

DISCUSSION QUESTIONS

5-1 Contrast formal with informal planning.

⭐ 5-2 Discuss why planning is beneficial.

5-3 Describe in detail the six-step strategic management process.

⭐ 5-4 What is a SWOT analysis, and why is it important to managers?

5-5 "Organizations that fail to plan are planning to fail." Agree or disagree? Explain your position.

5-6 Under what circumstances do you believe MBO would be most useful? Discuss.

5-7 Describe how managers can plan in today's dynamic environment.

5-8 What types of planning do you do in your personal life? Describe these plans in terms of being (a) strategic or operational, (b) short term or long term, (c) specific or directional, and (d) single-use or standing.

5-9 Do a personal SWOT analysis. Assess your personal strengths and weaknesses (skills, talents,). What are you good at? What are you not so good at? What do you enjoy doing? Not enjoy doing? Then, identify career opportunities and threats by researching job prospects in the industry you're interested in. Look at trends and projections. You might want to check out the information the Bureau of Labor Statistics provides on job prospects. Once you have all this information, write a specific career action plan. Outline five-year career goals and what you need to do to achieve those goals.

5-10 "The concept of competitive advantage is as important for not-for-profit organizations as it is for for-profit organizations." Do you agree or disagree with this statement? Explain, using examples to make your case.

Writing Assignments

5-11 Will planning become more or less important to managers in the future? Why?

5-12 How could the Internet be helpful to managers as they follow the steps in the strategic management process?

Management Skill Builder | **BEING A GOOD GOAL SETTER**

It's been said that if you don't know where you're going, any road will get you there. It has also been said that the shortest distance between two points is a straight line. These two "adages" emphasize the importance of goals. Managers are typically judged on their ability to achieve goals. If individuals or units in the organization lack goals, there can be no direction or unity of effort. So successful managers are good at setting their own goals and helping others set goals.

✪ PERSONAL INVENTORY ASSESSMENT PERSONAL INVENTORY ASSESSMENT

Tolerance of Ambiguity Scale

Managers often have to deal with ambiguous situations, which can make planning very challenging. In this PIA, you'll assess your level of tolerance for ambiguity.

Skill Basics

In addition to your own focus on goals, employees should also have a clear understanding of what they're attempting to accomplish. Managers have the responsibility to help employees with this understanding as they set work goals. You can be more effective at helping employees set goals if you use the following eight suggestions:

• *Identify an employee's key job tasks.* Goal setting begins by defining what it is that you want your employees to accomplish. The best source for this information is each employee's job description.

• *Establish measurable, specific, and challenging goals for each key task.* Identify the level of performance expected of each employee. Specify the target toward which the employee is working.

• *Specify the deadlines for each goal.* Putting deadlines on each goal reduces ambiguity. Deadlines, however, should not be set arbitrarily. Rather, they need to be realistic given the tasks to be completed.

• *Allow the employee to participate actively.* When employees participate in goal setting, they're more likely to accept the goals. However, it must be sincere participation. That is, employees must perceive that you are truly seeking their input, not just going through the motions.

- *Prioritize goals.*   When you give someone more than one goal, it's important to rank the goals in order of importance. The purpose of prioritizing is to encourage the employee to take action and expend effort on each goal in proportion to its importance.

- *Rate goals for difficulty and importance.*   Goal setting should not encourage people to choose easy goals. Instead, goals should be rated for their difficulty and importance. When goals are rated, individuals can be given credit for trying difficult goals, even if they don't fully achieve them.

- *Build in feedback mechanisms to assess goal progress.*   Feedback lets employees know whether their level of effort is sufficient to attain the goal. Feedback should be both self-generated and supervisor-generated. Feedback should also be frequent and recurring.

- *Link rewards to goal attainment.*   It's natural for employees to ask, "What's in it for me?" Linking rewards to the achievement of goals will help answer that question.

Based on E. A. Locke and G. P. Latham, *Goal-Setting: A Motivational Technique That Works!* (Upper Saddle River, NJ: Prentice Hall, 1984); and E. A. Locke and G. P. Latham, "Building a Practically Useful Theory of Goal Setting and Task Motivation," *American Psychologist*, September 2002, 705–17.

Practicing the Skill

Read through this scenario and follow the directions at the end of it:

You worked your way through college while holding down a part-time job bagging groceries at the Food Town supermarket chain. You liked working in the food industry, and when you graduated, you accepted a position with Food Town as a management trainee. Three years have passed and you've gained experience in the grocery store industry and in operating a large supermarket. Several months ago, you received a promotion to store manager at one of the chain's locations. One of the things you've liked about Food Town is that it gives store managers a great deal of autonomy in running their stores. The company provides very general guidelines to its managers. Top management is concerned with the bottom line; for the most part, how you get there is up to you. Now that you're finally a store manager, you want to establish an MBO-type program in your store. You like the idea that everyone should have clear goals to work toward and then be evaluated against those goals.

Your store employs 70 people, although except for the managers, most work only 20 to 30 hours per week. You have six people reporting to you: an assistant manager; a weekend manager; and grocery, produce, meat, and bakery managers. The only highly skilled jobs belong to the butchers, who have strict training and regulatory guidelines. Other less-skilled jobs include cashier, shelf stocker, maintenance worker, and grocery bagger.

Specifically describe how you would go about setting goals in your new position. Include examples of goals for the jobs of butcher, cashier, and bakery manager.

Winwood Performance Plus

To: Hannah Paul, Human Resources Manager

From: Eric Winwood, CEO

Subject: Environmental Issues

Experiential Exercise

Hannah, as you know, our entertainment consulting business has had a remarkable couple of years. The success we've achieved wouldn't be possible without the hard work our associates do, and I'm honored to be surrounded by such committed and talented individuals. I feel that our next push as a company should be to become more environmentally responsible. All of us (me included) generate a lot of paper as we do our work, so I think our first step (and main focus right now) should be on controlling paper waste. I would like you to create a company-wide program for controlling paper waste. Before we get our associates involved, I'd like you to set some goals and develop some plans for this program. Get me your report (keep it to one page, please) outlining these goals and plans as soon as you can.

This fictionalized company and message were created for educational purposes only, and not meant to reflect positively or negatively on management practices by any company that may share this name.

CASE APPLICATION #1

Fast Fashion

When Amancio Ortega, a former Spanish bathrobe maker, opened his first Zara clothing store, his business model was simple: sell high-fashion look-alikes to price-conscious Europeans.[50] After succeeding in this, he decided to tackle the outdated clothing industry in which it took six months from a garment's design to consumers being able to purchase it in a store. What Ortega envisioned was "fast fashion"—getting designs to customers quickly. And that's exactly what Zara has done, using technology and an army of designers!

The company has been described as having more style than Gap, faster growth than Target, and logistical expertise rivaling Walmart's. Zara, which is owned by the Spanish fashion retail group Inditex SA, recognizes that success in the fashion world is based on a simple rule—get trendy, desired products to market quickly. Accomplishing this, however, isn't so simple. It involves a clear and focused understanding of fashion, technology, and their market, *and* the ability to adapt quickly to trends.

Inditex, the world's largest fashion retailer by sales worldwide, has eight retail brands: Zara, Zara Home, Pull and Bear, Massimo Dutti, Stradivarius, Bershka, Oysho, and Uterqüe. The company has over 5,600 stores in 88 countries, although Zara pulls in over two-thirds of the company's revenues. Despite its global presence, Zara is not yet a household name in the United States, with just over 50 stores open, including a flagship store in New York City.

What is Zara's secret to excelling at fast fashion? It takes approximately two weeks to get a new design from drawing board to store floor. And stores are stocked with new designs twice a week as clothes are shipped directly to the stores from the factory. Thus, each aspect of Zara's business contributes to the fast turnaround. Sales managers at "the Cube"—what employees call their futuristic-looking headquarters—sit at a long row of computers and scrutinize sales at every store. They see the hits and the misses almost instantaneously. They ask the in-house designers, who work in teams, sketching out new styles and deciding which fabrics will provide the best combination of style and price, for new designs. Once a design is drawn, it's sent electronically to Zara's factory across the street, where a clothing sample is made. To minimize waste, computer programs arrange and rearrange clothing patterns on the massive fabric rolls before a laser-guided machine does the cutting. Zara produces most of its designs close to home—in Morocco, Portugal, Spain, and Turkey. Finished garments are returned to the factory within a week. Finishing touches (buttons, trim, detailing, etc.) are added, and each garment goes through a quality check. Garments that don't pass are discarded, while those that do pass are individually pressed. Then, garment labels (indicating to which country garments will be shipped) and security tags are added. The bundled garments proceed along a moving carousel of hanging rails via a maze of tunnels to the warehouse, a four-story, 5-million-square-foot building (about the size of 90 football fields). As the merchandise bundles move along the rails, electronic bar code tags are read by equipment that send them to the right "staging area," where specific merchandise is first sorted by country and then by individual store, ensuring that each store gets exactly the shipment it's supposed to. From there, merchandise for European stores is sent to a loading dock and packed on a truck with other shipments in order of delivery. Deliveries to other locations go by plane. Some 60,000 items each hour—more than 2.6 million items a week—move through this ultrasophisticated distribution center. And this takes place with only a handful of workers who monitor the entire process. The company's just-in-time production (an idea borrowed from the auto industry) gives it a competitive edge in terms of speed and flexibility.

Despite Zara's success at fast fashion, its competitors are working to be faster. But CEO Pablo Isla isn't standing still. To maintain Zara's leading advantage, he's introducing new methods that enable store managers to order and display merchandise faster and is adding new cargo routes for shipping goods. And the company has finally made the jump into online retailing. One analyst forecasts that the company could quadruple sales in the United States, with a majority of that coming from online sales.

Zara's Secret to FAST FASHION

Discussion Questions

5-14 How is strategic management illustrated by this case story?

5-15 How might SWOT analysis be helpful to Inditex executives? To Zara store managers?

5-16 What competitive advantage do you think Zara is pursuing? How does it exploit that competitive advantage?

5-17 Do you think Zara's success is due to external or internal factors or both? Explain.

5-18 What strategic implications does Zara's move into online retailing have? (Hint: Think in terms of resources and capabilities.)

CASE APPLICATION #2

Crisis Planning at Live**strong** Foundation

In 1996, Lance Armstrong, the now-disgraced pro cyclist, was diagnosed with testicular cancer. Only 25 years old when he found out he had cancer, Armstrong chose to focus on being a survivor, not a victim. During his personal battle with cancer, he soon realized there was a critical lack of resources for individuals facing this disease. He decided to start a foundation devoted to helping others manage their lives on the cancer journey. Since 1998, the Live**strong** Foundation has served millions of people affected by cancer. But in October 2012, everything turned upside down for the organization. That's when the U.S. Anti-Doping Agency released its report that "concluded once and for all that Lance Armstrong, the cancer charity's founder and chairman, was guilty of doping during his legendary cycling career."[51]

Doug Ulman, CEO and president of the Live**strong** Foundation at the time, said he remembers that day clearly. In fact, he had anticipated for months that this day would come. As good friends, Ulman had believed Armstrong's statements of innocence over the years. But now, "there was no more hiding."[52] After the news broke, Ulman called a meeting of every one of the foundation's 100-person staff, all squeezing into the foundation's boardroom. There, shoulder to shoulder and crammed together, the suspicions and tingling uncertainties all of a sudden became all too real. When Ulman announced that the organization could no longer "defend" its founder, it was a defining, watershed moment. Live**strong**, the once highflying charity which had raised half a billion dollars over the years, was now facing a crisis—maybe even a life-or-death crisis—of its own. Now, Live**strong** would be operating in "life without Lance" mode.

Although it might be tempting to write off Live**strong** as a hopeless case, Ulman and the rest of Livestrong's staff have worked hard to keep the foundation viable and focused on its purpose. It's not to ignore the challenges facing the organization, because those challenges are significant. But in managing through the crisis, Ulman had to keep staff morale up *and* make plans to transform and distance itself from Mr. Armstrong.[53] One piece of advice he received from a crisis-communications firm was to take the opportunity to get the foundation's message out. Like many of the cancer sufferers it helps, Live**strong** wanted to come out on the other side stronger than ever. It's not been easy. The foundation has lost some of its biggest sponsors, including Nike and RadioShack. Revenues fell in 2012 and 2013. But in addition to his "crisis management" responsibilities, Ulman has been formulating plans and strategies. He says, "It's so ironic—we are in the business of survivorship, that's what we do. Now we find ourselves dealing with the same circumstances in a totally different place."[54]

A new phase in Live**strong**'s history began in early 2015.[55] The foundation's Board of Directors announced a new president and CEO, Chandini Portteus. She comes to Live**strong** from Susan G. Komen, the most widely-known, largest, and best-funded breast cancer organization in the United States. With her extensive knowledge and skills in fundraising, global programming, and advocacy, Live**strong** has an individual well-versed in the challenges of leading this organization into the future.

Surviving a **Crisis**…possible only with **PLANNING**

Discussion Questions

5-19 Could an organization even plan for this type of situation? If yes, how? If not, why not?

5-20 How would goals be useful in this type of situation? What types of goals might be necessary?

5-21 What types of plans will be useful to Live**strong**? Explain why you think these plans would be important.

5-22 What lessons about planning can managers learn from what Live**strong** has endured?

CASE APPLICATION #3

Eyeing the Future

Fanatically focusing on execution *and* brand. That's how analysts describe the strategic approach of Warby Parker, a New York City eyewear startup that's quickly disrupting the old-fashioned eyewear business. Co-founded in 2010 by David Gilboa and Neil Blumenthal (who are also now co-CEOs), Warby Parker has shown itself to be a fierce and successful competitor. Why? "One word, deliberate."[56] They are disciplined about their brand, but embrace and exploit technology in disrupting the staid and conservative way eyewear has traditionally been sold. So what *does* Warby Parker do?

To appreciate what Warby Parker is doing, we need to look back at how the idea for the company came about. After leaving a $700 pair of Prada frames in a seat-back pocket on a flight while backpacking in Southeast Asia, Gilboa began questioning why he had a $200 iPhone in his pocket that had the technology to do a number of really cool things and yet replacing that pair of glasses—a technology that's hundreds of years old—would cost way more than that $200 iPhone.[57] Like many other entrepreneurs, he believed there had to be a better way. His research exposed an industry that was a virtual monopoly with a very powerful eyewear supplier, thus the reason for the high-priced eyewear. Gilboa and a friend, who were both in Wharton's MBA program, weren't even sure they could take on such a powerful competitor until they teamed up with Blumenthal (also at Wharton). Blumenthal was rumored to know "more than pretty much anyone else in the world about how to work outside of the traditional eyeglass-supply chains."[58] Well, it didn't take long for the crew to start selling eyewear online from a Philadelphia apartment.

Today, Warby Parker designs and manufactures its own trendy, stylish frames and sells them directly to consumers over the Internet for an affordable $95 a pair. That price also includes prescription lenses, shipping, and a donation to VisionSpring, a not-for-profit where Blumenthal served as a director. The company has begun opening brick-and-mortar stores, with 11 open currently. Other growth plans include expanding their product mix, diversifying their frame selection into areas such as kids' frames and glasses with progressive lenses, and exploring revolutionary technologies that would do eye exams online. Warby Parker was named *Fast Company*'s Most Innovative Company of 2015 and was honored as a finalist in the 2014 *USA Today* Entrepreneur of the Year.[59] Another thing Warby Parker does is its "Buy a Pair, Give a Pair" program, which benefits visually-impaired individuals in developing countries. Meanwhile, to carry on the company's success, Gilboa and Blumenthal will continue being disciplined in all they do, fanatically focusing attention on execution and brand. That future vision should help Warby Parker continue on its successful journey.

Future Vision

Discussion Questions

5-23 What role do you think goals might play in planning for Warby Parker's future? List some goals you think might be important. (Make sure these goals have the characteristics of well-written goals.)

5-24 What types of plans would be needed in an industry such as this one? (For instance, long-term or short-term, or both?) Explain why you think these plans would be important.

5-25 What contingency factors might affect the planning Warby Parker executives do? How might those contingency factors affect the planning?

5-26 What competitive advantage(s) do you think Warby Parker has? What competitive challenges do you think the company faces?

Endnotes

1. M. C. Mankins and R. Steele, "Stop Making Plans—Start Making Decisions," *Harvard Business Review*, January 2006, 76–84; L. Bossidy and R. Charan, *Execution: The Discipline of Getting Things Done* (New York: Crown/Random House, 2002); P. Roberts, "The Art of Getting Things Done," *Fast Company*, June 2000, 162; H. Mintzberg, *The Rise and Fall of Strategic Planning* (New York: Free Press, 1994); G. Hamel and C. K. Prahalad, *Competing for the Future* (Boston: Harvard Business School Press, 1994); and D. Miller, "The Architecture of Simplicity," *Academy of Management Review*, January 1993, 116–38.

2. See, for example, F. Delmar and S. Shane, "Does Business Planning Facilitate the Development of New Ventures?" *Strategic Management Journal* (December 2003): 1165–85; R. M. Grant, "Strategic Planning in a Turbulent Environment: Evidence from the Oil Majors," *Strategic Management Journal* (June 2003): 491–517; P. J. Brews and M. R. Hunt, "Learning to Plan and Planning to Learn: Resolving the Planning School/Learning School Debate," *Strategic Management Journal* (December 1999): 889–913; C. C. Miller and L. B. Cardinal, "Strategic Planning and Firm Performance: A Synthesis of More Than Two Decades of Research," *Academy of Management Journal* (March 1994): 1649–85; N. Capon, J. U. Farley, and J. M. Hulbert, "Strategic Planning and Financial Performance: More Evidence," *Journal of Management Studies* (January 1994): 22–38; D.K. Sinha, "The Contribution of Formal Planning to Decisions," *Strategic Management Journal* (October 1990): 479–92; J. A. Pearce II, E. B. Freeman, and R. B. Robinson Jr., "The Tenuous Link between Formal Strategic Planning and Financial Performance," *Academy of Management Review*, October 1987, 658–75; L. C. Rhyne, "Contrasting Planning Systems in High, Medium, and Low Performance Companies," *Journal of Management Studies* (July 1987): 363–85; and J. A. Pearce II, K. K. Robbins, and R. B. Robinson Jr., "The Impact of Grand Strategy and Planning Formality on Financial Performance," *Strategic Management Journal* (March–April 1987): 125–34.

3. I. Boudway, "Holy Cow! The Chicago Cubs Finally Have a Winning Business Plan," http://www.bloomberg.com/news/articles/2015-04-01/the-chicago-cubs-finally-have-a-winning-business-plan, April 1, 2015.

4. S. Lohr, "IBM Scores Weather Data Deal and Starts Internet of Things Unit," *New York Times Online*, March 31, 2015.

5. M. Shiraki, "Toyota to End Expansion Freeze, Invest $1.3 Billion in Two New Mexico, China Plants," http://www.reuters.com/article/2015/04/03/us-toyota-factory-mexico-china-idUSKBN0MU05L20150403, April 3, 2015.

6. M. Snider, "ESPN.com Gets a Fresh Look for Its Big 2-0," *USA Today*, April 1, 2015, 1A.

7. B. Horovitz, "Breakfast Biscuits Take on a New Shape: Biscuit Taco," *USA Today*, March 25, 2015, 7B.

8. C. Rauwald, "Mercedes-Benz Plans First Pickup with Luxury Pushing Limits," http://www.bloomberg.com/news/articles/2015-03-27/mercedes-benz-plans-first-pickup-truck-as-luxury-pushes-limits, March 27, 2015.

9. A. J. Karr, "December Comp Crux," *Women's Wear Daily*, January 7, 2011, 4; A. Steigrad, "Specialty Retailers Show Weak Spots in Quarter," *Women's Wear Daily*, August 20, 2010, 14; K. Peterson, "Buckle Bends as Claiborne, Orbitz Climb, Ambow Sinks," *Wall Street Journal*, August 6, 2010, C6; N. Casey, "Teen Idols: Aeropostale, Buckle Post Big Gains as Rivals Swoon," *Wall Street Journal*, May 22, 2009, B8; V. Dagher, "Hot Topic Goes Cold, Buckle Wears a Smile," *Wall Street Journal*, May 22, 2009, C6; and J. B. Stewart, "A Retailer Bucks a Trend with Sales Success in Its Jeans," *Wall Street Journal*, May 13, 2009, D1.

10. M. Gruber, F. Heinemann, M. Brettel, and S. Hungeling, "Configurations of Resources and Capabilities and Their Performance Implications: An Exploratory Study on Technology Ventures," *Strategic Management Journal* (December 2010): 1337–56; T. H. Poister, "The Future of Strategic Planning in the Public Sector: Linking Strategic Management and Performance," *Public Administration Review*, December 2010, S246–S254; J. González-Benito and Isabel Suárez-González, "A Study of the Role Played by Manufacturing Strategic Objectives and Capabilities in Understanding the Relationship between Porter's Generic Strategies and Business Performance," *British Journal of Management* vol. 21 (2010): 1027–43; J. A. Parnell and E. B. Dent, "The Role of Luck in the Strategy-Performance Relationship," *Management Decision* vol. 47, no. 6 (2009): 1000–21; H. J. Cho and V. Pucik, "Relationship between Innovativeness, Quality, Growth, Profitability, and Market Value," *Strategic Management Journal* (June 2005): 555–75; W. F. Joyce, "What Really Works," *Organizational Dynamics*, May 2005, 118–29; M. A. Roberto, "Strategic

Decision-Making Processes," *Group & Organization Management*, December 2004, 625–58; A. Carmeli and A. Tischler, "The Relationships between Intangible Organizational Elements and Organizational Performance," *Strategic Management Journal* (December 2004): 1257–78; D. J. Ketchen, C. C. Snow, and V. L. Street, "Improving Firm Performance by Matching Strategic Decision-Making Processes to Competitive Dynamics," *Academy of Management Executive*, November 2004, 29–43; E. H. Bowman and C. E. Helfat, "Does Corporate Strategy Matter?" *Strategic Management Journal* 22 (2001): 1–23; P. J. Brews and M. R. Hunt, "Learning to Plan and Planning to Learn: Resolving the Planning School-Learning School Debate," *Strategic Management Journal* 20 (1999): 889–913; D. J. Ketchen Jr., J. B. Thomas, and R. R. McDaniel Jr., "Process, Content and Context; Synergistic Effects on Performance," *Journal of Management* 22, no. 2 (1996): 231–57; C. C. Miller and L. B. Cardinal, "Strategic Planning and Firm Performance: A Synthesis of More Than Two Decades of Research," *Academy of Management Journal* (December 1994): 1649–65; and N. Capon, J. U. Farley, and J. M. Hulbert, "Strategic Planning and Financial Performance: More Evidence," *Journal of Management Studies* (January 1994): 105–10.

11. From vision statement of Avon Products Inc. Copyright © by Avon Products Inc. Reprinted by permission.

12. C. K. Prahalad and G. Hamel, "The Core Competence of the Corporation," *Harvard Business Review*, May–June 1990, 79–91.

13. M. Snider, "ESPN.com Gets a Fresh Look for Its Big 2-0"; "ESPN Falls to 3rd in Online Sports Site Rankings," The Wrap Media <www.thewrap.com>, February 8, 2012; B. Barnes, "Across U.S., ESPN Aims to Be the Home Team," *New York Times Online*, July 20, 2009; and T. Lowry, "In the Zone," *Bloomberg Business-Week*, October 17, 2005, 66–77.

14. Managers and Technology box based on D. McGinn, "From Harvard to Las Vegas," *Newsweek*, April 18, 2005, E8–E14; G. Lindsay, "Prada's High-Tech Misstep," *Business 2.0*, March 2004, 72–75; G. Loveman, "Diamonds in the Data Mine," *Harvard Business Review*, May 2003, 109–13; and L. Gary, "Simplify and Execute: Words to Live by in Times of Turbulence," *Harvard Management Update*, January 2003, 12.

15. N. A. Shepherd, "Competitive Advantage: Mapping Change and the Role of the Quality Manager of the Future," *Annual Quality Congress*, May 1998, 53–60; T. C. Powell,

"Total Quality Management as Competitive Advantage: A Review and Empirical Study," *Strategic Management Journal* (January 1995): 15–37; and R. D. Spitzer, "TQM: The Only Source of Sustainable Competitive Advantage," *Quality Progress*, June 1993, 59–64.

16. C. H. Green, "Competitive Theory and Business Legitimacy," *BusinessWeek Online*, June 23, 2010; S. Parthasarathy, "Business Strategy" *Financial Management*, June 2010, 32–33; M. E. Porter, *On Competition, Updated and Expanded Edition* (Boston: Harvard Business School, 2008); O. Ormanidhi and O. Stringa, "Porter's Model of Generic Competitive Strategies," *Business Economics*, July 2008, 55–64; M. E. Porter, "The Five Competitive Forces That Shape Strategy," *Harvard Business Review*, January 2008, 78–93; N. Argyres and A. M. McGahan, "Introduction: Michael Porter's Competitive Strategy," *Academy of Management Executive*, May 2002, 41–42; and N. Argyres and A. M. McGahan, "An Interview with Michael Porter," *Academy of Management Executive*, May 2002, 43–52.

17. R. Pear, "A.M.A. to Develop Measure of Quality of Medical Care," *New York Times Online*, February 21, 2006; and A. Taylor III, "Double Duty," *Fortune*, March 7, 2005, 104–10.

18. T. Mullaney, "'Social Business' Launched This Burger," *USA Today*, May 17, 2012, 1A+.

19. B. Roberts, "Social Media Gets Strategic," *HR Magazine*, October 2012, 30.

20. B. Acohido, "Social-Media Tools Boost Productivity," *USA Today*, August 13, 2012, 1B+.

21. Ibid.

22. A. McAfee and E. Brynjolfsson, "Big Data: The Management Revolution," *Harvard Business Review*, October 2012, 62.

23. K. Cukier and V. Mayer-Schönberger, "The Financial Bonanza of Big Data," *Wall Street Journal*, March 8, 2013, A15.

24. "In-Store Cell Phone Tracking Pits Consumers against Retailers: Transparency Is Vital if Retailers Want to Build Trust with Customers," adage.com, April 17, 2014; "New Study: Consumers Overwhelmingly Reject In-Store Tracking by Retailers," www.prweb.com, March 27, 2014; A. Farnham, "Retailers Snooping on Holiday Shoppers Raises Privacy Concerns," abcnews.go.com/Business/, December 10, 2013; V. Kopytoff, "Stores Sniff out Smartphones to Follow Shoppers," *MIT Technology Review*, www.technologyreview.com, November 12, 2013; "How Stores Spy on You," www.consumerreports.org, March 2013; J. O'Donnell and S. Meehan,

"Retailers Want to Read Your Mind," *USA Today,* March 2, 2012, 1B+; and C. Duhigg, "How Companies Learn Your Secrets," *New York Times Online,* February 16, 2012.

25. McDonald's Annual Report 2007, www.mcdonalds.com (April 21, 2008).

26. S. Zesiger Callaway, "Mr. Ghosn Builds His Dream Car," *Fortune,* February 4, 2008, 56–58.

27. See, for instance, J. Pfeffer, *Organizational Design* (Arlington Heights, IL: AHM Publishing, 1978), 5–12; and C. K. Warriner, "The Problem of Organizational Purpose," *Sociological Quarterly* (Spring 1965): 139–46.

28. D. Drickhamer, "Braced for the Future," *Industry Week,* October 2004, 51–52.

29. P. N. Romani, "MBO by Any Other Name Is Still MBO," *Supervision,* December 1997, 6–8; and A. W. Schrader and G. T. Seward, "MBO Makes Dollar Sense," *Personnel Journal* (July 1989): 32–37.

30. From the Past to the Present box based on P. F. Drucker, *The Practice of Management* (New York: Harper & Row, 1954); J. F. Castellano and H. A. Roehm, "The Problem with Managing by Objectives and Results," *Quality Progress,* March 2001, 39–46; J. Loehr and T. Schwartz, "The Making of a Corporate Athlete," *Harvard Business Review,* January 2001, 120–28; A. J. Vogl, "Drucker, of Course," *Across the Board,* November–December 2000, 1. For information on goals and goal setting, see, for example, E. A. Locke, "Toward a Theory of Task Motivation and Incentives," *Organizational Behavior and Human Performance,* May 1968, 157–89; E. A. Locke, K. N. Shaw, L. M. Saari, and G. P. Latham, "Goal Setting and Task Performance: 1969–1980," *Psychological Bulletin,* July 1981, 12–52; E. A. Locke and G. P. Latham, *A Theory of Goal Setting and Task Performance* (Upper Saddle River, NJ: Prentice Hall, 1990); P. Ward and M. Carnes, "Effects of Posting Self-Set Goals on Collegiate Football Players' Skill Execution During Practice and Games," *Journal of Applied Behavioral Analysis,* Spring 2002, 1–12; D. W. Ray, "Productivity and Profitability," *Executive Excellence,* October 2001, 14; D. Archer, "Evaluating Your Managed System," *CMA Management,* January 2000, 12–14; and C. Antoni, "Management by Objectives: An Effective Tool for Teamwork," *International Journal of Human Resource Management* (February 2005): 174–84. For information on participation in goal setting, see, for example, T. D. Ludwig and E. S. Geller, "Intervening to Improve the Safety of Delivery Drivers: A Systematic Behavioral Approach," *Journal of Organizational Behavior Management* (April 4, 2000): 11–24; P. Latham

and L. M. Saari, "The Effects of Holding Goal Difficulty Constant on Assigned and Participatively Set Goals," *Academy of Management Journal* (March 1979): 163–68; M. Erez, P. C. Earley, and C. L. Hulin, "The Impact of Participation on Goal Acceptance and Performance: A Two Step Model," *Academy of Management Journal* (March 1985): 50–66; and G. P. Latham, M. Erez, and E. A. Locke, "Resolving Scientific Disputes by the Joint Design of Crucial Experiments by the Antagonists: Application to the Erez Latham Dispute Regarding Participation in Goal Setting," *Journal of Applied Psychology* (November 1988): 753–72. For information on effectiveness of MBO, see, for example, F. Dahlsten, A. Styhre, and M. Williander, "The Unintended Consequences of Management by Objectives: The Volume Growth Target at Volvo Cars," *Leadership & Organization Development Journal* (July 2005): 529–41; J. R. Crow, "Crashing with the Nose Up: Building a Cooperative Work Environment," *Journal for Quality and Participation* (Spring 2002): 45–50; and E. C. Hollensbe and J. P. Guthrie, "Group Pay-for-Performance Plans: The Role of Spontaneous Goal Setting," *Academy of Management Review,* October 2000, 864–72.

31. R. Rodgers and J. E. Hunter, "Impact of Management by Objectives on Organizational Productivity," *Journal of Applied Psychology* (April 1991): 322–36.

32. G. P. Latham, "The Motivational Benefits of Goal-Setting," *Academy of Management Executive,* November 2004, 126–29.

33. For additional information on goals, see, for instance, P. Drucker, *The Executive in Action* (New York: HarperCollins Books, 1996), 207–14; and E. A. Locke and G. P. Latham, *A Theory of Goal Setting and Task Performance* (Upper Saddle River, NJ: Prentice Hall, 1990).

34. J. L. Roberts, "Signed, Sealed, Delivered?" *Newsweek,* June 20, 2005, 44–46.

35. Several of these factors were suggested by R. K. Bresser and R. C. Bishop, "Dysfunctional Effects of Formal Planning: Two Theoretical Explanations," *Academy of Management Review,* October 1983, 588–99; and J. S. Armstrong, "The Value of Formal Planning for Strategic Decisions: Review of Empirical Research," *Strategic Management Journal* (July–September 1982): 197–211.

36. K. Garber, "Powering the Information Age," *U.S. News & World Report,* April 2009, 46–48; and S. Hamm, "It's Too Darn Hot," *BusinessWeek,* March 31, 2008, 60–63.

37. "As Q4 Approaches, Which of the Following Is Most Challenging for You as a Leader?" SmartBrief on Leadership, smartbrief.com/leadership, October 15, 2013.

38. A. Campbell, "Tailored, Not Benchmarked: A Fresh Look at Corporate Planning," *Harvard Business Review Online,* https://hbr.org/1999/03/tailored-not-benchmarked-a-fresh-look-at-corporate-planning, April 1999.

39. Ibid.

40. J. H. Sheridan, "Focused on Flow," *IW,* October 18, 1999, 46–51.

41. A. Taylor III, "Hyundai Smokes the Competition," *Fortune,* January 18, 2010, 62–71.

42. Brews and Hunt, "Learning to Plan and Planning to Learn: Resolving the Planning School/Learning School Debate."

43. R. J. Newman, "Coming and Going," *U.S. News and World Report,* January 23, 2006, 50–52; T. Atlas, "Bangalore's Big Dreams," *U.S. News and World Report,* May 2, 2005, 50–52; and K. H. Hammonds, "Smart, Determined, Ambitious, Cheap: The New Face of Global Competition," *Fast Company,* February 2003, 90–97.

44. See, for example, P. Tarraf and R. Molz, "Competitive Intelligence," *SAM Advanced Management Journal* (Autumn 2006): 24–34; W. M. Fitzpatrick, "Uncovering Trade Secrets: The Legal and Ethical Conundrum of Creative Competitive Intelligence," *SAM Advanced Management Journal* (Summer 2003): 4–12; L. Lavelle, "The Case of the Corporate Spy," *BusinessWeek,* November 26, 2001, 56–58; C. Britton, "Deconstructing Advertising: What Your Competitor's Advertising Can Tell You about Their Strategy," *Competitive Intelligence,* January/February 2002, 15–19; and L. Smith, "Business Intelligence Progress in Jeopardy," *InformationWeek,* March 4, 2002, 74.

45. S. Greenbard, "New Heights in Business Intelligence," *Business Finance,* March 2002, 41–46; K. A. Zimmermann, "The Democratization of Business Intelligence," *KN World,* May 2002, 20–21; and C. Britton, "Deconstructing Advertising: What Your Competitor's Advertising Can Tell You about Their Strategy," *Competitive Intelligence,* January–February 2002, 15–19.

46. C. Hausman, "Business-Ethics News Featured in World-Press Reports," *Ethics Newsline,* March 14, 2011; and L. Weathersby, "Take This Job and ***** It," *Fortune,* January 7, 2002, 122.

47. P. Lattiman, "Hilton and Starwood Settle Dispute," *New York Times Online,* December 22, 2010; "Starwood vs. Hilton," *Hotels' Investment Outlook,* June 2009, 14; R. Kidder, "Hotel Industry Roiled by Corporate Espionage Claim," *Ethics Newsline,* www.globalethicslorg/news-line; Reuters, "Hilton Hotels Is Subpoenaed in Espionage Case," *New York Times Online,* April 22, 2009; T. Audi, "U.S. Probes Hilton over Theft Claims," *Wall Street Journal,* April 22, 2009, B1; and T. Audi, "Hilton Is Sued over Luxury

Chain," *Wall Street Journal,* April 17, 2009, B1.

48. B. Rosner, "HR Should Get a Clue: Corporate Spying Is Real," *Workforce,* April 2001, 72–75.

49. K. Western, "Ethical Spying," *Business Ethics,* September–October 1995, 22–23.

50. C. Bjork, "Zara Builds Its Business around RFID," *Wall Street Journal,* September 17, 2014, B1+; D. Roman and W. Kemble-Diaz, "Owner of Fast-Fashion Retailer Zara Keeps up Emerging-Markets Push," *Wall Street Journal,* June 14, 2012, B3; Press Releases, "Inditex Achieves Net Sales of 9,709 Million Euros, an Increase of 10 percent," <www.inditex.com>, February 22, 2012; C. Bjork, "'Cheap Chic' Apparel Sellers Heat up U.S. Rivalry on Web," *Wall Street Journal,* September 6, 2011, B1+; A. Kenna, "Zara Plays Catch-up with Online Shoppers," *Bloomberg Business-Week,* August 29–September 4, 2011, 24–25; K. Girotra and S. Netessine, "How to Build Risk into Your Business Model," *Harvard Business Review,* May 2011, 100–05; M. Dart and R. Lewis, "Break the Rules the Way Zappos and Amazon Do," *Bloomberg BusinessWeek Online,* April 29, 2011; K. Cappell, "Zara Thrives by Breaking All the Rules," *BusinessWeek,* October 20, 2008, 66; and C. Rohwedder and K. Johnson, "Pace-Setting Zara Seeks More Speed to Fight Its Rising Cheap-Chic Rivals," *Wall Street Journal,* February 20, 2008, B1+.

51. I. Lapowsky, "Livestrong without Lance," http://www.inc.com/magazine/201404/issie-lapowsky/what-livestrong-is-like-without-lance-armstrong.html, April 1, 2014.

52. Ibid.

53. V. O'Connell, "Livestrong Seeks Life after Lance Armstrong," *Wall Street Journal,* March 6, 2013, B7.

54. Ibid.

55. "Chandini Portteus Named New President and CEO for LIVESTRONG," LIVESTRONG Staff, http://blog.livestrong.org/2015/03/24/chandini-portteus-named-new-president-and-ceo-for-livestrong/, March 24, 2015.

56. K. Weisul, "How Neil Blumenthal Took the Risk Out of Warby Parker," http://www.inc.com/kimberly-weisul/how-warby-parker-took-the-risk-out-of-its-business.html, May 28, 2015; and M. Chafkin, "Warby Parker Sees the Future of Retail," http://www.fastcompany.com/3041334/most-innovative-companies-2015/warby-parker-sees-the-future-of-retail, February 17, 2015.

57. M. Diebel, "A Visionary Approach to Selling Eyewear," *USA Today,* December 1, 2014, 3B.

58. Chafkin, "Warby Parker Sees the Future of Retail."

59. Chafkin, "Warby Parker Sees the Future of Retail"; and Diebel, "A Visionary Approach to Selling Eyewear."

Organizational Structure and Design

6

Management Myth

Myth

Bureaucracies are inefficient.

Tom Wang/Alamy

Management **DEBUNKED?** Myth

People commonly assume that bureaucracies—or mechanistic structures—are inefficient. Critics claim these organizations are slow, rule-bound, and have too much "red tape." The media makes you think bureaucracies are extinct—replaced by empowered teams and loosely structured and adaptive organizations. Although many organizations today *do* look like that, the truth is that bureaucracies are still alive and well. Most medium-sized and large organizations are structured as a bureaucracy because its traits—specialization, formal rules and regulations, clear chain of command, and departmentalization—help efficiently structure people and tasks.

WELCOME

to the fascinating world of organization structure and design in the twenty-first century! In this chapter, we present the basics of organizing. We define the concepts and their key components and how managers use these to create a structured environment in which organizational members can do their work efficiently and effectively. Once the organization's goals, plans, and strategies are in place, managers must develop a structure that will best facilitate the attainment of those goals. ●

Learning Outcomes

6-1 Describe six key elements in organizational design. p. 163

6-2 Identify the contingency factors that favor either the mechanistic model or the organic model of organizational design. p. 172

6-3 Compare and contrast traditional and contemporary organizational designs. p. 176

6-4 Discuss the design challenges faced by today's organizations. p. 181

What Are the Six Key Elements in Organizational Design?

6-1 Describe six key elements in organizational design.

A short distance south of McAlester, Oklahoma, employees in a vast factory complex make products that must be perfect. These people "are so good at what they do and have been doing it for so long that they have a 100 percent market share."[1] They make bombs for the U.S. military, and doing so requires a work environment that's an interesting mix of the mundane, structured, and disciplined, coupled with high levels of risk and emotion. The work gets done efficiently and effectively here. Work also gets done efficiently and effectively at Cisco Systems, although not in such a structured and formal way. At Cisco, some 70 percent of the employees work from home at least 20 percent of the time.[2] Both of these organizations get needed work done, although each does so using a different structure.

Getting work done **efficiently & effectively.**

Organizing is all about that! Recall from Chapter 1 that we defined **organizing** as the function of management that determines what needs to be done, how it will be done, and who is to do it; in other words, the function that creates the organization's structure. When managers develop or change the organization's structure, they're engaging in **organization design**. This process involves making decisions about how specialized jobs should be, the rules to guide employees' behaviors, and at what level decisions are to be made. Although organization design decisions are typically made by top-level managers, it's important for everyone involved to understand the process. Why? Because each of us works in some type of organization structure, and we need to know how and why things get done. In addition, given the changing environment and the need for organizations to adapt, you should begin understanding what tomorrow's structures may look like—those will be the settings you'll be working in.

Few topics in management have undergone as much change in the past few years as that of organizing and organizational structure. Managers are reevaluating traditional approaches and exploring new structural designs that best support and facilitate employees doing the organization's work—designs that can achieve efficiency but are also flexible.

The basic concepts of organization design formulated by management writers such as Henri Fayol and Max Weber offered structural principles for managers to follow. (Rewind to History Module, p. 27.) Over 90 years have passed since many of those principles were originally proposed. Given that length of time and all the changes that have taken place, you'd think that those principles would be mostly worthless today. Surprisingly, they're not. They still provide valuable insights into designing effective and efficient organizations. Of course, we've also gained a great deal of knowledge over the years as to their limitations. In the following sections, we discuss the *six basic elements of organizational structure*: work specialization, departmentalization, authority and responsibility, span of control, centralization versus decentralization, and formalization.

(1) What Is Work Specialization?

TRADITIONAL VIEW. At the Wilson Sporting Goods factory in Ada, Ohio, workers make every football used in the National Football League and most of those used in college and high school football games. To meet daily output goals, the workers specialize in job tasks such as molding, stitching and sewing, lacing, and so forth.[3] This is an example of **work specialization**, which is dividing work activities into separate job tasks. (That's why it's also known as division of labor.) Individual employees "specialize" in doing part of an activity rather than the entire activity in order to increase work output.

organizing
The function of management that creates the organization's structure

organization design
When managers develop or change the organization's structure

work specialization
Dividing work activities into separate job tasks; also called division of labor

Exhibit 6–1 Economies and Diseconomies of Work

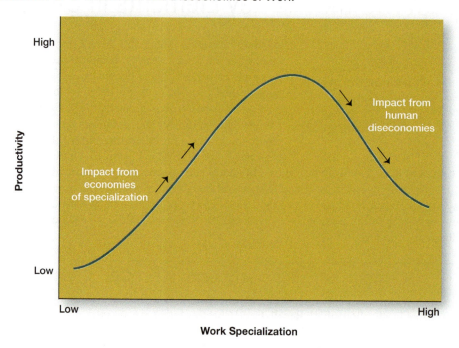

Work specialization allows organizations to efficiently use the diversity of skills that workers have. In most organizations, some tasks require highly developed skills; others can be performed by employees with lower skill levels. If all workers were engaged in all the steps of, say, a manufacturing process, all would need the skills necessary to perform both the most demanding and the least demanding jobs. Thus, except when performing the most highly skilled or highly sophisticated tasks, employees would be working below their skill levels. In addition, skilled workers are paid more than unskilled workers, and, because wages tend to reflect the highest level of skill, all workers would be paid at highly skilled rates to do easy tasks—an inefficient use of resources. This concept explains why you rarely find a cardiac surgeon closing up a patient after surgery. Instead, surgical residents learning the skill usually stitch and staple the patient after the surgeon has finished the surgery.

 Early proponents of work specialization believed that it could lead to great increases in productivity. At the beginning of the twentieth century, that generalization was reasonable. Because specialization was not widely practiced, its introduction almost always generated higher productivity. But a good thing can be carried too far. At some point, the human diseconomies—boredom, fatigue, stress, low productivity, poor quality, increased absenteeism, and high turnover—outweigh the economic advantages (see Exhibit 6–1).[4]

TODAY'S VIEW. Most managers today see work specialization as an important organizing mechanism because it helps employees be more efficient. For example, McDonald's uses high specialization to get its products made and delivered to customers efficiently. However, managers also have to recognize its limitations. That's why companies such as Avery-Dennison, Ford Australia, Hallmark, and American Express use minimal work specialization and instead give employees a broad range of tasks to do.

(2) What Is Departmentalization?

TRADITIONAL VIEW. Early management writers argued that after deciding what job tasks will be done by whom, common work activities needed to be grouped back together so work was done in a coordinated and integrated way. How jobs are grouped together is called **departmentalization**. There are five common forms (see Exhibit 6–2), although an organization may use its own unique classification. No single method of departmentalization

departmentalization
How jobs are grouped together

was advocated by the early writers. The method or methods used would reflect the grouping that best contributed to the attainment of the goals of the organization and the individual units.

How are **activities** grouped?

1. One of the most popular ways to group activities is by functions performed, or **functional departmentalization**. A manager might organize the workplace by separating engineering, accounting, information systems, human resources, and purchasing specialists into departments. Functional departmentalization can be used in all types of organizations. Only the functions change to reflect the organization's objectives and activities. The major advantage to functional departmentalization is the achievement of economies of scale by placing people with common skills and specializations into common units.

2. **Product departmentalization** focuses attention on major product areas in the corporation. Each product is under the authority of a senior manager who is a specialist in, and is responsible for, everything having to do with his or her product line. One company that uses product departmentalization is Nike. Its structure is based on its varied product lines, which include athletic and dress/casual footwear, sports apparel and accessories, and performance equipment. If an organization's activities were service related rather than product related, each service would be autonomously grouped. The advantage of product grouping is that it increases accountability for product performance, because all activities related to a specific product are under the direction of a single manager.

3. The particular type of customer an organization seeks to reach can also dictate employee grouping. The sales activities in an office supply firm, for instance, can be divided into three departments that serve retail, wholesale, and government customers. A large law office can segment its staff on the basis of whether it serves corporate or individual clients. The assumption underlying **customer departmentalization** is that customers in each department have a common set of problems and needs that can best be met by specialists.

4. Another way to departmentalize is on the basis of geography or territory—**geographic departmentalization**. The sales function might have western, southern, Midwestern, and eastern regions. If an organization's customers are scattered over a large geographic area, this form of departmentalization can be valuable. For instance, the organization structure of Coca-Cola reflects the company's operations in two broad geographic areas—the

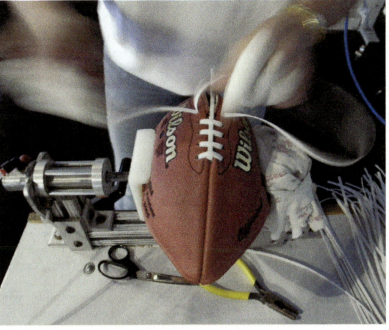

AFP/Newscom

Lacing is one of 13 separate tasks involved in hand-crafting a Wilson Sporting Goods football. The company uses work specialization in dividing job activities as an organizing mechanism that helps employees boost their productivity and makes efficient use of workers' diverse skills.

Exhibit 6–2 Types of Departmentalization

• **Functional**	Groups employees based on work performed (e.g., engineering, accounting, information systems, human resources)
• **Product**	Groups employees based on major product areas in the corporation (e.g., women's footwear, men's footwear, and apparel and accessories)
• **Customer**	Groups employees based on customers' problems and needs (e.g., wholesale, retail, government)
• **Geographic**	Groups employees based on location served (e.g., North, South, Midwest, East)
• **Process**	Groups employees based on the basis of work or customer flow (e.g., testing, payment)

functional departmentalization
Grouping activities by functions performed

product departmentalization
Grouping activities by major product areas

customer departmentalization
Grouping activities by customer

geographic departmentalization
Grouping activities on the basis of geography or territory

process departmentalization
Grouping activities on the basis of work or customer flow

cross-functional teams
Teams made up of individuals from various departments and that cross traditional departmental lines

chain of command
The line of authority extending from upper organizational levels to lower levels, which clarifies who reports to whom

authority
The rights inherent in a managerial position to give orders and expect the orders to be obeyed

responsibility
An obligation to perform assigned duties

North American sector and the international sector (which includes the Pacific Rim, the European Community, Northeast Europe and Africa, and Latin America).

5. The final form of departmentalization is called **process departmentalization**, which groups activities on the basis of work or customer flow—like that found in many government offices or in health care clinics. Units are organized around common skills needed to complete a certain process. If you've ever been to a state office to get a driver's license, you've probably experienced process departmentalization. With separate departments to handle applications, testing, information and photo processing, and payment collection, customers "flow" through the various departments in sequence to get their licenses.

TODAY'S VIEW.   Most large organizations continue to use most or all of the departmental groups suggested by the early management writers. Black & Decker, for instance, organizes its divisions along functional lines, its manufacturing units around processes, its sales around geographic regions, and its sales regions around customer groupings. However, many organizations use **cross-functional teams**, which are teams made up of individuals from various departments and that cross traditional departmental lines. These teams have been useful especially as tasks have become more complex and diverse skills are needed to accomplish those tasks.[5]

Also, today's competitive environment has refocused the attention of management on its customers. To better monitor the needs of customers and to be able to respond to changes in those needs, many organizations are giving greater emphasis to customer departmentalization.

(3) What Are Authority and Responsibility?

TRADITIONAL VIEW.   To understand authority and responsibility, you also have to be familiar with the **chain of command**, the line of authority extending from upper organizational levels to lower levels, which clarifies who reports to whom. Managers need to consider it when organizing work because it helps employees with questions such as "Who do I report to?" or "Who do I go to if I have a problem?" So, what *are* authority and responsibility?

Harley-Davidson uses cross-functional teams from the conception and design of its motorcycles to their production and product launch. Harley's teams of buyers, suppliers, marketers, operations personnel, engineers, and employees from other departments work together to provide customers with quality products.

Authority comes from **the position, not the person.**

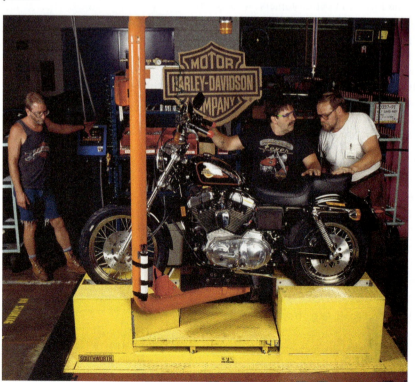

H. Mark Weidman Photography/Alamy

Authority refers to the rights inherent in a managerial position to give orders and expect the orders to be obeyed. Authority was a major concept discussed by the early management writers as they viewed it as the glue that held an organization together.[6] It was delegated downward to lower-level managers, giving them certain rights while prescribing certain limits within which to operate. Each management position had specific inherent rights that incumbents acquired from the position's rank or title. Authority, therefore, is related to one's position within an organization and has nothing to do with the personal characteristics of an individual manager. When a position of authority is vacated, the person who has left the position no longer has any authority. The authority remains with the position and its new incumbent.

When managers delegate authority, they must allocate commensurate **responsibility**. That is, when employees are given rights, they also assume a corresponding obligation to perform. And they'll be held accountable for their

Exhibit 6–3 Chain of Command and Line Authority

performance! Allocating authority without responsibility and accountability creates opportunities for abuse. Likewise, no one should be held responsible or accountable for something over which he or she has no authority.

WHAT ARE THE DIFFERENT TYPES OF AUTHORITY RELATIONSHIPS? The early management writers distinguished between two forms of authority: line authority and staff authority. **Line authority** entitles a manager to direct the work of an employee. It is the employer–employee authority relationship that extends from the top of the organization to the lowest echelon, according to the chain of command, as shown in Exhibit 6–3. As a link in the chain of command, a manager with line authority has the right to direct the work of employees and to make certain decisions without consulting anyone. Of course, in the chain of command, every manager is also subject to the direction of his or her superior.

Keep in mind that sometimes the term *line* is used to differentiate line managers from staff managers. In this context, *line* refers to managers whose organizational function contributes directly to the achievement of organizational objectives. In a manufacturing firm, line managers are typically in the production and sales functions, whereas managers in human resources and payroll are considered staff managers with staff authority. Whether a manager's function is classified as line or staff depends on the organization's objectives. For example, at Staff Builders, a supplier of temporary employees, interviewers have a line function. Similarly, at the payroll firm of ADP, payroll is a line function.

As organizations get larger and more complex, line managers may find that they don't have the time, expertise, or resources to get their jobs done effectively. In response, they create **staff authority** functions to support, assist, advise, and generally reduce some of their informational burdens. The hospital administrator who cannot effectively handle the purchasing of all the supplies the hospital needs creates a purchasing department, a staff department. Of course, the head of the purchasing department has line authority over the purchasing agents who work for him. The hospital administrator might also find that she is overburdened and needs an assistant. In creating the position of her assistant, she has created a staff position. Exhibit 6–4 illustrates line and staff authority.

WHAT IS UNITY OF COMMAND? An employee who has to report to two or more bosses might have to cope with conflicting demands or priorities.[7] Accordingly, the early writers believed that each employee should report to only one manager, a term called **unity of command**. In those

line authority
Authority that entitles a manager to direct the work of an employee

staff authority
Positions with some authority that have been created to support, assist, and advise those holding line authority

unity of command
Structure in which each employee reports to only one manager

Exhibit 6–4 **Line versus Staff Authority**

rare instances when the unity of command had to be violated, a clear separation of activities and a supervisor responsible for each was always explicitly designated.

One boss or more?

Unity of command was logical when organizations were relatively simple. Under some circumstances it is still sound advice and organizations continue to adhere to it. But advances in technology, for instance, allow access to organizational information that was once accessible only to top managers. And employees can interact with anyone else in the organization without going through the formal chain of command. Thus, in some instances, strict adherence to unity of command creates a degree of inflexibility that hinders an organization's performance.

TODAY'S VIEW. The early management writers loved the idea of authority. They assumed that the rights inherent in one's formal position in an organization were the sole source of influence, and they believed that managers were all-powerful. This assumption might have been true 60—even 30—years ago. Organizations were simpler. Staff was less important. Managers were only minimally dependent on technical specialists. Under such conditions, influence is the same as authority. And the higher a manager's position in the organization, the more influence he or she had. However, *those conditions no longer exist.* Researchers and practitioners of management now recognize that you don't have to be a manager to have power and that power is not perfectly correlated with one's level in the organization.

Authority is an important concept in organizations, but an exclusive focus on authority produces a narrow, unrealistic view of influence. Today, we recognize that *authority is but one element in the larger concept of power.*

HOW DO AUTHORITY AND POWER DIFFER? Authority and power are often considered the same thing, but they're not. Authority is a right. Its legitimacy is based on an authority figure's position in the organization. Authority goes with the job. **Power**, on the other hand, refers to an individual's capacity to influence decisions. Authority is part of the larger concept of power. That is, the formal rights that come with an individual's position in the organization are just one means by which an individual can affect the decision process.

power
An individual's capacity to influence decisions

Exhibit 6–5 Authority versus Power

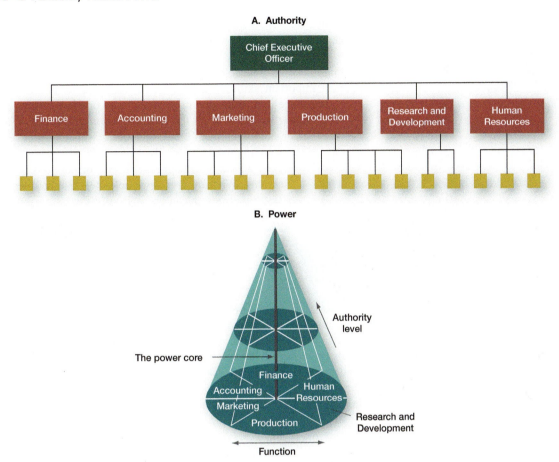

Exhibit 6–5 visually depicts the difference between authority and power. The two-dimensional arrangement of boxes in part A portrays authority. The area in which the authority applies is defined by the horizontal dimension. Each horizontal grouping represents a functional area. The influence one holds in the organization is defined by the vertical dimension in the structure. The higher one is in the organization, the greater one's authority.

Power, on the other hand, is a three-dimensional concept (the cone in part B of Exhibit 6–5). It includes not only the functional and hierarchical dimensions but also a third dimension called centrality. Although authority is defined by one's vertical position in the hierarchy, power is made up of both one's vertical position and one's distance from the organization's power core or center.

Think of the cone in Exhibit 6–5 as an organization. The center of the cone is the power core. The closer you are to the power core, the more influence you have on decisions. The existence of a power core is, in fact, the only difference between A and B in Exhibit 6–5. The vertical hierarchy dimension in A is merely one's level on the outer edge of the cone. The top of the cone corresponds to the top of the hierarchy, the middle of the cone to the middle of the hierarchy, and so on. Similarly, the functional groups in A become wedges in the cone. Each wedge represents a functional area.

The cone analogy explicitly acknowledges two facts: (1) The higher one moves in an organization (an increase in authority), the closer one moves to the power core; and (2) it is not necessary to have authority in order to wield power because one can move horizontally inward toward the power core without moving up. For instance, assistants often are powerful in a company even though they have little authority. As gatekeepers for their bosses, these assistants have considerable influence over whom their bosses see and when they see them. Furthermore, because they're regularly relied upon to pass information on to their bosses,

Melissa Brenner, senior vice president of marketing for the National Basketball Association, has expert power. Her expertise in using Facebook, Instagram, and other social media in innovative ways is helping the NBA achieve its goal of enhancing fans' engagement and enjoyment of the game throughout the world.

Jennifer S. Altman/Getty Images

they have some control over what their bosses hear. It's not unusual for a $105,000-a-year middle manager to tread carefully in order not to upset the boss's $45,000-a-year administrative assistant. Why? Because the assistant has power. This individual may be low in the authority hierarchy but close to the power core.

Likewise, low-ranking employees who have relatives, friends, or associates in high places might also be close to the power core. So, too, are employees with scarce and important skills. The lowly production engineer with 20 years of experience in a company might be the only one in the firm who knows the inner workings of all the old production machinery. When pieces of this old equipment break down, only this engineer understands how to fix them. Suddenly, the engineer's influence is much greater than it would appear from his or her level in the vertical hierarchy. What do these examples tell us about power? They indicate that power can come from different areas. French and Raven identified five sources, or bases, of power: coercive, reward, legitimate, expert, and referent.[8] We summarize them in Exhibit 6–6.

(4) What Is Span of Control?

TRADITIONAL VIEW. How many employees can a manager efficiently and effectively supervise? This question of **span of control** received a great deal of attention from early management writers. Although they came to no consensus on a specific number, most favored small spans—typically no more than six workers—in order to maintain close control.[9] However, several writers did acknowledge level in the organization as a contingency variable. They argued that as a manager rises in an organization, he or she has to deal with a greater number of unstructured problems, so top managers need a smaller span than do middle managers, and middle managers require a smaller span than do supervisors. Over the last decade, however, we've seen some change in theories about effective spans of control.[10]

TODAY'S VIEW. Many organizations are increasing their spans of control. The span for managers at such companies as General Electric and Kaiser Aluminum has expanded significantly in the past decade. It has also expanded in the federal government, where efforts to increase the span of control are being implemented to save time in making decisions.[11] The span of control is increasingly being determined by looking at contingency variables.

How Many People **Can I** Effectively and Efficiently Manage?

Most effective and efficient span depends on:

- Employee experience and training (more they have, larger span)
- Similarity of employee tasks (more similarity, larger span)
- Complexity of those tasks (more complex, smaller span)

Exhibit 6–6 Types of Power

Coercive power	Power based on fear.
Reward power	Power based on the ability to distribute something that others value.
Legitimate power	Power based on one's position in the formal hierarchy.
Expert power	Power based on one's expertise, special skill, or knowledge.
Referent power	Power based on identification with a person who has desirable resources or personal traits.

span of control
The number of employees a manager can efficiently and effectively supervise

- Physical proximity of employees (closer proximity, larger span)
- Amount and type of standardized procedures (more standardized, larger span)
- Sophistication of the organization's management information system (more sophisticated, larger span)
- Strength of the organization's value system (stronger the value system, larger span)
- Preferred managing style of the manager[12] (personal preference of more or fewer employees to manage)

(5) How Do Centralization and Decentralization Differ?

TRADITIONAL VIEW. One of the questions that needs to be answered when organizing is "At what level are decisions made?" **Centralization** is the degree to which decision making takes place at upper levels of the organization. **Decentralization** is the degree to which lower-level managers provide input or actually make decisions. Centralization-decentralization is not an either-or concept. Rather, it's a matter of degree. What we mean is that no organization is completely centralized or completely decentralized. Few, if any, organizations could effectively function if all their decisions were made by a select few people (centralization) or if all decisions were pushed down to the level closest to the problems (decentralization). Let's look, then, at how the early management writers viewed centralization as well as at how it exists today.

Early management writers proposed that centralization in an organization depended on the situation.[14] Their goal was the optimum and efficient use of employees. Traditional organizations were structured in a pyramid, with power and authority concentrated near the top of the organization. Given this structure, historically centralized decisions were the most prominent, but organizations today have become more complex and responsive to dynamic changes in their environments. As such, many managers believe that decisions need to be made by those individuals closest to the problems, regardless of their organizational level. In fact, the trend over the past several decades—at least in U.S. and Canadian organizations—has been a movement toward more decentralization in organizations.[15]

TODAY'S VIEW. Today, managers often choose the amount of centralization or decentralization that will allow them to best implement their decisions and achieve organizational goals.[16] What works in one organization, however, won't necessarily work in another, so managers must determine the amount of decentralization for each organization and work units within it. When managers empower employees and delegate to them the authority to make decisions on those things that affect their work and to change the way that they think about work, that's decentralization. Notice, however, that it doesn't imply that top-level managers no longer make decisions.

(6) What Is Formalization?

TRADITIONAL VIEW. **Formalization** refers to how standardized an organization's jobs are and the extent to which employee behavior is guided by rules and procedures. Highly formalized organizations have explicit job descriptions, numerous organizational rules, and clearly defined procedures covering work processes. Employees have little discretion over what's done, when it's done, and how it's done. However, where formalization is low, employees have more discretion in how they do their work. Early management writers expected organizations to be fairly formalized, as formalization went hand-in-hand with bureaucratic-style organizations. (Today's View is on p. 175.)

A Question of Ethics

How would you like to know all the closely held company secrets of your employer?[13] A small but growing number of private-sector businesses are revealing to employees details about everything from company financials to staff performance reviews to individual pay. Advocates of this approach say it's a good way to build trust among employees and a good way to make employees aware of how their individual contributions are affecting the overall company as a whole. And it can make them more motivated in how they work. However, critics say that such open management can be expensive and time consuming. For instance, employees may need to be "taught" how to read financial statements. And employees who have access to all the details may want to weigh in on all the decisions, slowing down the decision-making process. As work becomes collaborative and as office workers become accustomed to sharing details of each other's lives, maybe the move toward greater workplace openness is inevitable.

*If your professor has assigned this, go to the Assignments section of **mymanagementlab.com** to complete these discussion questions.*

⭐ **Talk About It 1:** What ethical issues might arise in an "open" company?

⭐ **Talk About It 2:** What are the implications for (a) managers and (b) employees?

centralization
The degree to which decision making takes place at upper levels of the organization

decentralization
The degree to which lower-level managers provide input or actually make decisions

formalization
How standardized an organization's jobs are and the extent to which employee behavior is guided by rules and procedures

What Contingency Variables Affect Structural Choice?

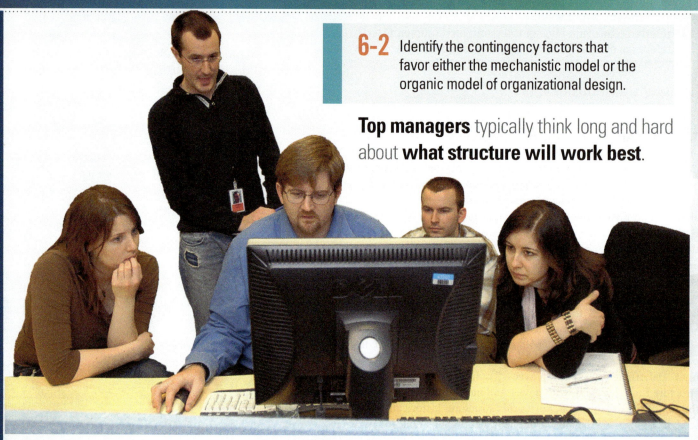

6-2 Identify the contingency factors that favor either the mechanistic model or the organic model of organizational design.

Top managers typically think long and hard about **what structure will work best**.

IF these are the contingency factors,
THEN this is the most appropriate structure.

The **"THEN"**: Appropriate Organizational Structure

MECHANISTIC

ORGANIC

MECHANISTIC	ORGANIC
☐ Rigid hierarchical relationships	☐ Collaboration (both vertical and horizontal)
☐ Fixed duties	☐ Adaptable duties
☐ Many rules	☐ Few rules
☐ Formalized communication channels	☐ Informal communication
☐ Centralized decision authority	☐ Decentralized decision authority
☐ Taller structures	☐ Flatter structures

Exhibit 6–7
Mechanistic versus Organic Organizations

mechanistic organization
A bureaucratic organization; a structure that's high in specialization, formalization, and centralization

organic organization
A structure that's low in specialization, formalization, and centralization

Mechanistic OR Organic[17]

Mechanistic organization (or bureaucracy)

- Rigid and tightly controlled structure
- Combines traditional aspects of all six elements of organization structure

- High specialization
- Rigid departmentalization
- Clear chain of command

- Narrow spans of control leading to taller structure
- Centralization
- High formalization

Organic organization

- Highly adaptive and flexible structure

- Collaboration (both vertical and horizontal)
- Adaptable duties
- Few rules

- Informal communication
- Decentralized decision authority
- Wider spans of control leading to flatter structures

- Loose structure allows for rapid adjustment to change[18]

⭐ **Watch It 1!**

If your professor has assigned this, go to **mymanagementlab.com** to watch a video titled *Elm City Market: Organizational Structure* and to respond to questions.

The "IF": 4 Contingency Variables

1 Strategy ⟶ Structure

- Based on work of Alfred Chandler[19]
- Goals are important part of organization's strategies; structure should facilitate goal achievement
- Simple strategy → simple structure
- Elaborate strategy → more complex structure
- Certain structural designs work best with different organizational strategies[20]
  — Passionate pursuit of innovation → organic
  — Passionate pursuit of cost control → mechanistic

Coloures-pic/Fotolia

❷ Size —→ Structure

- Considerable evidence that size (number of employees) affects structure[21]
- Magic number seems to be 2,000 employees
- **LARGE** organizations (> 2,000 employees)—mechanistic
- When an organization reaches this number, size is *less influential;* adding more employees has little impact as structure is already fairly mechanistic

ORGANIC

fewer than 2,000 employees can be organic

MECHANISTIC

more than 2,000 employees forces organizations to become more mechanicstic

> A smaller organization with a more organic structure becomes more mechanistic if a significant number of new employees are added to it.

❸ Technology —→ Structure

- Technology is used—by every organization—to convert inputs into outputs

(See Exhibit 6–8 in the From Past to Present box on p. 175.)

Your smartphone or tablet
standardized assembly line

Your résumé
custom design and print

Your bottle of ibuprofen
continuous-flow production process

❹ Environment —→ Structure

- Environment is a constraint on managerial discretion
- Environment also has a major effect on an organization's structure
  — Stable environment: Mechanistic structure
  — Dynamic/uncertain environment: Organic structure
- Helps explain why so many managers today have restructured their organizations to be lean, fast, and flexible.[22]

✪ **Try It!**

If your professor has assigned this, go to the Assignments section of **mymanagementlab.com** to complete the **Simulation:** *Organizational Structure*.

TODAY'S VIEW. Although some formalization is necessary for consistency and control, many organizations today rely less on strict rules and standardization to guide and regulate employee behavior. For instance, consider the following situation:

> A customer comes into a branch of a large national drug store chain and drops off a roll of film for same-day developing 37 minutes after the store's cut-off time. Although the sales clerk knows he's supposed to follow the rules, he also knows he could get the film developed with no problem and wants to accommodate the customer. So he accepts the film and hopes that his manager won't find out.[23]

Did this employee do something wrong? He did "break" the rule. But by "breaking" the rule, he actually brought in revenue and provided good customer service.

◄◄◄ From the Past to the Present ►►►

- Initial research on Technology → Structure done by Joan Woodward.[24]

- Woodward, a British management scholar, studied small manufacturing firms in southern England to determine the extent to which structural design elements were related to organizational success.[25]

- No consistent pattern found UNTIL firms divided into three distinct technologies that had increasing levels of complexity and sophistication.

  - Least complex and sophisticated: **Unit production**—the production of items in units or small batches

  - **Mass production**—large-batch manufacturing

  - Most complex and sophisticated: **process production**—continuous-process production

- One of the earliest *contingency* studies.

- Her answer to the "it depends on" question: Appropriate organizational design depends on what the organization's

technology is. These design decisions can influence an organization's sustainability efforts.

- More recent studies also have shown that organizations adapt their structures to their technology depending on *how routine their technology is* for transforming inputs into outputs.

  - More routine technology, more likely to have mechanistic structure

  - More nonroutine technology, more likely to have organic structure

> ### How does technology affect organization design?

If your professor has assigned this, go to the Assignments section of **mymanagementlab.com** *to complete these discussion questions.*

✪ **Talk About It 3:** Why is (a) mechanistic structure more appropriate for an organization with routine technology and (b) organic structure more appropriate for an organization with nonroutine technology?

✪ **Talk About It 4:** Does Woodward's framework still apply to today's organizations? Why or why not?

Exhibit 6–8 Woodward's Findings on Technology and Structure

	UNIT PRODUCTION	MASS PRODUCTION	PROCESS PRODUCTION
Structural characteristics:	Low vertical differentiation	Moderate vertical differentiation	High vertical differentiation
	Low horizontal differentiation	High horizontal differentiation	Low horizontal differentiation
	Low formalization	High formalization	Low formalization
Most effective structure:	Organic	Mechanistic	Organic

Considering there are numerous situations where rules may be too restrictive, many organizations have allowed employees some latitude, giving them sufficient autonomy to make those decisions that they feel are best under the circumstances. It doesn't mean throwing out all organizational rules because there always *will* be rules that are important for employees to follow—and these rules should be explained so employees understand why it's important to adhere to them. But for other rules, employees may be given some leeway.[26]

What Are Some Common Organizational Designs?

6-3 Compare and contrast traditional and contemporary organizational designs.

In making structural decisions, managers have some common designs from which to choose: traditional and more contemporary. Let's look at some.

What Traditional Organizational Designs Can Managers Use?

When designing a structure, managers may choose one of the traditional organizational designs. These structures—simple, functional, and divisional—tend to be more mechanistic in nature. (See Exhibit 6–9 for a summary of the strengths and weaknesses of each.)

WHAT IS THE SIMPLE STRUCTURE?   Most companies start as entrepreneurial ventures using a **simple structure**, which is an organizational design with low departmentalization, wide spans of control, authority centralized in a single person, and little formalization.[27] The simple structure is most widely used in smaller businesses and its strengths should be obvious. It's fast, flexible, and inexpensive to maintain, and accountability is clear. However, it becomes increasingly inadequate as an organization grows, because its few policies or rules to guide operations

simple structure
An organizational design with low departmentalization, wide spans of control, authority centralized in a single person, and little formalization

Exhibit 6–9 Traditional Organization Designs

Source: Robbins, Stephen P., Coulter, Mary, *Management*, 13th Ed., © 2016, p. 304. Reprinted and electronically reproduced by permission of Pearson Education, Inc., New York, NY.

and its high centralization result in information overload at the top. As size increases, decision making becomes slower and can eventually come to a standstill as the single executive tries to continue making all the decisions. If the structure is not changed and adapted to its size, the firm can lose momentum and is likely to eventually fail. The simple structure's other weakness is that it's risky: Everything depends on one person. If anything happens to the owner-manager, the organization's information and decision-making center is lost. As employees are added, however, most small businesses don't remain as simple structures. The structure tends to become more specialized and formalized. Rules and regulations are introduced, work becomes specialized, departments are created, levels of management are added, and the organization becomes increasingly bureaucratic. Two of the most popular bureaucratic design options grew out of functional and product departmentalizations and are called the functional and divisional structures.

WHAT IS THE FUNCTIONAL STRUCTURE? A **functional structure** is an organizational design that groups similar or related occupational specialties together. You can think of this structure as functional departmentalization applied to the entire organization. For example, Revlon, Inc., is organized around the functions of operations, finance, human resources, and product research and development.

The strength of the functional structure lies in the advantages that accrue from work specialization. Putting like specialties together results in economies of scale, minimizes duplication of personnel and equipment, and makes employees comfortable and satisfied because it gives them the opportunity to talk the same language as their peers. The most obvious weakness of the functional structure, however, is that the organization frequently loses sight of its best interests in the pursuit of functional goals. No one function is totally responsible for results, so members within individual functions become insulated and have little understanding of what people in other functions are doing.

WHAT IS THE DIVISIONAL STRUCTURE? The **divisional structure** is an organizational structure made up of separate business units or divisions.[28] In this structure, each division has limited autonomy, with a division manager who has authority over his or her unit and is responsible for performance. In divisional structures, however, the parent corporation typically acts as an external overseer to coordinate and control the various divisions, and often provides support services such as financial and legal. Health care giant Johnson & Johnson, for example, has three divisions: pharmaceuticals, medical devices and diagnostics, and consumer products. In addition, it has several subsidiaries that also manufacture and market diverse health care products.

The chief advantage of the divisional structure is that it focuses on results. Division managers have full responsibility for a product or service. The divisional structure also frees the headquarters staff from being concerned with day-to-day operating details so that they can pay attention to long-term and strategic planning. The major disadvantage of the divisional structure is duplication of activities and resources. Each division, for instance, may have a marketing research department. If there weren't any divisions, all of an organization's marketing research might be centralized and done for a fraction of the cost that divisionalization requires. Thus, the divisional form's duplication of functions increases the organization's costs and reduces efficiency.

What Contemporary Organizational Designs Can Managers Use?

Lean. Flexible. Innovative.

Managers are finding that the traditional designs often aren't appropriate for today's increasingly dynamic and complex environment. Instead, organizations need to be lean, flexible, and innovative; that is, more organic. So managers are finding creative ways to

functional structure
An organizational design that groups similar or related occupational specialties together

divisional structure
An organizational structure made up of separate business units or divisions

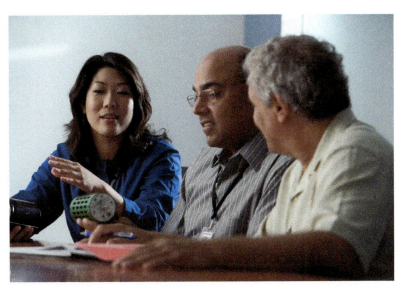

A team-based structure at W. L. Gore & Associates is key to the company's success as a technology-driven firm and contributes to its high associate satisfaction and retention. Bill Gore created work teams when he started the company in 1958, and today all 9,000 Gore associates located in 30 countries work in cross-functional and self-managed teams.

PRNewsFoto/W. L. Gore & Associates/AP Images

team structure
A structure in which the entire organization is made up of work teams

structure and organize work by using designs such as team-based structures, matrix and project structures, and boundaryless structures.[29] (See Exhibit 6–10 for a summary of these designs.)

WHAT ARE TEAM STRUCTURES? Larry Page and Sergey Brin, co-founders of Google, have created a corporate structure that "tackles most big projects in small, tightly focused teams."[30] A **team structure** is one in which the entire organization is made up of work teams that do the organization's work.[31] In this structure, employee empowerment is crucial because there is no line of managerial authority from top to bottom. Rather, employee teams design and do work in the way they think is best, but are also held responsible for all work performance results in their respective areas. In large organizations, the team

Exhibit 6–10 Contemporary Organization Designs

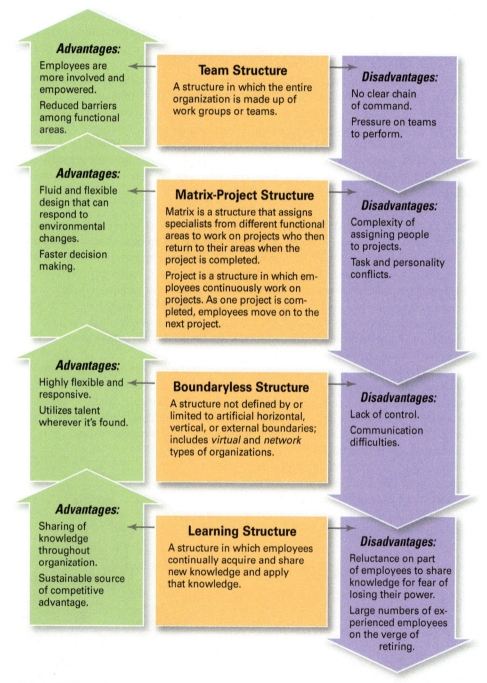

Advantages:
Employees are more involved and empowered.
Reduced barriers among functional areas.

Team Structure
A structure in which the entire organization is made up of work groups or teams.

Disadvantages:
No clear chain of command.
Pressure on teams to perform.

Advantages:
Fluid and flexible design that can respond to environmental changes.
Faster decision making.

Matrix-Project Structure
Matrix is a structure that assigns specialists from different functional areas to work on projects who then return to their areas when the project is completed.
Project is a structure in which employees continuously work on projects. As one project is completed, employees move on to the next project.

Disadvantages:
Complexity of assigning people to projects.
Task and personality conflicts.

Advantages:
Highly flexible and responsive.
Utilizes talent wherever it's found.

Boundaryless Structure
A structure not defined by or limited to artificial horizontal, vertical, or external boundaries; includes *virtual* and *network* types of organizations.

Disadvantages:
Lack of control.
Communication difficulties.

Advantages:
Sharing of knowledge throughout organization.
Sustainable source of competitive advantage.

Learning Structure
A structure in which employees continually acquire and share new knowledge and apply that knowledge.

Disadvantages:
Reluctance on part of employees to share knowledge for fear of losing their power.
Large numbers of experienced employees on the verge of retiring.

structure complements what is typically a functional or divisional structure. This allows the organization to have the efficiency of a bureaucracy while providing the flexibility of teams. For instance, companies such as Amazon, Boeing, Hewlett-Packard, Louis Vuitton, Motorola, and Xerox extensively use employee teams to improve productivity.

Although team structures have been positive, simply arranging employees into teams is not enough. Employees must be trained to work on teams, receive cross-functional skills training, and be compensated accordingly. Without a properly implemented team-based pay plan, many of the benefits of a team structure may be lost.[32] We'll cover teams more thoroughly in Chapter 10.

WHAT ARE MATRIX AND PROJECT STRUCTURES?   In addition to team-based structures, other popular contemporary designs are the matrix and project structures. The **matrix structure** assigns specialists from different functional departments to work on projects led by a project manager. When employees finish work on an assigned project, they go back to their functional departments. One unique aspect of this design is that it creates a *dual chain of command* since employees in a matrix organization have two managers: their functional area manager and their product or project manager, who share authority. (See Exhibit 6–11.) The project manager has authority over the functional members who are part of his or her project team in areas related to the project's goals. However, any decisions about promotions, salary recommendations, and annual reviews typically remain the functional manager's responsibility. To work effectively, both managers have to communicate regularly, coordinate work demands on employees, and resolve conflicts together.

The primary strength of the matrix is that it can facilitate coordination of a multiple set of complex and interdependent projects while still retaining the economies that result from keeping functional specialists grouped together. The major disadvantages of the matrix are the confusion it creates and its propensity to foster power struggles. When you dispense with the chain of command and unity of command principles, you significantly increase ambiguity. Confusion can arise over who reports to whom. The confusion and ambiguity, in turn, are what trigger the power struggles.

> **matrix structure**
> A structure in which specialists from different functional departments are assigned to work on projects led by a project manager

Exhibit 6–11 Sample Matrix Structure

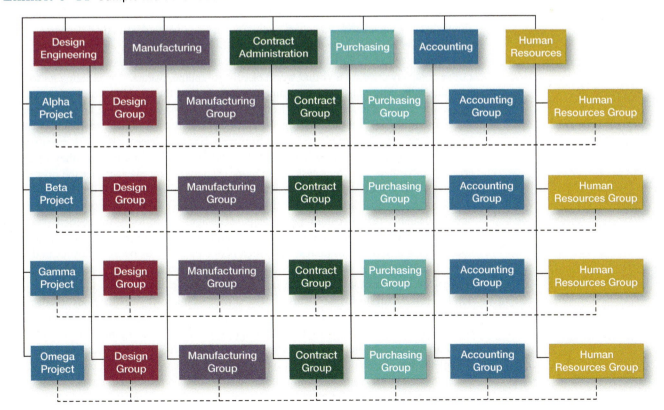

Instead of a matrix structure, many organizations are using a **project structure**, in which employees continuously work on projects. Unlike the matrix structure, a project structure has no formal departments where employees return at the completion of a project. Instead, employees take their specific skills, abilities, and experiences to other projects. Also, all work in project structures is performed by teams of employees. For instance, at design firm IDEO, project teams form, disband, and form again as the work requires. Employees "join" project teams because they bring needed skills and abilities to that project. Once a project is completed, however, they move on to the next one.[33]

Project structures tend to be more flexible organizational designs.

- Advantages:
  - Employees can be deployed rapidly to respond to environmental changes.
  - No departmentalization or rigid organizational hierarchy to slow down decisions or actions.
  - Managers serve as facilitators, mentors, and coaches and work to eliminate or minimize organizational obstacles and ensure that teams have the resources they need to effectively and efficiently complete their work.
- Disadvantages:
  - Complexity of assigning people to projects.
  - Inevitable task and personality conflicts that arise.

WHAT IS A BOUNDARYLESS ORGANIZATION? Another contemporary organizational design is the **boundaryless organization**, which is an organization whose design is not defined by, or limited to, the horizontal, vertical, or external boundaries imposed by a predefined structure.[34] Former GE chairman Jack Welch coined the term because he wanted to eliminate vertical and horizontal boundaries within GE and break down external barriers between the company and its customers and suppliers. Although the idea of eliminating boundaries may seem odd, many of today's most successful organizations are finding that they can operate most effectively by remaining flexible and *un*structured: that the ideal structure for them is *not* having a rigid, bounded, and predefined structure.[35]

What do we mean by "boundaries"? There are two types: (1) *internal*—the horizontal ones imposed by work specialization and departmentalization and the vertical ones that separate employees into organizational levels and hierarchies; and (2) *external*—the boundaries that separate the organization from its customers, suppliers, and other stakeholders. To minimize or eliminate these boundaries, managers might use virtual or network structural designs.

A **virtual organization** consists of a small core of full-time employees and outside specialists temporarily hired as needed to work on projects.[36] An example is when Second Life, a company creating a virtual world of colorful online avatars, was building its software. Founder Philip Rosedale hired programmers from around the world and divided up the work into about 1,600 individual tasks, "from setting up databases to fixing bugs." The process worked so well, the company used it for all sorts of work.[37] Another example is Nashville-based Emma Inc., an e-mail marketing firm with 100 employees who work from home or offices in Austin, Denver, New York, and Portland.[38] The biggest challenge they've faced is creating a "virtual" culture, a task made more challenging by the fact that the organization is virtual. The inspiration for this structural approach comes from the film industry. There, people are essentially "free agents" who move from project to project applying their skills—directing, talent casting, costuming, makeup, set design, and so forth—as needed.

Another structural option for managers wanting to minimize or eliminate organizational boundaries is a **network organization**, which is one that uses its own employees to do some work activities and networks of outside suppliers to provide other needed product components or work processes.[39] This organizational form is sometimes called a modular organization by manufacturing firms.[40] This structural approach allows organizations to concentrate on what they do best by contracting out other activities to companies that do those activities best. Many companies are using such an approach for certain organizational work activities. For instance, the head of development for Boeing's 787 airplane manages thousands of employees and some 100 suppliers at more than 100 sites in different countries.[41] Sweden's Ericsson contracts its manufacturing and even some of its research and development to more cost-effective contractors in New Delhi, Singapore, California, and other global locations.[42]

project structure
A structure in which employees continuously work on projects

boundaryless organization
An organization whose design is not defined by, or limited to, boundaries imposed by a predefined structure

virtual organization
An organization that consists of a small core of full-time employees and outside specialists temporarily hired as needed to work on projects

network organization
An organization that uses its own employees to do some work activities and networks of outside suppliers to provide other needed product components or work processes

And at Penske Truck Leasing, dozens of business processes such as securing permits and titles, entering data from drivers' logs, and processing data for tax filings and accounting have been outsourced to Mexico and India.[43]

✪ Write It!

If your professor has assigned this, go to the Assignments section of **mymanagementlab.com** to complete *MGMT 2: Organizational Structures*.

What Are Today's Organizational Design Challenges?

6-4 Discuss the design challenges faced by today's organizations.

Changing the **Way Work** Is Done

As managers look for organizational designs that will best support and facilitate *employees doing their work efficiently and effectively*, there are certain challenges they must contend with. These include keeping employees connected, managing global structural issues, building a learning organization, and designing flexible work arrangements.

How Do You Keep Employees Connected?

Many organizational design concepts were developed during the twentieth century when work tasks were fairly predictable and constant, most jobs were full-time and continued indefinitely, and work was done at an employer's place of business under a manager's supervision.[44] That's not what it's like in many organizations today, as you saw in our preceding discussion of virtual and network organizations. A major structural design challenge for managers is finding a way to keep widely dispersed and mobile employees connected to the organization. The Technology and the Manager's Job box describes ways that information technology can help.

How Do Global Differences Affect Organizational Structure?

Are there global differences in organizational structures? Are Australian organizations structured like those in the United States? Are German organizations structured like those in France or Mexico? Given the global nature of today's business environment, this is an issue with which managers need to be familiar. Researchers have concluded that the structures and strategies of organizations worldwide are similar, "while the behavior within them is maintaining its cultural uniqueness."[45] What does this mean for designing effective and efficient structures? When designing or changing structure, managers may need to think about the cultural implications of certain design elements. For instance, one study showed that formalization—rules and bureaucratic mechanisms—may be more important in less economically developed countries and less important in more economically developed countries where employees may have higher levels of professional education and skills.[46] Other structural design elements may be affected by cultural differences as well.

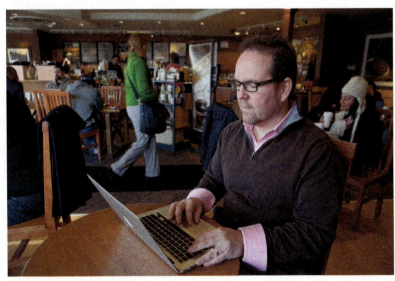

Tim Kilroy, a salesman for the online advertising agency Triggit, works remotely on his computer from a Starbucks coffee shop or his home in Massachusetts. With almost half of his clients located in other countries, Kilroy uses mobile computing and communication technology to stay connected to his company and to his widely dispersed clients.

Melanie Stetson Freeman/AP Images

learning organization
An organization that has developed the capacity to continuously learn, adapt, and change

How Do You Build a Learning Organization?

Doing business in an intensely competitive global environment, British retailer Tesco realized how important it was for its stores to run well behind the scenes. And it does so using a proven "tool" called Tesco in a Box, which promotes consistency in operations as well as being a way to share innovations. Tesco is an example of a **learning organization**, an organization that has developed the capacity to continuously learn, adapt, and change.[47] The concept of a learning organization doesn't involve a specific organizational design per se, but instead describes an organizational mind-set or philosophy that has significant design implications. In a learning organization, employees are practicing knowledge management by continually acquiring and sharing new knowledge and are willing to apply that knowledge in making decisions or performing their work. Some organizational design theorists even go so far as to say that an organization's ability to learn and to apply that learning as they perform the organization's work may be the only sustainable source of competitive advantage.

✪ Watch It 2!

If your professor has assigned this, go to the Assignments section of **mymanagementlab.com** to complete the video exercise titled *CH2MHill: Adaptive Organizational Design*.

Technology and the Manager's Job
♻ THE CHANGING WORLD OF WORK

It's fair to say that the world of work will never be like it was 10 years ago.[48] IT has opened up new possibilities for employees to do their work in locations as remote as Patagonia or in the middle of downtown Seattle. Although organizations have always had employees who traveled to distant corporate locations to take care of business, these employees no longer have to find the nearest pay phone or wait to get back to "the office" to see what problems have cropped up. Instead, mobile computing and communication have given organizations and employees ways to stay connected, be more productive, and be more environmentally friendly. Let's look at some of the technologies that are changing the way work is done.

- Handheld devices with e-mail, calendars, and contacts can be used anywhere there's a wireless network. And these devices can be used to log into corporate databases and company intranets.
- Employees can videoconference using broadband networks and Web cams.
- Many companies are giving employees key fobs with constantly changing encryption codes that allow them to log onto the corporate network to access e-mail and company data from any computer hooked up to the Internet.

- Cell phones switch seamlessly between cellular networks and corporate Wi-Fi connections.

The biggest issue in doing work anywhere, anytime is security. Companies must protect their important and sensitive information. However, software and other disabling devices have minimized security issues considerably. Even insurance providers are more comfortable giving their mobile employees access to information. For instance, Health Net Inc. gave BlackBerrys to many of its managers so they can tap into customer records from anywhere. One tech company CEO said that all types of organizations should start thinking about identifying and creating innovative apps that their workers could use in doing their jobs more efficiently and effectively and get those to them.

If your professor has assigned this, go to the Assignments section of **mymanagementlab.com** *to complete these discussion questions.*

✪ **TALK ABOUT IT 5:** What benefits do you see with being able to do work anywhere, anytime? (Think in terms of benefits for an organization and for its human resources.)

✪ **TALK ABOUT IT 6:** What other issues, besides security, do you see with being able to do work anywhere, anytime? (Again, think about this for an organization and for its employees.)

Exhibit 6–12 Characteristics of a Learning Organization

Sources: Based on P. M. Senge, *The Fifth Discipline: The Art and Practice of Learning Organizations* (New York: Doubleday, 1990); and R. M. Hodgetts, F. Luthans, and S. M. Lee, "New Paradigm Organizations: From Total Quality to Learning to World Class," *Organizational Dynamics*, Winter 1994, 4–19.

What would a learning organization look like? As you can see in Exhibit 6–12, the important characteristics of a learning organization revolve around (1) organizational design, (2) information sharing, (3) leadership, and (4) culture.

(1) What types of organizational design elements would be necessary for learning to take place? In a learning organization, it's critical for members to share information and collaborate on work activities throughout the entire organization—across different functional specialties and even at different organizational levels—through minimizing or eliminating the existing structural and physical boundaries. In this type of boundaryless environment, employees are free to work together and collaborate in doing the organization's work the best way they can, and to learn from each other. Because of this need to collaborate, teams also tend to be an important feature of a learning organization's structural design. Employees work in teams on whatever activities need to be done, and these employee teams are empowered to make decisions about doing their work or resolving issues. Empowered employees and teams have little need for "bosses" who direct and control. Instead, managers serve as facilitators, supporters, and advocates for employee teams.

(2) Learning can't take place without information. For a learning organization to "learn," information must be shared among members; that is, organizational employees must engage in knowledge management by sharing information openly, in a timely manner, and as accurately as possible. Because few structural and physical barriers exist in a learning organization, the environment is conducive to open communication and extensive information sharing.

(3) Leadership plays an important role as an organization moves toward becoming a learning organization. What should leaders do in a learning organization? One of their most important functions is facilitating the creation of a shared vision for the organization's future and then keeping organizational members working toward that vision. In addition, leaders should support and encourage the collaborative environment that's critical to learning. Without strong and committed leadership throughout the organization, it would be extremely difficult to be a learning organization.

(4) The organization's culture is important to being a learning organization. In a learning culture, everyone agrees on a shared vision and everyone recognizes the inherent interrelationships among the organization's processes, activities, functions, and external environment. It also fosters a strong sense of community, caring for each other, and trust. In a learning organization, employees feel free to communicate openly, share, experiment, and learn without fear of criticism or punishment.

telecommuting
A work arrangement in which employees work at home and are linked to the workplace by computer

How Can Managers Design Efficient and Effective Flexible Work Arrangements?

Accenture consultant Keyur Patel's job arrangement is becoming the norm, rather than the exception.[49] During a recent consulting assignment, he had three clocks on his desk: one set to Manila time (where his software programmers were), one to Bangalore (where another programming support team worked), and the third for San Francisco, where he was spending four days a week helping a major retailer implement IT systems to track and improve sales. And his cell phone kept track of the time in Atlanta, his home, where he headed on Thursday evenings.

For this new breed of professionals, life is a blend of home and office, work and leisure. Thanks to technology, work can now be done anywhere, anytime. As organizations adapt their structural designs to these new realities, we see more of them adopting flexible working arrangements. Such arrangements not only exploit the power of technology, but also give organizations the flexibility to deploy employees when and where needed. In this section, we're going to take a look at some different types of flexible work arrangements, including telecommuting; compressed workweeks, flextime, and job sharing; and contingent workforce. As with the other structural options we've looked at, managers must evaluate these in light of the implications for decision making, communication, authority relationships, work task accomplishment, and so forth.

WHAT'S INVOLVED IN TELECOMMUTING? Information technology has made telecommuting *possible* and external environmental changes have made it *necessary* for many organizations. **Telecommuting** is a work arrangement in which employees work at home and are linked to the workplace by computer. Needless to say, not every job is a candidate for telecommuting. But many are.

Working from home used to be considered a "cushy perk" for a few lucky employees and such an arrangement wasn't allowed very often. Now, many businesses view telecommuting as a business necessity. For instance, at SCAN Health Plan, the company's chief financial officer said that getting more employees to telecommute provided the company a way to grow without having to incur any additional fixed costs such as office buildings, equipment, or parking lots.[50] In addition, some companies view the arrangement as a way to combat high gas prices and to attract talented employees who want more freedom and control over their work.

Despite its apparent appeal, many managers are reluctant to have their employees become "laptop hobos."[51] They argue that employees might waste time surfing the Internet or playing online games instead of working, ignore clients, and desperately miss the camaraderie and social exchanges of the workplace. In addition, managers worry about how they'll "manage" these employees. How do you interact with an employee and gain his or her trust when they're not physically present? And what if their work performance isn't up to par? How do you make suggestions for improvement? Another significant challenge is making sure that company information is kept safe and secure when employees are working from home.

Employees often express the same concerns about working remotely, especially when it comes to the isolation of not being "at work." At Accenture, where employees are scattered around the world, the chief human resources officer says that it isn't easy to maintain that esprit de corps.[52] However, the company put in place a number of programs and processes to create that sense of belonging for its workforce including Web conferencing tools, assigning each employee

Airbnb, the global travel rental firm, uses telecommuters and a contingency workforce of part-time, temporary, and freelance workers. Flexible work arrangements, including those for employees shown here at Airbnb's office in Dublin, enable the company to connect people in more than 34,000 cities and 190 countries either online or from a mobile phone or tablet.

View Pictures/Newscom

to a career counselor, and holding quarterly community events at its offices. In addition, the telecommuter employee may find that the line between work and home becomes even more blurred, which can be stressful.[53] These are important organizing issues and ones that managers and organizations must address when moving toward having employees telecommute.

HOW CAN ORGANIZATIONS USE COMPRESSED WORKWEEKS, FLEXTIME, AND JOB SHARING?   During the most recent economic crisis in the United Kingdom, accounting firm KPMG needed to reduce costs and decided to use flexible work options as a way of doing so.[54] The company's program, called Flexible Futures, offered employees four options to choose from: a four-day workweek with a 20 percent salary reduction; a two-to-twelve-week sabbatical at 30 percent of pay; both options; or continue with their regular schedule. Some 85 percent of the UK employees agreed to the reduced-work-week plan. "Since so many people agreed to the flexible work plans, KPMG was able to cap the salary cut at about 10 percent for the year in most cases." The best thing, though, was that as a result of the plan, KPMG didn't have to do large-scale employee layoffs.

As this example shows, organizations sometimes find they need to restructure work using other forms of flexible work arrangements. (1) One approach is a **compressed workweek** in which employees work longer hours per day but fewer days per week. The most common arrangement is four 10-hour days (a 4–40 program). (2) Another alternative is **flextime** (also known as **flexible work hours**), which is a scheduling system in which employees are required to work a specific number of hours a week but are free to vary those hours within certain limits. In a flextime schedule, most companies designate certain common core hours when all employees are required to be on the job, but starting, ending, and lunch-hour times are flexible. 3. Another type of job scheduling is called **job sharing**—the practice of having two or more people split a full-time job. Organizations might offer job sharing to professionals who want to work but don't want the demands and hassles of a full-time position. For instance, at Ernst & Young, employees in many of the company's locations can choose from a variety of flexible work arrangements including job sharing. Many companies use job sharing during economic downturns to avoid employee layoffs.[55]

WHAT IS A CONTINGENT WORKFORCE?   "When Julia Lee first heard of Tongal, she thought it was a scam. Tongal pays people—anyone with a good idea, really—to create online videos for companies such as Mattel, Allstate, and Popchips."[56] Tongal divides projects into stages and pays cash for the top-five ideas. On Lee's first submission—which only took three hours of work—she got $1,000. On another, she earned $4,000. In a year's time, she's earned some $6,000 for about 100 hours of work. Tongal isn't the only business doing this. The idea of breaking up a job into small pieces and using the Internet to find workers to do those tasks was pioneered by LiveOps and followed by Amazon.com's Mechanical Turk and many others.

Switch on. Switch off.

"Companies want a workforce they can switch on and off as needed."[57] Although this quote may shock you, the truth is that the labor force already has begun shifting away from traditional full-time jobs toward **contingent workers**—temporary, freelance, or contract workers whose employment is *contingent* upon demand for their services. In today's economy, many organizations have responded by converting full-time permanent jobs into contingent jobs. It's predicted that by the end of the next decade the number of contingent employees will have grown to about 40 percent of the workforce. (It's at 30 percent today.)[58] In fact, one compensation and benefits expert says that "a growing number of workers will need to structure their careers around this model."[59] That's likely to include you!

compressed workweek
A workweek where employees work longer hours per day but fewer days per week

flextime (also known as flexible work hours)
A work scheduling system in which employees are required to work a specific number of hours per week but can vary when they work those hours within certain limits

job sharing
When two or more people split a full-time job

contingent workers
Temporary, freelance, or contract workers whose employment is *contingent* upon demand for their services

What are the implications for managers and organizations? Since contingent employees are not "employees" in the traditional sense of the word, managing them has its own set of challenges and expectations. Managers must recognize that because contingent workers lack the stability and security of permanent employees, they may not identify with the organization or be as committed or motivated. Managers may need to treat contingent workers differently in terms of practices and policies. However, with good communication and leadership, an organization's contingent employees can be just as valuable a resource to an organization as permanent employees are. Today's managers must recognize that it will be their responsibility to motivate their entire workforce, full-time and contingent, and to build their commitment to doing good work![60]

No matter what structural design managers choose for their organizations, the design should help employees do their work in the best, most efficient and effective way they can. The structure needs to help, not hinder, organizational members as they carry out the organization's work. After all, the structure is simply a means to an end.

MyManagementLab®

Go to **mymanagementlab.com** to complete the problems marked with this icon .

6 Review

CHAPTER SUMMARY

6-1 Describe six key elements in organizational design.

The first element, *work specialization*, refers to dividing work activities into separate job tasks. The second, *departmentalization,* is how jobs are grouped together, which can be one of five types: functional, product, customer, geographic, or process. The third—*authority, responsibility, and power*—all have to do with getting work done in an organization. Authority refers to the rights inherent in a managerial position to give orders and expect those orders to be obeyed. Responsibility refers to the obligation to perform when authority has been delegated. Power is the capacity of an individual to influence decisions and is not the same as authority. The fourth, *span of control*, refers to the number of employees a manager can efficiently and effectively manage. The fifth, *centralization and decentralization*, deals with where the majority of decisions are made—at upper organizational levels or pushed down to lower-level managers. The sixth, *formalization*, describes how standardized an organization's jobs are and the extent to which employees' behavior is guided by rules and procedures.

6-2 Identify the contingency factors that favor either the mechanistic model or the organic model of organizational design.

A *mechanistic* organization design is quite bureaucratic whereas an *organic* organization design is more fluid and flexible. The *strategy*-determines-structure factor says that as organizational strategies move from single product to product diversification, the structure will move from organic to mechanistic. As an organization's *size* increases, so does the need for a more mechanistic structure. The more nonroutine the *technology*, the more organic a structure should be. Finally, stable *environments*

are better matched with mechanistic structures, but dynamic ones fit better with organic structures.

6-3 Compare and contrast traditional and contemporary organizational designs.

Traditional structural designs include simple, functional, and divisional. A *simple structure* is one with low departmentalization, wide spans of control, authority centralized in a single person, and little formalization. A *functional structure* is one that groups similar or related occupational specialties together. A *divisional structure* is one made up of separate business units or divisions. Contemporary structural designs include *team-based structures* (the entire organization is made up of work teams); *matrix and project structures* (where employees work on projects for short periods of time or continuously); and *boundaryless organizations* (where the structural design is free of imposed boundaries). A boundaryless organization can either be a virtual or a network organization.

6-4 Discuss the design challenges faced by today's organizations.

One design challenge lies in keeping employees connected, which can be accomplished through using information technology. Another challenge is understanding the global differences that affect organizational structure. Although structures and strategies of organizations worldwide are similar, the behavior within them differs, which can influence certain design elements. Another challenge is designing a structure around the mind-set of being a learning organization. Finally, managers are looking for organizational designs with efficient and effective flexible work arrangements. They're using options such as telecommuting, compressed workweeks, flextime, job sharing, and contingent workers.

DISCUSSION QUESTIONS

6-1 Discuss what is meant by the term *organization design.*

6-2 Describe the traditional and contemporary views of each of the six key elements of organizational design.

6-3 *Can* an organization's structure be changed quickly? Why or why not? *Should* it be changed quickly? Why or why not?

6-4 "An organization can have no structure." Do you agree or disagree with this statement? Explain.

6-5 Contrast mechanistic and organic organizations.

6-6 Explain the contingency factors that affect organizational design.

6-7 With the availability of information technology that allows employees to work anywhere, anytime, is organizing still an important managerial function? Why or why not?

6-8 Researchers are now saying that efforts to simplify work tasks actually have negative results for both companies and their employees. Do you agree? Why or why not?

6-9 "The boundaryless organization has the potential to create a major shift in the way we work." Do you agree or disagree with this statement? Explain.

6-10 Draw an organization chart of an organization with which you're familiar (where you work, a student organization to which you belong, your college or university, etc.). Be very careful in showing the departments (or groups) and especially be careful to get the chain of command correct. Be prepared to share your chart with the class.

Writing Assignments

6-11 It's stated in the chapter that contemporary organization design should be lean, flexible, and innovative. What are the implications of those requirements?

6-12 If organizing is about getting work done efficiently and effectively, what organizing challenges might lower-level managers have to address? (Hint: Think in terms of the six key elements of organization design.)

Management Skill Builder | INCREASING YOUR POWER

Managerial jobs come with the power of authority. But sometimes that authority isn't enough to get things done. And other times you may not want to use your formal authority as a means of getting people to do what you want. You may, for instance, want to rely more on your persuasive skills than the power of your title. So effective managers increase their power by developing multiple sources of influence.

✪ PERSONAL INVENTORY ASSESSMENT PERSONAL INVENTORY ASSESSMENT

Gaining Power and Influence

As you saw in this chapter, power is an important component of an organization's structure. Use this PIA to identify ways that you gain power and influence.

Skill Basics

You can increase the likelihood that you'll survive and thrive in your organization if you learn how to develop a power base. Remember, because you have power doesn't mean you have to use it. But it's nice to be able to call upon it when you do need it. Four sources of power can be derived from your job. Another three sources are based on your personal unique characteristics.

• All management jobs come with the power to coerce, reward, and impose authority. *Coercive power* is based on

fear. If you can dismiss, suspend, demote, assign unpleasant work tasks, or write a negative performance review on someone, you hold coercive power over that person. Conversely, if you can give someone something of positive value or remove something of negative value—like control pay rates, raises, bonuses, promotions, or work assignments—you have *reward power*. And all managerial positions provide some degree—though within specific limitations—to exert authority over subordinates. If you can tell someone to do something and they see this request to be within your formal job description, you have *authority power* over them.

- In addition to coercive, reward, and authoritative power, many managerial positions also possess *information power* that comes from access to and control over information. If you have data or knowledge that others need, and which only you have access to, it gives you power. Of course, you don't have to be a manager to have information power. Many employees are quite skilled at operating in secrecy, hiding technical short-cuts, or avoiding showing others exactly what they do—all with the intention of keeping important knowledge from getting into others' hands.

- You don't have to be a manager or control information to have power in an organization. You can also exert influence based on your expertise, admiration that others might have for you, and through charismatic qualities. If you have a special skill or unique knowledge that others in the organization depend on, you hold *expert power*. In our current age of specialization, this source of power is increasingly potent. If others identify with you and look up to you to the extent that they want to please you, you have *referent power*. It develops out of admiration and the desire to be like someone else. The final source of influence is *charismatic power*, which is an extension of referent power. If others will follow you because they admire your heroic qualities, you have charismatic power over them.

- Based on these sources of power, we can say that you can increase your power in organizations by (1) taking on managerial responsibilities, (2) gaining access to important information, (3) developing an expertise that the organization needs, or (4) displaying personal characteristics that others admire.

Based on J. R. P. French, Jr. and B. Raven, "The Bases of Social Power," in D. Cartwright (ed.), *Studies in Social Power* (Ann Arbor: University of Michigan Institute of Social Research, 1959), 150–67; B. J. Raven, "The Bases of Power: Origin and Recent Developments," *Journal of Social Issues* 49 (1993): 227–51; E. A. Ward, "Social Power Bases of Managers: Emergence of a New Factor," *Journal of Social Psychology* (February 2001): 144–47; and B. H. Raven, "The Bases of Power and the Power/Interaction Model of Interpersonal Influence," *Analyses of Social Issues and Public Policy*, December 2008, 1–22.

Practicing the Skill

Read through this scenario and follow the directions at the end of it:

Margaret is a supervisor in the online sales division of a large clothing retailer. She has let it be known that she is devoted to the firm and plans to build her career there. Margaret is hard-working and reliable, has volunteered for extra projects, has taken in-house development courses, and joined a committee dedicated to improving employee safety on the job. She undertook an assignment to research ergonomic office furniture for the head of the department and gave up several lunch hours to consult with the head of human resources about her report. Margaret filed the report late, but she explained the delay by saying that her assistant lost several pages that she had to redraft over the weekend. The report was well received, and several of Margaret's colleagues think she should be promoted when the next opening arises.

Evaluate Margaret's skill in building a power base. What actions has she taken that are helpful to her in reaching her goal? Is there anything she should have done differently?

Experiential Exercise

Ontario Electronics Ltd.

To: Claude Fortier, Special Assistant to the President

From: Ian Campbell, President

Subject: Learning Organizations

First of all, thanks for keeping everything "going" while I attended the annual meeting of the Canadian Electronics Manufacturers Industry Association last week. Our luncheon speaker on the final day talked about how important it is for organizations to be responsive to customer and marketplace needs. One approach she discussed for doing this was becoming a learning organization. I'm now convinced that our company's future may well depend on how well we're able to "learn."

I'd like you to find some current information on learning organizations. Although I'm sure you'll be able to find numerous articles about the topic, limit your report to five of what you consider to be the best sources of information on the topic. Write a one-paragraph summary for each of these five articles, being sure to note all the bibliographic information in case we need to find the article later. Since I'd like our executive team to move on this idea fairly quickly, please have your report back to me by the end of the week.

This fictionalized company and message were created for educational purposes only, and not meant to reflect positively or negatively on management practices by any company that may share this name.

CASE APPLICATION #1

You Work Where?

Yahoo!, a pioneer in Web search and navigation, struggles to remain relevant in the face of competition from the likes of Google, Facebook, and Twitter.[61] It missed the two biggest Internet trends—social networking and mobile. However, in July 2012, after the company did its own search, it snagged a gem as the company's new CEO—Marissa Mayer, one of the top executives at Google. Mayer had been one of the few public faces of Google and was responsible for the look and feel of Google's most popular products. Guiding Yahoo! as it tries to regain its former prominence is proving to be the challenge that experts predicted, but they're also saying that if anyone could take on the challenge of making Yahoo! an innovator once again, Mayer is the person.

Two of her initial decisions included free food at the office and new smartphones for every employee, something that Google does. However, in February 2013, Mayer launched an employee initiative that has generated lots of discussion—positive and negative. She decided that as of June 2013, Yahoo! employees who worked remotely had to come back to the office. The memo from the vice president of people and development (code for head of Human Resources) clarified that the new initiative was a response to productivity issues that often can arise when employees work from home. With a new boss and a renewed commitment to making Yahoo! a strong company in a challenging industry, employees were expected to be physically present in the workplace, hopefully leading to developing a strong common bond and greater productivity. The announcement affects not only those who work from home full time—mainly customer service reps—but also those employees who have arranged to work from home one or two days a week. Yahoo! isn't the only company asking remote workers to return. Bank of America, which had a popular remote work program, decided late in 2012 that employees in certain roles had to come back to the office.

Before Mayer became CEO at Yahoo!, it was a wonder anything ever got done there. What she found wasn't even remotely like the way employees functioned at Google. At Yahoo!, few people were physically at work in the office cubicles throughout the building. Few cars or bikes or other vehicles could be found in the facility's parking lots. Even more disturbing: some of the employees who were physically there at work did as little work as needed and then took off early. She also discovered that other employees who worked from home did little but collect a paycheck or maybe work on a sideline business they had started. Even at the office, one former manager described morale as being as low as it could be because employees thought the company was failing. These were some of the reasons that Mayer abolished Yahoo!'s work-from-home policy. If Yahoo! was to again become the nimble company it had once been, a new culture of innovation, communication, and collaboration was needed. And that meant employees had to be at work; physically at work together. Restoring Yahoo!'s "cool"—from its products to its deteriorating morale and culture—would be difficult if the organization's people weren't there. That's why Mayer's decision at Yahoo! created such an uproar. Yahoo!'s only official statement on the new policy said, "This isn't a broad industry view on working from home. This is about what is right for Yahoo!, right now."

> ### Where **IS** work done most efficiently and effectively?

Where work is done most efficiently and effectively—office, home, combination—is an important workplace issue. The three main managerial concerns are productivity, innovation, and collaboration. Do flexible arrangements lead to greater productivity or inhibit innovation and collaboration? Another concern is that employees, especially younger ones, expect to be able to work remotely. Yes, the trend has been toward greater workplace flexibility, but does that flexibility lead to a bloated, lazy, and unproductive remote workforce? These are the challenges of designing work structures.

Discussion Questions

6-14 Evaluate Yahoo!'s new work initiative. Did it have to be an "all or nothing" proposition? Discuss.

6-15 What can managers and organizations do to help employees who work from home be efficient and effective?

6-16 Take the three main concerns—productivity, innovation, and collaboration. From the perspective of management, how do you think flexible arrangements stack up? How about from the employee's perspective?

6-17 Is "face-time" (that is, showing up at work to be seen by your boss and others) critical to one's career? Discuss.

6-18 Is being able to work remotely important to you? Why or why not?

CASE APPLICATION #2

Lift Off

Over the years, NASA (National Aeronautics and Space Administration) has provided us with some spectacular moments—from Neil Armstrong's first steps on the moon to the Hubble Telescope's mesmerizing photos of distant stars and galaxies.[62] As stated in NASA's Strategic Plan 2014, its vision is: "We reach for new heights and reveal the unknown for the benefit of humankind." And its mission is: "Drive advances in science, technology, aeronautics, and space exploration to enhance knowledge, education, innovation, economic vitality, and stewardship of Earth." These have guided (and continue to guide) its management team as decisions are made about projects, missions, and programs. When the space shuttle program—NASA's main project mission—ended in 2011, the organization struggled for a time with its purpose and identity. In fact, one agency program manager at that time described NASA's future as nothing but uncertainty. However, despite the ambiguity, NASA's leaders have been charting a new trajectory. Possible new goals include getting to an asteroid by 2025 and putting astronauts on Mars by 2030. (Here's a bit of trivia for you: Mars is 225,300,000 kilometers—140,000,000 miles—from earth.) And critical to achieving these goals is the necessity to guide this complex, technical organization and figure out how to best manage the vast array of knowledge resources that are so crucial to its future.

NASA, established by the National Aeronautics and Space Act on July 29, 1958, has led U.S. efforts in space exploration, including the Apollo lunar landing missions, the Skylab space station, and the reusable manned spacecraft—which we know better as the Space Shuttle. It's a unique organization where equipment costs millions of dollars and where people's lives can be at stake. Over the years, NASA has had many successful endeavors (and some tragic failures). Getting men on the moon, not once, but six times, reflects outstanding technological prowess, far superior to any other country. Being able to put a rocket into space with a shuttle that then comes back to earth and lands on its own is a reflection of the incredibly talented and knowledgeable employees that NASA has. Now, NASA is taking the first steps to develop new technologies and capabilities to send astronauts further into space than ever before.

It achieved a major milestone in early December 2014 with the successful test flight of Orion, a spacecraft designed for ultra-long-distance journeys. Accomplishments such as these are possible only because of the people in NASA who bring their knowledge, talents, skills, and creativity to that organization. And "managing" those people requires an "organization" structure that allows, enhances, and encourages the sharing of knowledge. It's not an easy thing to design and do.

One word that aptly describes NASA's organization environment is *complexity*. Not only is there technical complexity (yes, we are talking rocket science, here!), but also numerous projects are going on, change is an ongoing reality, and demands arise from numerous stakeholders both inside and outside the organization. And within this complexity, the challenge is finding a way to share the incredible wealth of knowledge within project teams and across the entire organization. How is NASA doing this?

Knowing how important it is to manage the organization's vast knowledge resources, NASA has identified knowledge-sharing activities currently being used and others that are needed. Some of these include: online tools such as collaboration and sharing sites, video libraries, portals, etc.; a search engine that allows tagging and classifications (taxonomy); a library of searchable case studies and publications; an index of defined processes or "lessons learned;" knowledge networks of location "experts," collaboration activities, collaborative workspaces, etc.; and forums, workshops and other social exchanges that bring people together. Through its knowledge management efforts, NASA administrators are showing that they understand how important it is for the organization's structure to contribute to efficiently and effectively managing its knowledge resources.

Managing the knowledge resources of **NASA**

Discussion Questions

6-19 Would you call NASA a learning organization? Why or why not?

6-20 In what ways is NASA's environment complex?

6-21 How does complexity affect structural choice?

6-22 Using Exhibit 6–12, what suggestions would you make to managers at NASA about being a learning organization?

CASE APPLICATION #3

A New Kind of Structure

Admit it. Sometimes the projects you're working on (school, work, or both) can get pretty boring and monotonous. Wouldn't it be great to have a magic button you could push to get someone else to do that boring, time-consuming stuff? At Pfizer, that "magic button" is a reality for a large number of employees.

As a global pharmaceutical company, Pfizer is continually looking for ways to help employees be more efficient and effective. The company's senior director of organizational effectiveness found that the "Harvard MBA staff we hired to develop strategies and innovate were instead Googling and making PowerPoints." Indeed, internal studies conducted to find out just how much time its valuable talent was spending on menial tasks was startling. The average Pfizer employee was spending 20 percent to 40 percent of his or her time on support work (creating documents, typing notes, doing research, manipulating data, scheduling meetings) and only 60 percent to 80 percent on knowledge work (strategy, innovation, networking, collaborating, critical thinking). And the problem wasn't just at lower levels. Even the highest-level employees were affected. Take, for instance, David Cain, an executive director for global engineering. He enjoys his job—assessing environmental real estate risks, managing facilities, and controlling a multimillion-dollar budget. But he didn't so much enjoy having to go through spreadsheets and put together PowerPoints. Now, however, with Pfizer's "magic button," those tasks are passed off to individuals outside the organization.

Just what is this "magic button"? Originally called the Office of the Future (OOF), the renamed PfizerWorks allows employees to shift tedious and time-consuming tasks with the click of a single button on their computer desktop. They describe what they need on an online form, which is then sent to one of two Indian service-outsourcing firms. When a request is received, a team member in India calls the Pfizer employee to clarify what's needed and by when. The team member then e-mails back a cost specification for the requested work. If the Pfizer employee decides to proceed, the costs involved are charged to the employee's department. About this unique arrangement, Cain said that he relishes working with what he prefers to call his "personal consulting organization."

The number 66,500 illustrates just how beneficial PfizerWorks has been for the company. That's the number of work hours estimated to have been saved by employees who've used PfizerWorks. What about Joe Cain's experiences? When he gave the Indian team a complex project researching strategic actions that worked when consolidating company facilities, the team put the report together in a month, something that would have taken him six months to do alone. He says, "Pfizer pays me not to work tactically, but to work strategically."

> Wouldn't you like a **MAGIC BUTTON** you could push to get someone else to do all your tedious and boring work?[63]

Discussion Questions

6-23 Describe and evaluate what Pfizer is doing with its PfizerWorks.

6-24 What structural implications—good and bad—does this approach have? (Think in terms of the six organizational design elements.)

6-25 Do you think this arrangement would work for other types of organizations? Why or why not? What types of organizations might it also work for?

6-26 What role do you think organizational structure plays in an organization's efficiency and effectiveness? Explain.

Endnotes

1. B. Fenwick, "Oklahoma Factory Turns Out US Bombs Used in Iraq," *Planet Ark* <www.planetark.com>, November 4, 2003; A. Meyer, "Peeking inside the Nation's Bomb Factory," *KFOR TV* <www.kfor.com>, February 27, 2003; G. Tuchman, "Inside America's Bomb Factory," *CNN* <cnn.usnews.com>, December 5, 2002; and C. Fishman, "Boomtown, U.S.A.," *Fast Company*, June 2002, 106–14.

2. D. Hudepohl, "Finesse a Flexible Work Schedule," *Wall Street Journal*, February 19, 2008, B8.

3. M. Boyle, "Super Bucks," *Fortune*, February 4, 2008, 8–9; and M. Hiestand, "Making a Stamp on Football," *USA Today*, January 25, 2005, 1C+.

4. S. E. Humphrey, J. D. Nahrgang, and F. P. Morgeson, "Integrating Motivational, Social, and Contextual Work Design Features: A Meta-Analytic Summary and Theoretical Expansion of the Work Design Literature," *Journal of Applied Psychology* (September 2007): 1332–56.

5. E. Kelly, "Keys to Effective Virtual Global Teams," *Academy of Management Executive*, May 2001, 132–33; and D. Ancona, H. Bresman, and K. Kaeufer, "The Comparative Advantage of X-Team," *MIT Sloan Management Review*, Spring 2002, 33–39.

6. R. S. Benchley, "Following Orders," *Chief Executive*, March 2002, 6.

7. R. Preston, "Inside Out," *Management Today*, September 2001, 37; and R. D. Clarke, "Over Their Heads," *Black Enterprise*, December 2000, 79.

8. See J. R. P. French and B. Raven, "The Bases of Social Power," in D. Cartwright and A. F. Zander, eds., *Group Dynamics: Research and Theory* (New York: Harper & Row, 1960), 607–23.

9. L. Urwick, *The Elements of Administration* (New York: Harper & Row, 1944), 52–53. See also, J. H. Gittel, "Supervisory Span, Relational Coordination, and Flight Departure Performance: A Reassessment of Post-Bureaucracy Theory," *Organizational Science*, July–August 2001, 468–83.

10. S. Harrison, "Is There a Right Span of Control? Simon Harrison Assesses the Relevance of the Concept of Span of Control to Modern Businesses," *Business Review*, February 2004, 10–13.

11. P. C. Light, "From Pentagon to Pyramids: Whacking at Bloat," *Government Executive*, July 2001, 100.

12. See, for instance, D. Van Fleet, "Span of Management Research and Issues," *Academy of Management Journal*, September 1983, 546–52; and S. H. Cady and P.

M. Fandt, "Managing Impressions with Information: A Field Study of Organizational Realities," *Journal of Applied Behavioral Science*, June 2001, 180–204.

13. Question of Ethics box based on R. E. Silverman, "Psst… This Is What Your Co-Worker Is Paid," *Wall Street Journal*, January 30, 2013, B6.

14. Henri Fayol, *General and Industrial Management*, trans. C. Storrs (London: Pitman Publishing, 1949), 19–42.

15. J. Zabojnik, "Centralized and Decentralized Decision Making in Organizations," *Journal of Labor Economics* (January 2002): 1–22.

16. See P. Kenis and D. Knoke, "How Organizational Field Networks Shape Interorganizational Tie-Formation Rates," *Academy of Management Review*, April 2002, 275–93.

17. T. Burns and G. M. Stalker, *The Management of Innovation* (London: Tavistock, 1961).

18. D. Dougherty, "Re-imagining the Differentiation and Integration of Work for Sustained Product Innovation," *Organization Science*, September–October 2001, 612–31.

19. A. D. Chandler Jr., *Strategy and Structure: Chapters in the History of the Industrial Enterprise* (Cambridge, MA: MIT Press, 1962).

20. See, for instance, L. L. Bryan and C. I. Joyce, "Better Strategy through Organizational Design," *McKinsey Quarterly* no. 2 (2007): 21–29; D. Jennings and S. Seaman, "High and Low Levels of Organizational Adaptation: An Empirical Analysis of Strategy, Structure, and Performance," *Strategic Management Journal* (July 1994): 459–75; D. C. Galunic and K. M. Eisenhardt, "Renewing the Strategy-Structure-Performance Paradigm," in B. M. Staw and L. L. Cummings (eds.), *Research in Organizational Behavior*, vol. 16 (Greenwich, CT: JAI Press, 1994), 215–55; R. Parthasarthy and S. P. Sethi, "Relating Strategy and Structure to Flexible Automation: A Test of Fit and Performance Implications," *Strategic Management Journal* 14, no. 6 (1993): 529–49; H. A. Simon, "Strategy and Organizational Evolution," *Strategic Management Journal* (January 1993): 131–42; H. L. Boschken, "Strategy and Structure: Re-conceiving the Relationship," *Journal of Management* (March 1990): 135–50; D. Miller, "The Structural and Environmental Correlates of Business Strategy," *Strategic Management Journal* (January–February 1987): 55–76; and R. E. Miles and C. C. Snow, *Organizational Strategy, Structure, and Process* (New York: McGraw-Hill, 1978).

21. See, for instance, P. M. Blau and R. A. Schoenherr, *The Structure of*

Organizations (New York: Basic Books, 1971); D. S. Pugh, "The Aston Program of Research: Retrospect and Prospect," in A. H. Van de Ven and W. F. Joyce (eds.), *Perspectives on Organization Design and Behavior* (New York: John Wiley, 1981), 135–66; and R. Z. Gooding and J. A. Wagner III, "A Meta-Analytic Review of the Relationship between Size and Performance: The Productivity and Efficiency of Organizations and Their Subunits," *Administrative Science Quarterly*, December 1985, 462–81.

22. See, for example, H. M. O'Neill, "Restructuring, Reengineering and Rightsizing: Do the Metaphors Make Sense?" *Academy of Management Executive* 8, no. 4 (1994): 9–30; R. K. Reger, J. V. Mullane, L. T. Gustafson, and S. M. Demarie, "Creating Earthquakes to Change Organizational Mindsets," *Academy of Management Executive* 8, no. 4 (1994): 31–41; and J. Tan, "Impact of Ownership Type on Environment–Strategy Linkage and Performance: Evidence from a Transitional Company," *Journal of Management Studies* (May 2002): 333–54.

23. E. W. Morrison, "Doing the Job Well: An Investigation of Pro-Social Rule Breaking," *Journal of Management* (February 2006): 5–28.

24. J. Woodward, *Industrial Organization: Theory and Practice* (London: Oxford University Press, 1965).

25. From the Past to the Present box based on J. Woodward, *Industrial Organization: Theory and Practice*. Also, see, for instance, C. Perrow, "A Framework for the Comparative Analysis of Organizations," *American Sociological Review*, April 1967, 194–208; J. D. Thompson, *Organizations in Action* (New York: McGraw-Hill, 1967); J. Hage and M. Aiken, "Routine Technology, Social Structure, and Organizational Goals," *Administrative Science Quarterly*, September 1969, 366–77; C. C. Miller, W. H. Glick, Y. D. Wang, and G. Huber, "Understanding Technology-Structure Relationships: Theory Development and Meta-Analytic Theory Testing," *Academy of Management Journal* (June 1991): 370–99; D. M. Rousseau and R. A. Cooke, "Technology and Structure: The Concrete, Abstract, and Activity Systems of Organizations," *Journal of Management* (Fall–Winter 1984): 345–61; and D. Gerwin, "Relationships between Structure and Technology," in P.C. Nystrom and W. H. Starbuck (eds.), *Handbook of Organizational Design*, vol. 2 (New York: Oxford University Press, 1981), 3–38.

26. Ibid.

27. H. Mintzberg, *Structure in Fives: Designing Effective Organizations* (Upper Saddle River, NJ: Prentice Hall, 1983), 157.

28. D. A. Garvin and L. C. Levesque, "The Multiunit Enterprise," *Harvard Business Review*, June 2008, 106–17; and R. J. Williams, J. J. Hoffman, and B. T. Lamont, "The Influence of Top Management Team Characteristics on M-Form Implementation Time," *Journal of Managerial Issues* (Winter 1995): 466–80.

29. See, for example, R. Greenwood and D. Miller, "Tackling Design Anew: Getting Back to the Heart of Organization Theory," *Academy of Management Perspectives*, November 2010, 78–88; G. J. Castrogiovanni, "Organization Task Environments: Have They Changed Fundamentally Over Time?" *Journal of Management* vol. 28, no. 2 (2002): 129–50; D. F. Twomey, "Leadership, Organizational Design, and Competitiveness for the 21st Century," *Global Competitiveness*, Annual 2002, S31–S40; M. Hammer, "Processed Change: Michael Hammer Sees Process as 'the Clark Kent of Business Ideas'—A Concept That Has the Power to Change a Company's Organizational Design," *Journal of Business Strategy* (November–December 2001): 11–15; T. Clancy, "Radical Surgery: A View from the Operating Theater," *Academy of Management Executive*, February 1994, 73–78; I. I. Mitroff, R. O. Mason, and C. M. Pearson, "Radical Surgery: What Will Tomorrow's Organizations Look Like?" *Academy of Management Executive*, February 1994, 11–21; and R. E. Hoskisson, C. W. L. Hill, and H. Kim, "The Multidivisional Structure: Organizational Fossil or Source of Value?" *Journal of Management* 19, no. 2 (1993): 269–98.

30. Q. Hardy, "Google Thinks Small," *Forbes*, November 14, 2005, 198–202.

31. See, for example, D. R. Denison, S. L. Hart, and J. A. Kahn, "From Chimneys to Cross-Functional Teams: Developing and Validating a Diagnostic Model," *Academy of Management Journal* (December 1996): 1005–23; D. Ray and H. Bronstein, *Teaming Up: Making the Transition to a Self-Directed Team-Based Organization* (New York: McGraw Hill, 1995); J. R. Katzenbach and D. K. Smith, *The Wisdom of Teams* (Boston: Harvard Business School Press, 1993); J. A. Byrne, "The Horizontal Corporation," *BusinessWeek*, December 20, 1993, 76–81; B. Dumaine, "Payoff from the New Management," *Fortune*, December 13, 1993, 103–10; and H. Rothman,

"The Power of Empowerment," *Nation's Business*, June 1993, 49–52.

32. C. Garvey, "Steer Teams with the Right Pay," *HR Magazine*, May 2002, 70–78.

33. P. Kaihla, "Best-Kept Secrets of the World's Best Companies," *Business 2.0*, April 2006, 83; C. Taylor, "School of Bright Ideas," *Time Inside Business*, April 2005, A8–A12; and B. Nussbaum, "The Power of Design," *BusinessWeek*, May 17, 2004, 86–94.

34. See, for example, G. G. Dess, A. M. A. Rasheed, K. J. McLaughlin, and R. L. Priem, "The New Corporate Architecture," *Academy of Management Executive*, August 1995, 7–20.

35. For additional readings on boundaryless organizations, see Rausch and Birkinshaw, June 2008; M. F. R. Kets de Vries, "Leadership Group Coaching in Action: The Zen of Creating High Performance Teams," *Academy of Management Executive*, February 2005, 61–76; J. Child and R. G. McGrath, "Organizations Unfettered: Organizational Form in an Information-Intensive Economy," *Academy of Management Journal* (December 2001): 1135–48; M. Hammer and S. Stanton, "How Process Enterprises Really Work," *Harvard Business Review*, November–December 1999, 108–18; T. Zenger and W. Hesterly, "The Disaggregation of Corporations: Selective Intervention, High-Powered Incentives, and Modular Units," *Organization Science* vol. 8 (1997): 209–22; R. Ashkenas, D. Ulrich, T. Jick, and S. Kerr, *The Boundaryless Organization: Breaking the Chains of Organizational Structure* (San Francisco: Jossey-Bass, 1997); R. M. Hodgetts, "A Conversation with Steve Kerr," *Organizational Dynamics*, Spring 1996, 68–79; and J. Gebhardt, "The Boundaryless Organization," *Sloan Management Review*, Winter 1996, 117–19. For another view of boundaryless organizations, see B. Victor, "The Dark Side of the New Organizational Forms: An Editorial Essay," *Organization Science*, November 1994, 479–82.

36. See, for instance, Y. Shin, "A Person-Environment Fit Model for Virtual Organizations," *Journal of Management* (December 2004): 725–43; D. Lyons, "Smart and Smarter," *Forbes*, March 18, 2002, 40–41; W. F. Cascio, "Managing a Virtual Workplace," *Academy of Management Executive*, August 2000, 81–90; G. G. Dess, A. M. A. Rasheed, K. J. McLaughlin, and R. L. Priem, "The New Corporate

Architecture"; H. Chesbrough and D. Teece, "When Is Virtual Virtuous: Organizing for Innovation," *Harvard Business Review*, January–February 1996, 65–73; and W. H. Davidow and M. S. Malone, *The Virtual Corporation* (New York: Harper Collins, 1992).

37. Q. Hardy, "Bit by Bit, Work Exchange Site Aims to Get Jobs Done," *New York Times Online*, November 6, 2011.

38. M. V. Rafter, "Cultivating a Virtual Culture," *Workforce Management Online*, April 5, 2012.

39. R. E. Miles, C. C. Snow, J. A. Matthews, G. Miles, and H. J. Coleman Jr., "Organizing in the Knowledge Age: Anticipating the Cellular Form," *Academy of Management Executive*, November 1997, 7–24; C. Jones, W. Hesterly, and S. Borgatti, "A General Theory of Network Governance: Exchange Conditions and Social Mechanisms," *Academy of Management Review*, October 1997, 911–45; R. E. Miles and C. C. Snow, "The New Network Firm: A Spherical Structure Built on Human Investment Philosophy," *Organizational Dynamics*, Spring 1995, 5–18; and R. E. Miles and C. C. Snow, "Causes of Failures in Network Organizations," *California Management Review* vol. 34, no. 4 (1992): 53–72.

40. G. Hoetker, "Do Modular Products Lead to Modular Organizations?" *Strategic Management Journal* (June 2006): 501–18; C. H. Fine, "Are You Modular or Integral?" *Strategy & Business*, Summer 2005, 44–51; D. A. Ketchen Jr. and G. T. M. Hult, "To Be Modular or Not to Be? Some Answers to the Question," *Academy of Management Executive*, May 2002, 166–67; M. A. Schilling, "The Use of Modular Organizational Forms: An Industry-Level Analysis," *Academy of Management Journal* (December 2001): 1149–68; D. Lei, M. A. Hitt, and J. D. Goldhar, "Advanced Manufacturing Technology: Organizational Design and Strategic Flexibility," *Organization Studies* vol. 17 (1996): 501–23; R. Sanchez and J. Mahoney, "Modularity Flexibility and Knowledge Management in Product and Organization Design," *Strategic Management Journal* vol. 17 (1996): 63–76; and R. Sanchez, "Strategic Flexibility in Product Competition," *Strategic Management Journal* vol. 16 (1995): 135–59.

41. C. Hymowitz, "Have Advice, Will Travel," *Wall Street Journal*, June 5, 2006, B1+.

42. S. Reed, A. Reinhardt, and A. Sains, "Saving Ericsson,"

BusinessWeek, November 11, 2002, 64–68.

43. P. Engardio, "The Future of Outsourcing," *BusinessWeek*, January 30, 2006, 50–58.

44. C. E. Connelly and D. G. Gallagher, "Emerging Trends in Contingent Work Research," *Journal of Management* (November 2004): 959–83.

45. N. M. Adler, *International Dimensions of Organizational Behavior*, 5th ed. (Cincinnati, OH: South-Western, 2008), 62.

46. Technology and the Manager's Job box based on R. Cheng, "So You Want to Use Your iPhone for Work? How the Smartest Companies Are Letting Employees Use Their Personal Gadgets to Do Their Jobs," *Wall Street Journal*, April 25, 2011, R1+; B. Roberts, "Mobile Workforce Management," *HR Magazine*, March 2011, 67–70; D. Darlin, "Software That Monitors Your Work, Wherever You Are," *New York Times Online* <www.nytimesonline.com> (April 12, 2009); D. Pauleen and B. Harmer, "Away from the Desk…Always," *Wall Street Journal*, December 15, 2008, R8; J. Marquez, "Connecting a Virtual Workforce," *Workforce Management Online* <www.workforce.com> (September 22, 2008); R. Yu, "Work Away from Work Gets Easier with Technology," *USA Today*, November 28, 2006, 8B; M. Weinstein, "GOing Mobile," *Training*, September 2006, 24–29; C. Cobbs, "Technology Helps Boost Multitasking," *Springfield, Missouri News-Leader*, June 15, 2006, 5B; C. Edwards, "Wherever You Go, You're on the Job," *BusinessWeek*, June 20, 2005, 87–90; and S. E. Ante, "The World Wide Work Space," *BusinessWeek*, June 6, 2005, 106–08.

47. P. Olson, "Tesco's Landing," *Forbes*, June 4, 2007, 116–18; and P. M. Senge, *The Fifth Discipline: The Art and Practice of Learning Organizations* (New York: Doubleday, 1990).

48. P. B. Smith and M. F. Peterson, "Demographic Effects on the Use of Vertical Sources of Guidance by Managers in Widely Differing Cultural Contexts," *International Journal of Cross Cultural Management* (April 2005): 5–26.

49. J. Marquez, "Connecting a Virtual Workforce," *Workforce Management Online*, February 3, 2009.

50. M. Conlin, "Home Offices: The New Math," *BusinessWeek*, March 9, 2009, 66–68.

51. Ibid.

52. J. Marquez, "Connecting a Virtual Workforce."

53. S. Jayson, "Working at Home: Family-Friendly," *USA Today*,

April 15, 2010, 1A+; T. D. Hecht and N. J. Allen, "A Longitudinal Examination of the Work-Nonwork Boundary Strength Construct," *Journal of Organizational Behavior* (October 2009): 839–62; and G. E. Kreiner, E. C. Hollensbe, and M. L. Sheep, "Balancing Borders and Bridges: Negotiating the Work-Home Interface via Boundary Work Tactics," *Academy of Management Journal* (August 2009): 704–30.

54. J. T. Marquez, "The Future of Flex," *Workforce Management Online*, January 2010.

55. S. Greenhouse, "Work-Sharing May Help Companies Avoid Layoffs," *New York Times Online*, June 16, 2009.

56. R. King, "Meet the Microworkers," *Bloomberg BusinessWeek Online*, February 1, 2011; and R. King, "Mechanical Serfdom Is Just That," *Bloomberg Business-Week Online*, February 1, 2011.

57. K. Bennhold, "Working (Part-Time) in the 21st Century," *New York Times Online*, December 29, 2010; and J. Revell, C. Bigda, and D. Rosato, "The Rise of Freelance Nation," *CNNMoney*, cnnmoney.com, June 12, 2009.

58. Revell, Bigda, and Rosato, "The Rise of Freelance Nation."

59. Ibid.

60. H. G. Jackson, "Flexible Workplaces: The Next Imperative," *HR Magazine*, March 2011, 8; E. Frauenheim, "Companies Focus Their Attention on Flexibility," *Workforce Management Online*, February 2011; P. Davidson, "Companies Do More with Fewer Workers," *USA Today*, February 23, 2011, 1B+; M. Rich, "Weighing Costs, Companies Favor Temporary Help," *New York Times Online*, December 19, 2010; and P. Davidson, "Temporary Workers Reshape Companies, Jobs," *USA Today*, October 13, 2010, 1B+.

61. C. C. Miller and N. Perlroth, "Yahoo Says New Policy Is Meant to Raise Morale," *New York Times Online*, March 5, 2013; C. Suddath, "Work-From-Home Truths, Half-Truths, and Myths," *Bloomberg BusinessWeek*, March 4–10, 2013, 75; Q. Fottrell, "The Home Office in the Spotlight," *Wall Street Journal*, February 27, 2013, B6; E. Weise, "Telecommuters to Yahoo: Boo," *USA Today*, February 26, 2013, 1A; R. E. Silverman and R. Bell, "Examining Marissa Mayer's Out-of-Office Message to Yahoo Employees," www.workforce.com, February 26, 2013; C. C. Miller and C. Rampell, "Yahoo Orders Home Workers Back to the Office," *New York Times Online*, February 25, 2013; and K. Swisher, "'Physically Together': Here's the Internal

Yahoo No-Work-from-Home Memo for Remote Workers and Maybe More," *allthingsd.com*, February 22, 2013.

62. D. Lumb, "NASA Chief Says Mars One Does Not Stand a Chance Without NASA," http://www.fastcompany.com/3045186/fastfeed/nasa-chief-says-mars-one-does-not-stand-a-chance-without-nasa, April 17, 2015; NASA Strategic Plan 2014, https://www.nasa.gov/sites/default/files/files/FY2014_NASA_SP_508c.pdf; S. Karlin, "Rebranding NASA for

a New Space Age," http://www.fastcocreate.com/3034276/re-branding-nasa-for-a-new-space-age, December 3, 2014; E. J. Hoffman and J. Boyle, "Managing Mission Knowledge at NASA," *T&D,* July 2014, 50–55; J. Dean, "Boldness of '81 Test Flight Unlikely to Be Repeated," *USA Today*, April 11, 2011, 7A; G. Griffin, "As Shuttle Retires, a Vote for Commercial Space Flight," *USA Today*, April 6, 2011, 9A; A. K. Donahue, "More to Learn from NASA about Learning, Unlearning, and Forgetting,"

Journal of Public Administration Research (April 2011): 391–95; and "NASA's Space-Shuttle Program Ends," *Fast Company*, February 2011, 22.

63. S. Silbermann, "How Culture and Regulation Demand New Ways to Sell," *Harvard Business Review,* July/August 2012, 104–05; P. Miller and T. Wedell-Wedellsborg, "How to Make an Offer That Managers Can't Refuse?" *IESE Insight,* second quarter, issue 9 (2011): 66–67; S. Hernández, "Prove Its Worth,"

IESE Insight, second quarter, issue 9 (2011): 68; T. Koulopoulos, "Know Thyself," *IESE Insight,* second quarter, issue 9 (2011): 69; M. Weinstein, "Retrain and Restructure Your Organization," *Training,* May 2009, 36; J. McGregor, "The Chore Goes Offshore," *BusinessWeek,* March 23 & 30, 2009, 50–51; "Pfizer: Making It 'Leaner, Meaner, More Efficient,'" *BusinessWeek Online*, March 2, 2009; and A. Cohen, "Scuttling Scut Work," *Fast Company,* February 2008, 42–43.

Managing Human Resources

7

Management
Myth
Myth

Managers don't need to know about human resources because that's the job of the HR department.

Management Myth DEBUNKED?

HR activities like selection and performance appraisal are frequently assumed to be the responsibility of only those who work in an organization's HR department. The truth is that *all* managers will have some responsibilities for staffing, appraising, and training people in their work unit. An HR department provides much needed advice, suggestions, and support activities, but managers *are* involved with human resource decisions in their work units.[1]

WITH an organization's structure in place, managers have to find people to fill the jobs that have been created or to remove people from jobs if business circumstances require it. That's where human resource management (HRM) comes in. It's an important task that involves having the *right number* of the *right people* in the *right place* at the *right time*. In this chapter, we'll look at the process managers use to do just that—a process that includes finding, interviewing, and assessing job applicants; helping new employees assimilate; recommending training; and assessing employee performance. In addition, we'll look at some contemporary HRM issues facing managers. ●

Learning Outcomes

7-1 Describe the key components of the human resource management process and the important influences on that process. p. 199

7-2 Discuss the tasks associated with identifying and selecting competent employees. p. 203

7-3 Explain how employees are provided with needed skills and knowledge. p. 210

7-4 Describe strategies for retaining competent, high-performing employees. p. 214

7-5 Discuss contemporary issues in managing human resources. p. 219

What Is the Human Resource Management Process and What Influences It?

7-1 Describe the key components of the human resource management process and the important influences on that process.

The quality of an organization *is* to a large degree determined by the quality of the people it employs. Success for most organizations depends on finding the employees with the skills to successfully perform the tasks required to attain the company's strategic goals. Staffing and HRM decisions and actions are critical to ensuring that the organization hires and keeps the right people.

Getting that done is what **human resource management (HRM)** is all about. The eight important HRM activities (the yellow boxes) are shown in Exhibit 7–1.

After an organization's strategy has been established and the organization structure designed, it's time to add the people—to acquire the talent! That's one of the most critical roles for HRM and one that has increased the importance of HR managers to the organization. The first three activities in

human resource management (HRM)
The management function concerned with getting, training, motivating, and keeping competent employees

Exhibit 7–1 The Human Resource Management Process

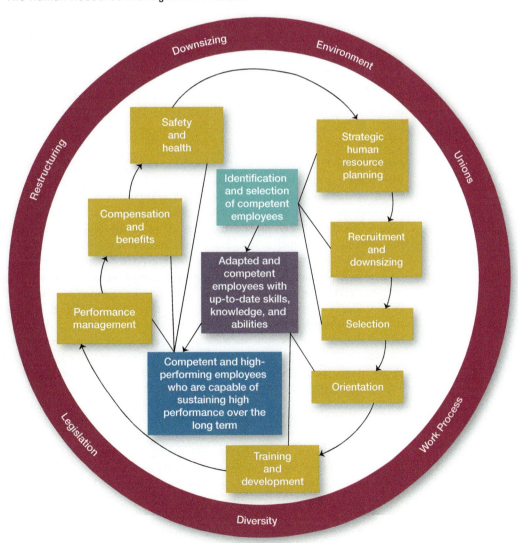

the HRM process represent employment planning: the addition of staff through recruitment, the reduction in staff through downsizing, and selection. When executed properly, these steps lead to the identification and selection of competent, talented employees who can assist an organization in achieving its strategic goals.

Once you select the people you want, you need to help them adapt to the organization and ensure that their job skills and knowledge are kept current. These next two activities in the HRM process are accomplished through orientation and training. The last steps in the HRM process are designed to identify performance goals, correct performance problems if necessary, and help employees sustain a high level of performance over their entire work life. The activities involved include performance appraisal, and compensation and benefits. (HRM also includes safety and health issues, but we're not covering those topics in this book.) All these activities, if properly executed, will staff an organization with competent, high-performing employees who are capable of sustaining their performance levels over the long run.

HRM = Right People, Right Place, Right Time

Notice in Exhibit 7–1 that the entire process is influenced by the external environment. Many of the factors we discussed in Chapter 2 directly affect all management practices, but their effect is keenly felt in managing the organization's human resources, because whatever happens to an organization ultimately influences what happens to its employees. So, before we review the HRM process, let's examine one external force that affects it—the legal environment.

What Is the Legal Environment of HRM?

HRM practices are governed by laws, which vary from country to country. State (or provincial) and local regulations further influence specific practices within countries. Consequently, it's impossible to provide you with all the information you need about the relevant regulatory environment. As a manager, it will be important for you to know what you legally can and cannot do wherever you're located.

WHAT ARE THE PRIMARY U.S. LAWS AFFECTING HRM? Since the mid-1960s, the federal government in the United States has greatly expanded its influence over HRM by enacting a number of laws and regulations (see Exhibit 7–2 for examples). Although we've not seen many laws enacted recently at the federal level, many states have enacted laws that add to the provisions of the federal laws. Today's employers must ensure that equal employment opportunities exist for job applicants and current employees. Decisions regarding who will be hired, for example, or which employees will be chosen for a management training program must be made without regard to race, sex, religion, age, color, national origin, or disability. Exceptions can occur only when special circumstances exist. For instance, a community fire department can deny employment to a firefighter applicant who is confined to a wheelchair, but if that same individual is applying for a desk job, such as a fire department dispatcher, the disability cannot be used as a reason to deny employment. The issues involved, however, are rarely that clear-cut. For example, employment laws protect most employees whose religious beliefs require a specific style of dress—robes, long shirts, long hair, and the like. However, if the specific style of dress may be hazardous or unsafe in the work setting (e.g., when operating machinery), a company could refuse to hire a person who would not adopt a safer dress code.

Trying to balance the "shoulds and should-nots" of these laws often falls within the realm of equal employment opportunity (EEO) initiatives and **affirmative action programs**. EEO strives to ensure that anyone has an equal opportunity based on his or her qualifications. And many organizations operating in the United States have affirmative action programs to ensure that decisions and practices enhance the employment, upgrading, and retention of members from protected groups such as minorities and females.

affirmative action programs
Programs that ensure that decisions and practices enhance the employment, upgrading, and retention of members of protected groups

Exhibit 7–2 Major HRM Laws

LAW OR RULING	YEAR	DESCRIPTION
Equal Employment Opportunity and Discrimination		
■ **Equal Pay Act**	1963	Prohibits pay differences for equal work based on gender
■ **Civil Rights Act, Title VII**	1964 (amended in 1972)	Prohibits discrimination based on race, color, religion, national origin, or gender
■ **Age Discrimination in Employment Act**	1967 (amended in 1978)	Prohibits discrimination against employees 40 years and older
■ **Vocational Rehabilitation Act**	1973	Prohibits discrimination on the basis of physical or mental disabilities
■ **Americans with Disabilities Act**	1990	Prohibits discrimination against individuals who have disabilities or chronic illnesses; also requires reasonable accommodations for these individuals
Compensation/Benefits		
■ **Worker Adjustment and Retraining Notification Act**	1990	Requires employers with more than 100 employees to provide 60 days' notice before a mass layoff or facility closing
■ **Family and Medical Leave Act**	1993	Gives employees in organizations with 50 or more employees up to 12 weeks of unpaid leave each year for family or medical reasons
■ **Health Insurance Portability and Accountability Act**	1996	Permits portability of employees' insurance from one employer to another
■ **Lilly Ledbetter Fair Pay Act**	2009	Changes the statute of limitations on pay discrimination to 180 days from each paycheck
■ **Patient Protection and Affordable Care Act**	2010	Health care legislation that puts in place comprehensive health insurance reforms
Health/Safety		
■ **Occupational Safety and Health Act (OSHA)**	1970	Establishes mandatory safety and health standards in organizations
■ **Privacy Act**	1974	Gives employees the legal right to examine personnel files and letters of reference
■ **Consolidated Omnibus Reconciliation Act (COBRA)**	1985	Requires continued health coverage following termination (paid by employee)

Source: Robbins, Stephen P., Coulter, Mary, *Management*, 13th Ed., © 2016, p. 341. Reprinted and electronically reproduced by permission of Pearson Education, Inc., New York, NY.

Operating within legal constraints, U.S. managers are not completely free to choose whom they hire, promote, or fire. Although laws and regulations have significantly helped to reduce employment discrimination and unfair employment practices, they have, at the same time, reduced management's discretion over HR decisions.

ARE HRM LAWS THE SAME GLOBALLY? No. As a global manager, you'll need to know applicable laws and regulations. Here's a quick overview of some HRM laws in other countries.

Canada:

• HRM laws closely parallel those in the United States. *Example:* Human Rights Act—a law that governs practices throughout the country—prohibits discrimination on the basis of race, religion, age, marital status, sex, physical or mental disability, or national origin.
• HRM environment involves more decentralized lawmaking at the provincial level. *Example:* Discrimination on the basis of language is not prohibited anywhere in Canada except in Quebec.

Mexico:

• Although once heavily unionized, unionization rates have been declining.
• Labor issues are governed by the Mexican Federal Labor Law.

◀◀◀ From the Past to the Present ▶▶▶

Hugo Munsterberg, a pioneer in the field of industrial psychology, is "generally credited with creating the field."[2] As an admirer of Frederick W. Taylor and the scientific management movement, Munsterberg stated that "Taylor had introduced most valuable suggestions which the industrial world cannot ignore." Drawing on Taylor's works, Munsterberg stressed "the importance of efficiently using workers to achieve economic production." His research and work in showing organizations ways to improve the performance and well-being of workers was fundamental to the emerging field of management in the early 1900s.

Today, industrial-organizational psychology is defined as the scientific study of the workplace. Industrial-organizational (I/O) psychologists use scientific principles and research-based designs to generate knowledge about workplace issues. (Check out the Society for Industrial and Organizational Psy-

Scientifically studying the WORKPLACE

chology at www.siop.org.) They study organizational topics such as job performance, job analysis, performance appraisal, compensation, work/life balance, work sample tests, employee training, employment law, personnel recruitment and selection, and so forth. Their research has contributed much to the field that we call human resource management. And all of this is due to the early work done by Hugo Munsterberg.

*If your professor has assigned this, go to the Assignments section of **mymanagementlab.com** to complete these discussion questions.*

⭐ **Talk About It 1:** Why is it important to scientifically study the workplace?

⭐ **Talk About It 2:** Do you think it's easier today to scientifically study the workplace than it was back in Munsterberg's days? Why or why not?

- *Example:* One hiring law states that employer has 28 days to evaluate a new employee's work performance; after that period, the employee has job security and termination is difficult and expensive.
- Violators face severe penalties, including criminal action, steep fines, and even jail sentences for employers who fail to pay, for example, the minimum wage.

Australia:

- Discrimination laws not enacted until the 1980s and generally apply to women (who need improved opportunities).
- Industrial relations specialists have important organizational roles, reducing the control line managers have over workplace labor issues.

General Electric is a multinational employer committed to observing all the different labor laws of the 100 countries in which it operates. Shown here are employees of GE's wind turbine factory in Vietnam, a country whose Labour Code of Vietnam was first passed in 1994 and provides strong protections for employees.

- Labor and industrial relations laws were overhauled in 1997 with the goal of increasing productivity and reducing union power.
- The Workplace Relations Bill gives employers greater flexibility to negotiate directly with employees on pay, hours, and benefits, and also simplifies federal regulation of labor–management relations.

Germany:

- Similar to most other Western European countries when it comes to HRM practices.
- Laws require companies to have representative participation—thus redistributing power within the organization and putting labor on a more equal footing with the interests of management and stockholders.

A Question of Ethics

Here's a challenging HR issue for managers: A business model that relies heavily on the appearance of employees AND balancing the rights of those employees. Hooters, the restaurant chain that hires attractive waitresses who are expected to wear (and look good) in tight tops and short shorts, uses that business model. However, when one of its waitresses in a St. Peters, Missouri, location had brain surgery to remove a tumor, her manager initially said the young woman could wear a "chemo cap" to cover her scar and her lack of hair.[3] However, a regional manager later said that was not sufficient and a wig was necessary. The employee told both her manager and the regional manager that she did not have a wig and could not afford to buy one because of the expense. The employee was able to borrow one and tried to wear it at work. However, it was too painful and kept her wound from healing, and she chose not to continue wearing it. Her manager then significantly reduced her hours, forcing her to quit because she could not earn sufficient income. The waitress filed a federal discrimination lawsuit against the restaurant chain in federal court saying she was forced out of her job for refusing to wear a wig. Hooters denies the allegations.

(Update: The young woman, who had worked at Hooters for almost eight years to pay for nursing school, is now a registered nurse. No information could be found on whether the case was settled.)

If your professor has assigned this, go to the Assignments section of **mymanagementlab.com** *to complete these discussion questions.*

⭐ **Talk About It 3:** How might this issue—balancing the rights of employees against a business model that's based on employee appearances—affect HR processes such as recruitment, selection, and performance management?

⭐ **Talk About It 4:** What possible HR ethical issue(s) do you see in this story?

- Two most common forms of representative participation are (1) **work councils**, which are groups of nominated or elected employees who must be consulted when management makes decisions involving personnel; and (2) **board representatives**, who are employees who sit on a company's board of directors and represent the interests of the firm's employees.

How Do Managers Identify and Select Competent Employees?

7-2 Discuss the tasks associated with identifying and selecting competent employees.

Every organization needs people to do whatever work is necessary for doing what the organization is in business to do. How do organizations get those people? And more importantly, what can they do to ensure they get competent, talented people? This first phase of the HRM process involves three tasks: **1** employment planning, **2** recruitment and downsizing, and **3** selection.

1 What Is Employment Planning?

Supply and Demand aren't just for economics—they're also important to HRM!

- Talent wars have come to Silicon Valley as Internet startups struggle to compete for scarce talent even as more-established companies such as Facebook, Twitter, and Google look to add employees as their businesses continue to grow.
- During the latest economic downturn, Boeing cut more than 3,000 jobs, mostly from its commercial airplanes unit. During the same time, it added 106 employees to its defense unit and was looking for several hundred more.[4]

Juggling the supply of human resources to meet demand is a challenge for many companies.

work councils
Groups of nominated or elected employees who must be consulted when management makes decisions involving personnel

board representatives
Employees who sit on a company's board of directors and represent the interest of employees

Employment planning is the process by which managers ensure that they have the right number and kinds of people in the right places at the right times, people who are capable of effectively and efficiently completing those tasks that will help the organization achieve its goals. Employment planning, then, translates the organization's mission and goals into an HR plan that will allow the organization to achieve those goals. The process can be condensed into two steps: (1) assessing current human resources and future human resource needs, and (2) developing a plan to meet those needs.

(1) HOW DOES AN ORGANIZATION DO A CURRENT HR ASSESSMENT?   Managers begin by reviewing the current human resource status. This review is typically done by generating a **human resource inventory**. It's not difficult to generate an inventory in most organizations since the information for it is derived from forms completed by employees. Such inventories might list the name, education, training, prior employment, languages spoken, capabilities, and specialized skills of each employee in the organization. This inventory allows managers to assess what talents and skills are currently available in the organization.

Another part of the current assessment is **job analysis**. Whereas the human resources inventory is concerned with telling management what individual employees can do, job analysis is more fundamental. It's typically a lengthy process, one in which workflows are analyzed and skills and behaviors that are necessary to perform jobs are identified. For instance, what does an international reporter who works for the *Wall Street Journal* do? What minimal knowledge, skills, and abilities are necessary for the adequate performance of this job? How do the job requirements for an international reporter compare with those for a domestic reporter or for a newspaper editor? Job analysis can answer these questions. Ultimately, the purpose of job analysis is to determine the kinds of skills, knowledge, and attitudes needed to successfully perform each job. This information is then used to develop or revise job descriptions and job specifications.

Why IS **JOB ANALYSIS** so important?

Job analysis results in: Job description → describes the job

&

Job specification → describes the person

A **job description** is a written statement that describes the job—what a job holder does, how it's done, and why it's done. It typically portrays job content, environment, and conditions of employment. The **job specification** states the minimum qualifications that a person must possess to perform a given job successfully. It focuses on the person and identifies the knowledge, skills, and attitudes needed to do the job effectively. The job description and job specification are important documents when managers begin recruiting and selecting. For instance, the job description can be used to describe the job to potential candidates. The job specification keeps the manager's attention on the list of qualifications necessary for an incumbent to perform a job and assists in determining whether candidates are qualified. Furthermore, hiring individuals on the basis of the information contained in these two documents helps ensure that the hiring process does not discriminate.

(2) HOW ARE FUTURE EMPLOYEE NEEDS DETERMINED?   Future human resource needs are determined by the organization's strategic goals and direction. Demand for human resources (employees) is a result of demand for the organization's products or services. On the basis of an estimate of total revenue, managers can attempt to establish the number and mix of people needed to reach that revenue. In some cases, however, the situation may be reversed. When particular skills are necessary and in scarce supply, the availability of needed human resources determines revenues. For example, managers of an upscale chain of assisted-living retirement facilities who find themselves with abundant business opportunities are limited in their ability to grow revenues by whether they can hire a qualified nursing staff to fully meet the needs of the residents. In most cases, however, the

employment planning
The process by which managers ensure they have the right numbers and kinds of people in the right places at the right time

human resource inventory
A report listing important information about employees such as name, education, training, skills, languages spoken, and so forth

job analysis
An assessment that defines jobs and the behaviors necessary to perform them

job description
A written statement that describes a job

job specification
A written statement of the minimum qualifications that a person must possess to perform a given job successfully

overall organizational goals and the resulting revenue forecast provide the major input in determining the organization's HR requirements.

After assessing both current capabilities and future needs, managers can estimate talent shortages—both in number and in kind—and highlight areas in which the organization is overstaffed. They can then develop a plan that matches these estimates with forecasts of future labor supply. Employment planning not only guides current staffing needs but also projects future employee needs and availability.

2A How Do Organizations Recruit Employees?

Once managers know their current staffing levels—understaffed or overstaffed—they can begin to do something about it. If vacancies exist, they can use the information gathered through job analysis to guide them in **recruitment**—that is, the process of locating, identifying, and attracting capable applicants. On the other hand, if employment planning indicates a surplus, managers may want to reduce the labor supply within the organization and initiate downsizing or restructuring activities.

Needed! **Outstanding Job Applicants!**
Now . . . how do we get those?

WHERE DOES A MANAGER RECRUIT APPLICANTS?   The Internet has become a popular approach for recruiting job applicants, although there are other sources to find them. Exhibit 7–3 offers some guidance. The source that's used should reflect the local labor market, the type or level of position, and the size of the organization.

Which recruiting sources tend to produce superior applicants? Most studies have found that employee referrals generally produce the best applicants.[5] Why? First, applicants referred by current employees are prescreened by those employees. Because the recommenders know both the job and the person being recommended, they tend to refer well-qualified applicants.[6] Second, because current employees often feel that their reputation in the organization is at stake with a referral, they tend to make referrals only when they are reasonably confident that the referral won't make them look bad. However, managers shouldn't always opt for the employee-referred applicant; such referrals may not increase the diversity and mix of employees.

Exhibit 7–3 Recruiting Sources

SOURCE	ADVANTAGES	DISADVANTAGES
Internet	Reaches large numbers of people; can get immediate feedback	Generates many unqualified candidates
Employee referrals	Knowledge about the organization provided by current employee; can generate strong candidates because a good referral reflects on the recommender	May not increase the diversity and mix of employees
Company Web site	Wide distribution; can be targeted to specific groups	Generates many unqualified candidates
College recruiting	Large centralized body of candidates	Limited to entry-level positions
Professional recruiting organizations	Good knowledge of industry challenges and requirements	Little commitment to specific organization

selection process
Screening job applicants to ensure that the most appropriate candidates are hired

> ✪ **Watch It 1!**
>
> If your professor has assigned this, go to the Assignments section of **mymanagementlab.com** to complete the video exercise titled *CH2MHill: Human Resource Management*.

2B How Does a Manager Handle Layoffs?

Coca-Cola laid off 1,600 to 1,800 of its corporate U.S. and international employees.[7] American Express cut costs by eliminating 4,000 jobs after failing to meet long-term revenue growth targets.[8] eBay cut 2,400 jobs (7 percent of its workforce) to adapt to changing conditions.[9]

In the past decade, and especially during the last few years, most global organizations, as well as many government agencies and small businesses, have been forced to shrink the size of their workforce or restructure their skill composition. Downsizing has become a relevant strategy for meeting the demands of a dynamic environment.

WHAT ARE DOWNSIZING OPTIONS? Obviously, people can be fired, but other restructuring choices may be more beneficial to the organization. Exhibit 7–4 summarizes a manager's major downsizing options. Keep in mind that, regardless of the method chosen, employees suffer. We discuss downsizing more fully—for both victims and survivors—later in this chapter.

3 How Do Managers Select Job Applicants?

Once the recruiting effort has developed a pool of applicants, the next step in the HRM process is to determine who is best qualified for the job. In essence, then, the **selection process** is a prediction exercise: It seeks to predict which applicants will be "successful" if hired; that is, who will perform well on the criteria the organization uses to evaluate its employees. In filling a network administrator position, for example, the selection process should be able to predict which applicants will be capable of properly installing, debugging, managing, and updating the organization's computer network. For a position as a sales representative, it should predict which applicants will be successful at generating high sales volumes. Consider, for a moment, that any selection decision can result in four possible outcomes. As shown in Exhibit 7–5, two outcomes would indicate correct decisions, and two would indicate errors.

Exhibit 7–4 Downsizing Options

OPTION	DESCRIPTION
Firing	Permanent involuntary termination
Layoffs	Temporary involuntary termination; may last only a few days or extend to years
Attrition	Not filling openings created by voluntary resignations or normal retirements
Transfers	Moving employees either laterally or downward; usually does not reduce costs but can reduce intraorganizational supply–demand imbalances
Reduced workweeks	Having employees work fewer hours per week, share jobs, or through furloughs perform their jobs on a part-time basis
Early retirements	Providing incentives to older and more-senior employees for retiring before their normal retirement date
Job sharing	Having employees, typically two part-timers, share one full-time position

Exhibit 7–5 Selection Decision Outcomes

	Reject	**Accept**
Successful	Reject error	Correct decision
Unsuccessful	Correct decision	Accept error

Later Job Performance

Selection Decision

A decision is correct when (1) the applicant who was predicted to be successful (was accepted) later proved to be successful on the job, or (2) the applicant who was predicted to be unsuccessful (was rejected) would not have been able to do the job if hired. In the former case, we have successfully accepted; in the latter case, we have successfully rejected. Problems occur, however, when we reject applicants who, if hired, would have performed successfully on the job (called *reject errors*) or accept those who subsequently perform poorly (*accept errors*). These problems are, unfortunately, far from insignificant. A generation ago, reject errors only meant increased selection costs because more applicants would have to be screened. Today, selection techniques that result in reject errors can open the organization to charges of employment discrimination, especially if applicants from protected groups are disproportionately rejected. Accept errors, on the other hand, have obvious costs to the organization, including the cost of training the employee, the costs generated or profits forgone because of the employee's incompetence, and the cost of severance and the subsequent costs of additional recruiting and selection screening. The *major intent of any selection activity is to reduce the probability of making reject errors or accept errors while increasing the probability of making correct decisions.* How? By using selection procedures that are both reliable and valid.

reliability
The degree to which a selection device measures the same thing consistently

validity
The proven relationship between a selection device and some relevant criterion

WHAT IS RELIABILITY? **Reliability** addresses whether a selection device measures the same characteristic consistently. For example, if a test is reliable, any individual's score should remain fairly stable over time, assuming that the characteristics it's measuring are also stable. The importance of reliability should be self-evident. No selection device can be effective if it's low in reliability. Using such a device would be the equivalent of weighing yourself every day on an erratic scale. If the scale is unreliable—randomly fluctuating, say, 10 to 15 pounds every time you step on it—the results will not mean much. To be effective predictors, selection devices must possess an acceptable level of consistency.

Employees who apply for management positions at this Sarku Japan fast-food restaurant must take written tests as part of the company's selection process. Properly designed written tests for intelligence, integrity, personality, and interests are popular selection devices that often are valid and reliable in helping to predict which applicants will be successful on the job.

WHAT IS VALIDITY? Any selection device that a manager uses—such as application forms, tests, interviews, or physical examinations—must also demonstrate **validity**. Validity

Michael S. Williamson/*The Washington Post*/Getty Images

is based on a proven relationship between the selection device used and some relevant measure. For example, we mentioned earlier a firefighter applicant who was wheelchair bound. Because of the physical requirements of a firefighter's job, someone confined to a wheelchair would be unable to pass the physical endurance tests. In that case, denying employment could be considered valid, but requiring the same physical endurance tests for the dispatching job would not be job related. Federal law prohibits managers from using any selection device that cannot be shown to be directly related to successful job performance. That constraint goes for entrance tests, too; managers must be able to demonstrate that, once on the job, individuals with high scores on such a test outperform individuals with low scores. Consequently, the burden is on the organization to verify that any selection device it uses to differentiate applicants is related to job performance.

Tests...not just **for school!**

HOW EFFECTIVE ARE TESTS AND INTERVIEWS AS SELECTION DEVICES?   Managers can use a number of selection devices to reduce accept and reject errors. The best-known devices include written and performance-simulation tests and interviews. Let's briefly review each device, giving particular attention to its validity in predicting job performance.

Typical *written tests* include tests of intelligence, aptitude, ability, and interest. Such tests have long been used as selection devices, although their popularity has run in cycles. Written tests were widely used after World War II, but beginning in the late 1960s, fell out of favor. They were frequently characterized as discriminatory, and many organizations could not validate that their written tests were job related. Today, written tests have made a comeback, although most of them are now Internet based.[10] Experts estimate that online personality tests are used by employers to assess personality, skills, cognitive abilities, and other traits of some 60 to 70 percent of prospective employees.[11] Managers are increasingly aware that poor hiring decisions are costly and that properly designed tests can reduce the likelihood of making such decisions. In addition, the cost of developing and validating a set of written tests for a specific job has declined significantly.

Research shows that tests of intellectual ability, spatial and mechanical ability, perceptual accuracy, and motor ability are moderately valid predictors for many semiskilled and unskilled operative jobs in an industrial organization.[12] However, an enduring criticism of written tests is that intelligence and other tested characteristics can be somewhat removed from the actual performance of the job itself.[13] For example, a high score on an intelligence test is not necessarily a good indicator that the applicant will perform well as a computer programmer. This criticism has led to an increased use of performance-simulation tests.

What better way to find out whether an applicant for a technical writing position at Apple can write technical manuals than to ask him or her to do it? That's why there's an increasing interest in **performance-simulation tests**. Undoubtedly, the enthusiasm for these tests lies in the fact that they're based on job analysis data and, therefore, should more easily meet the requirement of job relatedness than do written tests. Performance-simulation tests are made up of actual job behaviors rather than substitutes. The best-known performance-simulation tests are work sampling (a miniature replica of the job) and assessment centers (simulating real problems one may face on the job). The former is suited to persons applying for routine jobs, the latter to managerial personnel.

The advantage of performance simulation over traditional testing methods should be obvious. Because its content is essentially identical to job content, performance simulation should be a better predictor of short-term job performance and should minimize potential employment discrimination allegations. Additionally, because of the nature of their content and the methods used to determine content, well-constructed performance-simulation tests are valid predictors.

The *interview*, along with the application form, is an almost universal selection device. Few of us have ever gotten a job without undergoing one or more interviews. The irony of this is that the value of an interview as a selection device has been the subject of considerable debate.[14]

performance-simulation tests
Selection devices based on actual job behaviors

Interviews can be reliable and valid selection tools, but too often they're not. To be effective predictors, interviews need to be:

- structured,
- well organized, and have
- interviewers asking relevant questions.[15]

But those conditions don't characterize many interviews. The typical interview in which applicants are asked a varying set of essentially random questions in an informal setting often provides little in the way of valuable information. All kinds of potential biases can creep into interviews if they're not well structured and standardized.

What does research tell us about interviewing?

- Prior knowledge about the applicant biases the interviewer's evaluation.
- The interviewer tends to hold a stereotype of what represents a good applicant.
- The interviewer tends to favor applicants who share his or her own attitudes.
- The order in which applicants are interviewed will influence evaluations.
- The order in which information is elicited during the interview will influence evaluations.
- Negative information is given unduly high weight.
- The interviewer may make a decision concerning the applicant's suitability within the first four or five minutes of the interview.
- The interviewer may forget much of the interview's content within minutes after its conclusion.
- The interview is most valid in determining an applicant's intelligence, level of motivation, and interpersonal skills.
- Structured and well-organized interviews are more reliable than unstructured and unorganized ones.[16]

How Can I Be a GOOD INTERVIEWER?

TIPS FOR MANAGERS: Make interviews more valid and reliable!

1. Review the job description and job specification to help in assessing the applicant.
2. Prepare a structured set of questions to ask all applicants for the job.
3. Review an applicant's résumé before meeting him or her.
4. Ask questions and listen carefully to the applicant's answer.
5. Write your evaluation of the applicant while the interview is still fresh in your mind.

One last popular modification to interviews has been the behavioral or situation interview.[17] In this type of interview, applicants are observed not only for what they say, but also how they behave. Applicants are presented with situations—often complex problems involving role playing—and are asked to "deal" with the situation. This type of interview provides an opportunity for interviewers to see how a potential employee will behave and how he or she will react under stress. Proponents of behavioral interviewing indicate such a process is much more indicative of an applicant's performance than simply having the individual tell the interviewer what he or she has done. In fact, research in this area indicates that behavioral interviews are nearly eight times more effective for predicting successful job performance.[18]

⭐ Watch It 2!

If your professor has assigned this, go to the Assignments section of **mymanagementlab.com** to complete the video exercise titled *Rudi's Bakery: Human Resource Management*.

HOW CAN YOU "CLOSE THE DEAL"?   Interviewers who treat the recruiting and hiring of employees as if the applicants must be sold on the job and exposed only to an organization's positive characteristics are likely to have a workforce that is dissatisfied and prone to high turnover.[19]

realistic job preview (RJP)
A preview of a job that provides both positive and negative information about the job and the company

Closing the **Deal!**

During the hiring process, every job applicant develops a set of expectations about the company and about the job for which he or she is interviewing. When the information an applicant receives is excessively inflated, a number of things happen that have potentially negative effects on the company: (1) Mismatched applicants are less likely to withdraw from the search process. (2) Inflated information builds unrealistic expectations so new employees are likely to become quickly dissatisfied and to resign prematurely. (3) New hires are prone to become disillusioned and less committed to the organization when they face the unexpected harsh realities of the job. (4) In many cases, these individuals feel that they were misled during the hiring process and may become problem employees.

To increase job satisfaction among employees and reduce turnover, managers should consider a **realistic job preview (RJP)**.[20] An RJP includes both positive and negative information about the job and the company. For example, in addition to the positive comments typically expressed in the interview, the applicant is told of the less attractive aspects of the job. For instance, he or she might be told that there are limited opportunities to talk to coworkers during work hours, that chances of being promoted are slim, or that work hours fluctuate so erratically that employees may be required to work during what are usually off hours (nights and weekends). Research indicates that applicants who have been given a realistic job preview hold lower and more realistic job expectations for the jobs they will be performing and are better able to cope with the frustrating elements of the job than are applicants who have been given only inflated information. The result is fewer unexpected resignations by new employees. For managers, realistic job previews offer a major insight into the HRM process.

Presenting only positive job aspects to an applicant may initially entice him or her to join the organization, but it may be a decision that both parties quickly regret.

It's just as important to *retain* **good people** as it is to *hire* them in the first place.

How Are Employees Provided with Needed Skills and Knowledge?

7-3 Explain how employees are provided with needed skills and knowledge.

If we've done our recruiting and selecting properly, we've hired competent individuals who can perform successfully on the job. But *successful performance requires more than possessing certain skills!* New hires must be acclimated to the organization's culture and be trained and given the knowledge to do the job in a manner consistent with the organization's goals. To achieve this, HRM uses orientation and training.

How Are New Hires Introduced to the Organization?

Once a job candidate has been selected, he or she needs to be introduced to the job and organization. This introduction is called **orientation**.[21] The major goals of orientation are to

- reduce the initial anxiety all new employees feel as they begin a new job;
- familiarize new employees with the job, the work unit, and the organization as a whole; and
- facilitate the outsider–insider transition.

Job orientation: (1) expands on the information the employee obtained during the recruitment and selection stages; (2) clarifies the new employee's specific duties and

orientation
Introducing a new employee to the job and the organization

responsibilities as well as how his or her performance will be evaluated; and (3) corrects any unrealistic expectations new employees might hold about the job.

Work unit orientation: (1) Familiarizes an employee with the goals of the work unit; (2) clarifies how his or her job contributes to the unit's goals; and (3) provides an introduction to his or her coworkers.

Organization orientation: (1) Informs the new employee about the organization's goals, history, philosophy, procedures, and rules; (2) clarifies relevant HR policies such as work hours, pay procedures, overtime requirements, and benefits; and (3) may include a tour of the organization's physical facilities.

Managers have an obligation to make the integration of a new employee into the organization as smooth and anxiety-free as possible. Successful orientation, whether formal or informal:

- Results in an outsider–insider transition that makes the new member feel comfortable and fairly well-adjusted.
- Lowers the likelihood of poor work performance.
- Reduces the probability of a surprise resignation by the new employee only a week or two into the job.[22]

Technology and the Manager's Job
SOCIAL AND DIGITAL HR

HR has gone social and digital.[23] Mobile devices are increasingly being used to provide training in bite-sized lessons using videos and games. For instance, the 75,000-plus associates of realty company Keller Williams use their smartphones and tablets to view two- to three-minute video lessons on sales and customer service. Then, there are the few tech-forward marketing firms that are using tweets rather than the conventional résumé/job interview process. These "Twitterviews" are used in talent selection. One individual said, "The Web is your résumé. Social networks are your mass references." Many other firms are using social media platforms to expand their recruiting reach. Not only are social media tools being used by corporations to recruit applicants, they're being used to allow employees to collaborate by sharing files, images, documents, videos, and other documents.

On the digital side, HR departments using software that automates many basic HR processes associated with recruiting, selecting, orienting, training, appraising performance, and storing and retrieving employee information have cut costs and optimized service. One HR area where IT has contributed is in pre-employment assessments. For instance, at KeyBank, a Cleveland-based financial services organization, virtual "job tryout simulations" have been used in order to reduce 90-day turnover rates and create more consistency in staffing decisions. These simulations create an interactive multimedia experience and mimic key job tasks for competencies such as providing client service, adapting to change, supporting team members, following procedures, and working efficiently. Before using these virtual assessments, the bank was losing 13 percent of new tellers and call center associates in their first 90 days. After implementing the virtual assessments, that number dropped to 4 percent.

Another area where IT has had a significant impact is in training. In a survey by the American Society for Training and Development, 95 percent of the responding companies reported using some form of e-learning. Using technology to deliver needed knowledge, skills, and attitudes has had many benefits. As one researcher pointed out, e-learning can reduce the cost of training, but more importantly, can improve the way an organization functions. And in many instances, it seems to do that! For example, when Hewlett-Packard looked at how its customer service was affected by a blend of e-learning and other instructional methods, rather than just classroom training, it found that its sales representatives could answer customer questions more quickly and accurately. And Unilever found that after e-learning training for sales employees, sales increased by several million dollars.

If your professor has assigned this, go to the Assignments section of **mymanagementlab.com** *to complete these discussion questions.*

⭐ **TALK ABOUT IT 5:** Does the use of all this technology make HR—which is supposed to be a "people-oriented" profession—less so? Why or why not?

⭐ **TALK ABOUT IT 6:** You want a job after graduating from college. Knowing that you're likely to encounter online recruitment and selection procedures, how can you best prepare for making yourself stand out in the process?

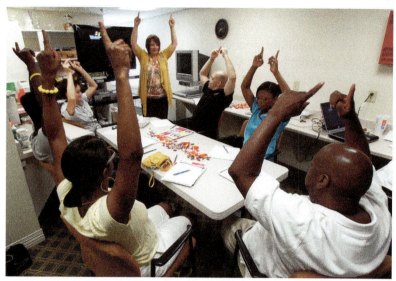

Fred Blocher/*Kansas City Star*/Getty Images

Employees at Villa Venture senior living community participate in a perception exercise during the Virtual Dementia Tour, a training tool that helps them understand Alzheimer's disease and other forms of dementia. The tour is a learning experience designed to improve employees' ability to care for victims of dementia.

What Is Employee Training?

On the whole, planes don't cause airline accidents, people do. Most collisions, crashes, and other airline mishaps—nearly three-quarters of them—result from errors by the pilot or air traffic controller, or from inadequate maintenance. Weather and structural failures typically account for the remaining accidents.[24] We cite these statistics to illustrate the importance of training in the airline industry. Such maintenance and human errors could be prevented or significantly reduced by better employee training, as shown by the unbelievably amazing "landing" of US Airways Flight 1549 in the Hudson River in January 2009 with no loss of life. Pilot Captain Chesley Sullenberger attributed the positive outcome to the extensive and intensive training that all pilots and flight crews undergo.[25]

Employee training is a learning experience that seeks a relatively permanent change in employees by improving their ability to perform on the job. Thus, training involves changing skills, knowledge, attitudes, or behavior.[26] This change may involve what employees know, how they work, or their attitudes toward their jobs, coworkers, managers, and the organization. It's been estimated, for instance, that U.S. business firms spend billions each year on formal courses and training programs to develop workers' skills.[27] Managers, of course, are responsible for deciding when employees are in need of training and what form that training should take.

Determining training needs typically involves answering several questions. If some of these questions sound familiar, you've been paying close attention. It's precisely the type of analysis that takes place when managers develop an organizational structure to achieve their strategic goals—only now the focus is on the people.[28]

employee training
A learning experience that seeks a relatively permanent change in employees by improving their ability to perform on the job

---

WHEN is training needed?

The questions in Exhibit 7–6 suggest the kinds of signals that can warn a manager when training may be necessary. The more obvious ones are related directly to productivity.

Exhibit 7–6 Determining Whether Training Is Needed

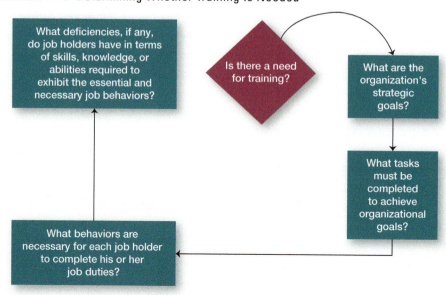

- What deficiencies, if any, do job holders have in terms of skills, knowledge, or abilities required to exhibit the essential and necessary job behaviors?
- Is there a need for training?
- What are the organization's strategic goals?
- What tasks must be completed to achieve organizational goals?
- What behaviors are necessary for each job holder to complete his or her job duties?

Indications that job performance is declining include decreases in production numbers, lower quality, more accidents, and higher scrap or rejection rates. Any of these outcomes might suggest that worker skills need to be fine-tuned. Of course, we're assuming that an employee's performance decline is in no way related to lack of effort. Managers, too, must also recognize that training may be required because the workplace is constantly evolving. Changes imposed on employees as a result of job redesign or a technological breakthrough also require training.

HOW ARE EMPLOYEES TRAINED? Most training takes place on the job. Why? It's simple and it usually costs less. However, on-the-job training can disrupt the workplace and result in an increase in errors while learning takes place. Also, some skill training is too complex to learn on the job and must take place outside the work setting.

Many different types of training methods are available. For the most part, we can classify them as traditional and technology-based. (See Exhibit 7–7.)

HOW CAN MANAGERS ENSURE THAT TRAINING IS WORKING? It's easy to generate a new training program, but if training efforts aren't evaluated, it may be a waste of resources. It would be nice if all companies could boast the returns on investments in training that Neil Huffman Auto Group executives do; they claim they receive $230 in increased productivity for every dollar spent on training.[29] But to make such a claim, training must be properly evaluated. (continued on p. 218)

 Try It!

If your professor has assigned this, go to the Assignments section of **mymanagementlab.com** to complete the **Simulation: *Human Resource Management***.

Exhibit 7–7 Training Methods

TRADITIONAL TRAINING METHODS

On-the-job—Employees learn how to do tasks simply by performing them, usually after an initial introduction to the task.

Job rotation—Employees work at different jobs in a particular area, getting exposure to a variety of tasks.

Mentoring and coaching—Employees work with an experienced worker who provides information, support, and encouragement; also called apprenticeships in certain industries.

Experiential exercises—Employees participate in role-playing, simulations, or other face-to-face types of training.

Workbooks/manuals—Employees refer to training workbooks and manuals for information.

Classroom lectures—Employees attend lectures designed to convey specific information.

TECHNOLOGY-BASED TRAINING METHODS

CD-ROM/DVD/videotapes/audiotapes/podcasts—Employees listen to or watch selected media that convey information or demonstrate certain techniques.

Videoconferencing/teleconferencing/satelliteTV—Employees listen to or participate as information is conveyed or techniques demonstrated.

E-learning—Employees participate in Internet-based learning, including simulations or other interactive modules.

Mobile learning—Employees participate in learning activities delivered via mobile devices.

Source: Robbins, Stephen P., Coulter, Mary, *Management*, 13th Ed., © 2016, p. 353. Reprinted and electronically reproduced by permission of Pearson Education, Inc., New York, NY.

Keeping Great People:
Two Ways Organizations Do This

1

Performance Management System

- *Desired* employee performance levels determined by organizations and managers
- *Actual* employee performance levels measured/appraised by managers
- *AKA* **performance management system**

Should people be **compared to one another** or **against a set of standards?**

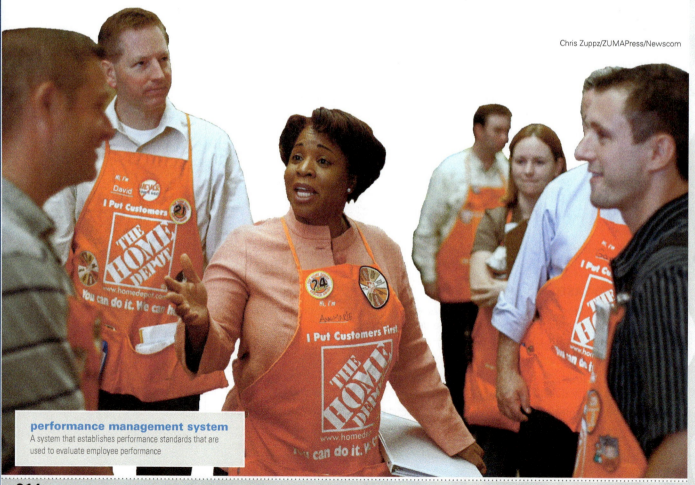

Chris Zuppz/ZUMAPress/Newscom

performance management system
A system that establishes performance standards that are used to evaluate employee performance

Exhibit 7–8 Specific Performance Appraisal Methods

Method	Advantage	Disadvantage
(a) Written essay—descriptions of employee's strengths and weaknesses	Simple to use	More a measure of evaluator's writing ability than of employee's actual performance
(b) Critical incidents—examples of critical behaviors that were especially effective or ineffective	Rich examples; behaviorally based	Time-consuming; lack quantification
(c) Adjective rating scales—lists descriptive performance factors (work quantity and quality, knowledge, cooperation, loyalty, attendance, honesty, initiative, and so forth) with numerical ratings	Provide quantitative data; less time-consuming than others	Do not provide depth of job behavior assessed
(d) BARS—rating scale + examples of actual job behaviors[30,31]	Focus on specific and measurable job behaviors	Time-consuming; difficult to develop measures
(e) MBO—evaluation of accomplishment of specific goals	Focuses on end goals; results oriented	Time-consuming
(f) 360-degree appraisal[32]—feedback from full circle of those who interact with employee	More thorough	Time-consuming
(g) Multiperson—evaluation comparison of work group	Compares employees with one another	Unwieldy with large number of employees

- **(a)** through **(f)** (see Exhibit 7–8) are ways to evaluate employee performance against a set of established standards or absolute criteria.

- **(g)** (see Exhibit 7–8) is a way to compare one person's performance with that of one or more individuals and is a relative, not absolute, measuring device.

Three approaches to multiperson comparison:

1 Group-order ranking

Evaluator places employees into a particular classification ("top fifth," "second fifth," etc.; "top third," "middle third," "bottom third"; or whatever classification is desired). Note: Number of employees placed in each classification must be as equal as possible.

2 Individual ranking approach

Evaluator lists employees in order from highest to lowest performance levels. Note: Only one can be "best." In the appraisal of whatever number of employees, the difference between the first and second employee is the same as that between any other two employees. And no "ties" allowed.

3 Paired comparison approach

Each employee is compared with every other employee in the comparison group and rated as either the superior or weaker member of the pair. Note: Each employee is assigned a summary ranking based on the number of superior scores he or she achieved. Each employee is compared against every other employee—an arduous task when assessing large numbers of employees.

360-degree appraisal
An appraisal device that seeks feedback from a variety of sources for the person being rated

— **Downsizing**—supervisors may have more employees to manage, making it difficult to have extensive knowledge of each one's performance.

— Project teams and employee involvement—others (not managers) may be better able to make accurate assessments.[34]

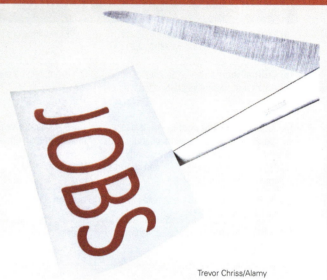

Lasse Kristensen/Alamy

Trevor Chriss/Alamy

When Employee's Performance Is Not Up to Par...

WHY?

Job mismatch (hiring error)

Inadequate training

Lack of desire to do job (**discipline** problem)

WHAT TO DO

→ Reassign individual to better-matched job

→ Provide training

→ Try **employee counseling**, a process designed to help employees overcome performance-related problems; attempt to uncover why employee has lost his/her desire or ability to work productively and find ways to fix the problem; or take disciplinary/punitive action (*verbal and written warnings, suspension, and even termination*).

2

Compensating Employees: Pay and Benefits

Compensation–Pay for doing a job

An **effective** and **appropriate** compensation system will:[35]

— Help attract and retain competent and talented individuals
— Impact strategic performance[36]
— Keep employees motivated

MOST of us work to have money

discipline
Actions taken by a manager to enforce an organization's standards and regulations

employee counseling
A process designed to help employees overcome performance-related problems

artpartner-images.com/Alamy

Determining Pay Levels

Who gets
$15.85
an hour?

Who gets
$325,000
a year?

A compensation system should reflect the changing nature of work and the workplace.

- Determining pay levels isn't easy, but employees expect appropriate compensation.

Different jobs require:

- Different kinds and levels of **knowledge, skills**, and **abilities** (**KSAs**) that have varying value to the organization
- Different levels of responsibility and authority

The **higher the KSAs** and the greater the authority and responsibility, **the higher the pay**.

Alternative approaches to determining compensation:

- **Skill-based pay systems**—reward employees for job skills and competencies they have. Job title doesn't define pay, skills do.[37] Usually more successful in manufacturing organizations than in service organizations or in organizations pursuing technical innovations.[38]
- **Variable pay systems**—individual's compensation is contingent on performance.

90%
of U.S. organizations use variable pay plans[39]

*Other **factors influencing compensation** and **benefit packages** include:*

Primary determinant of pay: the kind of job an employee performs

skill-based pay
A pay system that rewards employees for the job skills they demonstrate

variable pay
A pay system in which an individual's compensation is contingent on performance

Exhibit 7–9 What Determines Pay and Benefits?

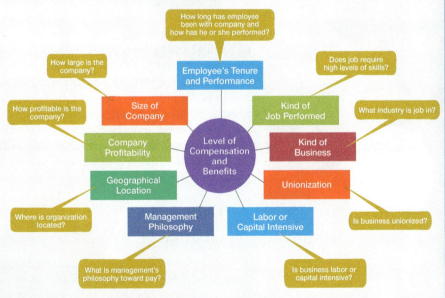

- How long has employee been with company and how has he or she performed?
- How large is the company?
- Does job require high levels of skills?
- How profitable is the company?
- What industry is job in?
- Employee's Tenure and Performance
- Size of Company
- Kind of Job Performed
- Company Profitability
- Kind of Business
- Level of Compensation and Benefits
- Geographical Location
- Unionization
- Where is organization located?
- Management Philosophy
- Labor or Capital Intensive
- Is business unionized?
- What is management's philosophy toward pay?
- Is business labor or capital intensive?

Compensation–Employee Benefits: Non-cash compensation from employers

- Compensation package is > just hourly wage or annual salary

- Also includes **employee benefits**—important and varied nonfinancial rewards designed to enrich employees' lives

- Benefit packages can vary widely and often reflect efforts to provide something that each employee values

- Some benefits—Social Security, workers' and unemployment compensation—are legally required, but organizations may provide others such as paid time off from work, life and disability insurance, retirement programs, and health insurance.[40]

employee benefits
Membership-based rewards designed to enrich employees' lives

J.R. Bale/Alamy

How can training programs be evaluated? Usually several managers, representatives from HRM, and a group of workers who have recently completed a training program are asked for their opinions. If the comments are generally positive, the program may get a favorable evaluation and it's continued until someone decides, for whatever reason, that it should be eliminated or replaced.

Such reactions from participants or managers, while easy to acquire, are the least valid. Their opinions are heavily influenced by factors that may have little to do with the training's effectiveness, such as difficulty, entertainment value, or the personality characteristics of the instructor. However, trainees' reactions to the training may, in fact, provide feedback on how worthwhile the participants viewed the training to be. Beyond general reactions, however, training must also be evaluated in terms of how much the participants learned; how well they are using their new skills on the job (did their behavior change?); and whether the training program achieved its desired results (reduced turnover, increased customer service, etc.).[41]

 Write It!
If your professor has assigned this, go to the Assignments section of **mymanagementlab.com** to complete *MGMT 9: Management & Human Resources (HR Decision Making)*.

What Contemporary HRM Issues Face Managers?

7-5 Discuss contemporary issues in managing human resources.

HR issues that face today's managers include downsizing, workforce diversity, sexual harassment, and HR costs.

How Can Managers Manage Downsizing?

downsizing
The planned elimination of jobs in an organization

layoff-survivor sickness
A set of attitudes, perceptions, and behaviors of employees who survive layoffs

Downsizing is the planned elimination of jobs in an organization. Because downsizing typically involves shrinking the organization's workforce, it's an important issue in HRM. When an organization has too many employees—which may happen when it's faced with an economic crisis, declining market share, overly aggressive growth, or when it's been poorly managed—one option for improving profits is to eliminate excess workers. Over the last few years, many well-known companies have gone through several rounds of downsizing—AmEx, Boeing, McDonald's, Volkswagen, Microsoft, Dell, General Motors, Unisys, Siemens, Merck, and Toyota, among others. How can managers best manage a downsized workforce?

After downsizing, disruptions in the workplace and in employees' personal lives are to be expected. Stress, frustration, anxiety, and anger are typical reactions. And it may surprise you to learn that *both* victims and survivors experience those feelings.[42] Many organizations have helped layoff victims by offering a variety of job-help services, psychological counseling, support groups, severance pay, extended health insurance benefits, and detailed communications. Although some individuals react negatively to being laid off (the worst cases involve individuals returning to their former organization and committing a violent act), offers of assistance reveal that an organization does care about its former employees. While those being laid off get to start over with a clean slate and a clear conscience, survivors don't. Unfortunately, the "survivors" who retain their jobs and have the task of keeping the organization going or even of revitalizing it seldom receive attention. One negative consequence appears to be what is being called **layoff-survivor sickness**, a set of attitudes, perceptions, and behaviors of employees who survive involuntary staff reductions.[43] Symptoms include job insecurity, perceptions of unfairness, guilt, depression, stress from increased workload, fear of change, loss of loyalty and commitment, reduced effort, and an unwillingness to do anything beyond the required minimum.

To show concern for job survivors, managers may want to provide opportunities for employees to talk to counselors about their guilt, anger, and anxiety.[44] Group discussions can be a way for the survivors to vent their feelings. Some organizations have used downsizing as the spark to implement increased employee participation programs such as empowerment and self-managed work teams. In short, to keep morale and productivity high, managers should make every attempt to ensure that those individuals still working in the organization know that they're valuable and much-needed resources. Exhibit 7–10 summarizes some ways that managers can reduce the trauma associated with downsizing.[45]

Exhibit 7–10 Tips for Managing Downsizing

- Communicate openly and honestly:
  - Inform those being let go as soon as possible
  - Tell surviving employees the new goals and expectations
  - Explain impact of layoffs
- Follow any laws regulating severance pay or benefits
- Provide support/counseling for surviving employees
- Reassign roles according to individuals' talents and backgrounds
- Focus on boosting morale:
  - Offer individualized reassurance
  - Continue to communicate, especially one-on-one
  - Remain involved and available

Diversity management at Target includes developing employee talent through mentoring. Target offers employees, such as executive team leader Chenille English-Boswell, shown here, group, virtual, and peer mentoring, as well as skip mentoring, whereby a senior leader mentors a team member several pay grades below the mentor.

How Can Workforce Diversity Be Managed?

Although we discussed the changing makeup of the workforce in Chapter 3, workforce diversity also affects such basic HRM activities as recruitment, selection, and orientation.[46]

Improving workforce diversity requires managers to widen their recruiting net. For example, the popular practice of relying on current employee referrals as a source of new job applicants tends to produce candidates who have similar characteristics to those of present employees. So managers have to look for applicants in places where they haven't typically looked before. To increase diversity, managers are increasingly turning to nontraditional recruitment sources such as women's job networks, over-50 clubs, urban job banks, disabled people's training centers, ethnic newspapers, and gay rights organizations. This type of outreach should enable an organization to broaden its pool of applicants.

Once a diverse set of applicants exists, efforts must be made to ensure that the selection process does not discriminate. Moreover, applicants need to be made comfortable with the organization's culture and be made aware of management's desire to accommodate their needs. For instance, at TGI Friday's, company managers work diligently to accommodate differences and create workplace choices for a diverse workforce; so, too, do companies such as Sodexo, Johnson & Johnson, EY, Mastercard Worldwide, and Procter & Gamble.[47]

Finally, orientation is often difficult for women and minorities. Many organizations, such as Lotus Development and Hewlett-Packard, provide special workshops to raise diversity consciousness among current employees as well as programs for new employees that focus on diversity issues. The thrust of these efforts is to increase individual understanding of the differences each of us brings to the workplace. A number of companies also have special mentoring programs to deal with the reality that lower-level female and minority managers have few role models with whom to identify.[48]

What Is Sexual Harassment?

Sexual harassment *is* a serious issue.

This is true in both public and private-sector organizations. Between 7,000 and 8,000 complaints are filed with the EEOC each year,[49] with more than 17 percent of those filed by males.[50] Settlements in some of these cases incurred a substantial cost to the companies in terms of litigation. It's estimated that sexual harassment is the single largest financial risk facing companies today—and can result in decreases (sometimes greater than 30 percent) in a company's stock price.[51] At Mitsubishi, for example, the company paid out more than $34 million to 300 women for the rampant sexual harassment to which they were exposed.[52] But it's more than just jury awards. Sexual harassment results in millions lost in absenteeism, low productivity, and turnover.[53] Sexual harassment, furthermore, is not just a U.S. phenomenon. It's a global issue. For instance, nearly 10 percent of workers responding to a global survey reported that they had been harassed sexually or physically at work. The survey covered countries such as India, China, Saudi Arabia, Sweden, France, Belgium, Germany, Great Britain, and Poland, among others.[54] Even though discussions of sexual harassment cases often focus on the large awards granted by a court, employers face other concerns. Sexual harassment creates an unpleasant work environment for organization members and undermines their ability to perform their jobs. But just what is sexual harassment?

Any unwanted action or activity of a sexual nature that explicitly or implicitly affects an individual's employment, performance, or work environment can be regarded as **sexual harassment**. It can occur between members of the opposite or of the same sex—between employees of the organization or between employee and nonemployee.[55] Although such

sexual harassment
Any unwanted action or activity of a sexual nature that explicitly or implicitly affects an individual's employment, performance, or work environment

an activity has been generally prohibited under Title VII (sex discrimination) in the United States, in recent years this problem has gained more recognition. By most accounts, prior to the mid-1980s, occurrences were generally viewed as isolated incidents, with the individual committing the act being solely responsible (if at all) for his or her actions.[56] Today, charges of sexual harassment continue to appear in the headlines on an almost regular basis.

Most of the challenges associated with sexual harassment involve determining what constitutes this illegal behavior.[57] The EEOC explains that it is unlawful to harass a person because of that person's sex. Harassment can include sexual harassment or unwelcome sexual advances, requests for sexual behavior, and other verbal or physical harassment of a sexual nature. However, harassment does *not* have to be of a sexual nature and can include offensive remarks about a person's sex. Simple teasing, offhand comments, or isolated incidents that are not serious are not prohibited by the law *unless* it becomes so frequent or so severe that it creates a hostile or offensive work environment or it results in an adverse employment decision (such as being demoted or fired).[58]

You gotta be attuned to what makes fellow **employees uncomfortable.**

For many organizations, it's the offensive or hostile environment issue that's problematic.[59] Managers need to know what constitutes such an environment. How do you determine whether something is offensive? For instance, do off-color jokes in the office create a hostile environment? How about classical artwork that shows nude men or women? The answer is it very well could! It depends on the people in the organization and the environment in which they work. The key is knowing what makes fellow employees uncomfortable—and if we don't know, we should ask![60] Also, managers must understand that the victim doesn't necessarily have to be the person harassed but could be *anyone* affected by the offensive conduct.[61]

Organizational success will, in part, reflect how sensitive each employee is toward another in the company. At DuPont, for example, the corporate culture and diversity programs are designed to eliminate sexual harassment through awareness and respect for all individuals.[62] It means understanding one another and, most importantly, respecting others' rights. Similar programs exist at FedEx, General Mills, and Levi-Strauss, among other companies.

If sexual harassment carries with it potential costs to the organization, what can a company do to protect itself?[63] The courts want to know two things: (1) Did the organization know about, or should it have known about, the alleged behavior? and (2) What did managers do to stop it?[64] With the number and dollar amounts of the awards today, it's even more important for organizations and managers to educate all employees on sexual harassment matters and to have mechanisms available to monitor employees. In addition, organizations need to ensure that no retaliatory actions—such as cutting back hours, assigning back-to-back work shifts without a rest break, etc.—are taken against a person who has filed harassment charges, especially in light of a U.S. Supreme Court ruling that broadened the definition of retaliation.[65]

Finally, in a sexual harassment matter, managers must remember that the harasser may have rights, too.[66] No action should be taken against someone until a thorough investigation has been conducted. Furthermore, the results of the investigation should be reviewed by an independent and objective individual before any action against the alleged harasser is taken. Even then, the harasser should be given an opportunity to respond to the allegation and have a disciplinary hearing if desired. Additionally, an avenue for appeal should also exist for the alleged harasser—an appeal heard by someone at a higher level of management who is not associated with the case.

How and Why Are Organizations Controlling HR Costs?

HR costs are skyrocketing, especially those associated with employee health care and employee pensions. Organizations are looking for ways to control these costs.

WHAT ABOUT EMPLOYEE HEALTH CARE COSTS? Employees at Paychex who undergo a confidential health screening and risk assessment, and those who smoke who agree to enroll in a smoking cessation program, can get free annual physicals, colonoscopies, and 100 percent coverage of preventive care as well as lower deductibles and costs. At Black and Decker Corporation, employees and dependents who certify in an honor system that they have been tobacco-free for at least six months pay $75 less per month for their medical and dental coverage. At Amerigas Propane, employees were given an ultimatum: get their medical checkups or lose their health insurance. Some 67 percent of employers are concerned about the effects of obesity on medical claims expenses.[67]

All these examples illustrate how companies are trying to control skyrocketing employee health-care costs. Since 2002, health-care costs have risen, hitting $3.8 trillion in 2013. The actual dollar amounts for 2014 were not available but increased by 5 percent over the previous year.[68] Two health areas of concern for organizations are employees who smoke and obese employees. Smokers cost companies an estimated $6,000 a year, with about a third of that being health-care costs.[69] The biggest health-care cost for companies, however, is obesity. Morbidly obese individuals cost employers more than $8,000 a year.[70] A study of manufacturing organizations found that presenteeism, which is defined as employees not performing at full capacity, was 1.8 percent higher for workers with moderate to severe obesity than for all other employees. The reason for the lost productivity is likely the result of reduced mobility because of body size or pain problems such as arthritis. Another study found that injuries sustained by obese workers often require substantially more medical care and are more likely to lead to permanent disabilities than similar injuries suffered by employees who were not obese.[71]

Is it any wonder that organizations are looking for ways to control their health-care costs? How? First, many organizations are providing opportunities for employees to lead healthy lifestyles. From financial incentives to company-sponsored health and wellness programs, the goal is to limit rising health-care costs. About 43 percent of companies use some type of positive incentives aimed at encouraging healthy behavior, up from 34 percent in 1996.[72] Another study indicated that nearly 90 percent of companies surveyed planned to aggressively promote healthy lifestyles to their employees during the next three to five years.[73] Many are starting sooner: Google, Yamaha Corporation of America, Caterpillar, and others are putting health food in company break rooms, cafeterias, and vending machines; providing deliveries of fresh organic fruit; and putting "calorie taxes" on fatty foods. At Wegmans Food Markets, employees are challenged to eat five cups of fruits and vegetables and walk 10,000 steps a day. And the "competition" between departments and stores has proved to be very popular and effective.[74] In the case of smokers, however, some companies have taken a more aggressive stance by increasing the amount smokers pay for health insurance or by firing them if they refuse to stop smoking.

WHAT ABOUT EMPLOYEE PENSION PLAN COSTS?   The other area where organizations are looking to control costs is employee pension plans. Corporate pensions have been around since the nineteenth century.[75] But the days when companies could afford to give employees a broad-based pension that provided them a guaranteed retirement income have changed. Pension commitments have become such an enormous burden that companies can no longer afford them. In fact, the corporate pension system has been described as "fundamentally broken."[76] It's not just struggling companies that have eliminated employee pension plans. Lots of reasonably sound companies—for instance, NCR, FedEx, Lockheed Martin, and Motorola—no longer provide pensions. Only 42 *Fortune* 100 companies now offer pension plans to their new hires. Even IBM, which closed its pension plan to new hires in December 2004, told employees that their pension benefits would be frozen.[77] Obviously, the pension issue is one that directly affects HR decisions. On the one hand, organizations want to attract talented, capable employees by offering them desirable benefits such as pensions. But on the other hand, organizations have to balance that with the costs of providing such benefits.

MyManagementLab®

Go to **mymanagementlab.com** to complete the problems marked with this icon

7 Review

7-1 Describe the key components of the human resource management process and the important influences on that process.

The HRM process consists of eight activities that will staff an organization with competent, high-performing employees who are capable of sustaining their performance level over the long term. The first three HR activities involve employment planning and include recruitment, downsizing, and selection. The next two steps involve helping employees adapt to the organization and ensuring that their skills and knowledge are kept current, and include the HR activities of orienting and training. The last steps involve identifying performance goals, correcting performance problems, and helping employees sustain high levels of performance. These are done using the HR activities of performance appraisal, compensation and benefits, and safety and health. The main influences on the HRM process are legal, although other environmental conditions such as restructuring, downsizing, diversity, and so forth can impact it as well.

7-2 Discuss the tasks associated with identifying and selecting competent employees.

The first task is employment planning, which involves job analysis and the creation of job descriptions and job specifications. Then, if job needs are indicated, recruitment involves attempts to develop a pool of potential job candidates. Downsizing is used to reduce the labor supply. Selection involves determining who is best qualified for the job. Selection devices need to be both reliable and valid. Managers may want to give potential employees a realistic job preview.

7-3 Explain how employees are provided with needed skills and knowledge.

New hires must be acclimated to the organization's culture and be trained and given the knowledge to do the job in a manner consistent with the organization's goals. Orientation—job, work unit, and organizational—provides new employees with information to introduce them to the job. Training is used to help employees improve their ability to perform on the job.

7-4 Describe strategies for retaining competent, high-performing employees.

Two HRM activities that play a role in this are managing employee performance and developing an appropriate compensation and benefits program. Managing employee performance involves establishing performance standards and then appraising performance to see if those standards have been met. There are various performance appraisal techniques managers can use. If an employee's performance is not up to par, managers need to assess why and take action. Compensation and benefits programs can help attract and retain competent and talented individuals. Managers have to determine who gets paid what and what benefits will be offered.

7-5 Discuss contemporary issues in managing human resources.

Downsizing is the planned elimination of jobs and must be managed from the perspective of layoff victims and job survivors. Workforce diversity must be managed through HRM activities including recruitment, selection, and orientation. Sexual harassment is a significant concern of organizations and managers, which means programs and mechanisms must be in place to educate all employees about it. Finally, organizations are looking for ways to control HR costs, especially health-care costs and pension costs.

DISCUSSION QUESTIONS

 7-1 How does HRM affect all managers?

 7-2 Discuss the external environmental factors that most directly affect the HRM process.

7-3 Some critics claim that corporate HR departments have outlived their usefulness and are not there to help employees but to shield the organization from legal problems. What do you think? What benefits are there to having a formal HRM process? What are the drawbacks?

7-4 Do you think it's ethical for a prospective employer to delve into an applicant's life by means of interviews, tests, and background investigations? What if those investigations involved looking at your Facebook page or personal blogs? Explain your position.

7-5 Discuss the advantages and drawbacks of the various recruiting sources.

7-6 Discuss the advantages and drawbacks of the various selection devices.

7-7 What are the benefits and drawbacks of realistic job previews? (Consider this question from both the perspective of the organization *and* the perspective of a potential employee.)

7-8 List the factors that influence employee compensation and benefits.

7-9 What, in your view, constitutes sexual harassment? Describe how companies can minimize sexual harassment in the workplace.

7-10 Research your chosen career by finding out what it's going to take to be successful in this career in terms of education, skills, experience, and so forth. Write a personal career guide that details this information.

Writing Assignments

7-11 How is technology changing how HRM is done?

7-12 How does HRM help achieve the goal of having the "the right numbers of the right people in the right place at the right time"?

Management Skill Builder | PROVIDING GOOD FEEDBACK

Everyone needs feedback! If you want people to do their best, they need to know what they're doing well and what they can do better. That's why providing feedback is such an important skill to have. But being effective at giving feedback is tricky! That's why we often see managers either (a) not wanting to give feedback or (b) giving feedback in such a way that it doesn't result in anything positive.

⭐ PERSONAL INVENTORY ASSESSMENT PERSONAL INVENTORY ASSESSMENT

Work Performance Assessment

As this chapter indicated, performance assessment is an important HR function. Use this PIA to assess work performance.

Skill Basics

You can feel more comfortable with and be more effective at providing feedback if you use the following specific suggestions:

1. *Be straightforward by focusing on specific behaviors.* Feedback should be specific rather than general. Avoid such statements as "You have a bad attitude" or "I'm really impressed with the good job you did." They're vague and although they provide information, they don't tell the recipient enough to correct the "bad attitude" or on what basis you concluded that a "good job" had been done so the person knows what behaviors to repeat or to avoid.

2. *Be realistic.* Focus your feedback on what can be changed. When people get comments on things over which they have no control, it can be frustrating.

3. *Keep feedback impersonal.* Feedback, particularly the negative kind, should be descriptive rather than judgmental or evaluative. No matter how upset you are, keep the feedback focused on job-related behaviors and never criticize someone personally because of an inappropriate action.

4. *Keep feedback goal oriented.* Feedback should not be given primarily to "blow off steam" or "unload" on another person. If you have to say something negative, make sure it's directed toward the recipient's goals. Ask yourself whom the feedback is supposed to help. If the answer is *you*, bite your tongue and hold the comment. Such feedback undermines your credibility and lessens the meaning and influence of future feedback.

5. *Know when to give feedback—make it well timed.* Feedback is most meaningful to a recipient when there's a very short interval between his or her behavior and the receipt of feedback about that behavior. Moreover, if you're particularly concerned with changing behavior, delays in providing feedback on the undesirable actions lessen the likelihood that the feedback will be effective in bringing about the desired change. Of course, making feedback prompt merely for the sake of promptness can backfire if you have insufficient information, if you're angry, or if you're otherwise emotionally upset. In such instances, "well timed" could mean "somewhat delayed."

6. *Ensure understanding.* Make sure your feedback is concise and complete so that the recipient clearly and fully understands the communication. It may help to have the recipient rephrase the content of your feedback to find out whether it fully captured the meaning you intended.

7. *Watch your body language, tone of voice, and facial expressions.* Your body language and tone of voice can speak louder than words. Think about what you want to communicate and make sure your body language supports that message.

Based on A. Tugend, "You've Been Doing a Fantastic Job. Just One Thing...," *New York Times Online*, April 5, 2013; C. R. Mill, "Feedback: The Art of Giving and Receiving Help," in L. Porter and C. R. Mill (eds.), *The Reading Book for Human Relations Training* (Bethel, ME: NTL Institute for Applied Behavioral Science, 1976), 18–19; and S. Bishop, *The Complete Feedback Skills Training Book* (Aldershot, UK: Gower Publishing, 2000).

Practicing the Skill

Read through this scenario and follow the directions at the end of it.

Craig is an excellent employee whose expertise and productivity have always met or exceeded your expectations. But recently he's been making work difficult for other members of your advertising team. Like his coworkers, Craig researches and computes the costs of media coverage for your advertising agency's clients. The work requires laboriously leafing through several large reference books to find the correct base price and add-on charges for each radio or television station and time slot, calculating each actual cost, and compiling the results in a computerized spreadsheet. To make things more efficient and convenient, you've always allowed your team members to bring the reference books they're using to their desks while they're using them. Lately, however, Craig has been piling books around him for days and sometimes weeks at a time. The books interfere with the flow of traffic past his desk and other people have to go out of their way to retrieve the books from Craig's pile. It's time for you to have a talk with Craig.

Prepare an outline of how you will address this issue with Craig. Using the suggestions in the Skill Basics, be as specific as possible in terms of what you will say and how you will approach this. If your professor chooses, be prepared to do some role-playing in class.

Experiential Exercise

Western Montana Power & Light

To: Sandra Gillies, Director of Human Resources

From: William Mulroney, CEO

Re: Sexual Harassment

Sandra, I think we might have a problem. It appears that some of our employees aren't clear about the practices and actions that do or do not constitute sexual harassment. We can't have any ambiguity or uncertainty about this, as you know. We need to immediately develop a training program for all our employees and develop a workable procedure to handle any complaints that might arise.

I want this issue of sexual harassment to be the primary topic at next month's executive board meeting. To facilitate discussion, please give me a bulleted list describing the content of an initial two-hour employee workshop on sexual harassment.

This fictionalized company and message were created for educational purposes only, and not meant to reflect positively or negatively on management practices by any company that may share this name.

CASE APPLICATION #1

Résumé Regrets

Human resource (HR) managers say that 53 percent of résumés and job applications contain falsification, and 21 percent of résumé falsification state a fraudulent degree. In this age of digital and social media, it's hard to imagine anyone falsifying their records, much less someone who's in a company's top position as CEO.[78]

After a thorough search, Scott Thompson was named as Yahoo!'s CEO in early 2012. Prior to his appointment at Yahoo!, Thompson was president of PayPal, and prior to that he was PayPal's chief technology officer. Thompson replaced Carol Bartz, a well-known computer industry executive, who, after two years on the job, had been unable to resolve Yahoo!'s troubles. In his first months on the job, Thompson formulated a strategic plan for turning around the company, including a massive layoff of employees. Then, the whole situation started to unravel. An activist investor sent a letter to Yahoo!'s board of directors expressing concern about an SEC regulatory filing signed by Thompson "that stated to the best of his knowledge its contents were accurate." That document said that Thompson had earned a college degree in accounting and computer science in 1979 from a small university south of Boston. The activist investor said he had reason to believe that the degree was in accounting only. And, come to find out, the university didn't have a computer science program until the early 1980s and school officials confirmed that Mr. Thompson received a bachelor's of science degree in business administration. The activist investor questioned if Thompson had embellished his academic credentials and if the board had failed to exercise due "diligence and oversight in one of its most important tasks—identifying and hiring the chief executive officer."

> ### Would **YOU** lie on a résumé to get a job you want? **70 percent** of college students said they would!

After all this came down, a person close to the company said that, "In the absence of evidence that Mr. Thompson actively misled Yahoo! about his résumé, Yahoo!'s directors likely won't force him out. Maintaining him as CEO of Yahoo! at this time is more important than whether he had a computer science degree or not." And at first, that was the stance Yahoo!'s board took. However, the controversy continued to grow. In a meeting with senior Yahoo! officials, Thompson said he "regretted not finding an error in his public biography." He then suggested that maybe an executive search firm might have inserted this information more than seven years earlier. Yet, this blame game backfired. Some of his comments ended up on tech blogs, which angered the search firm, which produced documents from Mr. Thompson showing his inaccurate biography. As one person close to the situation said, "The cover-up became worse than the crime." Not long after, Thompson ended up resigning his position. Although the board did not give him severance pay, he did get to keep $7 million of the cash and stock he received when appointed to the position. Not a bad haul for only four months' work. (Epilogue: Thompson was replaced by Marissa Mayer, whom we introduced in Case Application #1 in Chapter 6.)

Discussion Questions

7-14 What does this story tell you about the importance of checking a job applicant's background?

7-15 What stakeholders are affected when an executive has inaccuracies in his or her résumé? How might they be affected?

7-16 Look at the statistics in the first paragraph of this story. Are you surprised by them? Why or why not?

7-17 What can you learn from this story (a) personally and (b) professionally?

CASE APPLICATION #2

Stopping Traffic

Things weren't turning out so good for J.C. Penney Co. and its CEO, Ron Johnson (now the former CEO).[79] Johnson arrived with much acclaim from being the head of Apple's successful retail operations. At Penney's, he immediately began one of retailing's most ambitious overhauls, trying to position the company for success in a very challenging and difficult industry. His plans included a "stores-within-a store" concept, no sales or promotions, and a three-tiered pricing plan. He suggested that Penney could use "a little bit of Apple's magic." From the start, analysts and experts questioned whether Penney's customers, who were accustomed to sales and coupons, would accept this new approach. Long story short…customers didn't. For the full fiscal year of 2013, Penney had a loss of $985 million (compared to a loss of $152 million in 2012). And even after Johnson's dismissal, the company's financial situation continued to decline. Now, you may be asking yourself, what does this story have to do with HRM? Well, a lot it turns out! When a company is struggling financially, it *is* going to impact its people.

And for J.C. Penney employees, that impact came in the form of a "traffic light" color-coded performance appraisal system. In a companywide broadcast, supervisors were told that they should categorize their employees by one of three colors: Green—their performance is okay; Yellow—they need some coaching to improve performance; and Red—their performance is not up to par and they need to leave. Many employees weren't even aware of the system and supervisors were given no guidance one way or the other regarding whether to tell them about it, although company headquarters chose not to disclose the light system to employees.

Although the uncertainties over how to inform or even whether to inform employees about this HR initiative were troubling, communication and HR experts say there are other problems with this green/yellow/red approach. One problem is that such a system can appear to be inconsiderate and uncaring when you realize that it's dealing with people's ability to make a living. What appears to be an easy-to-understand and simplistic approach using the familiar green, yellow, and red colors doesn't translate well to what will be a tremendously personal and difficult situation for many employees, especially those with a "red" appraisal. Another problem is that labeling employees can create difficult interpersonal situations. The labels can become a source of humor and teasing, which can deteriorate into hurt feelings and even feelings of being discriminated against. Despite its simplicity and a belief that a color-coding system is so easy to use, it's going to be problematic. This doesn't mean that employers don't evaluate employees. But companies should be open about the process and the expectations. Employees should know that they're being rated, what the criteria are, and, if they have a poor rating, what options they have for improving. There should also be a fair process of appeal or protest if an employee feels the rating was unfair.

> Red, Yellow, and Green have a whole new meaning at **J.C. Penney** Co.[80]

Discussion Questions

⭐ **7-18** Many managers say that evaluating an employee's performance is one of their most difficult tasks. Why do you think they feel that way?

⭐ **7-19** What can organizations (and managers) do to make performance appraisal an effective process?

⭐ **7-20** What's your impression of a color-coded system like that used by J.C. Penney? As a store department supervisor, how would you have approached this?

7-21 What could J.C. Penney executives have done to make this process more effective?

CASE APPLICATION #3

Spotting Talent

Attracting and selecting the right talent is critical to a company's success. For tech companies, the process is even more critical since it's the knowledge, skills, and abilities of their employees that determines these companies' efficiency, innovation, and, ultimately, financial achievements.[81] So, how *do* companies like Google and Facebook, and even IBM and Microsoft, attract the talent they need? As you'll see, these companies use some unique approaches.

Modis, a global provider of IT staffing and recruiting, has an interesting philosophy about searching for talented tech types. As pressure has mounted on businesses to find qualified employees, the search for the "perfect" candidate has become increasingly competitive. This company calls its search for the perfect candidate "the quest for the 'purple squirrel.'"Sometimes you just have to realize that, like the purple squirrel, the "perfect" candidate isn't available or doesn't exist. But that doesn't mean you don't try to find the best available talent.

Beware the PURPLE SQUIRREL!

How do some of the big tech names spot talent?

For "mature" tech companies like IBM, Microsoft, and Hewlett-Packard (H-P), the challenge can be especially difficult since they don't have the allure of startups or the younger, "sexier" tech companies. So these businesses have to really step up their game. Take IBM, for instance. After its Watson computer beat two former *Jeopardy* champions in a televised match, the company hauled the machine to Carnegie Mellon, a top school, where students got a chance to challenge the computer. IBM's goal: lure some of those students to consider a career at IBM. H-P is using the pizza party/tech talk approach at various schools, trying to lure younger students before other tech companies and startups snatch them away. Microsoft, which was once one of those startups, has sent alumni back to schools to promote why Microsoft is a great place to take their talents. And it also hosts game nights, final-exam study parties, app-building sessions, and other events to try to lure students.

For companies like Facebook and Google, the search for talent is still challenging because of the increasing demand for and limited supply of potential employees. So even these companies have to be creative in spotting talent. Google, for instance, found that they had been looking at résumés too narrowly by focusing (as expected) on education, GPA, and even SAT scores trying to find those candidates with the highest IQs. But they found that some of those so-called geniuses weren't as effective on the job as expected. So, they started looking at résumés differently. Rather than looking at résumés starting at the top and reading to the bottom, it began to look from the bottom-up, trying to find some rare, special attribute that set an applicant apart as a unique talent. Facebook found that old-fashioned hiring channels weren't getting the talent it needed fast enough. So it tried online puzzles and programming challenges to attract and spot talent. It was an easy, fast, and cheap approach to get submissions from potential candidates. Despite these unique approaches, it's also true that younger tech companies, like these and many others, have a built-in appeal for candidates primarily because they're what's "in" and what's "hot" right now. Also, in many of the younger tech companies, there's no entrenched bureaucracy or cultural restrictions. If an employee wants to come to work in cargo shorts, T-shirts, and flip-flops, they do. In fact, what attracts many talented employees to companies like these is the fact that they can set their own hours, bring their pets to work, have access to free food and drinks, and a variety of other perks.

Discussion Questions

7-22 What does this case imply about the supply and demand for employees and what implications does that have for businesses?

7-23 What's the meaning behind the search for the "purple squirrel" in relation to spotting talent? Is this relevant to non-tech companies as well? Discuss.

7-24 Do you think that mature tech companies are always going to have a more difficult time attracting tech talent? Explain.

7-25 What do you think of the recruiting approaches that Google and Facebook have tried?

Endnotes

1. Material for this chapter is drawn from D. A. DeCenzo and S. P. Robbins, *Fundamentals of Human Resources Management*, 10th ed. (Hoboken, NJ: John Wiley & Sons, 2010).

2. From the Past to the Present box based on D. A. Wren and A. G. Bedeian, *The Evolution of Management Thought*, 6th ed. (Hoboken, NJ: John Wiley & Sons, 2009), 198–200; "Building Better Organizations: Industrial-Organizational Psychology in the Workplace," *Society for Industrial and Organizational Psychology*, www.siop.org (July 13, 2009); M. Munsterberg, *Hugo Munsterberg: His Life and Work* (New York: Appleton-Century-Crofts, 1922); and H. Munsterberg, *Psychology and Industrial Efficiency* (Boston: Houghton Mifflin Company, 1913).

3. M. Wilson, "Hooters Manager Asks Waitress to Wear a Wig after Brain Surgery," http://www.hrcommunication.com/Main/Articles/Hooters_manager_asks_waitress_to_wear_a_wig_after_8781.aspx, April 10, 2013; A. Langfield, "Hooters Sued by Former Waitress in Dispute over Wig," NBC News, http://www.cnbc.com/id/100627864, April 9, 2013; and R. Patrick, "Suit Says Hooters Waitress Forced out after Surgery," *St. Louis Post Dispatch,* http://www.stltoday.com/news/local/crime-and-courts/suit-says-hooters-waitress-forced-out-after-surgery/article_db861563-d08b-5cb7-9cc9-91150b39351b.html, April 6, 2013.

4. P. W. Tam and S. Woo, "Talent War Crunches Start-Ups," *Wall Street Journal*, February 28, 2011, B1+; and C. Tuna, "Many Companies Hire as They Fire," *Wall Street Journal*, May 11, 2009, B6.

5. J. J. Salopek, "Employee Referrals Remain a Recruiter's Best Friend," *Workforce Management Online*, December 2010; L. G. Klaff, "New Internal Hiring Systems Reduce Cost and Boost Morale," *Workforce Management*, March 2004, 76–79; M. N. Martinez, "The Headhunter Within," *HR Magazine*, August 2001, 48–55; "Even Non-Recruiting Companies Must Maintain Hiring Networks," *HR Focus*, November 2001, 8; and L. Greenhalgh, A. T. Lawrence, and R. I. Sutton, "Determinants of Work Force Reduction Strategies in Declining Organizations," *Academy of Management Review*, April 1988, 241–54.

6. J. J. Salopek, "Employee Referrals Remain a Recruiter's Best Friend"; "Employee Referral Programs: Highly Qualified New Hires Who Stick Around," *Canadian HR Reporter*, June 4, 2001, 21; and C. Lachnit, "Employee Referral Saves Time, Saves Money, Delivers Quality," *Workforce*, June 2001, 66–72.

7. B. Horovitz, "Layoffs Sting Icons Coca-Cola and McDonalds," *USA Today,* January 9, 2015, 5B.

8. B. Tuttle, "Why These 5 Companies Are Laying Off Thousands of Workers," http://time.com/money/3678511/ebay-amex-baker-hughes-layoffs/, January 22, 2015.

9. Ibid.

10. J. Mooney, "Pre-Employment Testing on the Internet: Put Candidates a Click Away and Hire at Modem Speed," *Public Personnel Management*, Spring 2002, 41–52.

11. I.. Weber and E. Dwoskin, "As Personality Tests Multiply, Employers Are Split," *Wall Street Journal,* September 30, 2014, A1+.

12. See, for instance, R. D. Arvey and J. E. Campion, "The Employment Interview: A Summary and Review of Recent Research," *Personnel Psychology*, Summer 1982, 281–322; and M. M. Harris, "Reconsidering the Employment Interview: A Review of Recent Literature and Suggestions for Future Research," *Personnel Psychology*, Winter 1989, 691–726; J. H. Prager, "Nasty or Nice: 56-Question Quiz," *Wall Street Journal*, February 22, 2000, A4; and M. K. Zachary, "Labor Law for Supervisors," *Supervision*, March 2001, 23–26.

13. See, for instance, G. Nicholsen, "Screen and Glean: Good Screening and Background Checks Help Make the Right Match for Every Open Position," *Workforce*, October 2000, 70.

14. R. A. Posthuma, F. P. Morgeson, and M. A. Campion, "Beyond Employment Interview Validity: A Comprehensive Narrative Review of Recent Research and Trends Over Time," *Personnel Psychology*, Spring 2002, 1–81.

15. A. I. Huffcutt, J. M. Conway, P. L. Roth, and N. J. Stone, "Identification and Meta-Analysis Assessment of Psychological Constructs Measured in Employment Interviews," *Journal of Applied Psychology* (October 2001): 897–913; and A. I. Huffcutt, J. A. Weekley, W. H. Wiesner, T. G. Degroot, and C. Jones, "Comparison of Situational and Behavioral Description Interview Questions for Higher-Level Positions," *Personnel Psychology*, Autumn 2001, 619–44.

16. See C. H. Middendorf and T. H. Macan, "Note-Taking in the Employment Interview: Effects on Recall and Judgments," *Journal of Applied Psychology* (April 2002): 293–303; D. Butcher, "The Interview Rights and Wrongs," *Management Today*, April 2002, 4; P. L. Roth, C. H. Can Iddekinge, A. I. Huffcutt, C. E. Eidson, and P. Bobko, "Corrections for Range Restriction in Structured Interview Ethnic Group Differences: The Value May Be Larger Than Researchers Thought," *Journal of Applied Psychology* (April 2002): 369–76; and E. Hermelin and I. T. Robertson, "A Critique and Standardization of Meta-Analytic Coefficients in Personnel Selection," *Journal of Occupational and Organizational Psychology* (September 2001): 253–77.

17. See J. Merritt, "Improv at the Interview," *BusinessWeek*, February 3, 2003, 63; P. J. Taylor and B. Small, "Asking Applicants What They Would Do versus What They Did Do: A Meta-Analysis Comparison of Situation and Past Behavior Employment Interview Questions," *Journal of Occupational and Organizational Psychology* (September 2002): 277–95; S. D. Mauer, "A Practitioner-Based Analysis of Interviewer Job Expertise and Scale Format as Contextual Factors in Situational Interviews," *Personnel Psychology*, Summer 2002, 307–28; and J. M. Barclay, "Improving Selection Interviews with Structure: Organizations' Use of Behavioral Interviews," *Personnel Review* 30, no. 1 (2001): 81–95.

18. J. Merritt, "Improv at the Interview," 63.

19. S. H. Applebaum and M. Donia, "The Realistic Downsizing Preview: A Management Intervention in the Prevention of Survivor Syndrome (Part II)," *Career Development International*, January 2001, 5–19.

20. D. Zielinski, "Effective Assessments," *HRMagazine*, January 2011, 61–64; W. L. Gardner, B. J. Reithel, R. T. Foley, C. C. Cogliser, and F. O. Walumbwa, "Attraction to Organizational Culture Profiles: Effects of Realistic Recruitment and Vertical and Horizontal Individualism-Collectivism," *Management Communication Quarterly*, February 2009, 437–72; and S. L. Premack and J. P. Wanous, "A Meta-Analysis of Realistic Job Preview Experiments," *Journal of Applied Psychology* (November 1985): 706–20.

21. C. Garvey, "The Whirlwind of a New Job," *HR Magazine*, June 2001, 110–18.

22. B. P. Sunoo, "Results-Oriented Customer Service Training," *Workforce* (May 2001): 84–90.

23. Technology and the Manager's Job box based on D. Zielinski, "Referral Booster," *HR Magazine*, March 2013, 63–65; B. Horovitz, "Tweet for This Job—And It Could Be Yours," *USA Today*, February 18, 2013, A 4; "Action Items," *HR Magazine*, January 2013, 33–35; B. Roberts, "From E-Learning to Mobile Learning," *HR Magazine*, August 2012, 61–65; D. Zielinski, "Effective Assessments"; R. E. DeRouin, B. A. Fritzsche, and E. Salas, "E-Learning in Organizations," *Journal of Management* (December 2005): 920–40; K. O'Leonard, *HP Case Study: Flexible Solutions for Multi-Cultural Learners* (Oakland: CA: Bersin & Associates, 2004); S. Greengard, "The Dawn of Digital HR," *Business Finance*, October 2003, 55–59; and J. Hoekstra, "Three in One," *Online Learning* vol. 5 (2001): 28–32.

24. See, for instance, E. G. Tripp, "Aging Aircraft and Coming Regulations: Political and Media Pressures Have Encouraged the FAA to Expand Its Pursuit of Real and Perceived Problems of Older Aircraft and Their Systems. Operators Will Pay," *Business and Commercial Aviation*, March 2001, 68–75.

25. "A&S Interview: Sully's Tale," *Air & Space Magazine*, www.airspacemag.com (February 18, 2009); A. Altman, "Chesley B. Sullenberger III," *Time*, www.time.com (January 16, 2009); and K. Burke, P. Donohue, and C. Siemaszko, "US Airways Airplane Crashes in Hudson River—Hero Pilot Chesley Sullenberger III Saves All Aboard," *New York Daily News*, www.nydailynews.com (January 16, 2009).

26. C. S. Duncan, J. D. Selby-Lucas, and W. Swart, "Linking Organizational Goals and Objectives to Employee Performance: A Quantitative Perspective," *Journal of American Academy of Business* (March 2002): 314–18.

27. "Training Expenditures," *Training* (November–December 2010): 19.

28. R. Langlois, "Fairmont Hotels: Business Strategy Starts with People," *Canadian HR Reporter*, November 5, 2001, 19.

29. M. Dalahoussaye, "Show Me the Results," *Training* (March 2002): 28.

30. A. Tziner, C. Joanis, and K. R. Murphy, "A Comparison of Three Methods of Performance Appraisal with Regard to Goal Properties, Goal Perception, and Rate Satisfaction," *Group and Organization Management*, June 2000, 175–90; and T. W. Kent and T. J. Davis, "Using Retranslation to Develop Operational Anchored Scales to Assess the Motivational Context of Jobs," *International Journal of Management* (March 2002): 10–16.

31. See also C. A. Ramus and U. Steger, "The Roles of Supervisory Support Behaviors and Environmental Policy in Employee 'Ecoinitiatives' at Leading-Edge European Companies," *Academy of Management Journal* (August 2000): 605–26.

32. See R. de Andrés, J. L. Garcia-Lapresta, and J. GonzálezPachón, "Performance Appraisal Based

on Distance Function Methods," *European Journal of Operational Research* (December 2010): 1599–607; and L. Atwater and J. Brett, "Feedback Format: Does It Influence Manager's Reaction to Feedback," *Journal of Occupational and Organizational Psychology* (December 2006): 517–32.

33. M. A. Peiperl, "Getting 360 Feedback Right," *Harvard Business Review*, January 2001, 142–47.

34. T. J. Maurer, D. R. D. Mitchell, and F. G. Barbeite, "Predictors of Attitudes Toward a 360-Degree Feedback System and Involvement in Post-Feedback Management Development Activity," *Journal of Occupational and Organizational Psychology* (March 2002): 87–107.

35. This section based on R. I. Henderson, *Compensation Management in a Knowledge-Based World*, 9th ed. (Upper Saddle River, NJ: Prentice Hall, 2003).

36. M. P. Brown, M. C. Sturman, and M. J. Simmering, "Compensation Policy and Organizational Performance: The Efficiency, Operational and Financial Implications of Pay Levels and Pay Structure," *Academy of Management Journal* (December 2003): 752–62; J. D. Shaw, N. P. Gupta, and J. E. Delery, "Pay Dispersion and Workforce Performance: Moderating Effects of Incentives and Interdependence," *Strategic Management Journal* (June 2002): 491–512; E. Montemayor, "Congruence between Pay Policy and Competitive Strategy in High-Performing Firms," *Journal of Management* vol. 22, no. 6 (1996): 889–908; and L. R. Gomez-Mejia, "Structure and Process of Diversification, Compensation Strategy, and Firm Performance," *Strategic Management Journal* 13 (1992): 381–97.

37. J. D. Shaw, N. Gupta, A. Mitra, and G. E. Ledford Jr., "Success and Survival of Skill-Based Pay Plans," *Journal of Management* (February 2005): 28–49; C. Lee, K. S. Law, and P. Bobko, "The Importance of Justice Perceptions on Pay Effectiveness: A Two-Year Study of a Skill-Based Pay Plan," *Journal of Management* vol. 26, no. 6 (1999): 851–73; G. E. Ledford, "Paying for the Skills, Knowledge and Competencies of Knowledge Workers," *Compensation and Benefits Review*, July–August 1995, 55–62; and E. E. Lawler III, G. E. Ledford Jr., and L. Chang, "Who Uses Skill-Based Pay and Why," *Compensation and Benefits Review*, March–April 1993, 22.

38. J. D. Shaw, N. Gupta, A. Mitra, and G. E. Ledford Jr., "Success and Survival of Skill-Based Pay Plans."

39. Information from Hewitt Associates Studies: "As Fixed Costs Increase, Employers Turn to Variable Pay Programs as Preferred Way to Reward Employees," August 21, 2007; "Hewitt Study Shows Pay-for-Performance Plans Replacing Holiday Bonuses," December 6, 2005; "Salaries Continue to Rise in Asia Pacific, Hewitt Annual Study Reports," November 23, 2005; and "Hewitt Study Shows Base Pay Increases Flat for 2006 with Variable Pay Plans Picking up the Slack," Hewitt Associates, LLC, www.hewittassociates.com (August 31, 2005).

40. "Mandated Benefits: 2002 Compliance Guide," *Employee Benefits Journal* (June 2002): 64; and J. J. Kim, "Smaller Firms Augment Benefits, Survey Shows," *Wall Street Journal*, June 6, 2002, D2.

41. See, for example, R. E. Catalano and D. L. Kirkpatrick, "Evaluating Training Programs: The State of the Art," *Training and Development Journal* (May 1968): 2–9.

42. P. P. Shah, "Network Destruction: The Structural Implications of Downsizing," *Academy of Management Journal* (February 2000): 101–12.

43. See, for example, K. A. Mollica and B. Gray, "When Layoff Survivors Become Layoff Victims: Propensity to Litigate," *Human Resource Planning*, January 2001, 22–32.

44. S. Berfield, "After the Layoff, the Redesign," *Business Week*, April 14, 2008, 54–56; L. Uchitelle, "Retraining Laid-off Workers, but for What?" *New York Times Online*, March 26, 2006; D. Tourish, N. Paulsen, E. Hobman, and P. Bordia, "The Downsides of Downsizing: Communication Processes and Information Needs in the Aftermath of a Workforce Reduction Strategy," *Management Communication Quarterly*, May 2004, 485–516; J. Brockner, G. Spreitzer, A. Mishra, W. Hochwarter, L. Pepper, and J. Weinberg, "Perceived Control as an Antidote to the Negative Effects of Layoffs on Survivors' Organizational Commitment and Job Performance," *Administrative Science Quarterly*, 49 (2004): 76–100; and E. Krell, "Defusing Downsizing," *Business Finance*, December 2002, 55–57.

45. And the Survey Says box based on "Find the Sharpest Needle in the Stack," *HR Magazine*, June 2012, 16; J. Yang and P. Trap, "If You Started a Job and You Didn't Like It, How Long Would You Stay?" *USA Today*, June 11, 2012, 1B; J. Yang and P. Trap, "Do You Use Social Networking Sites to Research Candidates?" *USA Today*, June 5, 2012, 1B; J. Yang and A. Gonzalez, "Top Actions Workers Feel Are Grounds for Termination," *USA Today*, May 7, 2012, 1B; L. Weber," Little Time for Resumes," *Wall Street Journal*, March 21, 2012, B8; J. Yang and P. Trap, "Top Reasons Why Someone Hired Would Not Work Out in the Position," *USA Today*, October 26,

2011, 1B; J. Yang and V. Salazar, "Are Annual Performance Reviews an Accurate Appraisal for Employees' Work?" *USA Today*, September 27, 2011, 1B; J. Yang and S. Ward, "What Are the Most Common Mistakes Candidates Make During Job Interviews?" *USA Today*, August 15, 2011, 1B; and P. Kujawa, "For Some Workers, the Piggy Bank Is Fat for Retirement," *Workforce Management Online*, July 16, 2012.

46. A. Joshi, "Managing the Organizational Melting Pot: Dilemmas of Workplace Diversity," *Administrative Science Quarterly*, December 2001, 783–84.

47. L. Dishman, "These Are the Companies Winning the Race to Increase Diversity," http://www.fastcompany.com/3045438/these-are-the-companies-winning-the-race-to-increase-diversity, April 25, 2015.

48. See, for instance, K. Iverson, "Managing for Effective Workforce Diversity," *Cornell Hotel and Restaurant Administration Quarterly*, April 2000, 31–38.

49. U.S. Equal Employment Opportunity Commission, "Charge Alleging Sexual Harassment: FY 2010–FY 2014," http://www1.eeoc.gov/eeoc/statistics/enforcement/sexual_harassment_new.cfm?renderforprint=1.

50. Ibid.

51. N. F. Foy, "Sexual Harassment Can Threaten Your Bottom Line," *Strategic Finance* (August 2000): 56–57.

52. "Federal Monitors Find Illinois Mitsubishi Unit Eradicating Harassment," *Wall Street Journal* (September 7, 2000): A8.

53. L. J. Munson, C. Hulin, and F. Drasgow, "Longitudinal Analysis of Dispositional Influences and Sexual Harassment: Effects on Job and Psychological Outcomes," *Personnel Psychology* (Spring 2000): 21.

54. B. Leonard, "Survey: 10% of Employees Report Harassment at Work," *HR Magazine*, October 2010, 18.

55. "Nichols v. Azteca Restaurant Enterprises," *Harvard Law Review*, May 2002, 2074; A. J. Morrell, "Non-Employee Harassment," *Legal Report* (January–February 2000): 1. See also S. Lim and L. M. Cortina, "Interpersonal Mistreatment in the Workplace: The Interface and Impact of General Incivility and Sexual Harassment," *Journal of Applied Psychology* (May 2005): 483–96.

56. Although the male gender is referred to here, it is important to note that sexual harassment may involve people of either sex or the same sex. (See, for instance, Oncale v. Sundowner Offshore Service, Inc., 118 S. Ct. 998.)

57. See also A. M. O'Leary-Kelly, L. Bowes-Sperry, C. A. Bates, and E. R. Lean, "Sexual Harassment at Work: A Decade (Plus) of

Progress," *Journal of Management* (June 2009): 503–36; M. Rotundo, D. H. Nguyen, and P. R. Sackett, "A Meta-Analytic Review of Gender Differences in Perceptions of Sexual Harassment," *Journal of Applied Psychology* (October 2001): 914–22.

58. "Sexual Harassment," http://www.eeoc.gov/laws/types/sexual_harassment.cfm, April 24, 2015.

59. R. L. Wiener and L. E. Hurt, "How Do People Evaluate Social Sexual Conduct at Work? A Psychological Model," *Journal of Applied Psychology* (February 2000): 75.

60. A. R. Karr, "Companies Crack Down on the Increasing Sexual Harassment by E-Mail," *Wall Street Journal*, September 21, 1999, A1; and A. Fisher, "After All This Time, Why Don't People Know What Sexual Harassment Means?" *Fortune*, January 12, 1998, 68.

61. Ibid.

62. "You and DuPont: Diversity," DuPont Company Documents (1999–2000), http://www.dupont.com/careers/you/diverse.html; and "DuPont Announces 2000 Dr. Martin Luther King, Days of Celebration," DuPont Company Documents, http://www.dupont.com/corp/whats-news/releases/00/001111.html (January 11, 2000).

63. It should be noted here that under the Title VII and the Civil Rights Act of 1991, the maximum award that can be given, under the Federal Act, is $300,000. However, many cases are tried under state laws that permit unlimited punitive damages.

64. J. W. Janove, "Sexual Harassment and the Big Three Surprises," *HR Magazine*, November 2001, 123–30; and L. A. Baar and J. Baar, "Harassment Case Proceeds Despite Failure to Report," *HR Magazine*, June 2005, 159.

65. S. Shellenbarger, "Supreme Court Takes on How Employers Handle Worker Harassment Complaints," *Wall Street Journal*, April 13, 2006, D1.

66. See, for instance, P. W. Dorfman, A. T. Cobb, and R. Cox, "Investigations of Sexual Harassment Allegations: Legal Means Fair—Or Does It?" *Human Resources Management*, Spring 2000, 33–39.

67. These examples taken from S. J. Wells, "Does Work Make You Fat?" *HR Magazine*, October 2010, 26–32; R. King, "Slimming Down Employees to Cut Costs"; C. Tkaczyk, "Lowering Health-Care Costs," *Fortune*, November 23, 2009, 16; and A. W. Matthews, "When All Else Fails: Forcing Workers into Healthy Habits," *Wall Street Journal*, July 8, 2009, D1+.

68. J. Tozzi, "U.S. Health-Care Spending Is on the Rise Again," http://www.bloomberg.com/news/articles/2015-02-18/u-s-health-care-spending-is-on-the-rise-again, February 18, 2015; and

D. Munro, "Annual U.S. Healthcare Spending Hits $3.8 Trillion," http://www.forbes.com/sites/danmunro/2014/02/02/annual-u-s-healthcare-spending-hits-3-8-trillion/, February 2, 2014.

69. S. Adams, "Every Smoker Costs an Employer $6,000 a Year. Really?" http://www.forbes.com/sites/susanadams/2013/06/05/every-smoker-costs-an-employer-6000-a-year-really/print/, June 5, 2013.

70. K. Kahn, "Obese Employees Cost Employers Thousands in Extra Medical Costs," http://www.cfah.org/hbns/2014/obese-employees-cost-employers-thousands-in-extra-medical-costs, May 13, 2014.

71. R. Ceniceros, "Obesity Can Exacerbate Workplace Injuries, Study Notes," *Workforce Management Online*, December 15, 2010; and "Obesity Weighs Down Production," *Industry Week*, March 2008, 22–23.

72. A. R. Carey and P. Trap, "Changes in Wellness Programs," *USA Today*, July 17, 2014, 1A.

73. G. Kranz, "Prognosis Positive: Companies Aim to Get Workers Healthy," *Workforce Management*, www.work-force.com (April 15, 2008).

74. S. J. Wells, "Does Work Make You Fat?"; and M. Conlin, "Hide the Doritos! Here Comes HR," *BusinessWeek*, April 28, 2008, 94–96.

75. J. Fox, "Good Riddance to Pensions," *CNN Money*, January 12, 2006.

76. M. Adams, "Broken Pension System in Crying Need of a Fix," *USA Today*, November 15, 2005, 1B+.

77. "Prevalence of Retirement Plans by Type in the Fortune 100," *Pension Benefits*, September 2010, 1–2; D. Kansas, "Has the 401(k) Failed?" *Fortune*, June 22, 2009, 94–98; S. Block, "Company Pensions Are Out on a Limb," *USA Today*, May 22, 2009, 1B+; A. Feldman, "Retiring the 401(k) Contribution," *BusinessWeek*, November 24, 2008, 32; J. Appleby, "Traditional Pensions Are Almost Gone. Is Employer-Provided Health Insurance Next?" *USA Today*, November 13, 2007, 1A+; S. Kelly, "FedEx, Goodyear Make Big Pension Plan Changes," *Workforce Management*, www.workforce.com (March 1, 2007); G. Colvin, "The End of a Dream," *Fortune*, www.cnnmoney.com (June 22, 2006); E. Porter and M. Williams Nash, "Benefits Go the Way of Pensions," *NY Times Online*, February 9, 2006; and J. Fox, "Good Riddance to Pensions."

78. A. Ford, "Liar, Liar. How Faux Credentials Felled Yahoo!'s CEO, among Others," *Time*, May 28, 2012, 18; G. Strauss and L. Petrecca, "CEOs Stumble over Ethics Violations, Mismanagement," *USA Today Online*, May 22, 2012; C. Hausman, "CEOs' Ethics in Spotlight," *Ethics Newsline*, May 21, 2012; A. Efrati and J. S. Lublin, "Yahoo CEO's Downfall," *Wall Street Journal*, May 15, 2012, B5; J. Pepitone, "Ousted Yahoo CEO Will Get No Severance," *CNNMoney.com*, May 15, 2012; S. Martin and J. Swartz, "Yahoo Ousts CEO In New Shake-Up," *USA Today*, May 14, 2012, 1B; A. Efrati and J. S. Lublin, "Thompson Resigns as CEO of Yahoo," *Wall Street Journal*, May 14, 2012, A1+; and A. Efrati and J. S. Lublin, "Resumé Trips up Yahoo's Chief," *Wall Street Journal*, May 5–6, 2012, A1+.

79. "Latest Layoffs at Penney Hit Back Office, District Office Workers," *Reuters*, www.reuters.com, March 7, 2013; K. Bhasin, "JCPenney Is Firing More Store Employees after a 'Secret Broadcast,'" *businessinsider.com*, March 7, 2013; M. Wilson, "JC Penney's Traffic-Light System under Fire," www.ragan.com, March 7, 2013; D. Mattioli, "Board's Patience with CEO Wears Thin at J.C. Penney," *Wall Street Journal*, March 6, 2013, B1; D. Mattioli, "J.C. Penney's Losses Snowball," *Wall Street Journal*, February 28, 2013, B1+; S. Clifford, "Chief Talks of Mistakes and Big Losses at J.C. Penney," *New York Times Online*, February 27, 2013; D. Mattioli, "For Penney's Heralded Boss, the Shine Is off the Apple," *Wall Street Journal*, February 25, 2013, A1+; and K. Bhasin, "Inside JCPenney: Widespread Fear, Anxiety, and Distrust of Ron Johnson and His New Management Team," *businessinsider.com*, February 22, 2013.

80. "Latest Layoffs at Penney Hit Back Office, District Office Workers," *Reuters*, www.reuters.com, March 7, 2013; K. Bhasin, "JCPenney Is Firing More Store Employees after a 'Secret Broadcast,'" *businessinsider.com*, March 7, 2013; M. Wilson, "JC Penney's Traffic-Light System under Fire," www.ragan.com, March 7, 2013; D. Mattioli, "Board's Patience with CEO Wears Thin at J.C. Penney," *Wall Street Journal*, March 6, 2013, B1; D. Mattioli, "J.C. Penney's Losses Snowball," *Wall Street Journal*, February 28, 2013, B1+; S. Clifford, "Chief Talks of Mistakes and Big Losses at J. C. Penney," *New York Times Online*, February 27, 2013; D. Mattioli, "For Penney's Heralded Boss, the Shine Is off the Apple," *Wall Street Journal*, February 25, 2013, A1+; and K. Bhasin, "Inside JCPenney: Widespread Fear, Anxiety, and Distrust of Ron Johnson and His New Management Team," *businessinsider.com*, February 22, 2013.

81. "Digital Report: Tug-of-War for Digital Talent," *Campaign Asia-Pacific*, June 2012, 12; N. Blacksmith and Y. Yang, "Executives: Your Company Isn't Attracting the Best Talent," *Gallup Management Journal Online*, May 29, 2012, 1; J. Cullen, "Stop Searching for the Elusive Purple Squirrel," *Computerworld*, April 9, 2012, 25; G. Anders, "The Rare Find," *Bloomberg BusinessWeek*, October 17–23, 2011, 106–12; and J. Light, "At Mature Techs, a Young Vibe," *Wall Street Journal*, June 13, 2011, B7.

Career Module
BUILDING YOUR CAREER

The term *career* has several meanings. In popular usage, it can mean advancement ("she is on a management career track"), a profession ("he has chosen a career in accounting"), or a lifelong sequence of jobs ("his career has included 12 jobs in six organizations"). For our purposes, we define a **career** as the sequence of work positions held by a person during his or her lifetime. Using this definition, it's apparent that we all have, or will have, a career. Moreover, the concept is as relevant to unskilled laborers as it is to software designers or physicians. But career development isn't what it used to be!

What Was Career Development Like, Historically?

Although career development has been an important topic in management courses for years, some dramatic changes have occurred in the concept. Career development programs used to be designed to help employees advance their work lives within a specific organization. The focus of such programs was to provide employees the information, assessment, and training needed to help them realize their career goals. Career development was also a way for organizations to attract and retain highly talented people. This approach has all but disappeared in today's workplace. Now, organizations that have such traditional career programs are few and far between. Downsizing, restructuring, and other organizational adjustments have brought us to one significant conclusion about career development: You—not the organization—will be responsible for designing, guiding, and developing your own career.

What Is Career Development Like, Now?

This idea of increased personal responsibility for one's career has been described as a **boundaryless career**. The challenge is that few hard-and-fast rules are available to guide you.

One of the first decisions you have to make is career choice. The optimum choice is one that offers the best match between what you want out of life and your interests, your abilities and personality, and market opportunities. Good career choices should result in a series of jobs that give you an opportunity to be a good performer, make you want to maintain your commitment to your career, lead to highly satisfying work, and give you the proper balance between work and personal life. A good career match, then, is one in which you are able to develop a positive self-concept, to do work that you think is important, and to lead the kind of life you desire. In a recent survey by Capital One Financial Corporation, 66 percent of college graduates said that a comprehensive benefits package (including, for example, health care, 401(k) program, child care, and domestic partner benefits) was the most important factor in their job search. Starting salary ranked second at 64 percent, with job location ranked third at 60 percent. Today's college grads are also looking to be rewarded or compensated (with comp time or matching donations, for instance) for their volunteer and philanthropic activities.

Once you've identified a career choice, it's time to initiate the job search. However, we aren't going to get into the specifics of job hunting, writing a résumé, or interviewing

career
The sequence of work positions held by a person during his or her lifetime

boundaryless career
When an individual takes personal responsibility for his or her own career

successfully, although those things are important. Let's fast-forward through all that and assume that your job search was successful. It's time to go to work! How do you survive and excel in your career?

How Can I Have a Successful Career?

What can you do to improve your chances for career success? You're already doing the *most* important thing: You're getting a college education! It's the surest way to increase your lifetime earnings. Currently, the average high school graduate earns $27,915 a year. His or her counterpart with a college degree earns $51,206. College graduates earn, on average, $800,000 more than high school graduates over their working career. Investing in your education and training is one of the best investments you'll make in your lifetime. What *else* can you do? The following suggestions are based on extensive research into career management.

Assess Your Personal Strengths and Weaknesses

Where do your natural talents lie? What can you do, relative to others, that gives you a competitive advantage? Are you particularly good with numbers? Have strong people skills? Good with your hands? Write better than most people? Everyone has some things that they do better than others and some areas where they're weak. Play to your strengths.

Identify Market Opportunities

Where are tomorrow's job opportunities? Regardless of your strengths, certain job categories are likely to decline in the coming decades—for instance, bank tellers, small farmers, movie projectionists, travel agents, and secretaries. In contrast, abundant opportunities are more likely to be created by an increasingly aging society, continued emphasis on technology, increased spending on education and training, and concern with personal security. These factors are likely to create excellent opportunities for jobs in gerontological counseling, network administration, training consultants, and security-alarm installers.

Take Responsibility for Managing Your Own Career

Historically, companies tended to assume responsibility for their employees' careers. Today, this is the exception rather than the rule. Employees are increasingly expected to take responsibility for their own careers.

Think of your career as your business and you're its CEO. To survive, you have to monitor market forces, head off competitors, and be ready to quickly take advantage of opportunities when they surface. You have to protect your career from harm and position yourself to benefit from changes in the environment.

Develop Your Interpersonal Skills

Interpersonal skills, especially the ability to communicate, top the list of almost every employer's "must have" skills. Whether it's getting a new job or a promotion, strong interpersonal skills are likely to give you a competitive edge.

Practice Makes Perfect

There's an increasing amount of evidence indicating that super-high achievers aren't fundamentally different from the rest of us. They just work harder and smarter. It's been found, based on studies of world-class performers in music, sports, chess, science, and business, that people like Tiger Woods, Mozart, and Bill Gates put in about 10,000 hours (or 10 years at 1,000 hours a year) of persistent, focused training and experience before they hit their peak performance level. If you want to excel in any field, you should expect to have to put in a lot of deliberate practice—consistently engaging in repeated activity specifically designed to improve performance beyond your current comfort and ability level.

Stay Up to Date

In today's dynamic world, skills can become obsolete quickly. To keep your career on track, you need to make learning a lifetime commitment. You should be continually "going to school"—if not taking formal courses, then reading books and journals to ensure that you don't get caught with obsolete skills.

Network

Networking refers to creating and maintaining beneficial relationships with others in order to accomplish your goals. It helps to have friends in high places. It also helps to have contacts who can keep you informed of changes that are going on in your organization and in your industry. Go to conferences. Maintain contact with former college friends and alumni. Get involved in community activities. Cultivate a broad set of relationships. And in today's increasingly interconnected world, join online business networking groups such as LinkedIn, Spoke, and Talkbiznow.

Stay Visible

Networking can increase your visibility. So, too, can writing articles in your professional journals, teaching classes or giving talks in your area of expertise, attending conferences and professional meetings, and making sure your accomplishments are properly promoted. You increase your mobility and value in the marketplace by keeping visible.

Seek a Mentor

Employees with mentors are likely to have enhanced mobility, increased knowledge of the organization's inside workings, greater access to senior executives, increased satisfaction, and increased visibility. For women and minorities, having mentors has been shown to be particularly helpful in promoting career advancement and success.

Leverage Your Competitive Advantage

Develop skills that will give you a competitive advantage in the marketplace. Especially focus on skills that are important to employers, skills that are scarce, and areas where you have limited competition. Try to avoid a worst-case scenario: You have a job that anyone can learn in 30 minutes. Remember that the harder it is for you to learn and develop a highly prized skill, the harder it'll also be for others to acquire it. Generally speaking, the more training necessary to do a job and the fewer people who have that training, the greater your security and influence.

Here's an insight from many years as a student and a professor: To succeed in school, you have to be a generalist and excel at everything. For instance, to earn a 4.0 GPA, you need to be a star in English, math, science, geography, languages, and so on. The "real world," on the other hand, rewards specialization. You don't have to be good at everything. You just need to be good at something that others aren't and that society values. You can be lousy in math or science and still be a very successful opera singer, artist, salesperson, or writer. You don't have to excel in English to be a computer programmer or electrician. The secret to life success is identifying your comparative advantage and then developing it. And as we've noted previously, you need to invest approximately 10,000 hours in honing your skills to achieve optimum proficiency.

Don't Shun Risks

Don't be afraid to take risks, especially when you're young and you don't have much to lose. Going back to school, moving to a new state or country, or quitting a job to start your own business can be the decision that will set your life in a completely new direction. Great accomplishments almost always require taking the path less traveled; and the road to nowhere is paved with fears of the unknown.

It's OK to Change Jobs

Past generations often believed "you don't leave a good job." That advice no longer applies. In today's fast-changing job market, staying put often only means that you're staying behind. Employers no longer expect long-term loyalty. And to keep your skills fresh, your income increasing, and your job tasks interesting, it will be increasingly likely that you'll need to change employers.

Opportunities, Preparation, and Luck = Success

Successful people are typically ambitious, intelligent, and hardworking. But they are also lucky. It's not by chance that many of the biggest technology success stories—Bill Gates and Paul Allen at Microsoft, Steve Jobs at Apple, Scott McNealy at Sun Microsystems, Eric Schmidt at Novell and Google—were born in a narrow three-year period between June 1953 and March 1956. They were smart. They were interested in computers and technology. But they were also lucky. They reached their teens and early 20s in 1975—at the dawn of the personal computer age. Those people with similar interests and talents but born in the mid-1940s were likely to have joined a firm like IBM out of college and been enamored with mainframe computers. Had they been born in the early 1960s, they would have missed getting in on the ground floor of the revolution.

Success is a matter of matching up opportunities, preparation, and luck. It's been suggested that few of us get more than a couple of special opportunities in our lifetime. If you're lucky, you will recognize those opportunities, have made the proper preparations, and then act on them.

You can't control when you were born, where you were born, your parents' finances, or the like. Those are the luck factors. But what you can control is your preparation and willingness to act when opportunity knocks.

Endnotes

1. Managing Your Career Module based on J. H. Greenhaus, V. M. Godstalk, and G. A. Callahan, *Career Management*, 3rd ed. (Cincinnati, OH: South-Western, 2000); K. A. Ericsson, "Deliberate Practice and the Modifiability of Body and Mind," *International Journal of Sports Psychology* (January–March 2007), pp. 4–34; J. P. Newport, "Mastery, Just 10,000 Hours Away," *Wall Street Journal*, March 14–15, 2009, p. W6; "Capital One Survey Highlights What Today's College Graduates Want from Employers," www.businesswire.com (June 10, 2008); M. Gladwell, *Outliers: The Story of Success* (New York: Little, Brown, 2008); R. N. Boles, *What Color Is Your Parachute? 2009: A Practical Manual for Job-Hunters and Career-Changers* (Berkeley, CA: Ten Speed Press, 2009); D. E. Super and D. T. Hall, "Career Development: Exploration and Planning," in M. R. Rosenzweig and L. W. Porter (eds.), *Annual Review of Psychology*, vol. 29 (Palo Alto, CA: Annual Reviews, 1978), p. 334; and M. B. Arthur and D. M. Rousseau, *The Boundaryless Career: A New Employment Principle for a New Organizational Era* (New York: Oxford University Press, 1996).

Managing Change and Innovation

8

Management **Myth** Myth

There's nothing managers can do to reduce the stress inherent in today's jobs.

Image Source/Alamy

Management **DEBUNKED!** Myth

It's an unusual employee today who isn't dealing with stress. Cutbacks, increased workloads, open workspace designs, work/life conflicts, and 24/7 communication access are just a few of the things that have increased job stress. However, organizations are not ignoring this problem. Smart managers are redesigning jobs, realigning schedules, and introducing employee assistance programs to help employees cope with the increasing stresses in their work and in balancing their work and personal lives.

STRESS

can be an unfortunate consequence of change and anxiety, both at work and personally. However, change is a constant for organizations and thus for managers and for employees. Large companies, small businesses, entrepreneurial startups, universities, hospitals, and even the military are changing the way they do things. Although change has always been part of a manager's job, it's become even more so in recent years. And because change can't be eliminated, managers must learn how to manage it successfully. In this chapter, we're going to look at organizational change efforts and how to manage those, the ways that managers can deal with the stress that exists in organizations, and how managers can stimulate innovation in their organizations. ●

Learning Outcomes

8-1 Define organizational change and compare and contrast views on the change process. p. 239

8-2 Explain how to manage resistance to change. p. 244

8-3 Describe what managers need to know about employee stress. p. 246

8-4 Discuss techniques for stimulating innovation. p. 250

What Is Change and How Do Managers Deal with It?

8-1 Define organizational change and compare and contrast views on the change process.

*If it weren't for change, a **manager's job** would be relatively easy.*

When John Lechleiter assumed the CEO's job at Eli Lilly, he sent each of his senior executives a clock ticking down the hours, minutes, and seconds until the day when one of the company's premier cash-generating drugs went off patent. It was a visual reminder of some major changes the executives had better be prepared for. By the end of 2016, Lilly was losing $10 billion in annual revenues as patents on three of its key drugs expired. Needless to say, the company has had to make some organizational changes as it picked up the pace of drug development.[1] Lilly's managers are doing what managers everywhere must do—implement change!

Change makes a manager's job more challenging. Without it, managing would be relatively easy. Planning would be easier because tomorrow would be no different from today. The issue of organization design would be solved because the environment would be free from uncertainty and there would be no need to adapt. Similarly, decision making would be dramatically simplified because the outcome of each alternative could be predicted with near pinpoint accuracy. It would also simplify the manager's job if competitors never introduced new products or services, if customers didn't make new demands, if government regulations were never modified, if technology never advanced, or if employees' needs always remained the same. But that's not the way it is.

Change is an organizational reality. Most managers, at one point or another, will have to change some things in their workplace. We call these changes **organizational change**, which is any alteration or adaptation of an organization's structure, technology, or people. (See Exhibit 8–1.) Let's look more closely at each.

1. **Changing *structure*:** Includes any change in authority relationships, coordination mechanisms, degree of centralization, job design, or similar organization structure variables. Examples might be restructuring work units, empowering employees, decentralizing, widening spans of control, reducing work specialization, or creating work teams. All of these may involve some type of structural change.
2. **Changing *technology*:** Encompasses modifications in the way work is done or the methods and equipment used. Examples might be computerizing work processes and procedures, adding robotics to work areas, installing energy usage monitors, equipping employees with mobile communication tools, implementing social media tools, or installing a new computer operating system.
3. **Changing *people*:** Refers to changes in employee attitudes, expectations, perceptions, or behaviors. Examples might be changing employee attitudes and behaviors to better support a new customer service strategy, using team building efforts to make a team more innovative, or training employees to adopt a "safety-first" focus.

organizational change
Any alteration of an organization's people, structure, or technology

Exhibit 8–1 Categories of Organizational Change

Structure	Technology	People
Authority relationships	Work processes	Attitudes
Coordinating mechanisms	Work methods	Expectations
Job redesign	Equipment	Perceptions
Spans of control		Behavior

Why Do Organizations Need to Change?

In Chapter 2 we pointed out that both external and internal forces constrain managers. These same forces also bring about the need for change. Let's briefly review these factors.

WHAT EXTERNAL FORCES CREATE A NEED TO CHANGE?   The external forces that create the need for organizational change come from various sources. In recent years, the *marketplace* has affected firms such as AT&T and Lowe's because of new competition. AT&T, for example, faces competition from local cable companies and from Internet services such as Hulu and Skype. Lowe's, too, must now contend with a host of aggressive competitors such as Home Depot and Menard's. *Government laws and regulations* are also an impetus for change. For example, when the Patient Protection and Affordable Care Act was signed into law, thousands of businesses were faced with decisions on how best to offer employees health insurance, revamp benefit reporting, and educate employees on the new provisions. Even today, organizations continue to deal with the requirements of improving health insurance accessibility.

Technology also creates the need for organizational change. The Internet has changed pretty much everything—the way we get information, how we buy products, and how we get our work done. Technological advancements have created significant economies of scale for many organizations. For instance, technology allows Scottrade to offer its clients the opportunity to make online trades without a broker. The assembly line in many industries has also undergone dramatic change as employers replace human labor with technologically advanced mechanical robots. Also, the fluctuation in *labor markets* forces managers to initiate changes. For example, the shortage of registered nurses in the United States has led many hospital administrators to redesign nursing jobs and to alter their rewards and benefits packages for nurses, as well as join forces with local universities to address the nursing shortage.

As the news headlines remind us, *economic* changes affect almost all organizations. For instance, prior to the mortgage market meltdown, low interest rates led to significant growth in the housing market. This growth meant more jobs, more employees hired, and significant increases in sales in other businesses that supported the building industry. However, as the economy soured, it had the opposite effect on the housing industry and other industries as credit markets dried up and businesses found it difficult to get the capital they needed to operate.

Challenged by changed consumer preferences, increased competition, and declining revenues, McDonald's has named internal manager Steve Easterbrook as its new CEO. As a change agent, Easterbrook's goal is to revitalize McDonald's "as a modern and progressive burger company delivering a contemporary customer experience."

WHAT INTERNAL FORCES CREATE A NEED TO CHANGE?   Internal forces can also create the need for organizational change. These internal forces tend to originate primarily from the internal operations of the organization or from the impact of external changes. (It's also important to recognize that such changes are a normal part of the organizational life cycle.)[2]

When managers redefine or modify an organization's *strategy*, that action often introduces a host of changes. For example, Nokia bringing in new equipment is an internal force for change. Because of this action, employees may face job redesign, undergo training to operate the new equipment, or be required to establish new interaction patterns within their work groups. Another internal force for change is that the *composition of an organization's workforce* changes in terms of age, education, gender, nationality, and so forth. A stable organization in

Hannelore Foerster/Getty Images

which managers have been in their positions for years might need to restructure jobs in order to retain more ambitious employees by affording them some upward mobility. The compensation and benefits systems might also need to be reworked to reflect the needs of a diverse workforce and market forces in which certain skills are in short supply. *Employee attitudes*, such as increased job dissatisfaction, may lead to increased absenteeism, resignations, and even strikes. Such events will, in turn, often lead to changes in organizational policies and practices.

Who Initiates Organizational Change?

Organizational changes need a **catalyst.**

People who act as catalysts and assume the responsibility for managing the change process are called **change agents**.[3] WHO can be a change agent?

- Any *manager* can. We assume organizational change is initiated and carried out by a manager within the organization.
- OR any *nonmanager*—for example, an *internal staff specialist* or an *outside consultant* whose expertise is in change implementation—can.

For major systemwide changes, an organization will often hire outside consultants for advice and assistance. Because these consultants come from the outside, they offer an objective perspective that insiders usually lack. However, the problem is that outside consultants may not understand the organization's history, culture, operating procedures, and personnel. They're also prone to initiating more drastic changes than insiders—which can be either a benefit or a disadvantage—because they don't have to live with the repercussions after the change is implemented. In contrast, internal managers who act as change agents may be more thoughtful (and possibly more cautious) because they must live with the consequences of their actions.

⭐ **Watch It 1!**

If your professor has assigned this, go to the Assignments section of **mymanagementlab.com** to complete the video exercise titled *Rudi's Bakery: Organizational Change and Development*.

How Does Organizational Change Happen?

We often use two metaphors in describing the change process.[4] These two metaphors represent distinctly different approaches to understanding and responding to change. Let's take a closer look at each one.

1 WHAT IS THE "CALM WATERS" METAPHOR? The **"calm waters" metaphor** envisions the organization as a large ship crossing a calm sea. The ship's captain and crew know exactly where they're going because they've made the trip many times before. Change appears as the occasional storm, a brief distraction in an otherwise calm and predictable trip. Until recently, the "calm waters" metaphor dominated the thinking of practicing managers and academics. The prevailing model for handling change in such circumstances is best illustrated in Kurt Lewin's three-step description of the change process.[5] (See Exhibit 8–2.)

According to Lewin, successful change requires unfreezing the status quo, changing to a new state, and freezing the new change to make it permanent. The status quo can be considered an equilibrium state. Unfreezing is necessary to move from this equilibrium. It can be achieved in one of three ways:

- Increase the driving forces, which direct behavior away from the status quo.
- Decrease the restraining forces, which hinder movement from the existing equilibrium.
- Do both.

change agents
People who act as change catalysts and assume the responsibility for managing the change process

"calm waters" metaphor
A description of organizational change that likens that change to a large ship making a predictable trip across a calm sea and experiencing an occasional storm

Exhibit 8–2 The Three-Step Change Process

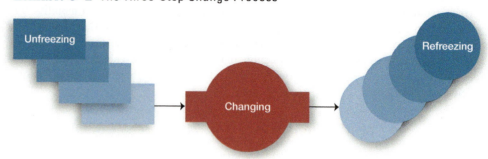

Once the situation has been "unfrozen," the change itself can be implemented. However, just introducing change doesn't mean it's going to take hold. The new situation needs to be "frozen" so that it can be sustained over time. Unless this last step is done, the change is likely to be short-lived, with employees reverting to the previous equilibrium state. The objective, then, is to freeze at the new equilibrium state and stabilize the new situation by balancing the driving and restraining forces. (Read more about Lewin and his organizational research in the From the Past to the Present box.)

Note how Lewin's three-step process treats change as a break in the organization's equilibrium state.[6] The status quo has been disturbed, and change is necessary to establish a new equilibrium state. Although this view might have been appropriate to the relatively calm environment faced by most organizations during the twentieth century, it's increasingly obsolete as a description of the kinds of "seas" that current managers have to navigate.

◀◀◀ From the Past to the Present ▶▶▶

Who Is Kurt Lewin?

- German-American psychologist, known for his research on group dynamics

- Often called the father of modern social psychology (an academic field of study that uses scientific methods to "understand and explain how the thought, feeling, and behavior of individuals are influenced by the actual, imagined, or implied presence of other human beings")[7]

What Did He Do?

- Described group behavior as an intricate set of symbolic interactions and forces that affect group structure and also modify individual behavior.

- One particular study that looked at modifying family food habits during World War II provided new and important insights into how best to introduce change.

Major Lessons from His Work:

- Change is more easily introduced *through group decision making* than through lectures and individual appeals

> Lewin's ideas have helped us better understand **ORGANIZATIONAL CHANGE.**

- Change is more readily accepted *when people feel they have an opportunity to be involved in the change* rather than being simply asked or told to change

- Use force field analysis to *look at the factors (forces) that influence* a change situation

  — Forces either *drive* or *block* movement toward a goal

  — Make change work and overcome resistance by *increasing the driving forces, decreasing the blocking forces*, or *doing both*

If your professor has assigned this, go to the Assignments section of **mymanagementlab.com** *to complete these discussion questions.*

⭐ **Talk About It 1:** Explain force field analysis and how it can be used in organizational change.

⭐ **Talk About It 2:** What advice do you see in this information about Lewin's ideas that managers might use?

2 WHAT IS THE "WHITE-WATER RAPIDS" METAPHOR? As former chair of Nielsen Media Research (the company best known for its TV ratings, which are frequently used to determine how much advertisers pay for TV commercials), Susan Whiting had to tackle significant industry changes. Video-on-demand services, streaming technologies, smartphones, tablet computers, and other changing technologies have made data collection much more challenging for the media research business. Here's what she had to say about the business environment: "If you look at a typical week I have, it's a combination of trying to *lead a company in change in an industry in change*."[8] That's a pretty accurate description of what change is like in our second change metaphor—white-water rapids. It's also consistent with a world that's increasingly dominated by information, ideas, and knowledge.[9]

In the **"white-water rapids" metaphor**, the organization is seen as a small raft navigating a raging river with uninterrupted white-water rapids. Aboard the raft are half a dozen people who have never worked together before, who are totally unfamiliar with the river, who are unsure of their eventual destination, and who, as if things weren't bad enough, are traveling at night. In the white-water rapids metaphor, change is the status quo and managing change is a continual process.

To get a feeling of what managing change might be like in a white-water rapids environment, consider attending a college that had the following rules: Courses vary in length. When you sign up, you don't know how long a course will run; it might go for 2 weeks or 30 weeks. Furthermore, the instructor can end a course at any time with no prior warning. If that isn't challenging enough, the length of the class changes each time it meets: Sometimes the class lasts 20 minutes; other times it runs for 3 hours. And the time of the next class meeting is set by the instructor during this class. There's one more thing. All exams are unannounced, so you have to be ready for a test at any time. To succeed in this type of environment, you'd have to respond quickly to changing conditions. Students who were overly structured or uncomfortable with change wouldn't succeed.

DOES EVERY MANAGER FACE A WORLD OF CONSTANT AND CHAOTIC CHANGE? Well, not *every* manager, but it *is* becoming more the norm. The stability and predictability of the calm waters metaphor don't exist. Disruptions in the status quo are not occasional and temporary, and they're not followed by a return to calm waters. Many managers never get out of the rapids. Like Susan Whiting, just described, they face constant forces in the environment (external *and* internal) that bring about the need for planned organizational change.

Most organizational **changes don't happen** by chance.

HOW DO ORGANIZATIONS IMPLEMENT PLANNED CHANGES? At the Wyndham Peachtree Conference Center in Georgia, businesses bring groups of employees to try their hand at the ancient Chinese water sport of dragon boat racing. Although the physical exercise is an added benefit, it's the team-building exercise in which participants learn about communication, collaboration, and commitment that's meant to be the longest-lasting benefit.[10]

Most organizational changes don't happen by chance. Often managers make a concerted effort to alter some aspect of the organization. Whatever happens—especially in terms of structure or technology—ultimately affects the organization's people. Efforts to assist organizational members with a planned change are referred to as **organization development (OD)**.

> **"white-water rapids" metaphor**
> A description of organizational change that likens that change to a small raft navigating a raging river
>
> **organization development (OD)**
> Efforts that assist organizational members with a planned change by focusing on their attitudes and values

As president and CEO of DeNA Company, a Japanese Internet firm, Isao Moriyasu manages in a white-water rapids environment where change is the status quo and managing change is a continual process. Moriyasu is rapidly acquiring firms and developing new services as DeNA expands from its base in Japan to countries worldwide.

Kiyoshi Ota/Bloomberg/Getty Images

survey feedback
A method of assessing employees' attitudes toward and perceptions of a change

process consultation
Using outside consultants to assess organizational processes such as workflow, informal intra-unit relationships, and formal communication channels

team-building
Using activities to help work groups set goals, develop positive interpersonal relationships, and clarify the roles and responsibilities of each team member

intergroup development
Activities that attempt to make several work groups more cohesive

In facilitating long-term, organization-wide changes, managers use OD to constructively change the attitudes and values of organization members so they can more readily adapt to and be more effective in achieving the new directions of the organization.[11] When OD efforts are planned, organization leaders are, in essence, attempting to change the organization's culture.[12] However, a fundamental issue of OD is its reliance on employee participation to foster an environment in which open communication and trust exist.[13] Persons involved in OD efforts acknowledge that change can create stress for employees. Therefore, OD attempts to involve organizational members in changes that will affect their jobs and seeks their input about how the change is affecting them (just as Lewin suggested).

Any organizational activity that assists with implementing planned change can be viewed as an OD technique. The more popular OD efforts in organizations rely heavily on group interactions and cooperation and include:

1. **Survey feedback**. Employees are asked their attitudes about and perceptions of the change they're encountering. Employees are generally asked to respond to a set of specific questions regarding how they view such organizational aspects as decision making, leadership, communication effectiveness, and satisfaction with their jobs, coworkers, and management.[14] The data that a change agent obtains are used to clarify problems that employees may be facing. As a result of this information, the change agent takes some action to remedy the problems.

2. **Process consultation**. Outside consultants help managers perceive, understand, and act on organizational processes they're facing.[15] These elements might include, for example, workflow, informal relationships among unit members, and formal communications channels. Consultants give managers insight into what is going on. It's important to recognize that consultants are not there to solve these problems. Rather, they act as coaches to help managers diagnose the interpersonal processes that need improvement. If managers, with the consultants' help, cannot solve the problem, the consultants will often help managers find experts who can.

3. **Team-building**. In organizations made up of individuals working together to achieve goals, OD helps them become a team. How? By helping them set goals, develop positive interpersonal relationships, and clarify the roles and responsibilities of each team member. It's not always necessary to address each area because the group may be in agreement and understand what's expected. The *primary* focus of team-building is to increase members' trust and openness toward one another.[16]

4. **Intergroup development**. Different groups focus on becoming more cohesive. That is, intergroup development attempts to change attitudes, stereotypes, and perceptions that one group may have toward another group. The goal? Better coordination among the various groups.

How Do Managers Manage Resistance to Change?

8-2 Explain how to manage resistance to change.

We know that it's better for us to eat healthy and to be physically active, yet few of us actually follow that advice consistently and continually. We resist making lifestyle changes. Volkswagen Sweden and ad agency DDB Stockholm did an experiment to see if they could get people to change their behavior and take the healthier option of using the stairs instead of riding an escalator.[17] How? They put a working piano keyboard on stairs in a Stockholm subway station (you can see a video of it on YouTube) to see if commuters would use it. The experiment was a resounding success as stair traffic rose 66 percent. The lesson: People *can change* if you make the change appealing!

Managers should be motivated to initiate change because they're concerned with improving their organization's effectiveness. But change isn't easy in any organization. It can be disruptive and scary. And people and organizations can build up inertia and not want to change.

People resist change even if **it might be beneficial!**

Let's look at why people in organizations resist change and what can be done to lessen that resistance.

Why Do People Resist Organizational Change?

It's often said that most people hate any change that doesn't jingle in their pockets. Resistance to change is well documented.[18] Why *do* people resist organizational change? The main reasons include:[19]

1. UNCERTAINTY. *Change replaces the known with uncertainty and we don't like uncertainty.* No matter how much you may dislike attending college (or certain classes), at least you know what's expected of you. When you leave college for the world of full-time employment, you'll trade the known for the unknown. Employees in organizations are faced with similar uncertainty. For example, when quality control methods based on statistical models are introduced into manufacturing plants, many quality control inspectors have to learn the new methods. Some may fear that they'll be unable to do so and may develop a negative attitude toward the change or behave poorly if required to use them.

2. HABIT. *We do things out of habit.* Every day when you go to school or work you probably get there the same way, if you're like most people. We're creatures of habit. Life is complex enough—we don't want to have to consider the full range of options for the hundreds of decisions we make every day. To cope with this complexity, we rely on habits or programmed responses. But when confronted with change, our tendency to respond in our accustomed ways becomes a source of resistance.

3. CONCERN OVER PERSONAL LOSS. *We fear losing something already possessed.* Change threatens the investment you've already made in the status quo. The more that people have invested in the current system, the more they resist change. Why? They fear losing status, money, authority, friendships, personal convenience, or other economic benefits that they value. This helps explain why older workers tend to resist change more than younger workers, since they generally have more invested in the current system and more to lose by changing.

4. CHANGE IS NOT IN ORGANIZATION'S BEST INTERESTS. *We believe that the change is incompatible with the goals and interests of the organization.* For instance, an employee who believes that a proposed new job procedure will reduce product quality can be expected to resist the change. Actually, this type of resistance can be beneficial to the organization if expressed in a positive way.

What Are Some Techniques for Reducing Resistance to Organizational Change?

At an annual 401(k) enrollment meeting, the CEO of North American Tool, frustrated at his employees' disinterest in maxing out their investments, brought in a big bag, unzipped it, and upended it over a table.[20] Cash poured out—$9,832 to be exact—the amount employees had failed to claim the prior year. He gestured at the money and said, "This is your money. It should be in your pocket. Next year, do you want it on the table or in your pocket?" When the 401(k) enrollment forms were distributed, several individuals signed up. Sometimes to get people to change, *you first have to get their attention.*

When managers see resistance to change as dysfunctional, what can they do? Several strategies have been suggested in dealing with resistance to change. These approaches include education and communication, participation, facilitation and support, negotiation, manipulation and co-optation, and coercion. These tactics are summarized here and described in Exhibit 8–4. Managers should view these techniques as tools and use the most appropriate one depending on the type and source of the resistance.

- *Education and communication* can help reduce resistance to change by helping employees see the logic of the change effort. This technique, of course, assumes that much of the resistance lies in misinformation or poor communication.

(*list continues on p. 250*)

What Reaction Do Employees Have to Organizational Change?

Yuri Arcurs/Alamy

| 8-3 | Describe what managers need to know about employee stress. |

Change often creates stress for employees!

Employee Stress Levels in Six Major Economies[21]	
United Kingdom	**35%** of employees
Brazil	**34%** of employees
Germany	**33%** of employees
United States	**32%** of employees
GLOBAL AVERAGE	**29%** of employees
China	**17%** of employees
India	**17%** of employees

1 What Is **Stress**?

- **Stress**—response to anxiety over intense demands, constraints, or opportunities.[22, 23]
- Not always bad; can be positive, especially when there's potential gain.
  — **Functional stress**—allows a person to perform at his or her highest level at crucial times.
- Often associated with **constraints** *(an obstacle that prevents you from doing what you desire)*, **demands** *(the loss of something desired)*, and **opportunities** *(the possibility of something new, something never done)*.
  Examples: Taking a test or having your annual work performance review.
- Although conditions may be right for stress to surface that doesn't mean it will.

stress
Response to anxiety over intense demands, constraints, or opportunities

For **potential stress** to become **actual stress**: • there is uncertainty over the outcome • the outcome is important.

What Are the **Symptoms of Stress?**

Exhibit 8–3 Symptoms of Stress

Physical

Changes in metabolism, increased heart and breathing rates, raised blood pressure, headaches, and potential of heart attacks.

SYMPTOMS OF STRESS

Psychological

Job-related dissatisfaction, tension, anxiety, irritability, boredom, and procrastination.

Behavioral

Changes in productivity, absenteeism, job turnover, changes in eating habits, increased smoking or consumption of alcohol, rapid speech, fidgeting, and sleep disorders.

Too much stress can also have tragic consequences. In Japan, there's a stress phenomenon called **karoshi** (pronounced kah-roe-she), which is translated as death from overwork.

karoshi
A Japanese term that refers to a sudden death caused by overworking

2

What Causes Stress? **Stressors**

Job-related factors:

- Examples: Pressures to avoid errors or complete tasks in a limited time period; changes in the way reports are filed; a demanding supervisor; unpleasant coworkers

  52% of employees say: Colleagues are a stressful part of their jobs.[24]

  1. **Task demands:** Stress due to an employee's job—job design (autonomy, task variety, degree of automation); working conditions (temperature, noise, etc.); physical work layout (overcrowded or in visible location with constant interruptions; work quotas, especially when excessive;[25] high level of task interdependence with others. (FYI: Autonomy lessens stress.)

  2. **Role demands:** Stress due to employee's particular role.
     - **Role conflicts:** expectations that may be hard to reconcile or satisfy.
     - **Role overload:** created when employee is expected to do more than time permits.
     - **Role ambiguity:** created when role expectations are not clearly understood—employee not sure what he or she is to do.

stressors
Factors that cause stress

role conflicts
Work expectations that are hard to satisfy

role overload
Having more work to accomplish than time permits

role ambiguity
When role expectations are not clearly understood

3. **Interpersonal demands:** Stress due to other employees—little or no social support from colleagues; poor interpersonal relationships.

4. **Organization structure:** Stress due to excessive rules; no opportunity to participate in decisions that affect an employee.

5. **Organizational leadership:** Stress due to managers' supervisory style in a culture of tension, fear, anxiety, unrealistic pressures to perform in the short run, excessively tight controls, and routine firing of employees who don't measure up.

Personal factors:
Life demands, constraints, opportunities of any kind

1 **Family issues, personal economic problems, and so forth.**
- Can't just ignore! Managers need to be understanding of these personal factors.[26]

2 **Employees' personalities —Type A or Type B.**
- **Type A personality**—chronic sense of time urgency, excessive competitive drive, and difficulty accepting and enjoying leisure time; more likely to shows symptoms of stress.
- **Type B personality**—little to no sense of time urgency or impatience.
- Stress comes from the hostility and anger associated with Type A behavior. Surprisingly, Type Bs are just as susceptible.

A Question of Ethics

One in five companies offers some form of stress management program.[27] Although such programs are available, many employees may choose not to participate. They may be reluctant to ask for help, especially if a major source of that stress is job insecurity. After all, there's still a stigma associated with stress. Employees don't want to be perceived as being unable to handle the demands of their job. Although they may need stress management now more than ever, few employees want to admit that they're stressed.

*If your professor has assigned this, go to the Assignments section of **mymanagementlab.com** to complete these discussion questions.*

⭐ **Talk About It 3:** What can be done about this paradox?

⭐ **Talk About It 4:** Do organizations even have an ethical responsibility to help employees deal with stress?

Type A personality
People who have a chronic sense of urgency and an excessive competitive drive

Type B personality
People who are relaxed and easygoing and accept change easily

Beyond Fotomedia GmbH/Alamy

How Can Stress Be Reduced?

1 General guidelines:

- Not all stress is dysfunctional.
- Stress can never be totally eliminated!
- Reduce dysfunctional stress by controlling job-related factors and offering help for personal stress.

2 Job-related factors:

- **Employee selection**—provide a realistic job preview and make sure an employee's abilities match the job requirements.

1bestofphoto/Alamy

- **On-the-job**—improve organizational communications to minimize ambiguity; use a performance planning program such as MBO to clarify job responsibilities, provide clear performance goals, and reduce ambiguity through feedback; redesign job, if possible, especially if stress can be traced to boredom (increase challenge) or to work overload (reduce the workload); allow employees to participate in decisions and to gain social support, which also lessen stress.[28]

3 Personal factors:

- Not easy for manager to control directly
- Ethical considerations

Does a manager have the **right to intrude**— even subtly—**in an employee's personal life**?

- If the manager believes it's ethical and the employee is receptive, consider employee assistance and wellness programs,[29] which are designed to assist employees in areas where they might be having difficulties (financial planning, legal matters, health, fitness, or stress).[30]

Samantha Craddock/Alamy

  - **Employee assistance programs (EAPs)[31]**—the rationale is to get a productive employee back on the job as quickly as possible.

  - **Wellness programs**—the rationale is to keep employees healthy.

---

employee assistance programs (EAPs)
Programs offered by organizations to help employees overcome personal and health-related problems

wellness programs
Programs offered by organizations to help employees prevent health problems

Exhibit 8–4 Techniques for Reducing Resistance to Change

TECHNIQUE	WHEN USED	ADVANTAGE	DISADVANTAGE
Education and communication	When resistance is due to misinformation	Clear up misunderstandings	May not work when mutual trust and credibility are lacking
Participation	When resisters have the expertise to make a contribution	Increase involvement and acceptance	Time-consuming; has potential for a poor solution
Facilitation and support	When resisters are fearful and anxiety-ridden	Can facilitate needed adjustments	Expensive; no guarantee of success
Negotiation	When resistance comes from a powerful group	Can "buy" commitment	Potentially high cost; opens doors for others to apply pressure too
Manipulation and co-optation	When a powerful group's endorsement is needed	Inexpensive, easy way to gain support	Can backfire, causing change agent to lose credibility
Coercion	When a powerful group's endorsement is needed	Inexpensive, easy way to gain support	May be illegal; may undermine change agent's credibility

- *Participation* involves bringing those individuals directly affected by the proposed change into the decision-making process. Their participation allows these individuals to express their feelings, increase the quality of the process, and increase employee commitment to the final decision.
- *Facilitation and support* involve helping employees deal with the fear and anxiety associated with the change effort. This help may include employee counseling, therapy, new skills training, or a short paid leave of absence.
- *Negotiation* involves exchanging something of value for an agreement to lessen the resistance to the change effort. This resistance technique may be quite useful when the resistance comes from a powerful source.
- *Manipulation and co-optation* refer to covert attempts to influence others about the change. They may involve twisting or distorting facts to make the change appear more attractive.
- *Coercion* involves the use of direct threats or force against those resisting the change.

⭐ **Try It!**
If your professor has assigned this, go to the Assignments section of **mymanagementlab.com** to complete the **Simulation: *Change*.**

How Can Managers Encourage Innovation in an Organization?

8-4 Discuss techniques for stimulating innovation.

"Innovation is the **key to continued** success."

"We innovate today to **secure the future**."

These two quotes (the first by Ajay Banga, the CEO of MasterCard, and the second by Sophie Vandebroek, chief technology officer of Xerox Innovation Group) reflect how important innovation is to organizations.[32] SUCCESS IN BUSINESS TODAY DEMANDS INNOVATION. In the dynamic, chaotic world of global competition, organizations must create new products and services and adopt state-of-the-art technology if they're going to compete successfully.[33]

What companies come to mind when you think of successful innovators? Maybe Apple with all its cool work and entertainment gadgets. Maybe Facebook for its 1 billion-plus users. Maybe Nissan for creating the Leaf, the first mass-market all-electric car. Or even maybe Foursquare, a startup that revved up the social-local-mobile trend by having users "check in" at locations, unlocking quirky badges and special offers from merchants.[34] What's the secret to the success of these innovator champions? What can other managers do to make their organizations more innovative? In the following pages, we'll try to answer those questions as we discuss the factors behind innovation.

K.C. Alfred/U-T San Diego/ZUMAPRESS/Alamy

Entrepreneur Nick Woodman channeled his creativity into a useful product. As founder of GoPro, Inc., Woodman designed a compact wearable camera that surfers, skydivers, and other sports enthusiasts can use to take high-quality photographs and videos. Woodman is shown here taking a photo of students with his wrist-strap GoPro during a college alumni event.

How Are Creativity and Innovation Related?

- **Creativity** refers to the ability to combine ideas in a unique way or to make unusual associations between ideas.[35] A creative organization develops unique ways of working or novel solutions to problems. For instance, at Mattel, company officials introduced "Project Platypus," a special group that brings people from all disciplines—engineering, marketing, design, and sales—and tries to get them to "think outside the box" in order to "understand the sociology and psychology behind children's play patterns." To help make this kind of thinking happen, team members embarked on such activities as imagination exercises, group crying, and stuffed-bunny throwing. What does throwing stuffed bunnies have to do with creativity? It's part of a juggling lesson where team members tried to learn to juggle two balls and a stuffed bunny. Most people can easily learn to juggle two balls but can't let go of that third object. Creativity, like juggling, is learning to let go—that is, to "throw the bunny."[36] Creativity by itself isn't enough, though.
- The outcomes of the creative process need to be turned into useful products or work methods, which is defined as **innovation**. Thus, the *innovative organization is characterized by its ability to channel creativity into useful outcomes*. When managers talk about changing an organization to make it more creative, they usually mean they want to stimulate and nurture innovation.

What's Involved in Innovation?

Some people believe that creativity is inborn; others believe that with training, anyone can be creative. The latter group views creativity as a fourfold process.[37]

1. *Perception* involves the way you see things. Being creative means seeing things from a unique perspective. One person may see solutions to a problem that others cannot or will not see at all. The movement from perception to reality, however, doesn't occur instantaneously.
2. Instead, ideas go through a process of *incubation*. Sometimes employees need to sit on their ideas, which doesn't mean sitting and doing nothing. Rather, during this incubation period, employees should collect massive amounts of data that are stored, retrieved, studied, reshaped, and finally molded into something new. During this period, it's common for years to pass. Think for a moment about a time you struggled for an answer on a test. Although you tried hard to jog your memory, nothing worked. Then suddenly, like a flash of light, the answer popped into your head. You found it!

creativity
The ability to produce novel and useful ideas

innovation
The process of taking a creative idea and turning it into a useful product, service, or method of operation

Technology and the Manager's Job

HELPING INNOVATION FLOURISH

When employees are busy doing their regular job tasks, how can innovation ever flourish? When job performance is evaluated by what you get done, how you get it done, and when you get it done, how can innovation ever happen? This has been a real challenge facing organizations wanting to be more innovative. One solution has been to give employees mandated time to experiment with their own ideas on company-related projects.[38] For instance, Google has its "20% Time" initiative, which encourages employees to spend 20 percent of their time at work on projects not related to their job descriptions. Other companies—Facebook, Apple, LinkedIn, 3M, Hewlett-Packard, among others—have similar initiatives. Hmmm...so having essentially one day a week to work on company-related ideas you have almost seems too good to be true. But, more importantly, does it really spark innovation? Well, it can. At Google, it led to the auto-complete system, Google News, Gmail, and Adsense. However, such "company" initiatives do face tremendous obstacles, despite how good they sound on paper. These challenges include:

- Strict employee monitoring in terms of time and resources leading to a reluctance to use this time since most employees have enough to do just keeping up with their regular tasks.
- When bonuses/incentives are based on goals achieved, employees soon figure out what to spend their time on.

- What happens to the ideas that employees do have?
- Unsupportive managers and coworkers who may view this as a "goof-around-for-free-day."
- Obstacles in the corporate bureaucracy.

So, how can companies make it work? Suggestions include: top managers need to support the initiatives/projects and make that support known; managers need to support employees who have that personal passion and drive, that creative spark—clear a path for them to pursue their ideas; perhaps allow employees more of an incentive to innovate (rights to design, etc.); and last, but not least, don't institutionalize it. Creativity and innovation, by their very nature, involve risk and reward. Give creative individuals the space to try and to fail and to try and to fail as needed.

*If your professor has assigned this, go to the Assignments section of **mymanagementlab.com** to complete these discussion questions.*

✪ **TALK ABOUT IT 5:** What benefits do you see with such mandated experiment time for (a) organizations? (b) individuals?

✪ **TALK ABOUT IT 6:** What obstacles do these initiatives face and how can managers overcome those obstacles?

3. *Inspiration* in the creative process is similar. Inspiration is the moment when all your efforts successfully come together. Although inspiration leads to euphoria, the creative work isn't complete. It requires an innovative effort.

4. *Innovation* involves taking that inspiration and turning it into a useful product, service, or way of doing things. Thomas Edison is often credited with saying that "Creativity is 1 percent inspiration and 99 percent perspiration." That 99 percent, or the innovation, involves testing, evaluating, and retesting what the inspiration found. It's usually at this stage that an individual involves others more in what he or she has been working on. Such involvement is critical because even the greatest invention may be delayed, or lost, if an individual cannot effectively deal with others in communicating and achieving what the creative idea is supposed to do.

How Can a Manager Foster Innovation?

The systems model (inputs → transformation process → outputs) can help us understand how organizations become more innovative.[39] If an organization wants innovative products and work methods (*outputs*), it has to take its *inputs* and *transform* them into those outputs. Those *inputs* include creative people and groups within the organization. But as we said earlier, having creative people isn't enough. The *transformation process* requires having the right environment to turn those inputs into innovative products or work methods. This "right" environment—that is, an environment that stimulates innovation—includes three variables: the organization's structure, culture, and human resource practices. (See Exhibit 8–5.)

Exhibit 8–5 Innovation Variables

Structural Variables
- Organic structures
- Abundant resources
- High interunit communication
- Minimal time pressure
- Work and nonwork support

Human Resource Variables
- High commitment to training and development
- High job security
- Creative people

STIMULATE INNOVATION

Cultural Variables
- Acceptance of ambiguity
- Tolerance of the impractical
- Low external controls
- Tolerance of risks
- Tolerance of conflict
- Focus on ends
- Open-system focus
- Positive feedback

⭐ **Watch It 2!**

If your professor has assigned this, go to the Assignments section of **mymanagementlab.com** to complete the video exercise titled **CH2MHill: Innovation**.

HOW DO STRUCTURAL VARIABLES AFFECT INNOVATION?   Research into the effect of structural variables on innovation shows five things.[40]

1. An organic-type structure positively influences innovation. Because this structure is low in formalization, centralization, and work specialization, it facilitates the flexibility and sharing of ideas that are critical to innovation.
2. The availability of plentiful resources provides a key building block for innovation. With an abundance of resources, managers can afford to purchase innovations, can afford the cost of instituting innovations, and can absorb failures.
3. Frequent communication between organizational units helps break down barriers to innovation.[41] Cross-functional teams, task forces, and other such organizational designs facilitate interaction across departmental lines and are widely used in innovative organizations.
4. Extreme time pressures on creative activities are minimized despite the demands of white-water-rapids-type environments. Although time pressures may spur people to work harder and may make them feel more creative, studies show that it actually causes them to be less creative.[42]
5. When an organization's structure explicitly supports creativity, employees' creative performance can be enhanced. Beneficial kinds of support include encouragement, open communication, readiness to listen, and useful feedback.[43]

HOW DOES AN ORGANIZATION'S CULTURE AFFECT INNOVATION?   Innovative organizations tend to have similar cultures.[44] They encourage experimentation; reward both

idea champions
Individuals who actively and enthusiastically support new ideas, build support for, overcome resistance to, and ensure that innovations are implemented

successes and failures; and celebrate mistakes. An innovative organization is likely to have the following characteristics.

- *Accepts ambiguity.* Too much emphasis on objectivity and specificity constrains creativity.
- *Tolerates the impractical.* Individuals who offer impractical, even foolish, answers to what-if questions are not stifled. What at first seems impractical might lead to innovative solutions.
- *Keeps external controls minimal.* Rules, regulations, policies, and similar organizational controls are kept to a minimum.
- *Tolerates risk.* Employees are encouraged to experiment without fear of consequences should they fail. Mistakes are treated as learning opportunities.
- *Tolerates conflict.* Diversity of opinions is encouraged. Harmony and agreement between individuals or units are *not* assumed to be evidence of high performance.
- *Focuses on ends rather than means.* Goals are made clear, and individuals are encouraged to consider alternative routes toward meeting the goals. Focusing on ends suggests that there might be several right answers to any given problem.
- *Uses an open-system focus.* Managers closely monitor the environment and respond to changes as they occur. For example, at Starbucks, product development depends on "inspiration field trips to view customers and trends." When Michelle Gass (now Kohl's Corporation's chief customer officer) was in charge of Starbucks marketing, she had her team travel to several trendy global cities to visit local Starbucks and other dining establishments to "get a better sense of local cultures, behaviors, and fashions."[45] Her rationale? Seeing and experiencing firsthand different ideas and different ways to think about things can be so much more valuable than reading about them.
- *Provides positive feedback.* Managers provide positive feedback, encouragement, and support so employees feel that their creative ideas receive attention. For instance, Mike Lazaridis, co-founder of Blackberry maker Research in Motion, said "I think we have a culture of innovation here, and [engineers] have absolute access to me. I live a life that tries to promote innovation."[46]

WHAT HUMAN RESOURCE VARIABLES AFFECT INNOVATION? In this category, we find that innovative organizations (1) actively promote the training and development of their members so their knowledge remains current, (2) offer their employees high job security to reduce the fear of getting fired for making mistakes, and (3) encourage individuals to become **idea champions**, actively and enthusiastically supporting new ideas, building support, overcoming resistance, and ensuring that innovations are implemented. Research finds that idea champions have common personality characteristics: extremely high self-confidence, persistence, energy, and a tendency toward risk taking. They also display characteristics associated with dynamic leadership. They inspire and energize others with their vision of the potential of an innovation and through their strong personal conviction in their mission. They're also good at gaining the commitment of others to support their mission. In addition, idea champions have jobs that provide considerable decision-making discretion. This autonomy helps them introduce and implement innovations in organizations.[47]

Netflix founder and CEO Reed Hastings has created a culture of innovation that encourages employees to become idea champions. Netflix gives employees the freedom to come up with new ideas and the responsibility to implement them by engaging employees from different departments and by forming groups to "socialize" their ideas.

Robin Utrecht/ABACAPRESS/Newscom

How Does Design Thinking Influence Innovation?

We introduced you to the concept of design thinking in a previous chapter. Well, undoubtedly, there's a strong connection between design thinking and innovation. "Design thinking can do for innovation what TQM did for quality."[48] Just as TQM provides a process for improving quality throughout an organization, design thinking can provide a process for coming up with things that don't exist. When a business approaches innovation with a design thinking mentality, the emphasis is on getting a deeper understanding of what customers need and want. It entails knowing customers as real people with real problems—not just as sales targets or demographic statistics. But it also entails being able to convert those customer insights into real and usable products. For instance, at Intuit, the company behind TurboTax software, founder Scott Cook felt the company was "lagging behind in innovation."[49] So he decided to apply design thinking. He called the initiative "Design for Delight," and it involved customer field research to understand their "pain points"—that is, what most frustrated them as they worked in the office and at home. Then, Intuit staffers brainstormed (they nicknamed it "painstorm") a wide array of possible ideas to address customer problems, which they would then try out with customers to find ones that worked best. For example, one pain point uncovered by an Intuit team was how customers could take pictures of tax forms to reduce typing errors. Some younger customers, used to taking photos with their smartphones, were frustrated that they couldn't just complete their taxes on their mobiles. To address this, Intuit developed a mobile app called SnapTax, which the company says has been downloaded more than a million times since it was introduced in 2010. That's how design thinking works in innovation.

MyManagementLab®

Go to **mymanagementlab.com** to complete the problems marked with this icon .

8 Review

CHAPTER SUMMARY

8-1 Define organizational change and compare and contrast views on the change process.

Organizational change is any alteration of an organization's people, structure, or technology. The "calm waters" metaphor of change suggests that change is an occasional disruption in the normal flow of events and can be planned and managed as it happens, using Lewin's three-step change process (unfreezing, changing, and freezing). The "white-water rapids" view of change suggests that change is ongoing, and managing it is a continual process.

8-2 Explain how to manage resistance to change.

People resist change because of uncertainty, habit, concern about personal loss, and the belief that a change is not in the organization's best interests. Techniques for managing resistance to change include education and communication (educating employees about and communicating to them the need for the change), participation (allowing employees to participate in the change process), facilitation and support (giving employees the support they need to implement the change), negotiation (exchanging something of value to reduce resistance), manipulation and co-optation (using negative actions to influence), selecting people who are open to and accept change, and coercion (using direct threats or force).

8-3 Describe what managers need to know about employee stress.

Stress is the adverse reaction people have to excessive pressure placed on them from extraordinary demands, constraints, or opportunities. The symptoms of stress can be physical, psychological, or behavioral. Stress can be caused by personal factors and by job-related factors. To help employees deal with stress, managers can address job-related factors by making sure an employee's abilities match the job requirements, improving organizational communications, using a performance planning program, or redesigning jobs. Addressing personal stress factors is trickier, but managers could offer employee counseling, time management programs, and wellness programs.

8-4 Discuss techniques for stimulating innovation.

Creativity is the ability to combine ideas in a unique way or to make unusual associations between ideas. Innovation is turning the outcomes of the creative process into useful products or work methods. An innovative environment encompasses structural, cultural, and human resource variables.

Important structural variables include an organic-type structure, abundant resources, frequent communication between organizational units, minimal time pressure, and support. Important cultural variables include accepting ambiguity, tolerating the impractical, keeping external controls minimal, tolerating risk, tolerating conflict, focusing on ends not means, using an open-system focus, and providing positive feedback. Important human resource variables include high commitment to training and development, high job security, and encouraging individuals to be idea champions.

Design thinking can also play a role in innovation. It provides a process for coming up with products that don't exist.

DISCUSSION QUESTIONS

 8-1 Why is managing change an integral part of every manager's job?

8-2 Contrast the calm waters and white-water rapids metaphors of change. Which of these would you use to describe your current life? Why is that one your choice?

8-3 Describe Lewin's three-step change process. How is it different from the change process needed in the white-water rapids metaphor of change?

8-4 How are opportunities, constraints, and demands related to stress? Give an example of each.

8-5 Organizations typically have limits to how much change they can absorb. As a manager, what signs would you look for that might suggest your organization has exceeded its capacity to change?

8-6 Why is organization development planned change? Explain how planned change is important for organizations in today's dynamic environment.

 8-7 How do creativity and innovation differ?

8-8 Research information on how to be a more creative person. Write down suggestions in a bulleted list format and be prepared to present your information in class.

8-9 How does an innovative culture make an organization more effective? Could an innovative culture ever make an organization less effective? Why or why not?

8-10 When you find yourself experiencing dysfunctional stress, write down what's causing the stress, what stress symptoms you're exhibiting, and how you're dealing with the stress. Keep this information in a journal and evaluate how well your stress reducers are working and how you could handle stress better. Your goal is to get to a point where you recognize that you're stressed and can take positive actions to deal with the stress.

Writing Assignments

8-11 Planned change is often thought to be the best approach to take in organizations. Can *unplanned* change ever be effective? Explain.

8-12 Describe the structural, cultural, and human resources variables that are necessary for innovation.

Management Skill Builder | STRESS MANAGEMENT

It's no secret that employees, in general, are more stressed out today than previous generations. Heavier workloads, longer hours, continual reorganizations, technology that breaks down traditional barriers between work and personal life, and reduced job security are among factors that have increased employee stress. This stress can lead to lower productivity, increased absenteeism, reduced job satisfaction, and higher quit rates. When stress is excessive, managers need to know how to reduce it.

✪ PERSONAL INVENTORY ASSESSMENT PERSONAL INVENTORY ASSESSMENT

Controlling Workplace Stress

As our debunked Management Myth pointed out, workplace stress is a reality *and* managers can do something about it. In this PIA, you'll assess how you control workplace stress.

Skill Basics

Eliminating all stress at work isn't going to happen and it shouldn't. Stress is an unavoidable consequence of life. It also has a positive side—when it focuses concentration and creativity. But when it brings about anger, frustration, fear, sleeplessness, and the like, it needs to be addressed.

Many organizations have introduced stress-reduction interventions for employees. These include improved employee selection and placement, helping employees set realistic goals, training in time management, redesign of jobs, increased involvement of employees in decisions that affect them, expanded social support networks, improved organizational communications, and organizationally supported wellness programs. But what can *you* do, on your own, to reduce stress if your employer doesn't provide such programs or if you need to take additional action? The following individual interventions have been suggested:

• *Implement time-management techniques*. Every person can improve his or her use of time. Time is a unique resource in that, if it's wasted, it can *never* be replaced. While people

talk about *saving time*, it can never actually be saved. And if it's lost, it can't be retrieved. The good news is that it's a resource we all have in equal amounts. Everyone gets the same 24 hours a day, 7 days a week to use. When tasks seem to exceed the hours you have available, stress often results. But effective management of time can reduce stress. Time-management training can, for example, teach you how to prioritize tasks by importance and urgency, schedule activities according to those priorities, avoid confusing actions with accomplishments, and understand your productivity cycle so you can handle the most demanding tasks during the high part of your cycle when you are most alert and productive.

• *Create personal goals*. Goal setting is designed to help you better prioritize your activities and better manage how you direct your efforts. Goals become, in effect, a personal planning tool. For instance, setting long-term goals provides general direction; while short-term goals—such as weekly or daily "to do" lists—reduce the likelihood that important activities will be overlooked and help you to maximize the use of your time.

- *Use physical exercise.* A large body of evidence indicates that noncompetitive physical exercise can help you to release tension that builds up in stressful situations. These activities include aerobics, walking, jogging, swimming, and riding a bicycle. Physical exercise increases heart capacity, lowers the at-rest heart rate, provides a mental diversion from work pressures, and offers a means to "let off steam."

- *Practice relaxation training.* You can teach yourself to reduce tension through meditation, deep-breathing exercises, and guided imaging. They work by taking your mind off the sources of stress, achieving a state of deep relaxation, and releasing body tension.

- *Expand your social support network.* Having friends, family, or work colleagues to talk to provides an outlet when stress levels become excessive. Expanding your social support network, therefore, can be a means for tension reduction. It provides you with someone to hear your problems and to offer a more objective perspective on the situation.[50]

Practicing the Skill

Read through this scenario and follow the directions at the end of it:

Dana had become frustrated in her job at Taylor Books—a chain of 22 bookstores in Georgia and Florida. After nearly 13 years as director of marketing, she felt she needed new challenges. When she was offered the job as senior account supervisor for Dancer Advertising in Tampa, she jumped at the opportunity. Now, after four months on the job, she's not so certain she made the right move.

At Taylor, she worked a basic 8-to-5 day. She was easily able to balance her work responsibilities with her personal responsibilities as a wife and mother of two children—ages 4 and 7. But her new job is very different. Clients call anytime—day, night, and weekends—with demands. People in Dancer's creative department are constantly asking for her input on projects. And Dana's boss expects her not only to keep her current clients happy, but also to help secure new clients by preparing and participating in presentations and working up budgets. Last month alone, Dana calculated that she spent 67 hours in the office plus another 12 at home working on Dancer projects. Short on sleep, frazzled by the hectic pace, having no time for her family or chores, she's lost five pounds and broken out in hives. Her doctor told her the hives were stress-induced and she needed to sort out her life.

Dana really likes her job as an account executive but feels the demands and pulls of the job are overwhelming. Yesterday she called her old boss at Taylor Books and inquired about coming back. His reply, "Dana, we'd love to have you back here but we filled your slot. We could find something for you in marketing but you wouldn't be director and the pay would be at least a third less."

If you were Dana, what would you do? Be specific.

Experiential Exercise

Performance Pros

To: Tina Sanchez, HR Director

From: Aaron Scott, President

Subject: Employee stress management program

Well, Tina, we've made it through the initial phases of our restructuring efforts. The changes haven't been easy on any of us. But we've still got a long way to go, and that's where I need your assistance. To help minimize the pressures on our software developers and sales staff, I think we need to develop an employee stress management program that we could implement immediately. Due to finances, we don't have a lot of excess funds to spend on fitness equipment, so you're going to have to work within that constraint. Could you put together a brief (no more than one page) outline of what you think this program should include? Also, note the benefit(s) you think each suggestion would provide. I'd like some time to review your suggestions over the weekend, so please get me your report as soon as possible.

This fictionalized company and message were created for educational purposes only, and not meant to reflect positively or negatively on management practices by any company that may share this name.

CASE APPLICATION #1

The Next Big Thing

It all started with a simple plan to make a superior T-shirt. As special teams captain during the mid-1990s for the University of Maryland football team, Kevin Plank hated having to repeatedly change the cotton T-shirt he wore under his jersey as it became wet and heavy during the course of a game.[51] He knew there had to be a better alternative and set out to make it. After a year of fabric and product testing, Plank introduced the first Under Armour compression product—a synthetic shirt worn like a second skin under a uniform or jersey. And it was an immediate hit! The silky fabric was light and made athletes feel faster and fresher, giving them, according to Plank, an important psychological edge. Today, Under Armour continues to passionately strive to make all athletes better by relentlessly pursuing innovation and design. A telling sign of the company's philosophy is found over the door of its product design studios: "We have not yet built our defining product."

Today, Baltimore-based Under Armour (UA) is a $3.08 billion company. In 19 years, it has grown from a college startup to a "formidable competitor of the Beaverton, Oregon, behemoth" (better known as Nike, a $27 billion company). The company has nearly 3 percent of the fragmented U.S. sports apparel market and sells products from shirts, shorts, and footwear to underwear, wearable fitness technology, and hats. In addition, more than 100 universities wear UA uniforms. The company's logo—an interlocking U and A—is becoming almost as recognizable as the Nike swoosh.

Starting out, Plank sold his shirts using the only advantage he had—his athletic connections. Drawing on his own personal team experiences, "he knew at least 40 NFL players well enough to call and offer them the shirt." He was soon joined by another Maryland player, Kip Fulks, who played lacrosse. Fulks used the same relationship-based "six-degrees strategy" in the lacrosse world. (Today, Fulks is the company's President of Footwear and Innovation.) Believe it or not, the strategy worked. UA sales quickly gained momentum. However, selling products to teams and schools would take a business only so far. That's when Plank began to look at the mass market. In 2000, he made his first deal with a big-box store, Galyan's (which was eventually bought by Dick's Sporting Goods). Today, over 66 percent of UA's sales come from wholesaling to retailers such as Dick's and the Sports Authority. But they haven't forgotten where they started, either. The company has all-school deals with eight Division 1 schools. Although that

Protecting Our House
THROUGH INNOVATION

doesn't seem like a lot of revenue, such deals do "deliver brand visibility...."

Despite their marketing successes, innovation continues to be the name of the game at UA. How important is innovation to the company's heart and soul? Consider what you have to do to enter its new products lab. "Place your hands inside a state-of-the-art scanner that reads—and calculates—the exact pattern of the veins on the back. If it recognizes the pattern—which it does for only 20 out of 5,000 employees—you're in. If it doesn't, the vault-like door won't budge." In the unmarked lab at the company's headquarters campus in Baltimore, products being developed include a shirt that can monitor an athlete's heart rate, a running shoe designed like your spine, and a sweatshirt that repels water almost as well as a duck. There's also work being done on a shirt that may help air condition your body by reading your vital signs.

So what's next for Under Armour? With a motto that refers to protecting this house, innovation will continue to be important. Building a business beyond what it's known for—that is, what athletes wear next to their skin—is going to be challenging. However, Plank is completely devoted to Under Armour's focus on finding ways to use technology in all the company's products to make athletes better. He says, "There's not a product we can't build."

Discussion Questions

⭐ **8-14** What do you think of UA's approach to innovation? Would you expect to see this type of innovation in an athletic wear company? Explain.

⭐ **8-15** What do you think UA's culture might be like in regards to innovation? (Hint: Refer to the list on p. 254.)

⭐ **8-16** How might design thinking help UA improve its innovation efforts?

8-17 What's your interpretation of the company's philosophy posted prominently over the door of its design studio? What does it say about innovation? What could other companies learn from the way UA innovates?

CASE APPLICATION

Making Over Avon

Have you heard of Avon products? Have you purchased Avon products? We're guessing that you've likely heard of Avon, but not as likely to have purchased any Avon products, especially if you're young and you live in North America.[52]

As the world's top direct seller of cosmetics and beauty-related items, Avon Products has built a global brand and a portfolio of products that are marketed primarily through direct selling. Despite being based in the United States, the company's North American revenues have continued to decline. Currently, 86 percent of Avon's sales come from other global regions. The company's CEO is looking at what organizational changes need to be made to address the performance problems.

Poor performance forces change

Avon, founded in 1886 (yes, you read that right!), has been quite successful, up until the last five years. It was a company that got its start by recruiting women as door-to-door sellers of perfume and branching out from there. Today, there are some 6 million active sales representatives in 60 countries or territories around the world. Brazil is the company's biggest market. However, as the industry has changed, as competitors have become more aggressive, and as technology has drastically changed the sales model, Avon has been struggling. One sticky problem the company dealt with was an expensive bribery probe centered on the company's Chinese operations. The company voluntarily reported itself in 2008 to the Securities and Exchange Commission and the U.S. Justice Department. It took some six years for Avon to finally resolve the investigation into payments and gifts provided to government officials in China, and in late 2014 Avon agreed to pay $135 million in fines and civil penalties related to violating the Foreign Corrupt Practices Act. Another problem concerned the global rollout of a sophisticated order management system that had been in the works since 2009. Avon had initiated a massive software upgrade that would make tracking orders and compensation easier for its reps. However, the program was scrapped in 2013 after a trial rollout in Canada. A filing with the SEC said that the pilot program caused "a significant business disruption in that market, and did not show a clear return on investment." The issue: the technology worked, but it was so hard for Avon's salespeople to use that many reps left the company. Although Avon finally completed the first major overhaul of its Web site in 10 years, it now finds itself competing against more nimble e-commerce competitors such as Birchbox, Cult

Beauty, Bliss, Doobop, and even Chanel and Clinique. On top of struggling to compete in online sales and lacking a cohesive social media strategy, Avon is being pummeled by other industry giants including L'Oreal, Unilever, and Coty, all of whom have increased their efforts to hold on to market share domestically and have made new forays into profitable developing markets where Avon has long had its strongest sales.

Changing an organization involves looking at external market conditions as well as the internal aspects. Avon's CEO, Sherilyn McCoy, who was brought on board from Johnson & Johnson in 2012, has been struggling to find the keys to a successful turnaround. Her attempts to shape up things at Avon have revolved around overhauling the company's top management through firings, hirings, and reassignments; addressing declining sales, especially in the North American market through expanding the range of products sold (think colorful vegetable peelers) and getting more sales representatives into the system quickly; and trying to pinpoint who and what Avon wants to be.

The world has changed. Now Avon has to try to find the right combination of people, products, and technology to once again prosper.

Discussion Questions

8-18 What external forces for change do you see described in this case? Would you describe Avon's environment as more "calm waters" or "white-water rapids?" Explain.

8-19 Why would it be important for the CEO to look at those external forces when planning organizational change?

8-20 Why might it be difficult to change a company that's over 130 years old?

8-21 Avon is truly a global company. How might this affect the CEO's efforts to implement organizational change?

CASE APPLICATION #3

Stress Kills

We know that too much stress can be bad for our health and well-being. That connection proved itself painfully and tragically at France Télécom.[53] Over the last seven years, there have been more than 50 suicides of people who worked for the company. The situation captured the attention

of the worldwide media, the public, and the French government because many of the suicides and more than a dozen failed suicide attempts were attributed to work-related problems. The masks worn by these protesting Telecom employees say "Lombard has killed me." Didier Lombard was the chairman of the board and chief executive officer of France Télécom when the suicides took place. Although France has a higher suicide rate than any other large Western country, this scenario was particularly troublesome. The spate of suicides highlighted a quirk at the heart of French society: "Even with robust labor protection, workers see themselves as profoundly insecure in the face of globalization, with many complaining about being pushed beyond their limits." France isn't the only country dealing with worker suicides. Workplace conditions at China's Foxconn, the world's largest maker of electronic components (including the iPhone, iPod, and iPad), were strongly criticized after 11 Foxconn employees committed suicide.

Here is what recent surveys are telling us about employee stress:

- 75 percent of Americans say their stress levels are high or moderate.
- 44 percent of Americans say their stress levels have gone up in the last five years.
- 81 percent of HR managers say that employee fatigue is a bigger problem than in past years.
- More than 50 percent of U.S. and Canadian workers say that they feel fatigued at the end of a workday. At least 40 percent of those workers say that their jobs made them depressed.
- 20 percent of UK workers say they have taken sick leave brought on by stress, but 90 percent have lied about the real reason for staying home.
- 30 percent of managers say they're more stressed at work today than a year ago.
- Reasons employees find work stressful: low pay, commuting, excessive workload, fear of being fired/laid off, annoying coworkers, and difficult bosses.

As you can see, stress and its effects on workers are (and should be) a serious concern for employers. When excessive pressure is placed on people from overwhelming demands or constraints, they often feel they've got no choices or options. At France Télécom, the wave of employee suicides was cause for concern. Trade union leaders blamed "the allegedly brutal management culture of a company which has transformed itself over a decade from a ponderous state utility to a leading telecommunications company." However, for months, France Télécom management "dismissed the suicides as a contagious fad among its workforce." Unions then criticized the company for its poor choice of language.

The Paris prosecutor's office opened an investigation of the company over accusations of psychological harassment. The judicial inquiry stemmed from a complaint by the union Solidaires Unitaires Démocratiques against France

Change → Stress → Serious Effects

Télécom's former chief executive and two members of his top management team. The complaint accused management of conducting a "pathogenic restructuring." Excerpts of the inspector's report, although not made public, were published in the French media. It described a situation in which the company used various forms of psychological pressure in an effort to eliminate 22,000 jobs over a two-year period. Company doctors alerted management about the possible psychological dangers of the stress that could accompany such drastic change. Despite these findings, a company lawyer denied that France Télécom had systematically pressured employees to leave.

Company executives realized that they needed to take drastic measures to address the issue. One of the first changes was a new CEO, Stéphane Richard, who said his priority "would be to rebuild the morale of staff who have been through trauma, suffering and much worse." The company also halted some workplace practices identified as being particularly disruptive, like involuntary transfers. It is also encouraging more supportive practices, including working from home. A company spokesperson says the company has completed two of six agreements with unions that cover a wide range of workplace issues like mobility and work/life balance and stress. Despite these measures, another France Télécom worker committed suicide. A union official suggested that "the man had struggled with being made to frequently change jobs." The worker had written to management on several occasions about the situation and was believed to have had no reply. France Télécom's CEO, Stéphane Richard, promised a thorough investigation into the suicide. "We need to analyze in great depth and detail what happened. It is my intention that this investigation will be particularly painstaking and transparent."

Discussion Questions

8-22 What is your reaction to the situation described in this case? What factors, both inside the company and externally, appear to have contributed to this situation?

8-23 What appeared to be happening in France Télécom's workplace? What stress symptoms might managers have looked for to be alerted to a problem?

8-24 Should managers be free to make decisions that are in the best interests of the company without worrying about employee reactions? Discuss. What are the implications for managing change?

8-25 What are France Télécom's executives doing to address the situation? Do you think it's enough? Are there other actions they might take? If so, describe those. If not, why not?

8-26 What could other companies and managers learn from this situation?

Endnotes

1. A. Weintraub and M. Tirrell, "Eli Lilly's Drug Assembly Line," *Bloomberg BusinessWeek*, March 8, 2010, 56–57.

2. K. Grzbowska, "The Social Aspect of Introducing Changes into the Organization," *International Journals of Human Resources Development and Management*, February 2, 2007, 67; and I. M. Jawahar and G. L. McLaughlin, "Toward a Descriptive Stakeholder Theory: An Organizational Life Cycle Approach," *Academy of Management Review*, July 2001, 397–415.

3. E. Shannon, "Agent of Change," *Time*, March 4, 2002, 17; B. Kenney, "SLA Head Shaffer Resigns Abruptly: Did 'Change Agent' Move Too Fast in Aggressive Restructuring?" *Library Journal*, March 15, 2002, 17–19; and T. Mudd, "Rescue Mission," *Industry Week*, May 1, 2000, 30–37.

4. The idea for these metaphors came from P. Vaill, *Managing as a Performing Art: New Ideas for a World of Chaotic Change* (San Francisco: Jossey Bass, 1989).

5. K. Lewin, *Field Theory in Social Science* (New York: Harper & Row, 1951).

6. R. E. Levasseur, "People Skills: Change Management Tools—Lewin's Change Model," *Interfaces*, August 2001, 71–74.

7. L. S. Lüscher and M. W. Lewis, "Organizational Change and Managerial Sensemaking: Working Through Paradox," *Academy of Management Journal* (April 2008), 221–40; F. Buckley and K. Monks, "Responding to Managers' Learning Needs in an Edge-of-Chaos Environment: Insights from Ireland," *Journal of Management* (April 2008): 146–63; and G. Hamel, "Take It Higher," *Fortune*, February 5, 2001, 169–70.

8. D. Lieberman, "Nielsen Media Has Cool Head at the Top," *USA Today*, March 27, 2006, 3B.

9. From the Past to the Present box based on D. A. Wren and A. G. Bedeian, *The Evolution of Management Thought*, 6th ed. (Hoboken, NJ: John Wiley & Sons, 2009); "Biography and Quotes of Kurt Lewin," *About.com, psychology. about.com* (July 15, 2009); and K. T. Lewin, "The Dynamics of Group Action," *Educational Leadership*, January 1944, 195–200.

10. L. Freifeld, "Paddle to Collaborate," *Training* (November–December 2010), 6.

11. S. Hicks, "What Is Organization Development?" *Training and Development* (August 2000): 65; and H. Hornstein, "Organizational Development and Change Management: Don't Throw the Baby Out with the Bath Water," *Journal of Applied Behavioral Science* (June 2001): 223–27.

12. J. Wolfram and S. Minahan, "A New Metaphor for Organization Development," *Journal of Applied Behavioral Science* (June 2006): 227–43.

13. See, for instance, H. B. Jones, "Magic, Meaning, and Leadership: Weber's Model and the Empirical Literature," *Human Relations*, June 2001, 753.

14. G. Akin and I. Palmer, "Putting Metaphors to Work for a Change in Organizations," *Organizational Dynamics*, Winter 2000, 67–79.

15. J. Grieves, "Skills, Values or Impression Management: Organizational Change and the Social Processes of Leadership, Change Agent Practice, and Process Consultation," *Journal of Management Development* (May 2000): 407.

16. M. McMaster, "Team Building Tips," *Sales & Marketing Management*, January 2002, 140; and "How To: Executive Team Building," *Training and Development* (January 2002): 16.

17. S. Shinn, "Stairway to Reinvention," *BizEd*, January–February 2010, 6; M. Scott, "A Stairway to Marketing Heaven," *BusinessWeek*, November 2, 2009, 17; and The Fun Theory, http://thefuntheory .com (November 10, 2009).

18. See, for example, J. Robison and D. Jones, "Overcoming the Fear of Change," *Gallup Management Journal Online*, January 7, 2011; J. D. Ford, L. W. Ford, and A. D'Amelio, "Resistance to Change: The Rest of the Story," *Academy of Management Review*, April 2008, 362–77; A. Deutschman, "Making Change: Why Is It So Hard to Change Our Ways?" *Fast Company*, May 2005, 52–62; S. B. Silverman, C. E. Pogson, and A. B. Cober, "When Employees at Work Don't Get It: A Model for Enhancing Individual Employee Change in Response to Performance Feedback," *Academy of Management Executive*, May 2005, 135–47; C. E. Cunningham, C. A. Woodward, H. S. Shannon, J. MacIntosh, B. Lendrum, D. Rosenbloom, and J. Brown, "Readiness for Organizational Change: A Longitudinal Study of Workplace, Psychological and Behavioral Correlates," *Journal of Occupational and Organizational Psychology* (December 2002): 377–92; M. A. Korsgaard, H. J. Sapienza, and D. M. Schweiger, "Beaten Before Begun: The Role of Procedural Justice in Planning Change," *Journal of Management* 28, no. 4 (2002): 497–516; R. Kegan and L. L. Lahey, "The Real Reason People Won't Change," *Harvard Business Review*, November 2001, 85–92; S. K. Piderit, "Rethinking Resistance and Recognizing Ambivalence: A Multidimensional View of Attitudes Toward an Organiza-tional Change," *Academy of Management Review*, October 2000, 783–94; C. R. Wanberg and J. T. Banas, "Predictors and Outcomes of Openness to Changes in a Reorganizing Workplace," *Journal of Applied Psychology* (February 2000): 132–42; A. A. Armenakis and A. G. Bedeian, "Organizational Change: A Review of Theory and Research in the 1990s," *Journal of Management* 25, no. 3 (1999): 293–315; and B. M. Staw, "Counterforces to Change," in P.S. Goodman and Associates (eds.), *Change in Organizations* (San Francisco: Jossey-Bass, 1982), 87–121.

19. A. Reichers, J. P. Wanous, and J. T. Austin, "Understanding and Managing Cynicism about Organizational Change," *Academy of Management Executive*, February 1997, 48–57; P. Strebel, "Why Do Employees Resist Change?" *Harvard Business Review*, May–June 1996, 86–92; and J. P. Kotter and L. A. Schlesinger, "Choosing Strategies for Change," *Harvard Business Review*, March–April 1979, 107–09.

20. D. Heath and C. Heath, "Passion Provokes Action," *Fast Company*, February 2011, 28–30.

21. S. D'Mello, "Stress: The Global Economic Downturn Has Taken Its Toll on Employees. What's the Impact for Organizations?" A 2011/2012 Kenexa® High Performance Institute Worktrends™ Report, http://khpi.com/documents/ KHPI-WorkTrends-Report-Stress, 2011/2012; and "Stress: By the Numbers," *AARP The Magazine*, September/October 2011, 30.

22. Adapted from the UK National Work-Stress Network, www. workstress.net.

23. R. S. Schuler, "Definition and Conceptualization of Stress in Organizations," *Organizational Behavior and Human Performance*, April 1980, 191.

24. J. Yang and S. Ward, "Which Is the More-Stress Inducing Aspect of Your Job?" *USA Today*, September 11, 2011, 1B.

25. See, for example, "Stressed Out: Extreme Job Stress: Survivors' Tales," *Wall Street Journal* January 17, 2001, B1.

26. See, for instance, S. Bates, "Expert: Don't Overlook Employee Burnout," *HR Magazine*, August 2003, 14.

27. Question of Ethics box based on D. Cole, "The Big Chill," *US News & World Report*, December 6, 2004, EE2–EE5.

28. H. Benson, "Are You Working Too Hard?" *Harvard Business Review*, November 2005, 53–58; B. Cryer, R. McCraty, and D. Childre, "Pull the Plug on Stress," *Harvard Business Review*, July 2003, 102–07; C. Daniels, "The Last Taboo"; C. L. Cooper and S. Cartwright, "Healthy Mind, Healthy Organization—A Proactive Approach to Occupational Stress," *Human Relations*, April 1994, 455–71; C. A. Heaney et al., "Industrial Relations, Worksite Stress Reduction and Employee Well-Being: A Participatory Action Research Investigation," *Journal of Organizational Behavior* (September 1993): 495–510; C. D. Fisher, "Boredom at Work: A Neglected Concept," *Human Relations*, March 1993, 395–417; and S. E. Jackson, "Participation in Decision Making as a Strategy for Reducing Job-Related Strain," *Journal of Applied Psychology* (February 1983): 3–19.

29. T. Barton, "Brave Face," *Employee Benefits*, January 2011, 41; and "Employee Assistance Programs," *HR Magazine*, May 2003, 143.

30. S. Barrett, "Employee Assistance Programs," *Employee Benefits*, January 2011, 49–52; "EAPs with the Most," *Managing Benefits Plans*, March 2003, 8; and K. Tyler, "Helping Employees Cope with Grief," *HR Magazine*, September 2003, 55–58.

31. N. Faba, "The EAP Problem," *Benefits Canada*, March 2011, 7; D. A. Masi, "Redefining the EAP Field," *Journal of Workplace Behavioral Health* (January–March 2011): 1–9; R. M. Weiss, "Brinksmanship Redux: Employee Assistance Programs' Precursors and Prospects," *Employee Responsibilities & Rights Journal* (December 2010): 325–43; and F. Hansen, "Employee Assistance Programs (EAPs) Grow and Expand Their Reach," *Compensation and Benefits Review*, March–April 2000, 13.

32. A. Saha-Bubna and M. Jarzemsky, "MasterCard President Is Named CEO," *Wall Street Journal*, April 13, 2010, C3; and S. Vandebook, "Quotable," *IndustryWeek*, April 2010, 18.

33. R. M. Kanter, "Think Outside the Building," *Harvard Business Review*, March 2010, 34; T. Brown, "Change By Design," *BusinessWeek*, October 5, 2009, 54–56; J. E. Perry-Smith and C. E. Shalley, "The Social Side of Creativity: A Static and Dynamic Social Network Perspective," *Academy of Management Review*, January 2003, 89–106; and P. K. Jagersma, "Innovate or Die: It's Not Easy, but It Is Possible to Enhance Your Organization's Ability to Innovate," *Journal of Business Strategy* (January–February 2003): 25–28.

34. Fast Company staff, "The World's 50 Most Innovative Companies," *Fast Company*, March 2011, 66+; and G. Colvin, "The World's Most Admired Companies," *Fortune*, March 21, 2011, 109+.

35. These definitions are based on T. M. Amabile, *Creativity in Context* (Boulder, CO: Westview Press, 1996).

36. C. Salter, "Mattel Learns to 'Throw the Bunny,'" *Fast Company*, November 2002, 22; and L. Bannon, "Think Tank in Toyland," *Wall Street Journal*, June 6, 2002, B1, B3.

37. C. Vogel and J. Cagan, *Creating Breakthrough Products: Innovation from Product Planning to Program Approval* (Upper Saddle River, NJ: Prentice Hall, 2002).

38. R. Tate, "Google Couldn't Kill 20 Percent Time Even If It Wanted To," wired.com, August 21, 2013; C. Mims, "Google Engineers Insist 20% Time Is Not Dead—It's Just Turned into 120% Time," qz.com, August 16, 2013; R. Neimi, "Inside the Moonshot Factory," *Bloomberg BusinessWeek*, May 22, 2013, 56–61; and A. Foege, "The Trouble with Tinkering Time," *Wall Street Journal*, January 19/20, 2013, C3.

39. R. W. Woodman, J. E. Sawyer, and R. W. Griffin, "Toward a Theory of Organizational Creativity," *Academy of Management Review*, April 1993, 293–321.

40. T. M. Egan, "Factors Influencing Individual Creativity in the Workplace: An Examination of Quantitative Empirical Research," *Advances in Developing Human Resources*, May 2005, 160–81; N. Madjar, G. R. Oldham, and M. G. Pratt, "There's No Place Like Home? The Contributions of Work and Nonwork Creativity Support to Employees' Creative Performance," *Academy of Management Journal* (August 2002): 757–67; T. M. Amabile, C. N. Hadley, and S. J. Kramer, "Creativity Under the Gun," *Harvard Business Review*, August 2002, 52–61; J. B. Sorensen and T. E. Stuart, "Aging, Obsolescence, and Organizational Innovation," *Administrative Science Quarterly*, March 2000, 81–112; G.R. Oldham and A. Cummings, "Employee Creativity: Personal and Contextual Factors at Work," *Academy of Management Journal* (June 1996): 607–34; and F. Damanpour, "Organizational Innovation: A Meta-Analysis of Effects of Determinants and Moderators," *Academy of Management Journal* (September 1991): 555–90.

41. P. R. Monge, M. D. Cozzens, and N. S. Contractor, "Communication and Motivational Predictors of the Dynamics of Organizational Innovations," *Organization Science*, May 1992, 250–74.

42. T. M. Amabile, C. N. Hadley, and S. J. Kramer, "Creativity Under the Gun."

43. N. Madjar, G. R. Oldham, and M. G. Pratt, "There's No Place Like Home? The Contributions of Work and Nonwork Creativity Support to Employees' Creative Performance."

44. See, for instance, J. E. Perry-Smith, "Social Yet Creative: The Role of Social Relationships in Facilitating Individual Creativity," *Academy of Management Journal* (February 2006): 85–101; C. E. Shalley, J. Zhou, and G. R. Oldham, "The Effects of Personal and Contextual Characteristics on Creativity: Where Should We Go from Here?" *Journal of Management* 30, no. 6 (2004): 933–58; J. E. Perry-Smith and C. E. Shalley, "The Social Side of Creativity: A Static and Dynamic Social Network Perspective"; J. M. George and J. Zhou, "When Openness to Experience and Conscientiousness Are Related to Creative Behavior: An Interactional Approach," *Journal of Applied Psychology* (June 2001): 513–24; J. Zhou, "Feedback Valence, Feedback Style, Task Autonomy, and Achievement Orientation: Interactive Effects on Creative Behavior," *Journal of Applied Psychology* 83 (1998): 261–76; T. M. Amabile, R. Conti, H. Coon, J. Lazenby, and M. Herron, "Assessing the Work Environment for Creativity," *Academy of Management Journal* (October 1996): 1154–84; S. G. Scott and R. A. Bruce, "Determinants of Innovative People: A Path Model of Individual Innovation in the Workplace," *Academy of Management Journal* (June 1994): 580–607; R. Moss Kanter, "When a Thousand Flowers Bloom: Structural, Collective, and Social Conditions for Innovation in Organization," in B. M. Staw and L. L. Cummings (eds.), *Research in Organizational Behavior*, vol. 10 (Greenwich, CT: JAI Press, 1988), 169–211; and Amabile, *Creativity in Context*.

45. J. McGregor, "The World's Most Innovative Companies," *BusinessWeek*, April 24, 2006, 70.

46. Ibid.

47. J. Ramos, "Producing Change That Lasts," *Across the Board*, March 1994, 29–33; T. Stjernberg and A. Philips, "Organizational Innovations in a Long-Term Perspective: Legitimacy and Souls-of-Fire as Critical Factors of Change and Viability," *Human Relations*, October 1993, 1193–2023; and J. M. Howell and C. A. Higgins, "Champions of Change," *Business Quarterly*, Spring 1990, 31–32.

48. J. Liedtka and T. Ogilvie, *Designing for Growth: A Design Thinking Tool Kit for Managers*, (New York: Columbia Business School Press, 2011).

49. R. E. Silverman, "Companies Change Their Way of Thinking," *Wall Street Journal*, June 7, 2012, B8; and R. L. Martin, "The Innovation Catalysts," *Harvard Business Review*, June 2011, 82–87.

50. Based on J. E. Newman and T. A. Beehr, "Personal and Organizational Strategies for Handling Job Stress," *Personnel Psychology*, Spring 1979, 1–38; M. T. Matteson and J. M. Ivancevich, "Individual Stress Management Interventions: Evaluation of Techniques," *Journal of Management Psychology* (January 1987): 24–30; and K. M. Richardson and H. R. Rothstein, "Effects of Occupational Stress Management Intervention Programs: A Meta-Analysis," *Journal of Occupational Health Psychology* (January 2008): 69–93.

51. S. Ember, "Under Armour Is Swinging for the Stars," *New York Times Online*, June 14, 2015; 2014 Annual Report, "Letter to the Shareholders," http://files.shareholder.com/downloads/UARM/165448209x0x816471/3BEBC664-8584-4F22-AC0B-844CB2949814/UA_2014_Annual_Report.PDF, January 31, 2015; B. Horovitz, "In Search of Next Big Thing," *USA Today*, July 9, 2012, 1B+; Press Release, "Under Armour Reports Fourth Quarter Net Revenues Growth of 34% and Fourth Quarter EPS Growth of 40%," *investor.underarmour.com*, January 26, 2012; D. Roberts, "Under Armour Gets Serious," *Fortune*, November 7, 2011, 153–62; E. Olson, "Under Armour Applies Its Muscle to Shoes," *New York Times Online*, August 8, 2011; M. Townsend, "Under Armour's Daring Half-Court Shot," *Bloomberg BusinessWeek*, November 1–7, 2010, 24–25; and E. Olson, "Under Armour Wants to Dress Athletic Young Women," *New York Times Online*, August 31, 2010.

52. N. Turner and L. Coleman-Lochner, "Avon Shares Fall on Report That Buyers Haven't Materialized," http://www.bloomberg.com/news/articles/2015-05-05/avon-shares-plummet-on-report-that-bidders-haven-t-materialized, May 5, 2015; L. Rupp and L. Coleman-Lochner, "Avon Profit Misses Estimates as North American Sales Suffer," http://www.bloomberg.com/news/articles/2015-04-30/avon-misses-earnings-estimates-as-north-american-sales-suffer, April 30, 2015; E. Byron and J. S. Lublin, "Lackluster Avon Explores Makeover," *Wall Street Journal*, April 28, 2015, A1+; B. Sutherland, "Overhaul of Avon U.S. May Be Better Than Selling the Unit," http://www.bloomberg.com/news/articles/2015-04-16/avon-u-s-overhaul-may-be-better-path-than-unit-sale-real-m-a, April 15, 2015; J. S. Lublin and E. Byron, "Avon Explores Strategic Alternatives," *Wall Street Journal*, http://www.wsj.com/articles/avon-explores-strategic-alternatives-1429030371, April 14, 2015; P. Wahba, "Avon's in a Ding-Dong Battle to Stay in Business," http://fortune.com/tag/avon/, April 14, 2015; P. J. Henning, "Foreign Bribery Cases That Can Drag on and On," *New York Times Online*, December 22, 2014; The Associated Press, "Avon Products Announces Another Round of Job Cuts," *New York Times Online*, June 24, 2014; D. Henschen, "Avon Pulls Plug on $125 Million SAP Project," http://www.informationweek.com/software/enterprise-applications/avon-pulls-plug-on-125-million-sap-project/d/d-id/1113061, December 12, 2013; and A. Martin, "Avon Chairwoman to Quit Earlier Than Expected," *New York Times Online*, October 5, 2012.

53. K. Dunn, "Employee Turnover and Suicide: It Turns out the Response to Either Is the Same," *HR Capitalist Online*, May 9, 2011; S. Mahoney, "Stress Less, Accomplish More," *Good Housekeeping*, May 2010, 57; A. Chrisafis, "France Telecom Worker Kills Himself in Office Car Park," www.guardian.co.uk (April 27, 2011); *Reuters*, "France Telecom to Probe Employee Suicide by Fire," www.trust.org (April 27, 2011); A. R. Carey and P. Trap, "Aspect of the Job That Workers Find the Most Stressful," *USA Today*, April 20, 2011, 1A; "Survey," *Shape*, April 2011, 48; M. V. Rafter, "The Yawning of New Era," *Workforce Management Online*, December 2010; C. Hausman, "Millions of U.K. Workers Lie to Bosses about Stress-Induced Days," *Global Ethics Online*, November 8, 2010; E. Holbrook, "Beneath the Bell Jar: Companies Confront a Rise in Workplace Suicides," *Risk Management*, November 2010, 6–8; "Survey: 30 Percent of Managers under More Stress," *Workforce Management Online*, September 22, 2010; M. Colchester, "France Télécom Faces Inquiry over Suicides," *New York Times Online*, April 12, 2010; M. Saltmarsh, "France Télécom Suicides Prompt an Investigation," *New York Times Online*, April 9, 2010; E. Frauenheim, "Suicides Spur Management Shake-Up at France Télécom," *Workforce Management*, March 2010, 6–8; C. Stievenard, "France's Approach to Workplace 'Bullying,'" *Workforce Management Online*, www.workforce.com (March 2010); R. Bender and M. Colchester, "Morale Is Priority for France Télécom," *Wall Street Journal*, February 4, 2010, B2; R. Bender and M. Colchester, "France Télécom Focuses on Morale," *Wall Street Journal Online*, online.wsj.com, February 4, 2010; *The Associated Press*, "Executive Quits after Suicides at France Télécom," *New York Times Online*, October 6, 2009; J. Lichfield and A. Mauviel, *The Independent*, www.independent.co.uk, September 30, 2009; and D. Jolly and M. Saltmarsh, "Suicides in France Put Focus on Workplace," *New York Times Online*, September 30, 2009.

Foundations of Individual Behavior

Management Myth
Myth
Myth

A good manager treats all employees the same.

OJO Images Ltd/Alamy

Management **DEBUNKED?** Myth

One thing you've probably realized over the years is how differently you and your friends interact with and react to life's situations. Some friends are laid-back; others are more anxious. Some are good at reading emotional clues; others are, well, clueless. The same is true of the people a manager manages. That's why a good manager works to get to know the unique individual characteristics of the people on his or her team to be able to effectively manage each of them.

MOST

organizations want to attract and retain employees with the right attitudes and personality. They want people who show up and work hard, get along with coworkers and customers, have good attitudes, and exhibit good work behaviors in other ways. But as you're probably already aware, people don't always behave like that "ideal" employee. They may job hop at the first opportunity or they may post critical comments in blogs. People differ in their behaviors and even the same person can behave one way one day and a completely different way another day. For instance, haven't you seen family members, friends, or coworkers behave in ways that prompted you to wonder: Why did they do that? In this chapter, we look at four psychological aspects—attitudes, personality, perception, and learning—and how these things can help managers understand the behavior of those people they work with. We conclude the chapter by looking at contemporary behavioral issues facing managers. ●

Learning Outcomes

What Are the Focus and Goals of Organizational Behavior?

9-1 Identify the focus and goals of organizational behavior (OB).

> Managers need good people skills.

The material in this and the next four chapters draws heavily on the field of study that's known as *organizational behavior (OB)*. Although it's concerned with the subject of **behavior**—that is, the actions of people—**organizational behavior** is the study of the actions of people at work.

One of the challenges in understanding organizational behavior is that it addresses issues that aren't obvious. Like an iceberg, OB has a small visible dimension and a much larger hidden portion. (See Exhibit 9–1.) What we see when we look at an organization is its visible aspects: strategies, objectives, policies and procedures, structure, technology, formal authority relationships, and chain of command. But under the surface are other elements that managers need to understand—elements that also influence how employees behave at work. As we'll show, OB provides managers with considerable insights into these important, but hidden, aspects of the organization.

behavior
The actions of people

organizational behavior
The study of the actions of people at work

What Is the Focus of OB?

Organizational behavior focuses on three major areas:

1. *Individual behavior.* Based predominantly on contributions from psychologists, this area includes such topics as attitudes, personality, perception, learning, and motivation.
2. *Group behavior*, which includes norms, roles, team building, leadership, and conflict. Our knowledge about groups comes basically from the work of sociologists and social psychologists.
3. *Organizational* aspects including structure, culture, and human resource policies and practices. We've addressed organizational aspects in previous chapters. In this chapter we'll look at individual behavior, and in the following chapter we'll look at group behavior.

Exhibit 9–1 Organization as Iceberg

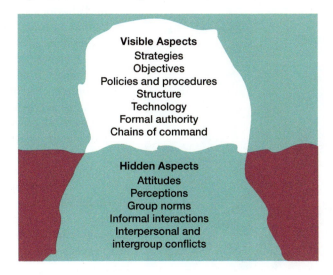

Visible Aspects
Strategies
Objectives
Policies and procedures
Structure
Technology
Formal authority
Chains of command

Hidden Aspects
Attitudes
Perceptions
Group norms
Informal interactions
Interpersonal and intergroup conflicts

employee productivity
A performance measure of both work efficiency and effectiveness

absenteeism
The failure to show up for work

turnover
Voluntary and involuntary permanent withdrawal from an organization

organizational citizenship behavior
Discretionary behavior that's not part of an employee's formal job requirements, but that promotes the effective functioning of the organization

job satisfaction
An employee's general attitude toward his or her job

workplace misbehavior
Any intentional employee behavior that is potentially harmful to the organization or individuals within the organization

What Are the Goals of Organizational Behavior?

The goals of OB are to *explain, predict,* and *influence* behavior. Managers need to be able to *explain* why employees engage in some behaviors rather than others, *predict* how employees will respond to various actions and decisions, and *influence* how employees behave.

SIX important employee behaviors that managers are specifically concerned with explaining, predicting, and influencing include the following:

(1) **Employee productivity**—a performance measure of both work efficiency and effectiveness. Managers want to know what factors will influence the efficiency and effectiveness of employees.

(2) **Absenteeism**—the failure to show up for work. It's difficult for work to get done if employees don't show up. Studies have shown that the total of all major types of absences cost organizations an average 35 percent of payroll, with unscheduled absences costing companies around $660 per employee per year.[1] Although absenteeism can't be totally eliminated, excessive levels have a direct and immediate impact on the organization's functioning.

(3) **Turnover**—the voluntary and involuntary permanent withdrawal from an organization. It can be a problem because of increased recruiting, selection, training costs, and work disruptions. Just like absenteeism, managers can never eliminate turnover, but it is something they want to minimize, especially among high-performing employees.

(4) **Organizational citizenship behavior**—discretionary behavior that's not part of an employee's formal job requirements, but which promotes the effective functioning of the organization.[2] Examples of good OCB include helping others on one's work team, volunteering for extended job activities, avoiding unnecessary conflicts, and making constructive statements about one's work group and the organization. Organizations need individuals who will do more than their usual job duties and the evidence indicates that organizations that have such employees outperform those that don't.[3] However, drawbacks to OCB arise if employees experience work overload, stress, and work-family conflicts.[4]

(5) **Job satisfaction**—an employee's general attitude toward his or her job. Although job satisfaction is an attitude rather than a behavior, it's an outcome that concerns many managers because satisfied employees are more likely to show up for work, have higher levels of performance, and stay with an organization.

Job satisfaction is an important concern of managers at Gilead Sciences, a biopharmaceutical firm that develops new medicines for HIV/AIDS and other unmet medical needs. Highly satisfied employees like research scientist Darryl Kato, shown here, are essential to Gilead in achieving its goal of improving the lives of people who suffer from life-threatening diseases.

David Paul Morris/Bloomberg/Getty Images

(6) **Workplace misbehavior**—any intentional employee behavior that is potentially harmful to the organization or individuals within the organization. Workplace misbehavior shows up in organizations in four ways: deviance, aggression, antisocial behavior, and violence.[5] Such behaviors can range from playing loud music just to irritate coworkers, to verbal aggression, to sabotaging work, all of which can create havoc in any organization.

In the following pages, you'll get a better understanding of how four psychological factors—employee attitudes, personality, perception, and learning—can help managers predict and explain these six employee behaviors.

What Role Do Attitudes Play in Job Performance?

9-2 Explain the role that attitudes play in job performance.

You sure have an attitude!

Attitudes are evaluative statements, either favorable or unfavorable, concerning objects, people, or events. They reflect how an individual feels about something. When a person says, "I like my job," he or she is expressing an attitude about work.

What Are the Three Components of an Attitude?

An attitude is made up of three components: cognition, affect, and behavior.[6]

- The **cognitive component** of an attitude is made up of the beliefs, opinions, knowledge, and information held by a person. For example, Brad feels strongly that smoking is unhealthy.
- The **affective component** is the emotional or feeling part of an attitude. This component would be reflected in the statement by Brad, "I don't like Erica because she smokes." Cognition and affect can lead to behavioral outcomes.
- The **behavioral component** of an attitude refers to an intention to behave in a certain way toward someone or something. So, to continue our example, Brad might choose to avoid Erica because of his feelings about her smoking habit.

Looking at attitudes as being made up of three components—cognition, affect, and behavior— helps to illustrate their complexity and helps us better understand what "precedes" someone's response, reaction, or behavior. But keep in mind that when people use the term "attitude"—as in, "that person has a bad attitude" or "I'm glad your attitude towards this is positive"—they're usually referring only to the actual affective (emotional) component. Remember that managers are trying to explain, predict, and influence people's behavior, and knowing that there's more to "attitude" than just the emotional part helps us better know how to do just that.

What Attitudes Might Employees Hold?

Naturally, managers are not interested in every attitude an employee might hold. Rather, they're specifically interested in the following:[7]

Job-Related Attitudes

- Job satisfaction is an employee's general attitude toward his or her job. When people speak of employee attitudes, more often than not they mean job satisfaction.
- **Job involvement** is the degree to which an employee identifies with his or her job, actively participates in it, and considers his or her job performance important for self-worth.
- **Organizational commitment** represents an employee's orientation toward the organization in terms of his or her loyalty to, identification with, and involvement in the organization.

A concept associated with job attitudes generating widespread interest is **employee engagement**, which happens when employees are connected to, satisfied with, and enthusiastic about their jobs.[8] Highly engaged employees are passionate about and deeply connected to their work. Disengaged employees have essentially "checked out" and don't care. They show up for work, but have no energy or passion for it. A global study of more than 12,000 employees found that the top five factors contributing to employee engagement were:[9]

1. Respect
2. Type of work
3. Work/life balance
4. Providing good service to customers
5. Base pay

Having highly engaged employees produces both benefits and costs. Highly engaged employees are two-and-a-half times more likely to be top performers than their less-engaged

attitudes
Evaluative statements, either favorable or unfavorable, concerning objects, people, or events

cognitive component
The part of an attitude made up of the beliefs, opinions, knowledge, and information held by a person

affective component
The part of an attitude that's the emotional or feeling part

behavioral component
The part of an attitude that refers to an intention to behave in a certain way toward someone or something

job involvement
The degree to which an employee identifies with his or her job, actively participates in it, and considers his or her job performance important for self-worth

organizational commitment
An employee's orientation toward the organization in terms of his or her loyalty to, identification with, and involvement in the organization

employee engagement
When employees are connected to, satisfied with, and enthusiastic about their jobs

cognitive dissonance
Any incompatibility or inconsistency between attitudes or between behavior and attitudes

coworkers. In addition, companies with highly engaged employees have higher retention rates, which help keep recruiting and training costs low. And both of these outcomes—higher performance and lower costs—contribute to superior financial performance.[10]

Do Individuals' Attitudes and Behaviors Need to Be Consistent?

What I believe is what I do ... I hope.

Did you ever notice how people change what they say so that it doesn't contradict what they do? Perhaps a friend of yours had consistently argued that American-manufactured cars were poorly built and that he'd never own anything but a foreign import. Then his parents gave him a late-model American-made car, and suddenly they weren't so bad. Or when going through sorority rush, a new freshman believes that sororities are good and that pledging a sorority is important. If she's not accepted by a sorority, however, she may say, "Sorority life isn't all it's cracked up to be anyway."

Research generally concludes that people seek consistency among their attitudes and between their attitudes and their behavior.[11] Individuals try to reconcile differing attitudes and align their attitudes and behavior so that they appear rational and consistent. How? By altering their attitudes or their behavior, *or* by developing a rationalization for the discrepancy.

What Is Cognitive Dissonance Theory?

Can we assume from this consistency principle that an individual's behavior can always be predicted if we know his or her attitude on a subject? The answer isn't a simple "yes" or "no." Why? Cognitive dissonance theory.

Cognitive dissonance theory, proposed by Leon Festinger in the 1950s, sought to explain the relationship between attitudes and behavior.[12] **Cognitive dissonance** is any incompatibility or inconsistency between attitudes or between behavior and attitudes. The theory argued that inconsistency is uncomfortable and that individuals will try to reduce the discomfort and, thus, the dissonance.

Of course, no one can avoid dissonance. You know you should floss your teeth every day, but don't do it. There's an inconsistency between attitude and behavior. How do people cope with cognitive dissonance? The theory proposed that how hard we try to reduce dissonance is determined by three things: (1) the *importance* of the factors creating the dissonance, (2) the degree of *influence* the individual believes he or she has over those factors, and (3) the *rewards* that may be involved in dissonance.

If the factors creating the dissonance are relatively unimportant, the pressure to correct the inconsistency will be low. However, if those factors are important, individuals may change their behavior, conclude that the dissonant behavior isn't so important, change their attitude, or identify compatible factors that outweigh the dissonant ones.

How much influence individuals believe they have over the factors also affects their reaction to the dissonance. If they perceive the dissonance is something about which they have no choice, they won't be receptive to attitude change or feel a need to do so. If, for example, the dissonance-producing behavior was required as a result of a manager's order, the pressure to reduce dissonance would be less than if the behavior had been performed voluntarily. Although dissonance exists, it can be rationalized and justified by the need to follow the manager's orders—that is, the person had no choice or control.

People may believe they are safe drivers yet create potentially unsafe road conditions by driving and texting at the same time. To reduce this cognitive dissonance, they may stop their habit of driving and texting or they may rationalize that it doesn't pose a threat to others' safety and that they are in control of the situation.

Robert Crum/Shutterstock

Finally, rewards also influence the degree to which individuals are motivated to reduce dissonance. Coupling high dissonance with high rewards tends to reduce the discomfort by motivating the individual to believe that there is consistency.

Let's look at an example. Tracey Ford, a corporate manager, believes strongly that no company should lay off employees. Unfortunately, Tracey has to make decisions that trade off her company's strategic direction against her convictions on layoffs. She knows that organizational restructuring means some jobs may no longer be needed. She also knows layoffs are in the best economic interest of her firm. What will she do? Undoubtedly, Tracey is experiencing a high degree of cognitive dissonance. Let's explain her behavior.

1. IMPORTANCE OF FACTORS: Because of the *importance* of the issues in this example, she can't ignore the inconsistency. To deal with her dilemma, she can follow several steps. She can change her behavior (lay off employees). Or she can reduce dissonance by concluding that the dissonant behavior is not so important after all ("I've got to make a living, and in my role as a decision maker, I often have to place the good of my company above that of individual organizational members"). She might also change her attitude ("There is nothing wrong in laying off employees"). Finally, another choice would be to seek out more consonant elements to outweigh the dissonant ones ("The long-term benefits to the surviving employees from our restructuring more than offset the associated costs").

2. DEGREE OF INFLUENCE: The *degree of influence* that Tracey believes she has also impacts how she reacts to the dissonance. If she perceives the dissonance to be uncontrollable—something about which she has no choice—she's less likely to feel she needs to change her attitude. If, for example, her boss told her that she had to lay off employees, the pressure to reduce dissonance would be less than if Tracey was performing the behavior voluntarily. Dissonance would exist but it could be rationalized and justified. This tendency illustrates why it's critical in today's organizations for leaders to establish an ethical culture. With the leaders' influence and support, employees won't feel as much dissonance when faced with decisions of whether to act ethically or unethically.[13]

3. REWARDS: Finally, *rewards* also influence how likely Tracy is to reduce dissonance. High dissonance, when accompanied by high rewards, tends to reduce the tension inherent in the dissonance. The reward reduces dissonance by adding to the consistency side of the individual's balance sheet. Tracey might feel because she is well compensated in her job that she sometimes has to make hard decisions, such as laying off employees.

So, what can we say about dissonance and employee behavior? These moderating factors suggest that although individuals experience dissonance, they won't necessarily move toward consistency, that is, toward reducing the dissonance. If the issues underlying the dissonance are of minimal importance, if an individual perceives that the dissonance is externally imposed and is substantially uncontrollable, or if rewards are significant enough to offset the dissonance, the individual will not be under great tension to reduce the dissonance.[14]

How Can an Understanding of Attitudes Help Managers Be More Effective?

Managers should be interested in their employees' attitudes because they influence behavior in the following ways:

1. *Satisfied and committed employees have lower rates of turnover and absenteeism.* If managers want to keep resignations and absences down—especially among their more productive employees—they'll want to do things that generate positive job attitudes.

2. Whether satisfied workers are productive workers is a debate that's been going on for almost 80 years. After the Hawthorne studies (see p. 29 in the

A Question of Ethics

Have you ever faked a smile? All of us have sometime, somewhere. Now research has shown that employees "fake a positive outlook when the boss is around."[15] Being ambivalent (or even negative) about your work or about working for your organization can be a definite detriment. Employers want to see passion. They want you to love your job and be excited about coming to work and about doing your job. And when you don't? If you want to keep your job, you fake it. But all that faking takes a toll.

*If your professor has assigned this, go to the Assignments section of **mymanagementlab .com** to complete these discussion questions.*

⭐ **Talk About It 1:** What ethical issues might arise under these circumstances for both employees and for managers?

⭐ **Talk About It 2:** Discuss ways that managers could create an environment where employees don't have to fake a positive outlook.

Management History Module), managers believed that happy workers were productive workers. Because it's not easy to determine whether job satisfaction "caused" job productivity or vice versa, some management researchers felt that the belief was generally wrong. However, we can say with some certainty that the correlation between satisfaction and productivity is fairly strong.[16] *Satisfied employees do perform better on the job.* So managers should focus on those factors that have been shown to be conducive to high levels of employee job satisfaction: making work challenging and interesting, providing equitable rewards, and creating supportive working conditions and supportive colleagues.[17] These factors are likely to help employees be more productive.

3. Managers should also survey employees about their attitudes. As one study put it, "*A sound measurement of overall job attitude is one of the most useful pieces of information an organization can have about its employees.*"[18] However, research has also shown that attitude surveys can be more effective at pinpointing employee dissatisfaction if done multiple times rather than just at one point in time.[19]

4. Managers should know that *employees will try to reduce dissonance*. If employees are required to do things that appear inconsistent to them or that are at odds with their attitudes, managers should remember that pressure to reduce the dissonance is not as strong when the employee perceives that the dissonance is externally imposed and uncontrollable. It's also decreased if rewards are significant enough to offset the dissonance. So the manager might point to external forces such as competitors, customers, or other factors when explaining the need to perform some work that the individual may have some dissonance about. Or the manager can provide rewards that an individual desires.

What Do Managers Need to Know About Personality?

9-3 Describe different personality theories.

Many colleges use roommate compatibility tests to assign rooms in on-campus housing.[20] If you've ever shared a living space with someone else (family or nonfamily), you know how important it can be for roommates to be compatible and to get along with each other. This compatibility is affected and influenced by our own and by other people's personalities.

Some of us are quiet and passive; others are loud and aggressive. When we describe people using terms such as *quiet, passive, loud, aggressive, ambitious, extroverted, loyal, tense,* or *sociable,* we're describing their personalities. An individual's **personality** is a unique combination of emotional, thought, and behavioral patterns that affect how a person reacts to situations and interacts with others. Personality is most often described in terms of measurable traits that a person exhibits. We're interested in looking at personality because just like attitudes, it affects how and why people behave the way they do.

> 78 percent of employers say that personality is the most important attribute in a job candidate.[21]

How Can We Best Describe Personality?

Your personality is your natural way of doing things and relating to others. *Your personality traits influence, among other things, how you interact with others and how you solve problems.* Literally dozens of behaviors are attributed to an individual's personality traits. But how can we best describe personality? Over the years, researchers have attempted to focus specifically on which personality traits and personality types would describe an individual's personality. Two widely recognized personality research efforts are the Myers-Briggs Type Indicator® and the Big Five model. In addition, we can't possibly describe personality and behavior without looking at emotions.

WHAT IS THE MYERS-BRIGGS TYPE INDICATOR? One of the more widely used methods of identifying personalities is the **Myers-Briggs Type Indicator (MBTI)**. The MBTI®

personality
A unique combination of emotional, thought, and behavioral patterns that affect how a person reacts to situations and interacts with others

Myers-Briggs Type Indicator (MBTI)
A personality assessment that uses four dimensions of personality to identify different personality types

assessment uses four dimensions of personality to identify 16 different personality types based on the responses to an approximately 100-item questionnaire. The MBTI personality assessment is used by some 80 percent of Fortune 1000 companies.[22]

The 16 personality types are based on four dimensions:

- *Extraversion versus Introversion (EI)*
  - The EI dimension describes an individual's orientation toward the external world of the environment (E) or the inner world of ideas and experiences (I).
- *Sensing versus Intuition (SN)*
  - The SN dimension indicates an individual's preference for gathering data while focusing on a standard routine based on factual data (S) to focusing on the big picture and making connections among the facts (N).
- *Thinking versus Feeling (TF)*
  - The TF dimension reflects one's preference for making decisions in a logical and analytical manner (T) or on the basis of values and beliefs and the effects the decision will have on others (F).
- *Judging versus Perceiving (JP)*
  - The JP dimension reflects an attitude toward how one deals with the external world—either in a planned and orderly way (J) or preferring to remain flexible and spontaneous (P).[23]

Let's give you some examples:

- ISTJ (Introversion - Sensing - Thinking - Judging)—quiet, serious, dependable, practical, and matter-of-fact
- ESFP (Extraversion - Sensing - Feeling - Perceiving)—outgoing, friendly, spontaneous, enjoys working with others, and learns best by trying a new skill with other people
- INFP (Introversion - Intuition - Feeling - Perceiving)—idealistic, loyal to personal values, and seeks to understand people and help them fulfill their potential
- ENTJ (Extraversion - Intuition - Thinking - Judging)—frank, decisive, and will assume leadership roles; also enjoys long-term planning and goal setting and is forceful in presenting ideas[24]

How can the MBTI assessment help managers? Proponents believe that it's important to know these personality types because they influence the way people interact and solve problems.[25] For example, if your boss prefers Intuition and you're a Sensing type, you'll deal with information in different ways. An Intuition preference indicates your boss is one who prefers gut reactions, whereas you, as a Sensing type, prefer to deal with the facts. To work well with your boss, you have to present more than just facts about a situation—you'll also have to discuss your gut feeling about the situation. The MBTI assessment has also been found to be useful in focusing on growth orientations for entrepreneurial types as well as profiles supporting emotional intelligence (something we'll look at shortly).[26]

WHAT IS THE BIG FIVE MODEL OF PERSONALITY?   Another way of viewing personality is through a five-factor model of personality—more typically called the **Big Five model**.[27] The Big Five factors are:

1 Extraversion	A personality dimension that describes the degree to which someone is sociable, talkative, and assertive.
2 Agreeableness	A personality dimension that describes the degree to which someone is good-natured, cooperative, and trusting.
3 Conscientiousness	A personality dimension that describes the degree to which someone is responsible, dependable, persistent, and achievement oriented.
4 Emotional stability	A personality dimension that describes the degree to which someone is calm, enthusiastic, and secure (positive) or tense, nervous, depressed, and insecure (negative).
5 Openness to experience	A personality dimension that describes the degree to which someone is imaginative, artistically sensitive, and intellectual.

Big Five model
A personality trait model that examines five traits: extraversion, agreeableness, conscientiousness, emotional stability, and openness to experience

The personality dimension of extraversion of the Big Five Model applies to entrepreneur Sara Blakely, founder of Spanx. Being sociable, talkative, and assertive contributed to Blakely's launch and development of her enormously successful undergarment venture. Blakely (at left) is shown here introducing her employee team to shoppers at a new Spanx store in Tampa.

The Big Five model provides more than just a personality framework. Research has shown that important relationships exist between these personality dimensions and job performance.[28] For example, one study reviewed five categories of occupations: professionals (e.g., engineers, architects, attorneys), police, managers, sales, and semi-skilled and skilled employees. Job performance was defined in terms of employee performance ratings, training competency, and personnel data such as salary level. The results of the study showed that conscientiousness predicted job performance for all five occupational groups.[29] Predictions for the other personality dimensions depended on the situation and the occupational group. For example, extraversion predicted performance in managerial and sales positions, in which high social interaction is necessary.[30] Openness to experience was found to be important in predicting training competency. Ironically, emotional security was not positively related to job performance. Although it would seem logical that calm and secure workers would be better performers, that wasn't the case. Perhaps it's a function of the likelihood that emotionally stable workers often keep their jobs and emotionally unstable people may not. Given that all those participating in the study were employed, the variance on that dimension was probably small.

WHAT IS EMOTIONAL INTELLIGENCE?   *People who understand their own emotions and are good at reading others' emotions may be more effective in their jobs.* That, in essence, is the theme of the underlying research on emotional intelligence.[31]

Emotional intelligence (EI) refers to an assortment of noncognitive skills, capabilities, and competencies that influences a person's ability to cope with environmental demands and pressures.[32] It's composed of five dimensions:

- *Self-awareness*. Being aware of what you're feeling.
- *Self-management*. Managing your own emotions and impulses.

emotional intelligence (EI)
The ability to notice and to manage emotional cues and information

---

Technology and the Manager's Job
INCREASED RELIANCE ON EMOTIONAL INTELLIGENCE

Even as technology allows more and more employees to move to off-site work arrangements, that doesn't mean that they won't be interacting with others. Nope... they'll still have ongoing contact with colleagues and customers. And whether it goes by the name of emotional intelligence, social intelligence, or something else, the ability to understand yourself and others will be a skill that organizations will seek when hiring employees. In fact, in a survey of critical skills for the workforce in 2020, social intelligence ranked second on a list of the most critical skills.[33] (FYI: the number-one skill was sense-making, that is, being able to determine the deeper meaning or significance of what's being expressed.) **The ability to get along with others—coworkers, colleagues, team members, bosses, and customers—will be critical to success in most jobs.** Those employees who have strong technical skills but are weak on emotional intelligence will find it increasingly difficult to find and hold a job.

If your professor has assigned this, go to the Assignments section of **mymanagementlab.com** *to complete these discussion questions.*

⭐ **TALK ABOUT IT 3:** Why do you think the ability to get along with others is so critical?

⭐ **TALK ABOUT IT 4:** How can you develop this ability?

- *Self-motivation*. Persisting in the face of setbacks and failures.
- *Empathy*. Sensing how others are feeling.
- *Social skills*. Adapting to and handling the emotions of others.

Several studies suggest that EI may play an important role in job performance.[34] For instance, one study looked at the characteristics of Bell Lab engineers who were rated as stars by their peers. The scientists concluded that these stars were better at relating to others. That is, it was EI, not academic IQ, that characterized high performers. A second study of Air Force recruiters generated similar findings: Top-performing recruiters exhibited high levels of EI. Using these findings, the Air Force revamped its selection criteria. A follow-up investigation found that future hires who had high EI scores were 2.6 times more successful than those with low scores. Organizations such as American Express have found that implementing emotional intelligence programs has helped increase its effectiveness; other organizations also found similar results showing that emotional intelligence contributes to team effectiveness.[35] For instance, at Cooperative Printing in Minneapolis, a study of its 45 employees concluded that EI skills were twice as important in "contributing to excellence as intellect and expertise alone."[36] A poll of human resources managers asked this question: How important is it for your workers to demonstrate EI to move up the corporate ladder? Forty percent of the managers replied "very important." Another 16 percent said moderately important. Other studies also indicated that emotional intelligence can be beneficial to quality improvements in contemporary organizations.[37]

The implication is that employers should consider emotional intelligence as a criterion in their selection process—especially for those jobs that demand a high degree of social interaction.[38]

Can Personality Traits Predict Practical Work-Related Behaviors?

In a word, "YES!" Five specific personality traits have proven most powerful in explaining individual behavior in organizations. Let's take a look.

1. Who has control over an individual's behavior? Some people believe that they control their own fate. Others see themselves as pawns of fate, believing that what happens to them in their lives is due to luck or chance. The **locus of control** in the first case is internal. In the second case, it is external; these people believe that their lives are controlled by outside forces.[39] A manager might also expect to find that externals blame a poor performance evaluation on their boss's prejudice, their coworkers, or other events outside their control, whereas "internals" explain the same evaluation in terms of their own actions.

2. The second characteristic is called **Machiavellianism ("Mach")**, after Niccolo Machiavelli, who provided instruction in the sixteenth century on how to gain and manipulate power. An individual who is high in Machiavellianism is pragmatic, maintains emotional distance, believes that ends can justify the means,[40] and may have beliefs that are less ethical.[41] The philosophy "if it works, use it" is consistent with a high Mach perspective. Do high Machs make good employees? That answer depends on the type of job and whether you consider ethical implications in evaluating performance. In jobs that require bargaining skills (a labor negotiator) or that have substantial rewards for winning (a commissioned salesperson), high Machs are productive. In jobs in which ends do not justify the means or that lack absolute standards of performance, it's difficult to predict the performance of high Machs.

3. People differ in the degree to which they like or dislike themselves. This trait is called **self-esteem (SE)**.[42] The research on SE offers some interesting insights into organizational behavior. For example, SE is directly related to expectations for success. High SEs believe that they possess the ability to succeed at work. Individuals with high SE will take more risks in job selection and are more likely to choose unconventional jobs than are people with low SE.[43] The most common finding on self-esteem is that low SEs are more susceptible to external influence than are high SEs. Low SEs are

locus of control
The degree to which people believe they control their own fate

Machiavellianism ("Mach")
A measure of the degree to which people are pragmatic, maintain emotional distance, and believe that ends justify means

self-esteem (SE)
An individual's degree of like or dislike for himself or herself

dependent on positive evaluations from others. As a result, they're more likely to seek approval from others and more prone to conform to the beliefs and behaviors of those they respect than are high SEs. In managerial positions, low SEs will tend to be concerned with pleasing others and, therefore, will be less likely to take unpopular stands than will high SEs. Not surprisingly, self-esteem has also been found to be related to job satisfaction. A number of studies confirm that high SEs are more satisfied with their jobs than are low SEs.

4. Another personality trait researchers have identified is called **self-monitoring**.[44] Individuals high in self-monitoring can show considerable adaptability in adjusting their behavior to external, situational factors.[45] They're highly sensitive to external cues and can behave differently in different situations. High self-monitors are capable of presenting striking contradictions between their public persona and their private selves. Low self-monitors can't alter their behavior. They tend to display their true dispositions and attitudes in every situation; hence, they exhibit high behavioral consistency between who they are and what they do. Evidence suggests that high self-monitors tend to pay closer attention to the behavior of others and are more capable of conforming than are low self-monitors.[46] We might also hypothesize that high self-monitors will be more successful in managerial positions that require individuals to play multiple, and even contradicting, roles.

5. The final personality trait influencing worker behavior reflects the willingness to take chances—the propensity for *risk taking.* A preference to assume or avoid risk has been shown to have an impact on how long it takes individuals to make a decision and how much information they require before making their choice. For instance, in one classic study, 79 managers worked on a simulated human resources management exercise that required them to make hiring decisions.[47] High-risk-taking managers made more rapid decisions and used less information in making their choices than did the low-risk-taking managers. Interestingly, the decision accuracy was the same for both groups.

Although it's generally correct to conclude that managers in organizations are risk averse, especially in large companies and government agencies,[48] individual differences are still found on this dimension.[49] As a result, it makes sense to recognize these differences and even to consider aligning risk-taking propensity with specific job demands. For instance, a high-risk-taking propensity may lead to effective performance for a stock trader in a brokerage firm since this type of job demands rapid decision making. The same holds true for the entrepreneur.[50] On the other hand, this personality characteristic might prove a major obstacle to accountants performing auditing activities, which might be better done by someone with a low-risk-taking propensity.

How Do We Match Personalities and Jobs?

We all want a job that **fits our personality.**

"What if you're not happy in your job? Is it possible that you're in the wrong career entirely?"[51] As you do your job day by day, you may realize that your tasks don't mesh well with your personality or talents. Wouldn't it seem to make more sense to strive for a match between your personality and your chosen job or career path?

Obviously, individual personalities differ. So, too, do jobs. How do we match the two? The best-documented personality–job fit theory was developed by psychologist John Holland.[52] His theory states that an employee's satisfaction with his or her job, as well as his or her likelihood of leaving that job, depends on the degree to which the individual's personality matches the job environment. Holland identified six basic personality types, as shown in Exhibit 9–2.

Holland's theory proposes that satisfaction is highest and turnover lowest when personality and occupation are compatible.[53] Social individuals should be in "people-type" jobs, and so forth. The key points of this theory include the following: (1) there do appear to be

self-monitoring
A personality trait that measures the ability to adjust behavior to external situational factors

Exhibit 9–2 Holland's Personality-Job Fit

TYPE	PERSONALITY CHARACTERISTICS	SAMPLE OCCUPATIONS
Realistic. Prefers physical activities that require skill, strength, and coordination	Shy, genuine, persistent, stable, conforming, practical	Mechanic, drill press operator, assembly-line worker, farmer
Investigative. Prefers activities involving thinking, organizing, and understanding	Analytical, original, curious, independent	Biologist, economist, mathematician, news reporter
Social. Prefers activities that involve helping and developing others	Sociable, friendly, cooperative, understanding	Social worker, teacher, counselor, clinical psychologist
Conventional. Prefers rule-regulated, orderly, and unambiguous activities	Conforming, efficient, practical, unimaginative, inflexible	Accountant, corporate manager, bank teller, file clerk
Enterprising. Prefers verbal activities that offer opportunities to influence others and attain power	Self-confident, ambitious, energetic, domineering	Lawyer, real estate agent, public relations specialist, small business manager
Artistic. Prefers ambiguous and unsystematic activities that allow creative expression	Imaginative, disorderly, idealistic, emotional, impractical	Painter, musician, writer, interior decorator

Source: Robbins, Stephen P., Coulter, Mary, *Management*, 13th Ed., © 2016, p. 444. Reprinted and electronically reproduced by permission of Pearson Education, Inc., New York, NY.

intrinsic differences in personality among individuals; (2) there are different types of jobs; and (3) people in job environments compatible with their personality types should be more satisfied and less likely to resign voluntarily than people in incongruent jobs.

Do Personality Attributes Differ Across Cultures?

Do personality frameworks, like the Big Five model, transfer across cultures? Are dimensions like locus of control relevant in all cultures? Let's try to answer these questions.

The five personality factors studied in the Big Five model appear in almost all cross-cultural studies.[54] A wide variety of diverse cultures, such as China, Israel, Germany, Japan, Spain, Nigeria, Norway, Pakistan, and the United States, have been the setting for these studies. Differences are found in the emphasis on dimensions. The Chinese, for example, use the category of conscientiousness more often and use the category of agreeableness less often than do Americans. But a surprisingly high amount of agreement is found, especially among individuals from developed countries. As a case in point, a comprehensive review of studies covering people from the European Community found that conscientiousness was a valid predictor of performance across jobs and occupational groups.[55] U.S. studies found the same results.

We know that there are certainly no common personality types for a given country. You can, for instance, find high risk takers and low risk takers in almost any culture. Yet a country's culture influences the *dominant* personality characteristics of its people. We can see this effect of national culture by looking at one of the personality traits we just discussed: locus of control.

National cultures differ in terms of the degree to which people believe they control their environment. For instance, North Americans believe that they can dominate their

Jean-Paul Pelissier/Thomson Reuters

Understanding the differences in the emphasis countries place on personality dimensions helps managers of global companies. For example, knowing that the trait of conscientiousness is a valid predictor of performance in European Community nations helps U.S.-based Burger King manage employees such as this BK employee in France.

environment; other societies, such as those in Middle Eastern countries, believe that life is essentially predetermined. Notice how closely this distinction parallels the concept of internal and external locus of control. On the basis of this particular cultural characteristic, we should expect a larger proportion of internals in the U.S. and Canadian workforces than in the workforces of Saudi Arabia or Iran.

As we have seen throughout this section, personality traits influence employees' behavior. For global managers, understanding how personality traits differ takes on added significance when looking at it from the perspective of national culture.

How Can an Understanding of Personality Help Managers Be More Effective?

Managers should be interested in their employees' personalities because those personalities influence their behavior in the following ways:

1. *Job-Person Compatibility*. Some 62 percent of companies are using personality tests when recruiting and hiring.[56] And that's where the major value in understanding personality differences probably lies. Managers are likely to have higher-performing and more-satisfied employees if consideration is given to matching personalities with jobs.
2. *Understanding Different Approaches to Work*. By recognizing that people approach problem solving, decision making, and job interactions differently, a manager can better understand why, for instance, an employee is uncomfortable with making quick decisions or why an employee insists on gathering as much information as possible before addressing a problem. For instance, managers can expect that individuals with an external locus of control may be less satisfied with their jobs than those with an internal locus and also that they may be less willing to accept responsibility for their actions.
3. *Being a Better Manager*. Being a successful manager and accomplishing goals means working well together with others both inside and outside the organization. In order to work effectively together, you need to understand each other. This understanding comes, at least in part, from an appreciation of personality traits and emotions. Also, one of the skills you have to develop as a manager is learning to fine-tune your emotional reactions according to the situation. In other words, you have to learn to recognize "when you have to smile and when you have to bark."[57]

⭐ **Watch It 1!**

If your professor has assigned this, go to the Assignments section of **mymanagementlab.com** to complete the video exercise titled *CH2MHill: Ability and Personality*.

⭐ **Watch It 2!**

If your professor has assigned this, go to the Assignments section of **mymanagementlab.com** to complete the video exercise titled *Rudi's Bakery: Ability and Personality*.

What Is Perception and What Influences It?

9-4 Describe perception and the factors that influence it.

We interpret what we see and call it reality.

perception
A process by which we give meaning to our environment by organizing and interpreting sensory impressions

"L ke y ur b ain, the n w L nd Rov r autom tic lly adj sts to anyth ng."[58] This advertisement for a Land Rover SUV illustrates the perceptual process at work. You were likely able to read the sentence even with the missing letters because you recognized the word patterns and organized and interpreted them in a way that made sense.

Perception is a process by which we give meaning to our environment by organizing and interpreting sensory impressions. Research on perception consistently demonstrates that individuals may look at the same thing yet perceive it differently. One manager, for instance, can interpret the fact that her assistant regularly takes several days to make important decisions as evidence that the assistant is slow, disorganized, and afraid to make decisions. Another manager with the same assistant might interpret the same tendency as evidence that the assistant is thoughtful, thorough, and deliberate. The first manager would probably evaluate her assistant negatively; the second manager would probably evaluate the person positively. The point is that none of us see reality. *We interpret what we see and call it reality.* And, of course, as the example shows, we behave according to our perceptions.

What Influences Perception?

How do we explain the fact that Cathy, a marketing supervisor for a large commercial petroleum products organization, age 52, noticed Bill's nose ring during his employment interview, and Sean, a human resources recruiter, age 23, didn't? A number of factors operate to shape and sometimes distort perception. These factors can reside in (1) the perceiver, (2) the object or target being perceived, or (3) the context of the situation in which the perception is made.

1. When an individual looks at a target and attempts to interpret what he or she sees, that individual's personal characteristics will heavily influence the interpretation. These personal characteristics include attitudes, personality, motives, interests, past experiences, and expectations.
2. The characteristics of the target being observed can also affect what is perceived. Loud people are more likely than quiet people to be noticed in a group. So, too, are extremely attractive or unattractive individuals. Because targets are not looked at in isolation, the relationship of a target to its background also influences perception (see Exhibit 9–3 for an example), as does our tendency to group close things and similar things together.
3. The context in which we see objects or events is also important. The time at which an object or event is seen can influence attention, as can location, lighting, temperature, and any number of other situational factors.

Exhibit 9–3 Perceptual Challenges—What Do You See?

Old woman or young woman?   Two faces or an urn?   A knight on a horse?

How Do Managers Judge Employees?

Much of the research on perception is directed at inanimate objects. Managers, though, are more concerned with people. Our perceptions of people differ from our perceptions of such inanimate objects as computers, robots, or buildings because we make inferences about the actions of people that we don't, of course, make about inanimate objects. When we observe people, we attempt to develop explanations of why they behave in certain ways. Our perception and judgment of a person's actions, therefore, will be significantly influenced by the assumptions we make about the person's internal state. Many of these assumptions have led researchers to develop attribution theory.

WHAT IS ATTRIBUTION THEORY?   **Attribution theory** has been proposed to explain how we judge people differently depending on what meaning we attribute to a given behavior.[59] Basically, the theory suggests that when we observe an individual's behavior, we attempt to determine whether it was internally or externally caused. *Internally caused behavior* is believed to be under the control of the individual. *Externally caused behavior* results from outside causes; that is, the person is seen as having been forced into the behavior by the situation. That determination, however, depends on three factors: (1) distinctiveness, (2) consensus, and (3) consistency.

1. *Distinctiveness* refers to whether an individual displays a behavior in many situations or whether it is particular to one situation. Is the employee who arrived late to work today also the person coworkers see as a goof-off? What we want to know is whether this behavior is unusual. If it is, the observer is likely to give the behavior an external attribution. If this action is not unique, it will probably be judged as internal.

2. If everyone who is faced with a similar situation responds in the same way, we can say the behavior shows *consensus*. Our tardy employee's behavior would meet this criterion if all employees who took the same route to work today were also late. If consensus is high, you would be expected to give an external attribution to the employee's tardiness, whereas if other employees who took the same route made it to work on time, you would conclude the reason to be internal.

3. Finally, a manager looks for *consistency* in an employee's actions. Does the individual engage in the behaviors regularly and consistently? Does the employee respond the same way over time? Coming in 10 minutes late for work is not perceived in the same way if, for one employee, it represents an unusual case (she hasn't been late for several months), but for another it is part of a routine pattern (he is late two or three times a week). The more consistent the behavior, the more the observer is inclined to attribute it to internal causes.

Exhibit 9–4 summarizes the key elements in attribution theory. It would tell us, for instance, that if an employee, Mr. Flynn, generally performs at about the same level on other

Exhibit 9–4 Attribution Theory

OBSERVATION	INTERPRETATION	ATTRIBUTION OF CAUSE
Does person behave this way in other situations?	**YES:** Low distinctiveness **NO:** High distinctiveness	Internal attribution External attribution
Do other people behave the same way in similar situations?	**YES:** High consensus **NO:** Low consensus	External attribution Internal attribution
Does person behave this way consistently?	**YES:** High consistency **NO:** Low consistency	Internal attribution External attribution

related tasks as he does on his current task (low distinctiveness), if other employees frequently perform differently—better or worse—than Mr. Flynn does on that current task (low consensus), and if Mr. Flynn's performance on this current task is consistent over time (high consistency), his manager or anyone else who is judging Mr. Flynn's work is likely to hold him primarily responsible for his task performance (internal attribution).

CAN ATTRIBUTIONS BE DISTORTED?

One of the more interesting findings drawn from attribution theory is that errors or biases distort attributions. For instance, substantial evidence supports the hypothesis that when we make judgments about the behavior of other people, we have a tendency to underestimate the influence of external factors and overestimate the influence of internal or personal factors.[60]

Michael Conroy/AP Images

Stereotyping generalizes that women lack the technical skills and emotional and physical strength required to succeed in auto racing. In announcing the formation of Grace Autosport, the first all-female IndyCar racing team, British race car driver Katherine Legge (right) purports that gender should not be a barrier to pursuing a successful career in motorsports.

This **fundamental attribution error** can explain why a sales manager may be prone to attribute the poor performance of her sales agents to laziness rather than to the innovative product line introduced by a competitor. Individuals also tend to attribute their own successes to internal factors such as ability or effort while putting the blame for failure on external factors such as luck (or an "unfair" test). This **self-serving bias** suggests that feedback provided to employees in performance reviews will be predictably distorted by them, whether it is positive or negative.

WHAT PERCEPTUAL SHORTCUTS DO WE USE? All of us, managers included, use a number of shortcuts to judge others. Perceiving and interpreting people's behavior is a lot of work, so we use shortcuts to make the task more manageable.[61] Such shortcuts can be valuable when they let us make accurate perceptions quickly and provide valid data for making predictions. However, they aren't perfect. They can and do get us into trouble. What are these perceptual shortcuts? (See Exhibit 9–5 for a summary.)

Exhibit 9–5 Perceptual Shortcuts

SHORTCUT	WHAT IT IS	DISTORTION
Selectivity	People assimilate certain bits and pieces of what they observe depending on their interests, background, experience, and attitudes	"Speed reading" others may result in an inaccurate picture of them
Assumed similarity	People assume that others are like them	May fail to take into account individual differences, resulting in incorrect similarities
Stereotyping	People judge others on the basis of their perception of a group to which the others belong	May result in distorted judgments because many stereotypes have no factual foundation
Halo effect	People form an impression of others on the basis of a single trait	Fails to take into account the total picture of what an individual has done

fundamental attribution error
The tendency to underestimate the influence of external factors and overestimate the influence of internal factors when making judgments about the behavior of others

self-serving bias
The tendency for individuals to attribute their successes to internal factors while putting the blame for failures on external factors

selective perception
The tendency for people to only absorb parts of what they observe, which allows us to "speed read" others

assumed similarity
An observer's perception of others influenced more by the observer's own characteristics than by those of the person observed

stereotyping
When we judge someone on the basis of our perception of a group to which that person belongs

halo effect
When we form a general impression of a person on the basis of a single characteristic

Individuals can't assimilate all they observe, so they're selective in their perception. They absorb bits and pieces. These bits and pieces are not chosen randomly; rather, they're selectively chosen depending on the interests, background, experience, and attitudes of the observer. **Selective perception** allows us to "speed read" others, but not without the risk of drawing an inaccurate picture.

It's easy to judge others if we assume that they're similar to us. In **assumed similarity**, or the "like me" effect, the observer's perception of others is influenced more by the observer's own characteristics than by those of the person observed. For example, if you want challenges and responsibility in your job, you'll assume that others want the same. People who assume that others are like them can, of course, be right, but not always.

When we judge someone on the basis of our perception of a group he or she is part of, we're using the shortcut called **stereotyping**. For instance, "Married people are more stable employees than single persons" or "Older employees are absent more often from work" are examples of stereotyping. To the degree that a stereotype is based on fact, it may produce accurate judgments. However, many stereotypes aren't factual and distort our judgment.

When we form a general impression about a person on the basis of a single characteristic, such as intelligence, sociability, or appearance, we're being influenced by the **halo effect**. This effect frequently occurs when students evaluate their classroom instructor. Students may isolate a single trait such as enthusiasm and allow their entire evaluation to be slanted by the perception of this one trait. If an instructor who is quiet, assured, knowledgeable, and highly qualified has a classroom teaching style that lacks enthusiasm, that instructor might be rated lower on a number of other characteristics.

◀◀◀ From the Past to the Present ▶▶▶

To better understand operant conditioning, we need to first look at a different perspective on learning—classical conditioning theory. In classical conditioning, something happens, and we react in a specific way. As such, it can explain simple reflexive behavior. For instance, classical conditioning can explain why a scheduled visit by the "top brass" brings flurried activities of cleaning, straightening, and rearranging at a local outlet of a major retail company. However, most behavior by people at work is voluntary rather than reflexive; that is, employees choose to arrive at work on time, ask their boss for help with some problem, or "goof off" when no one is watching.

Learn how to SHAPE SOMEONE'S BEHAVIOR!

A better explanation for behavior is operant conditioning, which says that people behave the way they do so they can get something they want or avoid something they don't want. It's voluntary or learned behavior, not reflexive or unlearned behavior. Harvard psychologist B. F. Skinner first identified the process of operant conditioning and his research widely expanded our knowledge of it.[62] He argued that creating pleasing consequences to follow specific forms of behavior would increase the frequency of that behavior. Skinner demonstrated that people will most likely engage in desired behaviors if they're positively reinforced for doing so, that rewards are most effective if they immediately follow the desired response (behavior), and that behavior that is not rewarded or is punished is less likely to be repeated. For example, a professor places a mark by a student's name each time the student makes a contribution to class discussions. Operant conditioning would argue that this practice is motivating because it conditions a student to expect a reward (earning class credit) each time she demonstrates a specific behavior (speaking up in class). Operant conditioning can be seen in work settings as well. And smart managers quickly recognize that they can use operant conditioning to shape employees' behaviors to get work done in the most effective and efficient manner possible.

*If your professor has assigned this, go to the Assignments section of **mymanagementlab.com** to complete these discussion questions.*

⭐ **Talk About It 5:** How do classical conditioning and operant conditioning differ?

⭐ **Talk About It 6:** What ethical concerns might arise in "shaping" someone's behavior?

How Do Learning Theories Explain Behavior?

Almost all behavior is learned.

9-5 Discuss learning theories and their relevance in shaping behavior.

What Is **Learning**?

- Considerably broader than average person's view that "it's what you do in school."
- Occurs all the time as we continually learn from our experiences.

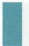

1 **Operant conditioning**—behavior is a function of its consequences.

- People learn to behave to get something they want or to avoid something they don't want.
- Voluntary or learned behavior, not reflexive or unlearned behavior.
- Tendency to repeat learned behavior is influenced by:

    - Reinforcement → strengthens a behavior and increases the likelihood it will be repeated.

    - Lack of reinforcement → weakens a behavior and lessens the likelihood it will be repeated.

- Examples of operant conditioning are everywhere—in any situation where *(explicitly or implicitly)* reinforcement *(rewards)* are contingent on some action on your part.

    - (For more information on operant conditioning, see the From the Past to the Present box on p. 285).

learning
A relatively permanent change in behavior that occurs as a result of experience

operant conditioning
A theory of learning that says behavior is a function of its consequences

Andres Rodriguez/Alamy

2 Social learning theory—learning both through observation and direct experience.[63]

- Influence of models, such as parents, teachers, peers, celebrities, managers, and so forth, is central to social learning.
- Four processes determine the amount of influence these models have:

1 Attentional processes. People learn from a model when they recognize and pay attention to its critical features.

2 Retention processes. A model's influence will depend on how well the individual remembers the model's action, even after the model is no longer readily available.

3 Motor reproduction processes. After a person has seen a new behavior by observing the model, the watching must become doing.

4 Reinforcement processes. Individuals will be motivated to exhibit the modeled behavior if positive incentives or rewards are provided. Reinforced behaviors will be given more attention, learned better, and performed more often.

Shaping Behavior
Putting Learning Theory into Practice

WHY

- Managers can teach employees to behave in ways that most benefit the organization.[64]

HOW

- Guide learning in graduated steps, that is, **shaping behavior**.

Vladimir Nenov/Alamy

social learning theory
A theory of learning that says people can learn through observation and direct experience

shaping behavior
The process of guiding learning in graduated steps, using reinforcement or lack of reinforcement

Four ways to shape behavior:

1 **Positive reinforcement:** Follow a desired behavior with something pleasant—a manager praising an employee for a job well done.

2 **Negative reinforcement:** Follow a desired behavior by terminating or withdrawing something unpleasant—a manager telling an employee he won't dock her pay if she starts coming to work on time. The only way for the employee to not have her pay docked is to come to work on time, which is the behavior the manager wants.

3 **Punishment** penalizes undesirable behavior—suspending an employee for two days without pay for showing up drunk.

4 **Extinction** is not reinforcing (ignoring) a behavior, making it gradually disappear.

Both positive and negative reinforcement result in learning. They strengthen a desired response and increase the probability of repetition.

Both punishment and extinction also result in learning; however, they weaken behavior and tend to decrease its subsequent frequency.

How Can an Understanding of Learning Help Managers Be More Effective?

Manage Employees' Learning

Employees are going to learn on the job. Are managers going to manage their learning through **(1)** the rewards they allocate and the examples they set, or **(2)** allow it to occur haphazardly?

Watch What You Reward:

If managers want behavior A, but reward behavior B, they shouldn't be surprised to find employees learning to engage in behavior B.

Watch What You Do:

Managers should expect that employees will look to them as models and do what they do.

Carlos's Premium Images/Alamy

How Can an Understanding of Perception Help Managers Be More Effective?

Managers should be interested in perception because it helps them understand employee behavior in the following ways:

1. Managers need to recognize that their employees react to perceptions, not to reality. So whether a manager's appraisal of an employee's performance is actually objective and unbiased or whether the organization's wage levels are among the highest in the community is less relevant than what employees perceive them to be. If individuals perceive appraisals to be biased or wage levels as low, they'll behave as if those conditions actually exist.
2. Employees organize and interpret what they see, so there is always the potential for perceptual distortion. The message is clear: Pay close attention to how employees perceive both their jobs and management actions. Remember, the valuable employee who quits because of an inaccurate perception is just as great a loss to an organization as the valuable employee who quits for a valid reason.

What Contemporary OB Issues Face Managers?

9-6 Discuss contemporary issues in OB.

By this point, you're probably well aware of why managers *need to understand* how *and* why *employees behave the way they do.* We conclude this chapter by looking at two OB issues having a major influence on managers' jobs today.

How Do Generational Differences Affect the Workplace?

They're young, smart, brash. They wear flip-flops to the office or listen to iPods at their desk. They want to work, but they don't want work to be their life. This is Generation Y, some 70 million of them, embarking on their careers, taking their place in an increasingly multi-generational workplace.[65]

JUST WHO IS GEN Y?   There's no consensus about the exact time span that Gen Y comprises, but most definitions include those individuals born from about 1982 to 1997. One thing is for sure—they're bringing new attitudes with them to the workplace. Gen Ys have grown up with an amazing array of experiences and opportunities. And they want their work life to provide that as well, as shown in Exhibit 9–6. For instance, Stella Kenyi, who is passionately interested in international development, was sent by her employer, the National Rural Electric Cooperative Association, to Yai, Sudan, to survey energy use.[66] At Best Buy's corporate offices, a senior scheduling specialist feels that as long as the results are there, why should it matter how it gets done, even if that involves playing a video game while on a phone call.[67] An assistant account executive from Atlanta described herself and fellow Gen Yers as tech-savvy risk takers—individuals who are quite willing to shake up how things currently stand. And from her perspective, appealing work environments are those that offer opportunities to work independently and creatively.[68]

DEALING WITH THE MANAGERIAL CHALLENGES. Managing Gen Y workers presents some unique challenges. Conflicts and resentment can arise over issues such as appearance, technology, and management style.

How flexible must an organization be in terms of "appropriate" office attire? It may depend on the type of work being done and the size of the organization. There are many organizations where jeans, T-shirts, and

Fab.com, a shopping portal for design products, understands the attitudes of Millennials and has created a casual and fun environment that appeals to them. Fab offers its tech-savvy employees, like those shown here at their office in Germany, opportunities to develop themselves and their careers in a fast-growing e-commerce firm.

Jens Kalaene/dpa/picture-alliance/Newscom

Exhibit 9–6 Gen Y Workers

Source: © Rainmaker Thinking, Inc. Reproduced with permission.

flip-flops are acceptable. However, in other settings, employees are expected to dress more conventionally. But even in those more conservative organizations, one possible solution to accommodate the more casual attire preferred by Gen Y is to be more flexible in what's acceptable. For instance, the guideline might be that when the person is not interacting with someone outside the organization, more casual wear (with some restrictions) can be worn.

What about technology? This generation has lived much of their lives with ATMs, DVDs, cell phones, e-mail, texting, laptops, and the Internet. When they don't have information they need, they just simply enter a few keystrokes to get it. Having grown up with technology, Gen Ys tend to be totally comfortable with it. They're quite content to meet virtually to solve problems, while bewildered baby boomers expect important problems to be solved with an in-person meeting. Baby boomers complain about Gen Y's inability to focus on one task, while Gen Ys see nothing wrong with multitasking. Again, flexibility from both is the key.

Finally, what about managing Gen Ys? Like the old car advertisement that used to say, "This isn't your father's Oldsmobile," we can say that "this isn't your father's or mother's way of managing." Gen Y employees want bosses who are open minded; experts in their field, even if they aren't tech-savvy; organized; teachers, trainers, and mentors; not authoritarian or paternalistic; respectful of their generation; understanding of their need for work/life balance; providing constant feedback; communicating in vivid and compelling ways; and providing stimulating and novel learning experiences.[69]

Gen Y employees have a lot to offer organizations in terms of their knowledge, passion, and abilities. Managers, however, have to recognize and understand the behaviors of this group in order to create an environment in which work can be accomplished efficiently, effectively, and without disruptive conflict.

How Do Managers Deal with Negative Behavior in the Workplace?

Jerry notices the oil is low in his forklift but continues to drive it until it overheats and can't be used. After enduring 11 months of repeated insults and mistreatment from her supervisor,

Maria quits her job. An office clerk slams her keyboard and then shouts profanity whenever her computer freezes up. Rudeness, hostility, aggression, and other forms of workplace negativity have become all too common in today's organizations. In a survey of U.S. employees, 10 percent said they witnessed rudeness daily within their workplaces and 20 percent said that they personally were direct targets of incivility at work at least once a week. In a survey of Canadian workers, 25 percent reported seeing incivility daily and 50 percent said they were the direct targets at least once per week.[70] And it's been estimated that negativity costs the U.S. economy some $300 billion a year.[71] What can managers do to manage negative behavior in the workplace?

The main thing is to recognize that it's there. Pretending that negative behavior doesn't exist or ignoring such misbehaviors will only confuse employees about what is expected and acceptable behavior. Although researchers continue to debate about the preventive or responsive actions to negative behaviors, in reality, both are needed.[72] Preventing negative behaviors by carefully screening potential employees for certain personality traits and responding immediately and decisively to unacceptable negative behaviors can go a long way toward managing negative workplace behaviors. But it's also important to pay attention to employee attitudes, since negativity will show up there as well. As we said earlier, when employees are dissatisfied with their jobs, they *will* respond somehow.

MyManagementLab®

Go to **mymanagementlab.com** to complete the problems marked with this icon .

9 Review

CHAPTER SUMMARY

9-1 Identify the focus and goals of organizational behavior (OB).

OB focuses on three areas: individual behavior, group behavior, and organizational aspects. The goals of OB are to explain, predict, and influence employee behavior. Six important employee behaviors are as follows: Employee productivity is a performance measure of both efficiency and effectiveness. Absenteeism is the failure to report to work. Turnover is the voluntary and involuntary permanent withdrawal from an organization. Organizational citizenship behavior (OCB) is discretionary behavior that's not part of an employee's formal job requirements, but it promotes the effective functioning of an organization. Job satisfaction is an individual's general attitude toward his or her job. Workplace misbehavior is any intentional employee behavior that's potentially harmful to the organization or individuals within the organization.

9-2 Explain the role that attitudes play in job performance.

Attitudes are evaluative statements concerning people, objects, or events. The cognitive component of an attitude refers to the beliefs, opinions, knowledge, or information held by a person. The affective component is the emotional or feeling part of an attitude. The behavioral component refers to an intention to behave in a certain way toward someone or something.

Four job-related attitudes include job satisfaction, job involvement, organizational commitment, and employee engagement. Job satisfaction refers to a person's general attitude toward his or her job. Job involvement is the degree to which an employee identifies with his or her job, actively participates in it, and considers his or her job performance to be important to his or her self-worth. Organizational commitment is the degree to which an employee identifies with a particular organization and its goals, and wishes to maintain membership in that organization. Employee engagement is when employees are connected to, satisfied with, and enthusiastic about their jobs.

According to cognitive dissonance theory, individuals try to reconcile attitude and behavior inconsistencies by altering their attitudes, altering their behavior, or rationalizing the inconsistency.

9-3 Describe different personality theories.

The MBTI measures four dimensions: social interaction, preference for gathering data, preference for decision making, and

style of making decisions. The Big Five Model consists of five personality traits: extraversion, agreeableness, conscientiousness, emotional stability, and openness to experience. Another way to view personality is through the five personality traits that help explain individual behavior in organizations: locus of control, Machiavellianism, self-esteem, self-monitoring, and risk taking.

Finally, how a person responds emotionally and how they deal with their emotions is a function of personality. A person who is emotionally intelligent has the ability to notice and to manage emotional cues and information.

9-4 Describe perception and the factors that influence it.

Perception is how we give meaning to our environment by organizing and interpreting sensory impressions.

Attribution theory helps explain how we judge people differently. It depends on three factors. Distinctiveness is whether an individual displays different behaviors in different situations (that is, is the behavior unusual). Consensus is whether others facing a similar situation respond in the same way. Consistency is when a person engages in behaviors regularly and consistently. Whether these three factors are high or low helps managers determine whether employee behavior is attributed to external or internal causes.

The fundamental attribution error is the tendency to underestimate the influence of external factors and overestimate the influence of internal factors. The self-serving bias is the tendency to attribute our own successes to internal factors and to put the blame for personal failure on external factors. Shortcuts used in judging others are selective perception, assumed similarity, stereotyping, and the halo effect.

9-5 Discuss learning theories and their relevance in shaping behavior.

Operant conditioning argues that behavior is a function of its consequences. Social learning theory says that individuals learn by observing what happens to other people and by directly experiencing something.

Managers can shape behavior by using positive reinforcement (reinforcing a desired behavior by giving something pleasant), negative reinforcement (reinforcing a desired response by withdrawing something unpleasant), punishment (eliminating undesirable behavior by applying penalties), or extinction (not reinforcing a behavior to eliminate it).

9-6 Discuss contemporary issues in OB.

The challenge of managing Gen Y workers is that they bring new attitudes to the workplace. The main challenges are over issues such as appearance, technology, and management style.

Workplace misbehavior can be dealt with by recognizing that it's there; carefully screening potential employees for possible negative tendencies; and most importantly, by paying attention to employee attitudes through surveys about job satisfaction and dissatisfaction.

DISCUSSION QUESTIONS

⭐ 9-1 How is an organization like an iceberg? Use the iceberg metaphor to describe the field of organizational behavior.

9-2 Does the importance of knowledge of OB differ based on a manager's level in the organization? If so, how? If not, why not? Be specific.

⭐ 9-3 Define the six important employee behaviors.

9-4 Clarify how individuals reconcile inconsistencies between attitudes and behaviors.

9-5 Describe what is meant by the term *emotional intelligence.* Provide an example of how it's used in contemporary organizations.

9-6 "Instead of worrying about job satisfaction, companies should be trying to create environments where performance is enabled." What do you think this statement means? Explain. What's your reaction to this statement? Do you agree? Disagree? Why?

9-7 How might a manager use personality traits to improve employee selection in his or her department? Emotional intelligence? Discuss.

9-8 Describe the implications of social learning theory for managing people at work.

9-9 A Gallup Organization survey shows that most workers rate having a caring boss even higher than they value money or fringe benefits. How should managers interpret this information? What are the implications?

9-10 Write down three attitudes you have. Identify the cognitive, affective, and behavioral components of those attitudes.

Writing Assignments

9-11 Why is it important for managers to have an understanding of organizational behavior?

9-12 Describe the key elements of attribution theory. Discuss how the fundamental attribution error and self-serving bias play a role.

Management Skill Builder | UNDERSTANDING EMPLOYEE EMOTIONS

Employees bring their emotions with them to work every day. Although managers would like to think that employees are always rational, they aren't. And any manager who deals with people by ignoring how emotions—such as fear, anger, love, hate, joy, and grief—shape employees' day-to-day behavior isn't likely to be very effective.

❋ PERSONAL INVENTORY ASSESSMENT PERSONAL INVENTORY ASSESSMENT

Understanding Employee Emotions

How emotionally intelligent are you? Take this PIA and find out how good you are at understanding employee emotions.

Skill Basics

Understanding another person's felt emotions is a difficult task. But we *can* learn to read others' emotions. How? By focusing on actual behaviors as well as verbal, nonverbal, and paralinguistic cues.[73]

- *Assess others' emotional intelligence (EI).* Some people are more in touch with their emotions than others. Those who understand and can manage their emotions are said to be high in EI. When people exhibit the following behaviors, you should find that they have less variance in their emotions and are easier to read. People high in EI understand the way they feel (self-aware), are sensitive to the feelings of others (empathetic), voluntarily help others (socially responsible), see things the way they are rather than the way they wish them to be (reality-oriented), reach out to others and show concern for others' interests (sociable), and manage their frustrations and anger (impulse control).

- *Ask about emotions.* The easiest way to find out what someone is feeling is to ask them. Saying something as simple as "Are you OK? What's the problem?" can frequently provide you with the information to assess an individual's emotional state. But relying on a verbal response has two drawbacks. First, almost all of us conceal our emotions to some extent for privacy and to reflect social expectations. So we might be unwilling to share our true feelings. Second, even if we want to convey our feelings verbally, we may be unable to do so. Some people have difficulty understanding their own emotions and, hence, are unable to express them verbally. So, at best, verbal responses provide only partial information.

- *Look for nonverbal cues.* You're talking with a coworker. Does the fact that his back is rigid, his teeth clenched, and his facial muscles tight tell you something about his emotional state? It probably should. Facial expressions, gestures, body movements, and physical distance are nonverbal cues that can provide additional insights into what a person is feeling. Facial expressions, for instance, are a window into a person's feelings. Notice differences in facial features: the height of the cheeks, the raising or lowering of the brow, the turn of the mouth, the positioning of the lips, and the configuration of muscles around the eyes. Even something as subtle as the distance at which someone chooses to position him- or herself from you can convey their feelings, or lack, of intimacy, aggressiveness, repugnance, or withdrawal.

- *Look for how things are said.* As Janet and I talked, I noticed a sharp change in the tone of her voice and the speed at which she spoke. I was tapping into the third source of information on a person's emotions—*paralanguage*. This is communication that goes beyond the specific spoken words. It includes pitch, amplitude, rate, and voice quality of speech. Paralanguage reminds us that people convey their feelings not only in *what* they say, but also in *how* they say it.

Practicing the Skill

Do the following:

Part A. Form groups of two. Each person is to spend a couple of minutes thinking (without sharing with the other person) of a time in the past when he or she was emotional about something. Examples might include being upset with a parent, sibling, or friend; being excited or disappointed about an academic or athletic achievement; being angry with someone over an insult or slight; being disgusted by something someone has said or done; or being happy because of something good that happened.

Part B. Now you'll conduct two role plays. Each will be an interview. In the first, one person will play the interviewer and the other will play the job applicant. The job is for a summer management internship with a large retail chain. Each role play will last no longer than 10 minutes. The interviewer is to conduct a normal job interview, except you are to continually rethink the emotional episode you envisioned in Part A. Try hard to convey this emotion while, at the same time, being professional in interviewing the job applicant.

Part C. Now reverse positions for the second role play. The interviewer becomes the job applicant, and vice versa. The new interviewer will conduct a normal job interview, except that he or she will continually rethink the emotional episode chosen in Part A.

Part D. Spend 10 minutes deconstructing the interview, with specific attention focused on what emotion(s) you think the other was conveying? What cues did you pick up? How accurate were you in reading those cues?

Continue to practice these skills in your everyday interactions with others. Pretty soon, you'll feel more competent at reading others' emotional cues.

Experiential Exercise

Wood Designs Plus

To: Ted Sigler, Director of HR

From: Michelle DePriest, President

Re: Hiring

Ted, as we discussed last Friday, our manufacturing operations have grown to the point where we need to add a couple of people to our executive team; specifically, a corporate controller and a national sales director. The controller will be responsible for establishing operational and financial standards (in other words, a lot of number-crunching using financial and manufacturing statistics) for our various work units. The national sales director will be responsible for working closely with our sales staff to further develop long-lasting and mutually beneficial relationships with our customers.

I recall something from a management class I took in college that certain personality types fit best with certain types of jobs. Could you do some research on this topic for me? Write up a short report (no more than a page) describing the personality type that might be an appropriate match for each of these new positions. Get this to me by the end of the week.

This fictionalized company and message were created for educational purposes only, and not meant to reflect positively or negatively on management practices by any company that may share this name.

CASE APPLICATION #1

Getting All Emotional at Google

As the number-one company on Fortune's *Best Company to Work For* list for six straight years, Google must be doing something right! Actually, it does many things right! One thing that you might be surprised at is a self-improvement course (one of many) that's offered to Google's employees. The course, first offered in 2007, is called simply Search Inside Yourself (SIY). And it's so popular that thousands of Googlers are on waiting lists to take the course!

SIY was developed by a Google engineer, Chade-Meng Tan. Tan has been around Google from almost the beginning—he was Google employee No. 107. His current work position carries the title "Jolly Good Fellow," and his job description says he wants to, "Enlighten minds, open hearts, create world peace."[74] Interesting concepts for a highly successful tech company, don't you think! But there's a serious side to what might seem to be a "fluff" topic. The SIY course was designed to show Googlers how to be more aware of their emotions, to be more compassionate toward others, to be able to build sustainable relationships (internally and externally), and, of course, to contribute to world peace. (We're not kidding!) SIY is based on the five dimensions of emotional intelligence —here's a little review for you: self-awareness, self-management, self-motivation, empathy, and social skills—and is broken into three parts. The first part of the course focuses on *attention training*—being able to center yourself calmly and clearly in the midst of whatever is going on around you…shouting, stress, conflict, or whatever. The second part involves *self-knowledge*—being aware of your emotions and eventually being able to master those emotions. And the third part is *creating mental habits*—being in control of your emotions and able to naturally think how to relate calmly and kindly to others. Although all this sounds very interesting *and* very useful, that isn't the most fascinating part of the story.

What is most interesting is the fact that this course is so popular among people who are extremely intelligent and very logical, practical, and straight-forward. After all, Google hires the best and the brightest engineers—people who have a lot of knowledge and training, but who may not always have the best social/people skills. So how did Tan appeal to those individuals? The appeal was that the course was designed for the intellectual intelligence side (the nerd side) by focusing on the neuroscience behind the touchy-feely behavioral self-control that is possible through emotional intelligence. And despite Google's need for very smart, competent, tech-oriented employees, the reality is that even its workplace has to be about people working together to solve problems and design new ways to keep moving the company forward. So, even for them, emotional intelligence skills are needed for successful collaboration.

Search Inside Yourself

Discussion Questions

⭐ **9-14** Why might emotional intelligence be important to Google's engineers?

9-15 What is the purpose of this Search Inside Yourself course?

⭐ **9-16** Describe each of the three parts of the SIY course. Which do you think would be the hardest to master? Why?

⭐ **9-17** How has Google made the SIY course appeal to its engineers?

CASE APPLICATION #2

Odd Couples

A 29-year-old and a 68-year-old. How much could they possibly have in common? And what could they learn from each other? At Randstad USA's Manhattan office, such employee pairings are common.[75] One such pair of colleagues sits inches apart facing each other. "They hear every call the other makes. They read every e-mail the other sends or receives. Sometimes they finish each other's sentences."

Randstad Holding NV, a Dutch company, has been using this pairing idea since its founding more than 40 years ago. The founder's motto was "Nobody should be alone." The original intent was to boost productivity by having sales agents share one job and trade off job responsibilities. Today, these partners in the home office have an arrangement where one is in the office one week while the other one is out making sales calls, then the next week, they switch. The company brought its partner arrangement to the United States in the late 1990s. But when it began recruiting new employees, the vast majority of whom were in their twenties, it realized the challenges and the potential of pairing different generations together. "Knowing that these Gen Yers need lots of attention in the workplace, Randstad executives figured that if they shared a job with someone whose own success depended on theirs, they were certain to get all the nurturing they required."

Pairing different generations together at work…and making it work!

Randstad doesn't simply pair up people and hope it works. There's more to it than that! The company looks for people who will work well with others by conducting extensive interviews and requiring job applicants to shadow a sales agent for half a day. "One question Randstad asks is: What's your most memorable moment while being on a team? If they respond 'When I scored the winning touchdown,' that's a deal killer. Everything about our organization is based on the team and group." When a new hire is paired with an experienced agent, both individuals have some adjusting. One of the most interesting elements of Randstad's program is that neither person is "the boss." And both are expected to teach the other.

Discussion Questions

⭐ **9-18** What possible OB topics do you see in this story? Explain.

9-19 What do you think about this pairing-up idea? Would you be comfortable with such an arrangement? Why or why not?

⭐ **9-20** What personality traits would be most needed for this type of work arrangement? Why?

⭐ **9-21** What types of issues might a Gen Y employee and an older, more-experienced employee face? How could two people in such a close-knit work arrangement deal with those issues? That is, how could both make the adjustment easier?

CASE APPLICATION

Employees First

"Employees first." That's the most important and crucial cultural value that HCL Technologies' former CEO Vineet Nayar believed would help his company succeed and take it into the future.[76] Although most managers think that customers should come first, Nayar's philosophy was that employee satisfaction needed to be the top priority.

As one of the largest companies in India, HCL sells various information technology consulting services, such as infrastructure consulting, product engineering, custom software development, and application and enterprise consulting. Luring and keeping top talent is one of the challenges HCL faces. And at its size, it doesn't have the atmosphere of a fun and quirky startup.

Part of that "employee first" philosophy is a no-layoff policy, which was difficult to uphold during the pressures of the economic downturn. Like its competitors, HCL had excess employees and had suspended raises. But HCL kept its promise and didn't lay off any HCLites (Nayar's name for HCL employees). As business has picked up, however, employees begin looking at competitors' job offers. During the first quarter alone of 2010, HCL lost 22 percent of its workforce. Maybe it's time to monitor and track employee satisfaction.

HCL Technologies is headquartered in the world's largest democracy, so it's quite fitting that the New Delhi–based company is attempting a radical experiment in workplace democracy. Nayar was committed to creating a company where the job of company leaders was to enable people to find their own destiny by gravitating to their strengths. One thing that Nayar did was to pioneer a culture in which employees were first. What has he done to put employees first? Part of the cultural initiative dealt with the organization's structure. HCL inverted its organizational structure and placed more power in the hands of frontline employees, especially those in direct contact with customers and clients. It increased its investment in employee development and improved communication through greater

What would an EMPLOYEES-FIRST culture look like?

transparency. Employees were encouraged to communicate directly with Nayar. Through a forum called U&I (You and I), Nayar fielded more than a hundred questions from employees every week. "I threw open the door and invited criticism," he said. However, the signature piece of the company's cultural mission is probably what HCL called "trust pay." In contrast to the industry standard in which the average employee's pay is 30 percent variable, HCL decided to pay higher fixed salaries and reduce the variable component.

Does the unique "employees first" culture at HCL Technologies attract unique employees? Rajeev Sawhney, HCL's European president, would say yes. He uses *Slumdog Millionaire,* the movie that won an Academy Award for Best Picture, as a parallel. "It (the movie) is a reflection of the Indian race. It shows the adversity that creates the desire in people to reach out and create.…With each adversity they face, there is a greater desire to reach out and do something more." Sawhney says that entrepreneurialism is a key value of the HCL culture. "You can still tell an HCL person from a mile off. I think there is a particular DNA for an HCL person. It includes a very high need for achievement and very persuasive skills. HCL people are very energetic; they want to do lots of things and to take risks on behalf of the company."

Discussion Questions

9-22 What is your impression of an "employees first" culture? Would this work in other organizations? Why or why not? What would it take to make it work?

9-23 How might an understanding of organizational behavior help CEO Vineet Nayar lead his company? Be specific. How about first-line company supervisors? Again, be specific.

9-24 What aspects of personality do you see in this story about HCL? How have the personality traits of HCL employees contributed to make HCL what it is?

9-25 Design an employee attitude survey for HCL's employees.

Endnotes

1. "Survey on the Total Financial Impact of Employee Absences," *Medical Benefits,* November 30, 2010, 9; and K. M. Kroll, "Absence-Minded," *CFO Human Capital,* 2006, 12–14.

2. D. W. Organ, *Organizational Citizenship Behavior: The Good Soldier Syndrome* (Lexington, MA: Lexington Books, 1988), 4. See also J. L. Lavell, D. E. Rupp, and J. Brockner, "Taking a Multifoci Approach to the Study of Justice, Social Exchange, and Citizenship Behavior: The Target Similarity Model," *Journal of Management* (December 2007): 841–66; and J. A. LePine, A. Erez, and D. E. Johnson, "The Nature and Dimensionality of Organizational Citizenship Behavior: A Critical Review and Meta-Analysis," *Journal of Applied Psychology* (February 2002): 52–65.

3. J. R. Spence, D. L. Ferris, D. J. Brown, and D. Heller, "Understanding Daily Citizenship Behaviors: A Social Comparison Approach," *Journal of Organizational Behavior* (May 2011): 547–71; L. M. Little, D. L. Nelson, J. C. Wallace, and P. D. Johnson, "Integrating Attachment Style, Vigor at Work, and Extra-Role Performance," *Journal of Organizational Behavior* (April 2011): 464–84; N. P. Podsakoff, P. M. Podsakoff, S. W. Whiting, and P. Mishra, "Effects of Organizational Citizenship Behavior on Selection Decisions in Employment Interviews," *Journal of Applied Psychology* (March 2011): 310–26; T. M. Glomb, D. P. Bhave, A. G. Miner, and M. Wall, "Doing Good, Feeling Good: Examining the Role of Organizational Citizenship Behaviors in Changing Mood," *Personnel Psychology,* Spring 2011, 191–223; T. P. Munyon, W. A. Hochwarter, P. L. Perrewé, and G. R. Ferris, "Optimism and the Nonlinear Citizenship Behavior—Job Satisfaction Relationship in Three Studies," *Journal of Management* (November 2010): 1505–28; R. Ilies, B. A. Scott, and T. A. Judge, "The Interactive Effects of Personal Traits and Experienced States on Intraindividual Patterns of Citizenship Behavior," *Academy of Management Journal* (June 2006): 561–75; P. Cardona, B. S. Lawrence, and P. M. Bentler, "The Influence of Social and Work Exchange Relationships on Organizational Citizenship Behavior," *Group & Organization Management,* April 2004, 219–47; M. C. Bolino and W. H. Turnley, "Going the Extra Mile: Cultivating and Managing Employee Citizenship Behavior," *Academy of Management Executive,* August 2003, 60–73; M. C. Bolino, W. H. Turnley, and J. J. Bloodgood, "Citizenship Behavior and the Creation of Social Capital in Organizations,"

Academy of Management Review, October 2002, 505–22; and P. M. Podsakoff, S. B. MacKenzie, J. B. Paine, and D. G. Bachrach, "Organizational Citizenship Behaviors: A Critical Review of the Theoretical and Empirical Literature and Suggestions for Future Research," *Journal of Management* 26, no. 3 (2000): 543–48.

4. M. C. Bolino and W. H. Turnley, "The Personal Costs of Citizenship Behavior: The Relationship between Individual Initiative and Role Overload, Job Stress, and Work-Family Conflict," *Journal of Applied Psychology* (July 2005): 740–48.

5. This definition adapted from R. W. Griffin and Y. P. Lopez, "Bad Behavior in Organizations: A Review and Typology for Future Research," *Journal of Management* (December 2005): 988–1005.

6. S. J. Becker, "Empirical Validation of Affect, Behavior, and Cognition as Distinct Components of Behavior," *Journal of Personality and Social Psychology* (May 1984): 1191–1205.

7. S. P. Robbins and T. A. Judge, *Essentials of Organizational Behavior,* 11th ed. (Upper Saddle River, NJ: Prentice Hall, 2010).

8. M. S. Christian, A. S. Garza, and J. E. Slaughter, "Work Engagement: A Quantitative Review and Test of Its Relations with Task and Contextual Performance," *Personnel Psychology,* Spring 2011, 89–136; V. T. Ho, S-S Wong, and C. H. Lee, "A Tale of Passion: Linking Job Passion and Cognitive Engagement to Employee Work Performance," *Journal of Management Studies* (January 2011): 26–47; D. R. May, R. L. Gilson, and L. M. Harter, "The Psychological Conditions of Meaningfulness, Safety and Availability and the Engagement of the Human Spirit at Work," *Journal of Occupational and Organizational Psychology* (March 2004): 11–37; R. T. Keller, "Job Involvement and Organizational Commitment as Longitudinal Predictors of Job Performance: A Study of Scientists and Engineers," *Journal of Applied Psychology* (August 1997): 539–45; W. Kahn, "Psychological Conditions of Personal Engagement and Disengagement at Work," *Academy of Management Journal* (December 1990): 692–794; and P. P. Brooke Jr., D. W. Russell, and J. L. Price, "Discriminant Validation of Measures of Job Satisfaction, Job Involvement, and Organizational Commitment," *Journal of Applied Psychology* (May 1988): 139–45. Also, see, for example, J. Smythe, "Engaging Employees to Drive Performance," *Communication World,* May–June 2008, 20–22; A. B. Bakker and W. B. Schaufeli, "Positive Organizational Behavior: Engaged Employees in

Flourishing Organizations," *Journal of Organizational Behavior* (February 2008): 147–54; U. Aggarwal, S. Datta, and S. Bhargava, "The Relationship between Human Resource Practices, Psychological Contract, and Employee Engagement—Implications for Managing Talent," *IIMB Management Review,* September 2007, 313–25; M. C. Christian and J. E. Slaughter, "Work Engagement: A Meta-Analytic Review and Directions for Research in an Emerging Area," *AOM Proceedings,* August 2007, 1–6; C. H. Thomas, "A New Measurement Scale for Employee Engagement: Scale Development, Pilot Test, and Replication," *AOM Proceedings,* August 2007, 1–6; A. M. Saks, "Antecedents and Consequences of Employee Engagement," *Journal of Managerial Psychology* 21, no. 7 (2006): 600–19; and A. Parsley, "Road Map for Employee Engagement," *Management Services,* Spring 2006, 10–11.

9. Mercer, *IndustryWeek,* April 2008, 24.

10. J. M. George, "The Wider Context, Costs, and Benefits of Work Engagement," *European Journal of Work & Organizational Psychology* (February 2011): 53–59; and "Employee Engagement Report 2011," Blessing White Research, http:// www.blessingwhite.com/eee__ report.asp (January 2011): 7–8.

11. A. J. Elliott and P. G. Devine, "On the Motivational Nature of Cognitive Dissonance: Dissonance as Psychological Discomfort," *Journal of Personality and Social Psychology* (September 1994): 382–94.

12. L. Festinger, *A Theory of Cognitive Dissonance* (Stanford, CA: Stanford University Press, 1957); C. Crossen, "Cognitive Dissonance Became a Milestone in 1950s Psychology," *Wall Street Journal,* December 4, 2006, B1; and Y. "Sally" Kim, "Application of the Cognitive Dissonance Theory to the Service Industry," *Services Marketing Quarterly,* April–June 2011, 96–112.

13. H. C. Koh and E. H. Y. Boo, "The Link between Organizational Ethics and Job Satisfaction: A Study of Managers in Singapore," *Journal of Business Ethics,* February 15, 2001, 309.

14. See, for example, W. D. Crano and R. Prislin, "Attitudes and Persuasion," *Annual Review of Psychology,* 2006, 345–74; and J. Jermias, "Cognitive Dissonance and Resistance to Change: The Influence of Commitment Confirmation and Feedback on Judgment Usefulness of Accounting Systems," *Accounting, Organizations, and Society,* March 2001, 141.

15. P. Jaskunas, "The Tyranny of the Forced Smile," *New York Times Online,* February 14, 2015; and R. E. Silverman, "Workers Really Do

Put on a Happy Face for the Boss," *Wall Street Journal,* January 29, 2015, D4.

16. T. A. Judge, C. J. Thoresen, J. E. Bono, and G. K. Patton, "The Job Satisfaction–Job Performance Relationship: A Qualitative and Quantitative Review," *Psychological Bulletin,* May 2001, 376–407.

17. L. Saari and T. A. Judge, "Employee Attitudes and Job Satisfaction," *Human Resource Management,* Winter 2004, 395–407; and T. A. Judge and A. H. Church, "Job Satisfaction: Research and Practice," in C. L. Cooper and E. A. Locke (eds.), *Industrial and Organizational Psychology: Linking Theory with Practice* (Oxford, UK: Blackwell, 2000).

18. D. A. Harrison, D. A. Newman, and P. L. Roth, "How Important Are Job Attitudes?: Meta-Analytic Comparisons of Integrative Behavioral Outcomes and Time Sequences," *Academy of Management Journal* (April 2006): 305–25.

19. G. Chen, R. E. Ployhart, H. C. Thomas, N. Anderson, and P. D. Bliese, "The Power of Momentum: A New Model of Dynamic Relationships between Job Satisfaction Change and Turnover Intentions," *Academy of Management Journal* (February 2011): 159–81.

20. I. Arnsdorf, "No More New Kid on Campus," *Wall Street Journal,* August 5, 2010, D1+.

21. "Personality Is More Important Than Hard Skills, Managers Say," *T&D,* July 2014, 19.

22. L. Evans, "Do You Have the Right Personality to Work from Home?" http://www.fastcompany. com/3046450/how-to-be-a-success-at-everything/do-you-have-the-right-personality-to-work-from-home, May 26, 2015.

23. CPP, Inc., Myers-Briggs Type Indicator® (MBTI®), http://www. cpp.com/products/mbti/index.asp (2011); and J. Llorens, "Taking Inventory of Myers-Briggs," *T&D,* April 2010, 18–19.

24. Ibid.

25. See, for instance, J. Overbo, "Using Myers-Briggs Personality Type to Create a Culture Adapted to the New Century," *T&D,* February 2010, 70–72; K. Garrety, R. Badham, V. Morrigan, W. Rifkin, and M. Zanko, "The Use of Personality Typing in Organizational Change: Discourse, Emotions, and the Reflective Subject," *Human Relations,* February 2003, 211–35.

26. P. Moran, "Personality Characteristics and Growth-Orientation of the Small Business Owner Manager," *Journal of Managerial Psychology* (July 2000): 651; and M. Higgs, "Is There a Relationship between the Myers-Briggs Type Indicator and Emotional Intelligence?" *Journal of Managerial Psychology* (September–October 2001): 488–513.

27. J. M. Digman, "Personality Structure: Emergence of the Five Factor Model," in M. R. Rosenzweig and L. W. Porter, eds., *Annual Review of Psychology*, vol. 41 (Palo Alto, CA: Annual Reviews, 1990), 417–40; O. P. John, "The Big Five Factor Taxonomy: Dimensions of Personality in the Natural Language and in Questionnaires," in L. A. Pervin, ed., *Handbook of Personality Theory and Research* (New York: Guilford Press, 1990), 66–100; and M. K. Mount, M. R. Barrick, and J. P. Strauss, "Validity of Observer Ratings of the Big Five Personality Factors," *Journal of Applied Psychology* (April 1996): 272–80.

28. See, for example, T. W. Yiu and H. K. Lee, "How Do Personality Traits Affect Construction Dispute Negotiation: Study of Big Five Personality Model," *Journal of Construction Engineering & Management* (March 2011): 169–78; H. J. Kell, A. D. Rittmayer, A. E. Crook, and S. J. Motowidlo, "Situational Content Moderates the Association between the Big Five Personality Traits and Behavioral Effectiveness," *Human Performance*, February 2010, 213–28; R. D. Meyer, R. S. Dalal, and S. Bonaccio, "A Meta-Analytic Investigation into the Moderating Effects of Situational Strength on the Conscientiousness–Performance Relationship," *Journal of Organizational Behavior* (November 2009): 1077–102; G. Vittorio, C. Barbaranelli, and G. Guido, "Brand Personality: How to Make the Metaphor Fit," *Journal of Economic Psychology* (June 2001): 377; G. M. Hurtz and J. J. Donovan, "Personality and Job Performance: The Big Five Revisited," *Journal of Applied Psychology* (December 2000): 869; W. A. Hochwarter, L. A. Witt, and K. M. Kacmar, "Perceptions of Organizational Politics as a Moderator of the Relationship between Conscientiousness and Job Performance," *Journal of Applied Psychology* (June 2000): 472; and M. R. Barrick and M. K. Mount, "The Big Five Personality Dimensions and Job Performance: A Meta-Analytic Study," *Personnel Psychology* 44 (1991): 1–26.

29. Barrick and Mount, "Autonomy as a Moderator of the Relationship between the Big Five Personality Dimensions and Job Performance."

30. See also M. R. Furtner and J. F. Rauthmann, "Relations between Self-Leadership and Scores on the Big Five," *Psychological Reports*, October 2010, 339–53; R. Barrick, M. Piotrowski, and G. L. Stewart, "Personality and Job Performance: Test of the Mediating Effects of Motivation Among Sales Representatives," *Journal of Applied Psychology* (February 2002): 43–52; and I. T. Robertson, H. Baron, P. Gibbons, R. MacIver, and G. Nyfield, "Conscientiousness and Managerial Performance," *Journal of Occupational and Organizational Psychology* (June 2000): 171–78.

31. See, for example, J. L. Kisamore, I. M. Jawahar, E. W. Liguori, T. L. Mharapara, and T. H. Stone, "Conflict and Abusive Workplace Behaviors: The Moderating Effects of Social Competencies," *Career Development International*, October 2010, 583–600; P. S. Mishra and A. K. Das Mohapatra, "Relevance of Emotional Intelligence for Effective Job Performance: An Empirical Study," *Vikalpa: The Journal for Decision Makers* (January–March 2010): 53–61; T-Y. Kim, D. M. Cable, S-P. Kim, and J. Wang, "Emotional Competence and Work Performance: The Mediating Effect of Proactivity and the Moderating Effect of Job Autonomy," *Journal of Organizational Behavior* (October 2009): 983–1000; J. M. Diefendorff and G. J. Greguras, "Contextualizing Emotional Display Rules: Examining the Roles of Targets and Discrete Emotions in Shaping Display Rule Perceptions," *Journal of Management* (August 2009): 880–98; J. Gooty, M. Gavin, and N. M. Ashkanasy, "Emotions Research in OB: The Challenges That Lie Ahead," *Journal of Organizational Behavior* (August 2009): 833–38; N. M. Ashkanasy and C. S. Daus, "Emotion in the Workplace: The New Challenge for Managers," *Academy of Management Executive*, February 2002, 76–86; N. M. Ashkanasy, C. E. J. Hartel, and C. S. Daus, "Diversity and Emotions: The New Frontiers in Organizational Behavior Research," *Journal of Management* 28, no. 3 (2002): 307–38; S. Fox, "Promoting Emotional Intelligence in Organizations: Make Training in Emotional Intelligence Effective," *Personnel Psychology*, Spring 2002, 236–40; B. E. Ashforth, "The Handbook of Emotional Intelligence: Theory, Development, Assessment, and Application at Home, School, and in the Work Place: A Review," *Personnel Psychology*, Autumn 2001, 721–24; and R. Bar-On and J. D. A. Parker, *The Handbook of Emotional Intelligence: Theory, Development, Assessment, and Application at Home, School, and in the Work Place* (San Francisco, CA: Jossey-Bass, 2000).

32. See, for instance, C. S. P. Fernandez, "Emotional Intelligence in the Workplace," *Journal of Public Health Management and Practice* (February 2007): 80–82.

33. "Critical Skills for Workforce 2020," *T&D,* September 2011, 19.

34. R. Pearman, "The Leading Edge: Using Emotional Intelligence to Enhance Performance," *T&D,* March 2011, 68–71; C. Prentice and B. King, "The Influence of Emotional Intelligence on the Service Performance of Casino Frontline Employees," *Tourism & Hospitality Research*, January 2011, 49–66; E. H. O'Boyle Jr., R. H. Humphrey, J. M. Pollack, T. H. Hawver, and P. A. Story, "The Relation between Emotional Intelligence and Job Performance: A Meta-Analysis," *Journal of*

Organizational Behavior Online, www.interscience.wiley.com, June 2010; and P. J. Jordan, N. M. Ashkanasy, and C. E. J. Hartel, "Emotional Intelligence as a Moderator of Emotional and Behavioral Reactions to Job Insecurity," *Academy of Management Review*, July 2002, 361–72.

35. C. Cherniss and R. D. Caplan, "A Case Study of Implementing Emotional Intelligence Programs in Organizations," *Journal of Organizational Excellence* (Winter 2001): 763–86; and S. B. Vanessa-Urch and W. Deuskat, "Building the Emotional Intelligence of Groups," *Harvard Business Review*, March 2001, 81–91.

36. "Can't We All Just Get Along," *BusinessWeek*, October 9, 2000, 18.

37. C. Moller and S. Powell, "Emotional Intelligence and the Challenges of Quality Management," *Leadership and Organizational Development Journal* (July–August 2001): 341–45.

38. See L. A. Downey, V. Papageorgiou, and C. Stough, "Examining the Relationship between Leadership, Emotional Intelligence, and Intuition in Female Managers," *Leadership & Organization Development Journal* (April 2006): 250–64.

39. See, for instance, J. Silvester, F. M. Anderson-Gough, N. R. Anderson, and A. R. Mohamed, "Locus of Control, Attributions and Impression Management in the Selection Interview," *Journal of Occupational and Organizational Psychology* (March 2002): 59–77; D. W. Organ and C. N. Greene, "Role Ambiguity, Locus of Control, and Work Satisfaction," *Journal of Applied Psychology* (February 1974): 101–02; and T. R. Mitchell, C. M. Smyser, and S. E. Weed, "Locus of Control: Supervision and Work Satisfaction," *Academy of Management Journal* (September 1975): 623–31.

40. I. Zettler, N. Friedrich, and B. E. Hilbig, "Dissecting Work Commitment: The Role of Machiavellianism," *Career Development International*, February 2011, 20–35; S. R. Kessler, A. C. Bandelli, P. E. Spector, W. C. Borman, C. E. Nelson, and L. M. Penney, "Re-Examining Machiavelli: A Three-Dimensional Model of Machiavellianism in the Workplace," *Journal of Applied Social Psychology* (August 2010): 1868–96; W. Amelia, "Anatomy of a Classic: Machiavelli's Daring Gift," *Wall Street Journal*, August 30–31, 2008, W10; S. A. Snook, "Love and Fear and the Modern Boss," *Harvard Business Review*, January 2008, 16–17; and R. G. Vleeming, "Machiavellianism: A Preliminary Review," *Psychology Reports*, February 1979, 295–310.

41. P. Harris, "Machiavelli and the Global Compass: Ends and Means in Ethics and Leadership," *Journal of Business Ethics* (June 2010): 131–38; and P. Van Kenhove, I. Vermeir, and S. Verniers, "An

Empirical Investigation of the Relationship between Ethical Beliefs, Ethical Ideology, Political Preference and Need for Closure," *Journal of Business Ethics*, August 15, 2001, 347.

42. Based on J. Brockner, *Self-Esteem at Work: Research, Theory, and Practice* (Lexington, MA: Lexington Books, 1988), chs. 1–4.

43. See, for instance, R. Vermunt, D. van Knippenberg, B. van Knippenberg, and E. Blaauw, "Self-Esteem and Outcome Fairness: Differential Importance of Procedural and Outcome Considerations," *Journal of Applied Psychology* (August 2001): 621; T. A. Judge and J. E. Bono, "Relationship of Core Self-Evaluation Traits—Self-Esteem, Generalized Self Efficacy, Locus of Control, and Emotional Stability—With Job Satisfaction and Job Performance," *Journal of Applied Psychology* (February 2001): 80; and D. B. Fedor, J. M. Maslyn, W. D. Davis, and K. Mathieson, "Performance Improvement Efforts in Response to Negative Feedback: The Roles of Source Power and Recipient Self-Esteem," *Journal of Management* (January–February 2001): 79–97.

44. M. Snyder, *Public Appearances, Private Realities: The Psychology of Self-Monitoring* (New York: W. H. Freeman, 1987).

45. See, for example, D. U. Bryant, M. Mitcham, A. R. Araiza, and W. M. Leung, "The Interaction of Self-Monitoring and Organizational Position on Perceived Effort," *Journal of Managerial Psychology* 26, no. 2 (2011): 138–54; B. B. Vilela and J. A. V. González, "Salespersons' Self-Monitoring: Direct, Indirect, and Moderating Effects on Salespersons' Organizational Citizenship Behavior," *Psychology & Marketing*, January 2010, 71–89; and P. M. Fandt, "Managing Impressions with Information: A Field Study of Organizational Realities," *Journal of Applied Behavioral Science* (June 2001): 180–205.

46. Ibid.

47. R. N. Taylor and M. D. Dunnette, "Influence of Dogmatism, Risk Taking Propensity, and Intelligence on Decision Making Strategies for a Sample of Industrial Managers," *Journal of Applied Psychology* (August 1974): 420–23.

48. I. L. Janis and L. Mann, *Decision Making: A Psychological Analysis of Conflict, Choice, and Commitment* (New York: Free Press, 1977).

49. See, for instance, C. P. Cross, L. T. Copping, and A. Campbell, "Sex Differences in Impulsivity: A Meta-Analysis," *Psychological Bulletin*, January 2011, 97–130; A. A. Schooler, K. Fujita, X. Zou, and S. J. Stroessner, "When Risk Seeking Becomes a Motivational Necessity," *Journal of Personality and Social Psychology* (August 2010): 215–31; A. Chatterjee and D. C. Hambrick, "Executive Personality, Capability Cues, and Risk-Taking: How Narcissistic CEOs React to Their Successes

and Stumbles," *Academy of Management Proceedings*, www.aomonline.org (2010); E. Soane, C. Dewberry, and S. Narendran, "The Role of Perceived Costs and Perceived Benefits in the Relationship between Personality and Risk-Related Choices," *Journal of Risk Research* (April 2010): 303–18; and N. Kogan and M. A. Wallach, "Group Risk Taking as a Function of Members' Anxiety and Defensiveness," *Journal of Personality* (March 1967): 50–63.

50. H. Zhao, S. E. Seibert, and G. T. Lumpkin, "The Relationship of Personality to Entrepreneurial Intentions and Performance: A Meta-Analytic Review," *Journal of Management* (March 2010): 381–404; and K. Hyrshy, "Entrepreneurial Metaphors and Concepts: An Exploratory Study," *Journal of Managerial Psychology* (July 2000): 653; and B. McCarthy, "The Cult of Risk Taking and Social Learning: A Study of Irish Entrepreneurs," *Management Decision*, August 2000, 563–75.

51. M. Goldman, "A Journey into Personality Self-Discovery, Vol. 2," *Bloomberg BusinessWeek Online*, March 22, 2011; M. Goldman, "A Journey into Personality Self-Discovery, Vol. 1," *Bloomberg BusinessWeek Online*, February 15, 2011; and P. Korkki, "The True Calling That Wasn't," *New York Times Online*, July 16, 2010.

52. J. L. Holland, *Making Vocational Choices: A Theory of Vocational Personalities and Work Environments* (Odessa, FL: Psychological Assessment Resources, 1997).

53. S. Bates, "Personality Counts: Psychological Tests Can Help Peg the Job Applicants Best Suited for Certain Jobs," *HR Magazine*, February 2002, 28–38; and K. J. Jansen and A. K. Brown, "Toward a Multi-Level Theory of Person Environment Fit," *Academy of Management Proceedings from the Fifty-Eighth Annual Meeting of the Academy of Management*, San Diego, CA (August 7–12, 1998), HR: FR1–FR8.

54. See, for instance, G. W. M. Ip and M. H. Bond, "Culture, Values, and the Spontaneous Self-Concept," *Asian Journal of Psychology*, vol. 1 (1995): 30–36; J. E. Williams, J. L. Saiz, D. L. FormyDuval, M. L. Munick, E. E. Fogle, A. Adom, A. Haque, F. Neto, and J. Yu, "Cross-Cultural Variation in the Importance of Psychological Characteristics: A Seven-Year Country Study," *International Journal of Psychology* (October 1995): 529–50; V. Benet and N. G. Walker, "The Big Seven Factor Model of Personality Description: Evidence for Its Cross-Cultural Generalizability in a Spanish Sample," *Journal of Personality and Social Psychology* (October 1995): 701–18; R. R. McCrae and P. To. Costa Jr., "Personality Trait Structure as a Human Universal," *American Psychologist*, 1997, 509–16; and M. J.

Schmit, J. A. Kihm, and C. Robie, "Development of a Global Measure of Personality," *Personnel Psychology*, Spring 2000, 153–93.

55. J. F. Salgado, "The Five Factor Model of Personality and Job Performance in the European Community," *Journal of Applied Psychology* (February 1997): 30–43. Note: This study covered the 15-nation European community and did not include the 10 countries that joined in 2004.

56. G. Kranz, "Organizations Look to Get Personal in '07," *Workforce Management*, www.workforce.com (June 19, 2007).

57. A. O'Connell, "Smile, Don't Bark in Tough Times," *Harvard Business Review*, November 2009, 27; and G. A. Van Kleef et al., "Searing Sentiment or Cold Calculation? The Effects of Leader Emotional Displays on Team Performance Depend on Follower Epistemic Motivation," *Academy of Management Journal*, June 2009, 562–80.

58. Reprinted by permission from Land Rover North America, LLC.

59. H. H. Kelley, "Attribution in Social Interaction," in E. Jones et al. (eds.), *Behavior* (Morristown, NJ: General Learning Press, 1972).

60. G. Miller and T. Lawson, "The Effect of an Informational Option on the Fundamental Attribution Error," *Personality and Social Psychology Bulletin*, June 1989, 194–204. See also G. Charness and E. Haruvy, "Self-Serving Bias: Evidence from a Simulated Labour Relationship," *Journal of Managerial Psychology* (July 2000): 655; and T. J. Elkins, J. S. Phillips, and R. Konopaske, "Gender-Related Biases in Evaluations of Sex Discrimination Allegations: Is Perceived Threat a Key?" *Journal of Applied Psychology* (April 2002): 280–93.

61. S. T. Fiske, "Social Cognition and Social Perception," *Annual Review of Psychology*, 1993, 155–94; G. N. Powell and Y. Kido, "Managerial Stereotypes in a Global Economy: A Comparative Study of Japanese and American Business Students' Perspectives," *Psychological Reports*, February 1994, 219–26; and J. L. Hilton and W. von Hippel, "Stereotypes," in J. T. Spence, J. M. Darley, and D. J. Foss (eds.), *Annual Review of Psychology*, vol. 47 (Palo Alto, CA: Annual Reviews Inc., 1996), 237–71.

62. B. F. Skinner, *Contingencies of Reinforcement* (East Norwalk, CT: Appleton-Century-Crofts, 1971).

63. A. Bandura, *Social Learning Theory* (Upper Saddle River, NJ: Prentice Hall, 1977).

64. For an interesting article on the subject, see D. Nitsch, M. Baetz, and J. C. Hughes, "Why Code of Conduct Violations Go Unreported: A Conceptual Framework to Guide Intervention and Future Research," *Journal of Business Ethics* (April 2005): 327–41.

65. R. J. Alsop, "The Last Word: Youth and Consequences," *Workforce Management Online*, February

2011; M. Fertik, "Managing Employees in Their Twenties," *Bloomberg BusinessWeek Online*, January 19, 2011; M. Richtel, "Growing Up Digital: Wired for Distraction," *New York Times Online*, November 21, 2010; N. Lublin, "In Defense of Millennials," *Fast Company*, October 2010, 72–74; A. D. Wright and T. D. Tapscott, "Millennials: Bathed in Bits," *HR Magazine*, July 2010, 40–41; S. Jayson, "A Detailed Look at Millennials"; T. Janisch, "Digital Marketplace: Welcoming Gen Y to the Workforce"; and S. Armour, "Generation Y: They've Arrived at Work with a New Attitude," *USA Today*, November 6, 2005, 1B+.

66. N. Ramachandran, "New Paths at Work," *US News & World Report*, March 20, 2006, 47.

67. D. Sacks, "Scenes from the Culture Clash," *Fast Company*, January–February 2006, 75.

68. S. Armour, "Generation Y: They've Arrived at Work with a New Attitude," 2B.

69. S. Armour, "Generation Y: They've Arrived at Work with a New Attitude"; B. Moses, "The Challenges of Managing Gen Y," *The Globe and Mail*, March 11, 2005, C1; and C. A. Martin, *Managing Generation Y* (Amherst, MA: HRD Press, 2001).

70. C. M. Pearson and C. L. Porath, "On the Nature, Consequences, and Remedies of Workplace Incivility: No Time for Nice? Think Again," *Academy of Management Executive*, February 2005, 7–18.

71. J. Robison, "Be Nice: It's Good for Business," *Gallup Brain*, http://brain.gallup.com (August 12, 2004).

72. M. Sandy Hershcovis and J. Barling, "Towards a Multi-Foci Approach to Workplace Aggression: A Meta-Analytic Review of Outcomes from Different Perpetrators," *Journal of Organizational Behavior* (January 2010): 24–44; R. E. Kidwell and S. R. Valentine, "Positive Group Context, Work Attitudes, and Organizational Behavior: The Case of Withholding Job Effort," *Journal of Business Ethics* (April 2009): 15–28; P. Bordia and S. L. D. Resubog, "When Employees Strike Back: Investigating Mediating Mechanisms between Psychological Contract Breach and Workplace Deviance," *Journal of Applied Psychology* (September 2008): 1104–17; and Y. Vardi and E. Weitz, *Misbehavior in Organizations* (Mahwah, NJ: Lawrence Erlbaum Associates, 2004), 246–47.

73. Based on V. P. Richmond, J. C. McCroskey, and S. K. Payne, *Nonverbal Behavior in Interpersonal Relations*, 2nd ed. (Englewood Cliffs, NJ: Prentice Hall, 1991), 117–38; R. Bar-On, *The Emotional Intelligence Inventory (EQ-I): Technical Manual* (Toronto: Multi-Health Systems, 1997); L. A. King, "Ambivalence over Emotional Expression and Reading Emotions in Situations and Faces," *Journal of*

Personality and Social Psychology (March 1998): 753–62; and M. Lewis, J. M. Haviland-Jones, and L. F. Barrett (eds.), *Handbook of Emotions*, 3rd ed. (New York: Guilford Press, 2011).

74. V. Giang, "Inside Google's Insanely Popular Emotional Intelligence Course," http://www.fastcompany.com/3044157/the-future-of-work/inside-googles-insanely-popular-emotional-intelligence-course, March 25, 2015; D. Baer, "Here's What Google Teaches Employees in Its 'Search Inside Yourself' Course," http://www.businessinsider.com/search-inside-yourself-googles-life-changing-mindfulness-course-2014-8, August 5, 2014; G. Gregoire, "Google's 'Jolly Good Fellow' on the Power of Emotional Intelligence," http://www.huffingtonpost.com/2013/09/29/googles-jolly-good-fellow_n_3975944.html, September 29, 2013; and N. Shachtman, "In Silicon Valley, Meditation Is No Fad. It Could Make Your Career," http://www.wired.com/2013/06/meditation-mindfulness-silicon-valley/, June 18, 2013.

75. K. J. O'Hara, "Measuring Sticks," *Smart Business Atlanta*, May 2010, 14–18; "Working in an Ideal World," *T&D*, December 2009, 21; D. Smith, "Surviving a Down Economy with an Upbeat Attitude," *T&D*, November 2009, 16–17; G. Mijuk, "Tough Times for Temp Agencies Likely to Prompt Consolidation," *Wall Street Journal*, March 17, 2009, B7; M. Laff, "Gen Y Proves Loyalty in Economic Downturn," *T&D*, December 2008, 18; and From "How One Company Bridges the Generation Gap," *Bloomberg Business*. Copyright © 2007 by Bloomberg Business. Reprinted with permission.

76. R. Mobbs, "The Employee Is Always Right," *In the Black*, April 2011, 12–15; V. Nayar, "Employee Happiness: Zappos vs. HCL," *Bloomberg BusinessWeek*, January 5, 2011; G. Hamel, "Extreme Makeover," *Leadership Excellence*, January 2011, 3–4; V. Nayar, "The World in 2036: Vineet Nayar Envisages Bottom-Up Leadership," *Economist*, November 27, 2010, 114; V. Nayar, "Employees First, Customers Second," *Chief Learning Officer*, October 2010, 20–23; V. Nayar, "Back to Front," *People Management*, August 12, 2010, 26–29; V. Nayar, "A Maverick CEO Explains How He Persuaded His Team to Leap into the Future," *Harvard Business Review*, June 2010, 110–13; B. Einhorn and K. Gokhale, "Bangalore's Paying Again to Keep the Talent," *Bloomberg BusinessWeek*, May 24, 2010, 14–16; M. Srivastava and S. Hamm, "Using the Slump to Get Bigger in Bangalore," *BusinessWeek*, September 3, 2009, 50–51; and S. Lauchlan, "HCL Takes On the World," *Computer Weekly*. Copyright © 2009 by Computer Weekly. Reprinted with Permission.

10

Management Myth Myth

Teams almost always outperform employees working individually.

Management

DEBUNKED?

Myth

Based on news reports, you'd think that every organization has restructured itself around teams. And it's widely believed that team-based organizations will always outperform more traditional organizations structured around individual efforts. As you'll see in this chapter, teams *can* be very effective devices for accomplishing tasks. But not always! For tasks that demand highly creative thinking, individuals often outperform teams. Additionally, teams can dilute responsibility, which can lead to taking outsized risks and allowing contributors to hide behind the work of others.

MANAGERS

today believe that the use of teams allows their organizations to increase sales or produce better products faster and at lower costs. Although the efforts to create teams aren't always successful, well-planned teams can reinvigorate productivity and better position an organization to deal with a rapidly changing environment.

You've probably had a lot of experience working in groups—class project teams, maybe an athletic team, a fundraising committee, or even a sales team at work. Work teams are one of the realities—and challenges—of managing in today's dynamic global environment. Many organizations have made the move to restructure work around teams rather than individuals. Why? What do these teams look like? And how can managers build effective teams? These are some of the questions we'll be answering in this chapter. Before we can understand teams, however, we first need to understand some basics about groups and group behavior. ●

Learning Outcomes

What Is a Group and What Stages of Development Do Groups Go Through?

10-1 Define *group* and describe the stages of group development.

Each person in this group had his or her assigned role: the Spotter, the Back Spotter, the Gorilla, and the Big Player. For over 10 years, this group—former MIT students who were members of a secret Black Jack Club—used their extraordinary mathematical abilities, expert training, teamwork, and interpersonal skills to take millions of dollars from some of the major casinos in the United States.[1] Although most groups aren't formed for such dishonest purposes, the success of this group at its task was impressive. Managers would like their work groups to be successful at their tasks also. The first step is understanding what a group is and how groups develop.

group
Two or more interacting and interdependent individuals who come together to achieve specific goals

forming stage
The first stage of group development in which people join the group and then define the group's purpose, structure, and leadership

What Is a Group?

A **group** is defined as two or more interacting and interdependent individuals who come together to achieve specific goals. *Formal groups* are work groups that are defined by the organization's structure and have designated work assignments and specific tasks directed at accomplishing organizational goals. Exhibit 10–1 provides some examples. *Informal groups* are social groups. These groups occur naturally in the workplace and tend to form around friendships and common interests. For example, five employees from different departments who regularly eat lunch together are an informal group.

What Are the Stages of Group Development?

Five Stages of Group Development

Research shows that groups develop through five stages.[2] As shown in Exhibit 10–2, these five stages are: *forming, storming, norming, performing,* and *adjourning.*

The **forming stage** has two phases. The first occurs as people join the group. In a formal group, people join because of some work assignment. Once they've joined, the second phase begins: defining the group's purpose, structure, and leadership. This phase involves a great deal

Exhibit 10–1 Examples of Formal Work Groups

- **Command groups**—Groups that are determined by the organization chart and composed of individuals who report directly to a given manager.
- **Task groups**—Groups composed of individuals brought together to complete a specific job task; their existence is often temporary because when the task is completed, the group disbands.
- **Cross-functional teams**—Groups that bring together the knowledge and skills of individuals from various work areas or groups whose members have been trained to do each other's jobs.
- **Self-managed teams**—Groups that are essentially independent and that, in addition to their own tasks, take on traditional managerial responsibilities, such as hiring, planning and scheduling, and evaluating performance.

storming stage
The second stage of group development, which is characterized by intragroup conflict

norming stage
The third stage of group development, which is characterized by close relationships and cohesiveness

performing stage
The fourth stage of group development, when the group is fully functional and works on the group task

adjourning stage
The final stage of group development for temporary groups, during which groups prepare to disband

Exhibit 10–2 Stages of Group Development

Stage I
Forming

Stage II
Storming

Stage III
Norming

Stage IV
Performing

Stage V
Adjourning

of uncertainty as members "test the waters" to determine what types of behavior are acceptable. This stage is complete when members begin to think of themselves as part of a group.

The **storming stage** is appropriately named because of the intragroup conflict. There's conflict over who will control the group and what the group needs to be doing. When this stage is complete, a relatively clear hierarchy of leadership and agreement on the group's direction will be evident.

The **norming stage** is one in which close relationships develop and the group becomes cohesive. The group now demonstrates a strong sense of group identity and camaraderie. This stage is complete when the group structure solidifies and the group has assimilated a common set of expectations (or norms) regarding member behavior.

Palmer Luckey (center), inventor of the Oculus Rift virtual reality headset, started a company to launch his product. Shown here in the forming stage of the start-up Oculus VR are hardware engineer Chris Dycus, foreground; Nate Mitchell, vice president of product, left; CEO Brendan Iribe, second from right; and Michael Antonov, chief software architect.

The fourth stage is the **performing stage**. The group structure is in place and accepted by group members. Their energies have moved from getting to know and understand each other to working on the group's task. This is the last stage of development for permanent work groups. However, for temporary groups—project teams, task forces, or similar groups that have a limited task to do—the final stage is the **adjourning stage**. In this stage, the group prepares to disband. Attention is focused on wrapping up activities instead of task performance. Group members react in different ways. Some are upbeat, thrilled about the group's accomplishments. Others may be sad over the loss of camaraderie and friendships.

Think of a class project you've been involved in and you've probably experienced these stages firsthand. Group members are selected or assigned and then meet for the first time. There's a "feeling out" period to assess what the group is

Ana Venegas/ZUMA Press/Newscom

going to do and how it's going to be done. This is usually followed by a battle for control: Who's going to be in charge? Once this issue is resolved and a "hierarchy" agreed on, the group identifies specific work that needs to be done, who's going to do each part of the project, and dates by which the assigned work needs to be completed. General expectations are established. These decisions form the foundation for what you hope will be a coordinated group effort culminating in a project that's been done well. Once the project is complete and turned in, the group breaks up. Of course, some groups don't get much beyond the forming or storming stages. These groups may have serious interpersonal conflicts, turn in disappointing work, and get lower grades.

So, *does a group become more effective as it progresses through the first four stages?* Some researchers say yes, but it's not that simple.[3] That assumption may be generally true, but what makes a group effective is a complex issue. Here's why:

- Under some conditions, high levels of conflict are conducive to high levels of group performance; that is, there might be situations in which groups in the storming stage outperform those in the norming or performing stages.
- Groups don't always proceed sequentially from one stage to the next. Sometimes, groups are storming and performing at the same time. Groups even occasionally regress to previous stages.
- Don't assume all groups precisely follow this process or that performing is always the most preferable stage.

Think of this group stages model as a general framework that underscores the fact that *groups are dynamic entities* and *managers need to know the stage a group is in.* Why? So they can understand the problems and issues that are most likely to surface.

What else do you need to know about groups? Let's look at some important aspects of group behavior.

⭐ Watch It 1!

If your professor has assigned this, go to the Assignments section of **mymanagementlab.com** to complete the video exercise titled *Rudi's Bakery: Work Teams.*

A Question of Ethics

When coworkers work closely on a team project, is there such a thing as TMI (too much information)?[4] At one company, a team that had just finished a major project went out to lunch to celebrate. During lunch, one colleague mentioned that he was training for a 20-mile bike race. In addition to a discussion of his new helmet and Lycra shorts, the person also described shaving his whole body to reduce aerodynamic drag. Afterwards, another team member said that she didn't want to hear that type of information from someone who was a colleague not a friend and wasn't sure why this individual even wanted to share such information with the rest of the work team. At other companies, managers often hear awkward and questionable comments from their younger Gen Y employees about activities like too much partying after work or on the weekend or that they're looking for another job at another company.

If your professor has assigned this, go to the Assignments section of **mymanagementlab.com** *to complete these discussion questions.*

⭐ **Talk About It 1:** What benefits/drawbacks arise from sharing information like this?

⭐ **Talk About It 2:** What are the ethical implications of sharing such personal information in the workplace?

5 Major Concepts of Group Behavior

1 Roles

Behavior patterns expected of someone who occupies a given position in a social unit

- We adjust our **roles** to the group we belong to at the time.
- Employees attempt to determine what behaviors are expected of them by: reading their job descriptions, getting suggestions from their bosses, *and* watching what their coworkers do.
  — Role conflict happens when an employee has conflicting role expectations.

Kwest/Shutterstock

2ª Norms

Acceptable standards shared by a group's members

*Each group has its own unique set of **norms**. Most organizations have common norms, which typically focus on:*

- Effort and performance
  — Probably most widespread norm
  — Can be extremely powerful in affecting an individual employee's performance
- Dress codes (what's acceptable to wear to work)

Mogen creative/Shutterstock

role	**norms**
Behavior patterns expected of someone who occupies a given position in a social unit	Standards or expectations that are accepted and shared by a group's members

2^b Conformity

Adjusting one's behavior to align with a group's norms

- We all want to be accepted by groups to which we belong, which makes us susceptible to conformity pressures.

- See the From Past to Present box (p. 308) for more information on **Solomon Asch's classic studies on conformity**.[5]

35% of participants in Asch's study would conform to group behavior or "follow the pack."

Kjpargeter/Shutterstock

3 Status Systems

A prestige grading, position, or rank within a group and an important factor in understanding behavior

- Human groupings have always had status hierarchies.

- A disparity between what individuals perceive their status to be and what others perceive it to be is a significant motivator with behavioral consequences.

- Anything can have status value if others in the group admire it.

- Group members have no problem placing people into status categories, and they usually agree about who's high, low, and in the middle.

- It's important for people to believe there's congruency (equity between perceived ranking of an individual and the status symbols he or she has) in an organization's status system to prevent disruptions to general "this is what I expect."

Vbar/Shutterstock

conformity
Adjusting one's behavior to align with a group's norms

status
A prestige grading, position, or rank within a group

4 Group Size

Group size affects a group's behavior, but the effect depends on what criteria you're using.[6]

Small Group Better At:

(5–7 members) <

- Completing tasks faster Lantapix/Shutterstock
- Figuring out what to do
- Getting job done

Large Group Better At:

(12 or more members) >

Lantapix/Shutterstock

- Problem solving
- Finding facts
- Gaining diverse input

Drawbacks of Large Groups:

- Individual productivity of each group member declines as the group expands, which is known as **social loafing**[7]—reducing effort because dispersion of responsibility encourages individuals to slack off.

    — When a group's results can't be attributed to any single person, individuals may be tempted to become "free riders" and coast on the group's efforts because they think their contributions can't be measured.

When using large work groups, managers should **find a way to identify individual efforts**.

5 Group Cohesiveness

The degree to which members are attracted to one another and share the group's goals

- Groups that experience a lot of internal disagreement and lack of cooperation are less effective than are groups in which individuals generally agree, cooperate, and like each other.

- The more that members are attracted to one another and the more that a group's goals align with each individual's goals, the greater the group's cohesiveness.

- Highly cohesive groups are more effective than are those with less cohesiveness.

However, the **relationship between cohesiveness and effectiveness is more complex**.[8]

— A key moderating variable is the degree to which the group's attitude aligns with its formal goals or those of the larger organization.[9] **See Exhibit 10–3**, which tells us that:

Cohesiveness

	High	**Low**
High	Strong increase in productivity	Moderate increase in productivity
Low	Decrease in productivity	No significant effect on productivity

Alignment of Group and Organizational Goals

Exhibit 10–3 Group Cohesiveness and Productivity

— **The more cohesive a group**, the more its members will follow its goals. If these goals are favorable, **a cohesive group is more productive than a less cohesive group**.

— If cohesiveness is high and attitudes are unfavorable, productivity decreases.

— If cohesiveness is low and goals are supported, productivity increases, but not as much as when both cohesiveness and support are high.

— When cohesiveness is low and goals are not supported, cohesiveness has no significant effect on productivity.

Andreanita/Fotolia

social loafing
The tendency for individuals to expend less effort when working collectively than when working individually

group cohesiveness
The degree to which group members are attracted to one another and share the group's goals

◂◂◂ From the Past to the Present ▸▸▸

- *DOES* the desire to be accepted as a part of a group leave one susceptible to conforming to the group's norms?
- *WILL* a group exert pressure that's strong enough to change a member's attitude and behavior?

That's what Solomon Asch wanted to know, and according to his research, the answer appears to be yes.[10]

Asch's Research:

- Study involved groups of seven or eight people who sat in a classroom and were asked to compare two cards held by an investigator. The object was for each group member to announce aloud which of the three lines matched the single line.
- One card had one line; the other had three lines of varying length. One of the lines on the three-line card was identical to the line on the one-line card and the difference in line length was quite obvious. (See Exhibit 10–4.)
- Under ordinary conditions, subjects made errors of less than 1 percent.

BUT … what happens if members of the group begin to give incorrect answers?

Will the pressure to conform cause an unsuspecting subject (USS) to alter his or her answers to align with those of the others?

Have YOU ever been **pressured by a group to conform?**

- The group was seated in a prearranged way so the USS was the last to announce his or her decision and so was unaware that the experiment was fixed.
- The experiment began with two sets of matching exercises in which all the subjects gave the right answers.
- On the third set, however, the first subject gave an obviously wrong answer—for example, saying C in Exhibit 10–4. The next subject gave the same wrong answer, and so did the others, until it was the unsuspecting subject's turn.
- The USS knew that "B" was the same as "X" but everyone else said "C".
- The decision confronting the USS was this: Do you publicly state a perception that differs from the pre-announced position of the others? Or do you give an answer that you strongly believe to be incorrect in order to have your response agree with the other group members?
- Asch's subjects conformed—that is, gave answers they knew were wrong but were consistent with the replies of other group members—in about 35 percent of many experiments and many trials.

Implications for Managers:

- The Asch study provides considerable insight into group behaviors. The tendency, as Asch showed, is for individual members to go along with the pack. To diminish the negative aspects of conformity, managers should create a climate of openness in which employees are free to discuss problems without fear of retaliation.

*If your professor has assigned this, go to the Assignments section of **mymanagementlab.com** to complete these discussion questions.*

⭐ **Talk About It 3:** *Does* the desire to be accepted as a part of a group leave one susceptible to conforming to the group's norms? *Will* a group exert pressure that's strong enough to change a member's attitude and behavior? Discuss.

⭐ **Talk About It 4:** What can you use from this discussion to help you be a better manager?

Exhibit 10–4 Examples of Cards Used in Asch's Study

How Are Groups Turned into Effective Teams?

10-3 Discuss how groups are turned into effective teams.

When companies like W. L. Gore, Volvo, and Kraft Foods introduced teams into their production processes, it made news because no one else was doing it. Today, it's just the opposite—the organization that *doesn't* use teams would be newsworthy. It's estimated that some 80 percent of *Fortune* 500 companies have at least half of their employees on teams. In fact, more than 70 percent of U.S. manufacturers use work teams.[11]

Teams are likely to continue to be popular. Why? Research suggests that teams typically outperform individuals when the tasks being done require multiple skills, judgment, and experience.[12] Organizations are using team-based structures because they've found that teams are more flexible and responsive to changing events than are traditional departments or other permanent work groups. Teams have the ability to quickly assemble, deploy, refocus, and disband. In this section, we'll discuss what a work team is, the different types of teams that organizations might use, and how to develop and manage work teams.

Work groups = Work teams?

Are Work Groups and Work Teams the Same?

At this point, you may be asking yourself: Are teams and groups the same thing? No. In this section, we clarify the difference between a work group and a work team.[13]

Most of you are probably familiar with teams especially if you've watched or participated in organized sports events. Work *teams* do differ from work *groups* and have their own unique traits (see Exhibit 10–5). Work groups interact primarily to share information and to make decisions to help each member do his or her job more efficiently and effectively. There's no need or opportunity for work groups to engage in collective work that requires joint effort. On the other hand, **work teams** are groups whose members work intensely on a specific, common goal using their positive synergy, individual and mutual accountability, and complementary skills.

These descriptions should help clarify why so many organizations have restructured work processes around teams. Managers are looking for that positive synergy that will help the organization improve its performance.[14] The extensive use of teams creates the potential for an organization to generate greater outputs with no increase in (or even fewer) inputs. For example, until the economic downturn hit, investment teams at Wachovia's Asset Management Division (which is now a part of Wells Fargo & Company) were able to significantly improve investment performance. As a result, these teams helped the bank improve its Morningstar financial rating.[15]

Exhibit 10–5 Groups versus Teams

Team-based work is a key ingredient to the success of Google. Throughout the company, small teams that require multiple skills work on a specific common goal using their positive synergy. Shown here is Google's food preparation team in Toronto, whose goal is to plan and prepare nutritious and delicious meals for fellow workers.

Mark Blinch/Reuters

Recognize, however, that such increases are simply "potential." Nothing inherently magical in the creation of work teams guarantees that this positive synergy and its accompanying productivity will occur. Accordingly, merely calling a group a team doesn't automatically increase its performance.[16] As we show later in this chapter, successful or high-performing work teams have certain common characteristics. If managers hope to gain increases in organizational performance, they will need to ensure that the teams possess those characteristics.

What Are the Different Types of Work Teams?

Teams can do a variety of things. They can design products, provide services, negotiate deals, coordinate projects, offer advice, and make decisions.[17] For instance, at Rockwell Automation's facility in North Carolina, teams are used in work process optimization projects. At Arkansas-based Acxiom Corporation, a team of human resource professionals planned and implemented a cultural change. And every summer weekend at any NASCAR race, you can see work teams in action during drivers' pit stops.[18] The four most common types of work teams are problem-solving teams, self-managed work teams, cross-functional teams, and virtual teams.

1. When work teams first became popular, most were **problem-solving teams**, which are teams from the same department or functional area involved in efforts to improve work activities or to solve specific problems. Members share ideas or offer suggestions on how work processes and methods can be improved. However, these teams are rarely given the authority to implement any of their suggested actions.

2. Although problem-solving teams were helpful, they didn't go far enough in getting employees involved in work-related decisions and processes. This need led to another type of team, a **self-managed work team**, which is a formal group of employees who operate without a manager and are responsible for a complete work process or segment. A self-managed team is responsible for getting the work done *and* for managing themselves, and usually includes planning and scheduling of work, assigning tasks to members, collective control over the pace of work, making operating decisions, and taking action on problems. For instance, teams at Corning have no shift supervisors and work closely with other manufacturing divisions to solve production-line problems and coordinate deadlines and deliveries. The teams have the authority to make and implement decisions, finish projects, and address problems.[19] Other organizations, such as Xerox, Boeing, PepsiCo, and Hewlett-Packard, also use self-managed teams. It's estimated that about 30 percent of U.S. employers now use this form of team; and among large firms, the number is probably closer to 50 percent.[20] Most organizations that use self-managed teams find them to be effective.[21]

3. The third type of team is the **cross-functional team**, which we introduced in Chapter 6 and defined as a work team composed of individuals from various specialties. Many organizations use cross-functional teams. For example, ArcelorMittal, the world's largest steel company, uses cross-functional teams of scientists, plant managers, and salespeople to review and monitor product innovations.[22] The concept of cross-functional teams is even being applied in health care. For instance, at Suburban Hospital in Bethesda, Maryland, intensive care unit (ICU) teams composed of a doctor trained in intensive care medicine, a pharmacist, a social worker, a nutritionist, the chief ICU nurse, a respiratory therapist, and a chaplain meet daily with every patient's bedside nurse to discuss and debate the best course of treatment. The hospital credits this team care approach with reducing errors, shortening the amount of time patients spend in ICU, and improving communication between families and the medical staff.[23]

problem-solving teams
A team from the same department or functional area that's involved in efforts to improve work activities or to solve specific problems

self-managed work team
A type of work team that operates without a manager and is responsible for a complete work process or segment

cross-functional team
A work team composed of individuals from various specialties

4. The final type of team is the **virtual team**, which is a team that uses technology to link physically dispersed members in order to achieve a common goal. For instance, a virtual team at Boeing-Rocketdyne played a pivotal role in developing a radically new product.[24] Another company, Decision Lens, uses a virtual team environment to generate and evaluate creative ideas.[25] In a virtual team, members collaborate online with tools such as wide-area networks, videoconferencing, fax, e-mail, or Web sites where the team can hold online conferences.[26] Virtual teams can do all the things that other teams can—share information, make decisions, and complete tasks; however, they lack the normal give-and-take of face-to-face discussions. That's why virtual teams tend to be more task-oriented, especially if the team members have never personally met.

> **virtual team**
> A type of work team that uses technology to link physically dispersed members in order to achieve a common goal

✪ Try It!

If your professor has assigned this, go to the Assignments section of **mymanagementlab.com** to complete the **Simulation: *Virtual Teams*.**

What Makes a Team Effective?

Making a Team Effective

Much research has been done on what it is that makes a team effective.[27] Out of these efforts, we now have a fairly focused model identifying those characteristics.[28] Exhibit 10–6 summarizes what we currently know about what makes a team effective. As we look at this model, keep in mind two things. **1** Teams differ in form and structure. This model attempts to generalize across all teams, so you should only use it as a guide.[29] **2** The model assumes that managers have already determined that teamwork is preferable to individual work. Creating "effective" teams in situations in which individuals can do the job better would be wasted effort.

┄┄ Technology and the Manager's Job ┄┄
KEEPING CONNECTED: IT AND TEAMS

Thirty percent of managers say their work teams are "digitally fluent" and communicate very well using new electronic channels.[30] Work teams need information to do their work. With work teams often being not just steps away, but continents away from each other, it's important to have a way for team members to communicate and collaborate. That's where IT comes in. Technology has enabled greater online communication and collaboration within teams of all types.[31]

The idea of technologically aided collaboration actually originated with online search engines. The Internet itself was initially intended as a way for groups of scientists and researchers to share information. Then, as more and more information was put "on the Web," users relied on a variety of search engines to help them find that information. Now, we see many examples of collaborative technologies such as wiki pages, blogs, and even multiplayer virtual reality games.

Today, online collaborative tools have given work teams more efficient and effective ways to get work done. For instance, engineers at Toyota use collaborative communication tools to share process improvements and innovations. These communication tools allow employees to collectively share common knowledge and innovate faster. Managers everywhere should look to the power of IT to help work teams improve the way work gets done.

If your professor has assigned this, go to the Assignments section of **mymanagementlab.com** *to complete these discussion questions.*

✪ **TALK ABOUT IT 5:** What challenges do managers face in managing teams that must rely on IT to communicate?

✪ **TALK ABOUT IT 6:** Using Exhibit 10–6, discuss how the four major components of team effectiveness would affect and be affected by a team's use of IT.

Exhibit 10–6 Team Effectiveness Model

Source: Stephen P. Robbins and Timothy A. Judge, *Organizational Behavior*, 14th edition, © 2011, p. 319. Reprinted and electronically reproduced by permission of Pearson Education, Inc., New York, NY.

One thing we need to clarify first before looking at the model is what we mean by team effectiveness. Typically, it includes objective measures of a team's productivity, managers' ratings of the team's performance, and aggregate measures of member satisfaction. As you can see from the model, the four key components of effective teams include the context, the team's composition, work design, and process variables.

WHAT FACTORS IN THE CONTEXT APPEAR TO MAKE A TEAM EFFECTIVE? Four contextual factors appear to be most significantly related to team performance. These factors include adequate resources, leadership and structure, a climate of trust, and performance evaluation and reward systems.

As part of the larger organization system, a team relies on resources outside the group to sustain it. If it doesn't have *adequate resources*, the team's ability to perform its job effectively is reduced. This factor appears to be so important to team performance that one research study concluded that effective work groups must have support from the organization.[32] Resources can include timely information, proper equipment, encouragement, adequate staffing, and administrative assistance.

If a team can't agree on who is to do what or ensure that all members contribute equally in sharing the workload, it won't function properly. Agreeing on the specifics of work and how all the team members' individual skills fit together requires *team leadership and structure*. This aspect can come from the organization or from the team itself. Even in self-managed teams, a manager's job is to be more of a coach by supporting the team's efforts and managing outside (rather than inside) the team.

Members of effective teams *trust* each other. And they also trust their leaders.[33] Why is trust important? It facilitates cooperation, reduces the need to monitor each other's behavior, and bonds members around the belief that others on the team won't take advantage of them.

Trusting the team leader is also important because it means the team is willing to accept and commit to the leader's goals and decisions.

The final contextual factor of an effective team is a *performance evaluation and reward system.* Team members have to be accountable both individually and jointly. So, in addition to evaluating and rewarding employees for their individual contributions, managers should consider group-based appraisals, profit-sharing, and other approaches that reinforce team effort and commitment.

WHAT TEAM COMPOSITION FACTORS LEAD TO EFFECTIVENESS? Several team composition factors are important to a team's effectiveness. They include team member abilities, personality, role allocation, diversity, size of teams, member flexibility, and member preferences.

Part of a team's performance depends on its members' *knowledge, skills, and abilities.*[34] Research has shown that to perform effectively, a team needs three different types of skills. First, it needs people with technical expertise. Next, it needs members with problem-solving and decision-making skills. Finally, a team needs people with interpersonal skills. A team can't achieve its performance potential if it doesn't have or can't develop all these skills. And the right mix of these skills is also critical. Too much of one at the expense of another will lead to lower team performance. However, a team doesn't necessarily need all these skills immediately. It's not uncommon for team members to take responsibility for learning the skills in which the group is deficient. That way a team can achieve its full potential.

As we saw in the last chapter, *personality* significantly influences individual behavior. It's also true for team behavior. Research has shown that three of the Big Five dimensions are relevant to team effectiveness.[35] For instance, high levels of both conscientiousness and openness-to-experience tend to lead to higher team performance. Agreeableness also appears to matter. And teams that had one or more highly disagreeable members performed poorly. Maybe you've had that not-so-good experience in group projects that you've been part of!

Nine potential team *roles* have been identified. (See Exhibit 10–7.) High-performing work teams have people who were selected to fulfill these roles based on their skills and preferences.[36] On many teams, individuals may play multiple roles. It's important for managers to understand the individual strengths a person will bring to a team and select team members with those strengths in mind to ensure that these roles are filled.

Team *diversity* is another factor that can influence team effectiveness. Although many of us hold the optimistic view that diversity is desirable, research seems to show the opposite. One review found that "Studies on diversity in teams from the last 50 years have shown that surface-level social-category differences such as race/ethnicity, gender, and age tend to … have negative effects" on the performance of teams.[37] Some evidence does show that the disruptive effects of diversity decline over time, but evidence does not confirm that diverse teams perform better eventually.

What *size* should a work team be in order to be effective? At Amazon, work teams have considerable autonomy to innovate and to investigate ideas. Jeff Bezos, founder and CEO, uses a "two-pizza" philosophy; that is, a team should be small enough that it can be fed with two pizzas. This "two-pizza" philosophy usually limits groups to five to seven people, depending, of course, on team member appetites![38] Generally speaking, the most effective teams have five to nine members. And experts suggest using the smallest number of people who can do the task.

Team *member preferences* need to be considered. Why? Some people just prefer not to work on teams. Given the option, many

The Microsoft Surface design team had the necessary technical and interpersonal skills to perform effectively in creating the company's new tablet computer. Shown here demonstrating the product's innovative design are, from left, team members Steven Sinofsky and Mike Angiulo and team leader Panos Panay.

Damian Dovarganes/Associated Press

Exhibit 10–7 Team Member Roles

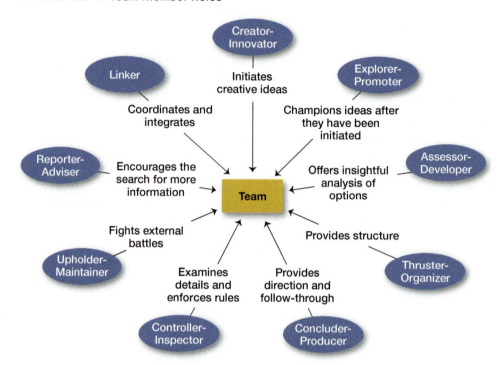

Source: Based on C. Margerison and D. McCann, *Team Management: Practical New Approaches* (London: Mercury Books, 1990).

employees will opt not to be part of a team. When people who would prefer to work alone are forced on a team, it creates a direct threat to the team's morale and to individual member satisfaction.[39]

HOW DOES WORK DESIGN AFFECT TEAM EFFECTIVENESS? Effective teams need to work together and take collective responsibility for completing tasks. An effective team must be more than a "team in name only."[40] Important work design elements include *autonomy*, using a *variety of skills*, being able to complete a *whole and identifiable* task or product, and working on a task or project that has a *significant impact* on others. Research indicates that these characteristics enhance team member motivation and increase team effectiveness.[41]

WHAT TEAM PROCESSES ARE RELATED TO TEAM EFFECTIVENESS? Five team process variables have been shown to be related to team effectiveness. These include a common purpose, specific team goals, team efficacy, managed conflict, and minimal social loafing.

An effective team has a *common plan and purpose*. This common purpose provides direction, momentum, and commitment for team members.[42] Members of successful teams put a lot of time and effort into discussing, shaping, and agreeing on a purpose that belongs to them both individually and as a team.

Teams also need *specific goals*. Such goals facilitate clear communication and help teams maintain their focus on getting results.

Team efficacy emerges when teams believe in themselves and believe they can succeed.[43] Effective teams have confidence in themselves and in their members.

Of team managers, 63.5 percent say they are somewhat effective at resolving conflict.[44]

Effective teams need some *conflict*. Conflict on a team isn't necessarily bad and can actually improve team effectiveness.[45] But it has to be the right kind of conflict. Relationship conflicts—those based on interpersonal incompatibilities, tension, and autonomy toward others—are almost always dysfunctional. However, task conflicts—those based on disagreements about task content—can be beneficial because they may stimulate discussion, promote critical assessment of problems and options, and can lead to better team decisions.

⭐ Write It 1!

If your professor has assigned this, go to the Assignments section of **mymanagementlab.com** and complete *BCOMM 2: Managing Conflict*.

Finally, effective teams work to minimize the tendency for *social loafing*, which we discussed earlier in this chapter. Successful teams make members individually and jointly accountable for the team's purpose, goals, and approach.[46]

How Can a Manager Shape Team Behavior?

A manager can do several things to shape a team's behavior including proper selection, employee training, and rewarding the appropriate team behaviors. Let's look at each.

WHAT ROLE DOES SELECTION PLAY?   Some individuals already possess the interpersonal skills to be effective team players. When hiring team members, managers should check whether applicants have the technical skills required to successfully perform the job *and* whether they can fulfill team roles.

Some applicants may have been socialized around individual contributions and, consequently, lack team skills, which could also be true for some current employees being moved into teams due to organizational restructuring. When faced with this situation, a manager can do several things. First, and most obvious, if team skills are woefully lacking, don't hire the person. If successful performance is going to require interaction, not hiring the individual is appropriate. On the other hand, an applicant who has some basic skills can be hired on a probationary basis and required to undergo training to shape him or her into a team player. If the skills aren't learned or practiced, then the individual may have to be let go.

> Fifty-seven percent of team leaders said if someone on their team hated their job, they would encourage them to find another job. Only 7 percent said they would change their role to make them happy.[47]

CAN INDIVIDUALS BE TRAINED TO BE TEAM PLAYERS?   Performing well in a team involves a set of behaviors.[48] As we discussed in the preceding chapter, new behaviors *can* be learned. Even people who feel strongly about the importance of individual accomplishment can be trained to become team players. Training specialists can conduct exercises so employees can experience what teamwork is all about. The workshops can cover such topics as team problem solving, communications, negotiations, conflict resolution, and coaching skills. In addition, it's not unusual for these individuals to be exposed to the five stages of team development that we discussed earlier.[49] At Verizon Communications, for example, trainers focus on how a team goes through various stages before it gels. And employees are reminded of the importance of patience, because teams take longer to do some things—such as make decisions—than do employees acting alone.[50]

The Container Store manager Jaimie Moeller (left) leads a team huddle with employees before they begin their work day. Because employees work as a team in serving customers, managers begin shaping team behavior when interviewing job candidates and hiring only a small percentage of applicants who are enthusiastic about working in a team-oriented environment.

ZUMA Press, Inc/Alamy

WHAT ROLE DO REWARDS PLAY IN SHAPING TEAM PLAYERS? An organization's reward system needs to encourage cooperative efforts rather than competitive ones. For instance, Lockheed Martin's aeronautics division organized its some 20,000 employees into teams. Rewards are structured to return a percentage increase in the bottom line to the team members on the basis of achievements of the team's performance goals.

Promotions, pay raises, and other forms of recognition should be given to employees who are effective collaborative team members. Taking this approach doesn't mean that individual contribution is ignored, but rather that it's balanced with selfless contributions to the team. Examples of behaviors that should be rewarded include training new colleagues, sharing information with teammates, helping resolve team conflicts, and mastering new skills in which the team is deficient.[51] Finally, managers can't forget the inherent rewards that employees can receive from teamwork. Work teams provide camaraderie. It's exciting and satisfying to be an integral part of a successful team. The opportunity to engage in personal development and to help teammates grow can be a satisfying and rewarding experience for employees.[52]

✪ Watch It 2!

If your professor has assigned this, go to the Assignments section of **mymanagementlab.com** to complete the video exercise titled *CH2MHill: Work Teams*.

What Current Issues Do Managers Face in Managing Teams?

10-4 Discuss contemporary issues in managing teams.

Few trends have influenced how work gets done in organizations as much as the use of work teams. The shift from working alone to working on teams requires employees to cooperate with others, share information, confront differences, and sublimate personal interests for the greater good of the team. Managers can build effective teams by understanding what influences performance and satisfaction. However, managers also face some current challenges in managing teams, including those associated with managing global teams and with understanding when teams aren't the answer.

✪ Write It 2!

If your professor has assigned this, go to the Assignments section of **mymanagementlab.com** and complete *MGMT 15: Team-Based Structures*.

What's Involved with Managing Global Teams?

Two characteristics of today's organizations are obvious: they're global and work is increasingly done by teams. Because of those reasons, any manager is likely to have to manage a global team. What do we know about managing global teams? We know there are both drawbacks and benefits in using global teams (see Exhibit 10–8). What are some of the challenges associated with managing global teams?

HOW DO TEAM COMPOSITION FACTORS AFFECT MANAGING A GLOBAL TEAM? In global organizations, understanding the relationship between team effectiveness and team composition is more challenging because of the unique cultural characteristics represented by members of a global team. In addition to recognizing team members' abilities, skills, knowledge, and personality, managers need to be familiar with and clearly understand the cultural characteristics of the groups and the group members they manage.[53] For instance,

Exhibit 10–8 Global Teams

DRAWBACKS	BENEFITS
• Disliking team members	• Greater diversity of ideas
• Mistrusting team members	• Limited groupthink
• Stereotyping	• Increased attention on understanding others' ideas, perspectives, etc.
• Communication problems	
• Stress and tension	

Source: Based on N. Adler, *International Dimensions of Organizational Behavior*, 4th ed. (Cincinnati, OH: Southwestern Cengage Publishing, 2002), 141–47.

is the global team from a culture in which uncertainty avoidance is high? If so, members will not be comfortable dealing with unpredictable and ambiguous tasks. Also, as managers work with global teams, they need to be aware of the potential for stereotyping, which can lead to problems.

HOW DOES TEAM STRUCTURE AFFECT MANAGING A GLOBAL TEAM? Some of the structural areas where we see differences in managing global teams include conformity, status, social loafing, and cohesiveness.

Are conformity findings generalizable across cultures? Research suggests that Asch's findings are culture-bound.[54] For instance, as might be expected, conformity to social norms tends to be higher in collectivistic cultures than in individualistic cultures. However, groupthink tends to be less of a problem in global teams because members are less likely to feel pressured to conform to the ideas, conclusions, and decisions of the group.[55]

Also, the importance of status varies among cultures. The French, for example, are extremely status conscious. Also, countries differ on the criteria that confer status. For instance, in Latin America and Asia, status tends to come from family position and formal roles held in organizations. In contrast, while status is important in countries like the United States and Australia, it tends to be less "in your face." And it tends to be given based on accomplishments rather than on titles and family history. Managers must understand who and what holds status when interacting with people from a culture different from their own. An American manager who doesn't understand that office size isn't a measure of a Japanese executive's position or who fails to grasp the importance the British place on family genealogy and social class is likely to unintentionally offend others and lessen his or her interpersonal effectiveness.

Social loafing has a Western bias. It's consistent with individualistic cultures, like the United States and Canada, which are dominated by self-interest. It's not consistent with collectivistic societies, in which individuals are motivated by group goals. For instance, in studies comparing employees from the United States with employees from the People's Republic of China and Israel (both collectivistic societies), the Chinese and Israelis showed no propensity to engage in social loafing. In fact, they actually performed better in a group than when working alone.[56]

Cohesiveness is another group structural element that may create special challenges for managers. In a cohesive group, members are unified and "act as one." There's a great deal of camaraderie and group identity is high. In global teams, however, cohesiveness is often more difficult to achieve because of higher levels of "mistrust, miscommunication, and stress."[57]

Jambu Palaniappan is a regional general manager in Eastern Europe, the Middle East, and Africa for Uber, a car service that is rapidly expanding throughout the world. In managing the market strategy, operations, and expansion teams that launch the service in different countries, he is challenged by the unique cultural characteristics of team members.

Mosa'ab Elshamy/AP Images

HOW DO TEAM PROCESSES AFFECT MANAGING A GLOBAL TEAM? The processes that global teams use to do their work can be particularly challenging for managers. For one thing, communication issues often arise because not all team members may be fluent in the team's working language, which can lead to inaccuracies, misunderstandings, and inefficiencies.[58] However, research has also shown that a multicultural global team is better able to capitalize on the diversity of ideas represented if a wide range of information is used.[59]

Managing conflict in global teams isn't easy, especially when those teams are virtual teams. Conflict can interfere with how information is used by the team. However, research shows that in collectivistic cultures, a collaborative conflict management style can be most effective.[60]

⭐ **Try It 2!**

If your professor has assigned this, go to the Assignments section of **mymanagementlab.com** to complete the **Simulation: *Teams***.

When Are Teams Not the Answer?

Teamwork takes more time and often more resources than does individual work.[61] Teams require managers to communicate more, manage conflicts, and run meetings. So, the benefits of using teams need to exceed the costs. And that's not always the case![62] In the rush to use teams, some managers have introduced them into situations in which it would have been better to have individuals do the work. So before implementing teams just because everyone's talking about their popularity, you should carefully evaluate whether the work requires or will benefit from a collective effort.

How do you know whether work is better done individually or by a group? Three "tests" have been suggested.[63] First, can the work be done better by more than one person? Task complexity would be a good indicator of a need for different perspectives. Simple tasks that don't require diverse input are probably better done by individuals. Second, does the work create a common purpose or set of goals for the people in the group that's more than the sum of individual goals? For instance, many car dealerships use teams to link customer-service personnel, mechanics, parts specialists, and sales representatives. Such teams can better meet the goal of outstanding customer satisfaction. The final test to assess whether teams or individuals are better suited for doing work is to look at the interdependence of the individuals. Using teams makes sense when there's interdependence between tasks; that is, when the success of everyone depends on the success of each person *and* the success of each person depends on the others. For example, soccer is an obvious team sport. Success requires a lot of coordination between interdependent players. On the other hand, swim teams aren't really teams, except on relays. They're groups of individuals, performing individually, whose total performance is merely the sum of their individual performances.

MyManagementLab®

Go to **mymanagementlab.com** to complete the problems marked with this icon .

10 Review

CHAPTER SUMMARY

10-1 Define *group* and describe the stages of group development.

A group is two or more interacting and interdependent individuals who come together to achieve specific goals. Formal groups are work groups that are defined by the organization's structure and have designated work assignments and specific tasks directed at accomplishing organizational goals. Informal groups are social groups.

The forming stage consists of two phases: joining the group and defining the group's purpose, structure, and leadership. The storming stage is one of intragroup conflict over who will control the group and what the group will be doing. The norming stage is when close relationships and cohesiveness develop as norms are determined. The performing stage is when group members work on the group's task. The adjourning stage happens when the group prepares to disband.

10-2 Describe the major concepts of group behavior.

A role refers to a set of behavior patterns expected of someone occupying a given position in a social unit. At any given time, employees adjust their role behaviors to the group of which they are a part. Norms are standards shared by group members. They informally convey to employees which behaviors are acceptable and which are unacceptable. Status is another factor to know because it can be a significant motivator and it needs to be congruent. Also, group size affects group behavior in a number of ways. Smaller groups are generally faster at completing tasks than are larger ones. However, larger groups are frequently better at fact finding because of their diversified input. As a result, larger groups are generally better at problem solving. Finally, group cohesiveness is important because of its impact on a group's effectiveness at achieving its goals.

10-3 Discuss how groups are turned into effective teams.

Effective teams have common characteristics. They have adequate resources, effective leadership, a climate of trust, and a performance evaluation and reward system that reflects team contributions. These teams have individuals with technical expertise as well as problem-solving, decision-making, and interpersonal skills and the right traits, especially conscientiousness and openness to new experiences. Effective teams also tend to be small, preferably of diverse backgrounds. They have members who fill role demands and who prefer to be part of a team. And the work that members do provides freedom and autonomy, the opportunity to use different skills and talents, the ability to complete a whole and identifiable task or product, and work that has a substantial impact on others. Finally, effective teams have members who believe in the team's capabilities and are committed to a common plan and purpose, specific team goals, a manageable level of conflict, and a minimal degree of social loafing.

10-4 Discuss contemporary issues in managing teams.

The challenges of managing global teams can be seen in team composition factors, especially the diverse cultural characteristics; in team structure, especially conformity, status, social loafing, and cohesiveness; in team processes, especially with communication and managing conflict; and in the manager's role in making it all work.

Managers also need to know when teams are not the answer. They can do this by assessing whether the work can be done better by more than one person; by whether the work creates a common purpose or set of goals for the members of the team; and by the amount of interdependence among team members.

DISCUSSION QUESTIONS

10-1 Think of a group to which you belong (or have belonged). Trace its development through the stages of group development as shown in Exhibit 10–2. How closely did its development parallel the group development model? How might the group development model be used to improve this group's effectiveness?

10-2 Contrast (a) self-managed and cross-functional teams, and (b) virtual and face-to-face teams.

10-3 How do you explain the popularity of work teams in countries such as the United States and Canada, whose national cultures place a high value on individualism?

⭐ 10-4 "All work teams are work groups, but not all work groups are work teams." Do you agree or disagree with this statement? Discuss.

10-5 Would you prefer to work alone or as part of a team? Why?

10-6 "To have a successful team, first find a great leader." What do you think of this statement? Do you agree? Why or why not?

10-7 What traits do you think good team players have? Do some research to answer this question and write a short report detailing your findings using a bulleted list format.

10-8 Contrast the pros and cons of diverse teams.

⭐ 10-9 How do you think scientific management theorists would react to the increased use of teams in organizations? How would behavioral science theorists react?

10-10 What challenges do managers face in managing global teams? How should those challenges be handled?

Writing Assignments

10-11 Why is it important for managers to know about the stages of group development?

10-12 What characteristics do effective teams need?

Management Skill Builder | DEVELOPING YOUR COACHING SKILLS

Organizations have become increasingly structured around teams. Twenty years ago, the individual was the basic building block of an organization; today it's teams. As the manager, you need to be able to effectively lead and coach a team. Without those skills, you're likely to have a short tenure in your management position.

⭐ PERSONAL INVENTORY ASSESSMENT

Diagnosing the Need for Team Building

Part of being a coach who wants to create and manage an effective team means knowing when a team needs help. Use this PIA to assess teams you're leading or are part of.

Skill Basics

Effective work team managers are increasingly being described as coaches rather than bosses. Just like coaches, they're expected to provide instruction, guidance, advice, and encouragement to help team members improve their job performance. You can learn to be a good team coach by practicing these behaviors:

• *Analyze ways to improve the team's performance and capabilities.* A coach looks for opportunities for team members to expand their capabilities and improve performance. How? You can use the following behaviors. Observe your team members' behaviors on a day-to-day basis. Ask questions of them: Why do you do a task this way? Can it be improved? What other approaches might be used? Show genuine interest

in team members as individuals, not merely as employees. Respect them individually. Listen to each employee.

• *Create a supportive climate.* It's the coach's responsibility to reduce barriers to development and to facilitate a climate that encourages personal performance improvement. How? You can use the following behaviors. Create a climate that contributes to a free and open exchange of ideas. Offer help and assistance. Give guidance and advice when asked. Encourage your team. Be positive and upbeat. Don't use threats. Ask, "What did we learn from this that can help us in the future?" Reduce obstacles. Assure team members that you value their contribution to the team's goals. Take personal responsibility for the outcome, but don't rob team members of their full responsibility. Validate team members' efforts when they succeed. Point to what was missing when they fail. Never blame team members for poor results.

- *Influence team members to change their behavior.* The ultimate test of coaching effectiveness is whether an employee's performance improves. You must encourage ongoing growth and development. How can you do this? Try the following behaviors. Recognize and reward small improvements and treat coaching as a way of helping employees to continually work toward improvement. Use a collaborative style by allowing team members to participate in identifying and choosing among improvement ideas. Break difficult tasks down into simpler ones. Model the qualities you expect from your team. If you want openness, dedication, commitment, and responsibility from your team members, demonstrate these qualities yourself.

Practicing the Skill

Read through this scenario and follow the directions at the end of it:

You're the leader of a five-member project team that's been assigned the task of moving your engineering firm into the growing area of high-speed intercity rail construction. You and your team members have been researching the field, identifying specific business opportunities, negotiating alliances with equipment vendors, and evaluating high-speed rail experts and consultants from around the world. Throughout the process, Tonya, a highly qualified and respected engineer, has challenged a number of things you've said during team meetings and in the workplace. For example, at a meeting two weeks ago, you presented the team with a list of 10 possible high-speed rail projects and started evaluating your organization's ability to compete for them. Tonya contradicted virtually all of your comments, questioned your statistics, and was quite pessimistic about the possibility of getting contracts on these projects. After this latest display of displeasure, two other group members, Bryan and Maggie, came to you and complained that Tonya's actions were damaging the team's effectiveness. You originally put Tonya on the team for her unique expertise and insight. You'd like to find a way to reach her and get the team on the right track to its fullest potential.

Form three-member teams in class. Each team should analyze this leader's problem and suggest solutions for coaching Tonya (and other team members, if you feel it's important). Each class team should be prepared to present its conclusions to the class.

Experiential Exercise

Colorado State High School Sports Association

To: Eric Gershman, Manager, Program Infractions Investigations

From: Audrey Costa, Director of Association Services

Subject: Conflicts on Investigation Teams

Eric, we've got a problem. I've been receiving complaints that the members of the five-person investigation teams we're sending out to high schools to investigate allegations of rules infractions are having conflicts. Because team members have to work closely together in interviewing people, interpreting the rules, and writing up reports, I'm worried that this conflict may be hurting the quality of the teams' investigation process. We've got to address this problem immediately in order to protect our reputation for being fair and reasonable in our rules enforcement. Please send me a bulleted list (no longer than a page) describing how you're going to address this problem and get it to me as soon as possible. Once I've had a chance to look it over, we'll get together to discuss it.

This fictionalized company and message were created for educational purposes only, and not meant to reflect positively or negatively on management practices by any company that may share this name.

CASE APPLICATION #1

Rx: Teamwork

The health-care industry is the fastest growing sector of the U.S. economy, with annual revenues projected at over $1.6 trillion (that's 12 zeroes!) and employing over 18 million workers.[64] Many challenges face the health-care industry, including changing laws/regulations, changing technologies, an aging population and increase in chronic disease, and labor shortages (physicians and nurses). But the goal is still the same—efficiently and effectively provide quality (appropriate and timely) health-care to patients. Given the challenges, health-care organizations are looking for better ways to do this. And one way is through using a "team-based care" approach, which research studies have shown can improve patient outcomes and reduce costs.

Many hospitals, clinics, and medical practices have adopted this team-care approach. What does that entail? A patient receives care from a team of medical professionals who divide up responsibilities for performing tasks that traditionally would have been done by a person's primary physician. Although supervising physicians still manage (oversee) patient care, tasks such as completing prescription refill requests, adjusting medication dosages, helping manage chronic diseases (for example, teaching someone diagnosed with diabetes how to take blood sugar counts and to administer insulin), and other routine tasks are now done by a team of health-care providers. For instance, at Kaiser Permanente, one of the largest not-for-profit managed health-care companies in the United States, a new program model called "complete care" was designed to enable health-care staffers to work together to make sure that no patient concern, need, preventive action, or matter was missed or overlooked.[65] As one individual described, staffers often literally chased patients down hallways to get them to schedule needed screenings. But the team approach is working. After a number of years using this model, research on Kaiser's team model showed significant gains in patient medical care across a wide range of standardized measures. Getting to that outcome wasn't easy, however. Departments that were accustomed to working on their own now had to work together. Instead of focusing on their own specialties, a team of specialists now worked together to provide patients with a well-rounded health-care experience. Physicians had to be retrained to view themselves as part of a team, supported by other professionals such as nurses, assistants, and other staff. As the health-care environment continues to be challenging, is teamwork the Rx?

TEAMING UP for better outcomes

Discussion Questions

10-14 What challenges are managers of health-care organizations facing?

10-15 How would the way health-care organization managers manage be different in a team-based model?

10-16 Explain how roles, norms, status systems, and group cohesiveness might influence the success of a team-based model?

10-17 What are some reasons you think a team-based model has led to improved patient outcomes and reduced costs?

CASE APPLICATION #2

The Cardinal Way

When you think of teams, do you automatically think of sports teams? For most of us, that was our first introduction to the concept of teams. Well, there's one sports team that is a perfect illustration of what an effective team is all about: the St. Louis Cardinals.[66] What can we learn about effective teams from them? Their record speaks for itself: the Cardinals, in the last four years (2011–2014), have won one World Series and two pennants, and achieved four consecutive playoff spots for the first time; in the last 15 years (2000–2014), the team has been to the playoffs 11 times, participated in more playoff games than any team since 2009, and had only one losing season; since 1960, the Cards have had consecutive losing seasons just once (yes, once) in 55 years, in the years 1994 and 1995. The Cardinals organization is a well-managed team, both on the field and behind the scenes. How have they managed these accomplishments? Here are some keys to their success:

WINNING Team—Winning **APPROACH**

- *Talent development.* The Cardinals organization finds ways to maximize its people and the skills they bring to the team. Their talent development process often grabs less-gifted minor league players (for less money) and transforms them into major-league contributors. How? Through its well-run farm system. Players in the Cards' AAA, AA, and A leagues are repeatedly reminded that this organization likes to win and knows it can win.

- *Intense focus on the fundamentals (the tasks) of the game.* The Cardinals play fundamentally sound baseball—they know their business and they execute. (Or, using the words of the Nike slogan, they "Just Do It!) Players and coaches religiously use the 86-page operations manual (titled, of course, "The Cardinal Way") as their guide. The manual includes such details as the position a catcher should take on a 3-2 count and the fine distinctions of 12 different ground balls a second baseman might face.

- *Coaches understand the importance of teaching the details.* Team players are "taught" and "coached" in real-time through a continual focus on improving their skills. Coaches help players learn from immediate game experiences. The pitching coaches and the batting coaches are right there refining players' behaviors during a game.

- *Culture of success, care, and support.* This is an organization with a deep history of success. There's an air of confidence that they're going to win. There's the expectation that they will play the game the right way. Traditions are celebrated and embraced. Team members genuinely care about each other. When a teammate was killed in a car accident at the end of the 2014 season, all pulled together in compassion and concern.

The Cardinal Way is, at its very heart, an organizational philosophy that guides all team members—from the team on the field to the coach staff to the front office staff to the marketing team and all others in the organization. Play ball!

Discussion Questions

10-18 How does the St. Louis Cardinals organization epitomize teamwork?

10-19 Do you think sports teams, like the St. Louis Cardinals, go through the stages of group development? Why or why not?

10-20 Using Exhibit 10–6 as your guide, discuss how the St. Louis Cardinals organization creates effective teams.

10-21 What could other organizations (even non-sports ones) learn from the St. Louis Cardinals?

CASE APPLICATION #3

Teaming Up for Take Off

The Boeing 737, a short- to medium-range twin-engine, narrow-body jet first rolled off the assembly line in 1967.[67] Now, almost half a century later, it's the best-selling jet airliner in the history of aviation. As airlines replace their aging narrow-body jet fleets, the burden is on Boeing to ramp up production to meet demand and to do so efficiently. Boeing managers face the challenge of producing more aircraft without increasing the size and scope of the manufacturing facility. Managing production of the multimillion-dollar product—a 737-800 is sold for $84.4 million—means "walking an increasingly fine line between generating cash and stoking an airplane glut." And Boeing is relying on its employee innovation teams to meet the challenge.

Boeing has been using employee-generated ideas since the 1990s, when its manufacturing facility in Renton, Washington, began adopting "lean" manufacturing techniques. Today, employee teams are continually looking for innovative ways—small and big—to be more efficient and effective. For instance, a member of one team thought of a solution to a problem of stray metal fasteners sometimes puncturing the tires as the airplane advanced down the assembly line. The solution? A canvas wheel cover that hugs the four main landing-gear tires. Another team figured out how to rearrange its work space to make four engines at a time instead of three. Another team of workers in the paint process revamped their work routines and cut 10 minutes to 15 minutes per worker off each job. It took five years for another employee team to perfect a process for installing the plane's landing gear hydraulic tubes, but it eventually paid off.

These employee teams are made up of seven to ten workers with diverse skills—from mechanics to assembly workers to engineers—and tend to focus on a specific part of a jet, such as the landing gear or the passenger seats or the galleys. These teams may meet as often as once a week. What's the track record of these teams? Today, it takes about 11 days for the final assembly of a 737 jet. That's down from 22 days about a decade ago. The near-term goal is to eventually shave off two more days.

Employee teams tackle INNOVATION CHALLENGE

Discussion Questions

⭐ **10-22** What type of team(s) do these employee teams appear to be? Explain.

⭐ **10-23** As this story illustrated, sometimes it may take a long time for a team to reach its goal. As a manager, how would you motivate a team to keep on trying?

⭐ **10-24** What role do you think a team leader needs to play in this type of setting? Explain.

⭐ **10-25** Using Exhibit 10–6, what characteristics of effective teams would these teams need? Explain.

Endnotes

1. B. Mezrich, *Bringing Down the House: The Inside Story of Six MIT Students Who Took Vegas for Millions* (New York: Free Press, 2002). The 2008 film *21* was a fictional work based loosely on the story.

2. B. W. Tuckman and M. C. Jensen, "Stages of Small-Group Development Revisited," *Group and Organizational Studies*, December 1977, 419–27; and M. F. Maples, "Group Development: Extending Tuckman's Theory," *Journal for Specialists in Group Work* (Fall 1988): 17–23.

3. L. N. Jewell and H. J. Reitz, *Group Effectiveness in Organizations* (Glenview, IL: Scott, Foresman, 1981); and M. Kaeter, "Repotting Mature Work Teams," *Training* (April 1994): 54–56.

4. Question of Ethics box based on S. Shellenbarger, "Office Oversharers: Don't Tell Us about Last Night," *Wall Street Journal,* June 25, 2014, D2; E. Bernstein, "Thank You for Not Sharing," *Wall Street Journal,* May 7, 2013, D1+; P. Klaus, "Thank You for Sharing. But Why at the Office?" *New York Times Online,* August 18, 2012; K. McCullum, "Hush, Hush," *OfficePro,* March–April 2011, 18–22; and E. Bernstein, "You Did What? Spare the Office the Details," *Wall Street Journal,* April 6, 2010, D1+.

5. S. E. Asch, "Effects of Group Pressure upon the Modification and Distortion of Judgments," in H. Guetzkow (ed.), *Groups, Leadership, and Men* (Pittsburgh, PA: Carnegie Press, 1951), 177–90.

6. See, for example, R. A. Henry, J. Kmet, and A. Landa, "Examining the Impact of Interpersonal Cohesiveness on Group Accuracy Interventions: The Importance of Matching versus Buffering," *Organizational Behavior and Human Decision Processes* (January 2002): 25–43.

7. Asch, "Effects of Group Pressure upon the Modification and Distortion of Judgments."

8. O. A. Alnuaimi, L. P. Robert Jr., and L. M. Maruping, "Team Size, Dispersion, and Social Loafing in Technology-Supported Teams: A Perspective on the Theory of Moral Disengagement," *Journal of Management Information Systems* (Summer 2010): 203–30; C. Cheshire and J. Antin, "None of Us Is as Lazy as All of Us," *Information, Communication & Society,* June 2010, 537–55; R. van Dick, J. Stellmacher, U. Wagner, G. Lemmer, and P. A. Tissington, "Group Membership Salience and Task Performance," *Journal of Managerial Psychology* 24, no. 7 (2009): 609–26; A. Jassawalla, H. Sashittal, and A. Malshe, "Students' Perceptions of Social Loafing: Its Antecedents and Consequences in Undergraduate Business Classroom Teams," *Academy of Management Learning & Education,* March 2009, 42–54; and R. Albanese and D. D. Van Fleet, "Rational Behavior in Groups: The Free Riding Tendency," *Academy of Management Review,* April 1985, 244–55.

9. L. Berkowitz, "Group Standards, Cohesiveness, and Productivity," *Human Relations,* November 1954, 509–19.

10. From the Past to the Present box based on S. S. Wang, "Under the Influence: How the Group Changes What We Think," *Wall Street Journal,* May 3, 2011, D1+; M. E. Shaw, *Group Dynamics: The Psychology of Small Group Behavior* (New York: McGraw-Hill, 1975); and E. J. Thomas and C. F. Fink, "Effects of Group Size," *Psychological Bulletin* (July 1963): 371–84.

11. Cited in T. Purdum, "Teaming, Take 2," *Industry Week,* May 2005, 43; and C. Joinson, "Teams at Work," *HR Magazine,* May 1999, 30.

12. See, for example, S. A. Mohrman, S. G. Cohen, and A. M. Mohrman Jr., *Designing Team-Based Organizations* (San Francisco: Jossey-Bass, 1995); P. MacMillan, *The Performance Factor: Unlocking the Secrets of Teamwork* (Nashville, TN: Broadman & Holman, 2001); and E. Salas, C. A. Bowers, and E. Eden (eds.), *Improving Teamwork in Organizations: Applications of Resource Management Training* (Mahwah, NJ: Lawrence Erlbaum, 2002).

13. Information for this section is based on J. R. Katzenbach and D. K. Smith, *The Wisdom of Teams* (Boston: Harvard Business School Press, 1993), 21, 45, 85; and D. C. Kinlaw, *Developing Superior Work Teams* (Lexington, MA: Lexington Books, 1991), 3–21.

14. S. Adams and L. Kydoniefs, "Making Teams Work: Bureau of Labor Statistics Learns What Works and What Doesn't," *Quality Progress* (January 2000): 43–49.

15. D. Hoffman, "At Wachovia, Fund Teams Work: Bank's Buddy System Improves Performance," *Investment News* (February 2001): 8.

16. T. Capozzoli, "How to Succeed with Self-Directed Work Teams," *Supervision* (February 2002): 25–27.

17. See, for instance, E. Sunstrom, DeMeuse, and D. Futrell, "Work Teams: Applications and Effectiveness," *American Psychologist,* February 1990, 120–33.

18. J. S. McClenahen, "Bearing Necessities," *Industry Week,* October 2004, 63–65; P. J. Kiger, "Acxiom Rebuilds from Scratch," *Workforce,* December 2002, 52–55; and

T. Boles, "Viewpoint—Leadership Lessons from NASCAR," *Industry Week, www.industryweek.com* (May 21, 2002).

19. M. Cianni and D. Wanuck, "Individual Growth and Team Enhancement: Moving Toward a New Model of Career Development," *Academy of Management Executive,* February 1997, 105–15.

20. C. Joinson, "Teams at Work," 30; and "Teams," *Training* (October 1996): 69.

21. J. P. Millikin, P. W. Hom, and C. C. Manz, "Self-Management Competencies in Self-Managing Teams: Their Impact on Multi-Team System Productivity," *Leadership Quarterly,* October 2010, 687–702; O. Turel and Y. Zhang, "Does Virtual Team Composition Matter? Trait and Problem-Solving Configuration Effects on Team Performance," *Behavior & Information Technology,* July–August 2010, 363–75; J. S. Bunderson and P. Boumgarden, "Structure and Learning in Self-Managed Teams: Why 'Bureaucratic' Teams Can Be Better Learners," *Organization Science,* May–June 2010, 609–24; and G. M. Spreitzer, S. G. Cohen, and G. E. Ledford Jr., "Developing Effective Self-Managing Work Teams in Service Organizations," *Group & Organization Management,* September 1999, 340–66.

22. "Meet the New Steel," *Fortune,* October 1, 2007, 68–71.

23. J. Appleby and R. Davis, "Teamwork Used to Save Money; Now It Saves Lives," *USA Today, www. usatoday. com* (March 1, 2001).

24. A. Malhotra, A. Majchrzak, R. Carman, and V. Lott, "Radical Innovation without Collocation: A Case Study at Boeing-Rocketdyne," *MIS Quarterly,* June 2001, 229–49.

25. A. Stuart, "Virtual Agreement," *CFO,* November 2007, 24.

26. Technology and the Manager's Job box based on K. Lee, "17 Tools for Remote Workers," http://www .fastcompany.com/3038333/17-tools-for-remote-workers, November 12, 2014; C. Mims, "Use of Voice Is Key to Managing Teams," *Wall Street Journal,* September 23, 2014, B1+; "Virtual Team Collaboration and Innovation in Organizations," *Team Performance Management,* March 2011, 109–19; M. Flammia, Y. Cleary, and D. M. Slattery, "Leadership Roles, Socioemotional Strategies, and Technology Use of Irish and US Students in Virtual Teams," *IEEE Transactions on Professional Communication,* June 2010, 89–101; P. Evans, "The Wiki Factor," *BizEd,* January–February 2006, 28–32; and M. McCafferty, "A Human Inventory," *CFO,* April 2005, 83–85.

27. See, for instance, D. C. Jones and T. Kato, "The Impact of Teams on Output, Quality, and Downtime: An Empirical Analysis Using Individual Panel Data," *Industrial and Labor Relations Review,* January 2011, 215–40; A. Gilley, J. W. Gilley, C. W. McConnell, and A. Veliquette, "The Competencies Used by Effective Managers to Build Teams: An Empirical Study," *Advances in Developing Human Resources,* February 2010, 29–45; M. A. Campion, G. J. Medsker, and C. A. Higgs, "Relations between Work Group Characteristics and Effectiveness: Implications for Designing Effective Work Groups," *Personnel Psychology,* Winter 1993, 823–50; and J. R. Hackman, "The Design of Work Teams," in J. W. Lorsch (ed.), *Handbook of Organizational Behavior* (Upper Saddle River, NJ: Prentice Hall, 1987), 315–42.

28. This model is based on M. A. Campion, E. M. Papper, and G. J. Medsker, "Relations between Work Team Characteristics and Effectiveness: A Replication and Extension," *Personnel Psychology,* Summer 1996, 429–52; D. E. Hyatt and T. M. Ruddy, "An Examination of the Relationship between Work Group Characteristics and Performance: Once More into the Breech," *Personnel Psychology,* Autumn 1997, 553–85; S. G. Cohen and D. E. Bailey, "What Makes Teams Work: Group Effectiveness Research from the Shop Floor to the Executive Suite," *Journal of Management* (September 1997): 239–90; L. Thompson, *Making the Team* (Upper Saddle River, NJ: Prentice Hall, 2000), 18–33; and J. R. Hackman, *Leading Teams: Setting the Stage for Great Performance* (Boston: Harvard Business School Press, 2002).

29. See M. Mattson, T. V. Mumford, and G. S. Sintay, "Taking Teams to Task: A Normative Model for Designing or Recalibrating Work Teams," paper presented at the National Academy of Management Conference, Chicago, August 1999; and G. L. Stewart and M. R. Barrick, "Team Structure and Performance: Assessing the Mediating Role of Intrateam Process and the Moderating Role of Task Type," *Academy of Management Journal* (April 2000): 135–48.

30. SmartPulse, "How Effectively Does Your Team Communicate Using New Electronic Channels?" Smart Brief on Leadership, www .smartbrief.com/leadership, October 7, 2014.

31. "Virtual Team Collaboration and Innovation in Organizations"; M. Flammia, Y. Cleary, and D. M. Slattery, "Leadership Roles, Socioemotional Strategies, and

Technology Use of Irish and U.S. Students in Virtual Teams"; A. Malhotra, A. Majchrzak, and B. Rosen, "Leading Virtual Teams," *Academy of Management Perspectives*, February 2007, 60–70; B. L. Kirkman and J. E. Mathieu, "The Dimensions and Antecedents of Team Virtuality," *Journal of Management* (October 2005): 700–18; J. Gordon, "Do Your Virtual Teams Deliver Only Virtual Performance?" *Training* (June 2005): 20–25; L. L. Martins, L. L. Gilson, and M. T. Maynard, "Virtual Teams: What Do We Know and Where Do We Go from Here?" *Journal of Management* (December 2004): 805–35; S. A. Furst, M. Reeves, B. Rosen, and R. S. Blackburn, "Managing the Life Cycle of Virtual Teams," *Academy of Management Executive*, May 2004, 6–20; B. L. Kirkman, B. Rosen, P. E. Tesluk, and C. B. Gibson, "The Impact of Team Empowerment on Virtual Team Performance: The Moderating Role of Face-to-Face Interaction," *Academy of Management Journal* (April 2004): 175–92; F. Keenan and S. E. Ante, "The New Teamwork," *Business Week e.biz*, February 18, 2002, EB12–EB16; and G. Imperato, "Real Tools for Virtual Teams," *Fast Company*, July 2000, 378–87.

32. R. I. Sutton, "The Boss as Human Shield," *Harvard Business Review*, September 2010, 106–09; and Hyatt and Ruddy, "An Examination of the Relationship between Work Group Characteristics and Performance," 577.

33. M. E. Palanski, S. S. Kahai, and F. J. Yammarino, "Team Virtues and Performance: An Examination of Transparency, Behavioral Integrity, and Trust," *Journal of Business Ethics* (March 2011): 201–16; H. H. Chang, S. S. Chuang, and S. H. Chao, "Determinants of Cultural Adaptation, Communication Quality, and Trust in Virtual Teams' Performance," *Total Quality Management and Business Excellence*, March 2011, 305–29; A. C. Costa and N. Anderson, "Measuring Trust in Teams: Development and Validation of a Multifaceted Measure of Formative and Reflective Indicators of Team Trust," *European Journal of Work & Organizational Psychology* (February 2011): 119–54; M. Mach, S. Dolan, and S. Tzafrir, "The Differential Effect of Team Members' Trust on Team Performance: The Mediation Role of Team Cohesion," *Journal of Occupational and Organizational Psychology* (September 2010): 771–94; B. A. DeJong and T. Elfring, "How Does Trust Affect the Performance of Ongoing Teams? The Mediating Role of Reflexivity, Monitoring, and Effort," *Academy of Management Journal* (June 2010): 535–49; M. Williams, "In Whom We Trust: Group Membership as an Affective Context for Trust De-

velopment," *Academy of Management Review*, July 2001, 377–96; and K. T. Dirks, "Trust in Leadership and Team Performance: Evidence from NCAA Basketball," *Journal of Applied Psychology* (December 2000): 1004–12.

34. R. R. Hirschfeld, M. J. Jordan, H. S. Field, W. F. Giles, and A. A. Armenakis, "Becoming Team Players: Team Members' Mastery of Team Knowledge as a Predictor of Team Task Proficiency and Observed Teamwork Effectiveness," *Journal of Applied Psychology* 91, no. 2 (2006): 467–74.

35. S. T. Bell, "Deep-Level Composition Variables as Predictors of Team Performance: A Meta-Analysis," *Journal of Applied Psychology* 92, no. 3 (2007): 595–615; and M. R. Barrick, G. L. Stewart, M. J. Neubert, and M. K. Mount, "Relating Member Ability and Personality to Work-Team Processes and Team Effectiveness," *Journal of Applied Psychology* (June 1998): 377–91.

36. M. Costello, "Team Weaver," *People Management*, January 2011, 26–27; and C. Margerison and D. McCann, *Team Management: Practical New Approaches* (London: Mercury Books, 1990).

37. K. H. T. Yu and D. M. Cable, "Unpacking Cooperation in Diverse Teams," *Team Performance Management*, March 2011, 63–82; A. Nederveen Pieterse, D. van Knippenberg, and W. P. van Ginkel, "Diversity in Goal Orientation, Team Reflexivity, and Team Performance," *Organizational Behavior and Human Performance*, March 2011, 153–64; M.-E. Roberge and R. van Dick, "Recognizing the Benefits of Diversity: When and How Does Diversity Increase Group Performance," *Human Resource Management Review*, December 2010, 295–308; and E. Mannix and M. A. Neale, "What Differences Make a Difference: The Promise and Reality of Diverse Teams in Organizations," *Psychological Science in the Public Interest*, October 2005, 31–55.

38. A. Deutschman, "Inside the Mind of Jeff Bezos," *Fast Company*, August 2004, 50–58.

39. Hyatt and Ruddy, "An Examination of the Relationship between Work Group Characteristics and Performance"; J. D. Shaw, M. K. Duffy, and E. M. Stark, "Interdependence and Preference for Group Work: Main and Congruence Effects on the Satisfaction and Performance of Group Members," *Journal of Management* (June 2000): 259–79; and S. A. Kiffin-Peterson and J. L. Cordery, "Trust, Individualism, and Job Characteristics of Employee Preference for Teamwork," *International Journal of Human Resource Management* (February 2003): 93–116.

40. J. S. Bunderson and P. Boumgarden, "Structure and Learning

in Self-Managed Teams: Why 'Bureaucratic' Teams Can Be Better Learners"; and R. Wageman, "Critical Success Factors for Creating Superb Self-Managing Teams," *Organizational Dynamics*, Summer 1997, 55.

41. Campion, Papper, and Medsker, "Relations between Work Team Characteristics and Effectiveness," 430; B. L. Kirkman and B. Rosen, "Powering Up Teams," *Organizational Dynamics*, Winter 2000, 48–66; and D. C. Man and S. S. K. Lam, "The Effects of Job Complexity and Autonomy on Cohesiveness in Collectivist and Individualist Work Groups: A Cross-Cultural Analysis," *Journal of Organizational Behavior* (December 2003): 979–1001.

42. A. Mehta, H. Feild, A. Armenakis, and N. Mehta, "Team Goal Orientation and Team Performance: The Mediating Role of Team Planning," *Journal of Management* (August 2009): 1026–46; K. Blanchard, D. Carew, and E. Parisi-Carew, "How to Get Your Group to Perform Like a Team," *Training and Development* (September 1996): 34–37; K. D. Scott and A. Townsend, "Teams: Why Some Succeed and Others Fail," *HR Magazine*, August 1994, 62–67; K. Hess, *Creating the High-Performance Team* (New York: Wiley, 1987); and Katzenbach and Smith, "The Wisdom of Teams," 43–64.

43. H. van Emmerik, I. M. Jawahar, B. Schreurs, and N. de Cuyper, "Social Capital, Team Efficacy and Team Potency: The Mediating Role of Team Learning Behaviors," *Career Development International* (February 2011): 82– 99; T. Lewis, "Assessing Social Identity and Collective Efficacy as Theories of Group Motivation at Work," *International Journal of Human Resource Management* (February 2011): 963–80; K. Tasa, G. J. Sears, and A. C. H. Schat, "Personality and Teamwork Behavior in Context: The Cross-Level Moderating Role of Collective Efficacy," *Journal of Organizational Behavior* (January 2011): 65–85; J. A. Goncalo, E. Polman, and C. Maslach, "Can Confidence Come Too Soon? Collective Efficacy, Conflict and Group Performance Over Time," *Organizational Behavior & Human Decision Processes*, September 2010, 13–24; K. Tasa, S. Taggar, and G. H. Seijts, "The Development of Collective Efficacy in Teams: A Multilevel and Longitudinal Perspective," *Journal of Applied Psychology* (January 2007): 17–27; C. B. Gibson, "The Efficacy Advantage: Factors Related to the Formation of Group Efficacy," *Journal of Applied Social Psychology* (October 2003): 2153–86; and D. I. Jung and J. J. Sosik, "Group Potency and Collective Efficacy: Examining Their Predictive Validity, Level of Analysis, and Effects

of Performance Feedback on Future Group Performance," *Group & Organization Management*, September 2003, 366–91.

44. SmartPulse, "How Effectively Do You Resolve Conflict with Others?" Smart Brief on Leadership, www.smartbrief.com, April 21, 2015.

45. K. C. Kostopoulos and N. Bozionelos, "Team Exploratory and Exploitative Learning: Psychological Safety, Task Conflict, and Team Performance," *Group & Organization Management*, June 2011, 385–415; K. J. Behfar, E. A. Mannix, R. S. Peterson, and W. M. Trochim, "Conflict in Small Groups: The Meaning and Consequences of Process Conflict," *Small Group Research*, April 2011, 127–76; R. S. Peterson and K. J. Behfar, "The Dynamic Relationship between Performance Feedback, Trust, and Conflict in Groups: A Longitudinal Study," *Organizational Behavior and Human Decision Processes*, September–November 2003, 102–12; and K. A. Jehn, "A Qualitative Analysis of Conflict Types and Dimensions in Organizational Groups," *Administrative Science Quarterly*, September 1997, 530–57.

46. O. A. Alnuaimi, L. P. Robert Jr., and L. M. Maruping, "Team Size, Dispersion, and Social Loafing in Technology-Supported Teams: A Perspective on the Theory of Moral Disengagement"; C. Cheshire and J. Antin, "None of Us Is as Lazy as All of Us"; R. van Dick, J. Stellmacher, U. Wagner, G. Lemmer, and P. A. Tissington, "Group Membership Salience and Task Performance"; A. Jassawalla, H. Sashittal, and A. Malshe, "Students' Perceptions of Social Loafing: Its Antecedents and Consequences in Undergraduate Business Classroom Teams"; K. H. Price, D. A. Harrison, and J. H. Gavin, "Withholding Inputs in Team Contexts: Member Composition, Interaction Processes, Evaluation Structure, and Social Loafing," *Journal of Applied Psychology* (December 2006): 1375–84; and R. Albanese and D. D. Van Fleet, "Rational Behavior in Groups: The Free Riding Tendency," *Academy of Management Review*, April 1985, 244–55.

47. SmartPulse, "If Someone on Your Team Hates Their Job, What Do You Do?" Smart Brief on Leadership, www.smartbrief.com/leadership, October 21, 2014.

48. "Helping Hands," *HR Magazine*, May 2011, 18; M. O'Neil, "Leading the Team," *Supervision*, April 2011, 8–10; J. Beeson, "Build a Strong Team," *Leadership Excellence*, February 2011, 15; S. Brutus and M. B. L. Donia, "Improving the Effectiveness of Students in Groups with a Centralized Peer Evaluation System," *Academy of Management Learning & Education*, December 2010, 652–62; and N. H. Woodward, "Make the Most

of Team Building," *HR Magazine*, September 2006, 73–76.

49. R. M. Yandrick, "A Team Effort," *HR Magazine*, June 2001, 136–41.

50. Ibid.

51. "How Should We Recognize Team Goals over Individual?" *Workforce Management Online*, February 2011; S. J. Goerg, S. Kube, and R. Zultan, "Treating Equals Unequally: Incentives in Teams, Workers' Motivation, and Production Technology," *Journal of Labor Economics* (October 2010):. 747–72; T. Taylor, "The Challenge of Project Team Incentives," *Compensation & Benefits Review*, September–October 2010, 411–19; M. J. Pearsall, M. S. Christian, and A. P. J. Ellis, "Motivating Interdependent Teams: Individual Rewards, Shared Rewards, or Something in Between?" *Journal of Applied Psychology* (January 2010): 183–91; M. A. Marks, C. S. Burke, M. J. Sabella, and S. J. Zaccaro, "The Impact of Cross-Training on Team Effectiveness," *Journal of Applied Psychology* (February 2000): 3–14; and M. A. Marks, S. J. Zaccaro, and J. E. Mathieu, "Performance Implications of Leader Briefings and Team Interaction for Team Adaptation to Novel Environments," *Journal of Applied Psychology* (December 2000): 971.

52. C. Garvey, "Steer Teams with the Right Pay: Team-Based Pay Is a Success When It Fits Corporate Goals and Culture, and Rewards the Right Behavior," *HR Magazine*, May 2002, 71–77.

53. F. Niederman and F. B. Tan, "Emerging Markets Managing Global IT Teams: Considering Cultural Dynamics,"

Communications of the ACM, April 2011, 24–27; R. M. B. Boyle and S. Nicholas, "Cross-Cultural Group Performance," *The Learning Organization*, March 2011, 94–101; G. K. Stahl, M. L. Maznevski, A. Voigt, and K. Jonsen, "Unraveling the Effects of Cultural Diversity in Teams: A Meta-Analysis of Research on Multicultural Work Groups," *Journal of International Business Studies* (May 2010): 690–709; and M. R. Haas, "The Double-Edged Sword of Autonomy and External Knowledge: Analyzing Team Effectiveness in a Multinational Organization."

54. R. Bond and P. B. Smith, "Culture and Conformity: A Meta-Analysis of Studies Using Asch's [1952, 1956] Line Judgment Task," *Psychological Bulletin*, January 1996, 111–37.

55. I. L. Janis, *Groupthink*, 2nd ed. (New York: Houghton Mifflin Company, 1982), 175.

56. See P. C. Earley, "Social Loafing and Collectivism: A Comparison of the United States and the People's Republic of China," *Administrative Science Quarterly*, December 1989, 565–81; and P. C. Earley, "East Meets West Meets Mideast: Further Explorations of Collectivistic and Individualistic Work Groups," *Academy of Management Journal* (April 1993): 319–48.

57. N. J. Adler, *International Dimensions of Organizational Behavior*, 4th ed. (Cincinnati, OH: South-western, 2002), 142.

58. K. B. Dahlin, L. R. Weingart, and P. J. Hinds, "Team Diversity and Information Use," *Academy of Management Journal* (December 2005): 1107–23.

59. Adler, *International Dimensions of Organizational Behavior*, 142.

60. S. Paul, I. M. Samarah, P. Seetharaman, and P. P. Mykytyn, "An Empirical Investigation of Collaborative Conflict Management Style in Group Support System-Based Global Virtual Teams," *Journal of Management Information Systems* (Winter 2005): 185–222.

61. This section is based on S. P. Robbins and T. A. Judge, *Organizational Behavior*, 14th ed. (Upper Saddle River, NJ: Pearson Prentice Hall, 2011).

62. C. E. Naquin and R. O. Tynan, "The Team Halo Effect: Why Teams Are Not Blamed for Their Failures," *Journal of Applied Psychology* (April 2003): 332–40.

63. A. B. Drexler and R. Forrester, "Teamwork—Not Necessarily the Answer," *HR Magazine*, January 1998, 55–58. See also R. Saavedra, P. C. Earley, and L. Van Dyne, "Complex Interdependence in Task-Performing Groups," *Journal of Applied Psychology* (February 1993): 61–72; and K. A. Jehn, G. B. Northcraft, and M. A. Neale, "Why Differences Make a Difference: A Field Study of Diversity, Conflict, and Performance in Work Groups," *Administrative Science Quarterly*, December 1999, 741–63.

64. "Health Care Industry Statistics," www.statisticbrain.com/health-care-industry-statistics/, February 3, 2015; and "Healthcare Workers," www.cdc.gov/niosh/topics/healthcare, December 12, 2014.

65. L. Landro, "The Teamwork Approach to Medical Care," *Wall Street Journal*, June 9, 2014, R3.

66. B. Nightengale, "Cardinals on 2015: 'We Can Do This for Oscar (Taveras)'," www.ustoday.

com/sports/, April 14, 2015; T. Ringolsby, "'Cardinal Way' Continues to Be Winning Formula," http://m.cardinals.mlb.com/news/article/97919236/tracy-ringolsby-cardinal-way-continues-to-be-winning-formula, October 7, 2014; A. Turock, "The Cardinal Way: Making Talent Development a Game-Changer Strategy," http://www.turock.com/the-cardinal-way-making-talent-development-a-game-changer-strategy/, March 27, 2014; T. Calandro, "The Cardinal Way: Built to Last," http://www.huffingtonpost.com/tony-calandro/the-cardinal-way-built-to_b_4164652.html, January 23, 2014; H. Megdal, "The Cardinal Way," http://www.sportsonearth.com/article/56835048/the-st-louis-cardinals-have-a-system-the-cardina_3, August 14, 2013; D. Goold, "Cardinal Way," http://www.stltoday.com/sports/baseball/professional/now-in-book-form-the-cardinal-way/article_1c76331b-077e-57aa-9333-86a85b1f5ac2.html, May 18, 2012; and D. O'Neill, "The 'Cardinal Way' Is Team's Foundation," http://www.stltoday.com/sports/baseball/professional/the-cardinal-way-is-team-s-foundation/article_a32b5806-a307-58b6-ae89-bac9e6ae0d2e.html, October 30, 2011.

67. D. Michaels and J. Ostrower, "Airbus, Boeing Walk a Fine Line on Jetliner Production," *Wall Street Journal*, July 16, 2012, B3; D. Kesmodel, "Boeing Teams Speed Up 737 Output," *Wall Street Journal*, February 7, 2012, B10; and A. Cohen, "Boeing Sees Demand for Existing, Reengined 737s," blog on *Seattle Post-Intelligencer Online*, October 26, 2011.

Motivating and Rewarding Employees

11

Motivation is all about "show me the money."

Maybe the greatest fallacy about motivation is that everyone is motivated by money. Many ineffective or inexperienced managers naively believe that money is a prime motivator. Then they proceed to ignore the many other actions and rewards they control that are as equally important as money, if not more so. As you'll see, one size doesn't fit all, and the secret to being an effective motivator is understanding each individual's unique needs.

SUCCESSFUL

managers need to understand that what motivates them personally may have little or no effect on others. Just because you're motivated by being part of a cohesive work team, don't assume everyone is. Or just because you're motivated by your job doesn't mean that everyone is. Or just because employees have access to free food, free massages, free laundry, and free M&Ms doesn't mean those extras are enough to keep them from looking elsewhere for career opportunities. Effective managers who get employees to put forth maximum effort know how and why those employees are motivated and tailor motivational practices to satisfy their needs and wants. Motivating and rewarding employees are some of the manager's most important and challenging activities. To get employees to put forth maximum work effort, managers need to know how and why they're motivated. ●

Learning Outcomes

11-1 Define and explain motivation. p. 331

11-2 Compare and contrast early theories of motivation. p. 332

11-3 Compare and contrast contemporary theories of motivation. p. 336

11-4 Discuss current issues in motivating employees. p. 343

What Is Motivation?

11-1 Define and explain motivation.

Several CEOs were attending a meeting where the topic was "What do employees want?"[1] Each CEO took turns describing the benefits they provided and how they gave out free M&Ms every Wednesday and offered their employees stock options and free parking spaces. However, the meeting's main speaker made the point that "employees don't want M&Ms; they want to love what they do." Half expecting his audience to laugh, the speaker was pleasantly surprised as the CEOs stood up one-by-one to agree. They all recognized that "the value in their companies comes from the employees who are motivated to be there."

These CEOs understand how important employee motivation is. Like them, all managers need to be able to motivate their employees, which requires understanding what motivation is. Let's begin by pointing out what motivation is not. Why? Because many people incorrectly view motivation as a personal trait; that is, they think some people are motivated and others aren't. Our knowledge of motivation tells us that we can't label people that way because individuals differ in motivational drive and their overall motivation varies from situation to situation. For instance, you're probably more motivated to work hard and do well in some classes than in others.

---

78 percent of managers say they do a fair job of motivating their people.[2]

Motivation refers to the process by which a person's efforts are energized, directed, and sustained toward attaining a goal.[3] This definition has three key elements: energy, direction, and persistence.

The (1) *energy* element is a measure of intensity or drive. A motivated person puts forth effort and works hard. However, the quality of the effort must be considered as well as its intensity. High levels of effort don't necessarily lead to favorable job performance unless the effort is channeled in a (2) *direction* that benefits the organization. Effort that's directed toward, and consistent with, organizational goals is the kind of effort we want from employees. Finally, motivation includes a (3) *persistence* dimension. We want employees to persist in putting forth effort to achieve those goals.

Motivating high levels of employee performance is an important organizational concern and managers keep looking for answers. For instance, a recent Gallup poll found that a large majority of U.S. employees—some 64 percent—are not excited about their work.[4] This level of disengagement has been described by researchers: "These employees are essentially 'checked out.' They're sleepwalking through their workday, putting time, but not energy or passion, into their work."[5] It's no wonder, then, that both managers and academics want to understand and explain employee motivation.

Let's start by looking at several early theories of motivation.

motivation
The process by which a person's efforts are energized, directed, and sustained toward attaining a goal

---

⭐ **Write It!**

If your professor has assigned this, go to the Assignments section of **mymanagementlab.com** to complete *MGMT 14: Theories of Motivation*.

4 Early Theories of Motivation (1950s & 1960s)

11-2 Compare and contrast early theories of motivation.

Know these early theories because they: ❶ *Represent the foundation from which contemporary theories grew,* and ❷ *Still are used by practicing managers to explain employee motivation.*

1 Maslow's Hierarchy of Needs Theory
(probably best-known motivation theory)[6]

- **Abraham Maslow**—a psychologist—proposed that within every person is a hierarchy of five needs:

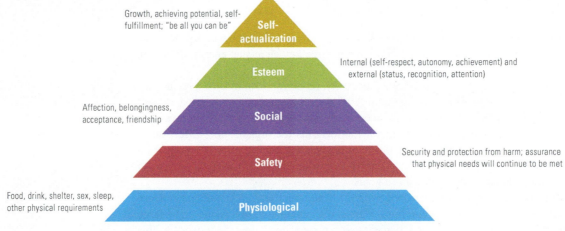

Growth, achieving potential, self-fulfillment; "be all you can be" — **Self-actualization**

Internal (self-respect, autonomy, achievement) and external (status, recognition, attention) — **Esteem**

Affection, belongingness, acceptance, friendship — **Social**

Security and protection from harm; assurance that physical needs will continue to be met — **Safety**

Food, drink, shelter, sex, sleep, other physical requirements — **Physiological**

Exhibit 11–1 Maslow's Hierarchy of Needs
Source: Maslow, Abraham H.; Frager, Robert D; Fadiman, James, *Motivation and Personality*, 3rd ed., ©1987. Reprinted and electronically reproduced by permission of Pearson Education, Inc., New York, NY.

- Each level must be substantially satisfied before the next need becomes dominant; an individual moves up the hierarchy from one level to the next.

- *Lower-order needs* are satisfied predominantly externally, and *higher-order needs* are satisfied internally.

HOW is Maslow's hierarchy used to motivate employees?

- Managers will do things to satisfy employees' needs.

- **Remember:** Once a need is substantially satisfied, it no longer motivates.

hierarchy of needs theory
Maslow's theory that there is a hierarchy of five human needs: physiological, safety, social, esteem, and self-actualization

- Widely popular among practicing managers probably because it's easy to understand and intuitive.[7]

- No empirical support provided for theory; other studies could not validate it.[8]

McGregor's Theory X and Theory Y

- Based on two assumptions about human nature.[9]
    - **Theory X**: a negative view of people that assumes workers have little ambition, dislike work, want to avoid responsibility, and need to be closely controlled to work effectively.
    - **Theory Y**: a positive view that assumes employees enjoy work, seek out and accept responsibility, and exercise self-direction.

- To maximize employee motivation, use Theory Y practices—allow employees to participate in decisions, create responsible and challenging jobs, and encourage good group relations.

- No evidence to confirm either set of assumptions or that being a Theory Y manager is the only way to motivate employees.

Marek/Fotolia

Herzberg's Two-Factor Theory

- **Frederick Herzberg's two-factor theory** (*also called motivation-hygiene theory*)—intrinsic factors are related to job satisfaction, while extrinsic factors are associated with job dissatisfaction.[10]
    - Popular theory from the 1960s to the early 1980s.
    - Criticized for being too simplistic.
    - Influenced today's approach to job design. (See From Past to Present box on p. 338.)

theory X	theory Y	two-factor theory
The assumption that employees dislike work, are lazy, avoid responsibility, and must be coerced to work	The assumption that employees are creative, enjoy work, seek responsibility, and can exercise self-direction	Herzberg's motivation theory, which proposes that intrinsic factors are related to job satisfaction and motivation, whereas extrinsic factors are associated with job dissatisfaction

- **Research focus**: When people felt exceptionally **good** (satisfied—see left-hand side of Exhibit 11–2) *or* **bad** (dissatisfied—see right-hand side of exhibit) about their jobs.
- Replies showed these were *two different factors!*
    - When people felt good about their work, they tended to cite intrinsic factors arising from the *job content (job itself),* such as achievement, recognition, and responsibility.
    - When they were dissatisfied, they tended to cite extrinsic factors arising from the *job context,* such as company policy and administration, supervision, interpersonal relationships, and working conditions.

Andersphoto/Fotolia

Exhibit 11–2 Herzberg's Two-Factor Theory

- Replies also gave us the new view of *Satisfaction vs. Dissatisfaction* (see Exhibit 11–3).

Exhibit 11–3 Contrasting Views of Satisfaction and Dissatisfaction

Source: Robbins, Stephen P., Coulter, Mary, *Management*, 13th Ed., © 2016, p. 465. Reprinted and electronically reproduced by permission of Pearson Education, Inc., New York, NY.

- Herzberg concluded that the traditional view—*the opposite of satisfaction is dissatisfaction*—was wrong.
- He believed that the factors that led to job satisfaction were separate and distinct from those that led to job dissatisfaction.

hygiene factors	**motivators**	**three-needs theory**
Factors that eliminate job dissatisfaction but don't motivate	Factors that increase job satisfaction and motivation	McClelland's theory, which says that three acquired (not innate) needs—achievement, power, and affiliation—are major motives at work

- Removing dissatisfying characteristics from a job didn't necessarily make that job more satisfying (or motivating); it simply made you "less" dissatisfied.

- Proposed a dual continuum: The opposite of "satisfaction" is "no satisfaction," and the opposite of "dissatisfaction" is "no dissatisfaction."

Olly/Fotolia

Motivating Employees:

1 When **hygiene factors** are adequate, people won't be dissatisfied, but they won't be motivated, either.

2 To motivate people, use the **motivators**.

4 McClelland's Three-Needs Theory

- David McClelland and his associates proposed the **three-needs theory**, which says **three** acquired (not innate) needs are major motives in work, including:[11]

1 **need for achievement (nAch)**, which is the drive to succeed and excel in relation to a set of standards

2 **need for power (nPow)**, which is the need to make others behave in a way that they would not have behaved otherwise

3 **need for affiliation (nAff)**, which is the desire for friendly and close interpersonal relationships

- nAch has been researched the most:

  - People with a high nAch are striving for personal achievement rather than for the trappings and rewards of success.

  - They have a desire to do something better or more efficiently than it's been done before.[12]

  - They prefer **1** jobs that offer personal responsibility for finding solutions to problems, **2** receiving rapid and unambiguous feedback on their performance in order to tell whether they're improving, and **3** moderately challenging goals.

  - High achievers avoid what they perceive to be very easy or very difficult tasks.

  - A high nAch doesn't necessarily lead to being a good manager, especially in large organizations. Why? Because high achievers focus on their own accomplishments, while good managers emphasize helping others accomplish their goals.[13]

  - Employees can be trained to stimulate their nAch by being in situations where they have personal responsibility, feedback, and moderate risks.[14]

- The best managers tend to be high in nPow and low in nAff.[15]

need for achievement (nAch)	**need for power (nPow)**	**need for affiliation (nAff)**
The drive to succeed and excel in relation to a set of standards	The need to make others behave in a way that they would not have behaved otherwise	The desire for friendly and close interpersonal relationships

⭐ **Watch It 1!**

If your professor has assigned this, go to the Assignments section of **mymanagementlab.com** to complete the video exercise titled *Rudi's Bakery: Motivation*.

How Do the Contemporary Theories Explain Motivation?

11-3 Compare and contrast contemporary theories of motivation.

At Electronic Arts (EA), one of the world's largest video game designers, employees put in grueling hours developing games. However, EA takes care of its game developers by providing them with workday intramural sports leagues, pinball arcades, group fitness classes, and an open invite to pets at work.[16] With a little over 8,000 workers in more than 20 countries, EA's managers need to understand employee motivation.

The theories we look at in this section—goal-setting, job design, equity, and expectancy—represent current explanations of employee motivation. Although maybe not as well known as those we just discussed, these are backed by research.[17]

What Is Goal-Setting Theory?

Goals CAN be **powerful motivators!**

goal-setting theory
The proposition that specific goals increase performance and that difficult goals, when accepted, result in higher performance than do easy goals

Before a big assignment or major class project presentation, has a teacher ever encouraged you to "Just do your best"? What does that vague statement "do your best" mean? Would your performance on a class project have been higher had that teacher said you needed to score a 93 percent to keep your A in the class? Research on goal-setting theory addresses these issues, and the findings, as you'll see, are impressive in terms of the effect that goal specificity, challenge, and feedback have on performance.[18]

Substantial research support has been established for **goal-setting theory**, which says that specific goals increase performance and that difficult goals, when accepted, result in higher performance than do easy goals. *What does goal-setting theory tell us?*

(a) Working toward a goal is a major source of job motivation. Studies on goal setting have demonstrated that specific and challenging goals are superior motivating forces.[19] Such goals produce a higher output than does the generalized goal of "do your best." The specificity of the goal itself acts as an internal stimulus. For instance, when a sales rep commits to making eight sales calls daily, this intention gives him a specific goal to try to attain.

Working toward a goal is a major source of motivation for Mary Kay Cosmetics beauty consultants who set their own sales goals and earn rewards for achieving them. Consultants Shannon Nelson (center) and her sister and mother are shown here with a Mustang Shannon earned for meeting an ambitious sales goal.

(b) Will employees try harder if they have the opportunity to participate in the setting of goals? Not always. In some cases, participatively set goals elicit superior performance; in other cases, individuals performed best when their manager assigned goals. However, participation is probably preferable to assigning goals when employees might resist accepting difficult challenges.[20]

(c) We know that people will do better if they get feedback on how well they're progressing toward their goals because feedback helps identify discrepancies between what they've done and what they want to do. But all feedback isn't equally effective. Self-generated feedback—where an employee monitors his or her own progress—has been shown to be a more powerful motivator than feedback coming from someone else.[21]

Three other contingencies besides feedback influence the goal-performance relationship: goal commitment, adequate self-efficacy, and national culture.

(1) First, goal-setting theory assumes that an individual is committed to the goal. Commitment is most likely when goals are made public, when the individual has an internal locus of control, and when the goals are self-set rather than assigned.[22]

(2) Next, **self-efficacy** refers to an individual's belief that he or she is capable of performing a task.[23] The higher your self-efficacy, the more confidence you have in your ability to succeed in a task. So, in difficult situations, we find that people with low self-efficacy are likely to reduce their effort or give up altogether, whereas those with high self-efficacy will try harder to master the challenge.[24] In addition, individuals with high self-efficacy seem to respond to negative feedback with increased effort and motivation, whereas those with low self-efficacy are likely to reduce their effort when given negative feedback.[25]

(3) Finally, the value of goal-setting theory depends on the national culture. It's well adapted to North American countries because its main ideas align reasonably well with those cultures. It assumes that subordinates will be reasonably independent (not a high score on power distance), that people will seek challenging goals (low in uncertainty avoidance), and that performance is considered important by both managers and subordinates (high in assertiveness). Don't expect goal setting to lead to higher employee performance in countries where the cultural characteristics aren't like this.

Exhibit 11–4 summarizes the relationships among goals, motivation, and performance. Our overall conclusion: *The intention to work toward hard and specific goals is a powerful motivating force.* Under the proper conditions, it can lead to higher performance. However, there's no evidence that such goals are associated with increased job satisfaction.[26]

How Does Job Design Influence Motivation?

Yes—you *can* **design jobs** that motivate!

Because managers want to motivate individuals on the job, we need to look at ways to design motivating jobs. If you look closely at what an organization is and how it works, you'll find that it's composed of thousands of tasks. These tasks are, in turn, aggregated into jobs. We use the term **job design** to refer to the way tasks are combined to form complete jobs. The jobs that people perform in an organization should not evolve by chance. Managers should design jobs deliberately and thoughtfully to reflect the demands of the changing environment, the organization's technology, and employees' skills, abilities, and preferences.[27] When jobs are designed like that, employees are motivated to work hard. What are the ways that managers can design motivating jobs? We can answer that with the **job characteristics model (JCM)**, developed by J. Richard Hackman and Greg R. Oldham.[28]

self-efficacy
An individual's belief that he or she is capable of performing a task

job design
The way tasks are combined to form complete jobs

job characteristics model (JCM)
A framework for analyzing and designing jobs that identifies five primary core job dimensions, their interrelationships, and their impact on outcomes

Exhibit 11–4 Goal-Setting Theory

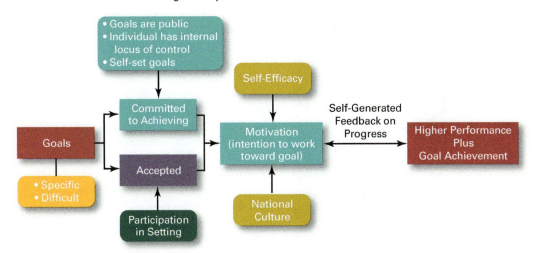

Deciding how work tasks should be performed has long been of interest to managers.[29] From scientific management's attempts to find the "one best way" to do work to the Hawthorne Studies that attempted to unravel patterns of human behavior at work, researchers have been curious about the ideal approach to work design. In the 1950s, Frederick Herzberg and his associates began research to "discover the importance of attitudes toward work and the experiences, both good and bad, that workers reported." He wanted to know the kinds of things that made people at their work happy and satisfied or unhappy and dissatisfied. What he discovered changed the way we view job design. The fact that job dissatisfaction and job satisfaction were the results of different aspects of the work environment was an important finding. Herzberg's two-factor theory gave practicing managers insights into both job context and job content. And if you wanted to motivate employees, you'd better focus more on the job content aspects (the motivators) than on the job context aspects (the hygiene factors).

Job Design: How *should* work tasks get done?

In addition, Herzberg's research stimulated additional interest in work design. The Job Characteristics model, for one, built upon Herzberg's findings in identifying the five core job dimensions, especially autonomy. As managers and organizations continue to search for work designs that will energize and engage employees, Herzberg's study of when people felt good and felt bad at work continues as a classic.

If your professor has assigned this, go to the Assignments section of **mymanagementlab.com** *to complete these discussion questions.*

⭐ **Talk About It 1:** Why do you think jobs need to be "designed"?

⭐ **Talk About It 2:** How can job design contribute to employee motivation?

According to Hackman and Oldham, any job can be described in terms of the following five core job dimensions:

1. *Skill variety*. The degree to which the job requires a variety of activities so the worker can use a number of different skills and talents
2. *Task identity*. The degree to which the job requires completion of a whole and identifiable piece of work
3. *Task significance*. The degree to which the job affects the lives or work of other people
4. *Autonomy*. The degree to which the job provides freedom, independence, and discretion to the individual in scheduling the work and in determining the procedures to be used in carrying it out
5. *Feedback*. The degree to which carrying out the work activities required by the job results in the individual's obtaining direct and clear information about the effectiveness of his or her performance

The job of this pediatric nurse caring for newborn babies at a children's hospital in Germany scores high on task significance as she uses her specialized knowledge and skills in caring for children from infancy through the late teen years, and their families. Task significance contributes to the meaningfulness of her job and high internal work motivation.

Ulrich Baumgarten/Getty Images

Exhibit 11–5 presents the model. Notice how the first three dimensions—skill variety, task identity, and task significance—combine to create meaningful work. What we mean is that *if these three characteristics exist in a job, we can predict that the person will view his or her job as being important, valuable, and worthwhile.* Notice, too, that jobs that possess autonomy give the job incumbent a feeling of personal responsibility for the results and that, if a job provides feedback, the employee will know how effectively he or she is performing.

From a motivational point of view, the JCM suggests that internal rewards are obtained when an employee *learns* (knowledge of results through feedback) that he or she *personally* (experienced responsibility through autonomy of work) has performed well on a task that he or she *cares* about (experienced

Exhibit 11–5 Job Characteristics Model

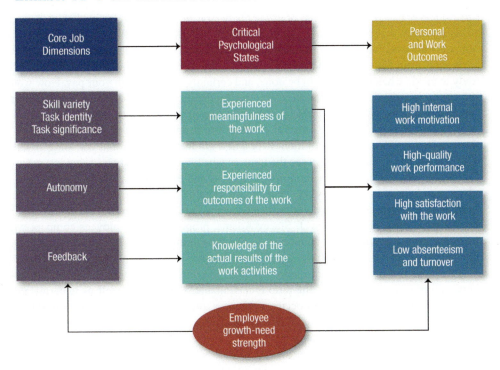

Source: Reprinted by permission from Judith D. Hackman (w/o) J. Richard Hackman.

job enrichment
The vertical expansion of a job by adding planning and evaluation responsibilities

meaningfulness through skill variety, task identity, and/or task significance). The more these three conditions characterize a job, the greater the employee's motivation, performance, and satisfaction and the lower his or her absenteeism and the likelihood of resigning. As the model shows, the links between the job dimensions and the outcomes are moderated by the strength of the individual's growth need (the person's desire for self-esteem and self-actualization). Individuals are more likely to experience the critical psychological states and respond positively when their jobs include the core dimensions than are individuals with a low growth need. This distinction may explain the mixed results with **job enrichment** (vertical expansion of a job by adding planning and evaluation responsibilities): Individuals with low growth need don't tend to achieve high performance or satisfaction by having their jobs enriched.

The JCM provides significant guidance to managers for job design for both individuals and teams.[30] The suggestions shown in Exhibit 11–6, which are based on the JCM, specify the types of changes in jobs that are most likely to improve each of the five core job dimensions.

Exhibit 11–6 Guidelines for Job Redesign

Source: Reprinted by permission from Judith D. Hackman (w/o) J. Richard Hackman.

What Is Equity Theory?

Have you ever wondered what kind of grade the person sitting next to you in class makes on a test or on a major class assignment? Sure you have—most of us do! Being human, we tend to compare ourselves with others. If someone offered you $55,000 a year on your first job after graduating from college, you'd probably jump at the offer and report to work enthusiastic, ready to tackle whatever needed to be done, and certainly satisfied with your pay. How would you react, though, if you found out a month into the job that a coworker—another recent graduate, your age, with comparable grades from a comparable school, and with comparable work experience—was getting $60,000 a year? You'd probably be upset! Even though in absolute terms, $55,000 is a lot of money for a new graduate to make (and you know it!), that suddenly isn't the issue. Now you see the issue as what you believe is *fair*—what is *equitable*. The term *equity* is related to the concept of fairness and equitable treatment compared with others who behave in similar ways. There's considerable evidence that employees compare themselves to others and that inequities influence how much effort employees exert.[31]

Equity theory, developed by J. Stacey Adams, proposes that employees compare what they get from a job (outcomes) in relation to what they put into it (inputs) and then compare their inputs-outcomes ratio with the inputs-outcomes ratios of relevant others (Exhibit 11–7). If an employee perceives her ratio to be equitable in comparison to those of relevant others, there's no problem. However, if the ratio is inequitable, she views herself as underrewarded or overrewarded. When inequities occur, employees attempt to do something about it.[32] The result might be lower or higher productivity, improved or reduced quality of output, increased absenteeism, or voluntary resignation.

The **referent**—the other persons, systems, or selves individuals compare themselves against in order to assess equity—is an important variable in equity theory.[33] Each of the three referent categories is important. (1) The "persons" category includes other individuals with similar jobs in the same organization but also includes friends, neighbors, or professional associates. Based on what they hear at work or read about in newspapers or trade journals, employees compare their pay with that of others. (2) The "system" category includes organizational pay policies, procedures, and allocation. (3) The "self" category refers to inputs-outcomes ratios that are unique to the individual. It reflects past personal experiences and contacts and is influenced by criteria such as past jobs or family commitments.

Originally, equity theory focused on **distributive justice**, which is the perceived fairness of the amount and allocation of rewards among individuals. More recent research has focused on looking at issues of **procedural justice**, which is the perceived fairness of the process used to determine the distribution of rewards. This research shows that distributive justice has a greater influence on employee satisfaction than procedural justice, while procedural justice tends to affect an employee's organizational commitment, trust in his or her boss, and intention to quit.[34] What are the implications for managers? They should consider openly sharing information on how allocation decisions are made, follow consistent and unbiased procedures, and engage in similar practices to increase the perception of procedural justice. By increasing the perception of procedural justice, employees are likely to view their bosses and the organization as positive even if they're dissatisfied with pay, promotions, and other personal outcomes.

Exhibit 11–7 Equity Theory Relationships

PERCEIVED RATIO COMPARISON*	EMPLOYEE'S ASSESSMENT
$\frac{\text{Outcomes A}}{\text{Inputs A}} < \frac{\text{Outcomes B}}{\text{Inputs B}}$	Inequity (underrewarded)
$\frac{\text{Outcomes A}}{\text{Inputs A}} = \frac{\text{Outcomes B}}{\text{Inputs B}}$	Equity
$\frac{\text{Outcomes A}}{\text{Inputs A}} > \frac{\text{Outcomes B}}{\text{Inputs B}}$	Inequity (overrewarded)

*Person A is the employee, and Person B is a relevant other or referent.

Exhibit 11–8 Expectancy Model

A = Effort–performance linkage (expectancy)
B = Performance–reward linkage (instrumentality)
C = Attractiveness (valence)

How Does Expectancy Theory Explain Motivation?

- How hard do I have to work to achieve a certain level of performance?
- Can I actually do that?
- What reward will I get for reaching it?
- How much do I want that reward?

The most comprehensive explanation of how employees are motivated is Victor Vroom's **expectancy theory**. Although the theory has its critics,[35] most research evidence supports it.[36]

Expectancy theory states that an individual tends to act in a certain way based on the expectation that the act will be followed by a given outcome and on the attractiveness of that outcome to the individual. It includes three variables or relationships (see Exhibit 11–8):

1. *Expectancy or effort-performance linkage* is the probability perceived by the individual that exerting a given amount of effort will lead to a certain level of performance.
2. *Instrumentality or performance-reward linkage* is the degree to which the individual believes that performing at a particular level is instrumental in attaining the desired outcome.
3. *Valence or attractiveness of reward* is the importance that the individual places on the potential outcome or reward that can be achieved on the job. Valence considers both the goals and needs of the individual.

This explanation of motivation might sound complicated, but it really isn't. It can be summed up in the questions: How hard do I have to work to achieve a certain level of performance, and can I actually achieve that level? What reward will performing at that level get me? How attractive is the reward to me, and does it help me achieve my own personal goals? Whether you are motivated to put forth effort (that is, to work hard) at any given time depends on your goals and your perception of whether a certain level of performance is necessary to attain those goals. Let's look at an example. Many years ago, when a woman went to work for IBM as a sales rep, her favorite work "reward" became having an IBM corporate jet fly to pick up her best customers and her and take them for a weekend of golfing at some fun location. But to get that particular "reward," she had to achieve at a certain level of performance, which involved exceeding her sales goals by a specified percentage. How hard she was willing to work (that is, how motivated she was to put forth effort) was dependent on the level of performance that had to be met and the likelihood that if she achieved at that level of performance she would receive that reward. Because she "valued" that reward, she always worked hard to exceed her sales goals. And the performance-reward linkage was clear because her hard work and performance achievements were always acknowledged by the company with the reward she valued (access to a corporate jet).

The key to expectancy theory is understanding an individual's goal and the linkage between effort and performance, between performance and rewards, and finally, between rewards and individual goal satisfaction. It emphasizes payoffs, or rewards. As a result, we have to believe that the rewards an organization offers align with what the individual wants. Expectancy theory recognizes that no universal principle explains what motivates individuals and thus stresses that managers understand why employees view certain outcomes as attractive or unattractive. After all, we want to reward individuals with those things they value positively. Also, expectancy theory emphasizes expected behaviors. Do employees know what is expected of

expectancy theory
The theory that an individual tends to act in a certain way based on the expectation that the act will be followed by a given outcome and on the attractiveness of that outcome to the individual

Foxconn chairman and founder Terry Gou (center) honored 140 employees in Shenzhen, China, for their excellent performance at an awards and recognition banquet for them and their relatives. Recognition programs that express appreciation for a job well done play a powerful role in motivating appropriate employee behavior.

them and how they'll be evaluated? Finally, the theory is concerned with perceptions. Reality is irrelevant. An individual's own perceptions of performance, reward, and goal outcomes, not the outcomes themselves, will determine his or her motivation (level of effort).

How Can We Integrate Contemporary Motivation Theories?

Many of the ideas underlying the contemporary motivation theories are complementary, and you'll understand better how to motivate people if you see how the theories fit together.[37] Exhibit 11–9 presents a model that integrates much of what we know about motivation. Its basic foundation is the expectancy model. Let's work through the model, starting on the left.

- The individual effort box has an arrow leading into it. This arrow flows from the individual's goals. Consistent with *goal-setting theory*, this goals-effort link is meant to illustrate that goals direct behavior.
- *Expectancy theory* predicts that an employee will exert a high level of effort if he or she perceives a strong relationship between effort and performance, performance and rewards, and rewards and satisfaction of personal goals. Each of these relationships is, in turn, influenced by certain factors. You can see from the model that the level of individual performance is determined not only by the level of individual effort but also by the individual's ability to perform and by whether the organization has a fair and objective performance evaluation system. The performance-reward relationship will be strong if the individual perceives that it is performance (rather than seniority, personal favorites, or some other criterion) that is rewarded. The final link in expectancy theory is the rewards-goal relationship.
- The *traditional need theories* come into play at this point. Motivation would be high to the degree that the rewards an individual received for his or her high performance satisfied the dominant needs consistent with his or her individual goals.

A closer look at the model also shows that it considers other theories.

- *Achievement-need* is seen, in that the high achiever isn't motivated by the organization's assessment of his or her performance or organizational rewards, hence the jump from effort to individual goals for those with a high nAch. Remember that high achievers are internally driven as long as the jobs they're doing provide them with personal responsibility, feedback, and moderate risks. They're not concerned with the effort-performance, performance-reward, or rewards-goals linkages.
- *Reinforcement theory* is seen in the model by recognizing that the organization's rewards reinforce the individual's performance. If managers have designed a reward system that is seen by employees as "paying off" for good performance, the rewards will reinforce and encourage continued good performance.
- Rewards also play a key part in *equity theory*. Individuals will compare the rewards (outcomes) they have received from the inputs or efforts they made with the inputs-outcomes ratio of relevant others. If inequities exist, the effort expended may be influenced.
- Finally, the *JCM* is seen in this integrative model. Task characteristics (job design) influence job motivation at two places. First, jobs that are designed around the five job dimensions are likely to lead to higher actual job performance because the individual's motivation will be stimulated by the job itself—that is, they will increase the linkage between effort and performance. Second, jobs that are designed around the five job dimensions also increase an employee's control over key elements in his or her work. Therefore, jobs that offer autonomy, feedback, and similar task characteristics help to satisfy the individual goals of employees who desire greater control over their work.

Exhibit 11–9 Integrating Contemporary Theories of Motivation

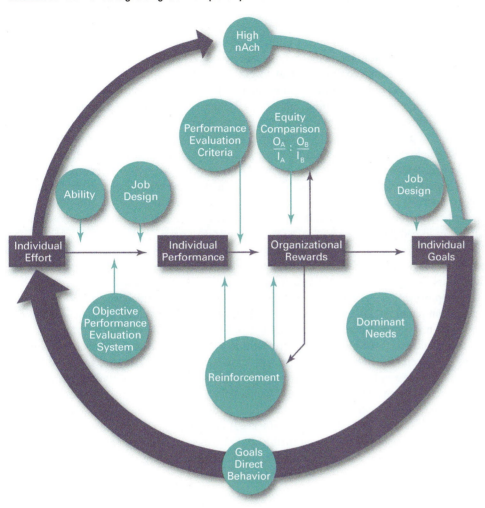

What Current Motivation Issues Do Managers Face?

11-4 Discuss current issues in motivating employees.

Understanding and predicting employee motivation is one of the most popular areas in management research. We've introduced you to several motivation theories. However, even current studies of employee motivation are influenced by some significant workplace issues—motivating in tough economic circumstances, managing cross-cultural challenges, motivating unique groups of workers, and designing appropriate rewards programs.

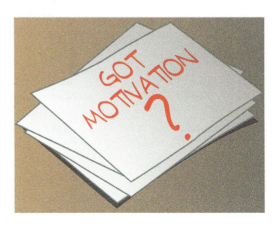

How Can Managers Motivate Employees When the Economy Stinks?

Zappos, the quirky Las Vegas–based online shoe retailer (now a part of Amazon.com), has always had a reputation for being a fun place to work.[38] However, during the economic recession, it, like many companies, had to cut staff—124 employees in total. CEO Tony Hsieh wanted to get out the news fast to lessen the stress for his employees. So he announced the layoff in an e-mail, on his blog, and on his Twitter account. Although some might think these are terrible ways to communicate that kind of news, most employees thanked him for being so open and so honest. The company also took good care of those being laid off. Laid-off employees with less than two years of service were paid through the end of the year. Longer-tenured employees got four weeks severance pay for every year of service. All got six months of continued paid health coverage and, at the request of the employees, got to keep their 40 percent merchandise discount through the Christmas season. Zappos had always been a model of how to nurture employees in good times; now it showed how to treat employees in bad times.

Economic recessions can be difficult for many organizations, especially when it comes to their employees. Layoffs, tight budgets, minimal or no pay raises, benefit cuts, no bonuses, long hours doing the work of those who had been laid off—this can be the reality that many employees face. As conditions deteriorate, employee confidence, optimism, and job engagement plummet as well. As you can imagine, it isn't an easy thing for managers to keep employees motivated under such challenging circumstances.

In an uncertain economy, managers have to be creative in keeping their employees' efforts energized, directed, and sustained toward achieving goals. They are forced to look at ways to motivate employees that don't involve money or that are relatively inexpensive.[39] So they use actions such as holding meetings with employees to keep the lines of communication open and to get their input on issues; establishing a common goal, such as maintaining excellent customer service, to keep everyone focused; creating a community feel so employees could see that managers cared about them and their work; and giving employees opportunities to continue to learn and grow. And, of course, an encouraging word always goes a long way, as well.

How Does Country Culture Affect Motivation Efforts?

The desire for **interesting work** seems to be global.

In today's global business environment, managers can't automatically assume that motivational programs that work in one geographic location are going to work in others. Most current motivation theories were developed in the United States by Americans and about Americans.[40] Maybe the most blatant pro-American characteristic in these theories is the strong emphasis on individualism and achievement. For instance, both goal-setting and expectancy theories emphasize goal accomplishment as well as rational and individual thought. Let's look at the cross-cultural transferability of the motivation theories.

Maslow's need hierarchy argues that people start at the physiological level and then move progressively up the hierarchy in order. This hierarchy, if it has any application at all, aligns with American culture. In countries such as Japan, Greece, and Mexico, where uncertainty avoidance characteristics are strong, security needs would be on top of the need hierarchy. Countries that score high on nurturing characteristics—Denmark, Sweden, Norway, the Netherlands, and Finland—would have social needs on top.[41] We would predict, for instance, that group work will be more motivating when the country's culture scores high on the nurturing criterion.

Another motivation concept that clearly has an American bias is the achievement need. The view that a high achievement need acts as an internal motivator presupposes two cultural characteristics—a willingness to accept a moderate degree of risk (which excludes countries with strong uncertainty avoidance characteristics) and a concern with performance (which applies almost singularly to countries with strong achievement characteristics).

This combination is found in the Anglo-American countries of the United States, Canada, and Great Britain.[42] On the other hand, these characteristics are relatively absent in countries such as Chile and Portugal.

Equity theory has a relatively strong following in the United States, which is not surprising given that U.S.–style reward systems are based on the assumption that workers are highly sensitive to equity in reward allocations. In the United States, equity is meant to closely link pay to performance. However, recent evidence suggests that in collectivist cultures, especially in the former socialist countries of Central and Eastern Europe, employees expect rewards to reflect their individual needs as well as their performance.[43] Moreover, consistent with a legacy of communism and centrally planned economies, employees exhibited a greater "entitlement" attitude—that is, they expected outcomes to be greater than their inputs.[44] These findings suggest that U.S.–style pay practices may need to be modified in some countries in order to be perceived as fair by employees.

Jae C. Hong/Associated Press

Like workers in most cultures, the desire for interesting work motivates Japan's Shigeru Miyamoto, the creator of many of Nintendo's characters including Mario, shown here. As a video game designer and producer, Miyamoto has also been motivated to achieve his goal of creating unique games that offer fun and joy to people of all ages throughout the world.

Despite these cross-cultural differences in motivation, a number of cross-cultural consistencies can be found. For instance, the desire for interesting work seems important to almost all workers, regardless of their national culture. In a study of seven countries, employees in Belgium, Britain, Israel, and the United States ranked "interesting work" number one among 11 work goals. It was ranked either second or third in Japan, the Netherlands, and Germany.[45] Similarly, in a study comparing job-preference outcomes among graduate students in the United States, Canada, Australia, and Singapore, growth, achievement, and responsibility were rated the top three and had identical rankings.[46] Both studies suggest some universality to the importance of intrinsic factors identified by Herzberg in his two-factor theory. Another recent study examining workplace motivation trends in Japan also seems to indicate that Herzberg's model is applicable to Japanese employees.[47]

How Can Managers *Motivate Unique Groups of Workers*?

Motivating employees has never been easy! Employees come into organizations with different needs, personalities, skills, abilities, interests, and aptitudes. They have different expectations of their employers and different views of what they think their employer has a right to expect of them. And they vary widely in what they want from their jobs. For instance, some employees get more satisfaction out of their personal interests and pursuits and only want a weekly paycheck—nothing more. They're not interested in making their work more challenging or interesting or in "winning" performance contests. Others derive a great deal of satisfaction in their jobs and are motivated to exert high levels of effort. Given these differences, how can managers do an effective job of motivating the unique groups of employees found in today's workforce? One thing is to understand the motivational requirements of these groups including (1) diverse employees, (2) professionals, and (3) contingent workers.

(1) MOTIVATING A DIVERSE WORKFORCE. To maximize motivation among today's workforce, managers need to think in terms of *flexibility*. For instance, studies tell us that men place more importance on having autonomy in their jobs than do women. In contrast, the opportunity to learn, convenient and flexible work hours, and good interpersonal relations are more important to women.[49] Having the opportunity to be independent and to be exposed to different experiences is important to Gen Y employees, whereas older workers may be more

A Question of Ethics

A scary thing is happening. Workers facing extraordinary work demands are turning to ADHD (attention deficit hyperactivity disorder) drugs to boost their energy. These pills are amphetamine-based stimulants that give users a boost of energy. Although some students may use these when studying for exams or putting the final touches on a research paper/presentation, experts now say that stimulant abuse is moving into the workplace. Many young workers using the drugs to increase their productivity say that "these drugs are used not to get high, but hired." Such seemingly harmless abuse can lead to serious consequences.[48]

*If your professor has assigned this, go to the Assignments section of **mymanagementlab .com** to complete these discussion questions.*

⭐ **Talk About It 3:** What do you think? Is this a problem of/for employee motivation? Explain.

⭐ **Talk About It 4:** Why is this a potential ethical issue? How might managers address this?

interested in highly structured work opportunities.[50] Managers need to recognize that what motivates a single mother with two dependent children who's working full time to support her family may be very different from the needs of a single part-time employee or an older employee who is working only to supplement his or her retirement income. A diverse array of rewards is needed to motivate employees with such diverse needs. Many of the work/life balance programs (see Chapter 7) that organizations have implemented are a response to the varied needs of a diverse workforce. In addition, many organizations have developed flexible work arrangements (see Chapter 6) that recognize different needs. These types of programs (including telecommuting, compressed workweeks, flextime, and job sharing) may become even more popular as employers look for ways to help employees cope with high fuel prices.

Do flexible work arrangements motivate employees? Although such arrangements might seem highly motivational, both positive and negative relationships have been found. For instance, one study of the impact of telecommuting on job satisfaction found that job satisfaction initially increased as the extent of telecommuting increased, but as the number of hours spent telecommuting increased, job satisfaction started to level off, decreased slightly, and then stabilized.[51]

(2) MOTIVATING PROFESSIONALS.   In contrast to a generation ago, the typical employee today is more likely to be a professional with a college degree than a blue-collar factory worker. What special concerns should managers be aware of when trying to motivate a team of engineers at Intel's India Development Center, software designers at SAS Institute in North Carolina, or a group of consultants at Accenture in Singapore?

Professionals are different from nonprofessionals.[52] They have a strong and long-term commitment to their field of expertise. To keep current in their field, they need to regularly update their knowledge, and because of their commitment to their profession they rarely define their workweek as 8 A.M. to 5 P.M. five days a week.

What motivates professionals? Money and promotions typically are low on their priority list. Why? They tend to be well paid and enjoy what they do. In contrast, job challenge tends to be ranked high. They like to tackle problems and find solutions. Their chief reward is the work itself. Professionals also value support. They want others to think that what they're working on is important. That may be true for all employees, but professionals tend to be focused on their work as their central life interest, whereas nonprofessionals typically have other interests outside of work that can compensate for needs not met on the job.

(3) MOTIVATING CONTINGENT WORKERS.   As full-time jobs have been eliminated through downsizing and other organizational restructurings, the number of openings for part-time, contract, and other forms of temporary work have increased. Contingent workers don't have the security or stability that permanent employees have, and they don't identify with the organization or display the commitment that other employees do. Temporary workers also typically get little or no benefits such as health care or pensions.[53]

There's no simple solution for motivating contingent employees. For that small set of individuals who prefer the freedom of their temporary status, the lack of stability may not be an issue. In addition, temporariness might be preferred by highly compensated physicians, engineers, accountants, or financial planners who don't want the demands of a full-time job. But these are the exceptions. For the most part, temporary employees are not temporary by choice.

What will motivate involuntarily temporary employees? An obvious answer is the opportunity to become a permanent employee. In cases in which permanent employees are selected from a pool of temps, the temps will often work hard in hopes of becoming permanent. A less obvious answer is the opportunity for training. The ability of a temporary employee to find a new job is largely dependent on his or her skills. If an employee sees that the job he or she is doing can help develop marketable skills, then motivation is increased. From an equity standpoint, when temps work alongside permanent employees who earn more and get benefits too for doing the same job, the performance of temps is likely to suffer. Separating such employees or perhaps minimizing interdependence between them might help managers counteract potential problems.[54]

How Can Managers *Design Appropriate Rewards Programs*?

At Blue Cross of California, doctors in its health maintenance organizations are paid bonuses on whether customers (patients) are satisfied. At FedEx, drivers are paid on the basis of the quantity of packages delivered and whether those packages are delivered on time.[55] There's no doubt that employee rewards programs play a powerful role in motivating appropriate employee behavior. Some of the more popular rewards programs include open-book management, employee recognition, and pay-for-performance.

HOW CAN OPEN-BOOK MANAGEMENT PROGRAMS MOTIVATE EMPLOYEES? Within 24 hours after managers of the Heavy Duty Division of Springfield Remanufacturing Company (SRC) gather to discuss a multipage financial document, every plant employee will have seen the same information. If the employees can meet shipment goals, they'll all share in a large year-end bonus.[56] Many organizations of various sizes involve their employees in workplace decisions by opening up the financial statements (the "books"). They share that information so that employees will be motivated to make better decisions about their work, be better able to understand the implications of what they do and how they do it, and see the ultimate impact on the bottom line. This approach is called **open-book management** and many organizations are using it.[57]

The goal of open-book management is to get employees to think like an owner by seeing the impact their decisions have on financial results. Because many employees don't have the knowledge or background to understand the financials, they have to be taught how to read and understand the organization's financial statements. Once employees have this knowledge, however, managers need to regularly share the numbers with them. By sharing this information, employees begin to see the link between their efforts, level of performance, and operational results.

HOW CAN MANAGERS USE EMPLOYEE RECOGNITION PROGRAMS? **Employee recognition programs** consist of personal attention and expressions of interest, approval, and appreciation for a job well done.[58] They can take numerous forms. For instance, Kelly Services introduced a new version of its points-based incentive system to better promote productivity and retention among its employees. The program, called Kelly Kudos, gives employees more choices of awards and allows them to accumulate points over a longer time

open-book management
A motivational approach in which an organization's financial statements (the "books") are shared with all employees

employee recognition programs
Programs that consist of personal attention and expressions of interest, approval, and appreciation for a job well done

gamification
Applying typical aspects of game playing to other areas of activity especially in a work setting

Technology and the Manager's Job
INDIVIDUALIZED REWARDS

Organizations have historically assumed that "one size fits all" when it comes to allocating rewards. Managers typically assumed that everyone wants more money and more vacation time. But as organizations become less bureaucratic and more capable of differentiating rewards, managers will be encouraged to differentiate rewards among employees as well as for individual employees over time.

Organizations control a vast number of potential rewards that employees might find appealing. A partial list would include increased base pay, bonuses, shortened workweeks, extended vacations, paid sabbaticals, flexible work hours, part-time employment, guaranteed job security, increased pension contributions, college tuition reimbursement, personal days off, help in purchasing a home, recognition awards, paid club memberships, and work-from-home options. And the latest twist in employee rewards comes through the use of social networking, mobile accessibility, and

gamification—that is, applying typical aspects of game playing to other areas of activity especially in a work setting—giving employees the opportunity to earn ongoing "badges" or "honors." These types of reward programs have the potential to engage and inspire employees. In the future, most organizations will structure individual reward packages in ways that will maximize employee motivation.

If your professor has assigned this, go to the Assignments section of mymanagementlab.com to complete these discussion questions.

⭐ **TALK ABOUT IT 5:** What are the positive aspects of having individualized rewards? (Think in terms of employees and managers.)

⭐ **TALK ABOUT IT 6:** What are the negative aspects of having individualized rewards? (Again, think in terms of employees and managers.)

pay-for-performance programs
Variable compensation plans that pay employees on the basis of some performance measure

period.[59] And it's working. Participants generate three times more revenue and hours than employees not receiving points. Most managers, however, use a far more informal approach. For example, when Julia Stewart—currently chairman and CEO of DineEquity, Inc.—was president of Applebee's Restaurants, she would frequently leave sealed notes on the chairs of employees after everyone had gone home.[60] These notes explained how important Stewart thought the person's work was or how much she appreciated the completion of a project. Stewart also relied heavily on voice mail messages left after office hours to tell employees how appreciative she was for a job well done. And recognition doesn't have to come only from managers. Some 35 percent of companies encourage coworkers to recognize peers for outstanding work efforts.[61] For instance, managers at Yum Brands Inc. (the Kentucky-based parent of food chains Taco Bell, KFC, and Pizza Hut) were looking for ways to reduce employee turnover. They found a successful customer-service program involving peer recognition at KFC restaurants in Australia. Workers there spontaneously rewarded fellow workers with "Champs cards, an acronym for attributes such as cleanliness, hospitality, and accuracy." Yum implemented the program in other restaurants around the world, and credits the peer recognition with reducing hourly employee turnover from 181 percent to 109 percent.[62]

A survey of organizations found that **84 percent had some type of program to recognize worker achievements.**[63]

And do employees think these programs are important? You bet! A survey of a wide range of employees asked them what they considered the most powerful workplace motivator. Their response? Recognition, recognition, and more recognition![64]

Consistent with reinforcement theory (see Chapter 9), rewarding a behavior with recognition immediately following that behavior is likely to encourage its repetition. And recognition can take many forms. You can personally congratulate an employee in private for a good job. You can send a handwritten note or e-mail message acknowledging something positive that the employee has done. For employees with a strong need for social acceptance, you can publicly recognize accomplishments. To enhance group cohesiveness and motivation, you can celebrate team successes. For instance, you can do something as simple as throw a pizza party to celebrate a team's accomplishments. Some of these things may seem simple, but they can go a long way in showing employees they're valued.

> ⭐ **Watch It 2!**
>
> If your professor has assigned this, go to the Assignments section of **mymanagementlab.com** to complete the video exercise titled *CH2MHill: Motivation*.

This baker at Zingerman's Deli in Ann Arbor, Michigan, is empowered with information that enables him to think and act like an owner. Embracing open-book management, Zingerman shares financial, product, customer service, and other information employees need to understand how the company works and how their decisions affect the company's profitability.

HOW CAN MANAGERS USE PAY-FOR-PERFORMANCE TO MOTIVATE EMPLOYEES?
Here's a survey statistic that may surprise you: 40 percent of employees see no clear link between performance and pay.[65] You have to think: What are the companies where these employees work paying for? They're obviously not clearly communicating performance expectations.[66] **Pay-for-performance programs** are variable compensation plans that pay employees on the basis of some performance measure.[67] Piece-rate pay plans, wage incentive plans, profit-sharing, and lump-sum bonuses are examples. What differentiates these forms of pay from more traditional compensation plans is that instead of paying a person for time on the job, pay is adjusted to reflect some performance measure. These performance measures might include such

things as individual productivity, team or work group productivity, departmental productivity, or the overall organization's profit performance.

Pay-for-performance is probably most compatible with expectancy theory. Individuals should perceive a strong relationship between their performance and the rewards they receive for motivation to be maximized. If rewards are allocated only on nonperformance factors—such as seniority, job title, or across-the-board pay raises—then employees are likely to reduce their efforts. From a motivation perspective, making some or all of an employee's pay conditional on some performance measure focuses his or her attention and effort toward that measure, then reinforces the continuation of the effort with a reward. If the employee, team, or organization's performance declines, so does the reward. Thus, there's an incentive to keep efforts and motivation strong.

Pay-for-performance programs are popular. Some 80 percent of large U.S. companies have some form of variable pay plan.[68] These types of pay plans have also been tried in other countries such as Canada and Japan. About 30 percent of Canadian companies and 22 percent of Japanese companies have company-wide pay-for-performance plans.[69]

Do pay-for-performance programs work? For the most part, studies seem to indicate that they do. For instance, one study found that companies that used pay-for-performance programs performed better financially than those that did not.[70] Another study showed that pay-for-performance programs with outcome-based incentives had a "positive impact on sales, customer satisfaction, and profits."[71] If an organization uses work teams, managers should consider group-based performance incentives that will reinforce team effort and commitment. But whether these programs are individual based or team based, managers need to ensure that they're specific about the relationship between an individual's pay and his or her expected level of appropriate performance. Employees must clearly understand exactly how performance—theirs and the organization's—translates into dollars on their paychecks.[72]

A FINAL NOTE ON EMPLOYEE REWARDS PROGRAMS. During times of economic and financial uncertainty, managers' abilities to recognize and reward employees are often severely constrained. It's hard to keep employees productive during challenging times, even though it's especially critical. It's not surprising, then, that employees feel less connected to their work. In fact, a recent study by the Corporate Executive Board found that declining employee engagement has decreased overall productivity by 3 to 5 percent.[73] But there are actions managers can take to maintain and maybe even increase employees' motivation levels. One is to clarify each person's role in the organization. Show them how their efforts are contributing to improving the company's overall situation. It's also important to keep communication lines open and use two-way exchanges between top-level managers and employees to soothe fears and concerns. The key with taking any actions is continuing to show workers that the company cares about them. As we said at the beginning of the chapter, the value in companies comes from employees who are motivated to be there. Managers have to give employees a reason to want to be there.

MyManagementLab®

Go to **mymanagementlab.com** to complete the problems marked with this icon .

11 Review

CHAPTER SUMMARY

11-1 Define and explain motivation.

Motivation is the process by which a person's efforts are energized, directed, and sustained toward attaining a goal.

The *energy* element is a measure of intensity or drive. The high level of effort needs to be *directed* in ways that help the organization achieve its goals. Employees must *persist* in putting forth effort to achieve those goals.

11-2 Compare and contrast early theories of motivation.

Individuals move up the hierarchy of five needs (physiological, safety, social, esteem, and self-actualization) as needs are substantially satisfied. A need that's substantially satisfied no longer motivates.

A Theory X manager believes that people don't like to work, or won't seek out responsibility, so they have to be threatened and coerced to work. A Theory Y manager assumes that people like to work and seek out responsibility, so they will exercise self-motivation and self-direction.

Herzberg's theory proposed that intrinsic factors associated with job satisfaction were what motivated people. Extrinsic factors associated with job dissatisfaction simply kept people from being dissatisfied.

Three-needs theory proposed three acquired needs that are major motives in work: need for achievement, need for affiliation, and need for power.

11-3 Compare and contrast contemporary theories of motivation.

Goal-setting theory says that specific goals increase performance, and difficult goals, when accepted, result in higher performance than do easy goals. Important points in goal-setting theory include intention to work toward a goal as a major source of job motivation; specific hard goals to produce higher levels of output than generalized goals; participation in setting goals as preferable to assigning goals, but not always; feedback to guide and motivate behavior, especially self-generated feedback; and contingencies that affect goal setting, such as goal commitment, self-efficacy, and national culture.

The job characteristics model is based on five core job dimensions (skill variety, task identity, task significance, autonomy, and feedback) that are used to design motivating jobs.

Equity theory focuses on how employees compare their inputs-outcomes ratios to relevant others' ratios. A perception of inequity will cause an employee to do something about it. Procedural justice has a greater influence on employee satisfaction than does distributive justice.

Expectancy theory says that an individual tends to act in a certain way based on the expectation that the act will be followed by a desired outcome. Expectancy is the effort-performance linkage (how much effort do I need to exert to achieve a certain level of performance); instrumentality is the performance-reward linkage (achieving at a certain level of performance will get me what reward); and valence is the attractiveness of the reward (Is the reward what I want?).

11-4 Discuss current issues in motivating employees.

During rough economic conditions, managers must look for creative ways to keep employees' efforts energized, directed, and sustained toward achieving goals.

Most motivational theories were developed in the United States and have a North American bias. Some theories (Maslow's need hierarchy, achievement need, and equity theory) don't work well for other cultures. However, the desire for interesting work seems important to all workers and Herzberg's motivator (intrinsic) factors may be universal.

Managers face challenges in motivating unique groups of workers. A diverse workforce is looking for flexibility. Professionals want job challenge and support, and are motivated by the work itself. Contingent workers want the opportunity to become permanent or to receive skills training.

Open-book management is when financial statements (the books) are shared with employees who have been taught what that information means. Employee recognition programs consist of personal attention, approval, and appreciation for a job well done. Pay-for-performance programs are variable compensation plans that pay employees on the basis of some performance measure.

DISCUSSION QUESTIONS

11-1 Most of us have to work for a living, and a job is a central part of our lives. So why do managers have to worry so much about employee motivation issues?

11-2 What is motivation? Explain the three key elements of motivation.

11-3 Contrast lower-order and higher-order needs in Maslow's needs hierarchy.

11-4 What role would money play in (a) the hierarchy of needs theory, (b) two-factor theory, (c) equity theory, (d) expectancy theory, and (e) motivating employees with a high nAch?

11-5 What are some of the possible consequences of employees perceiving an inequity between their inputs and outcomes and those of others?

11-6 What are some advantages of using pay-for-performance programs to motivate employee performance? Are there drawbacks? Explain.

11-7 Many job design experts who have studied the changing nature of work say that people do their best work when they're motivated by a sense of purpose rather than by the pursuit of money. Do you agree? Explain your position. What are the implications for managers?

11-8 As a manager, what will you need to know about goal-setting theory as a motivation tool?

11-9 Can an individual be too motivated? Discuss.

11-10 What challenges do managers face in motivating today's workforce?

Writing Assignments

11-11 What economic and cross-cultural challenges face when motivating employees?

11-12 What are the three variables in expectancy theory and how do they explain motivation?

Management Skill Builder | BEING A GOOD MOTIVATOR

Great managers are great motivators. They're able to find the magic "potion" that stimulates employees to reach their full potential. The fact that there are hundreds of business books on motivation and dozens of experts who make a living by putting on motivation seminars only confirms the importance of this topic to managerial effectiveness.

⭐ PERSONAL INVENTORY ASSESSMENT

Work Motivation Indicator

How motivated are you? Use this PIA to assess your own level of work motivation. You could also use it to assess others' levels of work motivation.

Skill Basics

Attempting to motivate others is a complex task. Unfortunately, no universal motivators are available that are guaranteed to work on anyone, anywhere. That said, we do know a lot about what works and doesn't work in terms of motivating others. The following suggestions summarize the essence of what we know is likely to be effective.[74]

- *Recognize individual differences*. People have different needs. Don't treat them all alike. Moreover, spend the time necessary to understand what's important to each person. This will allow you to individualize goals, level of involvement, and rewards to align with individual needs.

- *Use goals and feedback*. People prefer to have goals. If you're in a position to assign or participate in setting goals for others, help them to set hard and specific goals. These are most likely to motivate. In addition, individuals are most likely to be motivated when they get feedback on how well they are faring in the pursuit of their goals.

- *Allow people to participate in decisions that affect them*. If you are in a position to influence the level of participation, actively seek input from the person you seek to motivate. Employees are especially likely to respond positively when allowed to participate in setting work goals, choosing their benefit packages, solving productivity and quality problems, and the like.

- *Link rewards to unsatisfied needs*. Recommendations #2 and #3 apply most directly to managers or team leaders trying to motivate their employees or team members. Effectively linking rewards to unsatisfied needs is a more generalizable action: It applies to motivating colleagues, friends, spouses, customers—as well as employees and team members. It builds on recommendation #1 and individual differences.

Depending on your position in an organization and your resources, the rewards you control will vary. For example, senior-level executives typically can control pay increases, bonuses, promotion decisions, job assignments, and training decisions. They also can usually control job design such as allowing employees more freedom and control over their work, improving working conditions, increasing social interactions in the workplace, or modifying the workload. But everyone can offer others rewards such as recognition or providing sympathetic and sensitive help with problems. The key is identifying what needs are dominant and unsatisfied, then choosing rewards that will help satisfy those needs.

- *Link rewards to performance*. The rewards you choose should be allocated so as to be contingent on performance. Importantly, the person you're trying to motivate must perceive a clear linkage. Regardless of how closely rewards are actually correlated to performance criteria, it's perception that counts. If individuals perceive this relationship to be low, motivation and performance will suffer.

- *Maintain equity*. Rewards should be perceived by people in the organization as equating with the inputs they bring to their job. At a simplistic level, it means that experience, skills, abilities, effort, and other obvious inputs should explain differences in performance and, hence, pay, job assignments, and other obvious rewards.

Practicing the Skill

Read through this scenario and follow the directions at the end of it:

Sean's first job out of college is as a supervisor for Lyle's Catering Services. One of Lyle's main businesses is managing the food service operations at colleges and hospitals.

Sean has been given responsibility for the cafeteria at St. Paul College. He has a staff of approximately 12 full-time and 15 part-time workers. The cafeteria is open 7 days a week, from 6:30 A.M. until 8 P.M.

Sean has been in the job eight months and has become frustrated by the high employee turnover. Just since he's been on the job, three full-time and six part-time people have quit. Sean went back and looked at the personnel records for the past five years and this pattern has been a constant. He's frustrated by the cost and time involved in continually hiring and training new people. He's decided he needs to do something.

Sean has begun informally talking to employees. None seem particularly enthusiastic about their jobs. Even some of the "old timers"—who've worked in the cafeteria for six years or more—have little enthusiasm for their work. In fact, the part-timers seem more motivated than the full-timers even though the average part-timer makes only $11.50 an hour versus the full-timers' $15.00.

The class should form into small groups. Assume you are Sean. How can you improve the staff's motivation and reduce the turnover rate?

La Mexican Kitchen

To: Linda Bustamante, Operations Manager

From: Matt Perkins, Shift Supervisor

Experiential Exercise

Linda, HELP! We're having a difficult time keeping our food servers with us. It seems like I just get them trained and they leave. And we both know that our servers are key to our company's commitment to excellent customer service. We can have the best food in town (and do!), but if our servers aren't motivated to provide excellent service, we won't have any customers.

Although these positions pay minimum wage, you and I both know a motivated server can make additional money from tips. But it seems that this isn't enough to motivate them to stay. So what would you recommend? Could you jot down some ideas about how to better motivate our food servers and send those to me? Thanks!

This fictionalized company and message were created for educational purposes only, and not meant to reflect positively or negatively on management practices by any company that may share this name.

CASE APPLICATION #1

One for the Money…

Does money buy happiness? Several of the 120 employees at Gravity Payments, a credit card processing company based in Seattle, are about to find out.[75]

The company's founder, 29-year-old Dan Price, made the news in the spring of 2015 when he decided to bump up the salary of 70 employees to a new "minimum wage" of $70,000. Now, everyone in the company will be making at least $70,000. Some employees at the company, where the average salary was $48,000, doubled their pay, and others got a nice salary increase—probably enough, you'd think, for employees to be pretty happy about!

Why did Price do it? He said that he had been thinking about employee pay for a while, especially after reading several news reports about the glaring pay disparities between corporate CEOs and employees, which he says struck him as "ridiculous" and "absurd." Also, Price had read an article on happiness by two Princeton researchers (one a Nobel Prize-winning psychologist) who had surveyed 450,000 U.S. residents on whether money could buy happiness—both as it affected overall happiness but also how it affected day-to-day life. The researchers concluded that people claimed to be happier with each doubling of income but only to a point. But

Money = Happiness, or Does It?

even more interesting was the dollar amount that respondents said would make their daily life more pleasant: about $75,000 a year. Price decided to offer his employees a minimum salary of $70,000. He felt that giving his employees this amount could enable many of them to buy homes and pay for their kids' educations.

To pay for the salary increase, Price is taking a pay cut from his annual $1 million salary down to $70,000. Also, the company will have to use 75 to 80 percent of its profits to help cover the cost. Some management consultants are questioning the move, wondering if it will affect employee productivity and pay off in the long run. Concerns about what happens to employee motivation include: Will employees be less motivated to work to be promoted to higher levels of responsibility, and would those employees who put in additional effort above and beyond their current tasks lose the incentive to do so ("why should I work harder if we all get the same pay"). And what happens to the CEO's motivation—would Price himself lose the incentive to want to grow the company? Then, there's also the question of what happens if the company's profitability starts to fall. Only time will tell if such issues are even relevant.

Discussion Questions

⭐ **11-14** Look back at the chapter-opening Management Myth and how it was "debunked." Evaluate this wage decision in light of that.

⭐ **11-15** Explain each of the employee productivity/motivation concerns. Which of these do you think is most critical? Why?

⭐ **11-16** Choose one of the contemporary motivation theories discussed in the chapter and write a description of it for Mr. Price, explaining how and why it would be a good alternative for employee motivation.

⭐ **11-17** What problem(s) might managers face under this new pay approach and how could they use knowledge about employee motivation to help them deal with those problem(s)?

CASE APPLICATION #2

Searching For?

Google gets more than 3,000 job applications a day.[76] And it's no wonder! With a massage every other week, onsite laundry, swimming pool and spa, free delicious all-you-can-eat gourmet meals, and fun diversions like a huge slide in the workplace, what more could an employee want? Sounds like an ideal job, doesn't it? However, some employees are demonstrating by their decisions to leave the company that all those perks (and these are just a few) aren't enough to keep them there.

Google has been in the top spot of *Fortune*'s list of "best companies to work for" for six years running. But make no mistake, Google's executives offer these fabulous perks for several reasons: to attract the best knowledge workers it can in an intensely competitive, cutthroat market; to help employees work long hours and not have to deal with time-consuming personal chores; to show employees they're valued; and to have employees remain Googlers (the name used for employees) for many years. Yet, employees continue to jump ship. One analyst commented that Google is so successful, hires the best and the brightest, and offers a wonderful work environment, but people leave.

For instance, Sean Knapp and two colleagues, brothers Bismarck and Belsasar Lepe, came up with an idea on how to handle Web video. They left Google, or as one person described it, ditched the good life to try their hands at starting their own company. When the threesome left the company, Google really wanted them and their project to stay. Google offered them whatever they wanted to keep them. But the trio realized they would do all the hard work and Google would own the product. So off they went, for the excitement of a startup.

If this were an isolated occurrence, it would be easy to write off. But it's not. Other talented Google employees have done the same thing. In fact, so many have left that they've formed an informal alumni club of ex-Googlers turned entrepreneurs.

Google is taking aggressive steps to retain its talent, especially those with startup ambitions. One thing the company has done is give several engineers who said they wanted to leave to pursue their own ideas the opportunity to pursue those ideas within Google. These employees work independently and can recruit other engineers. In addition, Google's resources, such as its code base and computer servers, are available to them. In addition, from the very beginning, Google's founders (Larry Page and Sergey Brin) believed in giving everyone time—called 20 percent time—to work on their own projects.

Other Googlers have left because they felt Google had gotten too big and turned into a slow-moving bureaucratic company. Again, the company battled to keep the talent. For instance, when a Google product manager told his bosses that he was leaving to take a job at Facebook, they offered him a huge raise. But he told them it wasn't about the money. So they offered him a promotion, the opportunity to work in a different area, or even to start his own company inside Google. Yet, the former employee says that Facebook offered an opportunity to do things quickly that couldn't (or wouldn't) happen at Google. However, there's one other thing that startups can offer experienced employees: They're "private companies that haven't gone public and can lure workers with pre-IPO (initial public offering) stock."

How do you **KEEP THE BEST?**

Discussion Questions

11-18 What's it like to work at Google? (Hint: Go to Google's Web site and find the section on Google Careers and go from there.) What's your assessment of the company's work environment?

11-19 Google is doing a lot for its employees, but obviously not enough to retain some talented employees. Using what you've learned from studying the various motivation theories, what does this situation tell you about employee motivation?

11-20 What do you think is Google's biggest challenge in keeping employees motivated?

11-21 If you were managing a team of Google employees, how would you keep them motivated?

11-22 Reread the chapter section on motivating professionals. Using this information, what would you tell managers at Google?

CASE APPLICATION #3

Passionate Pursuits

At its headquarters in Ventura, California, Patagonia's office space feels more like a national park lodge than the main office of a $600 million retailer.[77] It has a Douglas fir staircase and a portrait of Yosemite's El Capitan. The company's café serves organic food and drinks. There's an infant and toddler child-care room for employees' children. An easy one-block walk from the Pacific Ocean, employees' surfboards are lined up by the cafeteria, ready at a moment's notice to catch some waves. (Current wave reports are noted on a whiteboard in the lobby.) After surfing or jogging or biking, employees can freshen up in the showers found in the restrooms. And no one has a private office. If an employee doesn't want to be disturbed, he or she wears headphones. Visitors are evident by the business attire they wear. The company encourages celebrations to boost employee morale. For instance, at the Reno store, the "Fun Patrol" organizes parties throughout the year.

Patagonia has long been recognized as a great workplace for mothers. And it's also earned a reputation for loyal employees, something that many retailers struggle with. Its combined voluntary and involuntary turnover in its retail stores was around 25 percent, while it was only 7 percent at headquarters. (The industry average for retail is around 44 percent.) Patagonia's CEO Casey Sheahan says the company's culture, camaraderie, and way of doing business is very meaningful to employees and they know that their work activities are helping protect and preserve the outdoors that they all love and enjoy. Managers are coached to define expectations, communicate deadlines, and then let employees figure out the best way to meet those.

Motivating employees the RIGHT WAY

Founded by Yvon Chouinard, an avid advocate of the natural environment, Patagonia's first and strongest passion is for the outdoors and the environment. And that attracts employees who are also passionate about those things. But Patagonia's executives do realize that they are first and foremost a business and, even though they're committed to doing the right thing, the company needs to remain profitable to be able to continue to do the things it's passionate about. But that hasn't seemed to be an issue since the recession in the early 1990s, when the company had to make its only large-scale layoffs in its history.

Discussion Questions

11-23 What would it be like to work at Patagonia? (Hint: Go to Patagonia's Web site and find the section on jobs in Company Info.) What's your assessment of the company's work environment?

11-24 Using what you've learned from studying the various motivation theories, what does Patagonia's situation tell you about employee motivation?

11-25 What do you think might be Patagonia's biggest challenge in keeping employees motivated?

11-26 If you were managing a team of Patagonia employees in the retail stores, how would you keep them motivated?

Endnotes

1. P. Bronson, "What Should I Do with My Life Now?" *Fast Company*, April 2009, 35–37.
2. SmartPulse, "How Well Do You Motivate Your People?" Smart Brief on Leadership, www.smartbrief.com/leadership, January 20, 2015.
3. R. M. Steers, R. T. Mowday, and D. L. Shapiro, "The Future of Work Motivation Theory," *Academy of Management Review*, July 2004, 379–87.
4. A. Adkins, "U.S. Employee Engagement Holds Steady at 31.7%," http://www.gallup.com/poll/183041/employee-engagement-holds-steady.aspx, May 7, 2015.
5. J. Krueger and E. Killham, "At Work, Feeling Good Matters," *Gallup Management Journal*, http://gmj.gallup.com (December 8, 2005).
6. "Maslow Motion," *New Statesman*, March 15, 2010, 37; "Dialogue," *Academy of Management Review*, October 2000, 696–701; M. L. Ambrose and C. T. Kulik, "Old Friends, New Faces: Motivation Research in the 1990s," *Journal of Management* 25, no. 3 (1999): 231–92; A. Maslow, D. C. Stephens, and G. Heil, *Maslow on Management* (New York: John Wiley & Sons, 1998); and A. Maslow, *Motivation and Personality* (New York: McGraw-Hill, 1954).
7. R. Coutts, "A Pilot Study for the Analysis of Dream Reports Using Maslow's Need Categories: An Extension to the Emotional Selection Hypothesis," *Psychological Reports*, October 2010, 659–73; E. A. Fisher, "Motivation and Leadership in Social Work Management: A Review of Theories and Related Studies," *Administration in Social Work*, October–December 2009, 347–67; and N. K. Austin, "The Power of the Pyramid: The Foundation of Human Psychology and, Thereby, of Motivation, Maslow's Hierarchy Is One Powerful Pyramid," *Incentive* (July 2002): 10.
8. See, for example, M. L. Ambrose and C. T. Kulik, "Old Friends, New Faces: Motivation Research in the 1990s"; J. Rowan, "Ascent and Descent in Maslow's Theory," *Journal of Humanistic Psychology* (Summer 1999): 125–33; J. Rowan, "Maslow Amended," *Journal of Humanistic Psychology* (Winter 1998): 81–92; R. M. Creech, "Employee Motivation," *Management Quarterly*, Summer 1995, 33–39; E. E. Lawler III and J. L. Suttle, "A Causal Correlational Test of the Need Hierarchy Concept," *Organizational Behav-*

ior and Human Performance, April 1972, 265–87; and D. T. Hall and K. E. Nongaim, "An Examination of Maslow's Need Hierarchy in an Organizational Setting," *Organizational Behavior and Human Performance*, February 1968, 12–35.
9. R. E. Kopelman, D. J. Prottas, and A. L. Davis, "Douglas McGregor's Theory X and Y: Toward a Construct-Valid Measure," *Journal of Managerial Issues* (Summer 2008): 255–71; and D. McGregor, *The Human Side of Enterprise* (New York: McGraw-Hill, 1960). For an updated description of Theories X and Y, see an annotated edition with commentary of *The Human Side of Enterprise* (McGraw-Hill, 2006); and G. Heil, W. Bennis, and D. C. Stephens, *Douglas McGregor, Revisited: Managing the Human Side of Enterprise* (New York: Wiley, 2000).
10. F. Herzberg, B. Mausner, and B. Snyderman, *The Motivation to Work* (New York: John Wiley, 1959); F. Herzberg, *The Managerial Choice: To Be Effective or to Be Human*, rev. ed. (Salt Lake City: Olympus, 1982); R. M. Creech, "Employee Motivation"; and M. L. Ambrose and C. T. Kulik, "Old Friends, New Faces: Motivation Research in the 1990s."
11. D. C. McClelland, *The Achieving Society* (New York: Van Nostrand Reinhold, 1961); J. W. Atkinson and J. O. Raynor, *Motivation and Achievement* (Washington, DC: Winston, 1974); D. C. McClelland, *Power: The Inner Experience* (New York: Irvington, 1975); and M. J. Stahl, *Managerial and Technical Motivation: Assessing Needs for Achievement, Power, and Affiliation* (New York: Praeger, 1986).
12. McClelland, *The Achieving Society*.
13. McClelland, *Power: The Inner Experience*; D. C. McClelland and D. H. Burnham, "Power Is the Great Motivator," *Harvard Business Review*, March–April 1976, 100–10.
14. D. Miron and D. C. McClelland, "The Impact of Achievement Motivation Training on Small Businesses," *California Management Review*, Summer 1979, 13–28.
15. "McClelland: An Advocate of Power," *International Management*, July 1975, 27–29.
16. J. Flint, "How to Be a Player," *Bloomberg BusinessWeek*, January 24–30, 2011, 108–09.
17. R. M. Steers, R. T. Mowday, and D. L. Shapiro, "The Future of Work Motivation Theory"; E. A. Locke and G. P. Latham, "What Should We Do about Motivation Theory? Six Recommendations

for the Twenty-First Century," *Academy of Management Review*, July 2004, 388–403; and M. L. Ambrose and C. T. Kulik, "Old Friends, New Faces: Motivation Research in the 1990s."
18. M. L. Ambrose and C. T. Kulik, "Old Friends, New Faces: Motivation Research in the 1990s."
19. J. C. Naylor and D. R. Ilgen, "Goal Setting: A Theoretical Analysis of a Motivational Technique," in B. M. Staw and L. L. Cummings (eds.), *Research in Organizational Behavior*, vol. 6 (Greenwich, CT: JAI Press, 1984), 95–140; A. R. Pell, "Energize Your People," *Managers Magazine*, December 1992, 28–29; E. A. Locke, "Facts and Fallacies about Goal Theory: Reply to Deci," *Psychological Science*, January 1993, 63–64; M. E. Tubbs, "Commitment as a Moderator of the Goal-Performance Relation: A Case for Clearer Construct Definition," *Journal of Applied Psychology* (February 1993): 86–97; M. P. Collingwood, "Why Don't You Use the Research?" *Management Decision*, May 1993, 48–54; M. E. Tubbs, D. M. Boehne, and J. S. Dahl, "Expectancy, Valence, and Motivational Force Functions in Goal-Setting Research: An Empirical Test," *Journal of Applied Psychology* (June 1993): 361–73; E. A. Locke, "Motivation Through Conscious Goal Setting," *Applied and Preventive Psychology*, vol. 5 (1996): 117–24; M. L. Ambrose and C. T. Kulik, "Old Friends, New Faces: Motivation Research in the 1990s; E. A. Locke and G. P. Latham, "Building a Practically Useful Theory of Goal Setting and Task Motivation: A 35-Year Odyssey," *American Psychologist*, September 2002, 705–17; Y. Fried and L. H. Slowik, "Enriching Goal-Setting Theory with Time: An Integrated Approach," *Academy of Management Review*, July 2004, 404–22; G. P. Latham, "The Motivational Benefits of Goal-Setting," *Academy of Management Executive*, November 2004, 126–29; and G. Yeo, S. Loft, T. Xiao, and C. Kiewitz, "Goal Orientation and Performance: Differential Relationships Across Levels of Analysis and as a Function of Task Demands," *Journal of Applied Psychology* (May 2009): 710–26.
20. J. A. Wagner III, "Participation's Effects on Performance and Satisfaction: A Reconsideration of Research and Evidence," *Academy of Management Review*, April 1994, 312–30; J. George-Falvey,

"Effects of Task Complexity and Learning Stage on the Relationship between Participation in Goal Setting and Task Performance," Academy of Management Proceedings on Disk, 1996; T. D. Ludwig and E. S. Geller, "Assigned versus Participative Goal Setting and Response Generalization: Managing Injury Control among Professional Pizza Deliverers," *Journal of Applied Psychology* (April 1997): 253–61; and S. G. Harkins and M. D. Lowe, "The Effects of Self-Set Goals on Task Performance," *Journal of Applied Social Psychology* (January 2000): 1–40.
21. J. M. Ivancevich and J. T. McMahon, "The Effects of Goal Setting, External Feedback, and Self-Generated Feedback on Outcome Variables: A Field Experiment," *Academy of Management Journal* (June 1982): 359–72; and E. A. Locke, "Motivation Through Conscious Goal Setting."
22. J. R. Hollenbeck, C. R. Williams, and H. J. Klein, "An Empirical Examination of the Antecedents of Commitment to Difficult Goals," *Journal of Applied Psychology* (February 1989): 18–23; see, also, J. C. Wofford, V. L. Goodwin, and S. Premack, "Meta-Analysis of the Antecedents of Personal Goal Level and of the Antecedents and Consequences of Goal Commitment," *Journal of Management* (September 1992): 595–615; Tubbs, "Commitment as a Moderator of the Goal-Performance Relation"; J. W. Smither, M. London, and R. R. Reilly, "Does Performance Improve Following Multisource Feedback? A Theoretical Model, Meta-Analysis, and Review of Empirical Findings," *Personnel Psychology*, Spring 2005, 171–203.
23. M. E. Gist, "Self-Efficacy: Implications for Organizational Behavior and Human Resource Management," *Academy of Management Review*, July 1987, 472–85; and A. Bandura, *Self-Efficacy: The Exercise of Control* (New York: Freeman, 1997).
24. E. A. Locke, E. Frederick, C. Lee, and P. Bobko, "Effect of Self-Efficacy, Goals, and Task Strategies on Task Performance," *Journal of Applied Psychology* (May 1984): 241–51; M. E. Gist and T. R. Mitchell, "Self-Efficacy: A Theoretical Analysis of Its Determinants and Malleability," *Academy of Management Review*, April 1992, 183–211; A. D. Stajkovic and F. Luthans, "Self-Efficacy and Work-Related Performance:

A Meta-Analysis," *Psychological Bulletin*, September 1998, 240–61; A. Bandura, "Cultivate Self-Efficacy for Personal and Organizational Effectiveness," in E. Locke (ed.), *Handbook of Principles of Organizational Behavior* (Malden, MA: Blackwell, 2004), 120–36; and F. Q. Fu, K. A. Richards, and E. Jones, "The Motivation Hub: Effects of Goal Setting and Self-Efficacy on Effort and New Product Sales," *Journal of Personal Selling & Sales Management* (Summer 2009): 277–92.

25. A. Bandura and D. Cervone, "Differential Engagement in Self-Reactive Influences in Cognitively Based Motivation," *Organizational Behavior and Human Decision Processes*, August 1986, 92–113; and R. Ilies and T. A. Judge, "Goal Regulation across Time: The Effects of Feedback and Affect," *Journal of Applied Psychology* (May 2005): 453–67.

26. See J. C. Anderson and C. A. O'Reilly, "Effects of an Organizational Control System on Managerial Satisfaction and Performance," *Human Relations*, June 1981, 491–501; and J. P. Meyer, B. Schacht-Cole, and I. R. Gellatly, "An Examination of the Cognitive Mechanisms by Which Assigned Goals Affect Task Performance and Reactions to Performance," *Journal of Applied Social Psychology* 18, no. 5 (1988): 390–408.

27. See, for example, R. W. Griffin, "Toward an Integrated Theory of Task Design," in L. L. Cummings and B. M. Staw (eds.), *Research in Organizational Behavior*, vol. 9 (Greenwich, CT: JAI Press, 1987), 79–120; and M. Campion, "Interdisciplinary Approaches to Job Design: A Constructive Replication with Extensions," *Journal of Applied Psychology* (August 1988): 467–81.

28. See J. R. Hackman and G. R. Oldham, "Motivation Through the Design of Work: Test of a Theory," *Organizational Behavior and Human Performance*, August 1976, 250–79; Y. Fried and G. R. Ferris, "The Validity of the Job Characteristics Model: A Review and Meta Analysis," *Personnel Psychology*, Summer 1987, 287–322; S. J. Zaccaro and E. F. Stone, "Incremental Validity of an Empirically Based Measure of Job Characteristics," *Journal of Applied Psychology* (May 1988): 245–52; and R. W. Renn and R. J. Vandenberg, "The Critical Psychological States: An Underrepresented Component in Job Characteristics Model Research," *Journal of Management* (February 1995): 279–303.

29. From the Past to the Present box based on C. M. Christensen, "How Will You Measure Your Life?"

Harvard Business Review, July–August 2010, 46–51; D. A. Wren and A. G. Bedeian, *The Evolution of Management Thought* (New York: John Wiley & Sons, Inc., 2009); F. Herzberg, *One More Time: How Do You Motivate Employees?* (Boston, MA: Harvard Business School Press, 2008); and F. Herzberg, B. Mausner, and B. B. Snyderman, *The Motivation to Work*.

30. G. Van Der Vegt, B. Emans, and E. Van Der Vliert, "Motivating Effects of Task and Outcome Interdependence in Work Teams," *Journal of Managerial Psychology* (July 2000): 829; and B. Bemmels, "Local Union Leaders' Satisfaction with Grievance Procedures," *Journal of Labor Research* (Summer 2001): 653–69.

31. J. S. Adams, "Inequity in Social Exchanges," in L. Berkowitz (ed.), *Advances in Experimental Social Psychology*, vol. 2 (New York: Academic Press, 1965): 267–300; and M. L. Ambrose and C. T. Kulik, "Old Friends, New Faces: Motivation Research in the 1990s."

32. See, for example, R. L. Bell, "Addressing Employees' Feelings of Inequity," *Supervision*, May 2011, 3–6; P. S. Goodman and A. Friedman, "An Examination of Adams' Theory of Inequity," *Administrative Science Quarterly*, September 1971, 271–88; M. R. Carrell, "A Longitudinal Field Assessment of Employee Perceptions of Equitable Treatment," *Organizational Behavior and Human Performance*, February 1978, 108–18; E. Walster, G. W. Walster, and W. G. Scott, *Equity: Theory and Research* (Boston: Allyn & Bacon, 1978); R. G. Lord and J. A. Hohenfeld, "Longitudinal Field Assessment of Equity Effects on the Performance of Major League Baseball Players," *Journal of Applied Psychology* (February 1979): 19–26; J. E. Dittrich and M. R. Carrell, "Organizational Equity Perceptions, Employee Job Satisfaction, and Departmental Absence and Turnover Rates," *Organizational Behavior and Human Performance*, August 1979, 29–40; and J. Greenberg, "Cognitive Reevaluation of Outcomes in Response to Underpayment Inequity," *Academy of Management Journal* (March 1989): 174–84.

33. P. S. Goodman, "An Examination of Referents Used in the Evaluation of Pay," *Organizational Behavior and Human Performance*, October 1974, 170–95; S. Ronen, "Equity Perception in Multiple Comparisons: A Field Study," *Human Relations*, April 1986, 333–46; R. W. Scholl, E. A. Cooper, and J. F. McKenna, "Referent Selection in Determining Equity

Perception: Differential Effects on Behavioral and Attitudinal Outcomes," *Personnel Psychology*, Spring 1987, 113–27; and C. T. Kulik and M. L. Ambrose, "Personal and Situational Determinants of Referent Choice," *Academy of Management Review*, April 1992, 212–37.

34. See, for example, R. C. Dailey and D. J. Kirk, "Distributive and Procedural Justice as Antecedents of Job Dissatisfaction and Intent to Turnover," *Human Relations*, March 1992, 305–16; D. B. McFarlin and P. D. Sweeney, "Distributive and Procedural Justice as Predictors of Satisfaction with Personal and Organizational Outcomes," *Academy of Management Journal* (August 1992): 626–37; M. A. Konovsky, "Understanding Procedural Justice and Its Impact on Business Organizations," *Journal of Management* 26, no. 3 (2000): 489–511; J. A. Colquitt, "Does the Justice of One Interact with the Justice of Many? Reactions to Procedural Justice in Teams," *Journal of Applied Psychology* (August 2004): 633–46; J. Brockner, "Why It's So Hard to Be Fair," *Harvard Business Review*, March 2006, 122–29; and B. M. Wiesenfeld, W. B. Swann Jr., J. Brockner, and C. A. Bartel, "Is More Fairness Always Preferred? Self-Esteem Moderates Reactions to Procedural Justice," *Academy of Management Journal* (October 2007): 1235–53.

35. See, for example, V. H. Vroom, "Organizational Choice: A Study of Pre- and Postdecision Processes," *Organizational Behavior and Human Performance*, April 1966, 212–25; L. W. Porter and E. E. Lawler III, *Managerial Attitudes and Performance* (Homewood, IL: Richard D. Irwin, 1968); W. Van Eerde and H. Thierry, "Vroom's Expectancy Models and Work-Related Criteria: A Meta-Analysis," *Journal of Applied Psychology* (October 1996): 575–86; and M. L. Ambrose and C. T. Kulik, "Old Friends, New Faces: Motivation Research in the 1990s."

36. Right or Wrong box based on Borders Group, Inc., 2010 Form 10-K, www.borders.com (June 6, 2011); J. Checkler, "Judge Clears Bonuses at Borders," *Wall Street Journal*, April 23–24, 2011, B3; "News Briefs," *Publishers Weekly*, April 11, 2011, 4+; P. Brickley, "Borders Seeks to Hand Out $8.3 Million in Bonuses," *Wall Street Journal*, March 26, 2011, B2; and J. A. Trachtenberg and M. Spector, "For Borders, a Scramble to Be Lean," *Wall Street Journal*, March 14, 2011, B1.

37. See, for instance, M. Siegall, "The Simplistic Five: An Integrative Framework for Teaching

Motivation," *The Organizational Behavior Teaching Review* 12, no. 4 (1987–1988): 141–43.

38. "100 Best Companies to Work For," *Fortune*, February 7, 2011, 91+; V. Nayar, "Employee Happiness: Zappos vs. HCL," *Businessweek.com*, January 5, 2011; D. Richards, "At Zappos, Culture Pays," *Strategy+Business Online*, Autumn 2010; T. Hseih, "Zappos's CEO on Going to Extremes for Customers," *Harvard Business Review*, July–August 2010, 41–45; A. Perschel, "Work-Life Flow: How Individuals, Zappos, and Other Innovative Companies Achieve High Engagement," *Global Business & Organizational Excellence*, July 2010, 17–30; and J. M. O'Brien, "Zappos Know How to Kick It," *Fortune*, February 2, 2009, 54–60.

39. T. Barber, "Inspire Your Employees Now," *Bloombeg BusinessWeek Online*, May 18, 2010; D. Mattioli, "CEOs Welcome Recovery to Look After Staff," *Wall Street Journal*, April 5, 2010, B5; J. Sullivan, "How Do We Keep People Motivated Following Layoffs?" *Workforce Management Online*, March 2010; S. Crabtree, "How to Bolster Employees' Confidence," *The Gallup Management Journal Online*, February 25, 2010; S. E. Needleman, "Business Owners Try to Motivate Employees," *Wall Street Journal*, January 14, 2010, B5; H. Mintzberg, "Rebuilding Companies as Communities," *Harvard Business Review*, July–August, 2009, 140–43; and R. Luss, "Engaging Employees through Periods of Layoffs," *Towers Watson*, www.towerswatson.com (March 3, 2009).

40. N. J. Adler with A. Gundersen, *International Dimensions of Organizational Behavior*, 5th ed. (Cincinnati, OH: Thomson Southwestern, 2008).

41. G. Hofstede, "Motivation, Leadership and Organization: Do American Theories Apply Abroad?" *Organizational Dynamics*, Summer 1980, 55.

42. Ibid.

43. J. K. Giacobbe-Miller, D. J. Miller, and V. I. Victorov, "A Comparison of Russian and U.S. Pay Allocation Decisions, Distributive Justice Judgments and Productivity under Different Payment Conditions," *Personnel Psychology*, Spring 1998, 137–63.

44. S. L. Mueller and L. D. Clarke, "Political-Economic Context and Sensitivity to Equity: Differences between the United States and the Transition Economies of Central and Eastern Europe," *Academy of Management Journal* (June 1998): 319–29.

45. I. Harpaz, "The Importance of Work Goals: An International Perspective," *Journal of International Business Studies* (First Quarter 1990): 75–93.

46. G. E. Popp, H. J. Davis, and T. T. Herbert, "An International Study of Intrinsic Motivation Composition," *Management International Review*, January 1986, 28–35.

47. R. W. Brislin, B. MacNab, R. Worthley, F. Kabigting Jr., and B. Zukis, "Evolving Perceptions of Japanese Workplace Motivation: An Employee-Manager Comparison," *International Journal of Cross-Cultural Management* (April 2005): 87–104.

48. A. Schwartz, "Workers Seeking Productivity in a Pill Are Abusing ADHD Drugs," *New York Times Online*, April 18, 2015.

49. J. R. Billings and D. L. Sharpe, "Factors Influencing Flextime Usage among Employed Married Women," *Consumer Interests Annual*, 1999, 89–94; and I. Harpaz, "The Importance of Work Goals: An International Perspective," *Journal of International Business Studies* (First Quarter 1990): 75–93.

50. N. Ramachandran, "New Paths at Work," *U.S. News & World Report*, March 20, 2006, 47; S. Armour, "Generation Y: They've Arrived at Work with a New Attitude," *USA Today*, November 6, 2005, B1+; and R. Kanfer and P. L. Ackerman, "Aging, Adult Development, and Work Motivation," *Academy of Management Review*, July 2004, 440–58.

51. T. D. Golden and J. F. Veiga, "The Impact of Extent of Telecommuting on Job Satisfaction: Resolving Inconsistent Findings," *Journal of Management* (April 2005): 301–18.

52. See, for instance, M. Alpert, "The Care and Feeding of Engineers," *Fortune*, September 21, 1992, 86–95; G. Poole, "How to Manage Your Nerds," *Forbes ASAP*, December 1994, 132–36; T. J. Allen and R. Katz, "Managing Technical Professionals and Organizations: Improving and Sustaining the Performance of Organizations, Project Teams, and Individual Contributors," *Sloan Management Review*, Summer 2002, S4–S5; and S. R. Barley and G. Kunda, "Contracting: A New Form of Professional Practice," *Academy of Management Perspectives*, February 2006, 45–66.

53. K. Bennhold, "Working (Part-Time) in the 21st Century," *New York Times Online*, December 29, 2010; and J. Revell, C. Bigda, and D. Rosato, "The Rise of Freelance Nation," *CNNMoney*, cnnmoney.com (June 12, 2009); and R. J. Bohner Jr. and E. R. Salasko, "Beware the Legal Risks of Hiring Temps," *Workforce*, October 2002, 50–57.

54. H. G. Jackson, "Flexible Workplaces: The Next Imperative," *HR Magazine*, March 2011, 8; E. Frauenheim, "Companies Focus Their Attention on Flexibility," *Workforce Management Online*, February 2011; P. Davidson, "Companies Do More with Fewer Workers," *USA Today*, February 23, 2011, 1B+; M. Rich, "Weighing Costs, Companies Favor Temporary Help," *New York Times Online*, December 19, 2010; P. Davidson, "Temporary Workers Reshape Companies, Jobs," *USA Today*, October 13, 2010, 1B+; J. P. Broschak and A. Davis-Blake, "Mixing Standard Work and Nonstandard Deals: The Consequences of Heterogeneity in Employment Arrangements," *Academy of Management Journal* (April 2006): 371–93; M. L. Kraimer, S. J. Wayne, R. C. Liden, and R. T. Sparrowe, "The Role of Job Security in Understanding the Relationship between Employees' Perceptions of Temporary Workers and Employees' Performance," *Journal of Applied Psychology* (March 2005): 389–98; and C. E. Connelly and D. G. Gallagher, "Emerging Trends in Contingent Work Research," *Journal of Management* (November 2004): 959–83.

55. C. Haddad, "FedEx: Gaining on the Ground," *BusinessWeek*, December 16, 2002, 126–28; and L. Landro, "To Get Doctors to Do Better, Health Plans Try Cash Bonuses," *Wall Street Journal*, September 17, 2004, A1+.

56. K. E. Culp, "Playing Field Widens for Stack's Great Game," *Springfield, Missouri, News-Leader*, January 9, 2005, 1A+.

57. P. M. Buehler, "Opening Up Management Communication: Learning from Open Book Management," *Supervision*, August 2010, 15–17; D. Drickhamer, "Open Books to Elevate Performance," *Industry Week*, November 2002, 16; J. Case, "Opening the Books," *Harvard Business Review*, March–April 1997, 118–27; J. P. Schuster, J. Carpenter, and M. P. Kane, *The Power of Open-Book Management* (New York: John Wiley, 1996); and J. Case, "The Open-Book Revolution," Inc., June 1995, 26–50.

58. J. Singer, "Healing Your Workplace," *Supervision*, March 2011, 11–13; P. Hart, "Benefits of Employee Recognition in the Workplace: Reduced Risk and Raised Revenues," *EHS Today*, February 2011, 49–52; and F. Luthans and A. D. Stajkovic, "Provide Recognition for Performance Improvement," in E. A. Locke (ed.), *Principles of Organizational Behavior* (Oxford, England: Blackwell, 2000), 166–80.

59. C. Huff, "Recognition That Resonates," *Workforce Management Online*, April 1, 2008.

60. J. Stewart, "I'm Standing up for the Industry. Are You?" *Restaurant Business*, February 2011, 36–37; and M. Littman, "Best Bosses Tell All," *Working Woman*, October 2000, 54.

61. E. White, "Praise from Peers Goes a Long Way," *Wall Street Journal*, December 19, 2005, B3.

62. Ibid.

63. K. J. Dunham, "Amid Sinking Workplace Morale, Employers Turn to Recognition," *Wall Street Journal*, November 19, 2002, B8.

64. See B. Nelson, "Try Praise," *Inc.*, September 1996, 115; and J. Wiscombe, "Rewards Get Results," *Workforce*, April 2002, 42–48. Cited in S. Caudron, "The Top 20 Ways to Motivate Employees," *Industry Week*, April 3, 1995, 15–16.

65. V. M. Barret, "Fight the Jerks," *Forbes*, July 2, 2007, 52–54.

66. E. Krell, "All for Incentives, Incentives for All," *HR Magazine*, January 2011, 35–38; and E. White, "The Best vs. the Rest," *Wall Street Journal*, January 30, 2006, B1+.

67. R. K. Abbott, "Performance-Based Flex: A Tool for Managing Total Compensation Costs," *Compensation and Benefits Review*, March–April 1993, 18–21; J. R. Schuster and P. K. Zingheim, "The New Variable Pay: Key Design Issues," *Compensation and Benefits Review*, March–April 1993, 27–34; C. R. Williams and L. P. Livingstone, "Another Look at the Relationship between Performance and Voluntary Turnover," *Academy of Management Journal* (April 1994): 269–98; A. M. Dickinson and K. L. Gillette, "A Comparison of the Effects of Two Individual Monetary Incentive Systems on Productivity: Piece Rate Pay versus Base Pay Plus Incentives," *Journal of Organizational Behavior Management* (Spring 1994): 3–82; and C. B. Cadsby, F. Song, and F. Tapon,

"Sorting and Incentive Effects of Pay for Performance: An Experimental Investigation," *Academy of Management Journal* (April 2007): 387–405.

68. E. White, "Employers Increasingly Favor Bonuses to Raises," *Wall Street Journal*, August 28, 2006, B3.

69. "More Than 20 Percent of Japanese Firms Use Pay Systems Based on Performance," *Manpower Argus*, May 1998, 7; and E. Beauchesne, "Pay Bonuses Improve Productivity, Study Shows," *Vancouver Sun*, September 13, 2002, D5.

70. H. Rheem, "Performance Management Programs," *Harvard Business Review*, September–October 1996, 8–9; G. Sprinkle, "The Effect of Incentive Contracts on Learning and Performance," *Accounting Review*, July 2000, 299–326; and "Do Incentive Awards Work?" *HRFocus*, October 2000, 1–3.

71. R.D. Banker, S.Y. Lee, G. Potter, and D. Srinivasan, "Contextual Analysis of Performance Impacts on Outcome-Based Incentive Compensation," *Academy of Management Journal* (August 1996): 920–48.

72. S. A. Jeffrey and G. K. Adomza, "Incentive Salience and Improved Performance," *Human Performance* 24, no. 1 (2011): 47–59; T. Reason, "Why Bonus Plans Fail," *CFO*, January 2003, 53; and "Has Pay for Performance Had Its Day?" *McKinsey Quarterly*, no. 4 (2002), accessed at www.forbes.com.

73. E. Frauenheim, "Downturn Puts New Emphasis on Engagement," *Workforce Management Online*, July 21, 2009; S. D. Friedman, "Dial Down the Stress Level," *Harvard Business Review*, December 2008, 28–29; and S. E. Needleman, "Allaying Workers' Fears During Uncertain Times," *Wall Street Journal*, October 6, 2008.

74. Based on V. H. Vroom, *Work and Motivation* (New York: John Wiley, 1964); J. S. Adams, "Inequity in Social Exchanges," in L. Berkowitz (ed.), *Advances in Experimental Social Psychology* (New York: Academic Press, 1965), 267–300; and E. A. Locke and G. P. Latham, *A Theory of Goal Setting and Task Performance* (Upper Saddle River, NJ: Prentice Hall, 1990).

75. L. Dishman, "Can a $70,000 Minimum Wage Work?" http://www.fastcompany.com/3045138/the-future-of-work/can-a-70000-minimum-wage-work, April 20,

2015; and P. Cohen, "One Company's New Minimum Wage: $70,000 a Year," *New York Times Online,* April 13, 2015.

76. J. D'onfro and K. Smith, "Google Employees Reveal Their Favorite Perks about Working for the Company," http://www.businessinsider .com/google-employees-favorite-perks-2014-7, July 1, 2014; J. B. Stewart, "Looking for a Lesson in Google's Perks," *New York Times Online,* March 15, 2013; "100 Best Companies to Work For," *Fortune,* February 4, 2013, 85+; S. Levy, "The Problem with Success," *Wall Street Journal,* April 7, 2011, A15; S. Levy, *In the Plex: How Google Thinks, Works, and Shapes Our Lives* (New York: Simon & Schuster, 2011); C. C. Miller and J. Wortham, "Silicon Valley Hiring

Perks: Meals, iPads, and a Cubicle for Spot," *New York Times Online,* March 26, 2011; J. Light, "Google Is No. 1 on List of Desired Employers," *Wall Street Journal,* March 21, 2011, B8; M Moskowitz, R. Levering, and C. Tkaczyk, "100 Best Companies to Work For," *Fortune,* February 7, 2011, 91+; C. C. Miller and M. Helft, "Google Shake-Up Is Effort to Revive Start-Up Spark," *New York Times Online,* January 20, 2011; C. C. Miller, "Google Grows and Works to Retain Nimble Minds," *New York Times Online,* November 28, 2010; A. Efrati and P-W. Tam, "Google Battles to Keep Talent," *Wall Street Journal,* November 11, 2010, B1+; L. Petrecca, "With 3,000 Applications a Day, Google Can Be Picky," *USA Today,* May

19, 2010, 2B; S. E. Ante and K. Weisul, "And Google Begat ...," *Bloomberg BusinessWeek,* March 8, 2010, 39–42; A. Lashinsky, "Where Does Google Go Next?" *CNNMoney.com,* May 12, 2008; and "Perk Place: The Benefits Offered by Google and Others May Be Grand, But They're All Business," *Knowledge @ Wharton,* http://knowledge.wharton.upenn .edu/article (March 21, 2007).

77. B. Schulte, "A Company That Profits as It Pampers Workers," http://www.washingtonpost .com/business/a-company-that-profits-as-it-pampers-workers/2014/10/22/d3321b34-4818-11e4-b72e-d60a9229cc10_story.html, October 25, 2014; D. Baer, "How Patagonia's New CEO Is Increasing Profits While Trying

to Save the World," http://www .washingtonpost.com/business/ a-company-that-profits-as-it-pampers-workers/2014/10/22/ d3321b34-4818-11e4-b72e-d60a9229cc10_story.html, February 28, 2014; "Patagonia CEO & President Casey Sheahan Talks Business, Conservation & Compassion," *offyonder.com,* February 13, 2012; T. Henneman, "Patagonia Fills Payroll with People Who Are Passionate," www .workforce.com, November 4, 2011; M. Hanel, "Surf's Up at Patagonia," *Bloomberg Business-Week,* September 5–11, 2011, 88–89; J. Wang, "Patagonia, From the Ground Up," *Entrepreneur,* June 2010, 26–32; and J. Laabs, "Mixing Business with Pleasure," *Workforce,* March 2000, 80–85.

Image Source/Alamy

Management Myth
Myth
Myth

Leadership can't be taught.

Many people incorrectly assume that leaders are born. For example, they point to kids who, as early as four or five years old, are leading other kids around on the playground and displaying leadership qualities. The evidence suggests that while there are certainly personality traits associated with leadership and that these traits are more due to nature than nurture, leadership *can* be taught.

WHAT does it take to be an effective leader in today's organizations? Should the workplace environment be one in which employees feel like they're heard and trusted? It's important for managers in all organizations to be seen as effective leaders. Why is leadership so important? Because it's the leaders in organizations who make things happen. But what makes leaders different from nonleaders? What's the most appropriate style of leadership? What makes leaders effective? These are just some of the topics we're going to address in this chapter. ●

Learning Outcomes

Who Are Leaders, and What Is Leadership?

12-1 Define *leader* and *leadership*.

Let's begin by clarifying who leaders are and what leadership is. Our definition of a **leader** is someone who can influence others and who has managerial authority. **Leadership** is what leaders do; that is, it's a process of leading a group and influencing that group to achieve its goals.

Are all managers leaders? Because leading is one of the four management functions, ideally all managers *should* be leaders. Thus, we're going to study leaders and leadership from a managerial perspective.[1] However, even though we're looking at these from a managerial perspective, we're aware that groups often have informal leaders who emerge. Although these informal leaders may be able to influence others, they have not been the focus of most leadership research and are not the types of leaders we're studying in this chapter.

Leaders and leadership, like motivation, are organizational behavior topics that have been researched a lot. Most of that research has been aimed at answering the question: "What is an effective leader?" We'll begin our study of leadership by looking at some early leadership theories that attempted to answer that question.

◄◄◄ From the Past to the Present ►►►

Both the Ohio State and Michigan studies added a lot to our understanding of effective leadership.[2] Prior to the completion of these studies, it was widely thought by researchers and practicing managers that one style of leadership was good and another bad. However, as the research showed, both leader behavior dimensions—job-centered and employee-centered in the Michigan studies, and initiating structure and consideration in the Ohio State studies—are necessary for effective leadership. That dual focus of "what" a leader does still holds today. Leaders are expected to focus on both the task and on the people he or she is leading. Even the later contingency leadership theories used the people/task distinction to define a leader's style. Finally, these early behavioral studies

> ### People—Task: Both are important to leaders.

were important for the rigorous methodology they used and for increasing awareness of how important leader behavior is. Although the behavioral theories may not have been the final chapter in the book on leadership, they provided us with important insights that became the foundation of contingency leadership theories.

*If your professor has assigned this, go to the Assignments section of **mymanagementlab.com** to complete these discussion questions.*

⭐ **Talk About It 1:** Is saying that the leader's "job" is to focus on the task and focus on the people too simplistic? Explain.

⭐ **Talk About It 2:** How did the behavioral theories serve as a springboard for the leadership research that followed?

What Do Early Leadership Theories Tell Us About Leadership?

12-2 Compare and contrast early leadership theories.

Leaders. Groups. **Long History!**

- Actual studies of leadership began in the twentieth century.

- Early leadership theories focused on:
  — The **person** (leader trait theories)
  — The **behaviors**—how the leader interacted with his or her group members (behavioral theories)

1   THE LEADER What Traits Do Leaders Have?

Sergiu Ungureanu/Shutterstock

- **WHAT DO YOU KNOW ABOUT LEADERSHIP?** When asked that question, most people cite a list of qualities they admire in leaders—intelligence, charisma, decisiveness, enthusiasm, strength, bravery, integrity, self-confidence, and so forth.

- That's the **trait theories of leadership** in a nutshell—the search for traits or characteristics that differentiate leaders from nonleaders.

- If this concept was valid, *all leaders would have to possess those unique and consistent characteristics*, making it easy to find leaders in organizations.

- But that's not going to happen: Despite the best efforts of researchers, they have yet to find a set of traits that would *always* differentiate a leader (the person) from a nonleader.

- Attempts to identify traits consistently associated with *leadership* (the process, not the person) have been more successful. See Exhibit 12–1 for those eight traits.[3]

> **trait theories of leadership**
> Theories that isolate characteristics (traits) that differentiate leaders from nonleaders

Exhibit 12–1 Traits Associated with Leadership

1 Drive.
Leaders exhibit a high effort level. They have a relatively high desire for achievement, they are ambitious, they have a lot of energy, they are tirelessly persistent in their activities, and they show initiative.

2 Desire to lead.
Leaders have a strong desire to influence and lead others. They demonstrate the willingness to take responsibility.

3 Honesty and integrity.
Leaders build trusting relationships with followers by being truthful, or nondeceitful, and by showing high consistency between word and deed.

4 Self-confidence.
Followers look to leaders who don't self-doubt. Leaders, therefore, need to show self-confidence in order to convince followers of the rightness of their goals and decisions.

5 Intelligence.
Leaders need to be intelligent enough to gather, synthesize, and interpret large amounts of information, and they need to be able to create visions, solve problems, and make correct decisions.

6 Job-relevant knowledge.
Effective leaders have a high degree of knowledge about the company, industry, and technical matters. In-depth knowledge allows leaders to make well-informed decisions and to understand the implications of those decisions.

7 Extraversion.
Leaders are energetic, lively people. They are sociable, assertive, and rarely silent or withdrawn.

8 Proneness to guilt.
Guilt proneness is positively related to leadership effectiveness because it produces a strong sense of responsibility for others.

Source: Based on S. A. Kirkpatrick and E. A. Locke, "Leadership: Do Traits Really Matter?" *Academy of Management Executive*, May 1991, 48–60; T. A. Judge, J. E. Bono, R. Ilies, and M. W. Gerhardt, "Personality and Leadership: A Qualitative and Quantitative Review," *Journal of Applied Psychology* (August 2002): 765–80.

What Now?

- TRAITS alone were not sufficient for identifying effective leaders? Why? Explanations based solely on traits ignored the interactions of leaders and their group members as well as situational factors.

- Possessing the appropriate traits only made it *more likely* that an individual would be an effective leader.

- Leadership research from the late 1940s to the mid-1960s turned to finding preferred behavioral styles that leaders demonstrated.

Was there something unique in what leaders did—in other words, in their behavior?

Vege/Fotolia

2 THE BEHAVIORS What Behaviors Do Leaders Exhibit?

- Would **behavioral theories of leadership** provide more definitive answers about the nature of leadership?

- If behavioral theories could identify critical behavioral determinants of leadership, people could be trained to be leaders—the premise behind management development programs.

UNIVERSITY OF IOWA[4]

Behavioral Dimension

Democratic style: involving subordinates, delegating authority, and encouraging participation

Autocratic style: dictating work methods, centralizing decision making, and limiting participation

Laissez-faire style: giving group freedom to make decisions and complete work

CONCLUSION

Democratic style of leadership was most effective, although later studies showed mixed results.

OHIO STATE[5]

Behavioral Dimension

Consideration: being considerate of followers' ideas and feelings

Initiating structure: structuring work and work relationships to meet job goals

CONCLUSION

High–high leader (high in consideration and high in initiating structure) achieved high subordinate performance and satisfaction, but not in all situations

UNIVERSITY OF MICHIGAN[6]

Behavioral Dimension

Employee oriented: emphasized interpersonal relationships and taking care of employees' needs

Production oriented: emphasized technical or task aspects of job

CONCLUSION

Employee-oriented leaders were associated with high group productivity and higher job satisfaction.

MANAGERIAL GRID[7]

Behavioral Dimension

Concern for people: measured leader's concern for subordinates on a scale of 1 to 9 (low to high)

Concern for production: measured leader's concern for getting job done on a scale 1 to 9 (low to high)

CONCLUSION

Leaders performed best with a 9,9 style (high concern for production and high concern for people).

What Now?

- Dual nature of leader behaviors—that is, focusing on the work to be done and focusing on the employees—is an important characteristic of each of these studies.

Coloures-pic/Fotolia

- Leadership researchers were discovering that predicting leadership success involved something more complex than isolating a few leader traits or preferable behaviors.

- They began looking at situational influences. *Specifically, which leadership styles might be suitable in different situations and what were these different situations?*

behavioral theories of leadership
Theories that isolate behaviors that differentiate effective leaders from ineffective leaders

managerial grid
A two-dimensional grid for appraising leadership styles

What Do the Contingency Theories of Leadership Tell Us?

12-3 Describe the four major contingency leadership theories.

"The corporate world is filled with stories of leaders who failed to achieve greatness because they failed to understand the context they were working in."[8] In this section we examine four contingency theories—Fiedler, Hersey-Blanchard, leader-participation, and path-goal. Each looks at defining leadership style and the situation, and attempts to answer the *if-then* contingencies (that is, *if* this is the context or situation, *then* this is the best leadership style to use).

Fiedler contingency model
Leadership theory proposing that effective group performance depends on the proper match between a leader's style and the degree to which the situation allowed the leader to control and influence

least-preferred coworker (LPC) questionnaire
A questionnaire that measures whether a leader was task or relationship oriented

What Was the First Comprehensive Contingency Model?

The first comprehensive contingency model for leadership was developed by Fred Fiedler.[9] The **Fiedler contingency model** proposed that effective group performance depended on properly matching the leader's style and the amount of control and influence in the situation. The model was based on the premise that a certain leadership style would be most effective in different types of situations. The keys were:

1. define those leadership styles and the different types of situations, and then
2. identify the appropriate combinations of style and situation.

Fiedler proposed that a key factor in leadership success was an individual's basic leadership style, either task oriented or relationship oriented. To measure a leader's style, Fiedler developed the **least-preferred coworker (LPC) questionnaire**. This questionnaire contained 18 pairs of contrasting adjectives—for example, pleasant–unpleasant, cold–warm, boring–interesting, or friendly–unfriendly. Respondents were asked to think of all the coworkers they had ever had and to describe that one person they *least enjoyed* working with by rating him or her on a scale of 1 to 8 for each of the sets of adjectives (the 8 always described the positive adjective out of the pair and the 1 always described the negative adjective out of the pair).

If the leader described the least preferred coworker in relatively positive terms (in other words, a "high" LPC score—a score of 64 or above), then the respondent was primarily interested in good personal relations with coworkers and the style would be described as *relationship oriented*. In contrast, if you saw the least preferred coworker in relatively unfavorable terms (a low LPC score—a score of 57 or below), you were primarily interested in productivity and getting the job done; thus, your style would be labeled as *task oriented*. Fiedler did acknowledge that a small number of people might fall in between these two extremes and not have a cut-and-dried leadership style. One other important point is that Fiedler assumed a person's leadership style was fixed regardless of the situation. In other words, if you were a relationship-oriented leader, you'd always be one, and the same for task-oriented.

After an individual's leadership style had been assessed through the LPC, it was time to evaluate the situation in order to be able to match the leader with the situation. Fiedler's research uncovered three contingency dimensions that defined the key situational factors in leader effectiveness. These were:

- *Leader-member relations*: the degree of confidence, trust, and respect employees had for their leader; rated as either good or poor.
- *Task structure*: the degree to which job assignments were formalized and structured; rated as either high or low.
- *Position power*: the degree of influence a leader had over activities such as hiring, firing, discipline, promotions, and salary increases; rated as either strong or weak.

Richard Branson, founder and CEO of Virgin Group, is a relationship-oriented leader. Pictured here with an in-flight teammate while showing the interior of a new Virgin airplane, Branson is fun loving, takes a personal interest in the needs of employees, emphasizes interpersonal relations, and accepts individual differences among workers.

David Woo/*Dallas Morning News*/Corbis

Exhibit 12–2 The Fiedler Model

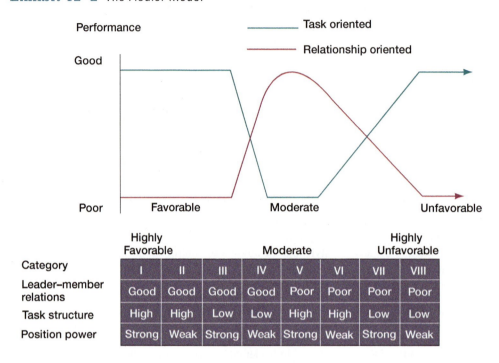

	Highly Favorable			Moderate			Highly Unfavorable	
Category	I	II	III	IV	V	VI	VII	VIII
Leader–member relations	Good	Good	Good	Good	Poor	Poor	Poor	Poor
Task structure	High	High	Low	Low	High	High	Low	Low
Position power	Strong	Weak	Strong	Weak	Strong	Weak	Strong	Weak

Each leadership situation was evaluated in terms of these three contingency variables, which when combined produced eight possible situations that were either favorable or unfavorable for the leader. (See the bottom of the chart in Exhibit 12–2). Situations I, II, and III were classified as highly favorable for the leader. Situations IV, V, and VI were moderately favorable for the leader. And situations VII and VIII were described as highly unfavorable for the leader.

Once Fiedler had described the leader variables and the situational variables, he had everything he needed to define the specific contingencies for leadership effectiveness. To do so, he studied 1,200 groups where he compared relationship-oriented versus task-oriented leadership styles in each of the eight situational categories. He concluded that task-oriented leaders performed better in very favorable situations and in very unfavorable situations. (See the top of Exhibit 12–2, where performance is shown on the vertical axis and situation favorableness is shown on the horizontal axis.) On the other hand, relationship-oriented leaders performed better in moderately favorable situations.

Because Fiedler treated an individual's leadership style as fixed, there were only two ways to improve leader effectiveness. First, you could bring in a new leader whose style better fit the situation. For instance, if the group situation was highly unfavorable but was led by a relationship-oriented leader, the group's performance could be improved by replacing that person with a task-oriented leader. The second alternative was to change the situation to fit the leader. This could be done by restructuring tasks; by increasing or decreasing the power that the leader had over factors such as salary increases, promotions, and disciplinary actions; or by improving the leader-member relations. Research testing the overall validity of Fiedler's model has shown considerable evidence to support the model.[10] However, his theory wasn't without criticisms. The major one is that it's probably unrealistic to assume that a person can't change his or her leadership style to fit the situation. Effective leaders can, and do, change their styles. Another is that the LPC wasn't very practical. Finally, the situation variables were difficult to assess.[11] Despite its shortcomings, the Fiedler model showed that effective leadership style needed to reflect situational factors.

How Do Followers' Willingness and Ability Influence Leaders?

situational leadership theory (SLT)
A leadership contingency theory that focuses on followers' readiness

Paul Hersey and Ken Blanchard developed a leadership theory that has had a strong following among management development specialists.[12] This model, called **situational leadership theory (SLT)**, is a contingency theory that focuses on followers' readiness. Before we proceed, there are two points we need to clarify: Why a leadership theory focuses on the followers, and what is meant by the term *readiness*.

The emphasis on the followers in leadership effectiveness reflects the reality that it *is* the followers who accept or reject the leader. Regardless of what the leader does, the group's effectiveness depends on the actions of the followers. This is an important dimension that has been overlooked or underemphasized in most leadership theories. And **readiness**, as defined by Hersey and Blanchard, refers to the extent to which people have the ability and willingness to accomplish a specific task.

LEADER

SLT uses the same two leadership dimensions that Fiedler identified: task and relationship behaviors. However, Hersey and Blanchard go a step further by considering each as either high or low and then combining them into four specific leadership styles described as follows:

- *Telling* (high task–low relationship): The leader defines roles and tells people what, how, when, and where to do various tasks.
- *Selling* (high task–high relationship): The leader provides both directive and supportive behavior.
- *Participating* (low task–high relationship): The leader and followers share in decision making; the main role of the leader is facilitating and communicating.
- *Delegating* (low task–low relationship): The leader provides little direction or support.

FOLLOWERS

The final component in the model is the four stages of follower readiness:

- *R1:* People are both *unable and unwilling* to take responsibility for doing something. Followers aren't competent or confident.
- *R2:* People are *unable but willing* to do the necessary job tasks. Followers are motivated but lack the appropriate skills.
- *R3:* People are *able but unwilling* to do what the leader wants. Followers are competent, but don't want to do something.
- *R4:* People are both *able and willing* to do what is asked of them.

Now—let's put the **two together!**

SLT essentially views the leader-follower relationship as like that of a parent and a child. Just as a parent needs to relinquish control when a child becomes more mature and responsible, so, too, should leaders. As followers reach higher levels of readiness, the leader responds not only by decreasing control over their activities but also decreasing relationship behaviors. The SLT says:

- If followers are at R1 (*unable* and *unwilling* to do a task), the leader needs to use the *telling style* and give clear and specific directions.
- If followers are at R2 (*unable* and *willing*), the leader needs to use the *selling style* and display high task orientation to compensate for the followers' lack of ability and high relationship orientation to get followers to "buy into" the leader's desires.
- If followers are at R3 (*able* and *unwilling*), the leader needs to use the *participating style* to gain their support.
- If followers are at R4 (both *able* and *willing*), the leader doesn't need to do much and should use the *delegating style*.

French entrepreneur Bertin Nahum is the founder and CEO of Medtech, a firm that develops, designs, and markets computer-assisted neurosurgical robotics. With high follower readiness of being able and willing, Nahum's managers and staff have the skills and experience to innovate and provide superior technical support.

Alain Robert/APERCU/SIPA/Newscom

SLT has intuitive appeal. It acknowledges the importance of followers and builds on the logic that leaders can compensate for ability and motivational limitations in their followers. However, research efforts to test and support the theory generally have been disappointing.[13] Possible explanations include internal inconsistencies in the model as well as problems with research methodology. Despite its appeal and wide popularity, we have to be cautious about any enthusiastic endorsement of SLT.

How Participative Should a Leader Be?

Back in 1973, Victor Vroom and Phillip Yetton developed a **leader-participation model** that related leadership behavior and participation to decision making.[14] Recognizing that task structures have varying demands for routine and nonroutine activities, these researchers argued that leader behavior must adjust to reflect the task structure. Vroom and Yetton's model was normative. That is, it provided a sequential set of rules to be followed in determining the form and amount of participation in decision making in different types of situations. The model was a decision tree incorporating seven contingencies (whose relevance could be identified by making yes or no choices) and five alternative leadership styles.

More recent work by Vroom and Arthur Jago has revised that model.[15] The new model retains the same five alternative leadership styles but expands the contingency variables to 12—from the leader's making the decision completely by himself or herself to sharing the problem with the group and developing a consensus decision. These variables are listed in Exhibit 12–3.

Research on the original leader-participation model was encouraging.[16] But unfortunately, the model is far too complex for the typical manager to use regularly. In fact, Vroom and Jago have developed a computer program to guide managers through all the decision branches in the revised model. Although we obviously can't do justice to this model's sophistication in this discussion, it has provided us with some solid, empirically supported insights into key contingency variables related to leadership effectiveness. Moreover, the leader-participation model confirms that leadership research should be directed at the situation rather than at the person. That is, it probably makes more sense to talk about autocratic and participative situations than autocratic and participative leaders. As House did in his path-goal theory, Vroom, Yetton, and Jago argue against the notion that leader behavior is inflexible. The leader-participation model assumes that the leader can adapt his or her style to different situations.[17]

> Only 53 percent of leaders are willing to step outside their leadership comfort zone and try new techniques.[18]

Exhibit 12–3 Contingency Variables in the Revised Leader-Participation Model

1. Importance of the decision
2. Importance of obtaining follower commitment to the decision
3. Whether the leader has sufficient information to make a good decision
4. How well structured the problem is
5. Whether an autocratic decision would receive follower commitment
6. Whether followers "buy into" the organization's goals
7. Whether there is likely to be conflict among followers over solution alternatives
8. Whether followers have the necessary information to make a good decision
9. Time constraints on the leader that may limit follower involvement
10. Whether costs to bring geographically dispersed members together are justified
11. Importance to the leader of minimizing the time it takes to make the decision
12. Importance of using participation as a tool for developing follower decision skills

Source: Stephen P. Robbins and Timothy A. Judge, *Organizational Behavior*, 13th ed., ©2009, p. 400. Reprinted and electronically reproduced by permission of Pearson Education, Inc., New York, NY.

How Do Leaders Help Followers?

Another approach to understanding leadership is **path-goal theory**, which states that the leader's job is to assist followers in attaining their goals and to provide direction or support needed to ensure that their goals are compatible with the goals of the group or organization. Developed by Robert House, path-goal theory takes key elements from the expectancy theory of motivation (see Chapter 11).[19] The term *path-goal* is derived from the belief that effective leaders clarify the path to help their followers get from where they are to the achievement of their work goals and make the journey along the path easier by reducing roadblocks and pitfalls.

House identified four leadership behaviors:

- *Directive leader*: Lets subordinates know what's expected of them, schedules work to be done, and gives specific guidance on how to accomplish tasks.
- *Supportive leader*: Shows concern for the needs of followers and is friendly.
- *Participative leader*: Consults with group members and uses their suggestions before making a decision.
- *Achievement-oriented leader*: Sets challenging goals and expects followers to perform at their highest level.

In contrast to Fiedler's view that a leader couldn't change his or her behavior, House assumed that leaders are flexible and can display any or all of these leadership styles depending on the situation.

As Exhibit 12–4 illustrates, path-goal theory proposes two situational or contingency variables that moderate the leadership behavior–outcome relationship:

1. those in the *environment* that are outside the control of the follower (factors including task structure, formal authority system, and the work group) and
2. those that are part of the personal characteristics of the *follower* (including locus of control, experience, and perceived ability).

Environmental factors determine the type of leader behavior required if subordinate outcomes are to be maximized; personal characteristics of the follower determine how the environment and leader behavior are interpreted. The theory proposes that a leader's behavior won't be effective if it's redundant with what the environmental structure is providing or is incongruent with follower characteristics. For example, some predictions from path-goal theory are:

- Directive leadership leads to greater satisfaction when tasks are ambiguous or stressful than when they are highly structured and well laid out. The followers aren't sure what to do, so the leader needs to give them some direction.

path-goal theory
A leadership theory that says the leader's job is to assist followers in attaining their goals and to provide direction or support needed to ensure that their goals are compatible with the organization's or group's goals

Exhibit 12–4 Path-Goal Model

Mary Barra, CEO of General Motors, is a participative leader. She involves employees in the decision-making process by encouraging them to voice their opinions, and she holds town hall meetings to gather advice. Barra's participative style results in highly engaged employees, organizational commitment, and effective work teams.

Epa european pressphoto agency b.v./Alamy

- Supportive leadership results in high employee performance and satisfaction when subordinates are performing structured tasks. In this situation, the leader only needs to support followers, not tell them what to do.
- Directive leadership is likely to be perceived as redundant among subordinates with high perceived ability or with considerable experience. These followers are quite capable so they don't need a leader to tell them what to do.
- The clearer and more bureaucratic the formal authority relationships, the more leaders should exhibit supportive behavior and deemphasize directive behavior. The organizational situation has provided the structure as far as what is expected of followers, so the leader's role is simply to support.
- Directive leadership will lead to higher employee satisfaction when there is substantive conflict within a work group. In this situation, the followers need a leader who will take charge.

- Subordinates with an internal locus of control will be more satisfied with a participative style. Because these followers believe that they control what happens to them, they prefer to participate in decisions.
- Subordinates with an external locus of control will be more satisfied with a directive style. These followers believe that what happens to them is a result of the external environment so they would prefer a leader who tells them what to do.
- Achievement-oriented leadership will increase subordinates' expectancies that effort will lead to high performance when tasks are ambiguously structured. By setting challenging goals, followers know what the expectations are.

Research findings on the path-goal model have been mixed because the theory has so many variables to examine. Although not every study has found support, we can still say that evidence supports the logic underlying the theory.[20] That is, an employee's performance and satisfaction are likely to be positively influenced when the leader chooses a leadership style that compensates for shortcomings in either the employee or the work setting. However, if the leader spends time explaining tasks that are already clear or when the employee has the ability and experience to handle them without interference, the employee is likely to see such directive behavior as redundant or even insulting.

> ⭐ **Try It!**
> If your professor has assigned this, go to the Assignments section of **mymanagementlab.com** to complete the **Simulation: *Leadership***.

What Is Leadership Like Today?

12-4 Describe modern views of leadership and the issues facing today's leaders.

What are the latest views of leadership, and what issues do today's leaders have to deal with? In this section, we're going to look at four contemporary views of leadership: leader-member exchange (LMX), transformational-transactional leadership, charismatic-visionary leadership, and team leadership. In addition, we'll discuss some issues that leaders have to face in leading effectively in today's environment.

What Do the Four Contemporary Views of Leadership Tell Us?

Remember our discussion at the beginning of this chapter where we said that leadership studies have long had the goal of describing what it takes to be an effective leader? That goal hasn't changed! Even the contemporary views of leadership are interested in answering that question. These views of leadership have a common theme: leaders who interact with, inspire, and support followers.

HOW DO LEADERS INTERACT WITH FOLLOWERS?   Have you ever been in a group in which the leader had "favorites" who made up his or her in-group? If so, that's the premise behind leader-member exchange (LMX) theory.[21] **Leader-member exchange (LMX) theory** says that leaders create in-groups and out-groups and those in the in-group will have higher performance ratings, less turnover, and greater job satisfaction.

LMX theory suggests that early on in the relationship between a leader and a given follower, a leader will implicitly categorize a follower as an "in" or as an "out." That relationship tends to remain fairly stable over time. Leaders also encourage LMX by rewarding those employees with whom they want a closer linkage and punishing those with whom they do not.[22] For the LMX relationship to remain intact, however, both the leader and the follower must "invest" in the relationship.

It's not exactly clear how a leader chooses who falls into each category, but evidence indicates that in-group members have demographic, attitude, personality, and even gender similarities with the leader or they have a higher level of competence than out-group members.[23] The leader does the choosing, but the follower's characteristics drive the decision.

> ### Ninety-two percent of executives see favoritism in who gets job promotions.[24]

Research on LMX has been generally supportive. It appears that leaders do differentiate among followers; that these disparities are not random; and followers with in-group status will have higher performance ratings, engage in more helping or "citizenship" behaviors at work, and report greater satisfaction with their boss.[25] These findings probably shouldn't be surprising when leaders are most likely to invest their time and other resources in those whom they expect to perform best.

HOW DO TRANSACTIONAL LEADERS DIFFER FROM TRANSFORMATIONAL LEADERS?
Many early leadership theories viewed leaders as **transactional leaders**; that is, leaders who lead primarily by using social exchanges (or transactions). Transactional leaders guide or motivate followers to work toward established goals by exchanging rewards for their productivity.[26] But another type of leader—a **transformational leader**—stimulates and inspires (transforms) followers to achieve extraordinary outcomes. How? By paying attention to the concerns and developmental needs of individual followers; changing followers' awareness of issues by helping those followers look at old problems in new ways; and being able to excite, arouse, and inspire followers to exert extra effort to achieve group goals.

Transactional and transformational leadership shouldn't be viewed as opposing approaches to getting things done.[27] Transformational leadership develops from transactional leadership. Transformational leadership produces levels of employee effort and performance that go beyond what would occur with a transactional approach alone. Moreover, transformational leadership is more than charisma since the transformational leader attempts to instill in followers the ability to question not only established views but those views held by the leader.[28]

The evidence supporting the superiority of transformational leadership over transactional leadership is overwhelmingly impressive. For instance, studies that looked at managers in different settings, including the military and business, found that transformational leaders were evaluated as more effective, higher performers, more promotable than their transactional counterparts, and more interpersonally sensitive.[29] In addition, evidence indicates that transformational leadership is strongly correlated with lower turnover rates and higher levels of productivity, work engagement, employee satisfaction, creativity, goal attainment, and follower well-being.[30]

HOW DO CHARISMATIC LEADERSHIP AND VISIONARY LEADERSHIP DIFFER?   Jeff Bezos, founder and CEO of Amazon.com, is a person who exudes energy, enthusiasm, and drive.[31] He's fun-loving (his legendary laugh has been described as a flock of Canada geese on nitrous oxide), but he has pursued his vision for Amazon with serious intensity and has

---

leader-member exchange (LMX) theory
A leadership theory that says leaders create in-groups and out-groups and those in the in-group will have higher performance ratings, less turnover, and greater job satisfaction

transactional leaders
Leaders who lead primarily by using social exchanges (or transactions)

transformational leaders
Leaders who stimulate and inspire (transform) followers to achieve extraordinary outcomes

charismatic leaders
Enthusiastic, self-confident leaders whose personalities and actions influence people to behave in certain ways

visionary leadership
The ability to create and articulate a realistic, credible, and attractive vision of the future that improves on the present situation

demonstrated an ability to inspire his employees through the ups and downs of a rapidly growing company. Bezos is what we call a **charismatic leader**—that is, an enthusiastic, self-confident leader whose personality and actions influence people to behave in certain ways.

Several authors have attempted to identify personal characteristics of the charismatic leader.[32] The most comprehensive analysis identified five such characteristics: they have a vision, the ability to articulate that vision, willingness to take risks to achieve that vision, sensitivity to both environmental constraints and follower needs, and behaviors that are out of the ordinary.[33]

It's good to be **charismatic!**

An increasing body of evidence shows impressive correlations between charismatic leadership and high performance and satisfaction among followers.[34] Although one study found that charismatic CEOs had no impact on subsequent organizational performance, charisma is still believed to be a desirable leadership quality.[35]

If charisma is desirable, can people learn to be charismatic leaders? Or are charismatic leaders born with their qualities? Although a small number of experts still think that charisma can't be learned, most believe that individuals can be trained to exhibit charismatic behaviors.[36] For example, researchers have succeeded in teaching undergraduate students to "be" charismatic. How? They were taught to articulate a far-reaching goal, communicate high performance expectations, exhibit confidence in the ability of subordinates to meet those expectations, and empathize with the needs of their subordinates; they learned to project a powerful, confident, and dynamic presence; and they practiced using a captivating and engaging voice tone. The researchers also trained the student leaders to use charismatic nonverbal behaviors including leaning toward the follower when communicating, maintaining direct eye contact, and having a relaxed posture and animated facial expressions. In groups with these "trained" charismatic leaders, members had higher task performance, higher task adjustment, and better adjustment to the leader and to the group than did group members who worked in groups led by noncharismatic leaders.

One last thing we should say about charismatic leadership is that it may not always be necessary to achieve high levels of employee performance. It may be most appropriate when the follower's task has an ideological purpose or when the environment involves a high degree of stress and uncertainty.[37] This aspect may explain why, when charismatic leaders surface, it's more likely to be in politics, religion, or wartime; or when a business firm is starting up or facing a survival crisis. For example, Martin Luther King Jr. used his charisma to bring about social equality through nonviolent means, and Steve Jobs achieved unwavering loyalty and commitment from Apple's technical staff in the early 1980s by articulating a vision of personal computers that would dramatically change the way people lived.

Although the term *vision* is often linked with charismatic leadership, **visionary leadership** is different: It's the ability to create and articulate a realistic, credible, and attractive vision of the future that improves on the present situation.[38] This vision, if properly selected and implemented, is so energizing that it "in effect jumpstarts the future by calling forth the skills, talents, and resources to make it happen."[39]

An organization's vision should offer clear and compelling imagery that taps into people's emotions and inspires enthusiasm to pursue the organization's goals. It should be able to generate possibilities that are inspirational and unique and offer new ways of doing things that are clearly better for the organization and its members. Visions that are clearly articulated and have powerful imagery are easily grasped and accepted. For instance, Michael Dell created a vision of a business that sells and delivers customized PCs directly to customers in less than a week. The late Mary Kay Ash's vision of women as entrepreneurs selling products that improved their self-image gave impetus to her cosmetics company, Mary Kay Cosmetics.

Amazon.com founder and CEO Jeff Bezos is a charismatic leader. Shown here displaying Amazon's Kindle Fire tablets, he is described as energetic, enthusiastic, optimistic, and self-confident. Bezos has the drive to set and pursue goals for risky new ventures and uses his charisma to inspire his employees to work hard to achieve them.

Reed Saxon/AP Images

☆ Watch It!

If your professor has assigned this, go to the Assignments section of **mymanagementlab.com** to complete the video exercise titled *CH2MHill: Power and Political Behavior*.

WHAT ABOUT LEADERS AND TEAMS?   Because leadership is increasingly taking place within a team context and more organizations are using work teams, the role of the leader in guiding team members has become increasingly important. The role of team leader *is* different from the traditional leadership role, as J. D. Bryant, a supervisor at Texas Instruments' Forest Lane plant in Dallas, discovered.[40] One day he was contentedly overseeing a staff of 15 circuit board assemblers. The next day he was told that the company was going to use employee teams and he was to become a "facilitator." He said, "I'm supposed to teach the teams everything I know and then let them make their own decisions." Confused about his new role, he admitted, "There was no clear plan on what I was supposed to do." What *is* involved in being a team leader?

> The most "dangerous" leadership trait: 32 percent of team members say *indecisiveness and over-cautiousness*; 26 percent say selfishness.[41]

Many leaders are not equipped to handle the change to employee teams. As one consultant noted, "Even the most capable managers have trouble making the transition because all the command-and-control type things they were encouraged to do before are no longer appropriate. There's no reason to have any skill or sense of this."[42] This same consultant estimated that "probably 15 percent of managers are natural team leaders; another 15 percent could never lead a team because it runs counter to their personality—that is, they're unable to sublimate their dominating style for the good of the team. Then there's that huge group in the middle: Team leadership doesn't come naturally to them, but they can learn it."[43]

The challenge for many managers is learning how to become an effective team leader. They have to learn skills such as patiently sharing information, being able to trust others and to give up authority, and understanding when to intervene. And effective team leaders have mastered the difficult balancing act of knowing when to leave their teams alone and when to get involved. New team leaders may try to retain too much control at a time when team members need more autonomy, or they may abandon their teams at times when the teams need support and help.[44]

One study looking at organizations that had reorganized themselves around employee teams found certain common responsibilities of all leaders. These responsibilities included coaching, facilitating, handling disciplinary problems, reviewing team and individual performance, training, and communication.[45] However, a more meaningful way to describe the team leader's job is to focus on two priorities: (1) managing the team's external boundary, and (2) facilitating the team process.[46] These priorities entail four specific leadership roles, as shown in Exhibit 12–5.

What Issues Do Today's Leaders Face?

It's not easy being a chief information officer (CIO) today. A person responsible for managing a company's information technology activities faces a lot of external and internal pressures. Technology changes rapidly—almost daily, it sometimes seems. Business costs continue to rise. Competitors develop new strategies. Economic conditions continue to confound even the experts. Rob Carter, CIO of FedEx, is on the hot seat facing such challenges.[47] He's responsible for all the computer and communication systems that provide around-the-clock and around-the-globe support for FedEx's products and services. If anything goes wrong, you know who takes the heat. However, Carter has been an effective leader in this seemingly chaotic environment.

A Question of Ethics

Have you ever watched the show *Undercover Boss?* It features a company's "boss" working undercover in his or her own company to find out how the organization really works. Typically, the executive works undercover for a week, and then the employees the leader has worked with are summoned to company headquarters and either rewarded or punished for their actions. Bosses from organizations ranging from Waste Management and White Castle to NASCAR and Stella and Dot have participated.

If your professor has assigned this, go to the Assignments section of **mymanagementlab.com** *to complete these discussion questions.*

☆ Talk About It 3: What do you think? Is it ethical for a leader to go undercover in his or her organization? Why or why not?

☆ Talk About It 4: What ethical issues could arise? How could managers deal with those issues?

Exhibit 12–5 Team Leader Roles

Leading effectively in today's environment is likely to involve such challenges for many leaders. Twenty-first-century leaders face some important leadership issues. In this section, we look at these issues, including empowering employees, cross-cultural leadership, and emotional intelligence and leadership.

Say What? Lead by NOT Leading

WHY DO LEADERS NEED TO EMPOWER EMPLOYEES? As we've described in different places throughout the text, managers are increasingly leading by not leading; that is, by empowering their employees. **Empowerment** involves increasing the decision-making discretion of workers. Millions of individual employees and employee teams are making the key operating decisions that directly affect their work. They're developing budgets, scheduling workloads, controlling inventories, solving quality problems, and engaging in similar activities that until very recently were viewed exclusively as part of the manager's job.[48] For instance, at The Container Store, any employee who gets a customer request has permission to take care of it. The company's chairman emeritus Garret Boone says, "Everybody we hire, we hire as a leader. Anybody in our store can take an action that you might think of typically being a manager's action."[49]

One reason more companies are empowering employees is the need for quick decisions by those people who are most knowledgeable about the issues—often those at lower organizational levels. If organizations want to successfully compete in a dynamic global economy, employees have to be able to make decisions and implement changes quickly. Another reason is that organizational downsizings left many managers with larger spans of control. In order to cope with the increased work demands, managers had to empower their people. Although empowerment is not a universal answer, it can be beneficial when employees have the knowledge, skills, and experience to do their jobs competently.

Technology also has contributed to the increases in employee empowerment. Managers face unique challenges in leading empowered employees who aren't physically present in the workplace as the Technology and the Manager's Job box discusses.

DOES NATIONAL CULTURE AFFECT LEADERSHIP? One general conclusion that surfaces from leadership research is that effective leaders do not use a single style. They adjust their style to the situation. Although not mentioned explicitly, national culture is certainly an important situational variable in determining which leadership style will be most effective. What works in China isn't likely to be

In China, the cultural value of collectivism affects the relationship between leaders and followers such as Yuki Tan, president of fashion retailer Folli Follie China, and store employees. During store visits, Tan displays her effective paternalistic leadership style of caring for her loyal, dependable, and hard-working employees.

Ton Koene/ZUMApress/Newscom

effective in France or Canada. For instance, one study of Asian leadership styles revealed that Asian managers preferred leaders who were competent decision makers, effective communicators, and supportive of employees.[50] Another study of leadership in Sub-Saharan Africa found that charismatic leaders can help overcome cultural problems of corruption, poverty, tribalism, and violence.[51]

National culture affects leadership style because it influences how followers will respond. Leaders can't (and shouldn't) just choose their styles randomly. They're constrained by the cultural conditions their followers have come to expect. Exhibit 12–6 provides some findings from selected examples of cross-cultural leadership studies. Because most leadership theories were developed in the United States, they have an American bias. They emphasize follower responsibilities rather than rights; assume self-gratification rather than commitment to duty or altruistic motivation; assume centrality of work and democratic value orientation; and stress rationality rather than spirituality, religion, or superstition.[52] However, the GLOBE research program, which we first introduced in Chapter 2, is the most extensive and comprehensive cross-cultural study of leadership ever undertaken. The GLOBE study has found that there are some universal aspects to leadership. Specifically, a number of elements of transformational leadership appear to be associated with effective leadership regardless of what country the leader is in.[53] These elements include vision, foresight, providing encouragement, trustworthiness, dynamism, positiveness, and proactiveness. The results led two members of the GLOBE team to conclude that "effective business leaders in any country are expected by their subordinates to provide a powerful and proactive vision to guide the company into the future, strong motivational skills to stimulate all employees to fulfill the vision, and excellent planning skills to assist in implementing the vision."[54] Some people suggest that the universal appeal of these transformational leader characteristics is due to the pressures toward common technologies and management practices, as a result of global competitiveness and multinational influences.

Becoming a STAR ★ leader

HOW DOES EMOTIONAL INTELLIGENCE AFFECT LEADERSHIP? We introduced emotional intelligence (EI) in our discussion of emotions in Chapter 9. We revisit the topic here because of recent studies indicating that EI—more than IQ, expertise, or any other single factor—is the best predictor of who will emerge as a leader.[55]

Exhibit 12–6 Cross-Cultural Leadership

- Korean leaders are expected to be paternalistic toward employees.
- Arab leaders who show kindness or generosity without being asked to do so are seen by other Arabs as weak.
- Japanese leaders are expected to be humble and speak frequently.
- Scandinavian and Dutch leaders who single out individuals with public praise are likely to embarrass, not energize, those individuals.
- Effective leaders in Malaysia are expected to show compassion while using more of an autocratic than a participative style.
- Effective German leaders are characterized by high performance orientation, low compassion, low self-protection, low team orientation, high autonomy, and high participation.

Sources: Based on J.-H. Shin, R. L. Heath, and J. Lee, "A Contingency Explanation of Public Relations Practitioner Leadership Styles: Situation and Culture," *Journal of Public Relations Research* (April 2011): 167–90; J. C. Kennedy, "Leadership in Malaysia: Traditional Values, International Outlook," *Academy of Management Executive*, August 2002, 15–17; F. C. Brodbeck, M. Frese, and M. Javidan, "Leadership Made in Germany: Low on Compassion, High on Performance," *Academy of Management Executive*, February 2002, 16–29; M. F. Peterson and J. G. Hunt, "International Perspectives on International Leadership," *Leadership Quarterly*, Fall 1997, 203–31; R. J. House and R. N. Aditya, "The Social Scientific Study of Leadership: Quo Vadis?" *Journal of Management* 23, no. 3 (1997): 463; and R. J. House, "Leadership in the Twenty-First Century," in A. Howard (ed.), *The Changing Nature of Work* (San Francisco: Jossey-Bass, 1995), 442.

Technology and the Manager's Job
VIRTUAL LEADERSHIP

How do you lead people who are physically separated from you and with whom your interactions are primarily written digital communications?[56] That's the challenge of being a virtual leader. And unfortunately, leadership research has been directed mostly at face-to-face and verbal situations. But we can't ignore the reality that today's managers and their employees are increasingly being linked by technology rather than by geographic proximity. So what guidance would be helpful to leaders who must inspire and motivate dispersed employees?

It's easy to soften harsh words in face-to-face communication with nonverbal action. A smile or a comforting gesture can go a long way in lessening the blow behind strong words like *disappointed, unsatisfactory, inadequate,* or *below expectations.* That nonverbal component doesn't exist in online interactions. The *structure* of words in a digital communication also has the power to motivate or demotivate the receiver. A manager who inadvertently sends a message in short phrases or in ALL CAPS may get a very different response than if the message had been sent in full sentences using appropriate punctuation.

To be an effective virtual leader, managers must recognize that they have choices in the words and structure of their digital communications. They also need to develop the skill of "reading between the lines" in the messages they receive. It's important to try and decipher the emotional content of a message as well as the written content. Also, virtual leaders need to think carefully about what actions they want their digital messages to initiate. Be clear about what's expected and follow up on messages.

For an increasing number of managers, good interpersonal skills may include the abilities to communicate support and leadership through digital communication and to read emotions in others' messages. In this "new world" of communication, writing skills are likely to become an extension of interpersonal skills.

If your professor has assigned this, go to the Assignments section of **mymanagementlab.com** *to complete these discussion questions.*

✪ **TALK ABOUT IT 5:** What challenges does a "virtual" leader face?

✪ **TALK ABOUT IT 6:** How can virtual leaders use technology to help them be more effective leaders?

As we said in our earlier discussion of trait research, leaders need basic intelligence and job-relevant knowledge. But IQ and technical skills are "threshold capabilities." They're necessary but not sufficient requirements for leadership. It's the possession of the five components of emotional intelligence—self-awareness, self-management, self-motivation, empathy, and social skills—that allows an individual to become a star performer. Without EI, a person can have outstanding training, a highly analytical mind, a long-term vision, and an endless supply of terrific ideas but still not make a great leader, especially as individuals move up in an organization. The evidence indicates that the higher the rank of a person considered to be a star performer, the more that EI capabilities surface as the reason for his or her effectiveness. Specifically, when star performers were compared with average ones in senior management positions, nearly 90 percent of the difference in their effectiveness was attributable to EI factors rather than basic intelligence.

Rudolph Giuliani's EI evolution

Example of EI and Leadership: The maturing of Rudolph Giuliani's leadership effectiveness closely followed the development of his emotional intelligence. For the better part of the eight years that he was mayor of New York, Giuliani ruled with an iron fist. He talked tough, picked fights, and demanded results. The result was a city that was cleaner, safer, and better governed—but also more polarized. Critics called Giuliani a tin-eared tyrant. In the eyes of many, something important was missing from his leadership. That something, his critics acknowledged, emerged as the World Trade Center collapsed. It was a newfound compassion to complement his command: a mix of resolve, empathy, and inspiration that brought comfort to millions.[57] It's likely that Giuliani's emotional capacities and compassion for others were stimulated by a series of personal hardships, including prostate cancer and the highly visible breakup of his marriage, both of which had taken place less than a year before the terrorist attacks on the World Trade Center.[58]

EI has been shown to be positively related to job performance at all levels. But it appears to be especially relevant in jobs that demand a high degree of social interaction. And of course, that's what leadership is all about. Great leaders demonstrate their EI by exhibiting all five of its key components: self-awareness, self-management, self-motivation, empathy, and social skills (see pp. 274–275).

Although there has been some controversy about the role of EI in leadership,[59] most research makes a case for concluding that EI is an essential element in leadership effectiveness.[60] As such, it could be added to the list of traits associated with leadership that we described earlier in the chapter.

credibility
The degree to which followers perceive someone as honest, competent, and able to inspire

trust
The belief in the integrity, character, and ability of a leader

Why Is Trust the Essence of Leadership?

12-5 Discuss trust as the essence of leadership.

Trust, or lack of trust, is an increasingly important issue in today's organizations.[61] In today's uncertain environment, leaders need to build, or even rebuild, trust and credibility. Before we can discuss ways leaders can do that, we have to know what trust and credibility are and why they're so important.

The main component of credibility is honesty. Surveys show that honesty is consistently singled out as the number one characteristic of admired leaders. "Honesty is absolutely essential to leadership. If people are going to follow someone willingly, whether it be into battle or into the boardroom, they first want to assure themselves that the person is worthy of their trust."[62] In addition to being honest, credible leaders are competent and inspiring. They are personally able to effectively communicate their confidence and enthusiasm. Thus, followers judge a leader's **credibility** in terms of his or her honesty, competence, and ability to inspire.

Trust is closely entwined with the concept of credibility, and, in fact, the terms are often used interchangeably. **Trust** is defined as the belief in the integrity, character, and ability of a leader. Followers who trust a leader are willing to be vulnerable to the leader's actions because they are confident that their rights and interests will not be abused.[63] Research has identified five dimensions that make up the concept of trust:

- *Integrity*: honesty and truthfulness
- *Competence*: technical and interpersonal knowledge and skills
- *Consistency*: reliability, predictability, and good judgment in handling situations
- *Loyalty*: willingness to protect a person, physically and emotionally
- *Openness*: willingness to share ideas and information freely[64]

Of these five dimensions, integrity seems to be the most critical when someone assesses another's trustworthiness.[65] Both integrity and competence were seen in our earlier discussion of leadership traits found to be consistently associated with leadership.

Workplace changes have reinforced why such leadership qualities are important. For instance, trends of employee empowerment and self-managed work teams have reduced many of the traditional control mechanisms used to monitor employees. If a work team is free to schedule its own work, evaluate its

PepsiCo CEO Indra Nooyi is a leader with high emotional intelligence. Shown here listening to an employee at the firm's yogurt plant, Nooyi possesses the five EI components that have contributed to her excellent performance in jobs that demand a high degree of social interaction with workers, customers, and business leaders throughout the world.

Donald Heupel/Corbis

own performance, and even make its own hiring decisions, trust becomes critical. Employees have to trust managers to treat them fairly, and managers have to trust employees to conscientiously fulfill their responsibilities.

Also, leaders have to increasingly lead others who may not be in their immediate work group or even may be physically separated—members of cross-functional or virtual teams, individuals who work for suppliers or customers, and perhaps even people who represent other organizations through strategic alliances. These situations don't allow leaders the luxury of falling back on their formal positions for influence. Many of these relationships, in fact, are fluid and fleeting. So the ability to quickly develop trust and sustain that trust is crucial to the success of the relationship.

Why is it important that followers trust their leaders?

Research has shown that trust in leadership is significantly related to positive job outcomes including job performance, organizational citizenship behavior, job satisfaction, and organizational commitment.[66] Given the importance of trust to effective leadership, leaders need to build trust with their followers. Some suggestions are shown in Exhibit 12–7.

Exhibit 12–7 Suggestions for Building Trust

1. **Practice openness.** Mistrust comes as much from what people don't know as from what they do know. Openness leads to confidence and trust. So keep people informed; make clear the criteria on how decisions are made; explain the rationale for your decisions; be candid about problems; and fully disclose relevant information.

2. **Be fair.** Before making decisions or taking actions, consider how others will perceive them in terms of objectivity and fairness. Give credit where credit is due; be objective and impartial in performance appraisals; and pay attention to equity perceptions in reward distributions.

3. **Speak your feelings.** Leaders who convey only hard facts come across as cold and distant. When you share your feelings, others will see you as real and human. They will know who you are and their respect for you will increase.

4. **Tell the truth.** If honesty is critical to credibility, you must be perceived as someone who tells the truth. Followers are more tolerant of being told something they "don't want to hear" than of finding out that their leader lied to them.

5. **Be consistent.** People want predictability. Mistrust comes from not knowing what to expect. Take the time to think about your values and beliefs. Then let them consistently guide your decisions. When you know your central purpose, your actions will follow accordingly, and you will project a consistency that earns trust.

6. **Fulfill your promises.** Trust requires that people believe that you're dependable. So you need to keep your word. Promises made must be promises kept.

7. **Maintain confidences.** You trust those whom you believe to be discreet and whom you can rely on. If people make themselves vulnerable by telling you something in confidence, they need to feel assured that you won't discuss it with others or betray that confidence. If people perceive you as someone who leaks personal confidences or someone who can't be depended on, you won't be perceived as trustworthy.

8. **Demonstrate confidence.** Develop the admiration and respect of others by demonstrating technical and professional ability. Pay particular attention to developing and displaying your communication, negotiating, and other interpersonal skills.

Sources: Based on P. S. Shockley-Zalabak and S. P Morreale, "Building High-Trust Organizations," *Leader to Leader*, Spring 2011, 39–45; J. K. Butler Jr., "Toward Understanding and Measuring Conditions of Trust: Evolution of a Condition of Trust Inventory," *Journal of Management* (September 1991): 643–63; and F. Bartolome, "Nobody Trusts the Boss Completely—Now What?" *Harvard Business Review*, March–April 1989, 135–42.

Now, more than ever, managerial and leadership effectiveness depends on the ability to gain the trust of followers.[67] Downsizing, corporate financial misrepresentations, and the increased use of temporary employees have undermined employees' trust in their leaders and shaken the confidence of investors, suppliers, and customers. A survey found that only 39 percent of U.S. employees and 51 percent of Canadian employees trusted their executive leaders.[68] Today's leaders are faced with the challenge of rebuilding and restoring trust with employees and with other important organizational stakeholders.

A Final Thought Regarding Leadership

Despite the belief that some leadership style will always be effective regardless of the situation, *leadership may not always be important*! Research indicates that, in some situations, any behaviors a leader exhibits are irrelevant. In other words, certain individual, job, and organizational variables can act as "substitutes for leadership," negating the influence of the leader.[69]

For instance, follower characteristics such as experience, training, professional orientation, or need for independence can neutralize the effect of leadership. These characteristics can replace the employee's need for a leader's support or ability to create structure and reduce task ambiguity. Similarly, jobs that are inherently unambiguous and routine or that are intrinsically satisfying may place fewer demands on the leadership variable. Finally, such organizational characteristics as explicit formalized goals, rigid rules and procedures, or cohesive work groups can substitute for formal leadership.

MyManagementLab®

Go to **mymanagementlab.com** to complete the problems marked with this icon .

12 Review

CHAPTER SUMMARY

12-1 Define *leader* and *leadership*.

A leader is someone who can influence others and who has managerial authority. Leadership is a process of leading a group and influencing that group to achieve its goals. Managers should be leaders because leading is one of the four management functions.

12-2 Compare and contrast early leadership theories.

Early attempts to define leader traits were unsuccessful, although later attempts found seven traits associated with leadership.

The University of Iowa studies explored three leadership styles. The only conclusion was that group members were more satisfied under a democratic leader than under an autocratic one. The Ohio State studies identified two dimensions of leader behavior—initiating structure and consideration. A leader high in both those dimensions at times achieved high group task performance and high group member satisfaction, but not always. The University of Michigan studies looked at employee-oriented leaders and production-oriented leaders. They concluded that leaders who were employee oriented could get high group productivity and high group member satisfaction. The Managerial Grid looked at leaders' concern for production and concern for people and identified five leader styles. Although it suggested that a leader who was high in concern for production and high in concern for people was the best, there was no substantive evidence for that conclusion.

As the behavioral studies showed, a leader's behavior has a dual nature: a focus on the task and a focus on the people.

12-3 Describe the four major contingency leadership theories.

Fiedler's model attempted to define the best style to use in particular situations. He measured leader style—relationship oriented or task oriented—using the least-preferred coworker questionnaire. Fiedler also assumed a leader's style was fixed. He measured three contingency dimensions: leader-member relations, task structure, and position power. The model suggests that task-oriented leaders performed best in very favorable and very unfavorable situations, and relationship-oriented leaders performed best in moderately favorable situations.

Hersey and Blanchard's situational leadership theory focused on followers' readiness. They identified four leadership styles: telling (high task–low relationship), selling (high task–high relationship), participating (low task–high relationship), and delegating (low task–low relationship). They also identified four stages of readiness: unable and unwilling (use telling style); unable but willing (use selling style); able but unwilling (use participative style); and able and willing (use delegating style).

The leader-participation model relates leadership behavior and participation to decision making. It uses a decision tree format with seven contingencies and five alternative leadership styles.

The path-goal model developed by Robert House identified four leadership behaviors: directive, supportive, participative, and achievement-oriented. He assumes that a leader can and should be able to use any of these styles. The two situational contingency variables were found in the environment and in the follower. Essentially the path-goal model says that a leader should provide direction and support as needed; that is, structure the path so the followers can achieve goals.

12-4 Describe modern views of leadership and the issues facing today's leaders.

Leader-member exchange (LMX) theory says that leaders create in-groups and out-groups and those in the in-group will have higher performance ratings, less turnover, and greater job satisfaction.

A transactional leader exchanges rewards for productivity where a transformational leader stimulates and inspires followers to achieve goals.

A charismatic leader is an enthusiastic and self-confident leader whose personality and actions influence people to behave in certain ways. People can learn to be charismatic. A visionary leader is able to create and articulate a realistic, credible, and attractive vision of the future.

A team leader has two priorities: manage the team's external boundary and facilitate the team process. Four leader roles are involved: liaison with external constituencies, troubleshooter, conflict manager, and coach.

The issues facing leaders today include employee empowerment, national culture, and emotional intelligence. As employees are empowered, the leader's role tends to be one of not leading. As leaders adjust their style to the situation, one of the most important situational characteristics is national culture. Finally, EI is proving to be an essential element in leadership effectiveness.

12-5 Discuss trust as the essence of leadership.

The five dimensions of trust include integrity, competence, consistency, loyalty, and truthfulness. Integrity refers to one's honesty and truthfulness. Competence involves an individual's technical and interpersonal knowledge and skills. Consistency relates to an individual's reliability, predictability, and good judgment in handling situations. Loyalty is an individual's willingness to protect and save face for another person. Openness means that you can rely on the individual to give you the whole truth.

DISCUSSION QUESTIONS

12-1 Define *leader* and *leadership* and discuss why managers should be leaders.

12-2 Discuss the strengths and weaknesses of the trait theory.

12-3 What does each of the behavioral leadership theories say about leadership?

12-4 What would a manager need to know to use Fiedler's contingency model? Be specific.

12-5 Do you think that most managers in real life use a contingency approach to increase their leadership effectiveness? Discuss.

12-6 "All managers should be leaders, but not all leaders should be managers." Do you agree or disagree with this statement? Support your position.

12-7 Do you think trust evolves out of an individual's personal characteristics or out of specific situations? Explain.

12-8 Do followers make a difference in whether a leader is effective? Discuss.

12-9 How can organizations develop effective leaders?

12-10 When might leaders be irrelevant?

Writing Assignments

12-11 What is the difference between trait theories and behavioral theories of leadership?

12-12 Why is trust the essence of leadership?

Management Skill Builder | BEING A GOOD LEADER

The terms *management* and *leadership* are frequently used interchangeably. That's a misnomer. The two aren't the same but they are related. Although you don't need to hold a management position to be a leader, you're unlikely to be an effective manager if you can't be an effective leader.

⭐ PERSONAL INVENTORY ASSESSMENT   PERSONAL INVENTORY ASSESSMENT

Leadership Style Indicator

What's your leadership style? Take this PIA and find out!

Skill Basics

Simply put, leadership style can be categorized as task- or people-oriented. Neither one is right for all situations. Although a number of situational variables influence the choice of an effective leadership style, four variables seem most relevant:[70]

- *Task structure.* Structured tasks have procedures and rules that minimize ambiguity. The more structured a job is, the less need there is for a leader to provide task structure.

- *Level of stress.* Situations differ in terms of time and performance stress. High-stress situations favor leaders with experience. Low stress favors a leader's intelligence.

- *Level of group support.* Members of close-knit and supportive groups help each other out. They can provide both task support and relationship support. Supportive groups make fewer demands on a leader.

- *Follower characteristics.* Personal characteristics of followers—such as experience, ability, and motivation—influence which leadership style will be most effective. Employees with extensive experience, strong abilities, and high motivation don't require much task behavior. They will be more effective with a people-oriented style. Conversely, employees with little experience, marginal abilities, and low motivation will perform better when leaders exhibit task-oriented behavior.

Practicing the Skill

Read through this scenario and follow the directions at the end of it:

You recently graduated from college with your degree in business administration. You've spent the past two summers working at Connecticut Mutual Insurance (CMI), filling in as an intern on a number of different jobs while employees took their vacations. You have received and accepted an offer to join CMI full time as supervisor of the policy renewal department.

CMI is a large insurance company. In the headquarters office alone, where you'll be working, there are more than 1,500 employees. The company believes strongly in the personal development of its employees. This belief translates into a philosophy, emanating from the top executive offices, of trust and respect for all CMI employees. The company is also regularly atop most lists of "best companies to work for," largely due to its progressive work/life programs and strong commitment to minimizing layoffs.

In your new job, you'll direct the activities of 18 policy-renewal clerks. Their jobs require little training and are highly routine. A clerk's responsibility is to ensure that renewal notices are sent on current policies, to tabulate any changes in premiums, to advise the sales division if a policy is to be canceled as a result of nonresponse to renewal notices, and to answer questions and solve problems related to renewals.

The people in your work group range in age from 19 to 62, with a median age of 25. For the most part they are high school graduates with little prior working experience. They earn between $2,350 and $3,200 a month. You will be replacing a long-time CMI employee, Jan Allison. Jan is retiring after 37 years with CMI, the past 14 spent as a policy-renewal supervisor. Because you spent a few weeks in Jan's group last summer, you're familiar with Jan's style and are acquainted with most of the department members. But people don't know you very well and are suspicious of the fact that you're fresh out of college and have little experience in the department. The reality is that you got this job because management wanted someone with a college degree to oversee the department. Your most vocal critic is Lillian Lantz. Lillian is well into her 50s, has been a policy renewal clerk for over a dozen years, and—as the "grand old lady" of the department—carries a lot of weight with group members. You know that it'll be very hard to lead this department without Lillian's support.

Using your knowledge of leadership concepts, which leadership style would you choose? And why?

Experiential Exercise

Preferred Bank Card, Inc.

To: Pat Muenks, VP Employee Relations

From: Jan Plemmons, Customer Service Director

About: Leadership Training

I agree completely with your recommendation that we need a leadership training program for our customer service team leaders. These leaders struggle with keeping our customer service reps focused on our goal of providing timely, accurate, and friendly service to our bank card holders who call in with questions or complaints.

Put together a one-page proposal that describes the leadership topics you think should be covered. Also, give me some suggestions for how we might present the information in a way that would be interesting. We need to get started on this immediately, so please get this report to me by early next week.

This fictionalized company and message were created for educational purposes only, and not meant to reflect positively or negatively on management practices by any company that may share this name.

CASE APPLICATION #1

Developing Gen Y Leaders

How important are excellent leaders to organizations? Well, the answer, in theory of course, would be very important. However, the answer as practiced by countless organizations might indicate otherwise. Only 38 percent of organizations have a formal frontline leadership development program in place.[71] It's important for organizations to commit to strong leadership development, and it's particularly important for organizations to begin grooming their Gen Y employees to move into critical leadership positions. Why? Within 10 years (by 2025), these Millennials are set to comprise 75 percent of the global workforce. That's why organizational leadership development programs are absolutely essential.[72] Let's look at what some companies are doing to prepare the next generation for leadership.

> **Excellent leaders have to be developed and cultivated.**

3M's leadership development program is so effective that it has been one of the "Top 20 Companies for Leadership" in six of the last seven years and ranks as one of the top 25 companies for grooming leadership talent according to consultant Hay Group.[73] What is 3M's leadership program all about? A few years ago, the company's former CEO and his top team spent 18 months developing a leadership model for the company. After numerous brainstorming sessions and much heated debate, the group finally agreed on six "leadership attributes" that they believed were essential for managers to have in order for the company to become skilled at executing strategy and being accountable. Those six attributes included the ability to: develop a plan and implement that plan; motivate and rouse others; be ethical and trustworthy and abide by the rules; achieve outcomes; strive for excellence; and be a capable and creative innovator. The company has continued to reinforce its pursuit of leadership excellence with these six attributes.

Other companies, such as Ernst & Young, start early in recruiting and investing in future leaders, often going after talented college freshmen who have leadership potential. They take the best talent and involve them in various leadership development programs both while in school and after graduation.[74] Deloitte, another company rated high for its leadership development programs, is deeply committed to helping its Millennial employees learn and absorb the leadership skills they will need to lead the company in the future.[75] It starts with a very specific recruiting strategy for hiring Millennials and continues with a yearlong "Welcome to Deloitte" program. This program is all about teaching this age group client-management skills and team-building skills, and offering professional development opportunities. And, not surprisingly, it's done largely through social media using interactive experiences such as role-plays, simulations, games, and a tool to help these employees track their first-year tasks.

At Facebook, the first Millennial-run organization to become a Fortune 500 company, leadership development is designed around the needs of a fast-moving, fast-growing company.[76] The head of leadership development at Facebook says that the only way leadership development works there is by making it consistent with the types of engineering tech types that comprise the company. Engineers are concerned only with "what works." And it's the same for any type of leadership development to be successful here; the focus has to be on *what works*. Also, since Facebook is an extremely flat organization with few levels of management, employees find out early on that in order to get anything done, they're going to have to be able to influence and inspire people. That's why leaders at Facebook don't have to be convinced of the need for people skills. They won't survive long without them.

Discussion Questions

12-14 Why do you think that there's a huge gap in theory (what we know we should do) and practice (what we're actually doing) of leadership development?

12-15 What are some reasons that companies might not be addressing Gen Y leadership development programs?

12-16 Take each of the six leadership attributes that 3M feels is important. Explain what you think each one involves. Then discuss how those attributes might be developed and measured.

12-17 Would any of those six leadership attributes be appropriate for any of the other companies mentioned? Explain.

12-18 Three different types of organizations are described here: 3M is primarily a manufacturing organization. Ernst & Young and Deloitte are professional services organizations. Facebook is a tech company. Compare and contrast their differing approaches to Gen Y leadership development.

CASE APPLICATION #2

Serving Up Leaders

Here's something to consider: $35 million; 5,000 live coffee plants; 1,000 lighting instruments; 120 speakers; 21 projection screens. These are just a few of the "numbers" describing the spectacle known as the Starbucks Leadership Lab.[77] For three days in the fall of 2012, some 9,600 Starbucks store managers trekked to a conference center in Houston to be immersed in a massive interactive experience. While there, these managers were steeped in the Starbucks brand.

The Leadership Lab was part leadership training and part trade show. The company's store managers were given a behind-the-scenes look and introduced up close and personal to what makes Starbucks go. From an exhibit featuring live coffee shrubs to a drying patio where they could get hands-on experience raking through coffee beans, to an enormous exhibit of used shoes with customer experiences noted on cards (sort of a "walk in my shoes" theme). Most of these experiences were designed to be instructive for the store managers. However, in addition, the store managers—who are on the "firing line" day in and day out—had the opportunity to interact with top managers of the company's roasting process, blend development, and customer service

functions. Managers also were encouraged to share what they had learned from the Leadership Lab by stopping at a station lined with laptops.

> ## Immerse yourself in a leadership experience.

The lights, the music, and the dramatic presentation were all designed to immerse the store managers in the Starbucks brand and culture. The goal was to "mobilize its employees to become brand evangelists." And since presentation is a significant component of what the Starbucks experience is built on—the sights, the sounds, the smells—the entire presentation at the Leadership Lab was well thought out and intentional.

Discussion Questions

⭐ **12-19** Describe the leadership lessons you think Starbucks Leadership Lab provided store managers.

⭐ **12-20** What role do you think an organization's culture plays in how its leaders lead? Relate this to the story told above.

⭐ **12-21** Using the behavioral theories as a guideline, what do you think would be more important to a Starbucks store manager: focus on task, focus on people, or both? Explain.

12-22 How might a Starbucks store manager use situational leadership theory? Path-goal theory? Transformational leadership?

CASE APPLICATION #3

Leadership Legacy

A lot has been written about the late Steve Jobs.[78] How he took Apple, a niche business, and turned it into the most valuable company in the world as measured by market capitalization. How he was extremely charismatic and extremely compelling in getting people to join with him and believe in his vision. But also how he was despotic, tyrannical, abrasive, uncompromising, and a perfectionist. So what *is* his leadership legacy?

Insanely Great Leadership

Everything that Jobs did and how he did it was motivated by his desire to have Apple make innovative products—products that were "insanely great"—"insanely" being one of his favorite descriptors. That singular focus shaped his leadership style, which has been described as autocratic and yet persuasive. As one reporter said, Jobs "violated every rule of management. He was not a consensus builder but a dictator who listened mainly to his own intuition. He was a maniacal micromanager. . . . He could be absolutely brutal in meetings."[79] His verbal assaults on staff could be terrifying. The story is told that when Apple launched its first version of the iPhone that worked on 3G mobile networks, it included MobileMe, an e-mail system that was supposed to provide seamless synchronization features similar to that used by the fanatical corporate users of BlackBerry phones. The problem? It didn't work well at all and product reviews were quite critical. Since "Steve Jobs doesn't tolerate duds,"[80] it wasn't long after the launch that he gathered the MobileMe team in an auditorium on Apple's campus. According to a participant in that meeting, Jobs walked in—in his trademark black mock turtleneck and jeans—and simply asked if anyone could tell him what MobileMe was designed to do. When he finally got an acceptable answer, he asked plainly why the *#$% it didn't do that. Then, for the next 30 minutes, Jobs blasted criticisms at the team. "You've tarnished Apple's reputation. You should hate each other for having let each other down."[81] Ouch. And this wasn't the only example of his taking employees to task. He was tough on the people around him. When asked about his tendency to be rough on people, Jobs responded, "Look at the results. These are all smart people I work with, and any of them could get a top job at another place if they were truly feeling brutalized. But they don't."[82]

On the other hand, Steve Jobs could be thoughtful, passionate, and "insanely" charismatic. He could encourage and get people to do what they didn't think was possible. And there's no arguing with the fact that the results from the company he co-founded have been market-changing. From the Macs and iPods to the iPhones and iPads, Apple's products have revolutionized industries and created a fan base of consumers who are very loyal to the Apple brand and employees who are very loyal to the company.

Discussion Questions

12-23 Think about what you thought you knew about Steve Jobs prior to reading this Case Application. How would you have described his leadership style?

12-24 After reading this Case Application, how would you describe his leadership style?

12-25 What were you most surprised about after reading this Case Application?

12-26 Would Steve Jobs's leadership approach work for others? Discuss.

Endnotes

1. Most leadership research has focused on the actions and responsibilities of managers and extrapolated the results to leaders and leadership in general.

2. From the Past to the Present box based on D. S. Derue, J. D. Nahrgang, N. Wellman, and S. E. Humphrey, "Trait and Behavioral Theories of Leadership: An Integration and Meta-Analytic Test of Their Relative Validity," *Personnel Psychology*, Spring 2011, 7–52; and D. A. Wren and A. G. Bedeian, *The Evolution of Management Thought*, 6th ed. (Hoboken, NJ: John Wiley & Sons, 2009), 345–46.

3. See D. S. Derue, J. D. Nahrgang, N. Wellman, and S. E. Humphrey, "Trait and Behavioral Theories of Leadership: An Integration and Meta-Analytic Test of Their Relative Validity," *Personnel Psychology*, Spring 2011, 7–52; T. A. Judge, J. E. Bono, R. Ilies, and M. W. Gerhardt, "Personality and Leadership: A Qualitative and Quantitative Review," *Journal of Applied Psychology* (August 2002): 765–80; and S. A. Kirkpatrick and E. A. Locke, "Leadership: Do Traits Matter?" *Academy of Management Executive*, May 1991, 48–60.

4. K. Lewin and R. Lippitt, "An Experimental Approach to the Study of Autocracy and Democracy: A Preliminary Note," *Sociometry* 1 (1938): 292–300; K. Lewin, "Field Theory and Experiment in Social Psychology: Concepts and Methods," *American Journal of Sociology* 44 (1939): 868–96; K. Lewin, R. Lippitt, and R. K. White, "Patterns of Aggressive Behavior in Experimentally Created Social Climates," *Journal of Social Psychology* 10 (1939): 271–301; and R. Lippitt, "An Experimental Study of the Effect of Democratic and Authoritarian Group Atmospheres," *University of Iowa Studies in Child Welfare* 16 (1940): 43–95.

5. R. M. Stogdill and A. E. Coons, eds., *Leader Behavior: Its Description and Measurement*, Research Monograph No. 88 (Columbus: Ohio State University, Bureau of Business Research, 1951). See also S. Kerr, C. A. Schriesheim, C. J. Murphy, and R. M. Stogdill, "Toward a Contingency Theory of Leadership Based upon the Consideration and Initiating Structure Literature," *Organizational Behavior and Human Performance* (August 1974): 62–82; and B. M. Fisher, "Consideration and Initiating Structure and Their Relationships with Leader Effectiveness: A Meta Analysis," in F. Hoy, ed., Proceedings of the 48th Annual Academy of Management Conference (Anaheim, CA, 1988), 201–05.

6. R. Kahn and D. Katz, "Leadership Practices in Relation to Productivity and Morale," in D. Cartwright and A. Zander, eds., *Group Dynamics: Research and Theory*, 2nd ed. (Elmsford, NY: Pow, Paterson, 1960).

7. R. R. Blake and J. S. Mouton, *The Managerial Grid III* (Houston: Gulf Publishing, 1984).

8. W. G. Bennis, "The Seven Ages of the Leader," *Harvard Business Review*, January 2004, 52.

9. F. E. Fiedler, *A Theory of Leadership Effectiveness* (New York: McGraw-Hill, 1967).

10. R. Ayman, M. M. Chemers, and F. Fiedler, "The Contingency Model of Leadership Effectiveness: Its Levels of Analysis," *Leadership Quarterly*, Summer 1995, 147–67; C. A. Schriesheim, B. J. Tepper, and L. A. Tetrault, "Lease Preferred Co-Worker Score, Situational Control, and Leadership Effectiveness: A Meta-Analysis of Contingency Model Performance Predictions," *Journal of Applied Psychology* (August 1994): 561–73; and L. H. Peters, D. D. Hartke, and J. T. Pohlmann, "Fiedler's Contingency Theory of Leadership: An Application of the Meta-Analysis Procedures of Schmidt and Hunter," *Psychological Bulletin*, March 1985, 274–85.

11. See B. Kabanoff, "A Critique of Leader Match and Its Implications for Leadership Research," *Personnel Psychology*, Winter 1981, 749–64; and E. H. Schein, *Organizational Psychology*, 3rd ed. (Upper Saddle River, NJ: Prentice Hall, 1980), 116–17.

12. P. Hersey and K. H. Blanchard, *Management of Organizational Behavior: Leading Human Resources*, 8th ed. (Englewood Cliffs, NJ: Prentice Hall, 2001); and P. Hersey and K. Blanchard, "So You Want to Know Your Leadership Style?" *Training and Development Journal* (February 1974): 1–15.

13. See, for instance, E. G. Ralph, "Developing Managers' Effectiveness: A Model with Potential," *Journal of Management Inquiry* (June 2004): 152–63; C. L. Graeff, "Evolution of Situational Leadership Theory: A Critical Review," *Leadership Quarterly* 8, no. 2 (1997): 153–70; and C. F. Fernandez and R. P. Vecchio, "Situational Leadership Theory Revisited: A Test of an Across-Jobs Perspective," *Leadership Quarterly* 8, no. 1 (1997): 67–84.

14. V. H. Vroom and P. W. Yetton, *Leadership and Decision Making* (Pittsburgh: University of Pittsburgh Press, 1973).

15. V. H. Vroom and A. G. Jago, *The New Leadership: Managing Participation in Organizations* (Upper Saddle River, NJ: Prentice Hall, 1988). See especially Chapter 8.

16. See, for example, R. H. G. Field and R. J. House, "A Test of the Vroom Yetton Model Using Manager and Subordinate Reports," *Journal of Applied Psychology* (June 1990): 362–66; J. T. Ettling and A. G. Jago, "Participation Under Conditions of Conflict: More on the Validity of the Vroom Yetton Model," *Journal of Management Studies* (January 1988): 73–83; C. R. Leana, "Power Relinquishment versus Power Sharing: Theoretical Clarification and Empirical Comparison of Delegation and Participation," *Journal of Applied Psychology* (May 1987): 228–33; and R. H. G. Field, "A Test of the Vroom Yetton Normative Model of Leadership," *Journal of Applied Psychology* (October 1982): 523–32.

17. For additional information about the exchanges that occur between the leader and the follower, see A. S. Phillips and A. G. Bedeian, "Leader Follower Exchange Quality: The Role of Personal and Interpersonal Attributes," *Academy of Management Journal* 37, no. 4 (1994): 990–1001; and T. A. Scandura and C. A. Schriesheim, "Leader Member Exchange and Supervisor Career Mentoring as Complementary Constructs in Leadership Research," *Academy of Management Journal* 37, no. 6 (1994): 1588–602.

18. SmartPulse, "How Willing Are You to Step Outside Your Leadership Style 'Comfort Zone' and Try New Techniques?" www.smartbrief.com/leadership, December 10, 2013.

19. R. J. House, "Path-Goal Theory of Leadership: Lessons, Legacy, and a Reformulated Theory," *Leadership Quarterly*, Fall 1996, 323–52; R. J. House and T. R. Mitchell, "Path-Goal Theory of Leadership," *Journal of Contemporary Business* (Autumn 1974): 86; and R. J. House, "A Path-Goal Theory of Leader Effectiveness," *Administrative Science Quarterly*, September 1971, 321–38.

20. A. Sagie and M. Koslowsky, "Organizational Attitudes and Behaviors as a Function of Participation in Strategic and Tactical Change Decisions: An Application of Path-Goal Theory," *Journal of Organizational Behavior* (January 1994): 37–47; and J. C. Wofford and L. Z. Liska, "Path-Goal Theories of Leadership: A Meta-Analysis," *Journal of Management* (Winter 1993): 857–76.

21. L. Ma and Q. Qu, "Differentiation in Leader-Member Exchange: A Hierarchical Linear Modeling Approach," *Leadership Quarterly*, October 2010, 733–44; C. P. Schriesheim, S. L. Castro, X. Zhou, and F. J. Yamarinno, "The Folly of Theorizing 'A' but Testing 'B': A Selective Level-of-Analysis Review of the Field and a Detailed Leader-Member Exchange Illustration," *Leadership Quarterly*, Winter 2001, 515–51; R. C. Liden, R. T. Sparrowe, and S. J. Wayne, "Leader-Member Exchange Theory: The Past and Potential for the Future," in G. R. Ferris (ed.), *Research in Personnel and Human Resource Management*, vol. 15 (Greenwich, CT: JAI Press, 1997), 47–119; G. B. Graen and M. Uhl-Bien, "Relationship-Based Approach to Leadership: Development of Leader-Member Exchange (LMX) Theory of Leadership Over 25 Years: Applying a Multi-Domain Perspective," *Leadership Quarterly*, Summer 1995, 219–47; and R. M. Dienesch and R. C. Liden, "Leader-Member Exchange Model of Leadership: A Critique and Further Development," *Academy of Management Review*, July 1986, 618–34.

22. J. B. Wu, A. S. Tsui, and A. J. Kinicki, "Consequences of Differentiated Leadership in Groups," *Academy of Management Journal* (February 2010): 90–106; S. S. Masterson, K. Lewis, and B. M. Goldman, "Integrating Justice and Social Exchange: The Differing Effects of Fair Procedures and Treatment on Work Relationships," *Academy of Management Journal* (August 2000): 738–48; S. J. Wayne, L. J. Shore, W. H. Bommer, and L. E. Tetrick, "The Role of Fair Treatment and Rewards in Perceptions of Organizational Support and Leader-Member Exchange," *Journal of Applied Psychology* (June 2002): 590–98; R. C. Liden, S. J. Wayne, and D. Stilwell, "A Longitudinal Study of the Early Development of Leader-Member Exchanges," *Journal of Applied Psychology* (August 1993): 662–74; and R. C. Liden and G. Graen, "Generalizability of the Vertical Dyad Linkage Model of Leadership," *Academy of Management Journal* (September 1980): 451–65.

23. V. L. Goodwin, W. M. Bowler, and J. L. Whittington, "A Social Network Perspective on LMX Relationships: Accounting for the Instrumental Value of Leader and Follower Networks," *Journal of Management* (August 2009): 954–80; R. Vecchio and D. M. Brazil, "Leadership and Sex-Similarity: A Comparison in a Military Setting," *Personnel Psychology*, vol. 60 (2007): 303–35; M. Uhl-Bien, "Relationship Development as a Key Ingredient for Leadership Development," in S. E. Murphy and R. E. Riggio (eds.), *Future of Leadership Development* (Mahwah, NJ: Lawrence Erlbaum, 2003), 129–47; R. C. Liden, S. J. Wayne, and D. Stilwell, "A

Longitudinal Study of the Early Development of Leader-Member Exchanges"; and D. Duchon, S. G. Green, and T. D. Taber, "Vertical Dyad Linkage: A Longitudinal Assessment of Antecedents, Measures, and Consequences," *Journal of Applied Psychology* (February 1986): 56–60.

24. P. Drexler, "The Upside of Favoritism," *Wall Street Journal*, June 8–9, 2013, C3.

25. See, for instance, F. O. Walumbwa, D. M. Mayer, P. Wang, H. Wang, K. Workman, and A. L. Christensen, "Linking Ethical Leadership to Employee Performance: The Roles of Leader-Member Exchange Theory, Self-Efficacy, and Organizational Identification," *Organizational Behavior & Human Decision Processes*, July 2011, 204–213; K. J. Harris, A. R. Wheeler, and K. M. Kacmar, "The Mediating Role of Organizational Embeddedness in the LMX-Outcomes Relationship," *Leadership Quarterly*, April 2011, 271–81; W. M. Bowler, J. R. B. Halbesleben, J. R. B. Paul, "If You're Close with the Leader, You Must Be a Brownnose: The Role of Leader-Member Relationships in Follower, Leader, and Coworker Attributions of Organizational Citizenship Behavior Motives," *Human Resource Management Review*, December 2010, 309–16; G. Sears and C. Holmvall, "The Joint Influence of Supervisor and Subordinate Emotional Intelligence on Leader-Member Exchange," *Journal of Business & Psychology* (December 2010): 593–605; V. Venkataramani, S. G. Green, and D. J. Schleicher, "Well-Connected Leaders' Social Network Ties on LMX and Members' Work Attitudes," *Journal of Applied Psychology* (November 2010): 1071–84; Z. Chen, W. Lam, and J. A. Zhong, "Leader-Member Exchange and Member Performance: A New Look at Individual-Level Negative Feedback-Seeking Behavior and Team-Level Empowerment Culture," *Journal of Applied Psychology* (January 2007): 202–12; R. Ilies, J. D. Nahrgang, and F. P. Morgeson, "Leader-Member Exchange and Citizenship Behaviors: A Meta-Analysis," *Journal of Applied Psychology* (January 2007): 269–77; and C. R. Gerstner and D. V. Day, "Meta-Analytic Review of Leader-Member Exchange Theory: Correlates and Construct Issues," *Journal of Applied Psychology* (December 1997): 827–44.

26. B. M. Bass and R. E. Riggio, *Transformational Leadership*, 2d ed. (Mahwah, NJ: Lawrence Erlbaum Associates, Inc., 2006), 3.

27. J. Seltzer and B. M. Bass, "Transformational Leadership: Beyond Initiation and Consideration," *Journal of Management* (December 1990): 693–703; and B. M. Bass, "Leadership: Good, Better, Best," *Organizational Dynamics*, Winter 1985, 26–40.

28. B. J. Avolio and B. M. Bass, "Transformational Leadership, Charisma, and Beyond," working paper, School of Management, State University of New York, Binghamton, 1985, 14.

29. R. S. Rubin, D. C. Munz, and W. H. Bommer, "Leading from within: The Effects of Emotion Recognition and Personality on Transformational Leadership Behavior," *Academy of Management Journal* (October 2005): 845–58; T. A. Judge and J. E. Bono, "Five-Factor Model of Personality and Transformational Leadership," *Journal of Applied Psychology* (October 2000): 751–65; B. M. Bass and B. J. Avolio, "Developing Transformational Leadership: 1992 and Beyond," *Journal of European Industrial Training* (January 1990): 23; and J. J. Hater and B. M. Bass, "Supervisors' Evaluation and Subordinates' Perceptions of Transformational and Transactional Leadership," *Journal of Applied Psychology* (November 1988): 695–702.

30. M. Tims, A. B. Bakker, and D. Xanthopoulou, "Do Transformational Leaders Enhance Their Followers' Daily Work Engagement?" *Leadership Quarterly*, February 2011, 121–31; X.-H. (Frank) Wang and J. M. Howell, "Exploring the Dual-Level Effects of Transformational Leadership on Followers," *Journal of Applied Psychology* (November 2010): 1134–44; A. E. Colbert, A. L. Kristof-Brown, B. H. Bradley, and M. R. Barrick, "CEO Transformational Leadership: The Role of Goal Importance Congruence in Top Management Teams," *Academy of Management Journal* (February 2008): 81–96; R. F. Piccolo and J. A. Colquitt, "Transformational Leadership and Job Behaviors: The Mediating Role of Core Job Characteristics," *Academy of Management Journal* (April 2006): 327–40; O. Epitropaki and R. Martin, "From Ideal to Real: A Longitudinal Study of the Role of Implicit Leadership Theories on Leader-Member Exchanges and Employee Outcomes," *Journal of Applied Psychology* (July 2005): 659–76; J. E. Bono and T. A. Judge, "Self-Concordance at Work: Toward Understanding the Motivational Effects of Transformational Leaders," *Academy of Management Journal* (October 2003): 554–71; T. Dvir, D. Eden, B. J. Avolio, and B. Shamir, "Impact of Transformational Leadership on Follower Development and Performance: A Field Experiment," *Academy of Management Journal* (August 2002): 735–44; N. Sivasubramaniam, W. D. Murry, B. J. Avolio, and D. I. Jung, "A Longitudinal Model of the Effects of Team Leadership and Group Potency on Group Performance," *Group and Organization Management* (March 2002): 66–96; J. M.

Howell and B. J. Avolio, "Transformational Leadership, Transactional Leadership, Locus of Control, and Support for Innovation: Key Predictors of Consolidated-Business-Unit Performance," *Journal of Applied Psychology* (December 1993): 891–911; R. T. Keller, "Transformational Leadership and the Performance of Research and Development Project Groups," *Journal of Management* (September 1992): 489–501; and Bass and Avolio, "Developing Transformational Leadership."

31. M. Thompson and B. Tracy, "Building a Great Organization," *Leader to Leader*, Fall 2010, 45–49; and F. Vogelstein, "Mighty Amazon," *Fortune*, May 26, 2003, 60–74.

32. J. M. Crant and T. S. Bateman, "Charismatic Leadership Viewed from Above: The Impact of Proactive Personality," *Journal of Organizational Behavior* (February 2000): 63–75; G. Yukl and J. M. Howell, "Organizational and Contextual Influences on the Emergence and Effectiveness of Charismatic Leadership," *Leadership Quarterly*, Summer 1999, 257–83; and J. A. Conger and R. N. Kanungo, "Behavioral Dimensions of Charismatic Leadership," in J. A. Conger, R. N. Kanungo and Associates, *Charismatic Leadership* (San Francisco: Jossey-Bass, 1988), 78–97.

33. J. A. Conger and R. N. Kanungo, *Charismatic Leadership in Organizations* (Thousand Oaks, CA: Sage, 1998).

34. F. Walter and H. Bruch, "An Affective Events Model of Charismatic Leadership Behavior: A Review, Theoretical Investigation, and Research Agenda," *Journal of Management* (December 2009): 1428–52; K. S. Groves, "Linking Leader Skills, Follower Attitudes, and Contextual Variables via an Integrated Model of Charismatic Leadership," *Journal of Management* (April 2005): 255–77; J. J. Sosik, "The Role of Personal Values in the Charismatic Leadership of Corporate Managers: A Model and Preliminary Field Study," *Leadership Quarterly*, April 2005, 221–44; A. H. B. deHoogh, D. N. den Hartog, P. L. Koopman, H. Thierry, P. T. van den Berg, J. G. van der Weide, and C. P. M. Wilderom, "Leader Motives, Charismatic Leadership, and Subordinates' Work Attitudes in the Profit and Voluntary Sector," *Leadership Quarterly*, February 2005, 17–38; J. M. Howell and B. Shamir, "The Role of Followers in the Charismatic Leadership Process: Relationships and Their Consequences," *Academy of Management Review*, January 2005, 96–112; J. Paul, D. L. Costley, J. P. Howell, P. W. Dorfman, and D. Trafimow, "The Effects of Charismatic Leadership on Followers' Self-Concept Accessibility," *Journal of Applied*

Social Psychology (September 2001): 1821–44; J. A. Conger, R. N. Kanungo, and S. T. Menon, "Charismatic Leadership and Follower Effects," *Journal of Organizational Behavior*, vol. 21 (2000): 747–67; R. W. Rowden, "The Relationship between Charismatic Leadership Behaviors and Organizational Commitment," *Leadership & Organization Development Journal* (January 2000): 30–35; G. P. Shea and C. M. Howell, "Charismatic Leadership and Task Feedback: A Laboratory Study of Their Effects on Self-Efficacy," *Leadership Quarterly*, Fall 1999, 375–96; S. A. Kirkpatrick and E. A. Locke, "Direct and Indirect Effects of Three Core Charismatic Leadership Components on Performance and Attitudes," *Journal of Applied Psychology* (February 1996): 36–51; D. A. Waldman, B. M. Bass, and F. J. Yammarino, "Adding to Contingent-Reward Behavior: The Augmenting Effect of Charismatic Leadership," *Group & Organization Studies*, December 1990, 381–94; and R. J. House, J. Woycke, and E. M. Fodor, "Charismatic and Noncharismatic Leaders: Differences in Behavior and Effectiveness," in Conger and Kanungo, *Charismatic Leadership*, 103–04.

35. B. R. Agle, N J. Nagarajan, J. A. Sonnenfeld, and D. Srinivasan, "Does CEO Charisma Matter? An Empirical Analysis of the Relationships among Organizational Performance, Environmental Uncertainty, and Top Management Team Perceptions of CEO Charisma," *Academy of Management Journal* (February 2006): 161–74.

36. R. Birchfield, "Creating Charismatic Leaders," *Management*, June 2000, 30–31; S. Caudron, "Growing Charisma," *Industry Week*, May 4, 1998, 54–55; and J. A. Conger and R. N. Kanungo, "Training Charismatic Leadership: A Risky and Critical Task," in Conger and Kanungo, *Charismatic Leadership*, 309–23.

37. J. G. Hunt, K. B. Boal, and G. E. Dodge, "The Effects of Visionary and Crisis-Responsive Charisma on Followers: An Experimental Examination," *Leadership Quarterly*, Fall 1999, 423–48; R. J. House and R. N. Aditya, "The Social Scientific Study of Leadership: Quo Vadis?" *Journal of Management* 23, no. 3 (1997): 316–23; and R. J. House, "A 1976 Theory of Charismatic Leadership."

38. This definition is based on M. Sashkin, "The Visionary Leader," in Conger and Kanungo et al., *Charismatic Leadership*, 124–25; B. Nanus, *Visionary Leadership* (New York: Free Press, 1992), 8; N. H. Snyder and M. Graves, "Leadership and Vision," *Business Horizons*, January–February 1994, 1; and J. R. Lucas, "Anatomy of a Vision Statement," *Management Review*, February 1998, 22–26.

39. Nanus, *Visionary Leadership*, 8.

40. S. Caminiti, "What Team Leaders Need to Know," *Fortune*, February 20, 1995, 93–100.

41. SmartPulse, "Which of These Characteristics Is the Most Dangerous Leadership Trait?" www.smartbrief.com/leadership, July 1, 2014.

42. S. Caminiti, "What Team Leaders Need to Know," *Fortune*, February 20, 1995, 93.

43. Ibid., 100.

44. D. S. DeRue, C. M. Barnes, and F. M. Morgeson, "Understanding the Motivational Contingencies of Team Leadership," *Small Group Research*, October 2010, 621–51; B. Meredith, "Leader Characteristics: Is There a Shift in Requirements?" *Leadership Excellence*, September 2010, 19; B. Neal, "Heroes and Sidekicks: Ensuring Proper Followership," *T&D*, September 2010, 76–77; R. D. Ramsey, "Preparing to Be Tomorrow's Leader Today," *Supervision*, January 2010, 79; N. Steckler and N. Fondas, "Building Team Leader Effectiveness: A Diagnostic Tool," *Organizational Dynamics*, Winter 1995, 20.

45. R. S. Wellins, W. C. Byham, and G. R. Dixon, *Inside Teams* (San Francisco: Jossey-Bass, 1994), 318.

46. Steckler and Fondas, "Building Team Leader Effectiveness," 21.

47. "The 100 Most Creative People in Business 2010," *Fast Company*, June 2010, 70–119; and G. Colvin, "The FedEx Edge," *Fortune*, April 3, 2006, 77–84.

48. J. Fabre, "The Importance of Empowering Front-Line Staff," *Supervision*, December 2010, 6–7; S. Raub and C. Robert, "Differential Effects of Empowering Leadership on In-Role and Extra-Role Employee Behaviors: Exploring the Role of Psychological Empowerment and Power Values," *Human Relations*, November 2010, 1743–70; N. D. Cakar and A. Erturk, "Comparing Innovation Capability of Small and Medium-Sized Enterprises: Examining the Effects of Organizational Culture and Empowerment," *Journal of Small Business Management* (July 2010): 325–59; A. Srivastava, K. M. Bartol, and E. A. Locke, "Empowering Leadership in Management Teams: Effects on Knowledge Sharing, Efficacy, and Performance," *Academy of Management Journal* (December 2006): 1239–51; P. K. Mills and G. R. Ungson, "Reassessing the Limits of Structural Empowerment: Organizational Constitution and Trust as Controls," *Academy of Management Review*, January 2003, 143–53; W. A. Rudolph and M. Sashkin, "Can Organizational Empowerment Work in Multinational Settings?" *Academy of Management Executive*, February 2002, 102–15; C. Gomez and B. Rosen, "The Leader-Member Link between Managerial Trust and Employee Empowerment," *Group & Organization Management*, March 2001, 53–69; C. Robert and T.

M. Probst, "Empowerment and Continuous Improvement in the United States, Mexico, Poland, and India," *Journal of Applied Psychology* (October 2000): 643–58; R. C. Herrenkohl, G. T. Judson, and J. A. Heffner, "Defining and Measuring Employee Empowerment," *Journal of Applied Behavioral Science* (September 1999): 373; R. C. Ford and M. D. Fottler, "Empowerment: A Matter of Degree," *Academy of Management Executive*, August 1995, 21–31; and W. A. Rudolph, "Navigating the Journey to Empowerment," *Organizational Dynamics*, Spring 1995, 19–32.

49. T. A. Stewart, "Just Think: No Permission Needed," *Fortune*, January 8, 2001, 190–92.

50. I. Wanasika, J. P. Howell, R. Littrell, and P. Dorfman, "Managerial Leadership and Culture in Sub-Saharan Africa," *Journal of World Business* (April 2011): 234–41.

51. F. W. Swierczek, "Leadership and Culture: Comparing Asian Managers," *Leadership & Organization Development Journal* (December 1991): 3–10.

52. House, "Leadership in the Twenty-First Century," 443; M. F. Peterson and J. G. Hunt, "International Perspectives on International Leadership," *Leadership Quarterly*, Fall 1997, 203–31; and J. R. Schermerhorn and M. H. Bond, "Cross-Cultural Leadership in Collectivism and High Power Distance Settings," *Leadership & Organization Development Journal* 18, no. 4/5 (1997): 187–93.

53. Wanasika, Howell, Littrell, and Dorfman, "Managerial Leadership and Culture in Sub-Saharan Africa"; R. J. House, P. J. Hanges, S. A. Ruiz-Quintanilla, P. W. Dorfman, et al., "Culture Specific and Cross-Culturally Generalizable Implicit Leadership Theories: Are the Attributes of Charismatic/Transformational Leadership Universally Endorsed?" *Leadership Quarterly*, Summer 1999, 219–56; and D. E. Carl and M. Javidan, "Universality of Charismatic Leadership: A Multi-Nation Study," paper presented at the National Academy of Management Conference, Washington, DC, August 2001.

54. D. E. Carl and M. Javidan, "Universality of Charismatic Leadership," 29.

55. This section is based on D. Goleman, R. E. Boyatzis, and A. McKee, *Primal Leadership: Realizing the Power of Emotional Intelligence* (Boston: Harvard Business School Press, 2002); D. R. Caruso, J. D. Mayer, and P. Salovey, "Emotional Intelligence and Emotional Leadership," in R. E. Riggio, S. E. Murphy, and F. J. Pirozzolo (eds.), *Multiple Intelligences and Leadership* (Mahwah, NJ: Lawrence Erlbaum, 2002), 55–74; J. M. George, "Emotions and Leadership: The Role of Emotional Intelligence," *Human Relations*, August 2000, 1027–55; D. Goleman,

"What Makes a Leader?" *Harvard Business Review*, November–December 1998, 93–102; and D. Goleman, *Working with Emotional Intelligence* (New York: Bantam, 1998).

56. Technology and the Manager's Job box based on K. D. Strang, "Leadership Substitutes and Personality Impact on Time and Quality in Virtual New Product Development Projects," *Project Management Journal* (February 2011): 73–90; A. Rapp, M. Ahearne, J. Mathieu, and T. Rapp, "Managing Sales Teams in a Virtual Environment," *International Journal of Research in Marketing* (September 2010): 213–24; M. Muethel and M. Hoegl, "Cultural and Societal Influences on Shared Leadership in Globally Dispersed Teams," *Journal of International Management* (September 2010): 234–56; J. Grenny, "Virtual Teams," *Leadership Excellence*, May 2010, 20; L. A. Hambley, T. A. O'Neill, and T. J. B. Kline, "Virtual Team Leadership: The Effects of Leadership Style and Communication Medium on Team Interaction Styles and Outcomes," *Organizational Behavior and Human Decision Processes*, May 2007, 1–20; and B. J. Avolio and S. S. Kahai, "Adding the 'E' to E-Leadership: How It May Impact Your Leadership," *Organizational Dynamics*, January 2003, 325–38.

57. "The Secret Skill of Leaders," *U.S. News & World Report* (January 14, 2002): 8. See, also, L. Gardner and C. Stough, "Examining the Relationship between Leadership and Emotional Intelligence in Senior Level Managers," *Leadership and Organization Development Journal*, January–February 2002, 68–79.

58. Ibid.

59. F. Walter, M. S. Cole, and R. H. Humphrey, "Emotional Intelligence: Sine Qua Non of Leadership or Folderol?" *Academy of Management Perspectives*, February 2011, 45–59.

60. See Walter, Cole, and Humphrey, "Emotional Intelligence: Sine Qua Non of Leadership or Folderol"; L. A. Zampetakis and V. Moustakis, "Managers' Trait Emotional Intelligence and Group Outcomes: The Case of Group Job Satisfaction," *Small Group Research*, February 2011, 77–102; H.-W. Vivian Tang, M.-S. Yin, and D. B. Nelson, "The Relationship between Emotional Intelligence and Leadership Practices," *Journal of Managerial Psychology* 25, no. 8 (2010): 899–926; P. K. Chopra and G. K. Kanji, "Emotional Intelligence: A Catalyst for Inspirational Leadership and Management Excellence," *Total Quality Management & Business Excellence*, October 2010, 971–1004; R. Boyatzis and A. McKee, "Intentional Change," *Journal of Organizational Excellence* (Summer 2006): 49– 60,

and R. Kerr; J. Garvin, N. Heaton, and E. Boyle, "Emotional Intelligence and Leadership Effectiveness," *Leadership and Organizational Development Journal* (April 2006): 265–79.

61. S. Simsarian, "Leadership and Trust Facilitating Cross-Functional Team Success," *Journal of Management Development* (March–April 2002): 201–15.

62. J. M. Kouzes and B. Z. Posner, *Credibility: How Leaders Gain and Lose It, and Why People Demand It* (San Francisco: Jossey-Bass, 1993), 14.

63. Based on F. D. Schoorman, R. C. Mayer, and J. H. Davis, "An Integrative Model of Organizational Trust: Past, Present, and Future," *Academy of Management Review*, April 2007, 344–54; G. M. Spreitzer and A. K. Mishra, "Giving Up Control without Losing Control," *Group & Organization Management*, June 1999, 155–87; R. C. Mayer, J. H. Davis, and F. D. Schoorman, "An Integrative Model of Organizational Trust," *Academy of Management Review*, July 1995, 712; and L. T. Hosmer, "Trust: The Connecting Link between Organizational Theory and Philosophical Ethics," *Academy of Management Review*, April 1995, 393.

64. P. L. Schindler and C. C. Thomas, "The Structure of Interpersonal Trust in the Workplace," *Psychological Reports*, October 1993, 563–73.

65. H. H. Tan and C. S. F. Tan, "Toward the Differentiation of Trust in Supervisor and Trust in Organization," *Genetic, Social, and General Psychology Monographs*, May 2000, 241–60.

66. J. H. Cho and E. J. Ringquist, "Managerial Trustworthiness and Organizational Outcomes," *Journal of Public Administration Research and Theory* (January 2011): 53–86; R. C. Mayer and M. B. Gavin, "Trust in Management and Performance: Who Minds the Shop While the Employees Watch the Boss?" *Academy of Management Journal* (October 2005): 874–88; and K. T. Dirks and D. L. Ferrin, "Trust in Leadership: Meta-Analytic Findings and Implications for Research and Practice," *Journal of Applied Psychology* (August 2002): 611–28.

67. R. Zemke, "The Confidence Crisis," *Training* (June 2004): 22–30; J. A. Byrne, "Restoring Trust in Corporate America," *BusinessWeek*, June 24, 2002, 30–35; S. Armour, "Employees' New Motto: Trust No One," *USA Today*, February 5, 2002, 1B; J. Scott, "Once Bitten, Twice Shy: A World of Eroding Trust," *New York Times*, April 21, 2002, WK5; J. Brockner, P. A. Siegel, J. P. Daly, T. Tyler, and C. Martin, "When Trust Matters: The Moderating Effect of Outcome Favorability," *Administrative Science Quarterly*, September

1997, 558; and J. Brockner, P. A. Siegel, J. P. Daly, T. Tyler, and C. Martin, "When Trust Matters: The Moderating Effect of Outcome Favorability," *Administrative Science Quarterly*, September 1997, 558.

68. "Weathering the Storm: A Study of Employee Attitudes and Opinions," *WorkUSA 2002 Study*, Watson Wyatt, www.watsonwyatt.com.

69. S. Kerr and J. M. Jermier, "Substitutes for Leadership: Their Meaning and Measurement," *Organizational Behavior and Human Performance*, December 1978, 375–403; J. P. Howell, P. W. Dorfman, and S. Kerr, "Leadership and Substitutes for Leadership," *Journal of Applied Behavioral Science* 22, no. 1 (1986): 29–46; J. P. Howell, D. E. Bowen, P. W. Dorfman, S. Kerr, and P. M. Podsakoff, "Substitutes for Leadership: Effective Alternatives to Ineffective Leadership," *Organizational Dynamics*, Summer 1990, 21–38; and P. M. Podsakoff, B. P. Niehoff, S. B. MacKenzie, and M. L. Williams, "Do Substitutes for Leadership Really Substitute for Leadership? An Empirical Examination of Kerr and Jermier's Situational Leadership Model," *Organizational Behavior and Human Decision Processes*, February 1993, 1–44.

70. Based on R. J. House and R. N. Aditya, "The Social Scientific Study of Leadership: Quo Vadis?" *Journal of Management* (June 1997): 409–73; and G. A. Yukl, *Leadership in Organizations*, 7th ed. (Upper Saddle River, NJ: Prentice Hall, 2010).

71. L. Patel, "Preparing Tomorrow's Executives," *T&D*, March 2014, 20.

72. A. Harjani, "From Brats to Bosses—Gen Y to Dominate by 2025," www.cnbc.com/id/101353573, January 22, 2014.

73. Best Companies for Leadership 2014, Hay Group, http://www.haygroup.com/bestcompaniesforleadership/downloads/Best_Companies_for_Leadership_2014_Executive_summary.pdf, 2014.

74. L. Lykins and A. Pace, "Mastering Millennial Leadership Development," *T&D*, May 2013, 42–45.

75. H. Stevens, "How Top-Ranked Companies Develop Leaders," http://www.clomedia.com/articles/5749-how-top-ranked-companies-develop-leaders, August 6, 2014.

76. D. Livermore, "What Facebook Tells Us about the Future of Leadership," http://www.management-issues.com/opinion/6776/what-facebook-tells-us-about-the-future-of-leadership/, October 15, 2013.

77. S. Kessler, "Take a Peek Inside Starbucks's $35 Million Leadership Lab," *fastcompany.com*, March 6, 2013; L. Sinclair, "Fast Company Goes Inside Starbucks' Leadership Lab," *sprudge.com*, November 5, 2012; and J. Jennings, "Successful Reinventors," *Leadership Excellence*, August 2012, 13.

78. D. Archer and A. Cameron, "Collaborative Leadership," www.trainingjournal.com, June 2012, 35–38; J. Katzenbach, "The Steve Jobs Way," *Strategy+Business Online*, April 23, 2012; W. Isaacson, "The Real Leadership Lessons of Steve Jobs," *Harvard Business Review*, April 2012, 93–102; R. Williams, "Why Steve Jobs Was Not a Leader," www.psychologytoday.com, April 7, 2012; R. Foroohar, "The Leadership Lessons of Steve Jobs," *business.time.com*, February 16, 2012; R. Foroohar, "What Would Steve Do?" www.time.com, February 27, 2012; F. E. Allen, "Steve Jobs Broke Every Leadership Rule. Don't Try It," www.forbes.com, August 27, 2011; J. Nocera, "What Makes Steve Jobs Great," *New York Times Online*, August 26, 2011; A. Sharma and D. Grant, "The Stagecraft of Steve Jobs," *Strategy+Business Online*, June 10, 2011; and A. Lashinsky, "How Apple Works: Inside the World's Biggest Startup," http://fortune.com/2011/05/09/inside-apple/, May 9, 2011.

79. J. Nocera, "What Makes Steve Jobs Great," *New York Times Online*, August 26, 2011.

80. A. Lashinsky, "How Apple Works: Inside the World's Biggest Startup," http://fortune.com/2011/05/09/inside-apple/, May 9, 2011.

81. Ibid.

82. W. Isaacson, "The Real Leadership Lessons of Steve Jobs," https://hbr.org/2012/04/the-real-leadership-lessons-of-steve-jobs, April 2012.

13

Management Myth

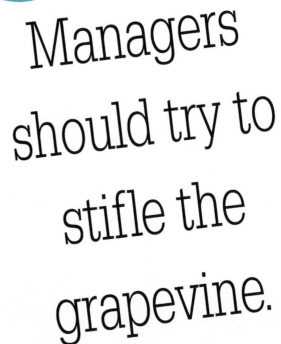

Managers should try to stifle the grapevine.

Management DEBUNKED? Myth

The grapevine is a well-known source for organizational gossip and news. For the inexperienced manager, it's seen as a destructive element in an organization's communication network. But the grapevine isn't going away. It's as natural to an organization as water is to an ocean. Astute managers acknowledge the existence of the grapevine and learn to use it in beneficial ways.

WELCOME to the world

of communication! In this "world," managers are going to have to understand both the importance and the drawbacks of communication—all forms of communication, even the grapevine. Communication takes place every day in every organization. In all areas. By all organizational members. In many different forms. Most of that communication tends to be work-related. But as we'll see, sometimes communication can cause some unintended consequences. In this chapter, we're going to look at basic concepts of interpersonal communication. We'll explain the communication process, methods of communicating, barriers to effective communication, and ways to overcome those barriers. In addition, we'll look at communication issues that today's managers face. ●

Learning Outcomes

13-1 Describe what managers need to know about communicating effectively. p. 395

13-2 Explain how technology affects managerial communication. p. 403

13-3 Discuss contemporary issues in communication. p. 406

How Do Managers Communicate Effectively?

13-1 Describe what managers need to know about communicating effectively.

Poor communication can cost a business up to $5,000 per employee each year![1]

The importance of effective communication for managers cannot be overemphasized for one specific reason: **EVERYTHING A MANAGER DOES INVOLVES COMMUNICATING.** Not *some* things but *everything*! A manager can't formulate strategy or make a decision without information. That information has to be communicated. Once a decision is made, communication must again take place. Otherwise, no one will know that a decision has been made. The best idea, the most creative suggestion, or the finest plan cannot take form without communication. Managers, therefore, need effective communication skills. We're not suggesting, of course, that good communication skills alone make a successful manager. We can say, however, that ineffective communication skills can lead to a continuous stream of problems for a manager.

✪ Write It 1!

If your professor has assigned this, go to the Assignments section of **mymanagementlab.com** to complete *BCOMM 3: Importance of Communication*.

How Does the Communication Process Work?

WHAT is communicated? The 3 I's: Information, Ideas, Instructions

Communication can be thought of as a process or flow. Communication problems occur when deviations or blockages disrupt that flow. Before communication can take place, a purpose, expressed as a message to be conveyed, is needed. It passes between a source (the sender) and a receiver. The message is encoded (converted to symbolic form) and is passed by way of some medium (channel) to the receiver, who retranslates (decodes) the message initiated by the sender. The result is **communication**, which is a transfer of understanding and meaning from one person to another.[2]

Exhibit 13–1 depicts the **communication process**. This model has seven parts: (1) the communication source or sender, (2) encoding, (3) the message, (4) the channel, (5) decoding, (6) the receiver, and (7) feedback.

1 and 2. The sender initiates a message by **encoding** a thought. Four conditions affect the encoded message: skill, attitudes, knowledge, and the social cultural system. Our message in our communication to you in this book depends on our writing *skills*; if we don't have the requisite writing skills, our message will not reach you in the form desired. Keep in mind that a person's total communicative success includes speaking, reading, listening, and reasoning skills as well. As we discussed in Chapter 9, our attitudes influence our behavior. We hold predisposed ideas on numerous topics, and our communications are affected by these *attitudes*. Furthermore, we're restricted in our communicative activity by the extent of our *knowledge* of the particular topic. We can't communicate what we don't know, and should our knowledge be too extensive, it's possible that our receiver will not understand our message. Clearly, the amount of knowledge the source holds about his or her subject will affect the message he or she seeks to transfer. And, finally, just as attitudes influence our behavior, so does our *position*

communication
A transfer of understanding and meaning from one person to another

communication process
The seven-part process of transferring and understanding of meaning

encoding
Converting a message into symbolic form

Exhibit 13–1 The Communication Process

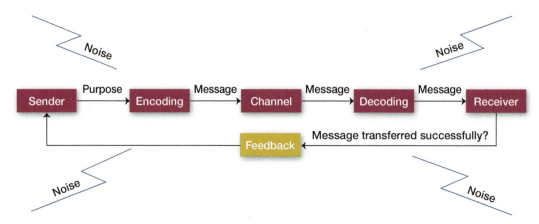

message
A purpose for communicating that's to be conveyed

channel
The medium by which a message travels

decoding
Translating a received message

feedback
Checking to see how successfully a message has been transferred

in the social cultural system in which we exist. Your beliefs and values, all part of your culture, act to influence you as a communication source.

3. The **message** is the actual physical product from the source that conveys some purpose. When we speak, the words spoken are the message. When we write, the writing is the message. When we paint, the picture is the message. When we gesture, the movements of our arms and the expressions on our faces are the message.[3] Our message is affected by the code or group of symbols we use to transfer meaning, the content of the message itself, and the decisions that we make in selecting and arranging both codes and content.[4]

4. The **channel** is the medium through which the message travels. It's selected by the source, who must determine whether to use a formal or an informal channel. Formal channels are established by the organization and transmit messages that pertain to the job-related activities of members. They traditionally follow the authority network within the organization. Other forms of messages, such as personal or social, follow the informal channels in the organization.

5 and 6. The receiver is the person to whom the message is directed. However, before the message can be received, the symbols in it must be translated into a form that can be understood by the receiver—the **decoding** of the message. Just as the encoder was limited by his or her skills, attitudes, knowledge, and social cultural system, the receiver is equally restricted. Accordingly, the source must be skillful in writing or speaking; the receiver must be skillful in reading or listening; and both must be able to reason. A person's knowledge, attitudes, and cultural background influence his or her ability to receive, just as they do the ability to send.

7. The final link in the communication process is a feedback loop. "If a communication source decodes the message that he encodes, if the message is put back into his system, we have feedback."[5] **Feedback** is the check on how successful we've been in transferring our messages as originally intended. It determines whether understanding has been achieved. Given the cultural diversity that exists in our workforce today, the importance of effective feedback to ensure proper communications cannot be overstated.[6]

Participating in a meeting at company headquarters, these employees of Alibaba, China's largest e-commerce firm, illustrate the channel part of the communication process. The meeting is a formal channel established by Alibaba during which employees transmit messages that pertain to their job-related activities.

Steven Shi/Reuters

Are Written Communications More Effective Than Verbal Ones?

Written communications include memos, letters, e-mail and other forms of digital communication, organizational periodicals, bulletin boards, or any other device that transmits written words or symbols. Why would a sender choose to use written communications?

Advantages: Well, they're tangible, verifiable, and more permanent than oral communication. Typically, both sender and receiver have a record of the communication. The message can be stored for an indefinite period of time. If questions arise about the content of the message, it's physically available for later reference. This feature is particularly important for complex or lengthy communications. For example, the marketing plan for a new product is likely to contain a number of tasks spread out over several months. By putting it in writing, those who have to carry out the plan can readily refer to the document over the life of the plan. A final benefit of written communication comes from the process itself. Written communications are more likely to be well thought out, logical, and clear. Except in rare instances, such as when presenting a formal speech, more care is taken with the written word than with the spoken word. Having to put something in writing forces a person to think more carefully about what he or she wants to convey.

Drawbacks: Of course, written messages have their drawbacks. Writing may be more precise, but it also consumes a great deal of time. You could convey far more information to your college instructor in a one-hour oral exam than in a one-hour written exam. In fact, you could probably say in 10 to 15 minutes what it takes you an hour to write. The other major disadvantage is the lack of feedback. Oral communications allow receivers to respond rapidly to what they think they hear. However, written communications don't have a built-in feedback mechanism. Sending a memo is no assurance that it will be received and, if it is received, no guarantee that the recipient will interpret it as the sender meant. The latter point is also relevant in oral communication, but it's easier in such cases merely to ask the receiver to summarize what you have said. An accurate summary presents feedback evidence that the message has been received and understood.

> ### ✪ Watch It 1!
>
> If your professor has assigned this, go to the Assignments section of **mymanagementlab.com** to complete the video exercise titled ***CH2MHill: Communication***.

Is the Grapevine an Effective Way to Communicate?

The **Grapevine**: Fruitful or Not?

The grapevine is the unofficial way that communication takes place in an organization. It's neither authorized nor supported by the organization. Rather, information is spread by word of mouth—and even through electronic means. Ironically, good information passes among us rapidly, but bad information travels even faster.[7] The grapevine gets information out to organizational members as quickly as possible.

The biggest question raised about the grapevine, however, focuses on the accuracy of the rumors. Research on this topic has found somewhat mixed results. In an organization characterized by openness, the grapevine may be extremely accurate. In an authoritative culture, the rumor mill may not be accurate. But even then, although the information flowing is inaccurate, it still contains some element of truth. Rumors about major layoffs, plant closings, and the like may be filled with inaccurate information regarding who will be affected or when it may occur. Nonetheless, the reports that something is about to happen are probably on target. (See the From the Past to the Present box on p. 398 for more about the grapevine.)

How Do Nonverbal Cues Affect Communication?

Some of the most meaningful communications are neither spoken nor written. They are nonverbal communications. A loud siren or a red light at an intersection tells you something without words. A college instructor doesn't need words to know that students are bored; their eyes get glassy or they begin to read the school newspaper during class. Similarly, when papers start to rustle and notebooks begin to close, the message is clear: Class time is about over. The size of a person's office and desk or the clothes he or she wears also convey

grapevine
An unofficial channel of communication

◀◀◀ From the Past to the Present ▶▶▶

One of the most famous studies of the grapevine was conducted by management researcher Keith Davis who investigated the communication patterns among 67 managerial personnel.[8] The approach he used was to learn from each communication recipient how he or she first received a given piece of information and then trace it back to its source. It was found that, while the grapevine was an important source of information, only 10 percent of the executives acted as liaison individuals (that is, passed the information on to more than one other person). For example, when one executive decided to resign to enter the insurance business, 81 percent of the executives knew about it, but only 11 percent transmitted this information to others. At the time, this study was interesting because of what it found, but more importantly because of what it showed about how the communication network worked.

Recent research by IBM and the Massachusetts Institute of Technology using a similar type of analysis focused more on people's social networks of contacts at work rather than on how information flowed through the organizational grapevine.

However, what was noticeably interesting about this study was that it found that employees who have strong communication ties with their managers tend to bring in more money than those who steer clear of the boss.

What managers can learn from both of these studies is that *it's important to understand the social and communication networks that employees use as they do their work.*

> ## The Grapevine:
> ## An important source
> ## of information

Know who the key contact points are so that if you ever need to find out or relay information, you know who to go to.

*If your professor has assigned this, go to the Assignments section of **mymanagementlab.com** to complete these discussion questions.*

⭐ **Talk About It 1:** Why is it important for managers to understand social and communication networks employees use?

⭐ **Talk About It 2:** What have been your experiences with the grapevine and what did you learn from those experiences about dealing with the grapevine as a source of communication?

---

messages to others. However, the best-known areas of nonverbal communication are body language and verbal intonation.

Body language refers to gestures, facial configurations, and other movements of the body.[9] A snarl, for example, says something different from a smile. Hand motions, facial expressions, and other gestures can communicate emotions or temperaments such as aggression, fear, shyness, arrogance, joy, and anger.[10]

It's not WHAT you say but **HOW you say it.**

Verbal intonation refers to the emphasis someone gives to words or phrases. To illustrate how intonations can change the meaning of a message, consider the student who asks the instructor a question. The instructor replies, "What do you mean by that?" The student's reaction will vary, depending on the tone of the instructor's response. A soft, smooth tone creates a different meaning from one that is abrasive with a strong emphasis on the last word. Most of us would view the first intonation as coming from someone who sincerely sought clarification, whereas the second suggests that the person is aggressive or defensive. The adage, "it's not what you say but how you say it," is something managers should remember as they communicate.

The fact that every oral communication also has a nonverbal message cannot be overemphasized.[11] Why? Because the nonverbal component is likely to carry the greatest impact. Research indicates that from 65 to 90 percent of the message of every face-to-face conversation is interpreted through body language. Without complete agreement between the spoken words and the body language that accompanies it, receivers are more likely to react to body language as the "true meaning."[12]

What Barriers Keep Communication from Being Effective?

A number of interpersonal and intrapersonal barriers affect why the message decoded by a receiver is often different from what the sender intended. We summarize the more prominent barriers to effective communication in Exhibit 13–2 and briefly describe them here.

body language
Nonverbal communication cues such as facial expressions, gestures, and other body movements

verbal intonation
An emphasis given to words or phrases that conveys meaning

HOW DOES FILTERING AFFECT COMMUNICATION?

Filtering refers to the way that a sender manipulates information so that it will be seen more favorably by the receiver. For example, when a manager tells his boss what he feels that boss wants to hear, he is filtering information. Does filtering happen much in organizations? Sure it does. As information is passed up to senior executives, it has to be condensed and synthesized by subordinates so upper management doesn't become overloaded with information. Those doing the condensing filter communications through their own personal interests and perceptions of what's important.

The extent of filtering tends to be the function of the organization's culture and number of vertical levels in the organization. More vertical levels in an organization mean more opportunities for filtering. As organizations become less dependent on strict hierarchical arrangements and instead use more collaborative, cooperative work arrangements, information filtering may become less of a problem. In addition, the ever-increasing use of e-mail to communicate in organizations reduces filtering because communication is more direct as intermediaries are bypassed. Finally, the organizational culture encourages or discourages filtering by the type of behavior it rewards. The more that organizational rewards emphasize style and appearance, the more managers will be motivated to filter communications in their favor.

Tomas van Houtryve/VII/Corbis

Employees gesture during a conversation in the break room at the offices of Facebook in Paris, France. Body language, which includes gestures such as hand motions, and facial expressions are areas of nonverbal communication that can express fear, shyness, arrogance, joy, anger, and other emotions and temperaments.

HOW DOES SELECTIVE PERCEPTION AFFECT COMMUNICATION?

The second barrier is selective perception. We've mentioned selective perception before in this book. We discuss it again here because the receivers in the communication process selectively see and hear based on their needs, motivations, experience, background, and other personal characteristics. Receivers also project their interests and expectations into communications as they decode them. The employment interviewer who expects a female job applicant

Exhibit 13–2 Barriers to Effective Communication

BARRIER	DESCRIPTION
Filtering	The deliberate manipulation of information to make it appear more favorable to the receiver.
Selective Perception	Receiving communications on the basis of what one selectively sees and hears depending on his or her needs, motivation, experience, background, and other personal characteristics.
Information Overload	When the amount of information one has to work with exceeds one's processing capacity.
Emotions	How the receiver feels when a message is received.
Language	Words have different meanings to different people. Receivers will use their definition of words being communicated.
Gender	How males and females react to communication may be different, and they each have a different communication style.
National Culture	Communication differences arising from the different languages that individuals use to communicate and the national culture of which they are a part.

filtering
Deliberately manipulating information to make it appear more favorable to the receiver

selective perception
Selectively perceiving or hearing a communication based on your own needs, motivations, experiences, or other personal characteristics

to put her family ahead of her career is likely to see that tendency in female applicants, regardless of whether the applicants would do so or not. As we said in Chapter 9, we don't see reality; rather, we interpret what we see and call it reality.

HOW DOES INFORMATION OVERLOAD AFFECT COMMUNICATION?   Individuals have a finite capacity for processing data. For instance, consider an international sales representative who returns home to find that she has more than 600 e-mails waiting for her. It's not possible to fully read and respond to each one of those messages without facing **information overload**. Today's typical executive frequently complains of information overload.[13] The demands of keeping up with e-mail, phone calls, faxes, meetings, and professional reading create an onslaught of data that is nearly impossible to process and assimilate. What happens when you have more information than you can sort out and use? You're likely to select out, ignore, pass over, or forget information. Or you may put off further processing until the overload situation is over. In any case, the result is lost information and less effective communication.

HOW DO EMOTIONS AFFECT COMMUNICATION?   How a receiver feels when a message is received influences how he or she interprets it. You'll often interpret the same message differently, depending on whether you're happy or distressed. Extreme emotions are most likely to hinder effective communications. In such instances, we often disregard our rational and objective thinking processes and substitute emotional judgments. It's best to avoid reacting to a message when you're upset because you're not likely to be thinking clearly.

HOW DOES LANGUAGE AFFECT COMMUNICATION?   Words mean different things to different people. "The meanings of words are not in the words; they are in us."[14] Age, education, and cultural background are three of the more obvious variables that influence the language a person uses and the definitions he or she applies to words. Columnist George F. Will and rapper Iggy Azalea both speak English. But the language one uses is vastly different from how the other speaks.

> Forty percent of employees say that buzzwords are very prevalent in normal conversations at work.[15]

In an organization, employees usually come from diverse backgrounds and, therefore, have different patterns of speech. Additionally, the grouping of employees into departments creates specialists who develop their own **jargon** or technical language.[16] In large organizations, members are also frequently widely dispersed geographically—even operating in different countries—and individuals in each locale will use terms and phrases that are unique to their area.[17] And the existence of vertical levels can also cause language problems. The language of senior executives, for instance, can be mystifying to regular employees not familiar with management jargon. Keep in mind that while we may speak the same language, our use of that language is far from uniform. Senders tend to assume that the words and phrases they use mean the same to the receiver as they do to them. This assumption, of course, is incorrect and creates communication barriers. Knowing how each of us modifies the language would help minimize those barriers.

HOW DOES GENDER AFFECT COMMUNICATION?   Effective communication between the sexes is important in all organizations if they are to meet organizational goals. But how can we manage the various differences in communication styles? To keep gender differences from becoming persistent barriers to effective communication, individuals must strive for acceptance, understanding, and a commitment to communicate adaptively with each other. Both men and women need to acknowledge differences are present in communication styles, that one style isn't better than the other, and that it takes real effort to talk successfully with each other.[18]

HOW DOES NATIONAL CULTURE AFFECT COMMUNICATION?   Finally, communication differences can also arise from the different languages that individuals use to

information overload
What results when information exceeds processing capacity

jargon
Technical language specific to a discipline or industry

communicate and the national culture of which they're a part.[19] For example, let's compare countries that place a high value on individualism (such as the United States) with countries where the emphasis is on collectivism (such as Japan).[20]

In the United States, communication patterns tend to be oriented to the individual and clearly spelled out. Managers in the United States rely heavily on memoranda, announcements, position papers, and other formal forms of communication to state their positions on issues. Supervisors here may hoard information in an attempt to make themselves look good (filtering) and as a way of persuading their employees to accept decisions and plans. And for their own protection, lower-level employees also engage in this practice.

In collectivist countries, such as Japan, there's more interaction for its own sake and a more informal manner of interpersonal contact. The Japanese manager, in contrast to the U.S. manager, engages in extensive verbal consultation with employees over an issue first and draws up a formal document later to outline the agreement that was made. The Japanese value decisions by consensus, and open communication is an inherent part of the work setting. Also, face-to-face communication is encouraged.[21]

Cultural differences can affect the way a manager chooses to communicate.[22] And these differences undoubtedly can be a barrier to effective communication if not recognized and taken into consideration.

✪ Write It 2!

If your professor has assigned this, go to the Assignments section of **mymanagementlab.com** to complete *BCOMM4: Multicultural Communication*.

How Can Managers Overcome Communication Barriers?

Given these barriers to communication, what can managers do to overcome them? The following suggestions should help make communication more effective (see also Exhibit 13–3).

WHY USE FEEDBACK?   Many communication problems are directly attributed to misunderstanding and inaccuracies. These problems are less likely to occur if the manager gets feedback, both verbal and nonverbal.

A manager can ask questions about a message to determine whether it was received and understood as intended. Or the manager can ask the receiver to restate the message in his or her own words. If the manager hears what was intended, understanding and accuracy should improve. Feedback can also be more subtle as general comments can give a manager a sense of the receiver's reaction to a message.

Feedback doesn't have to be verbal. If a sales manager e-mails information about a new monthly sales report that all sales representatives will need to complete and some of them don't turn it in, the sales manager has received feedback. This feedback suggests

Exhibit 13–3 Overcoming Barriers to Effective Communication

Use Feedback	Check the accuracy of what has been communicated—or what you think you heard.
Simplify Language	Use words that the intended audience understands.
Listen Actively	Listen for the full meaning of the message without making premature judgment or interpretation—or thinking about what you are going to say in response.
Constrain Emotions	Recognize when your emotions are running high. When they are, don't communicate until you have calmed down.
Watch Nonverbal Cues	Be aware that your actions speak louder than your words. Keep the two consistent.

Anthony Devlin/PA Wire URN:11384241/AP Images

Ana Botin, executive chairman of Spain's Banco Santander, is respected as an empathetic listener and a good communicator and consensus builder. Shown here communicating with employees at a bank in London, Botin asks questions and listens to feedback from employees, customers, and shareholders that helps her plan the company's strategy.

that the sales manager needs to clarify the initial communication. Similarly, managers can look for nonverbal cues to tell whether someone's getting the message.

WHY SHOULD SIMPLIFIED LANGUAGE BE USED? Because language can be a barrier, managers should consider the audience to whom the message is directed and tailor the language to them. Remember, effective communication is achieved when a message is both received and *understood*. For example, a hospital administrator should always try to communicate in clear, easily understood terms and to use language tailored to different employee groups. Messages to the surgical staff should be purposefully different from those directed to the marketing team or office employees. Jargon can facilitate understanding if it's used within a group that knows what it means, but can cause problems when used outside that group.

Do you **really listen** OR do you just **hear?**

WHY MUST WE LISTEN ACTIVELY? When someone talks, we hear. But too often we don't listen. Listening is an active search for meaning, whereas hearing is passive. In listening, the receiver is also putting effort into the communication.

Many of us are poor listeners. Why? Because it's difficult, and most of us would rather do the talking. Listening, in fact, is often more tiring than talking. Unlike hearing, **active listening**, which is listening for full meaning without making premature judgments or interpretations, demands total concentration. The average person normally speaks at a rate of about 125 to 200 words per minute. However, the average listener can comprehend up to 400 words per minute.[23] The difference leaves lots of idle brain time and opportunities for the mind to wander.

Active listening is enhanced by developing empathy with the sender—that is, by putting yourself in the sender's position. Because senders differ in attitudes, interests, needs, and expectations, empathy makes it easier to understand the actual content of a message. An empathetic listener reserves judgment on the message's content and carefully listens to what is being said. The goal is to improve one's ability to get the full meaning of a communication without distorting it by premature judgments or interpretations. Other specific behaviors that active listeners use include making eye contact, exhibiting affirmative nods and appropriate facial expressions, avoiding distracting actions or gestures that suggest boredom, asking questions, paraphrasing using your own words, avoiding interrupting the speaker, not talking too much, and making smooth transitions between being a speaker and a listener.

WHY MUST WE CONSTRAIN EMOTIONS? It would be naïve to assume that managers always communicate in a rational manner. We know that emotions can cloud and distort communication. A manager who's upset over an issue is more likely to misconstrue incoming messages and fail to communicate his or her outgoing messages clearly and accurately. What to do? The simplest answer is to calm down and get emotions under control before communicating.

WHY THE EMPHASIS ON NONVERBAL CUES? If actions speak louder than words, then it's important to make sure your actions align with and reinforce the words that go along with them. An effective communicator watches his or her nonverbal cues to ensure that they convey the desired message.

active listening
Listening for full meaning without making premature judgments or interpretations

Technology and Managerial Communication

IT is where it's at!

13-2 Explain how technology affects managerial communication.

- Information technology (IT) has radically changed the way organizational members work and communicate.

  — Improves manager's ability to monitor individual and team performance

  — Allows employees to have more complete information to make faster decisions

  — Provides employees more opportunities to collaborate and share information

  — Allows employees to be fully accessible 24/7

Steven Senne/AP Images

2 IT developments *have had a significant effect on managerial communication…*

1 Networked Communication

In a networked communication system

- Organizational computers are linked through compatible hardware and software, creating an integrated organizational network.

- Employees communicate with each other and get information wherever they are.

xstock/Shutterstock

Networked Communication Applications

- **E-mail**—instantaneous transmission of messages on networked computers.

  - ➕ Messages read at receiver's convenience
  - ➕ Fast, cheap, efficient, and convenient
  - ➕ Print documents, if needed
  - ➖ Slow and cumbersome

  Cemil Adakale/Fotolia

- **Instant messaging (IM)**—interactive, real-time communication among computer users who are logged on to the computer network at the same time.

  - ➕ Instantaneous communication without waiting for colleagues to read e-mail
  - ➖ Users must be logged on at the same time
  - ➖ Potential network and data security breaches

- **Voice mail**—a system that digitizes a spoken message, transmits it over the network, and stores it for a receiver to retrieve later.[24]

  - ➕ Information transmitted without receiver being physically present
  - ➕ Message can be saved, deleted, or re-routed
  - ➖ No immediate feedback

- **Fax machines**—transmit documents containing both text and graphics over ordinary telephone lines.

  - ➕ Printed form of information easily and quickly shared by organization members
  - ➖ Privacy can be compromised

  HSN/Fotolia

- **Electronic data interchange (EDI)**—organizations exchange business transaction documents such as invoices or purchase orders, using direct computer-to-computer networks.

  - ➕ Saves time and money by eliminating printing and handling of paper documents

- **Teleconference and videoconference meetings**—confer simultaneously by telephone, e-mail, or video screens.

  - ➕ Participants don't need to be in same physical location to share information and collaborate
  - ➕ Saves travel money

  Arekmalang/Fotolia

- **Organizational intranet**—an organizational communication network using Internet technology that's accessible only to organizational employees.

  - ➕ Share information and collaborate on documents and projects
  - ➕ Access company policy manuals and employee-specific materials[25]
  - ➖ Possible network and data security breaches

- Organizational **extranet**—an organizational communication network using Internet technology that allows authorized organizational users to communicate with certain outsiders such as customers or vendors.

  ➕ Faster and more convenient communication   ➖ Concerns about network and data security breaches

- **Internet-based voice/video communication**—Internet based communication services (such as Skype, Viber, FaceTime, Vonage, Yahoo!).

  ➕ Fast and convenient communication   ➖ Concerns about network and data security breaches

2 Wireless Communication

Wireless communication systems have benefits:

- Employees can be connected without being physically "plugged in" at work!
- Mobile technology is extremely popular!
- Improving the way you work is the payoff!

Monkey Business/Fotolia

Wireless Communication Applications

- People don't have to be physically "at the office" in order to communicate, collaborate, and share information with managers and colleagues.[26]
- Managers and employees "keep in touch" using smartphones, tablet computers, notebook computers, and mobile pocket communication devices.
- And wireless communication works—anywhere. People can send and receive information from the summit of Mt. Everest to the remotest locations on the planet.

Oleksiy Mark/Fotolia

┊┊┊┊ Technology and the Manager's Job ┊┊┊┊
OFFICE OF TOMORROW

The office of tomorrow is still likely to resemble in some ways the office of today. There probably won't be mail delivery by robots on hovercraft nor any teleportation devices. Most of the changes, however, will likely be in the *way* we communicate.[27] Employees will rely on multiple channels of communication with heavy reliance on social networks, text messaging, instant messaging, mobile technology, and dashboard apps that allow employees to message each other directly. Smartphones will be as powerful as today's mainframes, meaning employees will be able to do heavy computing on the go. Software will be able to track where employees are and blend that data with information about current projects and suggest potential collaborators. E-mail is likely to decline in popularity, largely because other channels are faster, more fluid, and more immediate.

Accurately forecasting tomorrow's technology is impossible. But several patterns seem to be evolving. For instance, the combining of functions in a single device is likely to result in employees having a single product that will combine phone, text messaging, Internet access, video camera, teleconferencing, and language translator. It will allow people to read proposals, legal papers, news, or almost any document digitally. It won't need a keyboard and will operate

> Over 83 percent of managers are using mobile technology to improve communication with employees.[28]

via voice commands. It's also likely not to be handheld but rather something akin to combining reading glasses and an earpiece. You'll read documents through the lenses of what look like normal reading glasses and the earpiece/microphone will make it hands-free. Google Glass is an example of this wearable technology.[29] As this type of technology becomes more common, organizations will have to address usage issues regarding information security and possible legal dilemmas.

Another outcome made possible by technology will be a significant decrease in business travel. Improvements in computer-mediated groupware will allow individuals to conduct meetings in environments that closely simulate face-to-face interactions. In these settings, real-time translations will be transcribed and displayed on screen and teleconferencers will be able to hear and see the words.

If your professor has assigned this, go to the Assignments section of **mymanagementlab.com** *to complete these discussion questions.*

✪ **TALK ABOUT IT 3:** Do you view communicating using technology as more of a help or a hindrance? Explain.

✪ **TALK ABOUT IT 4:** What issues does wearable technology present in the workplace? What do you think managers will need to do to deal with these issues?

✪ **Try It!**
If your professor has assigned this, go to the Assignments section of **mymanagementlab.com** to complete the **Simulation:** *Communication*.

What Communication Issues Do Managers Face Today?

13-3 Discuss contemporary issues in communication.

"Pulse lunches." That's what managers at Citibank's offices throughout Malaysia used to address pressing problems of declining customer loyalty and staff morale and increased employee turnover. By connecting with employees and listening to their concerns—that is, taking their "pulse"—during informal lunch settings, managers were able to make changes that boosted both customer loyalty and employee morale by more than 50 percent and reduced employee turnover to nearly zero.[30]

Being an effective communicator in today's organizations means being connected—most importantly to employees and customers, but in reality, to any of the organization's stakeholders. In this section, we examine five communication issues of particular significance to today's managers: managing communication in an Internet world, managing the organization's knowledge resources, communicating with customers, getting employee input, and communicating ethically.

How Do We Manage Communication in an Internet World?

Lars Dalgaard, founder and chief executive of SuccessFactors, a human resource management software company, recently sent an e-mail to his employees banning in-house e-mail for a week. His goal? Getting employees to "authentically address issues amongst each other."[31] And he's not alone. Other companies have tried the same thing. As we discussed earlier, e-mail can consume employees, but it's not always easy for them to let go of it, even when they know it can be "intexticating." But e-mail is only one communication challenge in this Internet world. A recent survey found that 20 percent of employees at large companies say they contribute regularly to blogs, social networks, wikis, and other Web services.[32] Managers are learning, the hard way sometimes, that all this new technology has created special communication challenges. The two main ones are (1) legal and security issues, and (2) lack of personal interaction.

This is **BIG!**

LEGAL AND SECURITY ISSUES.   Chevron paid $2.2 million to settle a sexual harassment lawsuit stemming from inappropriate jokes being sent by employees over company e-mail. UK firm Norwich Union had to pay £450,000 in an out-of-court settlement after an employee sent an e-mail stating that its competitor, Western Provident Association, was in financial difficulties. Whole Foods Market was investigated by federal regulators and its board after CEO John P. Mackey used a pseudonym to post comments on a blog attacking the company's rival Wild Oats Markets.[33]

Although e-mail, blogs, tweets, and other forms of online communication are quick and easy ways to communicate, managers need to be aware of potential legal problems from inappropriate usage. Electronic information is potentially admissible in court. For instance, during the Enron trial, prosecutors entered into evidence e-mails and other documents they say showed that the defendants defrauded investors. Says one expert, "Today, e-mail and instant messaging are the electronic equivalent of DNA evidence."[34] But legal problems aren't the only issue; security concerns are an issue as well.

A survey addressing outbound e-mail and content security found that 26 percent of the companies surveyed saw their businesses affected by the exposure of sensitive or embarrassing information.[35] Managers need to ensure that confidential information is kept confidential. Employee e-mails and blogs should not communicate—inadvertently or purposely—proprietary information. Corporate computer and e-mail systems should be protected against hackers (people who try to gain unauthorized access to computer systems) and spam (electronic junk mail). These serious issues must be addressed if the benefits of communication technology are to be realized.

PERSONAL INTERACTION.   It may be called social media, but another communication challenge posed by the Internet age we live and work in is the lack of personal interaction.[36] Even when two people are communicating face-to-face, understanding is not always achieved. However, it can be especially challenging to achieve understanding and collaborate on getting work done when communication takes place in a virtual environment. In response, some companies have banned e-mail on certain days, as we saw earlier. Others have simply encouraged employees to collaborate more in person. Yet, sometimes and in some situations, personal interaction isn't physically possible—your colleagues work across the continent or even across the globe. In those instances, real-time collaboration software (such as private workplace wikis,

Internal social media enable these IBM employees in Dublin, Ireland, to communicate and collaborate with colleagues at IBM offices throughout the world. They use IBM Connections, a social network platform, and Sametime 8.5.2, IBM's internal instant messaging system, to share knowledge, improve decision making, and accelerate innovation.

Artur Widak/ZUMA Press/Newscom

blogs, instant messengers, and other types of groupware) may be a better communication choice than sending an e-mail and waiting for a response.[37] Instead of fighting it, some companies are encouraging employees to utilize the power of social networks to collaborate on work and to build strong connections. This trend is especially appealing to younger workers who are comfortable with this communication medium. Some companies have gone as far as to create their own in-house social networks. For instance, employees at Starcom MediaVest Group tap into SMG Connected to find colleague profiles that outline their jobs, list the brands they admire, and describe their values. A company vice president says, "Giving our employees a way to connect over the Internet around the world made sense because they were doing it anyway."[38]

EMPLOYEES AND SOCIAL MEDIA

77 percent say they use social media to connect with colleagues.

35 percent say that social media has damaged a work relationship.

61 percent say that social media has led to new or better work relationships.

32 percent say they use social media to enhance work-related projects or solve problems.[39]

How Does Knowledge Management Affect Communication?

Part of a manager's responsibility in fostering an environment conducive to learning and effective communications is to create learning capabilities throughout the organization. These opportunities should extend from the lowest to the highest levels in all areas. How can managers create such an environment? An important step is recognizing the value of knowledge as a major resource, just like cash, raw materials, or office equipment. To illustrate the value of knowledge, think about how you register for your college classes. Do you talk to others who have had a certain professor? Do you listen to their experiences with this individual and make your decision based on what they have to say (their knowledge about the situation)? If you do, you're tapping into the value of knowledge. But in an organization, just recognizing the value of accumulated knowledge or wisdom isn't enough. Managers must deliberately manage that base of knowledge. **Knowledge management** involves cultivating a learning culture in which organizational members systematically gather knowledge and share it with others in the organization so as to achieve better performance.[40] For instance, accountants and consultants at Ernst & Young document best practices that they've developed, unusual problems they've dealt with, and other work information. This "knowledge" is then shared with all employees through computer-based applications and through community-of-interest teams that meet regularly throughout the company. Many other organizations, including General Electric, Toyota, and Hewlett-Packard, have recognized the importance of knowledge management within a learning organization (see Chapter 6, pp. 182–183). Today's technologies are helping improve knowledge management and facilitating organizational communications and decision making.

What's Involved with Managing the Organization's Knowledge Resources?

Kara Johnson is a materials expert at product design firm IDEO. To make finding the right materials easier, she built a master library of samples linked to a database that explains their properties and manufacturing processes.[41] What Johnson is doing is managing knowledge and making it easier for others at IDEO to learn and benefit from her knowledge. That's what today's managers need to do with the organization's knowledge resources—make it easy for employees to communicate and share their knowledge so they can learn from each other ways to do their jobs more effectively and efficiently. One way organizations can do this is to build online information databases that employees can access. For example, William Wrigley Jr. Co. launched an interactive Web site that allows sales agents to access marketing data and other product information. The sales agents can question company experts about products or search an online knowledge bank. In its first year, Wrigley estimates that the site cut research

knowledge management
Cultivating a learning culture in which organizational members systematically gather knowledge and share it with others

time of the sales force by 15,000 hours, making them more efficient and effective.[42] This one example, among many others, shows how managers can use communication tools to manage this valuable organizational resource called knowledge.

In addition to online information databases for sharing knowledge, companies can create **communities of practice**, which are groups of people who share a concern, a set of problems, or a passion about a topic, and who deepen their knowledge and expertise in that area by interacting on an ongoing basis. To make these communities of practice work, however, it's important to maintain strong human interactions through communication using such essential tools as interactive Web sites, e-mail, and videoconferencing. In addition, these groups face the same communication problems that individuals face—filtering, emotions, defensiveness, overdocumentation, and so forth. However, groups can resolve these issues by focusing on the same suggestions we discussed earlier.

communities of practice
Groups of people who share a concern, a set of problems, or a passion about a topic and who deepen their knowledge and expertise in that area by interacting on an ongoing basis

What Role Does Communication Play in Customer Service?

You've been a customer many times; in fact, you probably find yourself in a customer service encounter several times a day. So what does a customer service encounter have to do with communication? As it turns out, a lot! *What* communication takes place and *how* it takes place can have a significant impact on a customer's satisfaction with the service and the likelihood of being a repeat customer. Managers in service organizations need to make sure that employees who interact with customers are communicating appropriately and effectively with those customers. How? By first recognizing the three components in any service delivery process: the customer, the service organization, and the individual service provider.[43] Each plays a role in whether communication is working. Obviously, managers don't have a lot of control over what or how the customer communicates, but they can influence the other two.

An organization with a strong service culture already values taking care of customers—finding out what their needs are, meeting those needs, and following up to make sure that their needs were met satisfactorily. Each of these activities involves communication, whether face-to-face, by phone or e-mail, or through other channels. In addition, communication is part of the specific customer service strategies the organization pursues. One strategy that many service organizations use is personalization. For instance, at Ritz-Carlton Hotels, customers are provided with more than a clean bed and room. Customers who have stayed at a location previously and indicated that certain items are important to them—such as extra pillows, hot chocolate, or a certain brand of shampoo—will find those items waiting in their room at arrival. The hotel's database allows service to be personalized to customers' expectations. In addition, all employees are asked to communicate information related to service provision. For instance, if a room attendant overhears guests talking about celebrating an anniversary, he or she is supposed to relay the information so something special can be done.[44] Communication plays an important role in the hotel's customer personalization strategy.

Communication also is important to the individual service provider or contact employee. The quality of the interpersonal interaction between the customer and that contact employee does influence customer satisfaction, especially when the service encounter isn't up to expectations.[45] People on the front line involved with those "critical service encounters" are often the first to hear about or notice service failures or breakdowns. They must decide *how* and *what* to communicate during these instances. Their ability to listen actively and communicate appropriately with the customer goes a long way in whether the situation is resolved to the customer's satisfaction or spirals out of control. Another important communication concern for the individual service provider is making sure that he or she has the information needed to deal with customers efficiently and effectively. If the service provider

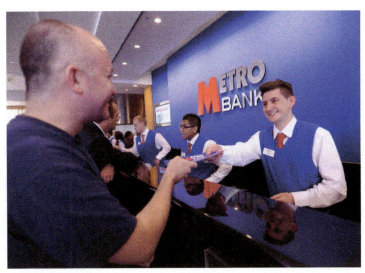

Communication is an important part of the customer service strategy of Metro Bank in London. Recognizing that *how* communication takes place has a great impact on customer satisfaction, the bank expects all employees to greet guests with a smile and a friendly greeting and teaches them how to treat guests with warmth, courtesy, and respect.

Facundo Arrizabalaga/EPA/Newscom

A Question of Ethics

Want to vent about your boss or your company? Now, there are apps to do just that: Yik Yak, Whisper, and Memo, among others.[47] In these apps, users post anonymous messages about their employers. Giving and receiving feedback can be a significant challenge for employees and managers. Yes, providing the opportunity for employees to offer honest feedback about their managers and workplace is commendable. But are apps that provide a platform for employees to do just that, but anonymously, the answer?

If your professor has assigned this, go to the Assignments section of **mymanagementlab.com** *to complete these discussion questions.*

⭐ **Talk About It 5:** How do these apps that let employees post anonymous feedback benefit employees? Managers?

⭐ **Talk About It 6:** What ethical dilemmas might arise because of these apps?

doesn't personally have the information, there should be some way to get the information easily and promptly.[46]

How Can We Get Employee Input and Why Should We?

Nokia's intranet soapbox, known as Blog-Hub, is open to employee bloggers around the world. There, employees have griped about their employer, but rather than shutting it down, Nokia managers want them to "fire away." They feel that Nokia's growth and success can be attributed to a "history of encouraging employees to say whatever's on their minds, with faith that smarter ideas will result."[48]

In today's challenging environment, companies need to get input from their employees. Have you ever worked somewhere that had an employee suggestion box? When an employee had an idea about a new way of doing something—such as reducing costs, improving delivery time, and so forth—it went into the suggestion box, where it usually sat until someone decided to empty the box. Businesspeople frequently joked about the suggestion box and cartoonists lambasted the futility of putting ideas in the employee suggestion box. Unfortunately, this attitude about suggestion boxes still persists in many organizations, but it shouldn't. Managers do business in a world today where you can't afford to ignore such potentially valuable information. Exhibit 13–4 lists some suggestions for letting employees know that their opinions matter.

Why Should Managers Be Concerned with Communicating Ethically?

Fifteen percent of employees say they wish their managers would improve their communication skills, especially in clarity and transparency.[49]

It's particularly important today that a company's communication efforts be ethical. **Ethical communication** "includes all relevant information, is true in every sense, and is not deceptive in any way."[50] On the other hand, unethical communication often distorts the truth or manipulates audiences. What are some ways that companies communicate unethically? It could be by omitting essential information. For instance, not telling employees that an impending merger is going to mean some of them will lose their jobs is unethical. It's also unethical to plagiarize, which is "presenting someone else's words or other creative product as your own."[51] It would also be unethical communication to selectively misquote,

ethical communication
Presented material that contains all relevant information, is true in every sense, and is not deceptive in any way

---

Exhibit 13–4 How to Let Employees Know Their Input Matters

- **Hold town-hall meetings** where information is shared and input solicited.
- **Provide information** about what's going on, good and bad.
- **Invest in training** so that employees see how they impact the customer experience.
- **Analyze problems together**—managers and employees.
- **Make it easy** for employees to give input by setting up different ways for them to do so (online, suggestion box, preprinted cards, and so forth).

Source: Robbins, Stephen P., Coulter, Mary, *Management*, 13th Ed., © 2016, p. 421. Reprinted and electronically reproduced by permission of Pearson Education, Inc., New York, NY.

misrepresent numbers, distort visuals, and fail to respect privacy or information security needs. For instance, although British Petroleum attempted to communicate openly and truthfully about the Gulf Coast oil spill, the public felt that much of the company's communication had some unethical elements to it.

So how can managers encourage ethical communications? One thing is to "establish clear guidelines for ethical behavior, including ethical business communication."[52] In a global survey by the International Association of Business Communicators, 70 percent of communication professionals said their companies clearly define what is considered ethical and unethical behavior.[53] If no clear guidelines exist, it's important to answer the following questions:

- Has the situation been defined fairly and accurately?
- Why is the message being communicated?
- How will the people who may be affected by the message or who receive the message be impacted?
- Does the message help achieve the greatest possible good while minimizing possible harm?
- Will this decision that appears to be ethical now seem so in the future?
- How comfortable are you with your communication effort? What would a person you admire think of it?[54]

Remember that as a manager, you have a responsibility to think through your communication choices and the consequences of those choices. If you always remember that, you're likely to have ethical communication.

MyManagementLab®

Go to **mymanagementlab.com** to complete the problems marked with this icon ⭐.

13 Review

CHAPTER SUMMARY

13-1 Describe what managers need to know about communicating effectively.

Communication is the transfer and understanding of meaning. The communication process consists of seven elements: First, a *sender* or source has a message. A *message* is a purpose to be conveyed. *Encoding* converts a message into symbols. A *channel* provides the medium along which a message travels. *Decoding* happens when the *receiver* retranslates a sender's message. Finally, *feedback* lets the sender know whether the communication was successful. The barriers to effective communication include filtering, emotions, information overload, defensiveness, language, and national culture. Managers can overcome these barriers by using feedback, simplifying language, listening actively, constraining emotions, and watching for nonverbal clues.

13-2 Explain how technology affects managerial communication.

Technology has radically changed the way organizational members communicate. It improves a manager's ability to monitor performance; it gives employees more complete information to make faster decisions; it provides employees more opportunities to collaborate and share information; and it makes it possible for people to be fully accessible, anytime anywhere.

IT has affected managerial communication through the use of networked computer systems and wireless capabilities.

13-3 Discuss contemporary issues in communication.

The two main challenges of managing communication in an Internet world are the legal and security issues and the lack of personal interaction.

Organizations can manage knowledge by making it easy for employees to communicate and share their knowledge so they can learn from each other ways to do their jobs more effectively and efficiently. One way is through online information databases, and another way is through creating communities of practice.

Communicating with customers is an important managerial issue because *what* communication takes place and *how* it takes place can significantly affect a customer's satisfaction with the service and the likelihood of being a repeat customer.

It's important for organizations to get input from their employees. Such potentially valuable information should not be ignored.

Finally, it's important that a company's communication efforts be ethical. Ethical communication can be encouraged through clear guidelines and through answering questions that force a communicator to think through the communication choices made and the consequences of those choices.

DISCUSSION QUESTIONS

13-1 Which type of communication do you think is most effective in a work setting? Why?

13-2 Why isn't effective communication synonymous with *agreement?*

⭐**13-3** Which do you think is more important for a manager: speaking accurately or listening actively? Why?

13-4 "Ineffective communication is the fault of the sender." Do you agree or disagree with this statement? Discuss.

⭐**13-5** Is information technology helping managers communicate more efficiently and effectively? Explain your answer.

13-6 How might a manager use the grapevine to his or her advantage? Support your response.

13-7 Research the characteristics of a good communicator. Write up your findings in a bulleted list report. Be sure to cite your sources.

13-8 Discuss the five contemporary communication issues facing managers.

13-9 For one day, track nonverbal communication that you notice in others. What types did you observe? Was the nonverbal communication always consistent with the verbal communication taking place? Describe.

Writing Assignments

13-10 What purposes does communication serve?

13-11 Describe three barriers to communication and how managers can overcome those barriers.

Management Skill Builder | BEING A GOOD LISTENER

Most of us like to talk more than we like to listen. In fact, it's been facetiously said that listening is just the price we have to pay to get people to allow us to talk. Managers must be effective communicators if they are to do their job well. Part of effective communication is conveying clear and understandable messages. But it's also using active listening skills to accurately decipher others' messages.

★ PERSONAL INVENTORY ASSESSMENT PERSONAL INVENTORY ASSESSMENT

Communication Styles

What type of communication style(s) do you use? Take this PIA and learn more about your communication style so you can become a better communicator.

Skill Basics

Too many people take listening skills for granted. They confuse hearing with listening. Hearing is merely picking up sound vibrations. Listening is making sense out of what we hear; and it requires paying attention, interpreting, and remembering. Active listening is hard work and requires you to "get inside" the speaker's head in order to understand the communication from his or her point of view.

Eight specific behaviors are associated with active listening. You can be more effective at active listening if you use these behaviors.[55]

- *Make eye contact.* We may listen with our ears, but others tend to judge whether we're really listening by looking at our eyes.

- *Exhibit affirmative nods and appropriate facial expressions.* The effective active listener shows interest in what's being said through nonverbal signals.

- *Avoid distracting actions or gestures.* When listening, don't look at your watch, shuffle papers, play with your pencil, or engage in similar distractions. They make the speaker feel that you're bored or uninterested.

- *Ask questions.* The critical listener analyzes what he or she hears and asks questions. This behavior provides clarification, ensures understanding, and assures the speaker that you're really listening.

- *Paraphrase.* Restate *in your own words* what the speaker has said. The effective active listener uses phrases such as "What I hear you saying is…" or "Do you mean…?" Paraphrasing is an excellent control device to check whether you're listening carefully and is also a control for accuracy of understanding.

- *Avoid interrupting the speaker.* Let the speaker complete his or her thoughts before you try to respond. Don't try to second-guess where the speaker's thoughts are going.

- *Don't overtalk.* Most of us would rather speak our own ideas than listen to what others say. Although talking might be more fun and silence might be uncomfortable, you can't talk and listen at the same time. The good active listener recognizes this fact and doesn't overtalk.

- *Make smooth transitions between the roles of speaker and listener.* In most work situations, you're continually shifting back and forth between the roles of speaker and listener. The effective active listener makes transitions smoothly from speaker to listener and back to speaker.

Practicing the Skill

Follow these directions:

Break into groups of two. This exercise is a debate. Person A can choose any contemporary issue. Some examples include business ethics, the value of unions, stiffer college grading policies, gun control, and money as a motivator. Person B then selects a position on this issue. Person A must automatically take the counterposition. The debate is to proceed for 8–10 minutes, with only one catch. Before each speaks, he or she must first summarize, in his or her own words and without notes, what the other has said. If the summary doesn't satisfy the speaker, it must be corrected until it does.

Experiential Exercise

Stone, Hartwick, and Mueller
Talent Management Associates

To: Chris Richards
From: Dana Gibson
Subject: Office gossip

I need some advice, Chris. As you know, my department and all its employees are being transferred from Los Angeles to Dallas. We've had to keep the information "under wraps" for competitive reasons. However, one of my employees asked me point blank yesterday about a rumor she's heard that this move is in the works. I didn't answer her question directly. But I'm afraid that the office grapevine is going to start spreading inaccurate information and then affect morale and productivity. What should I do now? Send me your written response soon (confidential, please!) about what you would do.

This fictionalized company and message were created for educational purposes only, and not meant to reflect positively or negatively on management practices by any company that may share this name.

CASE APPLICATION #1

Social Benefit or Social Disaster?

Tweets. Twittering. Prior to 2006, the only definition we would have known for these words would have involved birds and the sounds they make. Now, practically everyone knows that Twitter is also an online service—with 974 million registered users, 302 million monthly active users, 500 million tweets daily, and 1.6 billion daily search queries—used to trade short messages of 140 characters or less via the Web, cell phones, and other devices.[56] According to its founders (Jack Dorsey, Biz Stone, and Evan Williams), Twitter is many things: a messaging service, a customer-service tool to reach customers, a

The Good and the Bad of TWITTER

real-time search tool, and microblogging. And as the numbers show, it's become quite popular!

One place where Twitter has caught on is the sports world, especially in college sports. For instance, Mike Riley, head football coach at the University of Nebraska, uses Twitter to keep fans informed. He understands the power of instant communication. Coach Hugh Freeze of the University of Mississippi was an early adopter of social media to communicate recruitment news. He's discovered that tweeting is an easy and fun way to communicate quick tidbits of information to fans, alumni boosters, and other interested people who subscribe to Twitter. And it's a convenient way for the football staff and football recruiting prospects to communicate with each other. There are pretty strict rules the NCAA has about contact allowed between potential recruits and coaches, but NCAA rules do allow unlimited direct messaging. However, coaches still are cautious about committing recruiting violations. So, using Twitter to announce their destinations on the recruiting trail, coaches can indirectly share their recruitment news without naming names.[57]

However, many universities and college coaches are monitoring and, in some cases, banning athletes' use of social media. A potentially precarious issue can arise if an athlete tweets some comment that could put the university in a negative light, offend boosters, or possibly violate an NCAA regulation. Here are a couple of tweeting slip-ups: A Western Kentucky running back was suspended after he tweeted critical comments about the team's fans; the NCAA pulled 15 football scholarships after an investigation based on a player's tweet; and a Lehigh University wide receiver was suspended for retweeting a racial slur. We even saw how tweeting backfired at the London Olympics. The first "casualty"—a Greek triple jumper—was banned from the Games over some racially charged tweets. That seems to be good reason for the managers (i.e., coaches and administrators) of these programs to attempt to control the information flow. But is banning the answer? Some analysts say no. They argue that those setting up rules and regulations don't understand what social media is all about and the value

it provides as a marketing and recruiting tool, and they argue that it's necessary to understand First Amendment rights (part of which includes freedom of speech). Rather than banning the use of social media, many universities are hiring companies to monitor athletes' posts. This, however, requires athletes to give access to their accounts, which some call an invasion of privacy. But as time goes on, social media conversations are becoming more common and more expected. By the time the Sochi Olympics rolled around, social media had changed the way Olympics news and views were conveyed.[58]

Discussion Questions

13-13 What are the advantages and drawbacks of universities using social media to communicate with various stakeholders—students, potential students, alumni, donors, etc.?

13-14 Do you think there are more or fewer communication barriers when using social media? Discuss.

13-15 What should managers do to be sure they communicate effectively when using social media?

13-16 Looking at the rules and regulations that universities are establishing, do you think that business organizations should have rules for employees using social media? What types of rules do you think would be necessary? Be as specific as possible.

13-17 What have been your experiences—both positive and negative—with social media? From your experiences, what guidelines could you suggest for managers and organizations?

CASE APPLICATION #2

Banning E-Mail. Banning Voice Mail.

It's estimated that the average corporate user sends and receives some 112 e-mails daily.[59] That's about 14 e-mails per hour, and even if half of those don't require a lot of time and concentration, that level of e-mail volume can be stressful and lead to unproductive time. Once imagined to be a time-saver, has the inbox become a burden? What about voice mails? Are phone messages even necessary for organizational communication? These and other concerns are forcing many organizations to take a closer look at how information is communicated.

What IS necessary for organizational communication?

Several years ago, U.S. Cellular's executive vice president implemented a ban on e-mail every Friday. In his memo announcing the change to employees, he told them to get out and meet the people they work with rather than sending an e-mail. That directive went over with a thud. One employee confronted him saying that Ellison didn't understand how much work had to get done and how much easier it was when using e-mail. Eventually, however, employees were won over. Forced to use the phone, one employee learned that a coworker he thought was across the country was, instead, across the hall. Now, other executives are discovering the benefits of banning e-mail.

Jessica Rovello, cofounder and president of Arkadium, which develops games, has described e-mail as "a form of business attention-deficit disorder." She found herself—and her employees—putting e-mail in the inbox ahead of everything else being worked on. What she decided to do was only check her e-mail four times a day and to turn off her e-mail notification. Another executive, Tim Fry of Weber Shandwick, a global public relations firm, spent a year preparing to "wean" his employees off their e-mail system. His goal: dramatically reduce how much e-mail employees send and receive. His approach started with the firm's interoffice communication system, which became an internal social network, with elements of Facebook, work group collaboration software, and an employee bulletin board. And then there's Thierry Breton, head of Europe's largest IT firm, Atos. He announced a "zero e-mail policy" to be replaced with a service more like Facebook and Twitter combined.

The latest casualty in organizational communication choices is voice mail. Under pressure to cut costs, several large financial institutions, including J.P. Morgan Chase & Co., Citigroup Inc., and Bank of America Corp., are deleting or cutting back on phone voice mail. Some company executives explaining their actions cite the reality that few people use voice mail anymore. The question remains, however, whether customers still expect to be able to maintain voice contact with their financial advisors.

Discussion Questions

⭐ **13-18** What do you think of this? Do you agree that e-mail and voice mail can be unproductive in the workplace?

13-19 Were you surprised at the volume of e-mail an average employee receives daily? What are the challenges of dealing with this volume of e-mail? How much e-mail would you say you receive daily? Has your volume of e-mail increased? Have you had to change your e-mail habits?

⭐ **13-20** What do you think of the e-mail "replacement" some businesses are using—more of a social media tool? In what ways might it be better? Worse?

⭐ **13-21** What role should customer service play in choosing which organizational communication methods to use?

CASE APPLICATION #3

Delivering Bad News

One thing that's always hard for managers/ executives to do is deliver bad news to employees.[60] However, that's all the more reason to be sure to think through those decisions. And not every CEO or executive has done that! Here are some recent examples. See what you think!

Choose your CHANNEL wisely!

- IBM CEO Ginni Rometty, after a disappointing earnings report, publicly reprimanded all the company's 434,000 employees through a five-minute internal video message. She specifically pointed to the sales staff for missing out on several large deals. When the press heard about it, many referred to it as a public spanking.[61]

- AOL's CEO, Tim Armstrong, broke the news about the company's decision to cut employee 401k benefits on television network CNBC. Only after informing Wall Street did Armstrong hold a companywide conference call with employees to discuss the announcement and explain the rationale. Employees complained about "secret" cuts on Twitter and other social media sites. And Armstrong only added fuel to the fire after he tried to blame the change on the new federal health-care law and medical expenses associated with two "distressed babies" of AOL employees.

After a week of bad publicity, Armstrong informed employees through e-mail that he was reversing his decision and apologized for his controversial comments.[62]

- Some 90 workers at Ford Motor Company's Chicago assembly plant got an automated phone message announcing they had just been laid off.[63]

Although each of the managers involved in these communications probably thought they were doing the right thing, the choices they made led to an outcome they weren't expecting.

Discussion Questions

13-22 What's your impression of what took place in these scenarios? Did the managers in each of these scenarios communicate effectively? Why or why not?

13-23 For each of the scenarios, discuss what might have been a better way to communicate the message.

13-24 How could the guidelines to ethical communication have been used in these situations?

13-25 What could other managers learn from this about communication or *mis*communication?

Endnotes

1. D. L. Berchelmann, "You're Doing It Wrong," https://texasceomagazine.com/departments/leadership-feedback/, December 13, 2014.

2. D. K. Berlo, *The Process of Communication* (New York: Holt, Rinehart & Winston, 1960), 30–32.

3. Ibid., 54.

4. See, for instance, "Get the Message: Communication Is Key in Managing Change within Organizations—Yet Ensuring Its Effectiveness at Times of High Concerns Can Be Tricky," *Employee Benefits*, February 2002, 58–60.

5. Ibid., 103.

6. L. R. Birkner and R. K. Birkner, "Communication Feedback: Putting It All Together," *Occupational Hazards*, August 2001, 9.

7. L. Hilton, "They Heard It through the Grapevine," *South Florida Business Journal*, August 18, 2000, 53.

8. From the Past to the Present box based on S. Baker, "Putting a Price on Social Connections," *Business-Week Online*, April 8, 2009; and K. Davis, "Management Communication and the Grapevine," *Harvard Business Review*, September–October 1953, 43–49.

9. L. Talley, "Body Language: Read It or Weep," *HR Magazine*, July 2010, 64–65; and M. Fulfer, "Nonverbal Communication: How to Read What's Plain as the Nose…Or Eyelid…Or Chin…On Their Faces," *Journal of Occupational Excellence* (Spring 2001): 19–38.

10. Ibid.; and T. Fernsler, "The Secrets and Science of Body Language," *Nonprofit World*, 25.

11. P. Mornell, "The Sounds of Silence," *Inc.*, February 2001, 117.

12. A. Warfield, "Do You Speak Body Language?" *Training and Development* (April 2001): 60.

13. S. Begley, "I Can't Think," *Newsweek*, March 7, 2011, 28–33; D. Dean and C. Webb, "Recovering from Information Overload," *McKinsey Quarterly*, Issue 1, 2011, 80–88; and "Information Overload," *Australian Business Intelligence*, April 16, 2002.

14. S. I. Hayakawa, *Language in Thought and Action* (New York: Harcourt Brace Jovanovich, 1949), 292.

15. SmartPulse, "How Prevalent Is the Use of Buzzwords in Your Organization?" Smart Brief on Leadership, www.smartbrief.com/leadership, July 29, 2014.

16. "Jargon Leaves Us Lost for Words," *Australian Business Intelligence*, August 23, 2002; and W. S. Mossberg, "A Guide to the Lingo You'll Want to Learn for Wireless Technology," *Wall Street Journal*, March 28, 2002, B1.

17. "Gobbledygook Begone," *Workforce*, February 2002, 12; and "Business-Speak," *Training and Development* (January 2002): 50–52.

18. J. Langdon, "Differences between Males and Females at Work," *USA Today*, www.usatoday.com (February 5, 2001); J. Manion, "He Said, She Said," *Materials Management in Health Care*, November 1998, 52–62; G. Franzwa and C. Lockhart, "The Social Origins and Maintenance of Gender Communication Styles, Personality Types, and Grid-Group Theory," *Sociological Perspectives* 41, no. 1 (1998): 185–208; and D. Tannen, *Talking From 9 to 5: Women and Men in the Workplace* (New York: Avon Books, 1995).

19. See, for example, M. K. Kozan, "Subcultures and Conflict Management Styles," *Management International Review*, January 2002, 89–106.

20. A. Mehrabian, "Communication without Words," *Psychology Today*, September 1968, 53–55.

21. See also W. L. Adair, T. Okumura, and J. M. Brett, "Negotiation Behavior when Cultures Collide: The United States and Japan," *Journal of Applied Psychology* (June 2001): 371.

22. C. H. Tinsley, "How Negotiators Get to Yes: Predicting the Constellation of Strategies Used across Cultures to Negotiate Conflict," *Journal of Applied Psychology* (August 2001): 583.

23. See, for instance, S. P. Robbins and P. L. Hunsaker, *Training in Interpersonal Skills*, 4th ed. (Upper Saddle River, NJ: Prentice Hall, 2006); M. Young and J. E. Post, "Managing to Communicate, Communicating to Manage: How Leading Companies Communicate with Employees," *Organizational Dynamics*, Summer 1993, 31–43; J. A. DeVito, *The Interpersonal Communication Book*, 6th ed. (New York: HarperCollins, 1992); and A. G. Athos and J. J. Gabarro, *Interpersonal Behavior* (Upper Saddle River, NJ: Prentice Hall, 1978).

24. See, for example, R. R. Panko, *Business Data Networks and Communications*, 4th ed. (Upper Saddle River, NJ: Prentice Hall, 2003).

25. "Virtual Paper Cuts," *Workforce*, July 2000, 16–18.

26. See, for instance, A. Cohen, "Wireless Summer," *Time*, May 29, 2000, 58–65; and K. Hafner, "For the Well Connected, All the World's an Office," *New York Times*, March 30, 2000, D1.

27. S. Kessler, "Slack with Friends, Lovers and Geeks: How the Hot Workplace App Is Getting Personal," http://www.fastcompany.com/3046889/tech-forecast/slack-with-friends-lovers-and-geeks-how-the-hot-workplace-app-is-getting-perso, June 3, 2015; M. Ravindranath, "Slack Takes on Internal Communication for Small Teams and Startups," http://www.washingtonpost.com/business/on-it/slack-takes-on-internal-communication-for-small-teams-and-start-ups/2014/11/01/ab1ad5b4-5eed-11e4-8b9e-2ccdac31a031_story.html, November 2, 2014; and G. Colvin, "Brave New Work: The Office of Tomorrow," *Fortune*, January 16, 2012, 49+.

28. SmartPulse, "Do You Use Emerging Mobile Technology…To Improve Your Communication with Your Employees?" Smart Brief on Exec Tech, www.smartbrief.com/exectech, February 22, 2015.

29. H. Tsukayama, "Everything You Need to Know about Google Glass," www.washingtonpost.com, February 27, 2014.

30. S. Luh, "Pulse Lunches at Asian Citibanks Feed Workers' Morale, Lower Job Turnover," *Wall Street Journal*, May 22, 2001, B11.

31. S. Shellenbager, "Backlash against Email Builds," *Wall Street Journal*, April 29, 2010, D6.

32. H. Green, "The Water Cooler Is Now on the Web," *BusinessWeek*, October 1, 2007, 78–79.

33. The Associated Press, "Whole Foods Chief Apologizes for Posts," *New York Times Online*, July 18, 2007; E. White, J. S. Lublin, and D. Kesmodel, "Executives Get the Blogging Bug," *Wall Street Journal*, July 13, 2007, B1+; C. Alldred, "U.K. Libel Case Slows E-Mail Delivery," *Business Insurance*, August 4, 1997, 51–53; and T. Lewin, "Chevron Settles Sexual Harassment Charges," *New York Times Online*, February 22, 1995.

34. J. Eckberg, "E-mail: Messages Are Evidence," *Cincinnati Enquirer*, www.enquirer.com (July 27, 2004).

35. M. Scott, "Worker E-Mail and Blog Misuse Seen as Growing Risk for Companies," *Workforce Management*, www.workforce.com (July 20, 2007).

36. K. Byron, "Carrying Too Heavy a Load? The Communication and Miscommunication of Emotion by Email," *Academy of Management Review*, April 2008, 309–27.

37. J. Marquez, "Virtual Work Spaces Ease Collaboration, Debate among Scattered Employees," *Workforce Management*, May 22, 2006, 38; and M. Conlin, "E-Mail Is So Five Minutes Ago," *BusinessWeek*, November 28, 2005, 111–12.

38. H. Green, "The Water Cooler Is Now on the Web"; E. Frauenheim, "Starbucks Employees Carve Out Own 'Space,'" *Workforce Management*, October 22, 2007, 32; and S. H. Wildstrom, "Harnessing Social Networks," *BusinessWeek*, April 23, 2007, 20.

39. S. Castellano, "The Social Media Skills Gap," *T&D*, July 2014, 14.

40. J. S. Brown and P. Duguid, "Balancing Act: How to Capture Knowledge without Killing It," *Harvard Business Review*, May–June 2000, 73–80; and J. Torsilieri and C. Lucier, "How to Change the World," *Strategy and Business*, October 2000, 17–20.

41. J. Scanlon, "Woman of Substance," *Wired*, July 2002, 27.

42. H. Dolezalek, "Collaborating in Cyberspace," *Training* (April 2003): 33.

43. B. A. Gutek, M. Groth, and B. Cherry, "Achieving Service Success through Relationship and Enhanced Encounters," *Academy of Management Executive*, November 2002, 132–44.

44. R. C. Ford and C. P. Heaton, "Lessons from Hospitality That Can Serve Anyone," *Organizational Dynamics*, Summer 2001, 30–47.

45. M. J. Bitner, B. H. Booms, and L. A. Mohr, "Critical Service Encounters: The Employee's Viewpoint," *Journal of Marketing* (October 1994): 95–106.

46. S. D. Pugh, J. Dietz, J. W. Wiley, and S. M. Brooks, "Driving Service Effectiveness through Employee-Customer Linkages," *Academy of Management Executive*, November 2002, 73–84.

47. J. Mahler, "Who Spewed That Abuse? Anonymous Yik Yak App Isn't Telling," *New York Times Online*, March 8, 2015; L. Gellman, "App Lets Workers Vent Anonymously," *Wall Street Journal*, January 21, 2015, B7; and K. Whitehouse, "Workplace Gossip App Draws Ire from Firms," *USA Today*, January 19, 2015, 3B.

48. J. Ewing, "Nokia: Bring on the Employee Rants," *BusinessWeek*, June 22, 2009, 50.

49. S. Vozza, "5 Things Your Employees Wish They Could Tell You," http://www.fastcompany.com/3045282/hit-the-ground-running/5-things-your-employees-wish-they-could-tell-you, April 27, 2015.

50. J. V. Thill and C. L. Bovee, *Excellence in Business Communication*, 9th ed. (Upper Saddle River, NJ: Prentice Hall, 2011), 24–25.

51. Ibid.

52. Ibid.

53. Ibid.

54. Ibid.

55. Based on K. J. Murphy, *Effective Listening* (New York: Bantam Books, 1987); and T. Drollinger, L. B. Comer, and P. T. Warrington, "Development and Validation of the Active Empathetic Listening Scale," *Psychology & Marketing*, February 2006, 161–80.

56. Twitter Usage, Company Facts, https://about.twitter.com/company, March 31, 2015; E. Sherman, "Many Twitter Users

Don't Tweet, Finds Report," http://www.cbsnews.com/news/many-twitter-users-dont-tweet-finds-report/, April 14, 2014; R. W. Ahrens, "Tweets Per Day," *USA Today,* March 20, 2013, 2A; M. Lopresti, "Elimination by Twitter," *USA Today,* July 26, 2012, 1C; K. Paulson, "College Athlete Tweet Ban? Free Speech Sacks That Idea," *USA Today,* April 16, 2012, 9A; L. East, "Les Miles' Tweets Entertain CWS Fans," *theadvocate.com/sports,* July 12, 2012; P. Thamel, "Tracking Twitter, Raising Red Flags," *New York Times Online,* March 30, 2012; L. Dugan, "Twitter to Surpass 500 Million Registered Users on Wednesday," *www.mediabistro .com,* February 21, 2012; C. Ho, "Companies Tracking College Athletes' Tweets, Facebook Posts Go After Local Universities," *Washington Post Online,* October 16, 2011; D. Rovell, "Coaches Ban of Twitter Proves College Sports Isn't about Education," *CNBC Sports Business Online,* August 8, 2011; Staff of Corporate Executive Board, "Corporate Confidential: How Twitter Changes

Everything," *BusinessWeek Online,* September 4, 2009; S. Johnson, "How Twitter Will Change the Way We Live," *Time,* June 15, 2009, 30–37; J. Swartz, "A World That's All a-Twitter," *USA Today,* May 26, 2009, 1B+; and K. Whiteside, "College Coaches Are Chirping about Twitter!" *USA Today,* April 29, 2009, 1C+.

57. G. Schroeder, "Coaches Using Twitter from Recruiting Trail," *USA Today,* February 2, 2015, 10C.

58. K. Whiteside, "Sochi-al Media's Golden Moment," *USA Today,* February 11, 2014, 1A+.

59. M. Nalsky, "How Quitting Email Helped My Company Communicate Better," http://thenextweb .com/entrepreneur/2014/11/09/ quitting-email-helped-company-team-communicate-better/, November 9, 2014; M. Prokopeak, "What If Email Got Pantsed?" www.workforce .com, October 14, 2013; C. Brown, A. Killick, and K. Renaud, "To Reduce E-mail, Start at the Top," *Harvard Business Review,* September 2013, 26; J. Wortham, "When E-Mail Turns from Delight to Deluge," *New York Times Online,* February

9, 2013; T. Provost, "Long Live E-Mail," *CFO,* January/February 2013, 29; M. V. Rafter, "Too Much Email on the Menu? Here Are Five Tips to Curb Company Consumption," *Workforce Management Online,* April 24, 2012; M. V. Rafter, "If Tim Fry Has His Way, He'll Eradicate Email for Good," *Workforce Management Online,* April 24, 2012; M. A. Field, "Turning Off Email, Turning Up Productivity," *Workforce Management Online,* February 29, 2012; "Internet 2011 in Numbers," *royalpingdom. com,* January 17, 2012; "Should Workplaces Curtail Email?" *New York Times Online,* December 7, 2011; W. Powers, "The Phony 'Zero Email' Alarm," *New York Times Online,* December 6, 2011; L. Suarez, "What We Would Miss," *New York Times Online,* December 5, 2011; P. Duncan, "Break Bad Habits," *New York Times Online,* December 5, 2011; N. Carr, "Put the Cost Back in Communication," *New York Times Online,* December 5, 2011; and P. Allen, "One of the Biggest Information Technology Companies in the World to Abolish E-mails," www .dailymail.com, November 30, 2011.

60. A. Gallo, "How to Deliver Bad News to Your Employees," https:// hbr.org/2015/03/how-to-deliver-bad-news-to-your-employees, March 30, 2015; and C. Suddath, "I'm Sorry to Have to Say This," *Bloomberg BusinessWeek,* May 13, 2013, 80.

61. C. Suddath, "I'm Sorry to Have to Say This"; S. E. Ante, "IBM's Chief to Employees: Think Fast, Move Faster," *Wall Street Journal Online,* April 24, 2013.

62. G. Kratsas, "AOL Firestorm Grows Despite CEO Apology," *USA Today,* February 10, 2014, 1B; N. Singer, "Revelations by AOL Boss Raise Fears over Privacy," *New York Times Online,* February 10, 2014; L. Kaufman, "Facing Criticism after Remarks, AOL Chief Reverses 401(k) Changes," *New York Times Online,* February 9, 2014; and A.-M. Squeo, "AOL 401K Blow-Up: Worst Way to Deliver Bad News to Employees," www.forbes.com, February 9, 2014.

63. M. Martinez, "Ford Lays Off 90 at Chicago Assembly with Robocall," www.detroitnews.com, November 4, 2014.

14

Management Myth

Myth

Myth

A lack of employee turnover is a sign of a good manager.

Management **DEBUNKED?** Myth

While high employee turnover is almost always dysfunctional, low turnover is not necessarily the best goal. An absence of turnover often can mean a complacent manager, one who's willing to accept mediocre employee performance. In an effective organizational control system, managers are encouraged to identify and remove marginal employees. Low levels of employee turnover can be functional only *if* the right people—those who are the weakest performers—are the ones leaving.

CONTROLLING

is the final step in the management process. Managers must monitor whether goals that were established as part of the planning process are being accomplished efficiently and effectively. That's what they do when they control. Appropriate controls can help managers look for specific performance gaps and areas for improvement. Things don't always go as planned. But that's why controlling is so important! In this chapter, we'll look at the fundamental elements of controlling, including the control process, the types of controls that managers can use, and contemporary issues in control. ●

Learning Outcomes

14-1 Explain the nature and importance of control. p. 423

14-2 Describe the three steps in the control process. p. 425

14-3 Discuss the types of controls organizations and managers use. p. 430

14-4 Discuss contemporary issues in control. p. 436

What Is Control and Why Is It Important?

14-1 Explain the nature and importance of control.

"Bailout" was the magic word that cost Domino's Pizza 11,000 free pizzas. The company had prepared an Internet coupon for an ad campaign that was considered but not approved. However, when someone apparently typed "bailout" into a Domino's promotional code window and found it was good for a free medium pizza, the word spread like wildfire on the Web. Somewhere, somehow, a lack of control cost the company big time.[1]

control
Management function that involves monitoring activities to ensure that they're being accomplished as planned and correcting any significant deviations

What Is Control?

> How do you know a control system is effective? Look at whether **goals are being achieved**!

Control is the management function that involves monitoring activities to ensure that they're being accomplished as planned and correcting any significant deviations. Managers can't really know whether their units are performing properly until they've evaluated what activities have been done and have compared the actual performance with the desired standard. An effective control system ensures that activities are completed in ways that lead to the attainment of the organization's goals. The effectiveness of a control system is determined by how well it facilitates goal achievement. The more a control system helps managers achieve their organization's goals, the better it is.

Why Is Control Important?

- A press operator at the Denver Mint noticed a flaw—an extra up leaf or an extra down leaf—on Wisconsin state quarters being pressed at one of his five press machines. He stopped the machine and left for a meal break. When he returned, he saw the machine running and assumed that someone had changed the die in the machine. However, after a routine inspection, the machine operator realized the die had not been changed. The faulty press had likely been running for over an hour and thousands of the flawed coins were now commingled with unblemished quarters. As many as 50,000 of the faulty coins entered circulation, setting off a coin collector buying frenzy.[3]
- At least 4 million records of federal government employees' personal data held by the Office of Personnel Management were hacked. Hackers appeared to be looking for Social Security numbers and other personal information.[4]
- After an above-ground radioactive release at a nuclear waste storage vault in New Mexico, a report blamed managers who failed to "understand and control the risks."[5]
- McDonald's Japan has apologized to customers and vowed to better control product safety after objects including a tooth and plastic were found in food.[6]
- After a number of negatively publicized incidents on its cruise ships, Carnival Corporation accelerated its schedule of maintenance and other renovations.[7]
- A technical error on Walmart's Web site led to certain products showing unbelievably low prices (for instance, a

A Question of Ethics

It's called the "walk of shame." Marching employees through stores in handcuffs to discourage theft and other infractions.[2] At a Target store in Pasadena, California, an employee who was subjected to the walk of shame was released and never charged with a crime. However, the emotional distress of the incident led to the individual later committing suicide. After the incident went public, other Target employees in other stores told of their experiences either witnessing or experiencing the walk of shame. Target Corporation denies that it has any such policy. The company also did not elaborate on what guidance it gives managers on how to handle suspected employee theft or other work violations that could potentially involve law enforcement.

*If your professor has assigned this, go to the Assignments section of **mymanagementlab.com** to complete these discussion questions.*

⭐ **Talk About It 1:** What do you think of this "supposed" practice—positive and negative? Discuss.

⭐ **Talk About It 2:** How could an organization make sure it's being ethical in controlling employees' behaviors *and* still achieving organizational goals?

treadmill for $33). The error was not the result of hacking, but rather an internal glitch, and was quickly corrected.[8]

- Clothing return fraud costs U.S. retailers almost $9 billion annually. To combat this, many high-end retailers have started placing large black plastic tags in highly visible places on dresses and other pricey clothing items.[9]
- No fast-food chain wants its employees doing gross stuff behind the scenes, but social media photos and videos of a Taco Bell employee licking a stack of taco shells, a Wendy's employee bending down under a Frosty machine with mouth wide open gobbling the treat, or a Domino's Pizza employee performing vulgar and unsanitary actions while preparing food have all shown up online.[10]

> ## 77 percent of executives say that the biggest threat to their organizations comes from within.[11]

Can you see now why controlling is such an important managerial function? Planning can be done, an organizational structure created to facilitate efficient achievement of goals, and employees motivated through effective leadership. But there's no assurance that activities are going as planned and that the goals employees and managers are working toward are, in fact, being attained. Control is important, therefore, because it's the only way that managers know whether organizational goals are being met and, if not, the reasons why. The value of the control function can be seen in three specific areas:

1. **Planning.**   In Chapter 5, we described goals, which provide specific direction to employees and managers, as the foundation of planning. However, just stating goals or having employees accept goals doesn't guarantee that the necessary actions to accomplish those goals have been taken. As the old saying goes, "The best-laid plans often go awry." The effective manager follows up to ensure that what employees are supposed to do is, in fact, being done and goals are being achieved. As the final step in the management process, controlling provides the critical link back to planning. (See Exhibit 14–1.) If managers didn't control, they'd have no way of knowing whether goals and plans were being achieved and what future actions to take.
2. **Empowering employees.**   The second reason controlling is important is because of employee empowerment. Many managers are reluctant to empower their employees because

Exhibit 14–1 Planning–Controlling Link

they fear something will go wrong for which they would be held responsible. But an effective control system can provide information and feedback on employee performance and minimize the chance of potential problems.

3. **Protecting the workplace.** The final reason that managers control is to protect the organization and its assets.[12] Organizations face threats from natural disasters, financial pressures and scandals, workplace violence, supply chain disruptions, security breaches, and even possible terrorist attacks. Managers must protect organizational assets in the event that any of these should happen. Comprehensive controls and backup plans will help minimize work disruptions.

Richard Graulich/ZUMA Press/Corbis

John Jamason, media and public information manager, talks to employees working in the social media monitoring room at the Palm Beach County Emergency Operations Center. Social media such as Facebook and Twitter help the center track and monitor information during storm emergencies to get help to people in need.

What Takes Place as Managers Control?

14-2 Describe the three steps in the control process.

When Maggine Fuentes joined Ohio-based Core Systems as HR manager, she knew that her top priority was reducing the number of employee injuries, which was well above the industry average. The high frequency and severity of the company's injury rates not only affected employee morale but also resulted in lost workdays and affected the bottom line.[13] Fuentes relied on the control process to turn this situation around.

The **control process** is a three-step process of (1) measuring actual performance, (2) comparing actual performance against a standard, and (3) taking managerial action to correct deviations or to address inadequate standards. (See Exhibit 14–2.) The control process assumes that performance standards already exist, and they do. They're the specific goals created during the planning process.

Specific goals ARE the performance standards.

1 What Is Measuring?

To determine actual performance, a manager must first get information about it. Thus, the first step in control is measuring.

HOW DO MANAGERS MEASURE? Four common sources of information frequently used to measure actual performance include personal observation, statistical reports, oral reports, and written reports. Each has its own particular strengths and weaknesses, but using a combination of them increases both the number of input sources and the probability of receiving reliable information.

Personal observation provides firsthand, intimate knowledge of the actual activity—information that is not filtered through others. It permits intensive coverage because minor as well as major performance activities can be observed, and it provides opportunities for the manager to read between the lines. **Management by walking around (MBWA)** is a phrase used to describe when a manager is out in the work area, interacting directly with employees

control process
A three-step process of measuring actual performance, comparing actual performance against a standard, and taking managerial action to correct deviations

management by walking around (MBWA)
When a manager is out in the work area interacting with employees

Exhibit 14–2 The Control Process

Greeting customers with a handshake, a smile, and a warm welcome is a practice Apple stores adopted from Ritz-Carlton, the luxury hotel chain known as the gold standard of customer service. Apple benchmarked with Ritz-Carlton because it wants its employees to excel at customer service that leads to customer loyalty.

and exchanging information about what's going on. Management by walking around can pick up factual omissions, facial expressions, and tones of voice that may be missed by other sources. Unfortunately, in a time when quantitative information suggests objectivity, personal observation is often considered an inferior information source. It is subject to perceptual biases; what one manager sees, another might not. Personal observation also consumes a good deal of time. Finally, this method suffers from obtrusiveness. Employees might interpret a manager's overt observation as a lack of confidence or a sign of mistrust.

The widespread use of computers has led managers to rely increasingly on *statistical reports* for measuring actual performance. This measuring device, however, isn't limited to computer outputs. It also includes graphs, bar charts, and numerical displays of any form that managers can use for assessing performance. Although statistical information is easy to visualize and effective for showing relationships, it provides limited information about an activity. Statistics report on only a few key areas and may often ignore other important, often subjective, factors.

Information can also be acquired through *oral reports*—that is, through conferences, meetings, one-to-one conversations, or telephone calls. In employee-oriented organizations where employees work closely together, this approach may

Nati Harnik/AP Images

be the best way to keep tabs on work performance. For instance, at the Ken Blanchard Companies in Escondido, California, managers are expected to hold one-on-one meetings with each of their employees at least once every two weeks.[14] The advantages and disadvantages of this method of measuring performance are similar to those of personal observation. Although the information is filtered, it is fast, allows for feedback, and permits expression and tone of voice as well as words themselves to convey meaning. Historically, one of the major drawbacks of oral reports has been the problem of documenting information for later reference. However, our technological capabilities have progressed in the past couple of decades to the point where oral reports can be efficiently taped and become as permanent as if they were written.

Actual performance may also be measured by *written reports*. Like statistical reports, they are slower yet more formal than firsthand or secondhand oral measures. This formality also often gives them greater comprehensiveness and conciseness than found in oral reports. In addition, written reports are usually easy to catalog and reference.

Given the varied advantages and disadvantages of each of these four measurement techniques, managers should use all four for comprehensive control efforts.

> Seventy-three percent of employers have taken efforts to address productivity killers at work.[15]

WHAT DO MANAGERS MEASURE? *What* managers measure is probably *more critical* to the control process than *how* they measure. Why? The selection of the wrong criteria can result in serious dysfunctional consequences. Besides, what we measure determines, to a great extent, what people in the organization will attempt to excel at.[16] For example, assume that your instructor has required a total of 10 writing assignments from the exercises at the end of each textbook chapter. But in the grade computation section of the syllabus, you notice that these assignments are not scored. In fact, when you ask your professor about this, she replies that these writing assignments are for your own enlightenment and do not affect your grade for the course; grades are solely a function of how well you perform on the three exams. We predict that you would, not surprisingly, exert most, if not all, of your effort toward doing well on the three exams.

Some control criteria are applicable to any management situation. For instance, because all managers, by definition, direct the activities of others, *criteria such as employee satisfaction or turnover and absenteeism rates* can be measured. Also, most managers have budgets for their area of responsibility set in monetary units (dollars, pounds, francs, lire, and so on). *Keeping costs within budget* is, therefore, a fairly common control measure. However, any comprehensive control system needs to recognize the diversity of activities among managers. For example, a production manager in a paper tablet manufacturing plant might use measures of the quantity of tablets produced per day, tablets produced per labor hour, scrap tablet rate, or percentage of rejects returned by customers. On the other hand, the manager of an administrative unit in a government agency might use number of document pages produced per day, number of orders processed per hour, or average time required to process service calls. Marketing managers often use measures such as percent of market held, number of customer visits per salesperson, or number of customer impressions per advertising medium.

As you might imagine, some activities are more difficult to measure in quantifiable terms. It is more difficult, for instance, for a manager to measure the performance of a medical researcher or a middle school counselor than of a person who sells life insurance. But most activities can be broken down into objective segments that allow for measurement. The manager needs to determine what value a person, department, or unit contributes to the organization and then convert the contribution into standards.

Most jobs and activities can be expressed in tangible and measurable terms. When a performance indicator cannot be stated in quantifiable terms, managers should look for and use subjective measures. Certainly, subjective measures have significant limitations. Still,

◄◄◄ From the Past to the Present ►►►

We introduced benchmarking in the planning chapter (Chapter 5) as a way for organizations to promote quality.[17] Not surprisingly, since planning and controlling are so closely linked, it also has implications for control. Benchmarking has been a highly utilized management tool. Although Xerox is often credited with the first widespread benchmarking effort in the United States, the practice can actually be traced back much further.

The benefits of benchmarking have long been recognized in the manufacturing industry. At the Midvale Steel Company plant where he was employed, Frederick W. Taylor (of scientific management fame) used concepts of benchmarking to find the "one best way" to perform a job and to find the best worker to perform the job. Even Henry Ford recognized the benefits. Based on the techniques used at Chicago slaughterhouses where carcasses were hung from hooks mounted on a monorail, with each man performing his job and then pushing the carcass to the next work station, Ford's assembly line used the same concept for producing cars, beginning in 1913. "The idea that revolutionized manufacturing was imported from another industry."

Benchmarking: How do we measure up?

Today, managers in diverse industries such as health care, education, and financial services are discovering what manufacturers have long recognized—the benefits of benchmarking. For instance, the American Medical Association developed more than 100 standard measures of performance to improve medical care. Carlos Ghosn, CEO of Nissan, benchmarked Walmart's operations in purchasing, transportation, and logistics. At its most basic, benchmarking means learning from others. However, as a tool for monitoring and measuring organizational and work performance, benchmarking can be used to identify specific performance gaps and potential areas of improvement.

*If your professor has assigned this, go to the Assignments section of **mymanagementlab.com** to complete these discussion questions.*

⭐ **Talk About It 3:** What are the benefits of benchmarking?

⭐ **Talk About It 4:** What are the challenges in doing it?

they are better than having no standards at all and ignoring the control function. If an activity is important, the excuse that it's difficult to measure is inadequate. In such cases, managers should use subjective performance criteria. Of course, any analysis or decisions made on the basis of subjective criteria should recognize the limitations of the data.

2 How Do Managers Compare Actual Performance to Planned Goals?

The comparing step determines the variation between actual performance and the standard. Although some variation in performance can be expected in all activities, it's critical to determine an acceptable **range of variation** (see Exhibit 14–3). Deviations outside this range need attention. Let's work through an example.

Chris Tanner is a sales manager for Green Earth Gardening Supply, a distributor of specialty plants and seeds in the Pacific Northwest. Chris prepares a report during the first week of each month that describes sales for the previous month, classified by product line. Exhibit 14–4 displays both the sales goals (standard) and actual sales figures for the month of June. After looking at the numbers, should Chris be concerned? Sales were a bit higher than originally targeted, but does that mean there were no significant deviations? That depends on what Chris thinks is *significant*—that is, outside the acceptable range of variation. Even though overall performance was generally quite favorable, some product lines need closer scrutiny. For instance, if sales of heirloom seeds, flowering bulbs, and annual flowers continue to be over what was expected, Chris might need to order more product from nurseries to meet customer demand. Because sales of vegetable plants were 15 percent below goal, Chris may need to run a special on them. As this example shows, both overvariance and undervariance may require managerial attention, which is the third step in the control process.

range of variation
The acceptable parameters of variance between actual performance and a standard

Exhibit 14–3 Acceptable Range of Variation

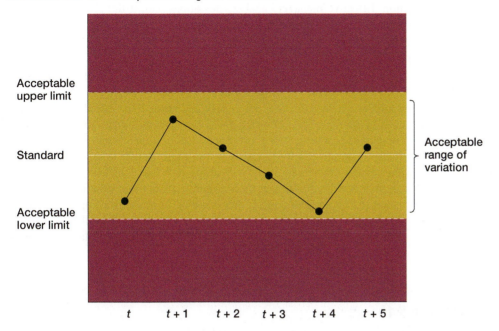

3 What Managerial Action Can Be Taken?

Managers can choose among **three possible courses of action**:

- Do nothing (self-explanatory)
- Correct actual performance
- Revise the standards

HOW DO YOU CORRECT ACTUAL PERFORMANCE?   Depending on what the problem is, a manager could take different corrective actions. For instance, if unsatisfactory work is the reason for performance variations, the manager could correct it through training programs, disciplinary action, changes in compensation practices, and so forth. One decision that a manager must make is whether to take **immediate corrective action**, which corrects problems at once to get performance back on track, or to use **basic corrective action**, which looks at how and why performance deviated before correcting the source of deviation. It's not unusual for managers to rationalize that they don't have time to find the source of a

immediate corrective action
Corrective action that addresses problems at once to get performance back on track

basic corrective action
Corrective action that looks at how and why performance deviated before correcting the source of deviation

Exhibit 14–4 Example of Determining Significant Variation: Green Earth Gardening Supply—June Sales

PRODUCT	STANDARD	ACTUAL	OVER (UNDER)
Vegetable plants	1,075	913	(612)
Perennial flowers	630	634	4
Annual flowers	800	912	112
Herbs	160	140	(20)
Flowering bulbs	170	286	116
Flowering bushes	225	220	(5)
Heirloom seeds	540	672	132
Total	3,600	3,777	177

problem (basic corrective action) and continue to perpetually "put out fires" with immediate corrective action. Effective managers analyze deviations and, if the benefits justify it, take the time to pinpoint and correct the causes of variance.

HOW DO YOU REVISE THE STANDARD? It's possible that the variance was a result of an unrealistic standard—too low or too high a goal. In such cases, it's the standard that needs corrective action, not the performance. If performance consistently exceeds the goal, then a manager should look at whether the goal is too easy and needs to be raised. On the other hand, managers must be cautious about revising a standard downward. It's natural to blame the goal when an employee or a team falls short. For instance, students who get a low score on a test often attack the grade cutoff standards as too high. Rather than accept the fact that their performance was inadequate, they will argue that the standards are unreasonable. Likewise, salespeople who don't meet their monthly quota often want to blame what they think is an unrealistic quota. The point is that when performance isn't up to par, don't immediately blame the goal or standard. If you believe the standard is realistic, fair, and achievable, tell employees that you expect future work to improve, and then take the necessary corrective action to help make that happen.

> ⭐ **Watch It 1!**
>
> If your professor has assigned this, go to the Assignments section of **mymanagementlab.com** to complete the video exercise titled *CH2MHill: Foundations of Control*.

What Should Managers Control?

14-3 Discuss the types of controls organizations and managers use.

Cost efficiency. The length of time customers are kept on hold. Customers being satisfied with the service provided. These are just a few of the important performance indicators that executives in the intensely competitive call-center service industry measure. To make good decisions, managers in this industry want and need this type of information so they can control work performance.

How do managers know what to control? In this section, we're first going to look at the decision of *what* to control in terms of when control takes place. Then, we're going to discuss some different areas in which managers might choose to establish controls.

When Does Control Take Place?

Management can implement controls *before* an activity commences, *during* the activity, or *after* the activity has been completed. The first type is called feedforward control, the second is concurrent control, and the last is feedback control (see Exhibit 14–5).

Exhibit 14–5 "When" Does Control Take Place?

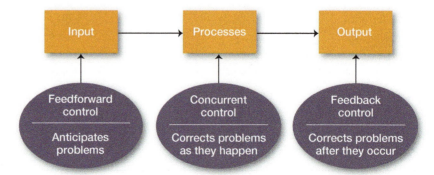

WHAT IS FEEDFORWARD CONTROL? The most desirable type of control—feedforward control—prevents problems because it takes place before the actual activity.[18] For instance, when McDonald's began doing business in Moscow, it sent company quality control experts to help Russian farmers learn techniques for growing high-quality potatoes and to help bakers learn processes for baking high-quality breads. Why? McDonald's demands consistent product quality no matter the geographical location. They want french fries in Moscow to taste like those in Omaha. Still another example of feedforward control is the scheduled preventive maintenance programs on aircraft done by the major airlines. These schedules are designed to detect and hopefully to prevent structural damage that might lead to an accident.

Elaine Thompson/AP Images

The key to feedforward controls is taking managerial action *before* a problem occurs. That way, problems can be prevented rather than having to correct them after any damage—poor-quality products, lost customers, lost revenue, etc.—has already been done. However, these controls require timely and accurate information that isn't always easy to get. Thus, managers frequently end up using the other two types of control.

Microsoft uses concurrent control to track its energy usage. Shown here at its operations center, control technician Ray Nichols monitors real-time data on heating, cooling, and other systems in the company's buildings that will help Microsoft achieve its goals of improving its carbon footprint and reducing its impact on the environment.

WHEN IS CONCURRENT CONTROL USED? Concurrent control, as its name implies, takes place while a work activity is in progress. For instance, the director of business product management at Google and his team keep a watchful eye on one of Google's most profitable businesses—online ads. They watch "the number of searches and clicks, the rate at which users click on ads, the revenue this generates—everything is tracked hour by hour, compared with the data from a week earlier and charted."[19] If they see something that's not working particularly well, they fine-tune it.

> Fifty-five percent of employees say that micromanaging decreases their productivity.[20]

Technical equipment (such as computers and computerized machine controls) can be designed to include concurrent controls. For example, you've probably experienced this with word-processing software that alerts you to a misspelled word or incorrect grammatical usage. Also, many organizational quality programs rely on concurrent controls to inform workers whether their work output is of sufficient quality to meet standards.

The best-known form of concurrent control, however, is direct supervision. For example, Nvidia's CEO Jen-Hsun Huang had his office cubicle torn down and replaced with a conference table so he's now available to employees at all times to discuss what's going on.[21] Even GE's CEO, Jeff Immelt, spends 60 percent of his workweek on the road talking to employees and visiting the company's numerous locations.[22] All managers can benefit from using concurrent control because they can correct problems before they become too costly. MBWA, which we described earlier in this chapter, is a great way for managers to do this.

WHY IS FEEDBACK CONTROL SO POPULAR? The most popular type of control relies on feedback. In feedback control, the control takes place *after* the activity is done. For instance, remember our earlier Denver Mint example. The flawed Wisconsin quarters were discovered with feedback control. The damage had already occurred even though the organization corrected the problem once it was discovered. And that's the major problem with this type of control. By the time a manager has the information, the problems have already occurred, leading to waste or damage. However, in many work areas—the financial area being one example—feedback is the only viable type of control. (Continued on p. 435)

feedforward control
Control that takes place before a work activity is done

concurrent control
Control that takes place while a work activity is in progress

feedback control
Control that takes place after a work activity is done

KEEPING TRACK:
What Gets Controlled?

Countless activities are taking place in different organizational locations and functional areas!

1 Keeping Track of an Organization's Finances

Want to earn a profit?
You need financial controls!

Traditional financial controls include:

- **Ratio analysis**. (See Exhibit 14–6.) Ratios are calculated using selected information from the organization's balance sheet and income statement.

Ekaterina Semenova/Fotolia

Exhibit 14–6 Popular Financial Ratios

OBJECTIVE	RATIO	CALCULATION	MEANING
Liquidity ratios: measure an organization's ability to meet its current debt obligations	Current ratio	$\dfrac{\text{Current assets}}{\text{Current liabilities}}$	Tests the organization's ability to meet short-term obligations
	Acid test	$\dfrac{\text{Current assets} - \text{Inventories}}{\text{Current liabilities}}$	Tests liquidity more accurately when inventories turn over slowly or are difficult to sell
Leverage ratios: examine the organization's use of debt to finance its assets and whether it's able to meet the interest payments on the debt	Debt to assets	$\dfrac{\text{Total debt}}{\text{Total assets}}$	The higher the ratio, the more leveraged the organization
	Times interest earned	$\dfrac{\text{Profits before interest and taxes}}{\text{Total interest charges}}$	Measures how many times the organization is able to cover its interest expenses
Activity ratios: assess how efficiently a company is using its assets	Inventory turnover	$\dfrac{\text{Sales}}{\text{Inventory}}$	The higher the ratio, the more efficiently inventory assets are being used
	Total asset turnover	$\dfrac{\text{Sales}}{\text{Total assets}}$	The fewer assets used to achieve a given level of sales, the more efficiently management is using the organization's total assets
Profitability ratios: measure how efficiently and effectively the company is using its assets to generate profits	Profit margin on sales	$\dfrac{\text{Net profit after taxes}}{\text{Total sales}}$	Identifies the profits that are being generated
	Return on investment	$\dfrac{\text{Net profit after taxes}}{\text{Total assets}}$	Measures the efficiency of assets to generate profits

- **Budget analysis.** Budgets are used for both planning and controlling.

  - **Planning tool**: indicates which work activities are important and what and how much resources should be allocated to those activities.

  - **Controlling tool**: provides managers with quantitative standards against which to measure and compare resource consumption. Significant deviations require action and a manager to examine what has happened and why and then take necessary action.

2 Keeping Track of Organization's Information

A **Information**—*a critical tool for controlling other organizational activities*

WHY Managers need **RIGHT INFORMATION** at the **RIGHT TIME** and in the **RIGHT AMOUNT** to help them monitor and measure organizational activities:

- about what is happening within their area of responsibility.

- about the standards in order to be able to compare actual performance with the standard.

- to help them determine if deviations are acceptable.

- to help them develop appropriate courses of action.

Morena/Shutterstock

Information is important!

HOW A **Management Information System (MIS)**

Dusit/Shutterstock

- Can be manual or computer-based, although most organizational MIS are computer-supported applications.

- System in MIS implies order, arrangement, and purpose.

- Focuses specifically on providing managers with information (processed and analyzed data), not merely data (raw, unanalyzed facts).

management information system (MIS)
A system used to provide management with needed information on a regular basis

B Information—*an organizational resource that needs controlling*

> **In 2014**—79,700 reported security incidents and 2,122 confirmed data breaches.[23]

- Information is critically important to everything an organization does—that information needs to be protected.

  - **Controls:** data encryption, system firewalls, data backups, and other techniques.[24]

  - Look for problems in places that might not even have been considered, like search engines.

  - Equipment such as laptop computers, tablets, and even RFID (radio-frequency identification) tags are vulnerable to viruses and hacking.

  - Monitor information controls regularly to ensure that all possible precautions are in place to protect important information.

Bedrin/Shutterstock

3 Keeping Track of Employee Performance

- Are employees doing their jobs as planned and meeting goals that have been set?

- If not, employee counseling or employee discipline may be needed.
  See p. 216 in Chapter 7.

> Over 81 percent of managers say they don't do very well at giving difficult feedback.[25]

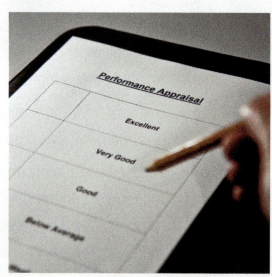
Mike Charles/Shutterstock

Keeping Track Using a Balanced Scorecard Approach

Balanced scorecard approach looks at more than the financial perspective[26] by typically looking at four areas that contribute to a company's performance:

1 Financial

2 Customer

3 Internal processes

4 People/innovation/ growth assets

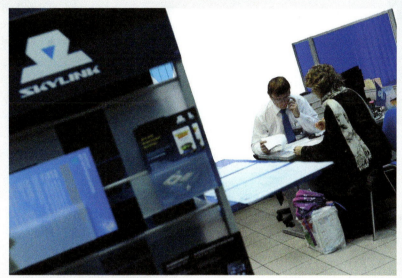

Sharifulin Valery/Itar-Tass Photos/Newscom

Managers should: **develop goals for each of the four areas** and **then measure whether goals are being met**.

> **balanced scorecard**
> A performance measurement tool that looks at more than just the financial perspective

Feedback controls do have two advantages.[27] First, feedback gives managers meaningful information on how effective their planning efforts were. Feedback that shows little variance between standard and actual performance indicates that the planning was generally on target. If the deviation is significant, a manager can use that information to formulate new plans. Second, feedback can enhance motivation. People want to know how well they're doing, and feedback provides that information.

 Try It!

If your professor has assigned this, go to the Assignments section of **mymanagementlab.com** to complete the **Simulation: *Controlling***.

What Contemporary Control Issues Do Managers Confront?

14-4 Discuss contemporary issues in control.

The employees of Integrated Information Systems Inc. didn't think twice about exchanging digital music over a dedicated office server they had set up. Like office betting on college and pro sports, it was technically illegal, but harmless—or so they thought. But after the company had to pay a $1 million settlement to the Recording Industry Association of America, managers wished they had controlled the situation better.[28] Control is an important managerial function. We're going to look at two control issues that managers face today: cross-cultural differences and workplace concerns.

✪ Watch It 2!

If your professor has assigned this, go to the Assignments section of **mymanagementlab.com** to complete the video exercise titled *Zane's Cycles: Foundations of Control*.

Do Controls Need to Be Adjusted for Cultural Differences?

The concepts of control that we've discussed are appropriate for organizational units that aren't geographically distant or culturally distinct. But what about global organizations? Would control systems be different, and what should managers know about adjusting controls for national differences?

Methods of controlling employee behavior and operations can be quite different in different countries. In fact, the differences in organizational control systems of global organizations are primarily in the measurement and corrective action steps of the control process. In a global corporation, for instance, managers of foreign operations tend not to be closely controlled by the home office if for no other reason than that distance keeps managers from being able to observe work directly. Because distance creates a tendency for formalized controls, the home office of a global company often relies on extensive, formal reports for control. The global company may also use information technology to control work activities. For instance, Seven and i Holdings (Japan's biggest retail conglomerate and parent company of the 7-Eleven convenience store chain in the United States) uses automated cash registers not only to record sales and monitor inventory but also to schedule tasks for store managers and to track their use of the built-in analytical graphs and forecasts. If managers don't use them enough, they're told to increase their activities.[29]

Technology's impact on control is most evident in comparisons of technologically advanced nations with countries that aren't as technologically advanced. Organizations in technologically advanced nations such as the United States, Japan, Canada, Great Britain, Germany, and Australia use indirect control devices—particularly computer-related reports and analyses—in addition to standardized rules and direct supervision to ensure that activities are going as planned. In less technologically advanced countries, direct supervision and highly centralized decision making are the basic means of control.

Also, constraints on what corrective action managers can take may affect managers in foreign countries because laws in some countries do not allow managers the option of closing facilities, laying off employees, or bringing in a new management

Yum! Brands, a global restaurant firm, established tighter control systems in China after learning that some of its poultry suppliers for its KFC restaurants violated company rules on the use of drugs to fatten chickens. Corrective actions of its control process included strengthening the oversight of its suppliers and establishing the principle of zero tolerance in food safety.

Zhou Junxiang/AP Images

Technology and the Manager's Job

MONITORING EMPLOYEES

Technological advances have made the process of managing an organization much easier.[30] And technological advancements have also provided employers a means of sophisticated employee monitoring. Although most of this monitoring is designed to enhance worker productivity, it could, and has been, a source of concern over worker privacy. These advantages bring with them difficult questions regarding what managers have the right to know about employees and how far they can go in controlling employee behavior, both on and off the job. Consider the following:

- The mayor of Colorado Springs, Colorado, reads the e-mail messages that city council members send to each other from their homes. He defended his actions by saying he was making sure that e-mails to each other were not being used to circumvent the state's "open meeting" law that requires most council business to be conducted publicly.

- The U.S. Internal Revenue Service's internal audit group monitors a computer log that shows employee access to taxpayers' accounts. This monitoring activity allows management to check and see what employees are doing on their computers.

- American Express has an elaborate system for monitoring telephone calls. Daily reports provided to supervisors detail the frequency and length of calls made by employees, as well as how quickly incoming calls are answered.

- Employers in several organizations require employees to wear badges at all times while on company premises. These badges contain a variety of data that allow employees to enter certain locations in the organization. Smart badges, too, can transmit where the employee is at all times!

Just how much control a company should have over the private lives of its employees also becomes an issue. Where should an employer's rules and controls end? Does the boss have the right to dictate what you do on your free time and in your own home? Could your boss keep you from engaging in riding a motorcycle, skydiving, smoking, drinking alcohol, or eating junk food? Again, the answers may surprise you. Today many organizations, in their quest to control safety and health insurance costs, are delving into their employees' private lives.

Although controlling employees' behaviors on and off the job may appear unjust or unfair, nothing in our legal system prevents employers from engaging in these practices. Rather, the law is based on the premise that if employees don't like the rules, they have the option of quitting. Managers, too, typically defend their actions in terms of ensuring quality, productivity, and proper employee behavior. For instance, an IRS audit of its southeastern regional offices found that 166 employees took unauthorized looks at the tax returns of friends, neighbors, and celebrities.

If your professor has assigned this, go to the Assignments section of ***mymanagementlab.com*** *to complete these discussion questions.*

⭐ **TALK ABOUT IT 5:** When does management's need for information about employee performance cross over the line and interfere with a worker's right to privacy?

⭐ **TALK ABOUT IT 6:** Is any action by management acceptable as long as employees are notified ahead of time that they will be monitored? Discuss.

---

team from outside the country. Finally, another challenge for global companies in collecting data is comparability. For instance, a company's manufacturing facility in Mexico might produce the same products as a facility in Scotland. However, the Mexican facility might be much more labor intensive than its Scottish counterpart (to take advantage of lower labor costs in Mexico). If top-level executives were to control costs by, for example, calculating labor costs per unit or output per worker, the figures would not be comparable. Managers in global companies must address these types of global control challenges.

What Challenges Do Managers Face in Controlling the Workplace?

Today's workplaces present considerable control challenges for managers. From monitoring employees' computer usage at work to protecting the workplace against disgruntled employees intent on doing harm, managers need controls to ensure that work can be done efficiently and effectively as planned.

Sixty-eight percent of employees admit to using company computers to check personal email.[31]

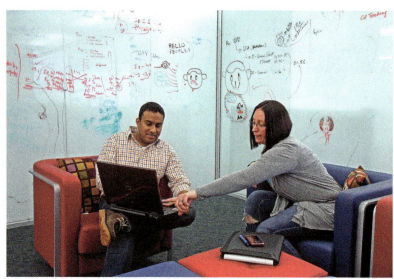

Miami Herald/MCT/Landov

At Citrix, a provider of virtualization, networking, and cloud technologies for businesses, employees are allowed to BYOD—Bring Your Own Device. Although more companies are adopting BYOD policies, the control risks are still very much the same. Even in a BYOD environment, workplace monitoring policies are very much needed.

IS MY WORK COMPUTER REALLY MINE? If you work, do you think you have a right to privacy at your job? What can your employer find out about you and your work? You might be surprised at the answers! Employers can (and do), among other things, read your e-mail (even those marked "personal or confidential"), tap your telephone, monitor your work by computer, store and review computer files, monitor you in an employee bathroom or dressing room, and track your whereabouts in a company vehicle. And these actions aren't that uncommon. In fact, some 30 percent of companies have fired workers for misusing the Internet and another 28 percent have terminated workers for e-mail misuse.[32]

Why do managers feel they need to monitor what employees are doing? A big reason is that employees are hired to work, not to surf the Web checking stock prices, watching online videos, playing fantasy baseball, or shopping for presents for family or friends. Recreational on-the-job Web surfing is thought to cost billions of dollars in lost work productivity annually. In fact, a survey of U.S. employers said that 87 percent of employees look at non-work-related Web sites while at work and more than half engage in personal Web site surfing every day.[33] Watching online video has become an increasingly serious problem not only because of the time being wasted by employees but also because it clogs already-strained corporate computer networks.[34] If you had to guess the video site viewed most often at work, what would you guess? If you said YouTube, you'd be absolutely correct![35] However, as innocent as it may seem (after all, it may be just a 30-second video), all this nonwork adds up to significant costs to businesses.

Another reason that managers monitor employee e-mail and computer usage is that they don't want to risk being sued for creating a hostile workplace environment because of offensive messages or an inappropriate image displayed on a coworker's computer screen. Concerns about racial or sexual harassment are one reason companies might want to monitor or keep backup copies of all e-mail. Electronic records can help establish what actually happened so managers can react quickly.[36]

Finally, managers want to ensure that company secrets aren't being leaked.[37] In addition to typical e-mail and computer usage, companies are monitoring instant messaging, blogs, and other social media outlets, and banning phone cameras in the office. Managers need to be certain that employees are not, even inadvertently, passing information on to others who could use that information to harm the company.

Because of the potentially serious costs and given the fact that many jobs now entail computers, many companies have workplace monitoring policies. Such policies should control employee behavior in a nondemeaning way, and employees should be informed about those policies.

⭐ **Write It!**

If your professor has assigned this, go to the Assignments section of **mymanagementlab.com** to complete *MGMT 3: Technology*.

IS EMPLOYEE THEFT ON THE RISE? Would you be surprised to find that up to 85 percent of all organizational theft and fraud is committed by employees, not outsiders?[38] And it's a costly problem—estimated to be about $4,500 per worker per year.[39] In a survey of U.S. companies, 20 percent said that workplace theft has become a moderate to very big problem.[40]

employee theft
Any unauthorized taking of company property by employees for their personal use

Employee theft is defined as any unauthorized taking of company property by employees for their personal use.[41] It can range from embezzlement to fraudulent filing of expense reports to removing equipment, parts, software, or office supplies from company premises. Although retail businesses have long faced serious potential losses from employee theft, loose financial controls at startups and small companies and the ready availability of information technology have made employee stealing an escalating problem in all kinds and sizes of organizations. It's a control issue that managers need to educate themselves about and be prepared to deal with it.[42]

> Global employee fraud is estimated to cost organizations $3.7 trillion a year.[43]

Why do employees steal? The answer depends on whom you ask.[44] Experts in various fields—industrial security, criminology, clinical psychology—have different perspectives. The industrial security people propose that people steal because the opportunity presents itself through lax controls and favorable circumstances. Criminologists say that it's because people have financial-based pressures (such as personal financial problems) or vice-based pressures (such as gambling debts). And the clinical psychologists suggest that people steal because they can rationalize whatever they're doing as being correct and appropriate behavior ("everyone does it," "they had it coming," "this company makes enough money and they'll never miss anything this small," "I deserve this for all that I put up with," and so forth).[45] Although each approach provides compelling insights into employee theft and has been instrumental in attempts to deter it, unfortunately, employees continue to steal. What can managers do?

The concept of feedforward, concurrent, and feedback control is useful for identifying measures to deter or reduce employee theft.[46] Exhibit 14–7 summarizes several possible managerial actions.

Exhibit 14–7   Controlling Employee Theft

FEEDFORWARD	CONCURRENT	FEEDBACK
Use careful prehiring screening.	Treat employees with respect and dignity.	Make sure employees know when theft or fraud has occurred—not naming names but letting people know this is not acceptable.
Establish specific policies defining theft and fraud and discipline procedures.	Openly communicate the costs of stealing.	Use the services of professional investigators.
Involve employees in writing policies.	Let employees know on a regular basis about their successes in preventing theft and fraud.	Redesign control measures.
Educate and train employees about the policies.	Use video surveillance equipment if conditions warrant.	Evaluate your organization's culture and the relationships of managers and employees.
Have a professional review of your internal security controls.	Install "lock-out" options on computers, telephones, and e-mail. Use corporate hotlines for reporting incidences. Set a good example.	

WHAT CAN MANAGERS DO ABOUT WORKPLACE VIOLENCE?   In January 2015, a cardiologist at Boston's Brigham and Women's Hospital was gunned down by a man whose mother had been operated on by the doctor and subsequently died. After killing the cardiologist, the man shot himself. In September 2014, a man who was recently fired walked into the UPS he had worked at and killed two individuals and then took his own life. In April 2014, an individual who worked as a baggage handler opened fire at a FedEx facility near Atlanta injuring six employees. In August 2010, a driver about to lose his job at Hartford Distributors in Hartford, Connecticut, opened fire killing eight other employees and himself. In July 2010, a former employee at a solar products manufacturer in Albuquerque, New Mexico, walked into the business and opened fire, killing two people and wounding four others. On November 6, 2009, in Orlando, Florida, an engineer who had been dismissed from his job for poor performance returned and shot and killed one person while wounding five others. This incident happened only one day after a U.S. Army psychiatrist went on a shooting rampage at Fort Hood Army post, killing 13 and wounding 27.[47] These are just a few of the deadly workplace attacks in recent years. Is workplace violence really an issue for managers? Yes. Despite these examples, thankfully, the number of workplace shootings has decreased.[48] However, the U.S. National Institute of Occupational Safety and Health still says that each year, some 2 million American workers are victims of some form of workplace violence. In an average week, one employee is killed and at least 25 are seriously injured in violent assaults by current or former coworkers. And according to a Department of Labor survey, 58 percent of firms reported that managers received verbal threats from workers.[49] Anger, rage, and violence in the workplace are intimidating to coworkers and adversely affect their productivity. The annual cost to U.S. businesses is estimated to be between $20 billion and $35 billion.[50] And office rage isn't a uniquely American problem. A survey of aggressive behavior in Britain's workplaces found that 18 percent of managers say they have personally experienced harassment or verbal bullying, and 9 percent claim to have experienced physical attacks.[51]

What factors are believed to contribute to workplace violence? Undoubtedly, employee stress caused by job uncertainties, declining value of retirement accounts, long hours, information overload, other daily interruptions, unrealistic deadlines, and uncaring managers play a role. Even office layout designs with small cubicles where employees work amidst the noise and commotion from those around them have been cited as contributing to the problem.[52] Other experts have described dangerously dysfunctional work environments characterized by the following as primary contributors to the problem:[53]

- Employee work driven by TNC (time, numbers, and crises)
- Rapid and unpredictable change where instability and uncertainty plague employees
- Destructive communication style where managers communicate in excessively aggressive, condescending, explosive, or passive-aggressive styles; excessive workplace teasing or scapegoating
- Authoritarian leadership with a rigid, militaristic mind-set of managers versus employees; employees not allowed to challenge ideas, participate in decision making, or engage in team-building efforts
- Defensive attitude with little or no performance feedback given; only numbers count; and yelling, intimidation, or avoidance as the preferred ways of handling conflict
- Double standards in terms of policies, procedures, and training opportunities for managers and employees
- Unresolved grievances due to an absence of mechanisms or only adversarial ones in place for resolving them; dysfunctional individuals protected or ignored because of long-standing rules, union contract provisions, or reluctance to take care of problems
- Emotionally troubled employees and no attempt by managers to get help for these people
- Repetitive, boring work and little chance for doing something else or for new people coming in
- Faulty or unsafe equipment or deficient training, which keeps employees from being able to work efficiently or effectively
- Hazardous work environment in terms of temperature, air quality, repetitive motions, overcrowded spaces, noise levels, excessive overtime, and so forth; to minimize costs, a failure

Exhibit 14–8 Controlling Workplace Violence

FEEDFORWARD	CONCURRENT	FEEDBACK
Ensure management's commitment to functional, not dysfunctional, work environments.	Use MBWA (managing by walking around) to identify potential problems; observe how employees treat and interact with each other.	Communicate openly about violent incidents and what's being done.
Provide employee assistance programs (EAPs) to help employees with behavioral problems.	Allow employees or work groups to "grieve" during periods of major organizational change.	Investigate incidents and take appropriate action.
Enforce organizational policy that any workplace rage, aggression, or violence will not be tolerated.	Be a good role model in how you treat others.	Review company policies and change, if necessary.
Use careful prehiring screening.	Use corporate hotlines or some other mechanism for reporting and investigating incidents.	
Never ignore threats.	Use quick and decisive intervention.	
Train employees about how to avoid danger if a situation arises.	Get expert professional assistance if violence erupts.	
Clearly communicate policies to employees.	Provide necessary equipment or procedures for dealing with violent situations (cell phones, alarm system, code names or phrases, and so forth).	

Sources: Based on M. Gorkin, "Five Strategies and Structures for Reducing Workplace Violence," *Workforce Management Online,* December 3, 2000; "Investigating Workplace Violence: Where Do You Start?" *Workforce Management Online,* December 3, 2000; "Ten Tips on Recognizing and Minimizing Violence," *Workforce Management Online,* December 3, 2000; and "Points to Cover in a Workplace Violence Policy," *Workforce Management Online,* December 3, 2000.

to hire additional employees when workload becomes excessive, leading to potentially dangerous work expectations and conditions

- Culture of violence perpetuated by a history of individual violence or abuse, violent or explosive role models, or tolerance of on-the-job alcohol or drug abuse

Reading through this list, you surely hope that workplaces where you'll spend your professional life won't be like this. However, the competitive demands of succeeding in a 24/7 global economy put pressure on organizations and employees in many ways.

What can managers do to deter or reduce possible workplace violence? Once again, the concept of feedforward, concurrent, and feedback control can help identify actions that managers can take.[54] Exhibit 14–8 summarizes several suggestions.

MyManagementLab®

Go to **mymanagementlab.com** to complete the problems marked with this icon .

14 Review

CHAPTER SUMMARY

14-1 Explain the nature and importance of control.

Control is the management function that involves monitoring activities to ensure that they're being accomplished as planned and correcting any significant deviations.

As the final step in the management process, controlling provides the link back to planning. If managers didn't control, they'd have no way of knowing whether goals were being met.

Control is important because (1) it's the only way to know whether goals are being met and, if not, why; (2) it provides information and feedback so managers feel comfortable empowering employees; and (3) it helps protect an organization and its assets.

14-2 Describe the three steps in the control process.

The three steps in the control process are measuring, comparing, and taking action. Measuring involves deciding how to measure actual performance and what to measure. Comparing involves looking at the variation between actual performance and the standard (goal). Deviations outside an acceptable range of variation need attention.

Taking action can involve doing nothing, correcting the actual performance, or revising the standards. Doing nothing is self-explanatory. Correcting the actual performance can involve different corrective actions, which can either be immediate or basic. Standards can be revised by either raising or lowering them.

14-3 Discuss the types of controls organizations and managers use.

Feedforward controls take place before a work activity is done. Concurrent controls take place while a work activity is being done. Feedback controls take place after a work activity is done.

Financial controls that managers can use include financial ratios (liquidity, leverage, activity, and profitability) and budgets. One information control managers can use is an MIS, which provides managers with needed information on a regular basis. Others include comprehensive and secure controls, such as data encryption, system firewalls, data backups, and so forth, that protect the organization's information. Also, balanced scorecards provide a way to evaluate an organization's performance in four different areas rather than just from the financial perspective.

14-4 Discuss contemporary issues in control.

Adjusting controls for cross-cultural differences may be necessary, primarily in the areas of measuring and taking corrective actions.

Workplace concerns include workplace privacy, employee theft, and workplace violence. For each of these, managers need to have policies in place to control inappropriate actions and ensure that work is getting done efficiently and effectively.

DISCUSSION QUESTIONS

14-1 What is the role of control in management?

14-2 Describe four methods managers can use to acquire information about actual work performance.

⭐ 14-3 How are planning and control linked? Is the control function linked to the organizing and leading functions of management? Explain.

⭐ 14-4 Contrast feedforward, concurrent, and feedback controls.

14-5 Why do you think feedback control is the most popular type of control? Justify your response.

14-6 In Chapter 8 we discussed the "white-water rapids" view of change. Do you think it's possible to establish and maintain effective standards and controls in this type of environment? Discuss.

14-7 Why is it that what is measured is more critical to the control process than how it is measured?

14-8 "Every individual employee in an organization plays a role in controlling work activities." Do you agree with this statement, or do you think control is something that only managers are responsible for? Explain.

14-9 What are some work activities in which the acceptable range of variation might be higher than average? What about lower than average? (Hint: Think in terms of the output from the work activities, whom it might affect, and how it might affect them.)

14-10 How could you use the concept of control in your personal life? Be specific. (Think in terms of feedforward, concurrent, and feedback controls as well as specific controls for the different aspects of your life—school, work, family relationships, friends, hobbies, etc.)

Writing Assignments

14-11 Why is it important for managers to understand the control process?

14-12 Discuss the various types of tools used to monitor and measure organizational performance.

Management Skill Builder | DISCIPLINING DIFFICULT EMPLOYEES

Almost all managers will, at one time or another, have to deal with employees who are difficult. There is no shortage of characteristics that can make someone difficult to work with. Some examples include being: short-tempered, demanding, abusive, angry, defensive, complaining, intimidating, aggressive, narcissistic, arrogant, and rigid. Successful managers have learned how to cope with difficult people.

⭐ PERSONAL INVENTORY ASSESSMENT

Workplace Discipline Indicator

P I A PERSONAL INVENTORY ASSESSMENT

Disciplining, especially with difficult employees, is usually not a manager's favorite thing to do. But it is important. Take this PIA and discover how you prefer to discipline employees.

Skill Basics

No single approach is always effective in dealing with difficult people. However, we can offer several suggestions that are likely to lessen the angst these people create in your life and may have some influence in reducing their difficult behavior.[55]

- *Don't let your emotions rule.* Our first response to a difficult person is often emotional. We get angry. We show frustration. We want to lash out at them or "get even" when we think they've insulted or demeaned us. This response is not likely to reduce your angst and may escalate the other person's negative behavior. So fight your natural tendencies and keep your cool. Stay rational and thoughtful. At worst, while this approach may not improve the situation, it is also unlikely to encourage and escalate the undesirable behavior.

- *Attempt to limit contact.* If possible, try to limit your contact with the difficult person. Avoid places where they hang out and limit nonrequired interactions. Also, use communication channels—like e-mail and text messaging—that minimize face-to-face contact and verbal intonations.

- *Try polite confrontation.* If you can't avoid the difficult person, consider standing up to them in a civil but firm manner. Let them know that you're aware of their behavior, that you find it unacceptable, and that you won't tolerate it. For people who are unaware of the effect their actions have on you, confrontation might awaken them to altering their behavior. For those who are acting purposefully, taking a clear stand might make them think twice about the consequences of their actions.

- *Practice positive reinforcement.* We know that positive reinforcement is a powerful tool for changing behavior. Rather than criticizing undesirable behavior, try reinforcing desirable behaviors with compliments or other positive comments. This focus will tend to weaken and reduce the exhibiting of the undesirable behaviors.

- *Recruit fellow victims and witnesses.* Finally, we know strength lies in numbers. If you can get others who are also offended by the difficult person to support your case, several positive things can happen. First, it's likely to lessen your frustrations because others will be confirming your perception and can offer support. Second, people in the organization with authority to reprimand are more likely to act when complaints are coming from multiple sources. And third, the difficult person is more likely to feel pressure to change when a group is speaking out against his or her specific behaviors than if the complaint is coming from a single source.

Practicing the Skill

Read through this scenario and follow the directions at the end of it:

Your career has progressed even faster than you thought possible. After graduating from college with an accounting degree, you passed your CPA exam and worked three years for a major accounting firm. Then you joined General Electric in their finance department. Two employers and four jobs later, you have just been hired by a Fortune 100 mining company as their vice president for finance. What you didn't expect in the new job was having to deal with Mark Hundley.

Mark is the vice president of company operations. He has been with the company for eight years. Your first impression of Mark was that he was a "know-it-all." He was quick to put you down and acted as if he was your superior rather than an equal. Based on comments you've heard around the offices, it seems you are not alone. Other executives all seemed to agree that Mark is a brilliant engineer and operations manager but very difficult to work with. Specific comments you've heard include "an abrasive attitude"; "talks down to people"; "arrogant"; "thinks everyone is stupid"; and "poor listener."

In your short time in the new job, you've already had several run-ins with Mark. You've even talked to your boss, the company president, about him. The president's response wasn't surprising: "Mark isn't easy to deal with. But no one knows this company's operations like he does. If he ever leaves, I don't know how we'd replace him. But, that said, he gives me a lot of grief. Sometimes he makes me feel like I work for him rather than the other way around." Describe what you could do to improve your ability to work with Mark.

Experiential Exercise

Collins State College, School of Accountancy

To: Matt Wrobeck, Ethics Committee Chair

From: Dr. Rebecca Rodriguez, Director

Re: Minimizing student cheating

Matt, you've probably heard that several of our faculty members want to develop some specific controls to minimize opportunities for our students to cheat on homework assignments and exams. As the ethics committee chair, I'd like you to work with them on developing some suggestions. As you look at this topic, please think in terms of ways to control cheating (1) before it happens, (2) while in-class exams or assignments are being completed, and (3) after it has happened.

Keep your list brief (around a page) and send it to me by the end of the week. I'd like to get this out to our entire faculty at our next scheduled monthly meeting.

This fictionalized organization and message were created for educational purposes only, and not meant to reflect positively or negatively on management practices by any company that may share this name.

CASE APPLICATION #1

Top Secret

"Prisons are easier to enter than Visa's top-secret Operations Center East (OCE), its biggest, newest and most advanced U.S. data center."[56] And Rick Knight, senior vice president at Visa and formerly the head of global operations and engineering, is responsible for its security and functioning. Why all the precautions? Because Visa acknowledges that (1) hackers are increasingly savvy, (2) data is an increasingly desirable black-market commodity, and (3) the best way to keep itself safe is with an information network in a fortress that instantly responds to threats.

In a year's time, Visa processes more than 91.6 billion retail electronic payments from around the globe. And every day, Visa's system connects up to 2.2 billion debit and credit cards, millions of acceptance locations, 2.1 million ATMs, and 14,400 financial institutions.[57] Visa, which completes an annual "stress test" of its system in preparation for the holiday season, recently processed a peak volume of 56,000 messages per second.[58] (Do some math on that and be amazed!) So what seems to us a simple swipe of a card or keying in our card numbers on an online transaction actually triggers a robust set of activities including the basic sales transaction processing, risk management, and information-based services. That's why OCE's workers have two jobs: "Keep hackers out and keep the network up, no matter what." And that's why Visa doesn't reveal the location of OCE—on the eastern seaboard is as specific as the description gets.

Beneath the road leading to the OCE, hydraulic posts can rise up fast enough to stop a car going 50 miles per hour. And a car won't be able to go that fast or it will miss a "vicious hairpin turn" and drive off into a drainage pond. Back in medieval days, that would have been known as the

Prisons are easier to enter than Visa's OCE!

castle moat, which was also designed as protection. There are also hundreds of security cameras and a superb security team of former military personnel. If you're lucky enough to be invited as a guest to OCE (which few people are), you'll have your photo taken and right index fingerprint encoded on a badge. Then you're locked into a "mantrap portal" where you put your badge on a reader that makes sure you are you, and then put it on another reader with your finger on a fingerprint detector. If you make it through, you're clear to enter the network operations center. With a wall of screens in front of them, each employee sits at a desk with four monitors. In a room behind the main center, three top-notch security experts keep an eye on things. Knight says that "about 60 incidents a day warrant attention."

Although hackers are a primary concern, OCE also worries about network capacity. Right now, maximum capacity is currently at 56,000 transactions per second. If the network goes over that capacity, the network wouldn't just stop processing one message, it would stop processing all of them. OCE is described as a "Tier-4" center, which is a certification from a data center organization. To achieve that certification, every (and yes, we mean every) mainframe, air conditioner, and battery has a backup.

Discussion Questions

14-14 Is Visa being overly cautious? Why or why not?

14-15 Why is this level of managerial controls necessary?

14-16 Which controls would be more important to Visa: feedforward, concurrent, or feedback? Explain.

14-17 What other managerial controls might be useful to the company?

CASE APPLICATION #2

If You Can't Say Something Nice, Don't Say Anything at All

Controlling employee performance is a vitally important responsibility of managers. After all, it's your employees who are working to accomplish established goals, and you want to see that those goals are being accomplished as planned. So wouldn't it seem that managing employees' performance would cover the good and the not-so-good? Well, some organizations are encouraging managers to lighten up on the harsh feedback and focus only on the positive.[59]

At consulting firm the Boston Consulting Group, managers now frequently praise employees, encourage them to celebrate even small victories, and conduct performance reviews focusing on an individual employee's strengths instead of any mistakes that may have happened. And managers are to bring up only one or two areas that require improvement and development. It never used to be this way. When employees didn't do a good job with a client's assignment, managers would focus on what went wrong and where and how the employee needed to improve and develop his or her skills. This shift towards more positive feedback occurred after the company noticed some employees leaving the company and other employees who were still upset for a period of time after a negative performance review. And BCG isn't the only company taking this approach. Others are increasing the use of positive feedback and minimizing any discussion of the areas that need improvement. At PricewaterhouseCoopers LLP, for instance, managers are asked to have discussions with employees about their future with the organization. These "career outlook" discussions focus more on where an employee fits in, rather than on where they screwed up. The company also encourages its staff to send shout-outs via e-cards praising colleagues or subordinates for work done. Managers have also allocated money to further reward positive accomplishments.

But there are companies not following this positivism trend. These companies take a more "tough-love" approach and don't shy away from giving negative feedback. For instance, at Netflix, CEO Reed Hasting's view is that they're a "pro sports team, not a Little League squad," noting that "adequate performance gets a generous severance package." Not everyone in the company is going to get a trophy. There's little doubt as to what that company's performance expectations are.

No Negativism Allowed!

Discussion Questions

⭐ **14-18** Is controlling employee performance an important responsibility of managers? Discuss.

⭐ **14-19** Why should managers focus on positive feedback?

⭐ **14-20** What are the risks associated with providing employees only positive feedback and providing limited feedback on areas of improvement?

14-21 Where would you be more comfortable? An organization with a performance review approach more like the Boston Consulting Group or more like Netflix? Why?

CASE APPLICATION #3

Too Relaxed

As yoga classes gained in popularity, one company that had benefited greatly was Lululemon. In fact, at one point, it was on *Fortune*'s Fastest-Growing Companies List three years in a row. Company executives had positioned the company as a lifestyle brand and customers were hooked and loyal. Then, a rare stumble happened. The company had to recall a large batch of its signature black "Luon" yoga pants because the fabric was too sheer.[60]

Lululemon was founded by Dennis (Chip) Wilson, who had noticed in his yoga class that other students' yoga pants became see-through when they bent over after class to roll up their mats. Having just sold his surf/skateboard/snowboard clothing company, he sensed an opportunity to pair his expertise in "technical" athletic wear with the surging demand by yoga enthusiasts. What he developed was revolutionary! Instead of following what others had done—essentially cutting down men's workout wear and then selling them in feminine colors—Wilson believed that women would prefer working out in clothes that actually fit them. So, in addition to fashionable styles, he concentrated on technical elements including seamless stitching and breathable fabrics. And surprise, surprise: women were willing to pay $100 or more for his company's workout clothes. Lululemon was off and running. Like many smaller companies, executives focused on the product and not so much on the "infrastructure" side of the business (human resources, IT, finance). That works … up to a point. When the chief information officer was hired, she actually found it fairly easy to implement the technology she felt was needed because there wasn't really anything in place to work around.

One area where former executives felt focus was lacking was in the production area. No rigorous manufacturing model was in place. There were no schedules or deadlines. The company countered that by saying it wanted to remain flexible. But the manufacturing weakness was also evident in the lack of people who had expertise in the technical aspects of clothing manufacturing, such as quality control or control over raw materials. Which brings us to the problem of sheer yoga pants—yoga pants being a core product of the company. As customers began returning the product and as the product complaint rate

Losing your pose...

hit 12 percent, Lululemon had no choice but to pull the pants off the store shelves. The CEO at that time said the pants had passed quality assurance tests, but admitted that the only way to actually quality test the product was to put them on and bend over. And the company hadn't done that … until it was too late.

That was in 2013, and the company is still trying to get back to where it was in terms of customer loyalty and sales numbers. Although the company's core business is still women, it is seeing strong growth in men's and girl's businesses. It's no longer one of the fastest-growing companies, but it has certainly learned something about the importance of control!

Discussion Questions

14-22 What type (or types) of control—feedforward, concurrent, or feedback—do you think would have been helpful in this situation? Explain your choice.

14-23 Using Exhibit 14–2, discuss if and how this situation could have been prevented.

14-24 Could Lululemon's controls have been more effective? How?

14-25 What role would information controls play in this situation? Customer interaction controls? What other controls do you think might have been useful?

Endnotes

1. "Domino's Delivered Free Pizzas," *Springfield, Missouri News-Leader*, April 3, 2009, p. 3B.
2. H. Peterson, "Target Workers Claim 'Walk of Shame' That Allegedly Led to a Suicide Is a Widespread Practice," http://www.businessinsider.com/target-workers-claim-walk-of-shame-is-widespread-2015-2, February 6, 2015; H. Peterson, "Target Cashier Jumped to His Death after Managers Allegedly Subjected Him to 'Walk of Shame,'" http://www.businessinsider.com/mother-blames-target-for-sons-suicide-2015-1, January 27, 2015; and ABC7 News Staff, "Lawsuit Claims Pasadena Target Employee Committed Suicide after Being Shamed," http://abc7.com/news/lawsuit-pasadena-target-employee-killed-self-after-being-shamed/488247/, January 23, 2015.
3. B. Hagenbaugh, "State Quarters Extra Leaf Grew Out of Lunch Break," *USA Today*, January 20, 2006, 1B.
4. D. E. Sanger and J. H. Davis, "Data Breach Linked to China Exposes Millions of Workers," *New York Times Online*, June 4, 2015.
5. J. R. Emshwiller, "Managers Blamed in Nuclear Leak," *Wall Street Journal*, April 25, 2014, A6.
6. Reuters, "McDonald's Japan Apologizes after Tooth, Plastic Found in Food," *New York Times Online*, January 7, 2015.
7. M. Murphy and S. Chaudhuri, "Carnival to Step Up Maintenance after Mishaps," *Wall Street Journal*, March 16–17, 2013, B3.
8. E. A. Harris, "Error Creates Deals Too Good to Be True on Walmart's Site," *New York Times Online*, November 6, 2013.
9. C. Timberlake, R. Dudley, and C. Burritt, "Don't Even Think about Returning This Dress," *Bloomberg BusinessWeek*, September 30–October 6, 2013, 29–31.
10. B. Horovitz, "Gross Photo with Wendy's Frosty Is Latest to Go Viral," *USA Today*, June 14, 2013, 2B; and S. Clifford, "Video Prank at Domino's Taints Brand," *New York Times Online*, April 16, 2009.
11. SmartPulse, "Where Does the Biggest Threat to Your Organizations Come From?" www.smartbrief.com/leadership, May 12, 2015.
12. J. F. Van Niekerk and R. Von Solms, "Information Security Culture: A Management Perspective," *Computers & Security*, June 2010, 476–86; T. Vinas and J. Jusko "5 Threats That Could Sink Your Company," *Industry Week*, September 2004, 52–61; "Workplace Security: How Vulnerable Are You?" special section in *Wall Street Journal*, September

29, 2003, R1–R8; P. Magnusson, "Your Jitters Are Their Lifeblood," *Business Week*, April 14, 2003, 41; and T. Purdum, "Preparing for the Worst," *Industry Week*, January 2003, 53–55.
13. A. Dalton, "Rapid Recovery," *Industry Week*, March 2005, 70–71.
14. B. Nelson, "Long-Distance Recognition," *Workforce*, August 2000, 50–52.
15. D. Auerbach, "Watch for Workplace Productivity Killers," *Springfield, Missouri, News-Leader*, July 13, 2014, 1G.
16. S. Kerr, "On the Folly of Rewarding A, While Hoping for B," *Academy of Management Journal* (December 1975): 769–83; and N. F. Piercy, D. W. Cravens, N. Lane, and D. W. Vorhies, "Driving Organizational Citizenship Behaviors and Salesperson In-Role Behavior Performance: The Role of Management Control and Perceived Organizational Support," *Journal of the Academy of Marketing Science* (Spring 2006): 244–62.
17. From the Past to the Present box based on H. Min and H. Min, "Benchmarking the Service Quality of Fast-Food Restaurant Franchises in the USA," *Benchmarking: An International Journal* (April 2011): 282–300; R. Pear, "A.M.A. to Develop Measure of Quality of Medical Care," *New York Times Online*, February 21, 2006; and A. Taylor III, "Double Duty," *Fortune*, March 7, 2005, 104–10; C. Bogan and D. Callahan, "Benchmarking in Rapid Time," *Industrial Management*, March–April 2001, 28–33; and L. D. McNary, "Thinking about Excellence and Benchmarking," *Journal for Quality and Participation* (July–August 1994).
18. H. Koontz and R. W. Bradspies, "Managing through Feedforward Control," *Business Horizons*, June 1972, 25–36.
19. M. Helft, "The Human Hands behind the Google Money Machine," *New York Times Online*, June 2, 2008.
20. J. Yang and S. Music, "Micromanaging," *USA Today*, August 8, 2014, 1B.
21. B. Caulfield, "Shoot to Kill," *Forbes*, January 7, 2008, 92–96.
22. T. Laseter and L. Laseter, "See for Yourself," *Strategy+Business*, www.strategy-business.com (November 29, 2007).
23. 2015 Data Breach Investigations Report, http://www.verizonenterprise.com/DBIR/2015/, May 31, 2015.
24. B. Grow, K. Epstein, and C.-C. Tschang, "The New E-Spionage Threat," *Business Week*, April 21, 2008, 32–41; S. Leibs, "Firewall of Silence," *CFO*, April 2008, 31–35; J. Pereira, "How Credit-Card

Data Went out Wireless Door," *Wall Street Journal*, May 4, 2007, A1+; and B. Stone, "Firms Fret as Office E-Mail Jumps Security Walls," *New York Times Online*, January 11, 2007.
25. SmartPulse, "How Well Do You Give Difficult Feedback?" Smart Brief on Leadership, www.smartbrief.com/leadership, December 3, 2014.
26. E. R. Iselin, J. Sands, and L. Mia, "Multi-Perspective Performance Reporting Systems, Continuous Improvement Systems, and Organizational Performance," *Journal of General Management* (Spring 2011): 19–36; L. Elmore, "The Balanced Business," *Women in Business*, Spring 2011, 14–16; D. Agostino and M. Arnaboldi, "How the BSC Implementation Process Shapes Its Outcome," *International Journal of Productivity & Performance Management* (January 2011): 99–114; R. S. Kaplan and D. P. Norton, "How to Implement a New Strategy without Disrupting Your Organization," *Harvard Business Review*, March 2006, 100–09; L. Bassi and D. McMurrer, "Developing Measurement Systems for Managers in the Knowledge Era," *Organizational Dynamics*, May 2005, 185–96; G. M. J. DeKoning, "Making the Balanced Scorecard Work (Part 1)," *Gallup Brain*, www.brain.gallup.com (July 8, 2004); G. M. J. DeKoning, "Making the Balanced Scorecard Work (Part 2)," *Gallup Brain*, www.brain.gallup.com (August 12, 2004); K. Graham, "Balanced Scorecard," *New Zealand Management*, March 2003, 32–34; K. Ellis, "A Ticket to Ride: Balanced Scorecard," *Training* (April 2001): 50; and T. Leahy, "Tailoring the Balanced Scorecard," *Business Finance*, August 2000, 53–56.
27. W. H. Newman, *Constructive Control: Design and Use of Control Systems* (Upper Saddle River, NJ: Prentice Hall, 1975), 33.
28. J. Yaukey and C. L. Romero, "Arizona Firm Pays Big for Workers' Digital Downloads," *Associated Press, Springfield, Missouri, News-Leader*, May 6, 2002, 6B.
29. Information on *Hoovers Online*, www.hoovers.com (June 17, 2011); and N. Shirouzu and J. Bigness, "7-Eleven Operators Resist System to Monitor Managers," *Wall Street Journal*, June 16, 1997, B1.
30. Technology and the Manager's Job box based on C. A. Ciocchetti, "The Eavesdropping Employer: A Twenty-First-Framework for Employee Monitoring," *American Business Law Journal* (Summer 2011): 285–369; G. M. Amsler, H. M. Findley, and E.

Ingram, "Performance Monitoring: Guidance for the Modern Workplace," *Supervision*, January 2011, 16–22; T. Harbert, "When IT Is Asked to Spy"; D. Searcey, "Employers Watching Workers Online Spurs Privacy Debate," *Wall Street Journal*, April 23, 2009, A13; D. Darlin, "Software That Monitors Your Work, Wherever You Are," *New York Times Online*, April 12, 2009; S. Boehle, "They're Watching You," *Training* (September 2008): 23+; S. Shellenbarger, "Work at Home? Your Employer May Be Watching You," *Wall Street Journal*, July 30, 2008, D1+; J. Jusko, "A Watchful Eye," *Industry Week*, May 7, 2001, 9; "Big Brother Boss," *U.S. News and World Report*, April 30, 2001, 12; and L. Guernsey, "You've Got Inappropriate E-Mail," *New York Times*, April 5, 2000, C1+.
31. A. R. Carey and P. Trap, "Wasting Work Time Online?" *USA Today*, October 18, 2014, 1A.
32. "2007 Electronic Monitoring & Surveillance Survey," *American Management Association*, www.amanet.org.
33. S. Armour, "Companies Keep an Eye on Workers' Internet Use," *USA Today*, February 21, 2006, 2B.
34. B. White, "The New Workplace Rules: No Video-Watching," *Wall Street Journal*, March 4, 2008, B1+.
35. Ibid.
36. N. Lugaresi, "Electronic Privacy in the Workplace: Transparency and Responsibility," *International Review of Law, Computers, & Technology*, July 2010, 163–73; P.-W. Tam, E. White, N. Wingfield, and K. Maher, "Snooping E-Mail by Software Is Now a Workplace Norm," *Wall Street Journal*, March 9, 2005, B1+; D. Hawkins, "Lawsuits Spur Rise in Employee Monitoring," *U.S. News & World Report*, August 13, 2001, 53; and L. Guernsey, "You've Got Inappropriate Mail," *New York Times*, April 5, 2000, C1+.
37. S. Armour, "More Companies Keep Track of Workers' E-Mail," *USA Today*, June 13, 2005, 4B; and E. Bott, "Are You Safe? Privacy Special Report," *PC Computing*, March 2000, 87–88.
38. A. M. Bell and D. M. Smith, "Theft and Fraud May Be an Inside Job," *Workforce Online*, www.workforce.com (December 3, 2000).
39. C. C. Verschoor, "New Evidence of Benefits from Effective Ethics Systems," *Strategic Finance*, May 2003, 20–21; and E. Krell, "Will Forensic Accounting Go Mainstream?" *Business Finance*, October 2002, 30–34.
40. B. Mirza, "Combat Costly Discrimination, Employee Fraud,

Theft," *HR Magazine*, February 2011, 14; and S. E. Needleman, "Businesses Say Theft by Their Workers Is Up," *Wall Street Journal*, December 11, 2008, B8.

41. J. Greenberg, "The STEAL Motive: Managing the Social Determinants of Employee Theft," in R. Giacalone and J. Greenberg (eds.), *Antisocial Behavior in Organizations* (Newbury Park, CA: Sage, 1997), 85–108.

42. M. S. Hershcovis, "Incivility, Social Undermining, Bullying… Oh My! A Call to Reconcile Constructs within Workplace Aggression Research," *Journal of Organizational Behavior* (April 2011): 499–519; B. E. Litzky, K. A. Eddleston, and D. L. Kidder, "The Good, the Bad, and the Misguided: How Managers Inadvertently Encourage Deviant Behaviors," *Academy of Management Perspective*, February 2006, 91–103; "Crime Spree," *BusinessWeek*, September 9, 2002, 8; B. P. Niehoff and R. J. Paul, "Causes of Employee Theft and Strategies That HR Managers Can Use for Prevention," *Human Resource Management*, Spring 2000, 51–64; and G. Winter, "Taking at the Office Reaches New Heights: Employee Larceny Is Bigger and Bolder," *New York Times*, July 12, 2000, C1+.

43. K. Aho, "A Highly Effective, Very Low-Tech Way to Stop Fraud," http://www.bloomberg.com/bw/articles/2014-08-11/to-stop-fraud-employee-tip-hotlines-are-remarkably-effective, August 11, 2014.

44. This section is based on J. Greenberg, *Behavior in Organizations*, 10th ed. (Upper Saddle River, NJ: Prentice Hall, 2011).

45. A. H. Bell and D. M. Smith, "Why Some Employees Bite the Hand That Feeds Them," *Workforce Online, www.workforce.com* (December 3, 2000).

46. B. E. Litzky et al., "The Good, the Bad, and the Misguided"; A. H. Bell and D. M. Smith, "Protecting the Company against Theft and Fraud"; J. D. Hansen, "To Catch a Thief," *Journal of Accountancy* (March 2000): 43–46; and J. Greenberg, "The Cognitive Geometry of Employee Theft," in *Dysfunctional Behavior in Organizations: Nonviolent and Deviant Behavior* (Stamford, CT: JAI Press, 1998), 147–93.

47. T. K. Garrett, "Subduing Violence at Work: Setting Policies to Help Safeguard the Workplace," http://www.workforce.com/articles/21201-subduing-violence-at-work-setting-policies-to-help-safeguard-the-workplace, March 18, 2015; G. Botelho, "Workplace Violence: Know the Numbers, Risk Factors and Possible Warning Signs," http://www.cnn.com/2014/09/27/us/workplace-violence-questions-answers/, September 28, 2014; L. Copeland and D. Stanglin, "'Rambo' Gunman Injures 6 at FedEx Facility," *USA Today Online*, April 29, 2014; R. Rivera and L. Robbins, "Troubles Preceded Connecticut Workplace Killing," *New York Times Online*, August 3, 2010; J. Griffin, "Workplace Violence News" [www.workplaceviolencenews.com], July 16, 2010; and J. Smerd, "Workplace Shootings in Florida, Texas Again Put Focus on Violence on the Job," *Workforce Management Online*, November 6, 2009.

48. "Workplace Homicides from Shootings," U.S. Bureau of Labor Statistics, http://www.bls.gov/iif/oshwc/cfoi/osar0016.htm, January 2013.

49. J. McCafferty, "Verbal Chills," *CFO*, June 2005, 17; S. Armour, "Managers Not Prepared for Workplace Violence," July 15, 2004, 1B+; and "Workplace Violence," OSHA Fact Sheet, U.S. Department of Labor, Occupational Safety and Health Administration, 2002.

50. "Ten Tips on Recognizing and Minimizing Violence," *Workforce Management Online*, December 3, 2000.

51. "Bullying Bosses Cause Work Rage Rise," *Management Issues News* [www.management-issues.com], January 28, 2003.

52. C. Cosh, "Keep a Close Eye Out for the Signs," *Macleans*, December 27, 2010, 24; and R. McNatt, "Desk Rage," *BusinessWeek*, November 27, 2000, 12.

53. M. Gorkin, "Key Components of a Dangerously Dysfunctional Work Environment," *Workforce Online*, www.workforce.com (December 3, 2000).

54. L. D. Lieber, "HR's Role in Preventing Workplace Violence"; C. Cosh, "Keep a Close Eye Out for the Signs"; "Ten Tips on Recognizing and Minimizing Violence"; A. C. Klotz and M. R. Buckley, "Where Everybody Knows Your Name: Lessons from Small Business about Preventing Workplace Violence," *Business Horizons*, November 2010, 571–79; M. Gorkin, "Five Strategies and Structures for Reducing Workplace Violence"; "Investigating Workplace Violence: Where Do You Start?"; and "Points to Cover in a Workplace Violence Policy"—all of these are articles from *Workforce Online*, www.workforce.com (December 3, 2000).

55. Based on N. Pelusi, "Dealing with Difficult People," *Psychology Today*, September–October 2006, 68–69; and R. I. Sutton, *The No Asshole Rule: Building a Civilized Workplace and Surviving One That Isn't* (New York: Business Plus, 2007).

56. J. Swartz, "Visa Stores Data Like Gold: In Its Own Fort Knox," *USA Today*, March 26, 2012, 4B; M. Fitzgerald, "Visa Is Ready for Anything," *FastCompany.com*, November 2011, 54–58; and "Visa Launches New Operating System, Data Center," *CardLine*, November 20, 2009, 37.

57. "Visa Inc. Corporate Overview," http://usa.visa.com/download/corporate/_media/visa-overview_may2014.pdf, May 2014.

58. J. Stewart, "Visa's Test Results: Record Peak Volume and Expected Smooth Sailing for Tokens," http://digitaltransactions.net/news/story/4831, August 25, 2014.

59. R. Feintzeig, "Everything Is Awesome! Why You Can't Tell Employees They're Doing a Bad Job," *Wall Street Journal Online*, February 10, 2015; TciiStrategic and Management Consultants, "Why Positive Feedback Is Crucial to High Performance," http://www.businesszone.co.uk/blogs/tcii/tcii-strategic-and-management-consultants/why-positive-feedback-crucial-high-performance, May 13, 2013; and C. M. Phoel, "Feedback That Works," *Harvard Business Review*, https://hbr.org/2009/04/feedback-that-works/, April 27, 2009.

60. Trefis Team, "Lululemon Grows on Higher-Than-Expected Men's, ivivva Businesses, But 2015 Outlook Disappoints," www.forbes.com, March 30, 2015; B. Kowitt and C. Leahey, "Lululemon: In an Uncomfortable Position," *Fortune*, September 16, 2013, 110-18; and S. Clifford, "Recall Is Expensive Setback for Maker of Yoga Pants," *New York Times Online*, March 21, 2013.

15

In the future of manufacturing, robots will replace almost all workers.

Ron Chapple Stock/Alamy

Recent headlines claiming that robots are making people obsolete in the workforce may be true in some jobs, but robots are more likely to *assist* people in doing their jobs rather than *replace* them completely. Robots will do menial or dangerous jobs and those made up entirely of repetitive tasks, so some types of jobs *are* likely to be replaced by technology. However, technology also means people can focus on more complex work that demands creativity and flexibility.

EVERY organization produces

something, whether it's a good or a service. Some, like Starbucks, produce both a good and a service. Technology has changed how production is done. This chapter focuses on how organizations do operations management. We also look at the important role that managers play in managing those operations. •

Learning Outcomes

Why Is Operations Management Important to Organizations?

15-1 Define operations management and explain its role.

You've probably never given much thought to how organizations "produce" the goods and services that you buy or use. But it's an important process. Without it, you wouldn't have a car to drive or McDonald's fries to snack on, or even a hiking trail in a local park to enjoy. *Organizations need to have well-thought-out and well-designed operating systems, organizational control systems, and quality programs to survive in today's increasingly competitive global environment. And it's the manager's job to manage those things.*

operations management
The study and application of the transformation process

What Is Operations Management?

The term **operations management** refers to the design, operation, and control of the transformation process that converts such resources as labor and raw materials into goods and services that are sold to customers. Exhibit 15–1 portrays a simplified overview of the transformation process of creating value by converting inputs into outputs. The system takes inputs—people, technology, capital, equipment, materials, and information—and transforms them through various processes, procedures, and work activities into finished goods and services. These processes, procedures, and work activities are found throughout the organization. For example, department members in marketing, finance, research and development, human resources, and accounting convert inputs into outputs such as sales, increased market share, high rates of return on investments, new and innovative products, motivated and committed employees, and accounting reports. As a manager, you'll need to be familiar with operations management concepts, regardless of the area in which you're managing, in order to achieve your goals more effectively and efficiently.

Why is operations management so important to **organizations and managers?**

1. It encompasses processes in services and manufacturing organizations.
2. It's important in effectively and efficiently managing productivity.
3. It plays a strategic role in an organization's competitive success.

1 How Do Service and Manufacturing Firms Differ?

With a menu that offers more than 250 items made fresh each day, The Cheesecake Factory restaurants rely on a finely tuned production system. One food-service consultant says, "They've evolved with this highly complex menu combined with a highly efficient kitchen."[1]

Exhibit 15–1 The Operations System

Kyodo/AP Images

Eri Otsubo is a flight attendant for Japan's Peach Aviation Ltd., a service firm that provides low-cost air transportation. Peach's operations system creates value by transforming inputs such as aircraft and crew members into the nonphysical output of air travel. Like other developed nations, Japan has a service-based economy.

All organizations produce goods or services through the **transformation process**. Simply stated, every organization has an operations system that creates value by transforming inputs into finished goods and services outputs. For manufacturers, the products are obvious: cars, cell phones, or food products. After all, **manufacturing organizations** produce physical goods. It's easy to see the operations management (transformation) process at work in these types of organizations because raw materials are turned into recognizable physical products. But that transformation process isn't as readily evident in **service organizations** because they produce nonphysical outputs in the form of services. For instance, hospitals provide medical and health care services that help people manage their personal health; taxi companies provide transportation services that move people from one location to another; cruise lines provide vacation and entertainment services; and residential plumbers and electricians ensure that we have electricity and running water where we live. All of these service organizations transform inputs into outputs. For example, look at your college. College administrators bring together inputs—instructors, books, multimedia classrooms, and similar resources—to transform students into educated and skilled individuals.

The reason we're making this point is that the U.S. economy, and to a large extent the global economy, is dominated by the creation and sale of services. Most of the world's developed countries are predominantly service economies.[2] In the United States, for instance, almost 78 percent of all economic activity is services, and in the European Union, it's nearly 73 percent. In lesser-developed countries, the services sector is less important. For instance, in Chad, it accounts for only 32 percent of economic activity; in Laos, only 44 percent; and in Bolivia, 48 percent.

2 How Do Businesses Improve Productivity?

One jetliner has some 4 million parts. Efficiently assembling such a finely engineered product requires intense focus. Boeing and Airbus, the two major global manufacturers, have copied techniques from Toyota. However, not every technique can be copied because airlines demand more customization than do car buyers and there are significantly more rigid safety regulations for jetliners than for cars.[3] At the Evans Findings Company in East Providence, Rhode Island, which makes the tiny cutting devices on dental-floss containers, one production shift each day is run without people.[4] The company's goal is to do as much as possible with no labor. And it's not because they don't care about their employees. Instead, like many U.S. manufacturers, Evans needed to improve productivity in order to survive, especially against low-cost competitors. So they turned to "lights-out" manufacturing, where machines are designed to be so reliable that they make flawless parts on their own, without people operating them.

Although most organizations don't make products that have 4 million parts and most organizations can't function without people, *improving productivity has become a major goal in virtually every organization*. For countries, high productivity can lead to economic growth and development. Employees can receive higher wages and company profits can increase without causing inflation. For individual organizations, increased productivity gives them a more competitive cost structure and the ability to offer more competitive prices.

Over the past decade, U.S. businesses have made dramatic improvements to increase their efficiency. For example, at Latex Foam International's state-of-the-art digital facility in Shelton, Connecticut, engineers monitor all of the factory's operations. The facility boosted capacity by 50 percent in a smaller space and achieved a 30 percent efficiency gain.[5] And it's not just in manufacturing that companies are pursuing productivity gains. Pella

transformation process
The process that converts resources into finished goods and services

manufacturing organizations
Organizations that produce physical goods

service organizations
Organizations that produce nonphysical products in the form of services

Corporation's purchasing office improved productivity by reducing purchase order entry times anywhere from 50 percent to 86 percent, decreasing voucher processing by 27 percent, and eliminating 14 financial systems. Its information technology department slashed e-mail traffic in half and implemented work design improvements for heavy PC users such as call center users. The human resources department cut the time to process benefit enrollment by 156.5 days. And the finance department now takes two days, instead of six, to do its end-of-month closeout.[6]

Organizations that hope to succeed globally are looking for ways to improve productivity. For example, McDonald's Corporation drastically reduced the time it takes to cook french fries—65 seconds as compared to the 210 seconds it once took, saving time and other resources.[7] The Canadian Imperial Bank of Commerce, based in Toronto, automated its purchasing function, saving several million dollars annually.[8] And Skoda, the Czech car company, improved its productivity through an intensive restructuring of its manufacturing process.[9]

Productivity = People + Operations variables

Productivity is a composite of people and operations variables. To improve productivity, managers must focus on both. The late W. Edwards Deming, a renowned quality expert, believed that managers, not workers, were the primary source of increased productivity. He outlined 14 points for improving management's productivity (see the From the Past to the Present box on p. 459 for more information). A close look at these suggestions reveals Deming's understanding of the interplay between people and operations. High productivity can't come solely from good "people management." The truly effective organization will maximize productivity by successfully integrating people into the overall operations system. For instance, at Simplex Nails Manufacturing in Americus, Georgia, employees were an integral part of the company's much-needed turnaround effort.[10] Some production workers were redeployed on a plant-wide cleanup and organization effort, which freed up floor space. The company's sales force was retrained and refocused to sell what customers wanted rather than what was in inventory. The results were dramatic. Inventory was reduced by more than 50 percent, the plant had 20 percent more floor space, orders were more consistent, and employee morale improved. Here's a company that understood the important interplay between people and the operations system.

3 What Role Does Operations Management Play in a Company's Strategy?

Modern manufacturing originated more than 110 years ago in the United States, primarily in Detroit's automobile factories. The success that U.S. manufacturers experienced during World War II led manufacturing executives to believe that troublesome production problems had been conquered. These executives focused, instead, on improving other functional areas such as finance and marketing and paid little attention to manufacturing.

However, as U.S. executives neglected production, managers in Japan, Germany, and other countries took the opportunity to develop modern, technologically advanced facilities that fully integrated manufacturing operations into strategic planning decisions. The competition's success realigned world manufacturing leadership. U.S. manufacturers soon discovered that foreign goods were being made not only less expensively but also with better quality. Finally, by the late 1970s, U.S. executives recognized that they were facing a true crisis and responded. They invested heavily in improving manufacturing technology, increased the corporate authority and visibility of manufacturing executives, and began incorporating existing and future production requirements into the organization's overall strategic plan. Today, successful organizations recognize the crucial role that operations management plays as part of the overall organizational strategy to establish and maintain global leadership.[11]

The strategic role that operations management plays in successful organizational performance can be seen clearly as more organizations move toward managing their operations from a value chain perspective, which we're going to discuss next.

What Is Value Chain Management and Why Is It Important?

 15-2 Define the nature and purpose of value chain management.

The following examples of *closely integrated work activities among many different players are brought to you by* ...
VALUE CHAIN MANAGEMENT!

- **BIG management assignment due in one week and your computer crashes! NO!!!** Your custom-designed dream computer is built to your exact specifications and delivered two days later. Management assignment **DONE!**

- **Zero inventory warehousing.** Order processing that involves only one change of hands. It's happening at Siemens AG's Computed Tomography manufacturing plant in Forchheim, Germany, because its 30 supplier partners share responsibility with the plant for overall process performance.

Marek Kosmal/Fotolia

- Black & Decker's handheld glue gun—**totally outsourced to the leading glue gun manufacturer**.[12]

1 What Is **Value Chain Management?**

Let's start from the beginning...

- Every organization needs customers to survive and prosper.

- Customers want value from the goods and services they purchase or use, and *they decide what has value*.

- Organizations must provide that value to attract and keep customers.

- **Value** is defined as the performance characteristics, features and attributes, and any other aspects of goods and services for which customers are willing to give up resources (usually money).

vege/Fotolia

value
The performance characteristics, features, attributes, and other aspects of goods and services, for which customers are willing to give up resources

- Value is provided to customers through transforming raw materials and other resources into some product or service that end users need or desire when, where, and how they want it.

That seemingly simple act of turning varied resources into something that customers value and are willing to pay for involves a vast array of interrelated work activities performed by different participants *(suppliers, manufacturers, and even customers)*—that is, it involves the **value chain**.[13]

- **Value chain management** (VCM) is *externally* oriented and focuses on both incoming materials and outgoing products and services. VCM is effectiveness oriented and aims to create the highest value for customers.[14]

  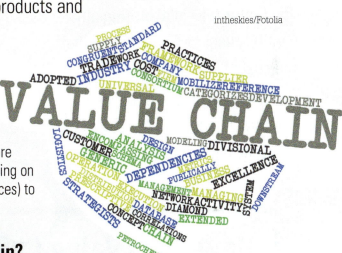

  intheskies/Fotolia

  - Contrast to supply chain management, which is efficiency oriented (its goal is to reduce costs and make the organization more productive) and *internally* oriented by focusing on efficient flow of incoming materials (resources) to the organization.

- **Who has the power in the value chain?**

  - Is it the supplier providing needed resources and materials? After all, suppliers have the ability to dictate prices and quality.

  - Is it the manufacturer that assembles those resources into a valuable product or service? A manufacturer's contribution in creating a product or service is critical.

  - Is it the distributor that makes sure the product or service is available where and when the customer needs it?

Actually, it's none of these!

> In value chain management, **CUSTOMERS are** the ones with the power.[15]

value chain
The entire series of work activities that add value at each step from raw materials to finished product

value chain management
The process of managing the sequence of activities and information along the entire value chain

- They define what value is and how it's created and provided.

- Using VCM, managers seek to find that unique combination in which customers are offered solutions that truly meet their needs and at a price that can't be matched by competitors.[16]

Goals of Value Chain Management

- Sequence of participants work together as a team, each adding some component of value—*such as faster assembly, more accurate information, or better customer response and service*—to the overall process.[17]

- The better the collaboration among the various chain participants, the better the customer solutions.

- When value is created for customers and their needs and desires satisfied, everyone along the chain benefits.[18]

Durand Florence/SIPA/Newscom

2 How Does Value Chain Management Benefit Businesses?

- Improved procurement (acquiring needed resources).

- Improved logistics (managing materials, service, and information).

- Improved product development (close relationships with customers leads to developing products they value).

- Enhanced customer order management *(managing every step to make sure customers are satisfied)*.[19]

nickylarson974/Fotolia

William Edwards Deming was an American statistician, professor, author, lecturer, and consultant.[20] He is widely credited with improving production in the United States during World War II, although he's probably best known for his work in Japan. From 1950 onward, he taught Japanese top managers how to improve product design and product quality, testing, and sales, primarily through applying statistical methods. Dr. Deming's philosophy was quite simple: Focus on increasing quality and reducing costs through continually improving how employees' work is done and by approaching manufacturing in an orderly, systematic, and logical way.

Deming: **Improving Managers' Productivity**

Putting that philosophy into practice required following Deming's 14 points for improving management's productivity. These suggestions are as follows:

- Plan for the long-term future.

- Never be complacent concerning the quality of your product.

- Establish statistical control over your production processes and require your suppliers to do so as well.

- Deal with the best and fewest number of suppliers.

- Find out whether your problems are confined to particular parts of the production process or stem from the overall process itself.

- Train workers for the job that you are asking them to perform.

- Raise the quality of your line supervisors.

- Drive out fear.

- Encourage departments to work closely together rather than to concentrate on departmental or divisional distinctions.

- Do not adopt strictly numerical goals.

- Require your workers to do quality work.

- Train your employees to understand statistical methods.

- Train your employees in new skills as the need arises.

- Make top managers responsible for implementing these principles.

These principles have withstood the test of time and are still applicable for managers looking to improve productivity.

*If your professor has assigned this, go to the Assignments section of **mymanagementlab.com** to complete these discussion questions.*

⭐ **Talk About It 1:** Why are (1) continual improvement and (2) thinking of manufacturing as a system so important to managing operations?

⭐ **Talk About It 2:** Explain why these 14 principles are still appropriate today.

How Is Value Chain Management Done?

15-3 Describe how value chain management is done.

The dynamic, competitive environment facing contemporary global organizations demands new solutions.[21] Understanding how and why value is determined by the marketplace has led some organizations to experiment with a new **business model**—that is, a strategic design for how a company intends to profit from its broad array of strategies, processes, and activities. For example, IKEA, the home furnishings manufacturer, transformed itself from a small, Swedish mail-order furniture operation into the world's largest retailer of home furnishings by reinventing the value chain in the home furnishings industry. The company offers customers well-designed products at substantially lower prices in return for the customers' willingness to take on certain key tasks traditionally done by manufacturers and retailers—such as getting the furniture home and assembling it.[22] The company's adoption of a unique business model and willingness to abandon old methods and processes have worked well. It also helped that IKEA recognized the importance of managing its value chain.

business model
A strategic design for how a company intends to profit from its broad array of strategies, processes, and activities

Exhibit 15–2 Requirements for Successful Value Chain Management

What Are the Requirements for Successful Value Chain Management?

So what does successful value chain management require? Exhibit 15–2 summarizes the six main requirements. Let's look at each of these elements more closely.

(1) COORDINATION AND COLLABORATION. For the value chain to achieve its goal of meeting and exceeding customers' needs and desires, comprehensive and seamless integration among all members of the chain is absolutely necessary. All partners in the value chain must identify things that they may not value but that customers do. Sharing information and being flexible as far as who in the value chain does what are important steps in building coordination and collaboration. This sharing of information and analysis requires open communication among the various value chain partners. For example, Furon Company, a manufacturer of specialty polymer products, believes that better communication with customers and with suppliers has facilitated timely delivery of goods and services and opened up additional business opportunities for all its value chain partners.[23]

Coca-Cola's CEO Muhtar Kent (at right) is shown here with officials of the firm's bottling partner Coca-Cola Hellenic at a new plant opening in Russia. Kent and other company managers are strongly committed to leading the firm's global value chain from producers of agricultural ingredients to bottling partners and retailers.

ZUMA Press, Inc./Alamy

(2) TECHNOLOGY INVESTMENT. Successful value chain management isn't possible without a significant investment in information technology. The payoff from this investment is that information technology can be used to restructure the value chain to better serve end users.[24] For example, Rollerblade, Inc., invested heavily in developing a Web site and used it to educate customers about its products. Although the company has chosen not to sell its products over the Web for fear of antagonizing its dealer network, managers remain flexible about the issue and would reconsider if they felt that value could be better delivered to customers by doing so.[25]

What types of technology are important? According to experts, the key tools include a supporting enterprise resource planning software (ERP) system that links all of an organization's activities, sophisticated work planning and scheduling software, customer relationship management systems, business intelligence capabilities, and e-business connections with trading network partners.[26] For instance, Dell Inc. manages its supplier relationships almost exclusively online. The company has one Web site for customers and one for suppliers. The supplier Web site is the primary mode of communication between Dell and its largest suppliers. The company's investment in this type of information technology allows it to meet customers' needs in a way that competitors haven't been able to match.[27]

(3) ORGANIZATIONAL PROCESSES. Value chain management radically changes organizational processes—that is, the way organizational work is done.[28] Managers must critically evaluate all organizational processes from beginning to end by looking at core competencies—the organization's unique skills, capabilities, and resources—to determine where value is being added. Non-value-adding activities are eliminated. Questions such as "Where can internal knowledge be leveraged to improve flow of material and information?" "How can we better configure our product to satisfy both customers and suppliers?" "How can the flow of material and information be improved?" and "How can we improve customer service?" should be asked for each process. For example, when managers at Deere & Company implemented value chain management in its Worldwide Commercial and Consumer Equipment Division, a thorough process evaluation revealed that work activities needed to be better synchronized and interrelationships between multiple links in the value chain better managed. They changed numerous work processes division-wide in order to improve these relationships.[29]

Three important conclusions can be made about how organizational processes must change:

- First, better demand forecasting is necessary and possible because of closer ties with customers and suppliers. For example, in an effort to make sure that Listerine was on the store shelves when customers wanted it, Walmart collaborated with product manufacturer Pfizer Consumer Healthcare on improving product demand forecast information. Through their mutual efforts, the partners boosted Walmart's sales of Listerine by $6.5 million. Customers also benefited because they were able to purchase the product when and where they wanted it.
- Second, selected functions may need to be done collaboratively with other partners in the value chain. This collaboration may even extend to sharing employees. For instance, Saint-Gobain Performance Plastics, headquartered in Northboro, Massachusetts, places its own employees in customer sites and brings employees of suppliers and customers to work on its premises. Saint-Gobain's CEO says this type of collaboration is essential.[30]
- Finally, new measures are needed for evaluating the performance of various activities along the value chain. Because the goal in value chain management is meeting and exceeding customers' needs and desires, managers need a better picture of how well value is being created and delivered to customers. For instance, when Nestlé USA implemented a value chain management approach, it redesigned its measurement system to focus on one consistent set of factors, including accuracy of demand forecasts and production plans, on-time delivery, and customer service levels. This redesign allowed management to more quickly identify problems and take actions to resolve them.[31]

(4) LEADERSHIP. The importance of leadership to value chain management is plain and simple—successful value chain management isn't possible without strong and committed leadership.[32] From top organizational levels to lower levels, managers must support, facilitate, and promote the implementation and ongoing practice of value chain management. Managers must make a serious commitment to identifying what value is, how that value can best be provided, and how successful those efforts have been. That type of organizational atmosphere or culture, in which all efforts are focused on delivering superb customer value, isn't possible without a serious commitment on the part of the organization's leaders.

Also, it's important that leaders outline expectations for what's involved in the organization's pursuit of value chain management. Ideally, articulating expectations should start with a vision or mission statement that expresses the organization's commitment to

organizational processes
The way organizational work is done

identifying, capturing, and providing the highest possible value to customers. For example, when American Standard Companies began its pursuit of value chain management, the CEO attended dozens of meetings across the country explaining the changing competitive environment and why the company needed to create better working relationships with its value chain partners.[33] Throughout the organization, then, managers should clarify expectations regarding each employee's role in the value chain. Being clear about expectations also extends to partners. For example, managers at American Standard identified clear requirements for suppliers and were prepared to drop any that couldn't meet them. The company was so serious about its expectations that it did cut hundreds of suppliers from air-conditioning, bath and kitchen, and vehicle control systems businesses. The upside, though, was that those suppliers that met the expectations benefited from more business and American Standard had partners that could deliver better value to customers.

Flexibility. **Flexibility.** Flexibility.

---

(5) EMPLOYEES/HUMAN RESOURCES.   We know from our discussions of management theories and approaches throughout this textbook that employees are the organization's most important resource. So, not surprisingly, employees play an important part in value chain management. Three main human resources requirements for value chain management are flexible approaches to job design, an effective hiring process, and ongoing training.

Flexibility is the key description of job design in a value chain management organization. Traditional functional job roles—such as marketing, sales, accounts payable, customer service representative, and so forth—are inadequate in a value chain management environment. Instead, jobs need to be designed around work processes that link all functions involved in creating and providing value to customers. This type of flexible job design supports the company's commitment to providing superb customer value.[34] In designing jobs for a value chain approach, the focus needs to be on how each activity performed by an employee can best contribute to the creation and delivery of customer value, which requires flexibility in what employees do and how they do it.

The fact that jobs in a value chain management organization must be flexible contributes to the second requirement: Flexible jobs require employees who are flexible. In a value chain organization, employees may be assigned to work teams that tackle a given process and are often asked to do different things on different days, depending on need. In an environment focusing on collaborative relationships that may change as customer needs change, employees' ability to be flexible is critical. Accordingly, the organization's hiring process must be designed to identify those employees who have the ability to quickly learn and adapt.

Finally, the need for flexibility also requires a significant investment in ongoing employee training. Whether the training involves learning how to use information technology software, how to improve the flow of materials throughout the chain, how to identify activities that add value, how to make better decisions faster, or how to improve any number of other potential work activities, managers must see to it that employees have the knowledge and tools they need to do their jobs. For example, at defense and electronics contractor Alenia Marconi Systems, based in Portsmouth, England, ongoing training is part of the company's commitment to efficiently and effectively meeting the needs of customers. Employees continually receive technical training as well as training in strategic issues, including the importance of emphasizing people and customers, not just sales and profits.[35]

(6) ORGANIZATIONAL CULTURE AND ATTITUDES.   The last requirement for value chain management is having a supportive organizational

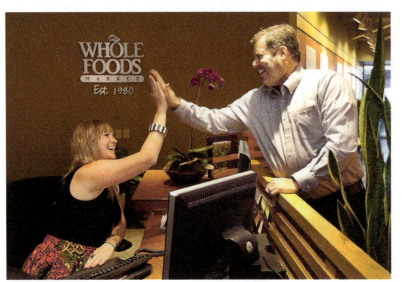

As the global VP for team member services for Whole Foods Market, Mark Ehrnstein ensures that the retailer's culture of sharing, respect, and trust extends to all value chain members. It encompasses the firm's core values of creating win-win partnerships with suppliers, delighting and nourishing customers, and supporting employee happiness and excellence.

Austin American-Statesman/MCT/Landov

culture and attitudes. Those cultural attitudes include sharing, collaborating, openness, flexibility, mutual respect, and trust. And these attitudes encompass not only the internal partners in the value chain but external partners as well. For instance, American Standard has chosen to practice these attitudes the old-fashioned way—with lots of face time and telephone calls. However, as we mentioned earlier, Dell has taken a completely different approach, as it works with its value chain partners almost exclusively through cyberspace.[36] Both approaches, however, reflect each company's commitment to developing long-lasting, mutually beneficial, and trusting relationships that best meet customers' needs.

What Are the Obstacles to Value Chain Management?

As desirable as value chain management may be, managers must tackle several obstacles in managing the value chain—organizational barriers, cultural attitudes, required capabilities, and people (see Exhibit 15–3).

ORGANIZATIONAL BARRIERS. Organizational barriers are among the most difficult obstacles to handle. These barriers include refusal or reluctance to share information, reluctance to shake up the status quo, and security issues. Without shared information, close coordination and collaboration is impossible. And the reluctance or refusal of employees to shake up the status quo can impede efforts toward value chain management and prevent its successful implementation. Finally, because value chain management relies heavily on a substantial information technology infrastructure, system security and Internet security breaches are issues that need to be addressed.

CULTURAL ATTITUDES. Unsupportive cultural attitudes—especially trust and control—also can be obstacles to value chain management. The trust issue is a critical one—both lack of trust and too much trust. To be effective, partners in a value chain must trust each other. There must be a mutual respect for, and honesty about, each partner's activities all along the chain. When that trust doesn't exist, the partners will be reluctant to share information, capabilities, and processes. But too much trust also can be a problem. Just about any organization is vulnerable to theft of intellectual property—that is, proprietary information that's critical to an organization's efficient and effective functioning and competitiveness. You need to be able to trust your value chain partners so your organization's valuable assets aren't compromised.[37] Another cultural attitude that can be an obstacle is the belief that when an organization collaborates with external and internal partners, it no longer controls its own destiny. However, this just isn't the case. Even with the intense collaboration that's important to value chain management, organizations still control critical decisions such as what customers value, how much value they desire, and what distribution channels are important.[38]

Exhibit 15–3 Obstacles to Successful Value Chain Management

A Question of Ethics

Okay—so here's an "unusual" ethics dilemma for you and it's a fitting conclusion in the last chapter of the textbook. Why? Because it illustrates that questions of ethics can pop up in the most ordinary of places. Suppose that you went to a popular shopping area where parking was extremely limited and the store owner had instituted "customers only" parking and you were lucky enough to find an open space. Then suppose that once you finished your business at that store—having spent a fair amount of money—you had other shopping to do in the same vicinity so you left your car in that same "customers only" parking space. You believed that what you did was okay since you "paid" for that spot with your purchase. But your significant other disagreed saying that since you had finished your business at that store, your car should be moved.[39]

*If your professor has assigned this, go to the Assignments section of **mymanagementlab.com** to complete these discussion questions.*

⭐ **Talk About It 3:** What is the "question of ethics" here? Why is it a "question of ethics"?

⭐ **Talk About It 4:** Who are the other stakeholders in this situation and how might this one seemingly simple decision affect them?

REQUIRED CAPABILITIES.   We know from our earlier discussion of requirements for the successful implementation of value chain management that value chain partners need numerous capabilities. Several of these—coordination and collaboration, the ability to configure products to satisfy customers and suppliers, and the ability to educate internal and external partners—aren't easy. But they're essential to capturing and exploiting the value chain. Many of the companies we've described throughout this section endured critical, and oftentimes difficult, self-evaluations of their capabilities and processes in order to become more effective and efficient at managing their value chains.

> Your people must be **committed to VCM.**

PEOPLE.   The final obstacles to successful value chain management can be an organization's people. Without their unwavering commitment to do whatever it takes, value chain management won't be successful. If employees refuse to be flexible in their work—how and with whom they work—collaboration and cooperation throughout the value chain will be hard to achieve. In addition, value chain management takes an incredible amount of time and energy on the part of an organization's employees. Managers must motivate those high levels of effort from employees, which isn't an easy thing to do.

⭐ **Try It!**

If your professor has assigned this, go to the Assignments section of **mymanagementlab.com** to complete the **Simulation:** *Operations Management*.

What Contemporary Issues Do Managers Face in Managing Operations?

15-4 Discuss contemporary issues in managing operations.

 Redesigned milk jugs that have been adopted by Walmart and Costco are cheaper to ship, better for the environment, cost less, and keep the milk fresher. Experts say this type of redesign is "an example of the changes likely to play out in the American economy over the next two decades. In an era of soaring global demand and higher costs for energy and materials, virtually every aspect of the economy needs to be re-examined and many products must be redesigned for greater efficiency."[40]

If you somehow thought that managing operations didn't really matter in today's online 24/7 global economy, think again. It does matter...a lot. We're going to look at three contemporary issues that managers face in managing operations.

1 What Role Does Technology Play in Operations Management?

As we know from our previous discussion of value chain management, today's competitive marketplace has put tremendous pressure on organizations to deliver products and services that customers value in a timely manner. Smart companies are looking at ways to harness technology to improve operations management. Many fast-food companies are competing to see who can provide faster and better service to drive-through customers. With drive-through now representing a huge portion of sales, faster and better delivery can be a significant competitive edge. For instance, Wendy's added awnings to some of its menu boards and replaced some of the text with pictures. Others use confirmation screens, a technology that helped McDonald's boost accuracy by more than 11 percent. And technology used by two national chains tells managers how much food they need to prepare by counting vehicles in the drive-through line and factoring in demand for current promotional and popular staple items.[41]

Although an organization's production activities are driven by the recognition that the customer is king, managers still need to be more responsive. For instance, operations managers need systems that can reveal available capacity, status of orders, and product quality while products are in the process of being manufactured, not just after the fact. To connect more closely with customers, production must be synchronized across the enterprise. To avoid bottlenecks and slowdowns, the production function must be a full partner in the entire business system.

What's making such extensive collaboration possible is technology. Technology is also allowing organizations to control costs particularly in the areas of predictive maintenance, remote diagnostics, and utility cost savings. For instance, Internet-compatible equipment contains embedded Web servers that can communicate proactively—that is, if a piece of equipment breaks or reaches certain preset parameters indicating that it's about to break, it asks for help. But technology can do more than sound an alarm or light up an indicator button. For instance, some devices have the ability to initiate e-mail or signal a pager at a supplier, the maintenance department, or contractor describing the specific problem and requesting parts and service. How much is such e-enabled maintenance control worth? It can be worth quite a lot if it prevents equipment breakdowns and subsequent production downtime.

Managers who understand the power of technology to contribute to more effective and efficient performance know that managing operations is more than the traditional view of simply producing the product. Instead, the emphasis is on working together with all the organization's business functions to find solutions to customers' business problems. (See the Technology and the Manager's Job box for more information on technology's role in the factory of the future.)

Technology and the Manager's Job
WELCOME TO THE FACTORY OF THE FUTURE!

What would the ideal factory of the future look like?[42] Experts at Georgia Tech's Manufacturing Research Center say that three important trends are driving what tomorrow's factories will look like. **①** One trend is *globalization of the supply chain.* In the factories of the future, design and business processes will be performed where it's most efficient and effective to do so. For example, parts for Boeing's 787 Dreamliner are produced around the world and then come together in Boeing's U.S. facilities. (See Case Application #2 on p. 477 for more info!) **②** The second trend is *technology that simultaneously dematerializes the product while vastly increasing complexity.* The challenge for managing operations is that despite simplicity in products, the production process is becoming more complex. **③** The third trend is *demographics and the impact on demand patterns.* Products will have shorter life cycles and more variety and choices. The key characteristic of the factory of the future will be its ability to change to accommodate whatever product is being produced in the needed time frame. And it will be particularly important that these factories be efficient and effective.

Given these trends, it's clear that technology will continue to play a key role in transformation processes that need to be collaborative, adaptive, flexible, and responsive. But keep in mind that technology is simply a tool. Future factories will also require a talented and skilled workforce and a clear understanding of managing operations processes. Those are the challenges facing managers who want their organizations to survive and thrive.

If your professor has assigned this, go to the Assignments section of **mymanagementlab.com** *to complete these discussion questions.*

⭐ **TALK ABOUT IT 5:** How will technology contribute to the operations management process? What are the downsides to using technology in the operations management process?

⭐ **TALK ABOUT IT 6:** In the factory of the future, what role does a manager play?

2 How Do Managers Control Quality?

$100 million—Apple's settlement with customers over poor quality.

Quality problems are expensive. For example, even though Apple has had phenomenal success with its iPod, the batteries in the first three versions died after four hours instead of lasting up to 12 hours, as buyers expected. Apple's settlement with consumers cost close to $100 million. At Schering-Plough, problems with inhalers and other pharmaceuticals were traced to chronic quality control shortcomings, for which the company eventually paid a $500 million fine. And the auto industry paid $14.5 billion to cover the cost of warranty and repair work in one year.[43]

Many experts believe that organizations unable to produce high-quality products won't be able to compete successfully in the global marketplace. What is quality? When you consider a product or service to have quality, what does that mean? Does it mean that the product doesn't break or quit working—that is, is it reliable? Does it mean that the service is delivered in a way that you intended? Does it mean that the product does what it's supposed to do? Or does quality mean something else? Exhibit 15–4 provides a description of several quality dimensions. We're going to define quality as the ability of a product or service to reliably do what it's supposed to do and to satisfy customer expectations.

HOW IS QUALITY ACHIEVED? How quality is achieved is an issue managers must address. A good way to look at quality initiatives is with the management functions—planning, organizing and leading, and controlling—that need to take place.

When *planning for quality,* managers must have quality improvement goals and strategies and plans to achieve those goals. Goals can help focus everyone's attention toward some objective quality standard. For instance, Caterpillar's goal is to apply quality improvement techniques to help cut costs.[44] Although this goal is specific and challenging, managers

Exhibit 15–4 *What Is Quality?*

PRODUCT QUALITY DIMENSIONS

1. Performance—Operating characteristics
2. Features—Important special characteristics
3. Flexibility—Meeting operating specifications over some period of time
4. Durability—Amount of use before performance deteriorates
5. Conformance—Match with preestablished standards
6. Serviceability—Ease and speed of repair or normal service
7. Aesthetics—How a product looks and feels
8. Perceived quality—Subjective assessment of characteristics (product image)

SERVICE QUALITY DIMENSIONS

1. Timeliness—Performed in promised period of time
2. Courtesy—Performed cheerfully
3. Consistency—Giving all customers similar experiences each time
4. Convenience—Accessibility to customers
5. Completeness—Full service, as required
6. Accuracy—Performed correctly each time

Sources: Based on J. W. Dean and J. R. Evans, *Total Quality: Management, Organization, and Society* (St. Paul, MN: West Publishing Company, 1994); H. V. Roberts and B. F. Sergesketter, *Quality Is Personal* (New York: The Free Press, 1993); D. Garvin, *Managed Quality: The Strategic and Competitive Edge* (New York: The Free Press, 1988); and M. A. Hitt, R. D. Ireland, and R. E. Hoskisson, *Strategic Management,* 4th ed. (Cincinnati: South-Western Publishing, 2001), 121.

---

and employees are partnering together to pursue well-designed strategies to achieve the goals, and are confident they can do so.

When *organizing and leading for quality,* it's important for managers to look to their employees. For instance, at the Moosejaw, Saskatchewan, plant of General Cable Corporation, every employee participates in continual quality assurance training. In addition, the plant manager believes wholeheartedly in giving employees the information they need to do their jobs better. He says, "Giving people who are running the machines the information is just paramount. You can set up your cellular structure, you can cross-train your people, you can use lean tools, but if you don't give people information to drive improvement, there's no enthusiasm." Needless to say, this company shares production data and financial performance measures with all employees.[45]

AFP/Stringer/Getty Images

Italian carmaker Ferrari competes successfully in the global marketplace by developing and producing high-quality cars in terms of design, performance, and reliability. Employees like this worker performing a quality check at the end of an assembly line apply the concept of excellence to the way they think, plan, act, and carry out their tasks.

Organizations with extensive and successful quality improvement programs tend to rely on two important people approaches: cross-functional work teams and self-directed or empowered work teams. Because achieving product quality is something that all employees from upper to lower levels must participate in, it's not surprising that quality-driven organizations rely on well-trained, flexible, and empowered employees.

Finally, managers must recognize when *controlling for quality* that quality improvement initiatives aren't possible without having some way to monitor and evaluate their progress. Whether it involves standards for inventory control, defect rate, raw materials procurement, or other operations management areas, controlling for quality is important. For instance, at the Northrup Grumman Corporation plant in Rolling Meadows, Illinois, several quality controls have been implemented, such as automated testing and IT that integrates product design and manufacturing and tracks process quality improvements. Also, employees are empowered to make accept/reject decisions about products throughout the manufacturing process. The plant manager explains, "This approach helps build quality into the product rather than trying to inspect quality into the product." But one of the most important things they do is "go to war" with their customers—soldiers preparing for war or live combat situations. Again, the plant manager says, "What discriminates us is that we believe if we can understand our customer's mission as well as they do, we can help them be more effective. We don't wait for our customer to ask us to do something. We find out what our customer is trying to do and then we develop solutions."[46]

Quality improvement success stories can be found globally. For example, at a Delphi assembly plant in Matamoros, Mexico, employees worked hard to improve quality and made significant strides. For instance, the customer reject rate on shipped products is now 10 ppm (parts per million), down from 3,000 ppm—an improvement of almost 300 percent.[47] Quality initiatives at several Australian companies, including Alcoa of Australia, Wormald Security, and Carlton and United Breweries, have led to significant quality improvements.[48] At Valeo Klimasystemme GmbH of Bad Rodach, Germany, assembly teams build different climate-control systems for high-end German cars including Mercedes and BMW. Quality initiatives by those teams have led to significant improvements.[49]

WHAT QUALITY GOALS MIGHT ORGANIZATIONS PURSUE?   To publicly demonstrate their commitment to quality, many organizations worldwide have pursued challenging quality goals. The two best-known are the following:

(1) **ISO 9000** is a series of international quality management standards established by the International Organization for Standardization (www.iso.org), which sets uniform guidelines for processes to ensure that products conform to customer requirements. These standards cover everything from contract review to product design to product delivery. The ISO 9000 standards have become the internationally recognized standard for evaluating and comparing companies in the global marketplace. In fact, this type of

ISO 9000
A series of international quality standards that set uniform guidelines for processes to ensure that products conform to customer requirements

Six Sigma
A quality standard that establishes a goal of no more than 3.4 defects per million units or procedures

project
A one-time-only set of activities with a definite beginning and ending point

project management
The task of getting project activities done on time, within budget, and according to specifications

certification can be a prerequisite for doing business globally. Achieving ISO 9000 certification provides proof that a quality operations system is in place. As of 2009, more than 1 million certifications had been awarded to organizations in 175 countries. Almost 40,000 U.S. businesses are ISO 9000 certified. More than 200,000 Chinese firms have received certification.[50]

(2) More than 30 years ago, Motorola further popularized the use of stringent quality standards through a trademarked quality improvement program called **Six Sigma**.[51] Very simply, Six Sigma is a quality standard that establishes a goal of no more than 3.4 defects per million units or procedures. What does the name mean? Sigma is the Greek letter that statisticians use to define a standard deviation from a bell curve. The higher the sigma, the fewer the deviations from the norm—that is, the fewer the defects. At One Sigma, two-thirds of whatever is being measured falls within the curve. Two Sigma covers about 95 percent. At Six Sigma, you're about as close to defect-free as you can get.[52] It's an ambitious quality goal! Although it's an extremely high standard to achieve, many quality-driven businesses are using it and benefiting from it. For instance, General Electric estimates that it has saved billions since 1995 by using Six Sigma, according to company executives.[53] Other examples of companies pursuing Six Sigma include ITT Industries, Dow Chemical, 3M Company, American Express, Sony Corporation, Nokia Corporation, and Johnson & Johnson. Although manufacturers seem to make up the bulk of Six Sigma users, service companies such as financial institutions, retailers, and health-care organizations are beginning to apply it. What impact can Six Sigma have? Let's look at an example.

It used to take Wellmark Blue Cross and Blue Shield, a managed-care health-care company, 65 days or more to add a new doctor to its medical plans. Thanks to Six Sigma, the company discovered that half the processes they used were redundant. With those unnecessary steps gone, the job now gets done in 30 days or less and with reduced staff. The company also has been able to reduce its administrative expenses by $3 million per year, an amount passed on to consumers through lower health premiums.[54]

Although it's important for managers to recognize that many positive benefits come from obtaining ISO 9000 certification or Six Sigma, *the key benefit comes from the quality improvement journey itself.* In other words, the goal of quality certification should be having work processes and an operations system in place that enable organizations to meet customers' needs and employees to perform their jobs in a consistently high-quality way.

3 How Are Projects Managed?

As we discussed in Chapter 6, many organizations are structured around projects. A **project** is a one-time-only set of activities with a definite beginning and ending point.[55] Projects vary in size and scope, from a NASA space shuttle launch to a wedding. **Project management** is the task of getting the activities done on time, within budget, and according to specifications.

Project management has actually been around for a long time in industries such as construction and movie making, but now it has expanded into almost every type of business. What explains the growing popularity of project management? It fits well with a dynamic environment and the need for flexibility and rapid response. Organizations are increasingly undertaking projects that are somewhat unusual or unique, have specific deadlines, contain complex interrelated tasks requiring specialized skills, and are temporary in nature. These types of projects don't lend themselves well to the standardized operating procedures that guide routine and continuous organizational activities.[56]

Project management in the music industry includes concert tours by artists such as country music singer Kenny Chesney. Managing a tour involves coordinating the timeline, activities, accommodations, and transportation for the musicians and crew members in different cities and performance venues from the first to the last concert date.

Eric Henderson/Reuters/Landov

Exhibit 15–5 A Sample Gantt Chart

In the typical project, team members are temporarily assigned to and report to a project manager who coordinates the project's activities with other departments and reports directly to a senior executive. The project is temporary: It exists only long enough to complete its specific objectives. Then it's wound down and closed up; members move on to other projects, return to their permanent departments, or leave the organization.

If you were to observe a group of supervisors or department managers for a few days, you would see them regularly detailing what activities have to be done, the order in which they are to be done, who is to do each, and when they are to be completed. The managers are doing what we call scheduling. The following discussion reviews some useful scheduling devices.

HOW DO YOU USE A GANTT CHART? The Gantt chart is a planning tool developed around the turn of the century by Henry Gantt. The idea behind the Gantt chart is relatively simple. It's essentially a bar graph, with time on the horizontal axis and the activities to be scheduled on the vertical axis. The bars show output, both planned and actual, over a period of time. The Gantt chart visually shows when tasks are supposed to be done and compares the assigned date with the actual progress on each. This simple but important device allows managers to detail easily what has yet to be done to complete a job or project and to assess whether it's ahead of, behind, or on schedule.

Exhibit 15–5 shows a Gantt chart that was developed for book production by a manager in a publishing firm. Time is expressed in months across the top of the chart. Major activities are listed down the left side. The planning comes in deciding what activities need to be done to get the book finished, the order in which those activities need to be done, and the time that should be allocated to each activity. The blue shading represents actual progress made in completing each activity.

A Gantt chart, then, actually becomes a managerial control device as the manager looks for deviations from the plan. In this case, most activities were completed on time. However, if you look at the "review first pages" activity, you will notice that it's actually almost two and a half weeks behind schedule. Given this information, the manager might want to take some corrective action to make up the lost time and to ensure that no further delays will occur. At this point, the manager can expect that the book will be published at least two weeks late if no corrective action is taken.

A modified version of the Gantt chart is a load chart. Instead of listing activities on the vertical axis, load charts list either whole departments or specific resources. This information allows managers to plan and control for capacity utilization. In other words, load charts schedule capacity by workstations. For example, Exhibit 15–6 shows a load chart for six production editors at the same publishing firm. Each editor supervises the design and production of several books. By reviewing the load chart, the executive editor who supervises the six production editors can see who is free to take on a new book. If everyone is fully scheduled, the executive editor might decide not to accept any new projects, to accept some new projects and delay others, to ask the editors to work overtime, or to employ more production editors.

PERT: Program Evaluation and Review Technique

Gantt chart
A planning tool that shows in bar graph form when tasks are supposed to be done and compares that with the actual progress on each

load chart
A modified version of a Gantt chart that lists either whole departments or specific resources

Exhibit 15–6 A Sample Load Chart

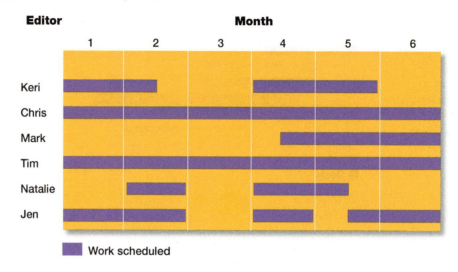

WHAT IS A PERT NETWORK ANALYSIS?   Gantt and load charts are helpful as long as the activities or projects being scheduled are few and independent of each other. But what if a manager had to plan a large project—such as a complex reorganization, the launching of a major cost-reduction campaign, or the development of a new product—that required coordinating inputs from marketing, production, and product design personnel? Such projects require coordinating hundreds or thousands of activities, some of which must be done simultaneously and some of which cannot begin until earlier activities have been completed. If you are constructing a shopping mall, you obviously cannot start erecting walls until the foundation has been laid. How, then, to schedule such a complex project? Use PERT.

PERT network analysis was originally developed in the late 1950s for coordinating the more than 3,000 contractors and agencies working on the Polaris submarine weapon system. This project was incredibly complicated, with hundreds of thousands of activities that had to be coordinated. PERT is reported to have cut two years off the completion date for the Polaris project.

A PERT network is a flowchart-like diagram that depicts the sequence of activities needed to complete a project and the time or costs associated with each activity. With a PERT network, a project manager must think through what has to be done, determine which events depend on one another, and identify potential trouble spots (see Exhibit 15–7). PERT also makes it easy to compare the effects alternative actions will have on scheduling and costs. PERT allows managers to monitor a project's progress, identify possible bottlenecks, and shift resources as necessary to keep the project on schedule.

To understand how to construct a PERT network, you need to know three terms: *events, activities,* and *critical path.* Let us define these terms, outline the steps in the PERT process, and then develop an example.

- **Events** are end points that represent the completion of major activities. Sometimes called milestones, events indicate that something significant has happened (such as receipt of purchased items) or an important component is finished. In PERT, events represent a point in time.
- **Activities,** on the other hand, are the actions that take place. Each activity consumes time, as determined on the basis of the time or resources required to progress from one event to another.
- The **critical path** is the longest or most time-consuming sequence of events and activities required to complete the project in the shortest amount of time.[57]

Let's apply PERT to a construction manager's task of building a 6,500-square-foot custom home.

PERT network analysis
A flowchart-like diagram that depicts the sequence of activities needed to complete a project and the time or costs associated with each activity

events
End points that represent the completion of major activities

activities
Actions that take place

critical path
The longest or most time-consuming sequence of events and activities required to complete a project in the shortest amount of time

Exhibit 15–7 Developing PERT Charts

Developing a PERT network requires the manager to identify all key activities needed to complete a project, rank them in order of dependence, and estimate each activity's completion time. This procedure can be translated into five specific steps:

1. Identify every significant activity that must be achieved for a project to be completed. The accomplishment of each activity results in a set of events or outcomes.
2. Ascertain the order in which these events must be completed.
3. Diagram the flow of activities from start to finish, identifying each activity and its relationship to all other activities. Use circles to indicate events and arrows to represent activities. The result is a flowchart diagram that we call the PERT network.
4. Compute a time estimate for completing each activity, using a weighted average that employs an optimistic time estimate (t_o) of how long the activity would take under ideal conditions, a most-likely estimate (t_m) of the time the activity normally should take, and a pessimistic estimate (t_p) that represents the time that an activity should take under the worst possible conditions. The formula for calculating the expected time (t_e) is then

$$t_e = \frac{t_o + 4t_m + t_p}{6}$$

5. Finally, using a network diagram that contains time estimates for each activity, the manager can determine a schedule for the start and finish dates of each activity and for the entire project. Any delays that occur along the critical path require the most attention because they delay the entire project. That is, the critical path has no slack in it; therefore, any delay along that path immediately translates into a delay in the final deadline for the completed project.

As a construction manager, you recognize that time really is money in your business. Delays can turn a profitable job into a money loser. Accordingly, you must determine how long it will take to complete the house. You have carefully dissected the entire project into activities and events. Exhibit 15–8 outlines the major events in the construction project and your estimate of the expected time required to complete each activity. Exhibit 15–9 depicts the PERT network based on the data in Exhibit 15–8.

HOW DOES PERT OPERATE? Your PERT network tells you that if everything goes as planned, it will take just over 32 weeks to build the house. This time is calculated by tracing the network's critical path: A B C D E I J K L M N P Q. Any delay in completing the events along this path will delay the completion of the entire project. For example, if it took six weeks instead of four to frame the house (event E), the entire project would be delayed by two weeks (or the time beyond that expected). But a one-week delay for installing the brick (event H) would have little effect because that event is not on the critical path. By using PERT, the construction manager would know that no corrective action would be needed. Further delays in installing the brick, however, could present problems—for such delays may, in actuality, result in a new critical path. Now back to our original critical path dilemma.

Notice that the critical path passes through N, P, and Q. Our PERT chart (Exhibit 15–9) tells us that these three activities take four weeks. Wouldn't path N O Q be faster? Yes. The PERT network shows that it takes only 3.5 weeks to complete that path. So why isn't N O Q on the critical path? Because activity Q cannot begin until both activities O and P are completed. Although activity O takes half a week, activity P takes one full week. So, the earliest we can begin Q is after one week. What happens to the difference between the critical activity (activity P) time and the noncritical activity (activity O) time? The difference, in this case half a week, becomes slack time. **Slack time** is the time difference between the critical path and all other paths. What use is there for slack? If the project manager notices some slippage on a critical activity, perhaps slack time from a noncritical activity can be borrowed and temporarily assigned to work on the critical one.

As you can see, PERT is both a planning and a control tool. Not only does PERT help us estimate the times associated with scheduling a project, but it also gives us clues about

slack time
The time difference between the critical path and all other paths

Exhibit 15–8 Major Activities in Building a Custom Home

EVENT	DESCRIPTION	TIME (WEEKS)	PRECEDING ACTIVITY
A	Approve design and get permits	3	None
B	Perform excavation/lot clearing	1	A
C	Pour footers	1	B
D	Erect foundation walls	2	C
E	Frame house	4	D
F	Install windows	0.5	E
G	Shingle roof	0.5	E
H	Install brick front and siding	4	F, G
I	Install electrical, plumbing, and heating and A/C rough-ins	6	E
J	Install insulation	0.25	I
K	Install sheetrock	2	J
L	Finish and sand sheetrock	7	K
M	Install interior trim	2	L
N	Paint house (interior and exterior)	2	H, M
O	Install all cabinets	0.5	N
P	Install flooring	1	N
Q	Final touch-up and turn over house to homeowner	1	O, P

Exhibit 15–9 A PERT Network for Building a Custom Home

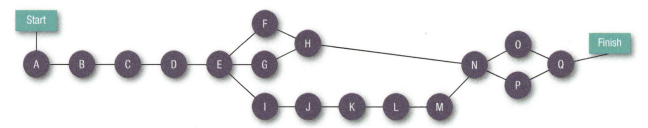

where our controls should be placed. Because any event on the critical path that is delayed will delay the overall project (making us not only late but also probably over budget), our attention needs to be focused on the critical activities at all times. For example, if activity F (installing windows) is delayed by a week because supplies have not arrived, that is not a major issue. It's not on the critical path. But if activity P (installing flooring) is delayed from one week to two weeks, the entire project will be delayed by one week. Consequently, anything that has the immediate potential for delaying a project (critical activities) must be monitored closely.

As we said in the beginning of this chapter, it's the manager's job to manage the organization's operating systems, organizational control systems, and quality programs. That's the only way organizations will survive in today's increasingly competitive global economy.

Go to **mymanagementlab.com** to complete the problems marked with this icon .

15 Review

CHAPTER SUMMARY

15-1 Define operations management and explain its role.

Operations management is the transformation process that converts resources into finished goods and services. Manufacturing organizations produce physical goods. Service organizations produce nonphysical outputs in the form of services. Productivity is a composite of people and operations variables. A manager should look for ways to successfully integrate people into the overall operations systems. Organizations must recognize the crucial role that operations management plays as part of their overall strategy in achieving successful performance.

15-2 Define the nature and purpose of value chain management.

The value chain is the sequence of organizational work activities that add value at each step from raw materials to finished product. Value chain management is the process of managing the sequence of activities and information along the entire product chain.

The goal of value chain management is to create a value chain strategy that meets and exceeds customers' needs and desires and allows for full and seamless integration among all members of the chain.

Four benefits from value chain management include improved procurement, improved logistics, improved product development, and enhanced customer order management.

15-3 Describe how value chain management is done.

The six main requirements for successful value chain management include coordination and collaboration, investment in technology, organizational processes, leadership, employees or human resources, and organizational culture and attitudes.

The obstacles to value chain management include organizational barriers (refusal to share information, reluctance to shake up the status quo, or security issues), unsupportive cultural attitudes, lack of required capabilities, and employees unwilling or unable to do it.

15-4 Discuss contemporary issues in managing operations.

Companies are looking at ways to harness technology to improve their operations management by extensive collaboration and cost control.

ISO 9000 is a series of international quality management standards that set uniform guidelines for processes to ensure that products conform to customer requirements. Six Sigma is a quality standard that establishes a goal of no more than 3.4 defects per million units or procedures.

Project management involves getting a project's activities done on time, within budget, and accomplished to specifications. A project is a one-time-only set of activities that has a definite beginning and ending point in time. Popular project scheduling tools include Gantt charts, load charts, and PERT network analysis.

DISCUSSION QUESTIONS

15-1 What is operations management and how is it used in both manufacturing and service organizations?

15-2 What strategic role does operations management play?

⭐ **15-3** How might operations management apply to other managerial functions besides control?

15-4 Do you think that manufacturing or service organizations have greater need of operations management? Explain.

⭐ **15-5** What is a value chain? What is value chain management? What is the goal of value chain management?

15-6 What types of organizational benefits does value chain management provide? What obstacles stand in the way of successful value chain management?

15-7 Explain why managing productivity is important in operations management.

15-8 Who has the power in the value chain? Explain your response.

15-9 Choose two tasks that you do every week (for example, shop for groceries, host a poker party, clean your house/apartment, do laundry). For each one, identify how you could (a) be more productive in doing that task, and (b) have higher-quality output from that task.

15-10 Select a company with which you're familiar. Describe its value chain. Be as specific as possible in your description. Evaluate how it "uses" the value chain to create value.

Writing Assignments

15-11 How could you use value chain management in your everyday life? Be specific.

15-12 How does technology affect operations management decisions?

Management Skill Builder | BEING A GOOD CONFLICT MANAGER

Managing any project will require good conflict management skills. You'll typically have to work across vertical and horizontal levels in the organization, deal with people over whom you have no formal authority, and have to negotiate schedules, deadlines, work assignments, and the like with people possibly both inside and outside the organization.

⭐ PERSONAL INVENTORY ASSESSMENT PERSONAL INVENTORY ASSESSMENT

Strategies for Handling Conflict

Conflict can arise any time you're working with a group of people on a project. Use this PIA to assess different strategies for handling conflict.

Practicing the Skill

To manage conflict effectively, you need to know yourself, as well as the conflicting parties; to understand the situation that has created the conflict; and to be aware of your options.[58]

• *What's your underlying conflict-handling style?* Most of us have the ability to vary our conflict response according to the situation, but each of us has a preferred style for handling conflicts. These styles include *collaborating* (accommodating various points of view to seek a win-win solution); *compromising* (we both give up something so there is no clear winner or loser); *accommodating* (self-sacrificing by putting others' interests above your own); *forcing* (satisfying your own interest regardless of the impact on others); and *avoiding* (withdrawing from or suppressing differences).

• *Selectively choose the conflicts you want to handle.* Not every conflict justifies your attention. Avoidance may appear to be a cop-out, but it can sometimes be the most appropriate response. Avoid trivial conflicts and save your efforts for the ones that count.

• *Evaluate the conflict parties.* Who is involved in the conflict? What interests do you or they represent? What are each party's values, personality, feelings, and resources?

• *Assess the source of the conflict.* The most common sources of interpersonal conflicts in organizations are communication differences, structural differences (i.e., rules, territorial battles, budget conflicts, questions of authority), and personality and value differences. Communication conflicts are typically the easiest to resolve, while personality and value differences the most difficult. Knowing the source of a conflict will narrow your choices of resolution techniques.

• *Select the best option.* In addition to the five preferred styles of handling conflict noted above, additional resolution techniques include expanding the scarce resource (such as a budget or promotion opportunities) that is causing the conflict; creating a shared goal that requires all parties to the conflict to cooperate on; behavioral-change intervention and counseling; and reorganizing jobs or departments.

Practicing the Skill

Follow the directions:

Form teams of three. Analyze each of the following scenarios and formulate a conflict-handling strategy:

Situation 1. You are a staff specialist and have been assigned two projects: one by your immediate supervisor and one by the supervisor of another department. There is adequate time to complete both projects by the deadline date; however, neither project would be completed with the degree of excellence required by your organization. What would you do?

Situation 2. You are the moderator of a group session with five other people. The purpose of the session is to formulate a plan that requires consent from all participants. One of the participants is so involved with the important details of the plan that he is delaying the group from reaching agreement. As moderator, what would you do in this situation?

Situation 3. Your boss has called you into his office and you find that he wants your opinion about the performance of one of your coworkers. The coworker is your best friend and neighbor, but you are inclined to believe that his performance is substandard. What would you tell the boss?

WestWood Travel Services

To: Ebben Crawford, Director of Operations

From: Anne Mendales, President

Subject: ISO 9001 Certification

Experiential Exercise

I've been doing a lot of reading on total quality management and I think we need to look at using TQM principles. Since our business has grown from one office with 12 employees to five offices with nearly 50 employees, I want to ensure that we're doing everything we can to meet our clients' needs, especially since we've lost some clients to competitors. Could you do an analysis describing how we might apply the concepts of customer focus, continuous process improvement, benchmarking, training, teamwork, and empowerment to our travel business to make us more competitive? Write up your analysis in a bulleted list format (no more than two pages please) and get it to me by the end of the week.

This fictionalized company and message were created for educational purposes only, and not meant to reflect positively or negatively on management practices by any company that may share this name.

CASE APPLICATION

Tragedy in Fashion

Although one fortunate and lucky young woman was pulled out alive after 17 days buried in the rubble, over 1,100 workers perished in a deadly factory building collapse in Dhaka, Bangladesh, in April 2013.[59] The Rana Plaza building collapse is now considered the deadliest disaster in the history of the clothing industry. As stated in this chapter, the dynamic competitive environment facing contemporary global organizations demands new solutions, but, as this story illustrates, sometimes those solutions have consequences—tragic consequences. As global apparel retailers reassess their operations management strategies, changes are likely to be forthcoming.

The **deadliest disaster** in the history of the clothing industry

Rock-bottom labor costs enticed global clothing giants to Bangladesh during the mid-2000s. Many of the retailers that have relied on these factories are known for cheap, "fast" apparel: H&M, Zara, Lee, Wrangler, J.C. Penney, and Walmart. And when you're selling many articles of clothing for $20 and under, it means your costs (especially when being shipped from another location halfway around the world) need to be tightly controlled. Also, the concept of fashion trends has changed over the last two decades. Where fashion used to be "good" for an entire season, now fashion styles, colors, shapes, and so forth, change, seemingly overnight.

Retailers like Zara and H&M have hooked customers on fast fashion—that is, clothes that go from concept and design to being in your local mall stores in a matter of weeks—and clothing has become a sort of "single-serving disposable item." Now consumers are wanting new and different items almost continuously. There's a "constant, ceaseless rotation through looks and styles." Providing for that demand has placed a significant strain on the operations system behind this fast, cheap fashion. Hasty expansion of factory capacity, lax governmental enforcement of permits and approvals, and a focus on keeping costs as low as possible in whatever ways needed have become the focus of factory work culture in this developing country. Because garment factories in Bangladesh don't have a lot of the more sophisticated machinery like China, their edge in the fashion industry had always been basic, simply-constructed clothing. And as the fashion industry's fashion emphasis changed, Bangladesh's importance to the global clothing trade rose. In fact, in six years, it rose from the 8th top clothing exporter to the 3rd (after China and Italy). Both Bangladeshi factory owners and the government were fully aware of the importance of this industry to the country.

Working conditions for factory employees in developing countries have long been less than desirable. Explosions and fires have been a continual problem, as have other unsafe work conditions. (Unfortunately, this isn't just a problem of the retail fashion industry.) Workplace protections are expensive, which doesn't work with consumers hooked on fashionable "cheap" clothing. However, with this latest tragic loss of life at this specific garment factory, the fashion industry's decisions— good and bad—are now on the world stage for everyone to see and criticize. Says one outspoken critic, "What happened in Bangladesh is a game-changer because of the gravity of the situation and tremendous loss of life." Now public policy and governmental groups around the world are turning up the heat on Bangladesh to reform its labor standards and are pressuring

global retailers to more carefully monitor their sourcing standards. Recently, several of the world's largest apparel companies agreed to a significant plan to help fund fire safety and building improvements. Part of this five-year agreement is to not hire/use manufacturers whose clothing factories fail to meet safety standards. Well-known European retailers who have signed on include Hennes & Mauritz AB (H&M), Inditex (the Spanish parent company of Zara), Tesco PLC, and others. Major U.S. retailers, including Walmart, Target, and Gap, chose not to sign that agreement because they felt it exposed them to unlimited liability. However, a group of nearly 20 U.S. North American retailers did sign a pact in which they agreed to inspect all the factories they do business with and to set up basic safety standards.[60] The Bangladeshi government also has pledged to raise wages for garment workers and to fix labor laws, making it easier for workers to form labor unions.

Discussion Questions

 15-14 Discuss this from a value chain management perspective. What happened? How did it happen? Why did it happen?

 15-15 How do incidents like this affect how managers work with a value chain?

15-16 Do some research on offshoring. What is it? What are the benefits and the drawbacks of offshoring as far as managing the operations system?

15-17 What can managers learn about managing operations from this situation?

15-18 Societal moral issue: Although enforcement of worker safety in Bangladesh is clearly lax, government officials clearly don't want global businesses withdrawing from the country (and moving the problem somewhere else) and driving it deeper into poverty. Discuss.

15-19 Personal moral issue: Would you pay a higher price for "ethical" clothing? Why or why not? Discuss.

CASE APPLICATION #2

Dreamliner Nightmare

The 787 Dreamliner was born out of desperation.[61] The year was 2003 and Boeing had just lost its title as the world's largest plane manufacturer to European rival Airbus. Boeing's then CEO had just resigned in a defense-contract scandal. And the company's stock price had plunged to its lowest price in a decade. Remember, this was two years after the 9/11 terrorist attacks and financially troubled airlines were reluctant to invest in new equipment. Boeing needed something revolutionary to win back customers.

That something was a technologically advanced aircraft that would be developed and built by a global network of suppliers. Major parts for the airplane would be preassembled all over the world and then shipped to Everett, Washington, where they would be "snapped together" in three days, compared with a month the traditional way. And it was Boeing's first aircraft built with lightweight composite materials (graphite, titanium, carbon fiber) rather than traditional metals, making the 787 a lighter and more efficient aircraft than previous models. Why was this so revolutionary? The 787 could fly farther, burn less fuel, and offer more passenger comforts than what was currently available. The 787 had built-in sensors designed to help counter the effects of turbulence, making for a smoother flight. And it was designed to have more humid air, quieter engines, improved lighting, and the largest windows in the industry. Of course, airlines were eager to save money and entice customers and ordered a record number of the planes. Despite its innovative features (or, as some critics said, maybe because of), the 787 faced many production setbacks and delays (the plane was originally scheduled to be delivered in May 2008). These delays were due to several issues, including design and manufacturing challenges—coordinating that many global suppliers, using new materials in the plane, and assembling the sophisticated components. However, three years after its first expected delivery date, Boeing handed over the first 787 on a rainy and blustery day in Everett, Washington, to Japan's All Nippon Airways Co. on September 26, 2011. The chief executive of Boeing's commercial airplanes division said "Today...will always be remembered as the dawn of a new day in commercial aviation."

> ### The Boeing 787: Developed and built by a global network of suppliers

In the 787's first year of service, at least four aircraft suffered some type of electrical problem. Although such problems are not unusual, especially in the first year of a newly designed aircraft, a number of incidents, including an electrical fire aboard an All Nippon Dreamliner plane and a similar fire aboard a landed 787 at Boston's Logan International Airport, led the Federal Aviation Administration (FAA) to order a review of the design and manufacture of the Dreamliner. There obviously was enough concern over what the FAA found because it proceeded to ground the entire Boeing 787 fleet. Aviation safety investigators focused their attention on the 787's lithium-ion batteries, manufactured by a Japanese company, GS Yuasa of Kyoto. Boeing's team immediately set to work to solve the issue because a grounded fleet is a BIG problem! In mid-March 2013, Boeing announced that it had come up with solutions for the Dreamliner problems. The 787's chief engineer said, "We may never get to a single root cause." But the engineers had looked at some 80 potential problems that could lead to a battery fire, categorized them into four groups, and come up with solutions for each group. A major part of the "fix" was a battery enclosure made of stainless steel, not designed to contain a fire, but to prevent the battery from ever having a fire to begin with by quickly starving any flame of oxygen. With the fix in place and approved by the FAA, a team of Dreamliner technicians fanned out around the globe modifying the 787's batteries. By the end of April 2013, the Dreamliner fleet went back into service.

Discussion Questions

⭐ **15-20** What role does innovation play in managing an organization's operations?

⭐ **15-21** What role does technology play in managing an organization's operations? (Take a look back at the Technology and the Manager's Job box on p. 465.)

⭐ **15-22** Describe the operations management issues that the Dreamliner team faced. Could these issues have been avoided? Why or why not?

⭐ **15-23** Is a global network of suppliers the future of operations management? Discuss.

15-24 What other lessons about operations management can you see in this story?

CASE APPLICATION #3

Stirring Things Up

The steaming cup of coffee placed in a customer's hand at any Starbucks store location starts as coffee beans (berries) plucked from fields of coffee plants.[62] From harvest to storage to roasting to retail to cup, Starbucks understands the important role each value chain participant plays.

Starbucks offers a selection of coffees from around the world, and its coffee buyers personally travel to the coffee-growing regions of Latin America, Africa/Arabia, and Asia/Pacific to select and purchase the highest-quality *arabica* beans. Once the beans arrive at any one of its six roasting facilities (in Washington, Pennsylvania, Nevada, South Carolina, Georgia, or Amsterdam), Starbucks' master professional roasters do their "magic" in creating the company's rich signature roast coffees. There are many potential challenges in "transforming" the raw material into the quality product and experience that customers expect at Starbucks—weather, shipping and logistics, technology, political instability, and so forth. All could potentially affect the company. Although those operations management challenges are significant, the most challenging issue facing Starbucks today is balancing its vision of the uniquely Starbucks' coffee experience with the realities of selling a $4 latte in today's world. Starbucks products have become an unaffordable luxury for many. As revenues and profits declined during the economic downturn, CEO Howard Schultz realized that Starbucks had to evaluate everything about how the company operated and to make changes where needed. Although it built its business as "the anti-fast-food joint," the recession and growing competition forced Starbucks to become more streamlined. Under one new initiative put into effect at its U.S. stores, employee time wasters such as bending over to scoop coffee from below the counter, idly standing by waiting for expired coffee to drain, or dawdling at the pastry case were discouraged. Instead, employees were to keep busy doing something, such as helping customers or cleaning. At one of the first stores to implement the "lean" techniques, the store manager looked for ways for her employees to be more efficient with simple things like keeping items in the same place, moving drink toppings closer to where drinks are handed to customers, and altering the order of assembly. After two months under the new methods, her store experienced a 10 percent increase in transactions.

Another thing that Schultz did that was quite unprecedented was to close every one of its stores for three hours on one Tuesday evening to train ALL of their over 135,000 baristas (a barista is a person who prepares and serves espresso-based coffee drinks). During that training, baristas were reminded that they played an important role in creating not only a fabulous product but a fabulous customer experience. Despite warnings that closing the stores would be a public relations nightmare and a financial mistake, the decision seemed to be a sound one. In the weeks following the retraining, quality scores for the company's beverages went up and stayed there.

Starbucks Value Chain: From Bean to Cup to You

Discussion Questions

15-25 Would you describe production/operations technology in Starbucks retail stores as unit, mass, or process? Explain your choice. (Hint: You may need to review this material found in Chapter 6.) How does its production/operations technology approach affect the way products are produced?

15-26 What uncertainties does Starbucks face in its value chain? Can Starbucks manage those uncertainties? If so, how? If not, why not?

15-27 Go to the company's Web site at www.starbucks.com and find the information on the company's environmental activities from bean to cup. Select one of the steps in the chain (or your professor may assign one). Describe what environmental actions it's taking. How might these affect the way Starbucks "produces" its products?

15-28 Research the concept of *lean organizations*. What benefits does "lean" offer? How might a business like Starbucks further utilize the concepts of being lean?

15-29 What lessons could other organizations learn from Starbucks' actions?

Endnotes

1. D. Eng, "Cheesecake Factory's Winning Formula," *Fortune*, May 2, 2011, 19–20; and D. McGinn, "Faster Food," *Newsweek*, April 19, 2004, E20–E22.

2. All of the following examples are from the World Factbook 2015, https://www.cia.gov/library/publications/the-world-factbook/geos/bl.html.

3. D. Michaels and J. L. Lunsford, "Streamlined Plane Making," *Wall Street Journal*, April 1, 2005, B1+.

4. T. Aeppel, "Workers Not Included," *Wall Street Journal*, November 19, 2002, B1+.

5. A. Aston and M. Arndt, "The Flexible Factory," *BusinessWeek*, May 5, 2003, 90–91.

6. P. Panchak, "Pella Drives Lean throughout the Enterprise," *IndustryWeek*, June 2003, 74–77.

7. J. Ordonez, "McDonald's to Cut the Cooking Time of Its French Fries," *Wall Street Journal*, May 19, 2000, B2.

8. C. Fredman, "The Devil in the Details," *Executive Edge*, April–May 1999, 36–39.

9. http://new.skoda-auto.com/Documents/AnnualReports/skoda_auto_annual_report_2007_%20EN_FINAL.pdf (July 8, 2008); and T. Mudd, "The Last Laugh," *IndustryWeek*, September 18, 2000, 38–44.

10. T. Vinas, "Little Things Mean a Lot," *IndustryWeek*, November 2002, 55.

11. P. Panchak, "Shaping the Future of Manufacturing," *IndustryWeek*, January 2005, 38–44; M. Hammer, "Deep Change: How Operational Innovation Can Transform Your Company," *Harvard Business Review*, April 2004, 84–94; S. Levy, "The Connected Company," *Newsweek*, April 28, 2003, 40–48; and J. Teresko, "Plant Floor Strategy," *IndustryWeek*, July 2002, 26–32.

12. T. Laseter, K. Ramdas, and D. Swerdlow, "The Supply Side of Design and Development," *Strategy & Business*, Summer 2003, 23; J. Jusko, "Not All Dollars and Cents," *IndustryWeek*, April 2002, 58; and D. Drickhamer, "Medical Marvel," *IndustryWeek*, March 2002, 47–49.

13. Q. H. Soon and Z. M. Udin, "Supply Chain Management from the Perspective of Value Chain Flexibility: An Exploratory Study," *Journal of Manufacturing Technology Management* (May 2011): 506–26; G. Soni and R. Kodali, "A Critical Analysis of Supply Chain Management Content in Empirical Research," *Business Process Management*, April 2011, 238–56; and J. H. Sheridan, "Managing the Value Chain," *IndustryWeek*, September 6, 1999, 1–4, available online in archives at www.industryweek.com.

14. "Supply Chain Management: A New Narrative," *Strategic Direction*, March 2011, 18–21; and J. H. Sheridan, "Managing the Value Chain."

15. S. Leibs, "Getting Ready: Your Suppliers," *IndustryWeek*, www.industryweek.com (September 6, 1999).

16. See, for example, J. Jusko, "Procurement—Not All Dollars and Cents," *IndustryWeek*, www.industryweek.com (April 4, 2002).

17. D. Bartholomew, "The Infrastructure," *IndustryWeek*, September 6, 1999, 1.

18. G. Taninecz, "Forging the Chain," *IndustryWeek*, May 15, 2000, 40–46.

19. T. Vinas, "A Map of the World: IW Value-Chain Survey," *IndustryWeek*, September 2005, 27–34.

20. From the Past to the Present box based on "Honorary Members Form Impressive Lineup of Quality Thinkers," *Quality Progress*, March 2011, 17; "W. Edwards Deming," *Quality Progress*, November 2010, 17; R. Aguayo, *Dr. Deming: The American Who Taught the Japanese about Quality* (New York: Fireside Press, 1991); M. Walton, *The Deming Management Method* (New York: Penguin Group, 1986); and W. E. Deming, "Improvement of Quality and Productivity through Action by Management," *National Productivity Review*, Winter 1981–1982, 12–22.

21. See J. H. Sheridan, "Now It's a Job for the CEO," *IndustryWeek*, March 20, 2000, 22–30.

22. R. Norman and R. Ramirez, "From Value Chain to Value Constellation," *Harvard Business Review on Managing the Value Chain* (Boston: Harvard Business School Press, 2000), 185–219.

23. S. Leibs, "Getting Ready: Your Customers," *IndustryWeek*, September 6, 1999, 4.

24. See, for example, C. Lunan, "Workers Doing More in Less Time," *Charlotte Observer*, June 1, 2002, D1.

25. S. Leibs, "Getting Ready: Your Customers," 3.

26. See, for instance, L. Harrington, "The Accelerated Value Chain: Supply Chain Management Just Got Smarter, Faster, and More Cost-Effective, Thanks to a Groundbreaking Alliance between Intel and Technologies," *IndustryWeek*, April 2002, 45–51.

27. Ibid.

28. Ibid.; and J. H. Sheridan, "Managing the Value Chain."

29. J. H. Sheriden, "Managing the Value Chain," 3.

30. S. Leibs, "Getting Ready: Your Customers," 4.

31. J. H. Sheriden, "Managing the Value Chain," 2–3; S. Leibs, "Getting Ready: Your Customers," 1, 4; and D. Bartholomew, "The Infrastructure," 6.

32. G. Taninecz, "Forging the Chain."

33. Ibid.

34. Ibid.

35. D. Drickhamer, "On Target," *IndustryWeek*, October 16, 2000, 111–12.

36. Ibid.

37. "Top Security Threats and Management Issues Facing Corporate America: 2003 Survey of Fortune 1000 Companies," *ASIS International* and *Pinkerton*, www.asisonline.org.

38. J. H. Sheridan, "Managing the Value Chain," 4.

39. Question of Ethics box based on C. Hausman, "Ethics of Using Store's Parking Lot Fuels Lively Debate in Newspaper Series," *Ethics Newsline Online*, April 25, 2011; J. Rose, "Ethics of Customer Parking in Portland: Circling the Block One More Time," *Oregonian Online*, April 21, 2011; and J. Rose, "The Ethics of 'Customer Only' Parking in the Pearl—and Beyond," *Oregonian Online*, April 16, 2011.

40. S. Rosenbloom, "Solution, or Mess? A Milk Jug for a Green Earth," *New York Times Online*, June 30, 2008.

41. K. T. Greenfeld, "Taco Bell and the Golden Age of Drive-Thru," *Bloomberg BusinessWeek Online*, May 5, 2011; and S. Anderson, Associated Press, "Restaurants Gear Up for Window Wars," *Springfield, Missouri, News-Leader*, January 27, 2006, 5B.

42. Technology and the Manager's Job box based on S. Minter, "What Is Advanced Manufacturing?" *IndustryWeek*, August 2009, 7; J. Bush, "Russia's Factories Shift Gears," *BusinessWeek*, May 18, 2009, 50–51; D. Blanchard, "A Manufacturer for All Seasons," *IndustryWeek*, December 2008, 7; J. Teresko, "Planning the Factory of the Future," *IndustryWeek*, December 2008, 22–24; and J. Teresko, "Winning with Digital Manufacturing," *IndustryWeek*, July 2008, 45–47.

43. D. Bartholomew, "Quality Takes a Beating," *IndustryWeek*, March 2006, 46–54; J. Carey and M. Arndt, "Making Pills the Smart Way," *BusinessWeek*, May 3, 2004, 102–03; and A. Barrett, "Schering's Dr. Feelbetter?" *BusinessWeek*, June 23, 2003, 55–56.

44. T. Vinas, "Six Sigma Rescue," *IndustryWeek*, March 2004, 12.

45. J. S. McClenahen, "Prairie Home Companion," *IndustryWeek*, October 2005, 45–46.

46. T. Vinas, "Zeroing In on the Customer," *IndustryWeek*, October 2004, 61–62.

47. W. Royal, "Spotlight Shines on Maquiladora," *IndustryWeek*, October 16, 2000, 91–92.

48. See B. Whitford and R. Andrew (eds.), *The Pursuit of Quality*

(Perth: Beaumont Publishing, 1994).

49. D. Drickhamer, "Road to Excellence," *IndustryWeek*, October 16, 2000, 117–18.

50. J. Heizer and B. Render, *Operations Management*, 10th ed. (Upper Saddle River, NJ: Prentice Hall, 2011), 193.

51. G. Hasek, "Merger Marries Quality Efforts," *IndustryWeek*, August 21, 2000, 89–92.

52. J. Jusko, "An Elite Crew," *IndustryWeek*, March 2011, 17–18; and M. Arndt, "Quality Isn't Just for Widgets," *BusinessWeek*, July 22, 2002, 72–73.

53. E. White, "Rethinking the Quality Improvement Program," *Wall Street Journal*, September 19, 2005, B3.

54. M. Arndt, "Quality Isn't Just for Widgets."

55. For a thorough overview of project management, see S. Berkun, *The Art of Project Management* (Upper Saddle River, NJ: Prentice Hall, 2005); or J. K. Pinto, *Project Management: Achieving Competitive Advantage and MS Project* (Upper Saddle River, NJ: Prentice Hall, 2007).

56. H. Maylor, "Beyond the Gantt Chart: Project Management Moving On," *European Management Journal* (February 2001): 92–101.

57. For additional information on CPM, see W. A. Haga and K. A. Marold, "A Simulation Approach to the PERT/CPM Time-Cost Trade-Off Problem," *Project Management Journal* (June 2004): 31–37.

58. Based on S. P. Robbins, *Managing Organizational Conflict* (Englewood Cliffs, NJ: Prentice Hall, 1974); K. W. Thomas, "Conflict and Conflict Management," in Marvin Dunnette (ed.), *Handbook of Industrial and Organizational Psychology* (Chicago: Rand McNally, 1976), 889–935; and K. Cloke and J. Goldsmith, *Resolving Conflicts at Work: Eight Strategies for Everyone on the Job*, rev. ed. (San Francisco: Jossey-Bass, 2006).

59. S. Banjoy and C. Passariello, "Promises in Bangladesh," *Wall Street Journal*, May 14, 2013, B1+; S. Greenhouse and J. Yardley, "Global Retailers Join Safety Plan for Bangladesh," *New York Times Online*, May 13, 2013; A. Zimmerman and N. Shah, "Taste for Cheap Clothes Fed Bangladesh Boom," *Wall Street Journal*, May 13, 2013, B1+; S. Zain Al-Mahmood, "Bangladesh to Raise Workers' Pay," *Wall Street Journal*, May 13, 2013, B4; J. Ali Manik and J. Yardley, "17 Days in Darkness, A Cry of 'Save Me,' and Joy," *New York Times Online*, May 10, 2013; S. Greenhouse, "Retailers Are Pressed on Safety at Factories," *New York Times Online*,

May 10, 2013; J. O'Donnell and C. Macleod, "Bangladesh Fire Adds Pressure on Retailers," *USA Today*, May 10, 2013, 1B+; S. Zain Al-Mahmood, K. Chu, and S. Banjo, "Bangladesh Shuts 3 Factories of Top Exporter," *Wall Street Journal*, May 10, 2013, A8; S. Clifford, "Some Retailers Say More about Their Clothing's Origins," *New York Times Online*, May 8, 2013; K. Chu, "Tough Options for Apparel Retailers," *Wall Street Journal*, May 8, 2013, B1+; "Clothing Retailers Evaluate Moral Choices in Contracting Work to Bangladesh," *www.globalethics.org*, May 6, 2013; S. Wright and F. Hossain, "Pressure on Bangladesh, Retailers to Fix Factories," *www.sfgate .com*, May 4, 2013; S. Zain Al-Mahmood, C. Passariello, and P. Rana, "The Global Garment Trail: From Bangladesh to a Mall Near You," *Wall Street Journal*, May 4/5, 2013, A1+; M. Mosk, "Big Retailers Reassess Practices after Bangladesh Building Collapse," abcnews.go.com, May 3, 2013; H. Malcolm, "Worker Safety Gains Steam," *USA Today*, May 2, 2013, 2B; E. L. Cline, "Ethical Fashion: Is the Tragedy in Bangladesh A Final Straw?" www.npr.org, May 2, 2013; M. Davies, "Can Bangladesh Clothing Factory Disasters Be Prevented? *www.bbc.co.uk*, May 2, 1013; S. Greenhouse, "Bangladesh Fears an Exodus of Apparel Firms," *New York Times Online*, May 2, 2013; D. Bobkoff, "Would You Pay a Higher Price for Ethical Clothing?" *www.npr .org*, May 1, 2013; S. Zain Al-Mahmood, "Doomed Factories Raced to Fill Orders," *Wall Street Journal*, April 30, 2013, A1+; "Deadly Bangladesh Collapse Focuses Spotlight on Ethics & Demand for Cheap Goods," *www.globalethics .org*, April 29, 2013; M. T. Anderson, "Clothed in Misery," *New York Times Online*, April 29, 2013; R. L. Brown, "Q&A: Who Ultimately Bears Responsibility for Bangladesh Factory Disasters," www.csmonitor.com, April 25, 2013; and J. Ali Manik, S. Greenhouse, and J. Yardley, "Western Firms Feel Pressure as Toll Rises in Bangladesh," *New York Times Online*, April 25, 2013.

60. A. D'innocenzio, "Gap, Walmart, Target Agree to Bangladesh Factory Safety Pact," http://www .mercurynews.com/ci_23634246/ gap-walmart-target-agree-bangladesh-factory-safety-pact, July 10, 2013.

61. J. Ostrower and H. Kachi, "Boeing's 787 Resumes Service," *Wall Street Journal*, April 29, 2013, B3; J. Ostrower and T. Stynes, "Boeing Steers Past 787 Woes," *Wall Street Journal*, April 25, 2013, B2; S. Jakab, "Dreamliner's Woes Fail to Ground Boeing," *Wall Street Journal*, April 24, 2013, C1; N. Clark, "Boeing Begins Modifying 787 Batteries," *New York Times Online*, April 22, 2013; A. Pasztor, "How Boeing Rescued the 787," *Wall Street Journal*, April 20/21, 2013, B1+; C. Drew and J. Mouawad, "Boeing Fix for Battery Is Approved by F.A.A.," *New York Times Online*, April 19, 2013; H. Tabuchi, "Boeing Presents Solution for Dreamliner Problems," *New York Times Online*, March 15, 2013; S. Mayerowitz, "Former Workers: Boeing Rushed Dreamliner Project," *Springfield, Missouri, News-Leader*, January 26, 2013, 7A; D. Michaels, "Innovation Is Messy Business," *Wall Street Journal*, January 24, 2013, B1+; S. Dubois, "Boeing's Dreamliner Mess: Simply Inevitable?" *management.fortune.com,* January 22, 2013; P. Kavilanz, "Dreamliner: Where in the World Its Parts Come From," *money.cnn. com,* January 18, 2013; "Boeing's Dreamliner Takes to the Skies," *USA Today*, October 21, 2011, 3B; P. Jonsson, "787 Dreamliner Takes Off at Last. When Can You Jump Aboard?" www.csmonitor.com, September 27, 2011; and W. J. Hennigan, "Boeing Delivers First 787 Dreamliner," *articles.latimes. com,* September 26, 2011.

62. B. Horovitz, "Starbucks CEO Reinvents the Spiel," *USA Today*, April 25, 2013, 3B; S. Jakab, "Starbucks Story Could Have a Bitter Edge," *Wall Street Journal*, April 25, 2013, C1; "Starbucks' Quest for Healthy Growth: An Interview with Howard Schultz," *McKinsey Quarterly*, no. 2 (2001): 34–43; "Return to Glory," *Retail Traffic*, May/June 2011, 38; J. Jannarone, "Grounds for Concern at Starbucks," *Wall Street Journal*, May 3, 2011, C10; M. Morrison, "Bang for Its Starbucks: Hits No. 3 Despite Limited Ad Spending," *Advertising Age*, May 2, 2011, 1+; W. Kendall, "A Long, Hard Grind," *Management Today*, May 2011, 27; "Howard Schultz, On Getting a Second Shot," *Inc.*, April 2011, 52–54; "Starbucks Corp. Plans Retail Push," *Nation's Restaurant News*, April 4, 2011, 6; "Starbucks Marks 40th Anniversary," *Beverage Industry*, April 2011, 8; R. Lowenstein, "When Latte Lost Its Luster," *Wall Street Journal*, March 29, 2011, A17; H. Schultz, "How Starbucks Got Its Mojo Back," *Newsweek*, March 21, 2011, 50–55; G. Charles, "Change Brewing at Starbucks," *Marketing*, January 2011, 14–15; "Starbucks Outlines Strategies for Growth," *Beverage Industry*, January 2011, 14; and H. Edwards, "Howard Schultz's Tall Order," *Marketing*, January 2011, 19; and S. Berfield, "Starbucks: Howard Schultz vs. Howard Schultz," *BusinessWeek Online*, August 6, 2009; J. Jargon, "Latest Starbucks Buzzword: 'Lean' Japanese Techniques," *Wall Street Journal*, August 4, 2009, A1.

Entrepreneurship Module
MANAGING ENTREPRENEURIAL VENTURES

Russell Simmons is an entrepreneur. He co-founded Def Jam Records because the emerging group of New York hip-hop artists needed a record company, and the big record companies refused to take a chance on unknown artists. Def Jam was just one piece of Simmons's corporation, Rush Communications, which also included a management company; a clothing company called Phat Farm; a movie production house; television shows; a magazine; and an advertising agency. In 1999, Simmons sold his stake in Def Jam to Universal Music Group, and in 2004, he sold Phat Farm. Today, Simmons is involved in UniRush, a Cincinnati company that sells a prepaid Visa debit card, and Russell Simmons ArgyleCulture, a clothing line. He also launched an advertising venture described as a digital solutions company, set up to work for ad agencies, not to be one. And in his latest announced venture, Simmons is bringing rap to Broadway. His show "The Scenario" is a musical featuring songs from more than 30 years of rap hits. *USA Today* named Simmons one of the top 25 Influential People, while *Inc.* magazine named him one of America's 25 Most Fascinating Entrepreneurs.

In this appendix, we're going to look at the activities engaged in by entrepreneurs like Russell Simmons. We'll start by looking at the context of entrepreneurship and then examining entrepreneurship from the perspective of the four managerial functions: planning, organizing, leading, and controlling.

What Is Entrepreneurship?

Entrepreneurship is the process of starting new businesses, generally in response to opportunities. For instance, Fred Carl, founder of the Viking Range Corporation, saw an opportunity to create an appliance that combined the best features of commercial and residential ranges.

Many people think that entrepreneurial ventures and small businesses are the same, but they're not. Entrepreneurs create **entrepreneurial ventures**—organizations that pursue opportunities, are characterized by innovative practices, and have growth and profitability as their main goals. On the other hand, a **small business** is an independent business having fewer than 500 employees that doesn't necessarily engage in any new or innovative practices and that has relatively little impact on its industry. A small business isn't necessarily entrepreneurial because it's small. To be entrepreneurial means that the business is innovative and seeking out new opportunities. Even though entrepreneurial ventures may start small, they pursue growth. Some new small firms may grow, but many remain small businesses, by choice or by default.

Who's Starting Entrepreneurial Ventures?

Call them accidental entrepreneurs, unintended entrepreneurs, or forced entrepreneurs: As the unemployment rate hovers around double digits, many corporate "refugees" are becoming entrepreneurs. These individuals are looking to entrepreneurship, not because they sense some great opportunity, but because there are no jobs. The Index of Entrepreneurial Activity by the Kauffman Foundation showed the rate at which new businesses formed in 2010 remained high, representing the "highest level of entrepreneurship over the past decade and a half." The report found that "the patterns provided some early evidence that 'necessity' entrepreneurship is increasing and 'opportunity' entrepreneurship is decreasing." But "accidental or by design," entrepreneurship is on the rise again.

entrepreneurship
The process of starting new businesses, generally in response to opportunities

entrepreneurial ventures
Organizations that pursue opportunities, are characterized by innovative practices, and have growth and profitability as their main goals

small business
An independent business having fewer than 500 employees that doesn't necessarily engage in any new or innovative practices and that has relatively little impact on its industry

As many entrepreneurs (successful and not-so-successful) would attest to, being an entrepreneur isn't easy. According to the Small Business Administration, only two-thirds of new businesses survive at least two years. The survival rate falls to 44 percent at four years, and to 31 percent at seven. But the interesting thing is that entrepreneurial venture survival rates are about the same in economic expansions and recessions.

What Do Entrepreneurs Do?

Describing what entrepreneurs do isn't an easy or simple task! No two entrepreneurs' work activities are exactly alike. In a general sense, entrepreneurs create something new, something different. They search for change, respond to it, and exploit it.

Initially, an entrepreneur is engaged in assessing the potential for the entrepreneurial venture and then dealing with startup issues. In exploring the entrepreneurial context, entrepreneurs gather information, identify potential opportunities, and pinpoint possible competitive advantage(s). Then, armed with this information, an entrepreneur researches the venture's feasibility—uncovering business ideas, looking at competitors, and exploring financing options.

After looking at the potential of the proposed venture and assessing the likelihood of pursuing it successfully, an entrepreneur proceeds to plan the venture. This process includes such activities as developing a viable organizational mission, exploring organizational culture issues, and creating a well-thought-out business plan. Once these planning issues have been resolved, the entrepreneur must look at organizing the venture, which involves choosing a legal form of business organization, addressing other legal issues such as patent or copyright searches, and coming up with an appropriate organizational design for structuring how work is going to be done.

Only after these startup activities have been completed is the entrepreneur ready to actually launch the venture. A launch involves setting goals and strategies, and establishing the technology-operations methods, marketing plans, information systems, financial-accounting systems, and cash flow management systems.

Once the entrepreneurial venture is up and running, the entrepreneur's attention switches to managing it. What's involved with actually managing the entrepreneurial venture? An important activity is managing the various processes that are part of every business: making decisions, establishing action plans, analyzing external and internal environments, measuring and evaluating performance, and making needed changes. Also, the entrepreneur must perform activities associated with managing people, including selecting and hiring, appraising and training, motivating, managing conflict, delegating tasks, and being an effective leader. Finally, the entrepreneur must manage the venture's growth, including such activities as developing and designing growth strategies, dealing with crises, exploring various avenues for financing growth, placing a value on the venture, and perhaps even eventually exiting the venture.

What Planning Do Entrepreneurs Need to Do?

Planning is important to entrepreneurial ventures. Once a venture's feasibility has been thoroughly researched, an entrepreneur then must look at planning the venture. The most important thing that an entrepreneur does in planning the venture is developing a **business plan**—a written document that summarizes a business opportunity and defines and articulates how the identified opportunity is to be seized and exploited. A written business plan can range from basic to thorough. The most basic type of business plan would simply include an *executive summary,* sort of a mini-business plan that's no longer than two pages. A *synopsis* type plan is a little more involved. It's been described as an "executive summary on steroids." In addition to the executive summary, it includes a business proposal that explains why the idea is relevant to potential investors. A *summary business plan* includes an executive summary and a page or so of explanation of each of the key components of a business plan. A *full business plan* is the traditional business plan, which we describe fully next. Finally, an *operational business plan* is the most detailed (50 or more pages) and is used by ventures already operating with an

business plan
A written document that summarizes a business opportunity and defines and articulates how the identified opportunity is to be seized and exploited

existing strategy. It's often used to "plan the business" but also can be used to raise additional money or to attract potential acquirers. It's important for entrepreneurs to know which type of business plan they need for their purposes.

What's in a Full Business Plan?

For many would-be entrepreneurs, developing and writing a business plan seems like a daunting task. However, a good business plan is valuable. It pulls together all the elements of the entrepreneur's vision into a single coherent document. The business plan requires careful planning and creative thinking. But if done well, it can be a convincing document that serves many functions. It serves as a blueprint and road map for operating the business. And the business plan is a "living" document, guiding organizational decisions and actions throughout the life of the business, not just in the startup stage.

If an entrepreneur has completed a feasibility study, much of the information included in it becomes the basis for the business plan. A good business plan covers six major areas: executive summary, analysis of opportunity, analysis of the context, description of the business, financial data and projections, and supporting documentation.

Executive summary. The executive summary summarizes the key points that the entrepreneur wants to make about the proposed entrepreneurial venture. These might include a brief mission statement; primary goals; brief history of the entrepreneurial venture, maybe in the form of a timeline; key people involved in the venture; nature of the business; concise product or service descriptions; brief explanations of market niche, competitors, and competitive advantage; proposed strategies; and selected key financial information.

Analysis of opportunity. In this section of the business plan, an entrepreneur presents the details of the perceived opportunity, which essentially includes (1) sizing up the market by describing the demographics of the target market; (2) describing and evaluating industry trends; and (3) identifying and evaluating competitors.

Analysis of the context. Whereas the opportunity analysis focuses on the opportunity in a specific industry and market, the context analysis takes a much broader perspective. Here, the entrepreneur describes the broad external changes and trends taking place in the economic, political-legal, technological, and global environments.

Description of the business. In this section, an entrepreneur describes how the entrepreneurial venture is going to be organized, launched, and managed. It includes a thorough description of the mission statement; a description of the desired organizational culture; marketing plans including overall marketing strategy, pricing, sales tactics, service-warranty policies, and advertising and promotion tactics; product development plans such as an explanation of development status, tasks, difficulties and risks, and anticipated costs; operational plans, including a description of proposed geographic location, facilities and needed improvements, equipment, and work flow; human resource plans, including a description of key management persons, composition of board of directors including their background experience and skills, current and future staffing needs, compensation and benefits, and training needs; and an overall schedule and timetable of events.

Financial data and projections. Every effective business plan contains financial data and projections. Although the calculations and interpretation may be difficult, they are absolutely critical. No business plan is complete without financial information. Financial plans should cover at least three years and contain projected income statements, pro forma cash flow analysis (monthly for the first year and quarterly for the next two), pro forma balance sheets, breakeven analysis, and cost controls. If major equipment or other capital purchases are expected, the items, costs, and available collateral should be listed. All financial projections and analyses should include explanatory notes, especially where the data seem contradictory or questionable.

Supporting documentation. This *is* an important component of an effective business plan. The entrepreneur should back up his or her descriptions with charts, graphs, tables, photographs, or other visual tools. In addition, it might be important to include information (personal and work-related) about the key participants in the entrepreneurial venture.

Just as the idea for an entrepreneurial venture takes time to germinate, so does the writing of a good business plan. It's important for an entrepreneur to put serious thought and consideration into the plan. It's not an easy thing to do. However, the resulting document should be valuable in current and future planning efforts.

What Issues Are Involved in Organizing an Entrepreneurial Venture?

Once the startup and planning issues for the entrepreneurial venture have been addressed, the entrepreneur is ready to begin organizing the entrepreneurial venture. The main organizing issues an entrepreneur must address include the legal forms of organization, organizational design and structure, and human resource management.

What Are the Legal Forms of Organization for Entrepreneurial Ventures?

The first organizing decision that an entrepreneur must make is a critical one. It's the form of legal ownership for the venture. The two primary factors affecting this decision are taxes and legal liability. An entrepreneur wants to minimize the impact of both of these factors. The right choice can protect the entrepreneur from legal liability as well as save tax dollars, in both the short run and the long run.

The three basic ways to organize an entrepreneurial venture are sole proprietorship, partnership, and corporation. However, when you include the variations of these basic organizational alternatives, you end up with six possible choices, each with its own tax consequences, liability issues, and pros and cons. These six choices are sole proprietorship, general partnership, limited liability partnership (LLP), C corporation, S corporation, and limited liability company (LLC).

The decision regarding the legal form of organization is important because it has significant tax and liability consequences. Although the legal form of organization can be changed, it's not easy to do. An entrepreneur needs to think carefully about what's important, especially in the areas of flexibility, taxes, and amount of personal liability, in choosing the best form of organization.

What Type of Organizational Structure Should Entrepreneurial Ventures Use?

The choice of an appropriate organizational structure is also an important decision when organizing an entrepreneurial venture. At some point, successful entrepreneurs find that they can't do everything. They need people. The entrepreneur must then decide on the most appropriate structural arrangement for effectively and efficiently carrying out the organization's activities. Without a suitable type of organizational structure, an entrepreneurial venture may soon find itself in a chaotic situation.

In many small firms, the organizational structure tends to evolve with very little intentional and deliberate planning by the entrepreneur. For the most part, the structure may be very simple—one person does whatever is needed. As an entrepreneurial venture grows and the entrepreneur finds it increasingly difficult to go it alone, employees are brought on board to perform certain functions or duties that the entrepreneur can't handle. As the company continues to grow, these individuals tend to perform those same functions. Soon, each functional area may require managers and employees.

As the venture evolves to a more deliberate structure, an entrepreneur faces a whole new set of challenges. All of a sudden, he or she must share decision making and operating responsibilities, which are typically the most difficult things for an entrepreneur to do—letting go and allowing someone else to make decisions. *After all*, he or she reasons, *how can anyone know this business as well as I do?* Also, what might have been a fairly informal, loose, and flexible atmosphere that worked well when the organization was small may no longer be effective. Many entrepreneurs are greatly concerned about keeping that "small company" atmosphere alive even as the venture grows and evolves into a more structured arrangement. But having a structured organization doesn't necessarily mean giving up flexibility, adaptability, and freedom. In fact, the structural design may be as fluid as the entrepreneur feels comfortable with and yet still have the rigidity it needs to operate efficiently.

Organizational design decisions in entrepreneurial ventures also revolve around the six elements of organizational structure discussed in Chapter 6: work specialization, departmentalization, chain of command, span of control, amount of centralization-decentralization, and amount of formalization. Decisions about these six elements will determine whether an entrepreneur designs a more mechanistic or organic organizational structure. When would each be preferable? A mechanistic structure would be preferable when cost efficiencies are critical to the venture's competitive advantage; when more control over employees' work activities is important; if the venture produces standardized products in a routine fashion; and when the external environment is relatively stable and certain. An organic structure would be most appropriate when innovation is critical to the organization's competitive advantage; for smaller organizations where rigid approaches to dividing and coordinating work aren't necessary; if the organization produces customized products in a flexible setting; and where the external environment is dynamic, complex, and uncertain.

What Human Resource Management (HRM) Issues Do Entrepreneurs Face?

As an entrepreneurial venture grows, additional employees must be hired to perform the increased workload. As employees are brought on board, two HRM issues of particular importance are employee recruitment and employee retention.

An entrepreneur wants to ensure that the venture has the people to do the required work. Recruiting new employees is one of the biggest challenges that entrepreneurs face. In fact, the ability of small firms to successfully recruit appropriate employees is consistently rated as one of the most important factors influencing organizational success.

Entrepreneurs, particularly, look for high-potential people who can perform multiple roles during various stages of venture growth. They look for individuals who "buy into" the venture's entrepreneurial culture—individuals who have a passion for the business. Unlike their corporate counterparts who often focus on filling a job by matching a person to the job requirements, entrepreneurs look to fill in critical skills gaps. They're looking for people who are exceptionally capable and self-motivated, flexible, multiskilled, and who can help grow the entrepreneurial venture. While corporate managers tend to focus on using traditional HRM practices and techniques, entrepreneurs are more concerned with matching characteristics of the person to the values and culture of the organization; that is, they focus on matching the person to the organization.

Getting competent and qualified people into the venture is just the first step in effectively managing the human resources. An entrepreneur wants to keep the people he or she has hired and trained. A unique and important employee retention issue entrepreneurs must deal with is compensation. Whereas traditional organizations are more likely to view compensation from the perspective of monetary rewards (base pay, benefits, and incentives), smaller entrepreneurial firms are more likely to view compensation from a total rewards perspective. For these firms, compensation encompasses psychological rewards, learning opportunities, and recognition in addition to monetary rewards (base pay and incentives).

What Issues Do Entrepreneurs Face in Leading an Entrepreneurial Venture?

Leading is an important function of entrepreneurs. As an entrepreneurial venture grows and people are brought on board, an entrepreneur takes on a new role—that of a leader. In this section, we want to look at what's involved with that. First, we're going to look at the unique personality characteristics of entrepreneurs. Then we're going to discuss the important role entrepreneurs play in motivating employees through empowerment and leading the venture and employee teams.

What Type of Personality Do Entrepreneurs Have?

Think of someone you know who is an entrepreneur. Maybe it's someone you personally know or maybe it's someone you've read about, like Bill Gates of Microsoft. How would you describe this person's personality? One of the most researched areas of entrepreneurship has been the search to determine what—if any—psychological characteristics entrepreneurs have in common; what types of personality traits entrepreneurs have that might distinguish them from nonentrepreneurs; and what traits entrepreneurs have that might predict who will be a successful entrepreneur.

Is there a classic "entrepreneurial personality"? Although trying to pinpoint specific personality characteristics that all entrepreneurs share has the same problem as identifying the trait theories of leadership—that is, being able to identify specific personality traits that *all* entrepreneurs share—this hasn't stopped entrepreneurship researchers from listing common traits. For instance, one list of personality characteristics included the following: high level of motivation, abundance of self-confidence, ability to be involved for the long term, high energy level, persistent problem solver, high degree of initiative, ability to set goals, and moderate risk-taker. Another list of characteristics of "successful" entrepreneurs included high energy level, great persistence, resourcefulness, the desire and ability to be self-directed, and relatively high need for autonomy.

Another development in defining entrepreneurial personality characteristics was the proactive personality scale to predict an individual's likelihood of pursuing entrepreneurial ventures. The **proactive personality** is a personality trait describing those individuals who are more prone to take actions to influence their environment—that is, they're more proactive. Obviously, an entrepreneur is likely to exhibit proactivity as he or she searches for opportunities and acts to take advantage of those opportunities. Various items on the proactive personality scale were found to be good indicators of a person's likelihood of becoming an entrepreneur, including gender, education, having an entrepreneurial parent, and possessing a proactive personality. In addition, studies have shown that entrepreneurs have greater risk propensity than do managers. However, this propensity is moderated by the entrepreneur's primary goal. Risk propensity is greater for entrepreneurs whose primary goal is growth versus those whose focus is on producing family income.

How Can Entrepreneurs Motivate Employees?

When you're motivated to do something, don't you find yourself energized and willing to work hard at doing whatever it is you're excited about? Wouldn't it be great if all of a venture's employees were energized, excited, and willing to work hard at their jobs? Having motivated employees is an important goal for any entrepreneur, and employee empowerment is an important motivational tool entrepreneurs can use.

Although it's not easy for entrepreneurs to do, employee empowerment—giving employees the power to make decisions and take actions on their own—is an important motivational approach. Why? Because successful entrepreneurial ventures must be quick and nimble, ready to pursue opportunities and go off in new directions. Empowered employees can provide that flexibility and speed. When employees are empowered, they often display stronger work motivation, better work quality, higher job satisfaction, and lower turnover.

Empowerment is a philosophical concept that entrepreneurs have to "buy into." It doesn't come easily. In fact, it's hard for many entrepreneurs to do. Their life is tied up in the business. They've built it from the ground up. But continuing to grow the entrepreneurial venture is eventually going to require handing over more responsibilities to employees. How can entrepreneurs empower employees? For many entrepreneurs, it's a gradual process.

proactive personality
A personality trait describing those individuals who are more prone to take actions to influence their environment

Entrepreneurs can begin by using participative decision making, in which employees provide input into decisions. Although getting employees to participate in decisions isn't quite taking the full plunge into employee empowerment, at least it's a way to begin tapping into the collective array of employees' talents, skills, knowledge, and abilities.

Another way to empower employees is through delegation—the process of assigning certain decisions or specific job duties to employees. By delegating decisions and duties, the entrepreneur is turning over the responsibility for carrying them out.

When an entrepreneur is finally comfortable with the idea of employee empowerment, fully empowering employees means redesigning their jobs so they have discretion over the way they do their work. It's allowing employees to do their work effectively and efficiently by using their creativity, imagination, knowledge, and skills.

If an entrepreneur implements employee empowerment properly—that is, with complete and total commitment to the program and with appropriate employee training—results can be impressive for the entrepreneurial venture and for the empowered employees. The business can enjoy significant productivity gains, quality improvements, more satisfied customers, increased employee motivation, and improved morale. Employees can enjoy the opportunities to do a greater variety of work that is more interesting and challenging.

How Can Entrepreneurs Be Leaders?

The last topic we want to discuss in this section is the role of an entrepreneur as a leader. In this role, the entrepreneur has certain leadership responsibilities in leading the venture and in leading employee work teams.

Today's successful entrepreneur must be like the leader of a jazz ensemble known for its improvisation, innovation, and creativity. Max DePree, former head of Herman Miller, Inc., a leading office furniture manufacturer known for its innovative leadership approaches, said it best in his book, *Leadership Jazz*, "Jazz band leaders must choose the music, find the right musicians, and perform—in public. But the effect of the performance depends on so many things—the environment, the volunteers playing the band, the need for everybody to perform as individuals and as a group, the absolute dependence of the leader on the members of the band, the need for the followers to play well…. The leader of the jazz band has the beautiful opportunity to draw the best out of the other musicians. We have much to learn from jazz band leaders, for jazz, like leadership, combines the unpredictability of the future with the gifts of individuals."

The way an entrepreneur leads the venture should be much like the jazz leader—drawing the best out of other individuals, even given the unpredictability of the situation. One way an entrepreneur does this is through the vision he or she creates for the organization. In fact, the driving force through the early stages of the entrepreneurial venture is often the visionary leadership of the entrepreneur. The entrepreneur's ability to articulate a coherent, inspiring, and attractive vision of the future is a key test of his or her leadership. But if an entrepreneur can do this, the results can be worthwhile. A study contrasting visionary and nonvisionary companies showed that visionary companies outperformed the nonvisionary ones by six times on standard financial criteria, and their stocks outperformed the general market by 15 times.

As we know from Chapter 6, many organizations—entrepreneurial and otherwise—are using employee work teams to perform organizational tasks, create new ideas, and resolve problems. The three most common types of employee work teams in entrepreneurial ventures are empowered teams (teams that have the authority to plan and implement process improvements), self-directed teams (teams that are nearly autonomous and responsible for many managerial activities), and cross-functional teams (work teams composed of individuals from various specialties who work together on various tasks).

Developing and using teams is necessary because technology and market demands are forcing entrepreneurial ventures to make products faster, cheaper, and better. Tapping into the collective wisdom of a venture's employees and empowering them to make decisions just may be one of the best ways to adapt to change. In addition, a team culture can improve the overall workplace environment and morale. For team efforts to work, however, entrepreneurs must shift from the traditional command-and-control style to a coach-and-collaboration style.

What Controlling Issues Do Entrepreneurs Face?

Entrepreneurs must look at controlling their venture's operations in order to survive and prosper in both the short run and long run. The unique control issues that face entrepreneurs include managing growth, managing downturns, exiting the venture, and managing personal life choices and challenges.

How Is Growth Managed?

Growth is a natural and desirable outcome for entrepreneurial ventures. Growth is what distinguishes an entrepreneurial venture. Entrepreneurial ventures pursue growth. Growing slowly can be successful, but so can rapid growth.

Growing successfully doesn't occur randomly or by luck. Successfully pursuing growth typically requires an entrepreneur to manage all the challenges associated with growing, which entails planning, organizing, and controlling for growth.

How Are Downturns Managed?

Although organizational growth is a desirable and important goal for entrepreneurial ventures, what happens when things don't go as planned—when the growth strategies don't result in the intended outcomes and, in fact, result in a decline in performance? There are challenges, as well, in managing the downturns.

Nobody likes to fail, especially entrepreneurs. However, when an entrepreneurial venture faces times of trouble, what can be done? How can downturns be managed successfully? The first step is recognizing that a crisis is brewing. An entrepreneur should be alert to the warning signs of a business in trouble. Some signals of potential performance decline include inadequate or negative cash flow, excess number of employees, unnecessary and cumbersome administrative procedures, fear of conflict and taking risks, tolerance of work incompetence, lack of a clear mission or goals, and ineffective or poor communication within the organization.

Although an entrepreneur hopes to never have to deal with organizational downturns, declines, or crises, these situations do occur. After all, nobody likes to think about things going bad or taking a turn for the worse. But that's exactly what the entrepreneur should do—think about it *before* it happens (remember feedforward control from Chapter 14). It's important to have an up-to-date plan for covering crises. It's like mapping exit routes from your home in case of a fire. An entrepreneur wants to be prepared before an emergency hits. This plan should focus on providing specific details for controlling the most fundamental and critical aspects of running the venture—cash flow, accounts receivable, costs, and debt. Beyond having a plan for controlling the venture's critical inflows and outflows, other actions would involve identifying specific strategies for cutting costs and restructuring the venture.

What's Involved with Exiting the Venture?

Getting out of an entrepreneurial venture may seem to be a strange thing for entrepreneurs to do. However, the entrepreneur may come to a point at which he or she decides it's time to move on. That decision may be based on the fact that the entrepreneur hopes to capitalize financially on the investment in the venture—called **harvesting**—or that the entrepreneur is facing serious organizational performance problems and wants to get out, or even on the entrepreneur's desire to focus on other pursuits (personal or business). The issues involved with exiting the venture include choosing a proper business valuation method and knowing what's involved in the process of selling a business.

Although the hardest part of preparing to exit a venture may involve valuing it, other factors are also important. These include being prepared, deciding who will sell the business, considering the tax implications, screening potential buyers, and deciding whether to tell employees before or after the sale. The process of exiting the entrepreneurial venture

harvesting
Exiting a venture when an entrepreneur hopes to capitalize financially on the investment in the venture

should be approached as carefully as the process of launching it. If the entrepreneur is selling the venture on a positive note, he or she wants to realize the value built up in the business. If the venture is being exited because of declining performance, the entrepreneur wants to maximize the potential return.

Why Is It Important to Think About Managing Personal Challenges as an Entrepreneur?

Being an entrepreneur is extremely exciting and fulfilling, yet extremely demanding. It involves long hours, difficult demands, and high stress. Yet, many rewards can come with being an entrepreneur as well. In this section, we want to look at how entrepreneurs can make it work—that is, how can they be successful and effectively balance the demands of their work and personal lives?

Entrepreneurs are a special group. They're focused, persistent, hardworking, and intelligent. Because they put so much of themselves into launching and growing their entrepreneurial ventures, many may neglect their personal lives. Entrepreneurs often have to make sacrifices to pursue their entrepreneurial dreams. However, they can make it work. They can balance their work and personal lives. But how?

One of the most important things an entrepreneur can do is *become a good time manager*. Prioritize what needs to be done. Use a planner (daily, weekly, monthly) to help schedule priorities. Some entrepreneurs don't like taking the time to plan or prioritize, or they think it's a ridiculous waste of time. Yet identifying the important duties and distinguishing them from those that aren't so important actually makes an entrepreneur more efficient and effective. In addition, part of being a good time manager is delegating those decisions and actions the entrepreneur doesn't have to be personally involved in to trusted employees. Although it may be hard to let go of some of the things they've always done, entrepreneurs who delegate effectively will see their personal productivity levels rise.

Another suggestion for finding that balance is to *seek professional advice* in those areas of business where it's needed. Although entrepreneurs may be reluctant to spend scarce cash, the time and energy saved and potential problems avoided in the long run are well worth the investment. Competent professional advisors can provide entrepreneurs with information to make more intelligent decisions. Also, it's important to *deal with conflicts* as they arise—both workplace and family conflicts. If an entrepreneur doesn't deal with conflicts, negative feelings are likely to crop up and lead to communication breakdowns. When communication falls apart, vital information may get lost, and people (employees *and* family members) may start to assume the worst. It can turn into a nightmare situation that feeds on itself. The best strategy is to deal with conflicts as they come up. Talk, discuss, argue (if you must), but an entrepreneur shouldn't avoid the conflict or pretend it doesn't exist.

Another suggestion for achieving that balance between work and personal life is to *develop a network of trusted friends and peers*. Having a group of people to talk with is a good way for an entrepreneur to think through problems and issues. The support and encouragement offered by these people can be an invaluable source of strength for an entrepreneur.

Finally, *recognize when your stress levels are too high*. Entrepreneurs *are* achievers. They like to make things happen. They thrive on working hard. Yet, too much stress can lead to significant physical and emotional problems (as we discussed in Chapter 8). Entrepreneurs have to learn when stress is overwhelming them and to do something about it. After all, what's the point of growing and building a thriving entrepreneurial venture if you're not around to enjoy it?

Endnotes

1. Entrepreneurship Module based on J. Newman, "Russell Simmons Is Ready to Bring Rap to Broadway," http://www.rollingstone.com/music/features/russell-simmons-is-ready-to-bring-rap-to-broadway-scenario-20150323, March 23, 2015; "Russell Simmons' New Venture Digital Marketing Launches 'Digital-Solutions' Shop Called Narrative," adage.com, April 10, 2013; T. Padgett, "Russell Simmons: Getting Rich Is So Simple," *CNNMoney.com,* April 29, 2011; R. Schmidt and P. O'Connor, "Def Jam's Founder Out-Lobbies Big Banks," *Bloomberg Business-Week,* June 28, 2010, 21–22; R. A. Smith, "From Phat to Skinny," *Wall Street Journal,* May 1, 2010, W7; J. Dean, "The Endless Flow of Russell Simmons," *Entrepreneur,* September 2009, 24–28; S. Page, "Top 25 Influential People," *USA Today,* September 4, 2007, A10; S. Berfield, "Hip-Hop Nation," *BusinessWeek,* June 13, 2005, 12; R. Kurtz, "Russell Simmons, Rush Communications," *Inc.,* April 2004, 137; J. Reingold, "Rush Hour," *Fast Company,* November 2003, 68–80; S. Berfield, "The CEO of Hip Hop," *BusinessWeek,* October 27, 2003, 90–98; J. L. Roberts, "Beyond Definition," *Newsweek,* July 28, 2003, 40–43; C. Dugas, "Hip-Hop Legend Far Surpassed Financial Goals," *USA Today,* May 15, 2003, 6B; "Jobless Entrepreneurship Tarnishes Steady Rate of U.S. Startup Activity, Kauffman Study Shows," www.kauffman.org/newsroom/ (March 7, 2011); "Frequently Asked Questions," *U.S. Small Business Administration,* www.sba.gov/advo (September 2008); D. E. Gumpert, "The Right Business Plan for the Job," *BusinessWeek Online,* January 7, 2008; W. H. Stewart, "Risk Propensity Differences between Entrepreneurs and Managers: A Meta-Analytic Review," *Journal of Applied Psychology* (February 2001): 145–53; I. O. Williamson, "Employer Legitimacy and Recruitment Success in Small Businesses," *Entrepreneurship Theory and Practice,* Fall 2000, 27–42; R. L. Heneman, J. W. Tansky, and S. M. Camp, "Human Resource Management Practices in Small and Medium-Sized Enterprises: Unanswered Questions and Future Research Perspectives," *Entrepreneurship Theory and Practice,* Fall 2000, 11–26; T. L. Hatten, *Small Business: Entrepreneurship and Beyond* (Upper Saddle River, NJ: Prentice Hall, 1997), 5; L. W. Busenitz, "Research on Entrepreneurial Alertness," *Journal of Small Business Management* (October 1996): 35–44; J. M. Crant, "The Proactive Personality Scale as Predictor of Entrepreneurial Intentions," *Journal of Small Business Management* (July 1996): 42–49; J. C. Collins and J. I. Porras, *Built to Last: Successful Habits of Visionary Companies* (New York: Harper Business, 1994); Max Depree, *Leadership Jazz: The Essential Elements of a Great Leader,* Dell.; P. B. Robinson, D. V. Simpson, J. C. Huefner, and H. K. Hunt, "An Attitude Approach to the Prediction of Entrepreneurship," *Entrepreneurship Theory and Practice,* Summer 1991, 13–31; P. F. Drucker, *Innovation and Entrepreneurship: Practice and Principles* (New York: Harper & Row, 1985); and J. W. Carland, F. Hoy, W. R. Boulton, and J. C. Carland, "Differentiating Entrepreneurs from Small Business Owners: A Conceptualization," *Academy of Management Review* 9, no. 2 (1984): 354–59.

Glossary

A

Absenteeism The failure to show up for work

Active listening Listening for full meaning without making premature judgments or interpretations

Activities Actions that take place

Adjourning stage The final stage of group development for temporary groups, during which groups prepare to disband

Affective component The part of an attitude that's the emotional or feeling part

Affirmative action programs Programs that ensure that decisions and practices enhance the employment, upgrading, and retention of members of protected groups

Assumed similarity An observer's perception of others influenced more by the observer's own characteristics than by those of the person observed

Attitudes Evaluative statements, either favorable or unfavorable, concerning objects, people, or events

Attribution theory A theory used to explain how we judge people differently, based on what meaning we attribute to a given behavior

Authority The rights inherent in a managerial position to give orders and expect the orders to be obeyed

B

Balanced scorecard A performance measurement tool that looks at more than just the financial perspective

Basic corrective action Corrective action that looks at how and why performance deviated before correcting the source of deviation

Behavior The actions of people

Behavioral component The part of an attitude that refers to an intention to behave in a certain way toward someone or something

Behavioral theories of leadership Theories that isolate behaviors that differentiate effective leaders from ineffective leaders

Benchmarking The search for the best practices among competitors or noncompetitors that lead to their superior performance

Big data The vast amount of quantifiable information that can be analyzed by highly sophisticated data processing

Big Five Model A personality trait model that examines five traits: extraversion, agreeableness, conscientiousness, emotional stability, and openness to experience

Board representatives Employees who sit on a company's board of directors and represent the interest of employees

Body language Nonverbal communication cues such as facial expressions, gestures, and other body movements

Boundaryless career When an individual takes personal responsibility for his or her own career

Boundaryless organization An organization whose design is not defined by, or limited to, boundaries imposed by a predefined structure

Bounded rationality Making decisions that are rational within the limits of a manager's ability to process information

Brainstorming An idea-generating process that encourages alternatives while withholding criticism

Break-even analysis A technique for identifying the point at which total revenue is just sufficient to cover total costs

Business model A strategic design for how a company intends to profit from its broad array of strategies, processes, and activities

Business plan A written document that summarizes a business opportunity and defines and articulates how the identified opportunity is to be seized and exploited

C

"Calm waters" metaphor A description of organizational change that likens that change to a large ship making a predictable trip across a calm sea and experiencing an occasional storm

Capabilities An organization's skills and abilities in doing the work activities needed in its business

Career The sequence of work positions held by a person during his or her lifetime

Centralization The degree to which decision making takes place at upper levels of the organization

Certainty A situation in which a decision maker can make accurate decisions because all outcomes are known

Chain of command The line of authority extending from upper organizational levels to lower levels, which clarifies who reports to whom

Change agents People who act as change catalysts and assume the responsibility for managing the change process

Channel The medium by which a message travels

Charismatic leaders Enthusiastic, self-confident leaders whose personalities and actions influence people to behave in certain ways

Code of ethics A formal document that states an organization's primary values and the ethical rules it expects managers and nonmanagerial employees to follow

Cognitive component The part of an attitude made up of the beliefs, opinions, knowledge, and information held by a person

Cognitive dissonance Any incompatibility or inconsistency between attitudes or between behavior and attitudes

Commitment concept The idea that plans should extend far enough to meet those commitments made when the plans were developed

Communication A transfer of understanding and meaning from one person to another

Communication process The seven-part process of transferring and understanding of meaning

Communities of practice Groups of people who share a concern, a set of problems, or a passion about a topic and who deepen their knowledge and expertise in that area by interacting on an ongoing basis

Competitive advantage What sets an organization apart; its distinctive edge

Competitive intelligence A type of environmental scanning that gives managers accurate information about competitors

Competitive strategy An organizational strategy for how an organization will compete in its business(es)

Compressed workweek A workweek where employees work longer hours per day but fewer days per week

Conceptual skills A manager's ability to analyze and diagnose complex situations

Concurrent control Control that takes place while a work activity is in progress

Conformity Adjusting one's behavior to align with a group's norms

Contingency approach (or situational approach) An approach to management that says that individual organizations, employees, and situations are different and require different ways of managing

Contingent workers Temporary, freelance, or contract workers whose employment is *contingent* upon demand for their services

Contingent workforce Part-time, temporary, and contract workers who are available for hire on an as-needed basis

Control Management function that involves monitoring activities to ensure that they're being accomplished as planned and correcting any significant deviations

Controlling Monitoring activities to ensure that they are accomplished as planned

Control process A three-step process of measuring actual performance, comparing actual performance against a standard, and taking managerial action to correct deviations

Core competencies The major value-creating capabilities of an organization

Corporate strategy An organizational strategy that specifies what businesses a company is in or wants to be in and what it wants to do with those businesses

Cost leadership strategy When an organization competes on the basis of having the lowest costs in its industry

Creativity The ability to produce novel and useful ideas

Credibility The degree to which followers perceive someone as honest, competent, and able to inspire

Critical path The longest or most time-consuming sequence of events and activities required to complete a project in the shortest amount of time

Cross-functional team A work team composed of individuals from various specialties

Customer departmentalization Grouping activities by customer

D

Decentralization The degree to which lower-level managers provide input or actually make decisions

Decisional roles Entailing making decisions or choices

Decision criteria Factors that are relevant in a decision

Decision implementation Putting a decision into action

Decision-making process A set of eight steps that includes identifying a problem, selecting a solution, and evaluating the effectiveness of the solution

Decision trees A diagram used to analyze a progression of decisions. When diagrammed, a decision tree looks like a tree with branches.

Decoding Translating a received message

Demographics The characteristics of a population used for purposes of social studies

Departmentalization How jobs are grouped together

Design thinking Approaching management problems as designers approach design problems

Differentiation strategy When an organization competes on the basis of having unique products that are widely valued by customers

Directional plans Plans that are flexible and set general guidelines

Discipline Actions taken by a manager to enforce an organization's standards and regulations

Distributive justice Perceived fairness of the amount and allocation of rewards among individuals

Divisional structure An organizational structure made up of separate business units or divisions

Division of labor (or job specialization) The breakdown of jobs into narrow repetitive tasks

Downsizing The planned elimination of jobs in an organization

E

Economic order quantity (EOQ) A model that seeks to balance the costs involved in ordering and carrying inventory, thus minimizing total costs associated with carrying and ordering costs

Effectiveness Doing the right things, or completing activities so that organizational goals are attained

Efficiency Doing things right, or getting the most output from the least amount of inputs

Electronic meeting A type of nominal group technique in which participants are linked by computer

Emotional intelligence (EI) The ability to notice and to manage emotional cues and information

Employee assistance programs (EAPs) Programs offered by organizations to help employees overcome personal and health-related problems

Employee benefits Membership-based rewards designed to enrich employees' lives

Employee counseling A process designed to help employees overcome performance-related problems

Employee engagement When employees are connected to, satisfied with, and enthusiastic about their jobs

Employee productivity A performance measure of both work efficiency and effectiveness

Employee recognition programs Programs that consist of personal attention and expressions of interest, approval, and appreciation for a job well done

Employee theft Any unauthorized taking of company property by employees for their personal use

Employee training A learning experience that seeks a relatively permanent change in employees by improving their ability to perform on the job

Employment planning The process by which managers ensure they have the right numbers and kinds of people in the right places at the right time

Empowerment The act of increasing the decision-making discretion of workers

Encoding Converting a message into symbolic form

Entrepreneurial ventures Organizations that pursue opportunities, are characterized by innovative practices, and have growth and profitability as their main goals

Entrepreneurship The process of starting new businesses, generally in response to opportunities

Environmental complexity The number of components in an organization's environment and the extent of knowledge that the organization has about those components

Environmental scanning An analysis of the external environment, which involves screening large amounts of information to detect emerging trends

Environmental uncertainty The degree of change and complexity in an organization's environment

Equity theory The theory that an employee compares his or her job's input-to-outcome ratio with that of relevant others and then corrects any inequity

Escalation of commitment An increased commitment to a previous decision despite evidence that it may have been a poor decision

Ethical communication Presented material that contains all relevant information, is true in every sense, and is not deceptive in any way

Ethics A set of rules or principles that defines right and wrong conduct

Ethnicity Social traits, such as one's cultural background or allegiance, that are shared by a human population

Events End points that represent the completion of major activities

Expectancy theory The theory that an individual tends to act in a certain way based on the expectation that the act will be followed by a given outcome and on the attractiveness of that outcome to the individual

Exporting Making products domestically and selling them abroad

External environment Factors, forces, situations, and events outside the organization that affect its performance

F

Family-friendly benefits Benefits that provide a wide range of scheduling options and allow employees more flexibility at work, accommodating their needs for work-life balance

Feedback Checking to see how successfully a message has been transferred

Feedback control Control that takes place after a work activity is done

Feedforward control Control that takes place before a work activity is done

Fiedler contingency model Leadership theory proposing that effective group performance depends on the proper match between a leader's style and the degree to which the situation allowed the leader to control and influence

Filtering Deliberately manipulating information to make it appear more favorable to the receiver

First-line managers Supervisors responsible for directing the day-to-day activities of non-managerial employees

Fixed-point reordering system A method for a system to "flag" the need to reorder inventory at some preestablished point in the process

Flextime (also known as flexible work hours) A work scheduling system in which employees are required to work a specific number of hours per week but can vary when they work those hours within certain limits

Focus strategy When an organization competes in a narrow segment or niche with either a cost focus or a differentiation focus

Foreign subsidiary A direct investment in a foreign country that involves setting up a separate and independent facility or office

Formal planning department A group of planning specialists whose sole responsibility is to help write the various organizational plans

Formalization How standardized an organization's jobs are and the extent to which employee behavior is guided by rules and procedures

Forming stage The first stage of group development in which people join the group and then define the group's purpose, structure, and leadership

Franchising An agreement in which an organization gives another organization the right, for a fee, to use its name and operating methods

Functional departmentalization Grouping activities by functions performed

Functional strategy Strategy used in an organization's various functional departments to support the competitive strategy

Functional structure An organizational design that groups similar or related occupational specialties together

Fundamental attribution error The tendency to underestimate the influence of external factors and overestimate the influence of internal factors when making judgments about the behavior of others

G

Gamification Applying typical aspects of game playing to other areas of activity especially in a work setting

Gantt chart A planning tool that shows in bar graph form when tasks are supposed to be done and compares that with the actual progress on each

General administrative theory Descriptions of what managers do and what constitutes good management practice

Geographic departmentalization Grouping activities on the basis of geography or territory

Global corporation An MNC that centralizes management and other decisions in the home country

Global sourcing Purchasing materials or labor from around the world, wherever it is cheapest

Global strategic alliance A partnership between an organization and foreign company partner(s) in which both share resources and knowledge in developing new products or building production facilities

Global village A boundaryless world where goods and services are produced and marketed worldwide

GLOBE The Global Leadership and Organizational Behavior Effectiveness research program, a program that studies cross-cultural leadership behaviors

Goals (objectives) Desired outcomes or targets

Goal-setting theory The proposition that specific goals increase performance and that difficult goals, when accepted, result in higher performance than do easy goals

Grapevine An unofficial channel of communication

Group Two or more interacting and interdependent individuals who come together to achieve specific goals

Group cohesiveness The degree to which group members are attracted to one another and share the group's goals

Groupthink When a group exerts extensive pressure on an individual to withhold his or her different views in order to appear to be in agreement

Growth strategy A corporate strategy in which an organization expands the number of markets served or products offered either through its current business(es) or through new business(es)

H

Halo effect When we form a general impression of a person on the basis of a single characteristic

Harvesting Exiting a venture when an entrepreneur hopes to capitalize financially on the investment in the venture

Hawthorne studies Research done in the late 1920s and early 1930s devised by Western Electric industrial engineers to examine the effect of different work environment changes on worker productivity, which led to a new emphasis on the human factor in the functioning of organizations and the attainment of their goals

Heuristics Judgmental shortcuts or "rules of thumb" used to simplify decision making

Hierarchy of needs theory Maslow's theory that there is a hierarchy of five human needs: physiological, safety, social, esteem, and self-actualization

Human resource inventory A report listing important information about employees such as name, education, training, skills, languages spoken, and so forth

Human resource management (HRM) The management function concerned with getting, training, motivating, and keeping competent employees

Hygiene factors Factors that eliminate job dissatisfaction but don't motivate

I

Idea champions Individuals who actively and enthusiastically support new ideas, build support for, overcome resistance to, and ensure that innovations are implemented

Immediate corrective action Corrective action that addresses problems at once to get performance back on track

Importing Acquiring products made abroad and selling them domestically

Industrial Revolution The advent of machine power, mass production, and efficient transportation beginning in the late eighteenth century in Great Britain

Informational roles Involving collecting, receiving, and disseminating information

Information overload What results when information exceeds processing capacity

Innovation The process of taking a creative idea and turning it into a useful product, service, or method of operation

Intergroup development Activities that attempt to make several work groups more cohesive

Interpersonal roles Involving people (subordinates and persons outside the organization) and other duties that are ceremonial and symbolic in nature

Interpersonal skills A manager's ability to work with, understand, mentor, and motivate others, both individually and in groups

Intuitive decision making Making decisions on the basis of experience, feelings, and accumulated judgment

ISO 9000 A series of international quality standards that set uniform guidelines for processes to ensure that products conform to customer requirements

J

Jargon Technical language specific to a discipline or industry

Job analysis An assessment that defines jobs and the behaviors necessary to perform them

Job characteristics model (JCM) A framework for analyzing and designing jobs that identifies five primary core job dimensions, their interrelationships, and their impact on outcomes

Job description A written statement that describes a job

Job design The way tasks are combined to form complete jobs

Job enrichment The vertical expansion of a job by adding planning and evaluation responsibilities

Job involvement The degree to which an employee identifies with his or her job, actively participates in it, and considers his or her job performance important for self-worth

Job satisfaction An employee's general attitude toward his or her job

Job sharing When two or more people split a full-time job

Job specification A written statement of the minimum qualifications that a person must possess to perform a given job successfully

Joint venture A specific type of strategic alliance in which the partners agree to form a separate, independent organization for some business purpose

K

Karoshi A Japanese term that refers to a sudden death caused by overworking

Knowledge management Cultivating a learning culture in which organizational members systematically gather knowledge and share it with others

L

Layoff-survivor sickness A set of attitudes, perceptions, and behaviors of employees who survive layoffs

Leader Someone who can influence others and who has managerial authority

Leader-member exchange (LMX) theory A leadership theory that says leaders create in-groups and out-groups and those in the in-group will have higher performance ratings, less turnover, and greater job satisfaction

Leader-participation model A leadership contingency theory that's based on a sequential set of rules for determining how much participation a leader uses in decision making according to different types of situations

Leadership The process of leading a group and influencing that group to achieve its goals

Leading Directing and coordinating the work activities of an organization's people

Learning A relatively permanent change in behavior that occurs as a result of experience

Learning organization An organization that has developed the capacity to continuously learn, adapt, and change

Least-preferred coworker (LPC) questionnaire A questionnaire that measures whether a leader was task or relationship oriented

Licensing An agreement in which an organization gives another the right, for a fee, to make or sell its products, using its technology or product specifications

Linear programming A mathematical technique that solves resource allocation problems

Line authority Authority that entitles a manager to direct the work of an employee

Load chart A modified version of a Gantt chart that lists either whole departments or specific resources

Locus of control The degree to which people believe they control their own fate

Long-term plans Plans with a time frame beyond three years

M

Machiavellianism ("Mach") A measure of the degree to which people are pragmatic, maintain emotional distance, and believe that ends justify means

Management The process of getting things done, effectively and efficiently, through and with other people

Management by objectives (MBO) A process of setting mutually agreed-upon goals and using those goals to evaluate employee performance

Management by walking around (MBWA) When a manager is out in the work area interacting with employees

Management information system (MIS) A system used to provide management with needed information on a regular basis

Managerial grid A two-dimensional grid for appraising leadership styles

Managerial roles Specific categories of managerial behavior; often grouped around interpersonal relationships, information transfer, and decision making

Managers Individuals in an organization who direct the activities of others

Manufacturing organizations Organizations that produce physical goods

Mass production Large-batch manufacturing

Matrix structure A structure in which specialists from different functional departments are assigned to work on projects led by a project manager

Means-ends chain An integrated network of goals in which higher-level goals are linked to lower-level goals, which serve as the means for their accomplishment

Mechanistic organization A bureaucratic organization; a structure that's high in specialization, formalization, and centralization

Message A purpose for communicating that's to be conveyed

Middle managers Individuals who are typically responsible for translating goals set by top managers into specific details that lower-level managers will see get done

Mission A statement of an organization's purpose

Motivation The process by which a person's efforts are energized, directed, and sustained toward attaining a goal

Motivators Factors that increase job satisfaction and motivation

Multidomestic corporation An MNC that decentralizes management and other decisions to the local country where it's doing business

Multinational corporation (MNC) Any type of international company that maintains operations in multiple countries

Myers-Briggs Type Indicator (MBTI) A personality assessment that uses four dimensions of personality to identify different personality types

N

Need for achievement (nAch) The drive to succeed and excel in relation to a set of standards

Need for affiliation (nAff) The desire for friendly and close interpersonal relationships

Need for power (nPow) The need to make others behave in a way that they would not have behaved otherwise

Network organization An organization that uses its own employees to do some work activities and networks of outside suppliers to provide other needed product components or work processes

Nominal group technique A decision-making technique in which group members are physically present but operate independently

Nonmanagerial employees People who work directly on a job or task and have no responsibility for overseeing the work of others

Nonprogrammed decision A unique and nonrecurring decision that requires a custom-made solution

Norming stage The third stage of group development, which is characterized by close relationships and cohesiveness

Norms Standards or expectations that are accepted and shared by a group's members

O

Omnipotent view of management The view that managers are directly responsible for an organization's success or failure

Open-book management A motivational approach in which an organization's financial statements (the "books") are shared with all employees

Open systems Systems that dynamically interact with their environment

Operant conditioning A theory of learning that says behavior is a function of its consequences

Operations management The study and application of the transformation process

Opportunities Positive trends in the external environment

Organic organization A structure that's low in specialization, formalization, and centralization

Organization A systematic arrangement of people brought together to accomplish some specific purpose

Organization design When managers develop or change the organization's structure

Organization development (OD) Efforts that assist organizational members with a planned change by focusing on their attitudes and values

Organizational behavior (OB) The field of study that researches the actions (behaviors) of people at work

Organizational change Any alteration of an organization's people, structure, or technology

Organizational citizenship behavior Discretionary behavior that's not part of an employee's formal job requirements, but that promotes the effective functioning of the organization

Organizational commitment An employee's orientation toward the organization in terms of his or her loyalty to, identification with, and involvement in the organization

Organizational culture The shared values, principles, traditions, and ways of doing things that influence the way organizational members act

Organizational processes The way organizational work is done

Organizing Determining what needs to be done, how it will be done, and who is to do it

Orientation Introducing a new employee to the job and the organization

P

Parochialism A narrow focus in which managers see things only through their own eyes and from their own perspective

Path-goal theory A leadership theory that says the leader's job is to assist followers in attaining their goals and to provide direction or support needed to ensure that their goals are compatible with the organization's or group's goals

Pay-for-performance programs Variable compensation plans that pay employees on the basis of some performance measure

Perception A process by which we give meaning to our environment by organizing and interpreting sensory impressions

Performance management system A system that establishes performance standards that are used to evaluate employee performance

Performance-simulation tests Selection devices based on actual job behaviors

Performing stage The fourth stage of group development, when the group is fully functional and works on the group task

Personality A unique combination of emotional, thought, and behavioral patterns that affect how a person reacts to situations and interacts with others

PERT network analysis A flowchart-like diagram that depicts the sequence of activities needed to complete a project and the time or costs associated with each activity

Planning Defining goals, establishing strategy, and developing plans to coordinate activities

Plans Documents that outline how goals are going to be met

Policy A guideline for making decisions

Political skills A manager's ability to build a power base and establish the right connections

Power An individual's capacity to influence decisions

Principles of management Fayol's fundamental or universal principles of management practice

Proactive personality A personality trait describing those individuals who are more prone to take actions to influence their environment

Problem A discrepancy between an existing and a desired state of affairs

Problem-solving team A team from the same department or functional area that's involved in efforts to improve work activities or to solve specific problems

Procedural justice Perceived fairness of the process used to determine the distribution of rewards

Procedure A series of interrelated, sequential steps used to respond to a structured problem

Process consultation Using outside consultants to assess organizational processes such as workflow, informal intra-unit relationships, and formal communication channels

Process departmentalization Grouping activities on the basis of work or customer flow

Process production Continuous flow or process production

Product departmentalization Grouping activities by major product areas

Programmed decision A repetitive decision that can be handled using a routine approach

Project A one-time-only set of activities with a definite beginning and ending point

Project management The task of getting project activities done on time, within budget, and according to specifications

Project structure A structure in which employees continuously work on projects

Q

Quantitative approach The use of quantitative techniques to improve decision making

Queuing theory Also known as waiting line theory, it is a way of balancing the cost of having a waiting line versus the cost of maintaining the line. Management wants to have as few stations open as possible to minimize costs without testing the patience of its customers.

R

Race The biological heritage (including physical characteristics, such as one's skin color and associated traits) that people use to identify themselves

Range of variation The acceptable parameters of variance between actual performance and a standard

Rational decision making Describes choices that are consistent and value-maximizing within specified constraints

Readiness The extent to which people have the ability and willingness to accomplish a specific task

Real goals Those goals an organization actually pursues as shown by what the organization's members are doing

Realistic job preview (RJP) A preview of a job that provides both positive and negative information about the job and the company

Recruitment Locating, identifying, and attracting capable applicants

Referent The persons, systems, or selves against which individuals compare themselves to assess equity

Reliability The degree to which a selection device measures the same thing consistently

Renewal strategy A corporate strategy that addresses declining organizational performance

Resources An organization's assets that it uses to develop, manufacture, and deliver products to its customers

Responsibility An obligation to perform assigned duties

Rights view of ethics View that says ethical decisions are made in order to respect and protect individual liberties and privileges

Ringisei Japanese consensus-forming group decisions

Risk A situation in which a decision maker is able to estimate the likelihood of certain outcomes

Role Behavior patterns expected of someone who occupies a given position in a social unit

Role ambiguity When role expectations are not clearly understood

Role conflicts Work expectations that are hard to satisfy

Role overload Having more work to accomplish than time permits

Rule An explicit statement that tells employees what can or cannot be done

S

Satisfice Accepting solutions that are "good enough"

Scientific management The use of scientific methods to define the "one best way" for a job to be done

Selection process Screening job applicants to ensure that the most appropriate candidates are hired

Selective perception Selectively perceiving or hearing a communication based on your own needs, motivations, experiences, or other personal characteristics

Self-efficacy An individual's belief that he or she is capable of performing a task

Self-esteem (SE) An individual's degree of like or dislike for himself or herself

Self-managed work team A type of work team that operates without a manager and is responsible for a complete work process or segment

Self-monitoring A personality trait that measures the ability to adjust behavior to external situational factors

Self-serving bias The tendency for individuals to attribute their successes to internal factors while putting the blame for failures on external factors

Service organizations Organizations that produce nonphysical products in the form of services

Sexual harassment Any unwanted action or activity of a sexual nature that explicitly or implicitly affects an individual's employment, performance, or work environment

Shaping behavior The process of guiding learning in graduated steps, using reinforcement or lack of reinforcement

Sharing economy An economic environment in which asset owners share with other individuals through a peer-to-peer service, for a set fee, their underutilized physical assets or their knowledge, expertise, skills, or time

Short-term plans Plans with a time frame of one year or less

Simple structure An organizational design with low departmentalization, wide spans of control, authority centralized in a single person, and little formalization

Single-use plan A one-time plan specifically designed to meet the needs of a unique situation

Situational leadership theory (SLT) A leadership contingency theory that focuses on followers' readiness

Six Sigma A quality standard that establishes a goal of no more than 3.4 defects per million units or procedures

Skill-based pay A pay system that rewards employees for the job skills they demonstrate

Slack time The time difference between the critical path and all other paths

Small business An independent business having fewer than 500 employees that doesn't necessarily engage in any new or innovative practices and has relatively little impact on its industry

Social learning theory A theory of learning that says people can learn through observation and direct experience

Social loafing The tendency for individuals to expend less effort when working collectively than when working individually

Social media Forms of electronic communication through which users create online communities to share ideas, information, personal messages, and other content

Social obligation When a business firm engages in social actions because of its obligation to meet certain economic and legal responsibilities

Social responsibility (corporate social responsibility, or CSR) A business firm's intention, beyond its legal and economic obligations, to do the right things and act in ways that are good for society

Social responsiveness When a business firm engages in social actions in response to some popular social need

Span of control The number of employees a manager can efficiently and effectively supervise

Specific plans Plans that are clearly defined and leave no room for interpretation

Stability strategy A corporate strategy in which an organization continues to do what it is currently doing

Staff authority Positions with some authority that have been created to support, assist, and advise those holding line authority

Stakeholders Any constituencies in an organization's environment that are affected by that organization's decisions and actions

Standing plans Plans that are ongoing and provide guidance for activities performed repeatedly

Stated goals Official statements of what an organization says, and wants its stakeholders to believe, its goals are

Status A prestige grading, position, or rank within a group

Stereotyping When we judge someone on the basis of our perception of a group to which that person belongs

Storming stage The second stage of group development, which is characterized by intragroup conflict

Strategic business units (SBUs) An organization's single businesses that are independent and formulate their own competitive strategies

Strategic management What managers do to develop an organization's strategies

Strategic management process A six-step process that encompasses strategy planning, implementation, and evaluation

Strategic plans Plans that apply to the entire organization and encompass the organization's overall goals

Strategies Plans for how the organization will do what it's in business to do, how it will compete successfully, and how it will attract its customers in order to achieve its goals

Strengths Any activities the organization does well or any unique resources that it has

Stress Response to anxiety over intense demands, constraints, or opportunities.

Stressors Factors that cause stress

Strong cultures Cultures in which the key values are deeply held and widely shared

Structured problem A straightforward, familiar, and easily defined problem

Survey feedback A method of assessing employees' attitudes toward and perceptions of a change

Sustainability A company's ability to achieve its business goals and increase long-term shareholder value by integrating economic, environmental, and social opportunities into its business strategies

SWOT analysis The combined external and internal analyses

Symbolic view of management The view that much of an organization's success or failure is due to external forces outside managers' control

Systems approach An approach to management that views an organization as a system, which is a set of interrelated and interdependent parts arranged in a manner that produces a unified whole

T

Tactical plans Plans that specify the details of how the overall goals are to be achieved

Team-building Using activities to help work groups set goals, develop positive interpersonal relationships, and clarify the roles and responsibilities of each team member

Team leaders Individuals who are responsible for managing and facilitating the activities of a work team

Team structure A structure in which the entire organization is made up of work teams

Technical skills Job-specific knowledge and techniques needed to perform work tasks

Technology Any equipment, tools, or operating methods that are designed to make work more efficient

Telecommuting A work arrangement in which employees work at home and are linked to the workplace by computer

Theory of justice view of ethics View that says ethical decisions are made in order to enforce rules fairly and impartially

Theory X The assumption that employees dislike work, are lazy, avoid responsibility, and must be coerced to work

Theory Y The assumption that employees are creative, enjoy work, seek responsibility, and can exercise self-direction

Threats Negative trends in the external environment

Three-needs theory McClelland's theory, which says that three acquired (not innate) needs—achievement, power, and affiliation—are major motives at work

360-degree appraisal An appraisal device that seeks feedback from a variety of sources for the person being rated

Top managers Individuals who are responsible for making decisions about the direction of the organization and establishing policies that affect all organizational members

Total quality management (TQM) A managerial philosophy devoted to continual improvement and responding to customer needs and expectations

Traditional goal setting Goals set by top managers flow down through the organization and become subgoals for each organizational area

Trait theories of leadership Theories that isolate characteristics (traits) that differentiate leaders from nonleaders

Transactional leaders Leaders who lead primarily by using social exchanges (or transactions)

Transformation process The process that converts resources into finished goods and services

Transformational leaders Leaders who stimulate and inspire (transform) followers to achieve extraordinary outcomes

Transnational (borderless) organization A structural arrangement for global organizations that eliminates artificial geographical barriers

Trust The belief in the integrity, character, and ability of a leader

Turnover Voluntary and involuntary permanent withdrawal from an organization

Two-factor theory Herzberg's motivation theory, which proposes that intrinsic factors are related to job satisfaction and motivation, whereas extrinsic factors are associated with job dissatisfaction

Type A personality People who have a chronic sense of urgency and an excessive competitive drive

Type B personality People who are relaxed and easygoing and accept change easily

U

Uncertainty A situation in which a decision maker has neither certainty nor reasonable probability estimates available

Unit production The production of items in units or small batches

Unity of command Structure in which each employee reports to only one manager

Unstructured problem A problem that is new or unusual for which information is ambiguous or incomplete

Utilitarian view of ethics View that says ethical decisions are made solely on the basis of their outcomes or consequences

V

Validity The proven relationship between a selection device and some relevant criterion

Value The performance characteristics, features, attributes, and other aspects of goods and services, for which customers are willing to give up resources

Value chain The entire series of work activities that add value at each step from raw materials to finished product

Value chain management The process of managing the sequence of activities and information along the entire value chain

Variable pay A pay system in which an individual's compensation is contingent on performance

Verbal intonation An emphasis given to words or phrases that conveys meaning

Virtual organization An organization that consists of a small core of full-time employees and outside specialists temporarily hired as needed to work on projects

Virtual team A type of work team that uses technology to link physically dispersed members in order to achieve a common goal

Visionary leadership The ability to create and articulate a realistic, credible, and attractive vision of the future that improves on the present situation

W

Weaknesses Activities the organization doesn't do well or resources it needs but doesn't possess

Wellness programs Programs offered by organizations to help employees prevent health problems

"White-water rapids" metaphor A description of organizational change that likens that change to a small raft navigating a raging river

Work councils Groups of nominated or elected employees who must be consulted when management makes decisions involving personnel

Workforce diversity Ways in which people in a workforce are similar and different from one another in terms of gender, age, race, sexual orientation, ethnicity, cultural background, and physical abilities and disabilities

Workplace misbehavior Any intentional employee behavior that is potentially harmful to the organization or individuals within the organization

Work specialization Dividing work activities into separate job tasks; also called division of labor

Work teams Groups whose members work intensely on specific, common goals using their positive synergy, individual and mutual accountability, and complementary skills

Index

Note: When page numbers are followed by the letter *e*, the reference appears in an exhibit.